HANDBOOK OF
Individual Therapy

edited by
Windy Dryden

SAGE Publications
London · Thousand Oaks · New Delhi

Previous editions have been published as *Individual Therapy in Britain* (1984), *Individual Therapy: A Handbook* (1990), and *Handbook of Individual Therapy* (1996)

This edition published 2002. Reprinted 2003.

SAGE Publications Ltd
6 Bonhill Street
London EC2A 4PU

SAGE Publications Inc
2455 Teller Road
Thousand Oaks, California 91320

SAGE Publications India Pvt Ltd
32, M-Block Market
Greater Kailash – I
New Delhi 110 048

British Library Cataloguing in Publication data

A catalogue record for this book is available from the British Library

ISBN 0 7619 6942 X
ISBN 0 7619 6943 8 (pbk)

Library of Congress Control Number: 2002101994

Typeset by Photoprint, Torquay, Devon
Printed in Great Britain by The Cromwell Press Ltd, Trowbridge, Wiltshire

HANDBOOK OF
Individual Therapy

For LOUISE

Contents

Preface

The first edition of this handbook was published in 1984 and attempted to fill a gap in the market at that time by having British authors write on well-established approaches to individual therapy for a British readership. The two subsequent editions published as six-year intervals carried on this tradition. In this, the fourth edition, the most successful elements of the previous editions have been retained. Contributors of chapters detailing specific therapeutic approaches were once again asked to keep to a common structure (Appendix 1) in writing their chapters (Chapters 2–14), there is a chapter placing therapy in a social context (Chapter 1) and chapters are included on research and training as they pertain to individual therapy (Chapters 15 and 16).

As before, I have sought feedback on the previous edition and have included a chapter on Cognitive-Analytic Therapy as a result of this feedback. All other chapters have been updated or completely rewritten. The book ends as the previous editions did with information on clinical services and training opportunities offered by every approach (see Appendix 2).

I welcome feedback on this handbook and hope that readers will once again join me in thanking all the contributors for a job very well done.

Windy Dryden, London

The Editor and Contributors

The Editor

Windy Dryden currently works at Goldsmiths College where he is the Pro-gramme Co-ordinator of the MSc in Rational Emotive Behaviour Therapy and the Diploma in Cognitive Approaches to Counselling and Psychotherapy. He is actively involved in the practice of REBT and in writing books on the subject for professionals and the general public.

The Contributors

Mark Aveline has been a consultant medical psychotherapist in Nottingham since 1974. His chief interests are in the development of a range of effective psychotherapies, suitable for NHS practice, and teaching the necessary skills at undergraduate, post-qualification and specialist levels. He employs group and focal therapy with an interpersonal emphasis and programming in 4th Dimen-sion, a relational database. Administrative responsibilities include: member of the Governing Board of the United Kingdom Council for Psychotherapy (1992–1998), chair of the Training Committee of the South Trent Training in Dynamic Psychotherapy (1984—), President of the British Association for Coun-selling and Psychotherapy (1994–2000), chair of the Psychotherapy Training Specialist Advisory Committee of the Royal College of Psychiatrists (1995–1998) and UK President of the Society for Psychotherapy Research (1996–1999) and International Vice-President (2001—). He is author of *From Medicine to Psycho-therapy* (Whurr, 1992) and co-editor of *Group Therapy in Britain* (Open University Press, 1988) and *Research Foundations for Psychotherapy Practice* (Wiley, 1995).

Michael Barkham is Professor of Clinical and Counselling Psychology and Director of the Psychological Therapies Research Centre at the University of Leeds and also Visiting Professor at the University of Northumbria at Newcastle. He has published widely on psychotherapy process and outcome as well as on issues of research methodology and the development of tools to help evaluate the outcomes of psychotherapy.

Gerhard Baumer studied psychology and trained as an Adlerian Psycho-therapist in Berlin. He has been working in private practice for 26 years and writes articles, gives lectures and runs workshops regularly in Germany and in Cambridge and Wendover, Buckinghamshire in England. He is an International Adlerian Trainer. He has co-authored a chapter in S. Palmer (ed.), *Introduction to Counselling and Psychotherapy* (Sage, 2000).

Ann Casement is a Jungian analyst in private practice and is a training analyst and supervisor for several psychotherapy organizations. She is a member of the

International Association for Analytical Psychology (IAAP) and sits on its Executive Committee. She is also a member of the British Psychological Society, an Associate Member of the Royal Society of Medicine and a fellow of the Royal Anthropological Institute. She writes for the *Economist* and various journals, and lectures and teaches in analytical psychology, psychotherapy and anthropology. She is a former chair of the United Kingdom Council for Psychotherapy. Her latest book is *Carl Gustav Jung* commissioned by Sage.

Cassie Cooper is a Kleinian psychotherapist/counselling psychologist. She is an external examiner and moderator for psychotherapy and counselling courses. She is the author of many papers on psychotherapy and counselling. Current publications include chapters in V.P. Varma (ed.), *Psychotherapy Today* (Constable, 1974), H. Cooper (ed.), *Soul Searching* (SCM, 1988), M. Jacobs (ed.), *Charlie, an Unwanted Child* (Open University Press, 1995), V.P. Varma (ed.), *Stresses in Psychologists* (Routledge, 1996), R. Woolfe and W. Dryden (eds), *Handbook of Counselling Psychology* (Sage, 1996) and I. Horton and V. Varma (eds), *The Needs of Counsellors & Psychotherapists*. She is the joint editor of the newsletter published by the Psychotherapy Section of the British Psychology Society.

Peggy Dalton is a member of PCP Education and Training and is involved in teaching personal construct psychology. She works independently as a psychotherapist and counsellor with children and young people as well as adults. She is joint author with Fay Fransella of *Personal Construct Counselling in Action* (Sage, 1990) and with Gavin Dunnett of *A Psychology for Living* (Wiley, 1992). Her most recent book, *Counselling People with Communication Problems* (Sage, 1994) focuses on her particular interest in speech, language and voice problems.

Emmy van Deurzen directs the New School of Psychotherapy and Counselling in London, where she is a Professor in Psychotherapy with Schiller International University. She is also Co-Director of the Centre for the Study of Conflict and Reconciliation at the University of Sheffield. She has written extensively on the application of philosophical ideas to psychotherapy and runs a private practice in Sheffield with Dilemma Consultancy in Human Relations. She founded the Society for Existential Analysis and created numerous courses in psychotherapy for academic institutions. Her book *Existential Counselling and Psychotherapy in Practice* saw its second edition in 2002. Other books are *Paradox and Passion in Psychotherapy* (Wiley, 1998) and *Everyday Mysteries* (Routledge, 1997).

Mark Dunn is Senior Principal Psychotherapist at the Munro Centre at Guy's Hospital, London. He heads a service providing outpatient psychotherapy, primarily CAT, on the NHS. He is an individual and group psychotherapist, clinical supervisor, trainer and training therapist with ACAT and Hon. tutor in Psychotherapy at the United Medical School of Guy's, St Thomas's and King's College Hospitals. He has a small private practice.

Fay Fransella is Director of the Centre for Personal Construct Psychology; Emeritus Reader in Clinical Psychology, University of London and Visiting Professor at the University of Hertfordshire, UK. The eight books she has authored include *Inquiring Man*, written with Don Bannister (Routledge, 3rd Edition, 1986), *Personal Construct Counselling in Action*, written with Peggy Dalton (Sage, 1990) and *George Kelly* (Sage, 1995). She runs a six-module distance learning personal construct psychology programme at intermediate and advanced levels.

Judith Hemming is a teaching and supervising member of the Gestalt Psycho-therapy and Training Institute and offers training and clinical supervision for several institutes in Britain and abroad. Formerly a teacher and teacher trainer, she has been in private practice in London for the last 20 years, having trained in Gestalt and other approaches in Britain and America since 1980. She specializes in, and has taught and written about Gestalt couples therapy, and for the past nine years has also been teaching Bert Hellinger's family systemic approach, integrating it with Gestalt practice and extending it into organizational settings. She is Deputy Editor of the *British Gestalt Journal*.

Robin Hobbes is a teaching and supervising transactional analyst and Co-Director of Elan Training and Development, a TA and Integrative Psychotherapy centre based in Manchester. He is a former chair of the British Institute of Transactional Analysis and of its Ethics Committee, on which he currently serves as a member. He offers individual therapy and individual and group supervision in which work he takes a transpersonal and integrative approach.

Alessandra Lemma is a consultant clinical psychologist and a psychoanalytic psychotherapist working with adults in the NHS as well as privately. She is an honorary senior lecturer at University College London where she teaches psycho-analysis. She has published widely in the fields of clinical psychology, psychother-apy and counselling.

Stirling Moorey is Consultant Psychiatrist in CBT at the Maudsley Hospital and Honorary Senior Lecturer at the Institute of Psychiatry. He is actively involved in teaching CBT and researching its application to psycho-oncology. Co-authored publications include *Psychological Therapy for Patients with Cancer* (Heine-mann, 1989) and *Evidence in the Psychological Therapies: A Critical Guide for Practitioners* (Routledge, 2001).

Malcolm Parlett is Visiting Professor of Gestalt Psychotherapy at the University of Derby, a teaching and supervising member (and co-founder) of the Gestalt Psychotherapy and Training Institute, Editor of the *British Gestalt Journal*, and a psychotherapist and organizational consultant in private practice. He is the author of many chapters and papers about Gestalt therapy. He is currently at work on researching 'five human abilities' which he suggests are at the root of necessary human development for adults living in the contemporary era.

David Pilgrim is Head of Adult and Forensic NHS Psychological Services in Preston, Lancashire and Professor of Mental Health in the Department of Sociology, Social Policy and Social Work Studies at the University of Liverpool. His books include *A Sociology of Mental Health and Illness* (Open University Press, 1999), *Mental Health Policy in Britain* (Palgrave, 2001) (both with Anne Rogers) and *Psychotherapy and Society* (Sage, 1997).

David Richards is Senior Lecturer at the University of Manchester's School of Nursing, Midwifery and Health Visiting. He is a mental health nurse and behavioural psychotherapist and is actively involved with the British Association for Behavioural and Cognitive Psychotherapy (BABCP), including having been Scientific Chair and Chair of the organization. He has published widely, focusing on the development of effective treatments for Post-traumatic Stress Disorder and self-help treatments in primary care.

Brian Thorne is Emeritus Professor of Counselling at the University of East Anglia, Norwich where he directs the Centre for Counselling Studies. He is also a Founder Member and Professional Fellow of the Norwich Centre. His books include *Person-Centred Therapy Today*, co-authored with Dave Mearns (Sage, 2000), *The Mystical Power of Person-Centred Therapy* (Whurr, 2002) and *Carl Rogers* (Sage, 1992). His current major interest is the relationship between therapy and both Western and Eastern spiritual traditions.

Keith Tudor is a qualified social worker and psychotherapist, and is UKCP registered both as a humanistic psychotherapist and as a group psychotherapist and facilitator. He is an experienced therapist, supervisor and trainer and a Director of Temenos in Sheffield. He is the author of over 50 papers and four books including an edited book on *Transactional Analysis Approaches to Brief Therapy* (Sage, 2001) and is the series editor of *Advancing Theory in Therapy* (Routledge).

Jenny Warner is a manager of children's speech and language therapy in the National Health Service. She has a psychology degree and is a practicing Adlerian counsellor and supervisor and an International Adlerian Trainer. She has written chapters in S. Palmer (ed.), *Introduction to Counselling and Psychotherapy* (Sage, 2000) and C. Feltham and I. Norton (eds), *Handbook of Counselling and Psychotherapy* (Sage, 2000).

1 The Cultural Context of British Psychotherapy

David Pilgrim

In order to understand psychotherapy in its British cultural context, this chapter will use an analytical framework drawn from social science (Mohan, 1996; Pilgrim and Rogers, 1999a). In this framework any phenomenon or topic can be examined at three levels of understanding. At the macro level there are elements which are global and transhistorical. These might include, in relation to psychotherapy, the transhistorical tension between somatic and conversational responses to madness and distress or the convergence of therapeutic forms of work across the world in mental health systems. At the meso level are cultural and national phenomena. At the micro level are the fine details of small groups and individual interactions, in particular local contexts. These might include the workings of psychological therapy services *in situ* or the personal context of psychotherapy in practice.

For reasons of space, not all three levels will be addressed. Given the title of this book, the meso factors will be my main concern. I have attempted a larger analysis of psychotherapy looking at all three levels elsewhere (Pilgrim, 1997). Also, some, but not much, will be said about the content of therapies (which is covered in the remaining chapters later). Instead my focus will be on the cultural history of psychological therapies in Britain. I am aware that the view set out below might be attacked for focusing on great figures. However, my stance and intentions are not personalistic. Instead I think that major figures articulate, champion and reinforce wider cultural forces. Consequently their products require analysis not as elite curios but as representative or dominant features of cultural phenomena. It will be clear that most of the discussion of named individuals is in relation to their work as part of a group co-producing a current of knowledge, reflecting and feeding back into British culture.

Three historical phases

For convenience, in order to break up what could be a continuous narrative, I have divided the discussion below into three historical phases. This does not imply that neat divisions exist between the periods and some reference to connecting events to and fro in time will be noted occasionally.

From 1920 to 1970: the twin towers of psychoanalysis and behaviourism

Currently, ordinary British people probably associate psychiatry, not just psycho-therapy, with psychoanalysis. Media stereotypes (from the Hollywood film indus-try to Radio 4's *In the Psychiatrist's Chair*) have sustained this image for the past half century. In fact, within British psychiatry, psychoanalysis has never had the strong organizational power base it developed in the USA. Despite our mislead-ing Americanized stereotype, a peculiar feature of Britain is that it has hosted some of the most important international 20th-century debates about psycho-analysis. These have had a major and a minor peak. The latter was evident between 1960 and 1975, when the British variant of 'anti-psychiatry' had, at its centre, the Scottish psychoanalyst Ronald Laing. He went from producing a near-orthodox extension of the work of Winnicott (Laing, 1960), to an anarchistic exploration of phenomenology, existentialism, Eastern mysticism and regressed perinatal experience. As a consequence, he soon fell over the humanistic edge of what psychoanalysis could accommodate (Pilgrim, 1997; Crossley, 1998). An international audience interested in the field of psychotherapy tracked this journey, probably with a mixture of delight and exasperation.

The major peak of hosted debate did not involve native British analysts but was linked overwhelmingly with the factional dispute between Melanie Klein and Anna Freud. Not only were the two protagonists émigrés but most psychoanalysts fleeing to London in the 1930s supported one or other of the women (the Austrians predominantly aligning themselves with Freud and the Germans with Klein) (Peters, 1996). This dispute between one part of the Jewish intellectual diaspora and another rumbled on until well after the war, with the eventual compromise of the British Institute of Psychoanalysis containing a Freudian group, a Kleinian group and a 'middle group'.

Freud's ideas were beginning to impact upon the medical and cultural life of most European countries before the First World War. The initial medical response in Britain was fairly hostile. The first British disciples of Freud were given a difficult time by their medical colleagues. At the turn of the century, Ernest Jones expected that British psychiatry, preoccupied with biological explanations and the institutional care of lunatics, would react badly to psychoanalysis. Until the outbreak of war he was absolutely right (Jones, 1913). When another Freudian, David Eder, had addressed the Neurological Section of the BMA in 1911, the small meeting of ten, including the chairman, stood up and left *en masse* in protest (Hobman, 1945). Indeed, had the 'Great War' never occurred, psycho-analysis might well have fizzled out in Britain.

Leading medical figures before the war were vehemently hostile to psycho-analysis (notably Mercier, Hughlings Jackson, Crichton-Browne, Albutt, Bolton and Armstrong-Jones). Even those medical men who were more psychological than biological in their approach (such as McDougall, Rivers and Crichton-Miller) were cautious about Freudian ideas, preferring to proceed pragmatically towards their therapeutic goals, mixing empathy, challenge and persuasion in with interpretation. None the less, the 'Great War' provided the political context in which some version of talking treatment became a practical necessity.

The therapeutic experiments in those days with shell-shocked soldier-patients at Maghull (now part of Ashworth Hospital) and Craiglockhart (explored in Pat Barker's *Regeneration* trilogy) established psychotherapy as a mainstream part of the mental health industry and it was to have a particular impact on psychiatric knowledge. The degeneracy theory of the Victorian period, linked explicitly to the eugenics movement, had to give way to more environmentalist explanations. 'England's finest blood' – commissioned officers and volunteers – were breaking down with embarrassing regularity in the war-strained trenches. The rate of breakdown in officers was higher than in lower ranks. Consequently, the strong eugenic line of Victorian psychiatry also fractured, as it was tantamount to treason (Stone, 1985). Shell-shock demonstrated that ordinary level-headed people with no apparent history of psychological vulnerability could be wrecked by a short traumatic period in their adult lives.

Although the notable organizational developments in talking treatments in the 20th century, such as the Tavistock Clinic and the Cassell and Henderson Hospitals, were psychodynamic in their orientation, psychoanalysis was only part of the picture. There were eclectic influences in play from early days. For example, when Hugh Crichton-Miller and his close supporters set up the Tavistock Clinic (then at 51 Tavistock Square) in 1920 there was immediate internal opposition to it becoming purely Freudian in orientation. Although the Tavistock eventually became dominated by psychoanalytical ideas, this was by no means the case at the outset (Dicks, 1970). The early Tavistock model put forward by Crichton-Miller coincided with an integrationist approach being developed by Meyer in the USA, during the 1920s, which was later to reinforce British eclecticism (see p. 7 below).

Thus, from its inception in Britain, psychoanalysis was accepted only partially. It has been either scorned or eclectically tolerated. It has survived in purer forms only in protected ghettos – specific identifiable institutions (such as the Tavistock Clinic) and localities (especially Hampstead) in the metropolis. Its dispersal elsewhere in Britain has been uneven and often linked to product champions leaving London (for example bound for Newcastle, Leeds or Edinburgh). This concentration means that there is a higher prevalence of private practitioners, as well as NHS workers in London than in regional Britain.

Although psychodynamic ideas have physically been dispersed unevenly in Britain, medical psychotherapy, where it has existed in the NHS, has been predominantly psychodynamic in its orientation. It is not only the institutional legacy in the Tavistock, the Cassell and the Henderson (now with branch offices in Birmingham and Crewe) which supports this claim but the network of NHS facilities of smaller outpatient psychotherapy departments. This network mainly contains medical psychotherapists and colleagues in social work, nursing and clinical psychology who tend broadly to share a psychodynamic orientation. Within British psychiatry medical psychotherapy is a minor specialty and the influence of psychoanalysis in the profession as a whole has been episodic. During wartime it has come to the fore. The First World War was a watershed, with a shift from events like the BMA walkout in 1911 to the flowering of the British Psychoanalytical Society, the Medical Section of the British Psychological Society and the Tavistock Clinic after 1919.

However, from the outset, the opponents of psychoanalysis could evoke a cautious native cultural impulse, which was fed by a mixture of emotional reserve and anti-intellectualism. As Porter (1996) notes, British middle-class values were driven by 'emotional reticence and the stiff upper lip'. Not only did these values discourage lay contact with psychiatry in general, but most psychiatrists themselves echoed doubts about the self-indulgence encouraged by their psychologically orientated medical colleagues. For example, Armstrong-Jones (1921) in a paper to the Medico-Psychological Association argued that psychoanalysis was arguably 'relevant to life in an Austrian or German frontier but not relevant to ordinary English life'. Similarly Crichton-Browne (cited in Turner, 1996) claimed that 'Freud resembled Socrates as much as a toadstool does a British Oak'. Turner (1996) discussing these two psychiatrists, along with other 'anti-psychoanalysts' of the time, notes that ethnocentricity was palpable in their commentary on Freud and his followers, although the extent to which anti-Semitism played a part is difficult to discern.

Hostility to psychoanalysis was not limited to medical patriarchs. For example, it characterized splits within the metropolitan avant-garde after the First World War. As Porter (1996) points out, in the Bloomsbury circle on one side were James and Alix Strachey who became analysts, as did Virginia Woolf's brother Adrian and his wife Karen. On the other side were G.E. Moore with his ultra-rational introspectionism, Roger Fry, Clive Bell and Virginia Woolf. The latter expressed her ardent contempt for those who 'dabble their fingers disapprovingly in the stuff of other's souls' (cited in Wootton, 1958). Thus the problems facing psychoanalysis were not only in relation to the little England (or Scottish) mentality of psychiatric patriarchs and an anti-intellectualism more prominent in common British culture than on the continent. From all sections of British society psychoanalysis was met with a good dose of distrust.

By the 1930s, psychoanalysis had been accommodated rather than embraced. The division in the Bloomsbury circle reflected a tension remaining today in Britain between its native philosophical traditions of rationalism and empiricism, and a temptation to incorporate and toy with exotic foreign products. Between the wars there was a friendly incorporation of German psychiatric thought, reinforced after 1945 by Eliot Slater after a research period in Munich. His style of research was informed by the work of the psychiatric geneticist Rudin, who was found guilty at the Nuremberg Tribunals at the end of the war. The pre-First World War campaign against psychoanalysis with its strong anti-German feel was not being reflected in relation to non-psychodynamic viewpoints – a point I will return to in conclusion. After 1945, many of the staff and ideas in emerging centres of excellence like the Institute of Psychiatry and its linked hospital the Maudsley were German or Austrian émigrés or, like Slater, were importing German ideas. The design and early clinical philosophy of the Maudsley had, from its inception in 1907, been shaped by a German model imported by Mott.

Despite the cultural ambivalence about psychoanalysis between the wars, as the Second World War approached, the psychoanalyst and director of the Tavistock Clinic, J.R. Rees, was appointed as head of the army psychiatric services and other analysts, notably Rickman, Bion, Bridger, Fuchs (Anglicized now as Foulkes) and Main, worked with military casualties, in Sheffield and Northfield. But during postwar periods British psychiatry has tended to return to business as usual, with its focus on the biological treatment of psychosis. Even social psychiatrists, who were less reductionist and more sensitive to environmental determinants, were hostile to psychoanalysis.

One of the main influences on British therapeutic community work came from someone who was less psychodynamic in his orientation. Maxwell Jones had worked separately from the Northfield experiments (at Belmont) within a social learning framework. He had had an incomplete period of analysis with Melanie Klein (never qualifying as a psychoanalyst) and his own model, more sociological than psychological, was more acceptable to anti-psychoanalytical elements in the profession of psychiatry, such as his mentor Aubrey Lewis. The latter was of the view that 'the claims of psycho-analysis to explain all human behaviour diverted attention from the social causes and effects of mental abnormality' (cited in Shepherd, 1980). Also, with the coming the NHS after 1948, the private practice model of therapy several times a week was always going to be at odds with pressures of equity of access to scarce outpatient facilities 'free at the time of need'.

By 1950, clinical psychoanalysis was being squeezed from at least four directions within the British mental health industry:

1   There was the resentful and dominant biological orthodoxy within psychiatry, whose authority psychotherapists had usurped during wartime and its immediate aftermath.
2   There was the emergence of social psychiatry attempting to operate within a traditional public health model of environmental factors causing or affecting illness outcomes. In 1948 a Medical Research Council unit in social psychiatry was funded at the Institute of Psychiatry. This was to be shaped by personnel and ideas which were at odds with a psychodynamic viewpoint.
3   The cash nexus, so important for analysts (for their living and its symbolic potential for interpretive work), was absent from work in the NHS.
4   There was the emergence of behaviour therapy. The NHS brought with it an opportunity for behavioural rather than psychodynamic psychotherapy to flourish. Unlike psychoanalytical therapy, behaviour therapy had no historical baggage, which fetishized the fee. It did not demand intense, lengthy (especially 'interminable') therapy and it could claim scientific credentials, which fitted well with British empiricism.

Whereas psychoanalysis originated on the continent and transferred with prestigious protagonists, behaviourism had had an immediate history in the USA and Russia. Prior to that it could claim two substantial British origins. The first was associationism within British philosophy, traceable to Locke, James Mill and others. Most importantly, Hartley was the philosophical bridge to the second area of British work, physiology. Not only was Hartley committed to the associationist view but he developed a theory which conceptually grounded mental events in neurophysiology. Physiological experiments with reflexes were conducted by

Whytt in Scotland in the mid-18th century and by Laycock an English physician a hundred years later.

In 1845 Laycock demonstrated a conditioned reflex nearly 20 years before his idea was elaborated by Sechenov in Russia (Hearnshaw, 1987). Sechenov's work was further developed by Bechterev and Pavlov before returning to British shores in the mid-20th century. Pavlov had lectured at Charing Cross Hospital in London in 1906 but his works were not available in English until the late 1920s. After that, his form of psychology was extended in the USA by Hull, a strand of behaviourism to be favoured in Britain later. However, by 1930 there was little sign of behaviourism having any impact in Britain or continental Europe, whereas in the USA it was already in the ascendant, having been championed persuasively by Watson.

Britain was not the single source of behaviourism, as precursor experiments with conditioning also occurred within French physiology in the early 19th century, with the work of Condillac and Cabanis (Flugel, 1933). However, the strong traditions of philosophical associationism and empirical physiology provided a scientific tradition within Britain, which was certainly at odds with the more speculative and hermeneutic character of depth psychology. In part this tradition may account for why a cognitive-behavioural approach currently dominates British clinical psychology as a safe native scientific orthodoxy (compared to other therapeutic orientations). There had been a minor early 19th-century theme within Scottish philosophy, in the works of Stewart, Brown and Hamilton, which prefigured the work of later depth psychologists (Ellenberger, 1970), but this did not translate into an early British prototype of psychoanalysis.

As Anderson (1969) noted about British culture, during the 20th century intellectual life was dominated by pragmatism and empiricism, with native thinkers eschewing attempts at theory building. Anderson traces the ways in which, across a variety of academic disciplines, theoretical renewals were generated by émigrés. Thus the immigrants in the Institutes of Psychoanalysis and Psychiatry north and south of the Thames were typical of a wider phenomenon in British culture. After the Second World War imported white-collar labourers revitalized the British academic system just as their blue-collar equivalents began to staff the transport system.

If psychoanalysis had had its major cultural moment after the First World War, the same could be said of behaviour therapy after 1945. Ironically the increasing focus upon neurosis arising from the shell-shock problem and the psychoanalytical work around it had produced a new terrain for psychological experts, such as the new behaviourists, to inhabit. In the Victorian period, mental abnormality basically meant 'lunacy'. By 1950 all this had changed. Now neurosis had been drawn into the psychiatric ambit, even if it was to be dubbed 'minor mental illness'. With the shell-shock problem, the eugenic orientation of 19th-century European and North American psychiatry had had to give way to a new eclecticism, which recognized the environmental antecedents of psychological abnormality.

Eventually a progressive orthodoxy of a 'biopsychosocial' model began to define this eclecticism in Britain (Clare, 1977; Goldberg and Huxley, 1980).

Crichton-Miller began this trend in Britain, but it was theoretically elaborated by the Swiss-born, but US-based, psychiatrist Adolf Meyer. His 'psychobiological' model emphasized that mental illness could be derived from several factors and was always experienced in a particular personal and social context (Meyer, 1952). His approach was championed by two particular British psychiatric leaders who had been his visiting students in America: Henderson, a Scot, and Lewis, an Australian immigrant to England. Henderson incorporated the Meyerian model in his writings and teaching of psychiatric trainees in Glasgow before the Second World War. Meyer stressed that clinicians and basic researchers in the biological and social sciences should form a creative partnership. It was this notion that found British substance when Aubrey Lewis became the founding Medical Director of the Institute of Psychiatry after the Second World War. One department in the new set-up was psychology, headed up by Hans Eysenck.

When a one-year training course was established for clinical psychologists at the Institute of Psychiatry at its inception in 1947, Eysenck was hostile to the idea of psychologists taking a therapeutic interest. He considered this to be incompatible with a disinterested scientific approach. He disapproved of therapeutic activity in his writings around 1950, suggesting that only psychometric and experimental approaches were to be used in the clinic. This view of the role of psychologists was also taken by Lewis, a political factor which may have influenced Eysenck. Such a rigid scientistic approach was strategically flawed. It would have left psychologists in a strictly limited handmaiden role to psychiatry. Moreover, it gave undue weight to one version of scientific psychology (differential psychology) to the exclusion of another (learning theory).

Eysenck saw few, if any, patients, and it was left to other Institute colleagues in the Clinical Section of the Department of Psychology to apply behaviourism to the problem of neurosis. Wolpe's South African work on reciprocal inhibition (Wolpe, 1958) was particularly influential in this group (Meyer, 1957; Yates, 1970). At the centre of the group was Monte Shapiro, the relatively unsung early leader of British clinical psychology. Eysenck's public posturing about an embryonic profession he related to only as a researcher, not as a clinician, gives a misleading impression of his political importance (Pilgrim and Treacher, 1992; Payne, 2000).

Within a short period it was evident that Eysenck's anti-therapy line was unsustainable and that his preference for 'disinterested' distance was being eclipsed by therapeutic concerns. He changed his mind and in a seminal paper given at the Royal Medico-Psychological Association in 1958, with Gwynne Jones, he argued that the therapeutic jurisdiction over neurosis should now be given over to psychologists (Eysenck, 1958). This was to set the scene for a formal phase of behaviour therapy in the young profession of clinical psychology until the 1970s, when it became more pluralistic (Pilgrim and Treacher, 1992). The offence it caused to Lewis and other psychiatrists was also to ensure a period of prolonged acrimony between psychologists and their medical colleagues.

Although two other courses other than that at the Institute of Psychiatry initiated the profession of British clinical psychology in the 1950s (at the Tavistock Clinic and Crichton Royal Hospital at Dumfries) only the first survived.

Not only did it survive but it came to dominate the profession, with most of the new courses throughout the UK being headed by its graduates up until the 1980s. Thus the psychodynamic view from the Tavistock and the psychometric one from Crichton Royal faded in salience in the norms of the profession of clinical psychology. For many years, clinical psychology and behaviour therapy became synonymous, even though clinical psychologists were not typically trained to the same level of competence as, for example, some nurse therapists under the direction of psychiatrists like Marks at the Institute of Psychiatry and Gelder at Oxford (Liddell, 1977).

Third force psychology, pluralism and eclecticism after 1970

Broadly, if the period between 1920 and 1950 established psychodynamic psychotherapy and that between 1950 and 1970 established behaviour therapy a new, more eclectic, phase in the mental health industry was emerging (internationally, not just in Britain). A number of factors accounted for this shift:

1 As was noted earlier, eclecticism was not new to British psychotherapy but could be found in the early days of the Tavistock Clinic.
2 Within academic psychiatry the biopsychosocial model was gaining increasing legitimacy. However, the academic advocates of this model did not ensure a change in the norms of their clinical colleagues. Clinical psychiatry was dominated by biological treatments and medical psychotherapy was reduced to a 'specialty' after the Royal Medico-Psychological Society became the Royal College of Psychiatrists in 1971.
3 The ultra-rationalism of behaviour therapy looked decidedly grey and conservative to many psychologists exposed to 'anti-psychiatric' ideas from the late 1960s onwards. This undermined the loyalty of younger clinical psychologists to the narrow project enunciated by Eysenck and Jones in 1958.
4 Whereas the twin towers of psychoanalysis and behaviourism were still attractive to many, Laing and his like-minded colleagues were importing a third current of continental thinking about inner life. This was to chime with the radical chic common to the 'counter-culture' of the period.

The green shoots of a model which drew upon Husserl's phenomenology and Sartre's existentialism were evident in *The Divided Self* (Laing, 1960). Leaving aside the merits or otherwise of these traditions (and whether they can be an amalgam model: one is a methodology, the other a philosophy) a third way was evident between psychoanalysis and behaviourism. This had already been dubbed 'third force psychology' by Maslow across the Atlantic.

The guardians of both psychoanalysis and behaviour therapy, though apparently in different universes of discourse, had one important common feature. Both groups were committed to the maintenance of a professionally dominated view of their world. Their authority rested in their esoteric knowledge – one of a dynamic unconscious, the other of a scientific package containing behavioural experimentation and the paraphernalia of statistics. Both in their own way believed that a known reality (psychopathology or conditioning history) existed in advance of therapy with individuals, which professionals understood with their preferred arcane body of knowledge.

Arguably the psychodynamic approach was more compatible with medical dominance. Analysts 'treat' their 'patients'. Non-medical colleagues in the culture are called 'lay analysts', denoting their suspect status. The unconscious life of individuals is 'psychopathology' and psychoanalysis continues to use the language of diagnosis, not just formulation. Indeed, in some cases, psychoanalysis has actively contributed to the extension of neo-Kraepelinian psychiatric knowledge (for example with the introduction of 'borderline personality' to the American Psychiatric Association's *Diagnostic and Statistical Manual*). To psychoanalysis we are all ill. On the one hand this obliterates the sharp divide between normal and abnormal mental life. On the other hand it makes us all potentially subject to the clinical gaze of a particular brand of therapeutic authority.

As for behaviour therapy – well it was still 'therapy' and its knowledge base emphasized reinforcement histories, stimulus-responses and conditioned reflexes. This authoritative world originated in Pavlov's and Skinner's laboratories and the haughty professional manipulation by Watson of an innocent child's fear. Also, like psychoanalysis, it legitimized psychiatric knowledge by claiming success in treating patients with particular diagnoses identified in *DSM* or International Classification of Diseases – a trend which continues today in works on cognitive-behaviour therapy.

What existentialism and phenomenology brought into therapeutic culture was a different possibility, which might subvert professional authority. Supposing the ultimate expert on madness or distress was not a professional but their client? However, this third position did not discard professional authority, only problematized it. The humanistic therapist may respect unique narratives but they still hold social power in relation to their clients because the relationship is not equal and reciprocal (Bannister, 1983). Ultimately, professional authority would be challenged by those rejecting therapy (e.g. Masson, 1985) not those who wished to humanize it. The humanized version of therapeutic authority was accepted and incorporated into the emerging mental health users' movement, with only a few among its ranks attacking therapy in principle.

During the 1970s, then, a wide range of humanistic styles of psychotherapy were grafted on to one or other of the dominant traditions of psychoanalysis and behaviourism or operated in a free-standing manner. These included personal construct therapy derived from the work of George Kelly, Rogers's client-centred counselling and the influences of the American existentialists May and Maslow. Others could be added, especially those who reacted against or modified psycho-analytical ideas – for example Ellis's rational-emotive therapy, the Gestalt therapy of Perls and, later, Ryle's cognitive-analytic therapy. These shifted the psycho-therapeutic discourse away from the forms of psychological determinism offered by behaviourism and psychoanalysis and towards an emphasis on client choice and responsibility.

After 1980: the return of professional authority and its postmodern critics

The countercultural period did not bring down the mental health industry. Psychiatry was reformed, not abolished. Biological psychiatry once more bounced back, driven by drug company research and its internal preoccupation with the somatic (especially genetic) basis for a medical mandate in clinical services. A 'decade of the brain' was announced triumphantly (Guze, 1989) after psychiatry's critics had been denounced by leading social psychiatrists (Wing, 1978). The subculture of psychotherapy contained by this reaction to 'anti-psychiatry' kept within its house factions of behaviourists, psychoanalysts and humanists. New hybrids which sprang up were met with tolerance, if not always with enthusiasm.

The enlargement of behaviour therapy to become cognitive-behaviour therapy was a compromise driven by pragmatism in the clinic, reinforced by the advantages of professional authority. Behaviour therapy had not delivered its promise by its own scientific criteria; Yates (1970) noted that only a minority of problems in the psychiatric clinic could be successfully treated using pure behavioural methods. Meichenbaum (1977) joined a throng of pragmatic clinicians including Beck and Lazarus who began to combine cognitive reappraisal with behavioural experimentation. This approach began to snowball during the 1970s into an apparently contradictory *rapprochement* between the declining hegemony of behaviourism and the emerging orthodoxy of cognitivism.

The early concerns of clinicians like Lazarus and Beck did not catch up with genuine cognitive psychology in the academy for a good few years, but eventually what was happening in therapy could be understood increasingly within a framework of cognitive science (e.g. Williams et al., 1988). Cognitive-behaviour therapy (CBT) marks a return to the tradition of British associationism of Locke, Mill and Hartley. As with those philosophers, it combines action with reflection and, for scientific and practical completeness, it is obliged to study feelings and thoughts as well as behaviour. Also, in the light of the challenge from humanistic anti-psychiatry about unique inner lives, subjectivity can be accommodated without scientific authority being lost or professional authority being compromised.

However, the theoretical disputes, notable between 1920 and 1970 but resolved for an interlude by eclecticism, were giving way to a different set of professional dynamics. What if psychological treatments in principle had to be justified? What if 'talking treatments' had lost the confidence of the state? This was precisely the scenario which was emerging during the 1970s after the Scientologists with their brand of psychotherapy (dianetics) had attempted to infiltrate and take over MIND (then the National Association of Mental Health). The official investigation into Scientology, the Foster Inquiry of 1973, was followed in 1978 by the Seighart Inquiry into the registration of psychotherapists. This new-found interest by the British state in psychotherapy in one sense was threatening but it also created a political opportunity for therapists to enhance their social standing and define the criteria by which they could legitimately corner the market in helpful conversations.

The first rumblings of rhetorics of professional justification for helpful conversations ('counselling', 'psychotherapy',' psychological therapy' and, latterly, 'counselling psychology' – take your pick), were started by Foster and Seighart during the 1970s. By 1980 psychotherapy in Britain was in a contradictory political space. It had been linked to a major leftist social movement ('anti-psychiatry'). At the same time, its energetic professional codification was turning it into a set of self-aggrandizing professional elites, with factions attempting to justify their theoretical and practical pre-eminence. This highly conservative tendency culminated in squabbles between and within bodies like the UKCP and the BCP, which were claiming a particular respectability for their own form of registration.

The professions based on core disciplines (medicine and psychology) aloofly considered that their own training negated the need for specialist registration. They just carried on protecting their traditional boundaries, functions and legitimacy. For example, at the time when psychotherapy registration was being mooted after the Seighart Report, clinical psychologists began a campaign inside the British Psychological Society for the registration of psychologists. In a more recent example, parliamentary proposals to set up a register of psychotherapists (the Elton Bill) have been met with generous approval by the Royal College of Psychiatrists because medical practitioners need not be registered.

Apart from these guild features of the professionalization debate, there are also logical problems about the nature of talking treatments. Psychotherapy is impossible to define in a succinct way because there are so many ways of conducting helpful conversations that the range of theorizations or the empirical investigations which support them become vast and often incommensurable. These different approaches vary in their emphasis in relation to inner life versus outward behaviour; the relationship between cognition, affect and behaviour; and their rootedness in a variety of medical, psychological or spiritual discourses. Today I can open my copy of the *Psychologist* and see advertisements for courses on CBT alongside those for 'Soul Therapy'. Making a connection between the two demands both intellectual tolerance and ingenuity.

Even within mainstream disciplines, like clinical psychology, practitioners cannot agree upon one style of therapy. CBT may predominate (for now) but many in the profession practise in a psychodynamic way or utilize postmodern approaches, such as solution-focused therapy or narrative therapy. Many just pick and mix. The pluralism and eclecticism established in the 1970s prefigured a longer-term trajectory of diversity. Indeed, one explanation of our current state of variegated confusion is that, like the rest of its social context, psychotherapy has irrevocably entered a postmodern space.

This current scenario is a jumble of coexisting types of therapy, coexisting disciplines and coexisting professionalization processes (of psychology, psychotherapy and counselling). In the latter regard, credentialism burgeons, an obsession with registration continues and relatively simple communicable models (for example person-centred counselling, cognitive-behaviour therapy or cognitive-analytical therapy) have become elaborate hierarchies of graded exclusive competence, defined by longer and longer training periods. This pattern can be added to the older psychoanalytical trajectory of 'more equals better' (in terms of the number and frequency of analytical sessions). A mathematical assumption operates in professionalization that moral worth and technical competence are correlated with the density and length of training. Whilst this makes intuitive sense, the empirical evidence to support it is weak.

At the same time, in relation to professional power, 'the cat is out of the bag and amongst the pigeons' (a view attributed to a leading psychiatric survivor, Peter Campbell). Consider Umberto Eco's epigram at the start of his *Foucault's Pendulum*: 'I have always thought that doubting was a scientific duty, but now I came to distrust the very master who had taught me to doubt'. Those seeking social closure, and with it an enlarged status and legitimacy for psychotherapy, no longer enjoy a world in which professionals expected, and tended to get, automatic respect and credibility from the laity. Instead, we are living in a time when professional authority is being questioned or even opposed. If we still use experts, we do so more cynically or cautiously than generations before us.

As far as mental health interventions are concerned, it is true that biological treatments have received the bulk of the anti-professional flak from the service users' movement but talking treatments have lost the romantic aura that surrounded them in the 1970s (Pilgrim and Rogers, 1999b). One section of the users' movement in Britain has targeted errant psychological therapists. Moreover, some therapists now set themselves against the shibboleth of professional registration, suggest alternatives to therapy or even argue for its abolition. Thus psychotherapy has changed its cultural position in the mental health industry: it is no longer the cowboy with the white hat but now plays a more dubious role. Twenty years ago it was seen by its advocates as a liberating alternative to the dehumanization of biological psychiatry. Now it faces similar hostility from its disaffected users and practitioners.

The professionalization debate has highlighted this state of precarious credibility. Why should potential clients trust psychological therapy services (private or public) given the following?

1 Professionals cannot always agree on what they are doing. Theoretical disputes still abound and good practice is defined and regulated by distant professional bodies, which advocate vastly different types of intervention. Client-defined outcomes, or ones regulated by local employers, are less salient or powerful in the therapy trade than the rules governed by these model-based or guild-based interests.

2 The evidence for the effectiveness of psychotherapy remains contested. At best it can claim to be effective on average compared to 'no treatment' but, within this overall picture, client outcomes include deterioration and stasis. Therapy can make some people with mental health problems more, not less, miserable ('deterioration effects').

3 One cause of deterioration effects is the existence of abusive and incompetent therapists. The physical condition of privacy (particularly in individual therapy) means that incompetence and abuse occur on a regular basis with no corrective feedback until a complaint is made.

4 Professional responses to this evidence of the iatrogenic damage caused by therapy have been opportunistic and cynical – professionals have simply suggested more guild credentialism, even though most abusive therapists are already highly trained, experienced and governed by a code of practice.

5 Professional bodies have been overly lenient to unethical practitioners, tending to favour temporary suspension and rehabilitation over expulsion. Consequently, professionals have often salvaged the careers of errant colleagues at the expense of justice for their victims and protection of their potential victims. Codes of practice set up the rules for dealing with unethical practice but rule enforcement has been less than robust, leaving complainants frustrated and contemptuous.

This list is deliberately critical, even bleak, but it summarizes the legitimation crisis (Habermas, 1975) facing the therapy industry. I am aware that mitigating points can be listed, about quality control in the public sector and the pursuit of core strategic conditions of change across models (Beutler and Baker, 1998). None the less, as I indicate in the list, the central problem is that client safety and therapeutic efficiency have been driven by a stubborn and unproven faith in credentialism, with the 'more equals better' assumption and other guild preferences for national collective advancement taking precedence over local quality assurance about practitioner competence, evidence-based practice, client feedback and robust disciplinary procedures (Hayes, 1998). Of greatest concern is the poor track record of national professional bodies in dealing with errant practitioners (Pilgrim and Guinan, 1999). The doubts expressed by critics of professionalization could be dispelled readily if those practitioners already under the ostensible regulatory control of respectable professional bodies, with their laudable codes of practice, were being effectively dealt with when malpractice came to light. At present this is not the case.

Conclusion

In light of the above criticisms, the widespread caution in British culture about mental health experts, dating back to the beginning of the 20th century, may have served the population well at times. A different conclusion is drawn by the Dutch sociologist and follower of the therapy trade, Abram de Swaan, when he argues that 'Granted all that is wrong with the helping professions. . .most Europeans and Americans may still be suffering more from a lack of what these have to offer than from an overdose' (de Swaan, 1990). Being part of, and thus too close to, this most recent period, I cannot decide which to favour: Dutch optimism or British caution.

I also do not know if de Swaan thought of the British as being Europeans when he made his point. As we know from our recent political debates, variants of the old *Times* headline 'FOG IN CHANNEL – EUROPE ISOLATED!' still resonate in our culture. The ethnocentrism of the early anti-psychoanalysts has not disappeared. If psychotherapy perennially retains an alien image (whether imported from Vienna, Paris or California) it may still be met, rightly or wrongly, with British suspicion. Maybe because of this traditional native distrust, once British associationism had set a number of hares running in the USA and Russia, most of the therapeutic currents discussed in this book were going to be elaborated predominantly by foreign labour, at home or abroad.

My final point concedes a contradiction about British culture: it is inconsistently xenophobic. The ethnocentric hostility to psychoanalysis was followed by an unopposed insinuation of other continental ideas into British psychiatry (for example in relation to the strong genetic research programme brought here just after the Nazi period). Britain has not been totally immune to foreign influence, which suggests that the episodic sniping at psychoanalysis may have been a particular case. What may have marked out psychoanalysis was that it was so grandly theoretical, offering not only a therapeutic rationale but also the arrogance of a complete conceptual superstructure for human science. The British antipathy to intellectual grandiosity probably meant that the cooler, piecemeal empiricism of genetic psychiatry, social psychiatry and behaviour therapy was more acceptable to mainstream mental health workers. The current scientific orthodoxies inside the Institute of Psychiatry reflect this legacy, as does the relative containment of psychodynamic approaches in north London and in specialist provincial outposts.

References

Anderson, P. (1969) 'Components of the national culture', *New Left Review*, 50, July/August.

Armstrong-Jones, R. (1921) 'Discussion', *Journal of Mental Science*, 67: 107.

Clare, A. (1977) *Psychiatry In Dissent*. London: Tavistock.

Bannister, D. (1983) 'The internal politics of psychotherapy', in D. Pilgrim (ed.), *Psychology and Psychotherapy*. London: Routledge & Kegan Paul.

Beutler, L.E. and Baker, M. (1998) 'The movement towards empirical validation: at what level should we analyze and who are the consumers?' in K.S. Dobson and K.D. Craig (eds), *Empirically Supported Therapies*. London: Sage.

Crossley, N. (1998) 'R.D. Laing and the British anti-psychiatry movement: a socio-historical analysis', *Social Science and Medicine*, 47(7): 877–89.

de Swaan, A. (1990) *The Management of Normality*. London: Routledge.

Dicks, H.V. (1970) *Fifty Years of the Tavistock Clinic*. London: Routledge & Kegan Paul.

Ellenberger, H. (1970) *The Discovery of the Unconscious*. Harmondsworth: Penguin.

Eysenck, H.J. (1958) 'The psychiatric treatment of neurosis'. Paper presented to the Royal Medico-Psychological Society, London.

Flugel, J.G. (1933) *A Hundred Years of Psychology*. London: Duckworth.

Goldberg, D. and Huxley, P. (1980) *Common Mental Disorders*. London: Tavistock.

Guze, S. (1989) 'Biological psychiatry: is there any other kind?' *Psychological Medicine*, 19: 315–23.

Habermas, J. (1975) *Legitimation Crisis*. Boston: Beacon Press.

Hayes, S.C. (1998) 'Scientific practice guidelines in a political, economic and professional context', in K.S. Dobson and K.D. Craig (eds), *Empirically Supported Therapies*. London: Sage.

Hearnshaw, L.S. (1987) *The Shaping of Modern Psychology*. London: Routledge & Kegan Paul.

Hobman, J.B. (1945) *David Eder, Memoirs of a Modern Pioneer*. London: Gollancz.

Jones, E. (1913) *Papers on Psychoanalysis*. London: Ballière Tindall & Cox.

Laing, R.D. (1960) *The Divided Self*. London: Tavistock.

Liddell, A. (1977) 'Clinical psychologists as behaviour therapists', *Bulletin of the British Psychological Society*, 30: 144.

Masson, J. (1985) *Against Therapy*. London: HarperCollins.

Meichenbaum, D. (1977) *Cognitive Behaviour Modification*. New York: Plenum.

Meyer, A. (1952) *The Collected Papers of Adolf Meyer*. Baltimore, MD: Johns Hopkins University Press.

Meyer, V. (1957) 'The treatment of two phobic patients on the basis of learning principles', *Journal of Abnormal and Social Psychology*, 55: 261–6.

Mohan, J. (1996) 'Accounts of the NHS reforms: macro-, meso- and micro-perspectives', *Sociology of Health and Illness*, 18(5): 675–98.

Payne, R.W. (2000) 'The beginnings of the clinical psychology programme at the Maudsley Hospital, 1947 to 1959', *Clinical Psychology Forum*, 145: 17–21.

Peters, U.H. (1996) 'The emigration of German psychiatrists to Britain', in H. Freeman and G.E. Berrios (eds), *150 Years of British Psychiatry: the Aftermath*. London: Athlone.

Pilgrim, D. (1997) *Psychotherapy and Society*. London: Sage.

Pilgrim, D. and Guinan, P. (1999) 'From mitigation to culpability: rethinking the evidence on therapist sexual abuse', *European Journal of Psychotherapy, Counselling and Health*, 4(1): 22–32.

Pilgrim, D. and Rogers, A. (1999a) 'The politics of mental health: a three tier analytical framework', *Politics and Policy*, 27(1): 13–24.

Pilgrim, D. and Rogers, A. (1999b) *A Sociology of Mental Health and Illness*, 2nd edn. Buckingham: Open University Press.

Pilgrim, D. and Treacher, A. (1992) *Clinical Psychology Observed*. London: Routledge.

Porter, R. (1996) 'Two cheers for psychiatry! The social history of mental disorder in twentieth century Britain', in H. Freeman and G.E. Berrios (eds), *150 Years of British Psychiatry: the Aftermath*. London: Athlone.

Shepherd, M. (1980) 'From social medicine to social psychiatry: the achievement of Sir Aubrey Lewis', *Psychological Medicine*, 10: 211–18.

Stone, M. (1985) 'Shellshock and the psychologists', in W. Bynum, R. Porter and M. Shepherd (eds), *The Anatomy of Madness*. London: Tavistock.

Turner, T. (1996) 'James Crichton-Browne and the anti-psychoanalysts', in H. Freeman and G.E. Berrios (eds), *150 Years of British Psychiatry: the Aftermath*. London: Athlone.

Williams, J.M.G., Watts, F., Macleod, C. and Mathews, A. (1988) *Cognitive Psychology and Emotional Disorders*. London: Wiley.

Wing, J. (1978) *Reasoning about Madness*. Oxford: Oxford University Press.

Wolpe, J. (1958) *Psychotherapy by Reciprocal Inhibition*. Stanford: Stanford University Press.

Wootton, B. (1958) *Social Science and Social Pathology*. London: Allen and Unwin.

Yates, A. (1970) *Behaviour Therapy*. New York: Wiley.

2 Psychodynamic Therapy: The Freudian Approach

Alessandra Lemma

Historical context and development in Britain

Historical context

Psychoanalysis may be seen as a set of hypotheses about the nature of human beings which developed out of 19th-century thought. Two basic strands of thinking underpinned the intellectual life of the 19th century. On the one hand there was determinism, which saw human behaviour as externally controlled. On the other hand there was subjectivism, focusing on our inner life, which was considered passionate, irrational and dark. Against this divided intellectual back-drop, psychoanalysis was conceived and went on to create an explanatory system – a deterministic system – of our inner, irrational, emotional life, which subsequently gave birth to a treatment method for psychological problems.

Psychoanalysis was originally the brainchild of Sigmund Freud, a cultured and gifted man and, importantly, a Jew. Freud's origins and cultural background are not without significance for an understanding of the personal, social and political factors motivating and shaping the development of his ideas (Robert, 1977; Roith, 1987). However, Freud failed to make links between his own Jewish origins and his theories even though he was acutely aware of the effect of his Jewish roots on the acclaim of his ideas. Indeed, when his friend and colleague, the Swiss psychiatrist Carl Jung – the only non-Jew then affiliated to the psychoanalytic movement – left Freud's following in 1914, Freud was concerned that psychoanalysis would be considered as no more than a 'Jewish national affair'.

Freud may well have wanted to play down the Jewish connection, but this fact was at the forefront of other people's minds. In the 1930s, with the rise of the Nazis, psychoanalysis was attacked: Freud's writings, together with those of Einstein, H. G. Wells, Thomas Mann and Proust were burned in public bonfires for their 'soul disintegrating exaggeration of the instinctual life' (Ferris, 1997). His position in Vienna became increasingly difficult. On 12 March 1938 German troops moved into Austria. On the 13th the Board of the Psycho-Analytic Society met for the last time. Freud likened their predicament to that of the rabbi Johannan ben Zakkai who fled Jerusalem after the Romans destroyed the temple and began a religious school in his place of refuge. Freud urged them to follow this example. In a strong vote of confidence the Board, before dissolving, agreed that the Society should reconstitute wherever Freud might end up.

Along with many of his colleagues Freud was forced into exile. Some fled to America, others to Palestine, Australia and South America. Others still, including Freud, found a home in Britain. Those analysts who remained in Germany practised but only under strict Nazi requirements. Classical Freudian analysis itself was deemed unacceptable. Along with Darwin, Freud was vilified for subverting the high values of fair-skinned races.

The very real persecution suffered by the psychoanalytic movement in its infancy left a deep scar. From the outset, Freud saw psychoanalysis as a cause to be defended against attack and select analytic institutes which emerged could be seen to be the 'bastions' of this defence (Kirsner, 1990). This had the unfortunate effect of keeping at bay other perspectives and related fields of enquiry, fearing their evaluation, criticism and attack.

The movement's paranoia, however, has not just been a feature of its relation-ship with the outside, non-analytic world. It has also been a striking feature of the quality of the relationships within the psychoanalytic establishment itself amongst its own rival theoretical offspring. The history of psychoanalysis is one of schisms. Indeed, psychoanalysis is an umbrella term covering a number of theoretical schools which, whilst all originating from and honouring some of Freud's original ideas and beliefs, have since evolved very different theories about personality development and different techniques for achieving the goals of psychoanalysis as a treatment for psychological problems.

Development in Britain

The British Psychoanalytic Society was established in 1913 by Ernest Jones. The development of psychoanalysis in Britain is a very good example of the difficulties of living in a pluralistic society (Hamilton, 1996). Since its inception, three distinct groups – the Contemporary Freudians, the Kleinians and the Independents – have had to live together in one society with the unavoidable tensions associated with living in close proximity to neighbours who do not necessarily share your same point of view. To regard oneself as belonging to any one of the three groups usually reflects the training therapist's allegiance, that is, the affiliation of the person with whom the trainee undertakes their training analysis.

For the last 20 years or so the British Freudians have formally referred to their group as the Contemporary Freudians. The new name reflects the advances in thinking that have taken place since Freud's time. The Contemporary Freudians are a rather heterogeneous group of practitioners who have been influenced by both object-relational and developmental perspectives within psychoanalysis, as well as including those who lean more specifically towards contemporary Kleinian thinking. There are also a small number of older British Freudians who were trained by, and remain loyal to, Anna Freud and who would be more appro-priately referred to as 'Classical Freudians'.

It is possible to obtain Freudian psychoanalysis in Britain through the Institute of Psychoanalysis or through other psychoanalytic training organizations. In the NHS, in the main, only once-weekly psychoanalytic psychotherapy is offered.

The three theoretical groups are represented in the various NHS-based psycho-therapy departments in Britain, but rarely within the same department. The Kleinians and Independents are, however, the more dominant in Britain.

Theoretical assumptions

Image of the person

Psychoanalysis, as originally conceived by Freud, reflects back to us a rather unflattering picture: we are beings driven by sexual and aggressive urges, we are envious, rivalrous and we harbour murderous impulses even towards those we consciously say we love. Much as we might like to believe that what we see, experience and know directly accounts for all that is important in life, Freud challenged our preferred belief in conscious thought as the ultimate datum of our experience. Rather, he suggested, we are driven by conflicting thoughts, feelings and wishes that are beyond our conscious awareness, but which none the less affect our behaviour – from behind the scenes as it were.

From the very start, psychoanalysis questioned the trustworthiness of human communication. It teaches us never to trust what appears obvious; it advocates an ironic, sceptical stance towards life and our conscious intentions. This is because, Freud suggested, we are beings capable of self-deception. Our mind appears to be structured in such a way that it allows for a part to be 'in the know' while another part is not 'in the know'. Not only can we be fooled but we can also be pulled in different directions, sometimes even oblivious to who or what may be responsible for this. An experience common to all of us is that of feeling, at least some of the time, conflict within ourselves or with others in our life. The idea of *psychic conflict* is central to psychoanalysis and to its view of human nature. It was one of Freud's great insights that our emotional experiences are dynamic, that is, the outcome of conflicting forces, ideas and wishes.

The topographical model of the mind

Freud proposed two models of the mind to account for the experience of conflict. The first is known as the *topographical model* consisting of three levels of consciousness. The first level, the *conscious*, corresponds to that which we are immediately aware of, whatever we may be concentrating on at any given moment – for instance, reading this chapter. Beneath the conscious level lies the second level, the *pre-conscious*, consisting of whatever we can recall without great difficulty. That is, the pre-conscious acts as a kind of storage bin for all those memories, ideas and sense impressions, that are readily available to us, but to which we are simply not attending all the time. Beneath the pre-conscious lies the *unconscious*.

Freud used the term unconscious in three different senses. First, he used it descriptively to denote that which is not in our consciousness at any given moment but is none the less available to us. This is roughly equivalent to the pre-conscious level and is no longer a controversial notion in contemporary psychology. Cognitive neuroscience has shown that most of the working brain is non-conscious in this sense; for example, memory can be acquired without any conscious awareness, and thinking, decision making and problem solving all involve unconscious aspects (Milner et al., 1998). Even our processing of emotional experience has been shown to occur unconsciously in an automatic way. Moreover, this type of processing has been found to be qualitatively different from conscious processing at the level of the neuro-mechanisms involved (Morris et al., 1998).

Secondly, Freud used the term unconscious in a systemic sense denoting his later understanding of the unconscious not as a gradation of consciousness but as a hypothetical system or structure of the mind. Finally he used it to denote the *dynamic unconscious*, that is, a constant source of motivation that makes things happen. In this sense what is stored in the unconscious is said not only to be inaccessible but also to have ended up in the unconscious because it was repressed. The unconscious contains sexual and aggressive drives, defences, memories and feelings that have been repressed.

The pre-conscious and the conscious systems both obey the usual rules of thinking, namely they are logical, reality tested and linear in time and causality. These rules are typical of what is referred to as *secondary process thinking*. The unconscious system obeys a different set of rules typical of *primary process thinking*. In this part of our mind information is not subjected to any kind of reality testing so that mutually exclusive 'truths' may coexist and contradictions abound. Because of these properties the unconscious mind has been likened in the classical Freudian model to an infantile and primitive part of us.

The structural model of the mind

In 1923 Freud revised the topographical model and replaced it with the *structural model*. This new model conceptualized the human psyche as an interaction of three forces: the *id*, *ego* and *superego*. These could be seen to be three different agencies of our personalities each with its own agenda and set of priorities. They were said to have their own separate origins and their own highly specific role in maintaining what might be regarded as 'normal' personality functioning.

According to Freud each one of us is endowed with a specific amount of *psychic energy*. The latter notion was used by Freud to explain the workings of our mental life and was characteristic of his tendency to draw analogies between psychological and physical events. Freud believed that we invest people, objects or ideas with psychic energy. *Cathexis* refers to the amount of psychic energy which becomes attached to the mental representative of a person or object, for example to the memories, thoughts or fantasies about a person. This investment of psychic energy is an indication of the emotional importance of the person or object to the individual in question.

In the newborn infant psychic energy is bound up entirely in the id, the mass of biological drives with which we are all born. The energy of the id is divided between two types of instincts: the Life and the Death instincts. The *Life instincts* are aimed at survival and self-propagation. Into this category fall our needs for food, warmth and, above all, sex. The energy of the Life instinct, the *libido*, was considered by Freud to be the driving force permeating our entire personalities and propelling us through life. In his earliest formulations Freud spoke as though our basic drive was entirely sexual and all other aims and desires arose by some modification of our sexual drive. Among Freudian therapists nowadays the term libido has lost a great deal of its original sexual connotations and refers essentially to the idea of drive energy; that is, the energy we may invest in our pursuit of particular interests in some topic or activity or in relationship with others.

In opposition to the Life instinct stands the *Death instinct*. Discussions of the Death instinct, including Freud's, tend to be rather vague. It is clear, however, that Freud saw the human organism as instinctively drawn back to a state in which all tension would be dissipated – in short, the state of death. This instinctive attraction towards death gives rise to self-directed aggressive tendencies. However, since self-destruction is opposed and tempered by the life-preserving energy of the libido, our aggression in most instances is redirected outward against the world. Aggressive instincts are a component of what drives behaviour. Our self-preservative instinct relies on a measure of aggression to fulfil its aims. In other words, it is imperative that we do not lose sight of aggression's 'propelling function' (Perelberg, 1999), which is essential to preserve life.

The Death instinct represents Freud's broadest philosophical speculation. Amongst Contemporary Freudians therefore, few still hold on to the notion of a Death instinct and find it much more useful to talk about, and to work with, such concepts as guilt, aggression, anger or conflict with the superego. Indeed the Kleinians have developed the notion further; they talk much more of patients 'turning away from life' or 'seeking a near-death state', which are seen as derivative of the operation of the Death instinct.

The instincts of the id are essentially biological. They are not amenable to reason, logic, reality or morality. They are, in a sense, reckless. They are concerned only with one thing: the reduction of whatever tensions our organism may experience. Our innate tendency to maximize pleasure and minimize pain was referred to by Freud as the *pleasure principle*. While the id knows what it wants and needs, it is in some respects 'blind' – blind to what constitutes safe or ethical ways of getting what it needs since it takes no account of reality. To fulfil this function Freud said that the mind developed a new psychic component, the *ego*, which he believed to emerge at about six months of age. The central function of the ego is to serve as a mediator between the id and reality. In contrast to the id's pleasure principle, the ego operates on what is called the *reality principle*, the foundation of which is a concern with safety.

Freud suggested that as we grow up we take into ourselves ideas and attitudes held by others around us. Parents are said to play an important role in curbing or inhibiting the id's excesses. As children we internalize our parents' standards and values and these come together to form the *superego*. This account of the formation of the superego is an instance of what is called *introjection*. The rules, the abstract moral principles and the ideal image of who we ought to be can be thought of as a person inside us who has strong views and is always ready to criticize if our behaviour is not up to standard. This person inside us is equivalent to our superego. While most of us have some awareness of the moral rules and standards which govern our behaviour the superego is only partly conscious.

The psychosexual stages of development

Freud's belief that our sexual life begins at birth led him to describe what are referred to as the stages of psychosexual development. He argued that we all progress through a series of stages, in each of which our psyche directs its sexual energy towards a different *erogenous zone*, that is, a part of our body which is a source of pleasure. Freud first proposed the *oral* stage (0–1 years) where satisfaction is predominantly derived by the infant via the mouth, for example from sucking the nipple or the thumb. Second, is the *anal* stage (1–3 years), where gratification is derived from gaining control over withholding or eliminating faeces. Everyday observations of toddlers highlight how, as they negotiate their increasing separateness from their parents, they come to view their faeces as their own possessions which they want to hold on to or give up in their own good time. The potential for battles and conflict between parent and child, for instance over toilet training, during this period is great. It is at this stage that defecation is said to symbolize giving and withholding. Metaphorically speaking, conflicts at the anal stage are seen to pose a major dilemma for all children with regard to the need to adapt to, or to resist, parental control.

The third stage (3–5 years), the *phallic* stage, sees the child beginning to be more aware of their genitals, with consequent curiosity and anxiety about sexual differences. The phallic stage is thought to be vital to our psychological development because it is this stage that provides the backdrop to the Oedipal drama. In Greek mythology, Oedipus unknowingly kills his father and marries his mother. Likewise, according to Freud, all children during the phallic stage long to do away with the parent of the same sex and take sexual possession of the parent of the opposite sex. The notion of an Oedipal phase places desire at the core of our psychology.

The resolution of the *Oedipus complex* is believed to be crucial to our development. Freud hypothesized that at the same time as the little boy harbours his incestuous desires towards his mother he also experiences *castration anxiety* – the child's fear that his father will punish him for his forbidden wishes by cutting off the guilty organ, his penis. Lacking penises, girls appear castrated to him and the little boy fears a similar fate. Girls, on the other hand, realizing that they have been born unequipped with penises, experience the female counterpart to castration anxiety, namely *penis envy*. They are said to harbour angry feelings towards the mother for having created them without a penis. While the boy's castration anxiety is what causes him to repress his longing for his mother, the girl's penis envy impels her towards her father, desiring a child by the father – the desire for a child being understood merely as a substitute for her former desire for a penis.

With time both the boy's and the girl's Oedipal desires recede and rather than remaining at war with the same-sex parent who is experienced as a rival, both settle for *identification* with the same-sex parent, incorporating their values, standards and sexual orientation. The resolution of the Oedipus complex was therefore linked by Freud to the development of the superego.

The Oedipal phase brings into relief feelings of rivalry and competitiveness and challenges the child with the negotiation of boundaries. Rivalry which is well managed by the parents can lead to constructive preoccupations in the child with fairness and justice (Raphael-Leff, 1991). From a developmental point of view, the child's recognition of the parents as sexual partners encourages an essential relinquishment of the idea of their sole and permanent possession. It involves awareness of the differences that exist between the relationship parents can enjoy with each other as distinct from that which the child is entitled to enjoy with them.

At its core, psychoanalysis is about the vagaries of our desire, our recalcitrant renunciations and the inevitability of loss. Whichever way you look at it, someone somewhere is always missing something in the psychoanalytic drama. Freud starkly reminded us that we simply cannot have it all our own way. Relinquishment and acceptance are common currency within psychoanalysis. The hard lessons begin at birth. As reality impinges on us, frustration, disappointment, loss and longing make their entry into the chronicles of our existence. The breast – that archetypal symbol of never-ending nourishment and care – eventually dries up. These very experiences, however painful, are those which have been singled out by psychoanalysis as privileged in our development towards adaptation to the so-called real world. Freud stressed the need to develop a capacity to delay gratification, to withstand absence and loss, all of which challenge our omnipotent feelings.

Conceptualization of psychological disturbance and health

Freud popularized *neurosis*. Even though clear demarcations hold a certain appeal, especially when we are dealing with human behaviours which have the potential to threaten our need to believe in a stable and orderly world, Freud challenged such demarcations in the context of mental health. He bluntly stated that we are all, to an extent, neurotic. He believed that it was not possible to distinguish so-called 'normal' from 'neurotic' people. Where there was a difference it was held to be one of degree rather than kind. Neurotic conflict is distinguished from the conflict that Freud postulated as being common to us all not by virtue of its content; rather it is the more accentuated nature of the conflict in the neurotic person which gives rise to considerable suffering.

The notion of a dynamic unconscious is central to an understanding of neurosis because Freud (1917) held that neurosis resulted from an unconscious conflict.

He argued that neurotic symptoms were born of unconscious conflict between the ego and the id and the resulting blocking or imbalance of energy flow. In addition, Freud thought that his neurotic patients were stuck somewhere in the past; their neurosis was understood to belie 'a kind of ignorance' about their emotional life. Because of fears and anxiety, neurotic individuals held on to their past, according to Freud, precluding development and change.

Freud's theory of psychosexual development is also integral to an under-standing of neurosis as he argued that the conflict underlying neurosis has an essentially sexual basis. At first, Freud believed that neurosis resulted from the repression of painful memories which, once recalled, frequently revealed trau-matic sexual experiences in childhood. Thereafter he came to believe that, in many cases at least, no such traumatic seductions had in fact taken place and this led to the development of the *wish theory* which stressed the role played by fantasy and desire. In this latest theory, Freud understood neurosis as resulting from repressed erotic impulses. This theory, however, proved to be something of a dead end. Indeed, in his later work, Freud emphasized far more the role of anxiety in neurosis. The experience of anxiety was seen to act as a warning signal in response to internal pressures (e.g. id wishes) or external pressures (e.g. actual trauma) on the ego. In neurotic conflict, the ego strives to keep the dangerous drive from gaining access to consciousness. This places the ego under consider-able pressure and impoverishes it so that the ego fails to keep up its defensive efforts, thereby allowing the drive's discharge in the disguised form of neurotic symptoms.

In order to protect the ego from the discomfort of anxiety, *defences* are called into place. Symptoms represent therefore *compromise formations* which express in disguised form unacceptable sexual and aggressive impulses, thus allowing us to carry on with our daily lives. Neurotic symptoms could perhaps be said to be creative insofar as they represent attempted solutions to conflicts which help us to restore a measure of psychic equilibrium.

Acquisition of psychological disturbance

Freud was a committed psycho-archaeologist who thought that the excavation of the past was essential to an understanding of ourselves. He found meaning in the seemingly irrational symptoms of his hysterical patients which had puzzled physicians before him. He understood these as resulting from painful memories which had been repressed into the unconscious and were struggling for expres-sion. Put simply, he suggested that we acquire psychological problems through forgetting what troubles us.

A central theme running throughout psychoanalytic theorizing is the impor-tance of our early experiences, from birth onwards, and their impact on the subsequent development of our personalities and consequently on the aetiology of psychological difficulties. What happens to us as children is seen to shape our personality in a very profound way. Indeed, all psychoanalytic theories have at their root the belief that the present can be understood in light of the past. Freud's original model of development and the acquisition of psychopathology was undoubtedly a deterministic one, which suggested that all events were determined by a sequence of causes and that nothing happened by accident. In the psychological realm this means that we can trace causal links between our behaviour in the here and now and our past, early, experiences.

The Contemporary Freudian understanding of how the mind works and how we can develop emotional problems has been greatly enhanced by the work of the late Joseph Sandler and his wife Anne-Marie Sandler (1984, 1997), both Contemporary Freudians. The Sandlers suggest that we all have formative interpersonal experiences which contribute to the development of *dynamic templates* or, if you like, schemata of self–other relationships. These templates are encoded in the *implicit memory system*, which stores non-conscious knowledge of 'how to do things' and relate to others. The Sandlers refer to this as the *past unconscious*. Its contents are not directly accessible in the form of autobiographical memories. The *present unconscious*, on the other hand, refers to our here-and-now unconscious strivings and responses. Although its contents may become conscious, they are still frequently subject to censorship before being allowed entry into consciousness. Our behaviour in the present is said to function according to rules and patterns of relating to the self and others which were set down very early on in our lives. The actual experiences which contributed to these 'rules' or templates are, however, thought to be irretrievable. According to this model, psychological disturbance may result from being locked into patterns of relating – with all the associated emotional states (e.g. depression), thoughts and wishes – which are ultimately limiting to the individual's development and mental health.

Perpetuation of psychological disturbance

Freud was only too well aware of the self-defeating patterns of behaviour that seem to prevent people from resolving their psychological problems. He believed that the persistence of psychological disturbance resulted from a fixation to particular periods in the patient's past as though the patient is really unable to free themselves from it and therefore to engage with the present in a more constructive way.

However distressing a symptom or a given life situation may be, there may yet be some *secondary gain*, a kind of payoff, for the individual which helps to explain the deadlock with regard to change. The forces underlying self-defeating and self-destructive behaviour are frequently so potent that their cost in terms of personal distress does not appear to act as a powerful enough deterrent. For instance, the suffering that symptoms impose may assuage a person's unconscious guilt and their 'need to suffer', as Freud put it, or the disabling nature of symptoms may help the person to side step other situations which are likely to generate conflict. In satisfying such unconscious needs the symptoms become powerfully reinforced.

Not only do some people remain in intolerable situations, and so perpetuate their psychological difficulties, but some actually appear to be compelled to repeat the same maladaptive patterns in their lives, as if they unconsciously search for situations that can bring only unhappiness and that often represent a re-enactment of earlier relationships and dynamics. Freud called this phenomenon the *compulsion to repeat*. While all therapists would agree that this is a commonly observed pattern, there is nevertheless considerable disagreement as to how one can explain it. Freud's own view was that the compulsion to repeat reflected an individual's attempt to master anxiety, relating to an earlier period, that would otherwise be too overwhelming. This was in keeping with his views on the nature of traumatic dreams where, for instance, following an accident the person may repeatedly dream about the accident. Freud understood such repetitive dreams as attempts to master the anxiety retrospectively.

The compulsion to repeat is a fascinating phenomenon as it challenges us with the existence of behaviour whose aim appears to be ostensibly self-destructive, even if it may well represent an unconscious attempt at mastery. The evidence of self-destructive tendencies in people reveals that vast quantities of the aggressive instinct are sometimes directed inwards and Freud therefore saw the compulsion to repeat as a manifestation of the Death instinct. Indeed it was this that led him to concede that there exists in us a compulsion to repeat which overrides the pleasure principle otherwise believed to rule our instinctual life.

Change

Freud's structural model of the mind, as we have seen, suggests that we live life in a perpetual state of intrapsychic conflict generated by the opposing demands of the id, ego and superego. The experience of conflict calls into place defences so as to protect the ego from anxiety. In so doing, however, the status quo is maintained since the individual fails to confront the source of the anxiety and simply invests emotional energy in the upkeep of the defences. If the resulting anxiety is severe enough to disrupt the person's functioning and defences fail, this can precipitate a kind of breakdown which may nevertheless, paradoxically, act as a spur to change. Indeed people often present for psychological help at times of stress either when their defensive strategies have failed them, or when the conflict becomes ego-dystonic, that is, it is not associated with any secondary gain but is experienced as wholly unpleasurable.

The early Freudians espoused a deterministic model of development which focused on what prevented people from changing, for example people's fixation at a given developmental stage, or the unconscious needs met by maintaining the status quo, thus precluding development and change. This model reflected a one-person psychology, that is, the emphasis was exclusively intrapsychic and favoured linear, causal explanations which had the appeal of simplicity. Far less attention was devoted to the much more interesting question of how people manage to change *in spite of* any predisposing factors that increase the likelihood of psychological problems and reduce the likelihood of change.

An overemphasis on the past as a major determining influence denies the inherent complexity of the human condition and the many forces and influences which shape us and produce change. Moreover, a strict deterministic stance is no longer tenable, as modern physics has highlighted the problems of such a position. Events are now no longer regarded as inexorably and absolutely determined: their occurrence is more a matter of high or low probability. Research indeed suggests that it is difficult to be very specific about the longer-term consequences of childhood events (see Lemma, 1995 for a review). This is particularly so since we all vary tremendously and people exposed to the same adverse experiences respond quite differently and show varying degrees of resilience in the face of adversity. To understand change we have to develop more complex models which allow us to take into account the influence of those experiences that can introduce change into an individual's life, such as, for example, the impact of other relationships besides those of early childhood. This has been one of the major contributions of relational, attachment-based models within psychoanalysis which have influenced the Contemporary Freudians. Now-adays, psychoanalysis espouses a two-person psychology reflecting the impor-tance of the attachments we develop throughout life and how these can contribute to revisions and changes to the early models of relationships we develop as a result of our experiences in our families of origin.

Even though we are not entirely determined by our past we can often trace in our own developmental histories some very interesting and meaningful relation-ships between the past and the present so that psychological events cannot be considered just to be haphazard. This notion, central to Freud's thinking, is at the core of the principle of *psychic determinism*: that is, in the mind nothing just happens by chance. Events in our mental life which may at first appear random or unrelated to that which preceded them are only apparently so. The notion of psychic determinism, however, does not imply a simple relationship of cause and effect in our mental life. Rather, it is generally recognized that a single event may be *overdetermined*, the end product of biological, developmental and environ-mental forces – all of which can contribute to psychological change or to arrests in development.

Practice

Goals of therapy

Any discussion on the goals of psychotherapy exposes an inherent problem that cuts across all the schools of psychoanalysis: what psychotherapists state publicly through their theories does not necessarily reflect what they believe implicitly and therefore what they actually do in practice with patients (Sandler and Dreyer, 1996).

At the level of public theories, the stated aims of the early Freudian approach were quite clear: the therapy would bring about a discharge of affect, a *catharsis*, and the role of the therapist was to interpret instinctual wishes and fantasies that had been repressed in the unconscious and the conflict with which they were associated. The overall aim within this context was to bring the latent instinctual wish to consciousness and overcome the resistance to their acceptance.

It is a well-known fact that psychoanalytic psychotherapists shirk from using the concept of cure in their written work. This dread of 'pathological therapeutic zeal' – to use Greenson's (1967) telling phrase – has been inherited from Freud, who was no therapeutic optimist. Moreover, Freud was far less interested in psychoanalysis as a therapeutic system than as a tool for understanding both individual and society. As far as he was concerned, psychoanalysis should be valued for its contributions to a science of human being rather than for any quick results as regards personality change or the alleviation of neurotic symptoms. Freud was indeed rather pessimistic, or one could perhaps more accurately say 'realistic', about the therapeutic benefits of psychoanalysis. In a hypothetical discussion with a patient, he stated that psychoanalysis could help transform 'hysterical misery' into 'common unhappiness'. This may not sound like a very enticing outcome for the majority of people, who harbour hopes of fundamental change and happiness. But Freudian psychoanalysis espouses a very particular philosophy of life, one within which life, as we have seen, is unavoidably lived in conflict. Repression is considered integral to our survival in a social world which confronts us daily with the impracticability of living our life under the sway of the pleasure principle. The aim of psychoanalysis as therapy was not, according to Freud, the reduction of suffering but was centred on the necessity of living with one's limitations and conflicts.

The aims of psychoanalytic treatment have shifted over the years along with the changing conceptualizations of the nature of psychological problems (Steiner, 1989). When Freud at first subscribed to a model of dammed-up libido where problems arose largely as a result of sexual inhibitions, the aim of psychoanalysis was to free the patients from their inhibitions so as to allow for a discharge of the libido. At that stage, the primary aim of treatment was therefore to make the unconscious conscious.

However, along with his later structural formulation of the mind in terms of id, ego and superego, Freud emphasized the need to modify defences, to reduce the pressures from the superego so that the patient could become less frightened of the superego and to strengthen the ego: 'where id was there shall ego be', as Freud put it. He believed that the therapist and the patient's weakened ego needed to become allies against the instinctual demands of the id and the conscientious demands of the superego (Freud, 1938). Within this model, psychological problems were thus understood to result from conflict. Those therapists who still subscribe to this model aim primarily to extend, through the psychoanalytic process, the patient's knowledge of themselves, in the hope that with such knowledge – their insight – they may be able to make choices which are not exclusively ruled by neurotic needs so that new compromises and more adaptive solutions can be explored.

The aims of Contemporary Freudians reflect some of these early thoughts insofar as improvement of reality testing and the acquisition of insight are still considered important aims. Most Contemporary Freudians have, however, incorporated ideas arising from both the Kleinian and Independent traditions which have elaborated treatment aims. This trend is perhaps best reflected in the work of Joseph and Anne-Marie Sandler (1997) who view the aim of psychoanalysis as that of helping the patient achieve psychic reintegration by reclaiming parts of the self which have been split off and projected into others because they could not be otherwise managed.

Notwithstanding the integration of various strands of analytic thinking, the broad therapeutic aims reflect something of Freud's original humbleness insofar as Freudian therapists recognize that psychic conflict cannot be completely eradicated, in the same way that the transference cannot be completely resolved. Insight is aimed for but it is no longer viewed as a strict requirement, just as retrieval of repressed childhood memories is no longer the main goal. Instead, the emphasis is on bringing about intrapsychic changes which could result in an improved resolution of conflicts and hopefully expand the individual's capacity for self-reflection.

Selection criteria

In Freud's time, the selection criteria for psychoanalysis were pretty straightforward: being a classical analyst meant accepting the view that psychoanalysis was only appropriate for those patients who suffered from neuroses, whose psychopathology was rooted in the Oedipal phase and who could reveal their infantile neurosis in the transference through the so-called *transference neurosis*. Although there still exists a minority of therapists aligning themselves with Freud's original views on the matter, the vast majority of Contemporary Freudians would feel somewhat restricted by this stance. Since the 1970s, cases of patients diagnosed as psychotic or personality disordered have been treated more frequently by psychoanalytic psychotherapists of all persuasions. However, perhaps it is amongst the Freudians that one is likely to find more diverse views on this matter.

Broadly speaking, the more contemporary Freudian approach shares selection criteria with the other schools of psychoanalysis. When assessing a patient with a view to psychoanalytic treatment, the assessor is likely to take into account the following:

- the patient's ability to get actively involved with the therapeutic process;
- the patient's interest in and capacity for self-reflection, however rudimentary;
- whether the patient has sufficient ego strength to withstand the inherent frustrations of the therapeutic relationship and to undertake self-exploration;
- whether the patient can tolerate frustration and anxiety and other strong affects without threats to the self (e.g. suicide), to others (e.g. violence) or to the therapy (e.g. forms of acting out);
- evidence of at least one positive relationship;
- the availability of other support systems in the patient's life.

In the NHS psychoanalytic psychotherapy is a very scarce resource, weighed down by long waiting lists. It is usually offered to those who present with moderate to severe difficulties which have taken a chronic course. Generally speaking, such an approach seems most indicated when the patient presents with

problems of a characterological nature or where there are interpersonal difficulties. Nowadays, the patient's formal diagnosis, for example whether they suffer
from borderline personality disorder or manic depression, is considered less
relevant than whether the patient shows some capacity for engaging with the
therapeutic process.

The drive towards evidence-based practice has encouraged many practitioners
to use research as a guideline for which treatment works best for a given
diagnostic group (Roth and Fonagy, 1996). Although this type of guidance is
immensely helpful and should be considered when formulating patients' problems
and deciding on treatment interventions, there is also recognition, especially
among psychoanalytic practitioners, of the limitations of such an approach. This
is because when we see a patient who presents with so-called depression or
anxiety, the individual formulation of the patient's difficulties is probably going to
be a far more reliable guide to what they need, and what help they can use, than
their formal diagnosis.

When considering the suitability of a *brief psychodynamic approach* several
factors need to be considered (Malan, 1979):

- There is a good history of interpersonal relationships even if conflicted.
- The patient's difficulties must lend themselves to focusing on one theme or core
  conflict.
- The conflict is at a neurotic, oedipal level (i.e. not indicative of borderline or pre-oedipal
  problems).
- During the assessment the patient responds to interpretations concerned with the
  identified focus.
- The patient is motivated to work with the chosen focus.
- The potential contra-indications for brief therapy (e.g. risk of impulsive behaviour), if
  present, are thought to be manageable.

Group psychoanalytic psychotherapy is also available: this does not identify
strictly with a Freudian approach, but reflects an integration of various strands of
analytic thinking. In a general sense the same criteria apply as for individual
psychotherapy. However, there are some instances when a group approach may
be the best treatment modality. For example, where a psychoanalytic approach is
thought to be indicated, but where there is a concern about the possibility of a
regressive transference (e.g. excessive dependency) or where the patient displays
an intolerance of dyadic intimacy and would find the intensity of a one-to-one
relationship overwhelming, a group approach might be recommended.

None of the above criteria would be sufficient in isolation to arrive at a decision;
these are some of the thoughts that an assessor would have in mind, but they
would always need to be considered in light of patients' problems and personal
history and along with their capacities and vulnerabilities. Moreover, none of the
criteria stated here have been backed up consistently by research findings; they
merely reflect common clinical thinking and practice in the author's experience of
working in the NHS.

Qualities of effective therapists

What makes a good Freudian therapist, as opposed to a Kleinian one for example, is not really a useful question. It is more helpful to think about what makes a good psychoanalytic psychotherapist generally speaking, as the label 'Freudian' probably adds little to our understanding of the very complex process of psychotherapy and the factors that facilitate it.

The most important qualities are *curiosity*, which fosters understanding that goes beyond the manifest meaning of what the patient tells the therapist, and *integrity* so that what the patient shares is handled sensitively and professionally with due respect for the patient's vulnerability in the context of the therapeutic relationship.

The greatest challenge for a psychoanalytic psychotherapist is to develop the capacity to monitor their own unconscious processes so as to safeguard the analytic space which exists for the patient. Ensuring that the therapist's own difficulties or frustrations do not impinge on the analytic space requires that the therapist him or herself has undergone a lengthy analysis so as to become aware of, as Freud called them, their 'blind spots'. In addition, engagement in this process hones the therapist-to-be's ear for unconscious communication as they learn to decipher their own.

A capacity for what Freud called *free-floating attention* is also needed. This denotes a capacity to be sensitively attuned and open to peripheral perceptions so as to catch the unconscious communications which are latent in the patient's material.

Aiming to maintain a *neutral stance*, a notion that we will look at further in the next section, is essential so as to allow the development of a space for thinking about problems with a patient without the encumbrance of moral dictates and judgements, though this does not mean that therapists operate without any ethical responsibilities.

Therapeutic relationship and style

The therapeutic relationship

Psychotherapy unfolds in a relational context: patient and therapist meet with both explicit and implicit aims and expectations. Both bring to the relationship their personal motivations and needs. The analytic relationship can become as complex as any intimate relationship: the patient may experience intense feelings of anger, hate, envy, love, sexual attraction and many others towards the therapist.

As Freud's understanding of the variables that facilitated change in psycho-analysis evolved, the relationship between therapist and patient gradually took centre stage. He noted affective changes in the patient's attachment to him developing in the course of treatment. These feelings were regarded as *trans-ference* coming about as a consequence of a 'false connection'. He came to see transferences as new editions of old impulses and fantasies aroused during the process of psychoanalysis, with the therapist replacing some earlier person.

At the root of the Freudian concept of transference lies the notion that the way in which we respond to particular people in the present is under the influence of our experiences in the past. In a general sense we approach new relationships according to patterns from the past, that is, we transfer to people in the present feelings and attitudes from the past which may not be appropriate. These represent a repetition, or a displacement, of reactions which originated in regard to significant figures in early childhood. This suggests that we may have developed habitual types of reacting to other people which have become part of our personality, such as a tendency to be afraid of authority so that certain feelings and modes of being may be repeatedly triggered in situations where we are faced with authority figures.

At first Freud thought that the transference was an unwanted complication in his new technique. But he soon capitalized on his former so-called error to formulate the major pillar of psychoanalytic technique: the analysis of transference. This was further divided into the positive and the negative transference – the positive and negative feelings which the patient transfers to the analyst.

In 1909 he remarked that transference was not just an obstacle to psychoanalysis but might play a positive role as a therapeutic agent. Later he concluded that it was in fact necessary for any psychoanalytic cure. Patients who were unable to develop a transferential relationship were not thought to be treatable by psychoanalysis. Despite this, Freud also warned practitioners of the powerful erotic charge of the transference, which creates the need for a professional ethic that prevents therapists from taking advantage of the seductive potential of the therapist/patient relationship.

Classical Freudians continue to understand the transference as a repetition of an earlier relationship. Contemporary Freudians, on the other hand, suggest that the intensity of the therapist–patient relationship arouses latent emotional experiences, but what transpires between patient and therapist is understood to be a *new* experience influenced by the past, not just a repetition.

Underpinning more contemporary views of transference continues to be a basic, and all too rarely challenged, assumption that can be traced throughout psychoanalytic theorizing, namely the existence of an objective reality known by the therapist and distorted by the patient (Stolorow and Attwood, 1992). One important implication of this position, with clinical ramifications, is a view of the therapeutic relationship, and of the process of psychotherapy itself, as one in which the impact of the observer on the observed as an ever-present influence on the therapeutic dyad is minimized.

In this theoretical climate the therapeutic functions of the so-called *real relationship* have been somewhat neglected. While most therapists readily acknowledge that a 'real' human relationship between therapist and patient is central to the therapeutic enterprise, clinicians have taken this for granted, thereby precluding a theoretical elaboration of its significance as part of the therapeutic process. The human foundation of psychoanalysis is largely underplayed in the literature. This appears to be partly because this awareness conflicts with the explicit conceptual formulations and 'rules' of the analytic process, that is, with the primacy of interpretations, transference and counter-transference reactions, and the importance, for example, of analytic neutrality, anonymity and unresponsiveness (Couch, 1979).

Few would, however, dispute the centrality of a bond or alliance between patient and therapist as a sine qua non of therapeutic work. Influential reviews of the psychotherapy outcome research literature underscore the importance of interpersonal factors as prominent ingredients of change in all therapies (Lambert et al., 1986; Horvath and Luborsky, 1993; Roth and Fonagy, 1996) and the studies have very consistently found a strong relationship between the therapeutic alliance and outcome that overrides technical differences between the therapies studied (e.g. Krupnick et al., 1996).

The notion of a *therapeutic* or *treatment alliance* has its origin in Freud's writings on technique although he never designated it as a distinctive concept. Originally it was encompassed within the general concept of transference. In 1913 Freud referred to the need to establish an 'effective transference' before the full work of psychoanalysis could begin. The essential distinction made by Freud at this time was between the patient's capacity to establish a friendly rapport with the therapist on the one hand, and the emergence of revived feelings and attitudes (i.e. the transference) which could become an obstacle to therapeutic progress on the other.

Some psychoanalytic theorists have been concerned with differentiating the treatment or therapeutic alliance from transference 'proper' (Sandler et al., 1973) – a trend reflected in the work of Greenson and Wexler (1969) in the way they regard the core of the alliance as being anchored in the 'real' or 'non-transferential' relationship. Zetzel (1956) made a notable contribution to this issue, stating that the presence of a real object relationship is necessary for the therapeutic alliance to develop, and, significantly, that these conditions are necessary for the psychoanalysis itself to proceed. This reflects a more general Freudian position which proposes that a part of the patient's ego is identified with the therapist's function and aims, while another part is engaged in resistance. The therapeutic alliance reflects the operation of the so-called *observing ego* which works alongside the therapist.

Although the analysis of transference is considered nowadays to be at the heart of analytic work, as we shall see in the next section, it is also a powerful dynamic. It is believed to be part of what drives the relationship. A patient can therefore also be a transference object for the therapist and can arouse in her feelings that are inappropriate to the present relationship. *Counter-transference*, the phenomenon accounting for the therapist's reactions to her patient, has been variously defined. At first Freud used this term to denote the therapist's blind spots and own transference to the patient. Subsequent formulations broadened the concept to the inappropriate emotional responses created in the therapist by the patient's transference material and role expectations. In more contemporary, especially Kleinian usage, it denotes all of the feelings aroused in the therapist by the patient. In other words, there has been a shift from seeing counter-transference as something which interferes with technique (the Classical Freudian position) to viewing such responses by the therapist as a means of understanding the patient's unconscious communications, thereby acting as a direct guide for analytic interpretations of the current material.

Style

Many myths abound about how a Freudian therapist behaves, not least of which is the idea that they say relatively little during sessions. On this, as indeed on many other variables, therapists will differ greatly along a continuum ranging from very passive/silent to very interactive. Some of the Classical Freudians are perhaps most identified with the silent end of the spectrum whereas there will be far more variability amongst the Contemporary Freudians on this question.

When we look at the pre-eminence of the interpretation of transference phenomena, it becomes possible to understand why therapists adopt a particular therapeutic style. Indeed, this emphasis is intimately linked to the analytic persona many therapists model themselves on: a relatively unobtrusive, neutral, anonymous professional who sacrifices her so-called 'normal' personality so as to receive the patient's projections, thereby providing fertile ground for the development of the transference. Therapists in training are typically encouraged to remain cordial yet aloof, and to avoid engaging in a conversational style with the patient or to disclose any personal information.

The notion of the therapist as a blank screen for the patient's projections is, however, difficult to uphold. This was Freud's (1912) own ideal as he described how the analyst should function as a 'mirror' to the patient's projections so that the reactions to the therapist could then be analysed to throw light on the patient's relationships more generally. However, the viability of the mirror-like attitude was gradually challenged (Balint and Balint 1939; Klauber, 1986; Greenberg, 1996).

The therapist as a person is a variable that cannot and should not be ignored. Moreover, it is a variable that – even if it were possible – we need not try to eliminate as it contributes to the analytic ambience of collaborative work which provides the essential backdrop to analytic work. Patients live in a real world as well as in their phantasy world and the exchanges with the therapist's humanity involve confrontations with their limitations as much as with their strengths. In other words, an important aspect of the therapeutic relationship is that it involves a confrontation with the reality of the therapist as real person, capable of spontaneous responses and, hence, inevitably fallible. The negotiation of disappointments and frustrations with a therapist who is real, in the sense just outlined, provides a potentially mutative interpersonal experience as long as this can be worked through. Just as a therapist compromises her potential effectiveness if she remains too fully a real person with no sensitivity to the distortions of projection, she will be equally ineffective if she remains solely a 'symbolic object' (Szasz, 1963). The therapeutic situation requires of the therapist that she function as both and of the patient that he perceive the therapist as both. Being neutral should not preclude an empathic, authentic, warm attitude. This was indeed

Freud's own style with his patients which he unfortunately never clearly articulated in his papers on technique, but which shines through in his case histories and in his patients' reports of their analyses with him (Couch, 1979).

Major therapeutic strategies and techniques

Free association and the use of the couch

In some key respects Freudian therapists remain true to Freud's own practice. While they were reclining back on the analytic couch, Freud encouraged his patients to share all their thoughts as they came to mind without any regard for logic or order. This was his fundamental rule and the cornerstone of his technique: *free association*. Freud was well aware of the demand he placed on his patients and he wrote, 'In confession, the sinner tells us what he knows; in analysis the neurotic has to tell more' (1926: 289). Freud insisted on the rule of free association because he realized that whatever the seemingly plausible reasons for the appearance in his patients' conscious minds of certain thoughts or images, these were used, as it were, by deeper forces pressing for expression. In encouraging patients simply to share everything that came to mind Freud hoped to be led to their inner conflicts through their associations. Whilst free-associating, patients certainly reveal a lot about themselves, their aspirations, fears, fantasies – often far more than would be the case if the therapist asked many questions or structured the therapeutic session more. Free association is, however, an ideal towards which the patient strives but in practice it is very difficult indeed to share all the contents of our thoughts. None the less the principle of free association underpins all current psychoanalytic practice.

When patients are seen more frequently than once weekly, the use of the couch remains standard practice. Typically the therapist sits out of the patient's sight, behind the couch. This way the usual conversational style that is encouraged by face-to-face communication, with its attendant non-verbal cues, is inhibited. Lying on the couch is thought to facilitate a more free-associative style. Also, the use of the couch has probably survived over the years because it benefits not only the patient but also the therapist, who does not have to be under the patient's constant visual scrutiny. This allows the therapist to think more freely and to become more sensitively attuned to the latent communications in the patient's manifest material.

Dream interpretation

Dream interpretation, once thought to be 'the royal road to the unconscious' (Freud, 1905), is nowadays viewed as less central to Freudian analytic technique. Dreams are believed to be carriers of unconscious meaning and are interpreted as they arise, but they no longer hold the centre stage that Freud awarded them. When they are worked with, the patient is asked to associate to elements of the dream, so as to access its latent meaning. It is through an understanding of the meaning of the patient's personal associations that the dream is eventually interpreted.

Interpretation of defence and of transference

Through its use of interpretation, psychoanalysis offers the patient a scheme or system of thought which enables them to make some sense out of their distress. Strictly speaking, to interpret in the analytic sense means to make an unconscious phenomenon conscious (Greenson, 1967). Interpretations help the patient to become aware of the unconscious meaning, source or cause of their feelings, thoughts and behaviours. To arrive at an interpretation the therapist may use clarificatory questions and prompts but these are usually kept to a minimum.

While interpretations seldom immediately get rid of symptoms, they do provide valuable relief from the patient's fear of chaos and meaninglessness. They offer the patient new concepts and information which allow for meaningful connections between symptoms and experiences that may have been, up until that point, mysterious. The creation of a powerful explanatory model acts as a means of reducing tension, replacing confusion with some degree of clarity.

The term 'interpretation' may give the misleading impression that when in analysis the patient tells the therapist their thoughts and dreams and the latter simply interprets these in light of the patient's past history. This makes it sound as though the patient is a passive recipient waiting for the therapist to dispense the 'truth' or the answer which will explain psychic pain away. Rather it is the patient ideally who arrives at their own interpretations through the process of exploring how they feel. The therapist will of course at times point out certain patterns, or emphasize something the patient has said which they appear to be glossing over but that may in fact be quite significant, while at other times they may highlight inconsistencies in thoughts or feelings which reflect underlying conflicts and defensive processes.

Throughout Freud's writings and those of his followers, we find numerous references to *defences*, whose aim is to ward off conflict and the ensuing anxiety. Classical Freudian therapists still believe that one of the core tasks of psychoanalysis is to undertake an *analysis of defence and resistance*. This focus is taken up to varying degrees by Contemporary Freudian therapists. It involves the clarification, confrontation, interpretation and working through of defences and resistances as they arise in the course of psychotherapy (Greenson, 1967).

The concept of defence mechanisms refers to a process designed to avoid danger and hence anxiety which is a product of perceived danger. Defences falsify reality in order to avoid situations which are perceived as threatening to the self. In 1926, Freud revised and broadened the concept of defence, which he had previously conceived as synonymous with *repression*, and recognized repression as just one of many defence mechanisms. Repression refers to the confinement to the unconscious of thoughts, images and memories which, if allowed into consciousness, would give rise to anxiety. Sometimes certain facts may be remembered but their connection to each other or their emotional significance is repressed as, for example, when someone recounts a traumatic experience with none of the expected accompanying emotions. Conflict may then arise when the person encounters a new experience which is somehow connected with what was previously repressed. In these cases we often find a tendency on the part of the repressed and unconscious to use this new experience as an opportunity for its outlet – it finds what is called a *derivative*. Because repressed material continues to exist in the unconscious and may develop such derivatives, repression is not a once and for all occurrence; it is a process that requires a constant input of psychic energy so as to maintain it (Fenichel, 1946).

Anna Freud developed much further the concept of defences and underlined the need for analysis to address the ego's defences against conflict so as to help patients obtain a more harmonious relationship between the psychic agencies and between them and the external world. Many defence mechanisms have been highlighted by psychoanalysis (e.g. projection, reaction formation, introjection, displacement, undoing isolation, identification with the aggressor). Anna Freud's (1936) book describes the most common ones.

The cornerstone of Contemporary Freudian analytic technique, like that of other schools of psychoanalysis, is the *interpretation of transference*. The outcome of therapy is held to be related by many, if not most, Contemporary Freudians to the successful elaboration and re-evaluation of patterns of relating which become accessible through an analysis of transference phenomena, that is, the enactment in the present of implicit schemata or dynamic templates of self–other relationships (Sandler and Sandler, 1997) and their interpretation. There appears to be a continuum along which therapists broadly situate themselves on this question. This ranges from those who believe in the 'total transference' and who focus almost exclusively on the here-and-now transference interpretation, and those who draw a clear distinction between real and distorted aspects of the relationship and whose range of interventions includes so-called 'extra-transference' interpretations (Hamilton, 1996). The latter position is the one typically associated with Classical Freudians and some Contemporary Freudians.

The change process in therapy

Contemporary Freudians believe that understanding how patients construe their early experiences is more important than the unravelling of what actually happened to them in the past. The emphasis in therapy is thus on the meaning attributed to an experience rather than on the fact of the experience itself. This is in keeping with research findings which suggest that autobiographical memory is unreliable and privy to the vicissitudes of our desire – in other words, we remember what we want to remember and this is not necessarily a factually accurate picture of what actually took place (see Fonagy and Target, 1997).

As we have seen, our early experiences are now thought to be encoded as procedures (i.e. how to do things and how to relate to others). This contributes to the development of templates for how relationships work and what may be expected of others and is expected of oneself. Following on from this assumption is the belief that therapeutic change results from the elaboration and re-evaluation of current models of relationships which are implicitly encoded as procedures.

Change is no longer thought to flow from uncovering repressed memories, as research suggests that it is not really possible to directly access unconscious memory. Rather, change occurs through an understanding of the vicissitudes of the new relationship created between the patient and the therapist, which is informed by the past and thus gives some clues as to the model of relationships that the patient operates from.

The capacity to make explicit, and to reflect on, implicit models of how relationships work has been shown, for example, to be critical in breaking the intergenerational transmission of insecure attachment patterns (Fonagy et al., 1993). The capacity for self-reflection is a vital moderating variable which can make a difference. People who lack this capacity are those more likely to develop psychological problems later in life, especially in the context of a history of a difficult childhood. Those who have endured very traumatic childhood experiences, but who nevertheless have developed the capacity for self-reflection, are more likely to break the intergenerational cycle of transmission of destructive patterns of behaviour and of relating. 'Self-reflective function', as it is referred to, can now be experimentally measured. It describes the capacity to process emotional experience, acting as a mediating device between our experience and the outcome that is translated into behaviour. It refers to our ability to relate to ourselves as thinking and feeling beings. It involves acknowledging mixed emotions, recognizing the irrationality of some of our beliefs and desires and the frequently pressing nature of our emotional states, along with our vulnerability in the face of such experiences.

Nowadays discussions on the nature of change often, but by no means exclusively, focus on the notion of *adaptation* rather than fundamental personality change or change in psychic structures. People are not necessarily thought to 'get better' as such; rather they are said to understand themselves better so that they have more options and are able to exercise the options open to them. This, in turn, may contribute to a subjective sense of well-being and a reduction in symptoms.

Limitations of the approach

Psychoanalysis is a rich, complex and stimulating theory and application, but it does not present a unified view either of the nature of our development or of the mutative factors in psychotherapy. It has a long, antagonistic relationship to empirical research. Psychoanalysis, however, badly needs the self-correcting methodology of empirical science so as to enable it to rationally decide between the rival theories which make up the umbrella term 'psychoanalysis'. Without a research perspective the danger is that psychoanalysis will continue to be a breeding ground for fanaticism and narrow-mindedness, which has in the past lent it the appearance of a cult or religion (Szasz, 1978). Not surprisingly, the easiest target for criticism has been the behaviour of some analysts who have acted more as true believers than as genuine enquirers.

Fortunately, over the last 20 years in particular, partly as a result of a *rapprochement* between the fields of child development and psychoanalysis, there has been an upsurge in empirical studies which have tried to substantiate some core psychoanalytic assumptions. There is now also increasing interest in the factors that are related to the successful outcome of psychotherapy (Stern et al., 1998). This will hopefully pave the way for research into other mutative factors in psychotherapy beyond the interpretation of transference which has perhaps been overvalued as the key to therapeutic change in more Contemporary Freudian thinking by contrast to a more Classical Freudian approach. Which interventions are the most facilitative of change remains a key research question. It would be of interest, for example, to study further the outcome of analytic approaches that focus more systematically on the interpretation of transference as opposed to approaches which make more use of reconstructive or supportive interpretations.

Recent psychoanalytic contributions have indeed challenged the pre-eminence of transference interpretation. This challenge is presented by those theoreticians and clinicians influenced by both dynamic and systemic ideas who underscore the need for the co-construction of new contexts by the meeting of two subjectivities (Beebe and Lachmann, 1988, 1994; Sameroff, 1983; Stern et al., 1998). The underlying assumption in these accounts is that both patient and therapist contribute to the regulation of the exchange, even if their respective contributions cannot be regarded as equal. From this perspective regulation is an emergent property of the dyadic system as well as a property of the individual. Within this context there is room for a variety of interventions, other than transference interpretations, which may have mutative potential.

A view commonly held by sceptics is that psychoanalytic treatment 'seems to produce a good many more converts than cures' (Crews, 1993: 55). Until recently, this criticism has been hard to refute as there has been a dearth of outcome research evaluating the effectiveness of psychoanalytic treatments. The stereotypical response by a significant number of psychoanalytic psychotherapists to outcome research is that it is not meaningful. Indeed, the evaluation of psychotherapy is inextricably linked to individual views on science and scientific method, on the nature of 'meaningful' questions, on how far the complex phenomena of psychotherapy can be scientifically investigated and, not least, on how one defines a successful outcome, that is whether one is 'cured'. While such arguments need to be considered there are obvious scientific, moral, political and financial reasons for at least attempting to carry out outcome research. The primary advantage of outcome studies is that they place into the empirical arena the many conflicting and hyperbolic claims made about the superiority of one approach over another. Furthermore, the value of knowing the relative efficacy of alternative techniques, the differences in the range or type of outcomes produced and the process through which such outcomes are achieved, encompasses critical theoretical and practical questions.

Psychoanalytic approaches undoubtedly have a place amongst a range of psychological therapies even though they have not been evaluated as extensively as other therapeutic modalities (Roth and Fonagy, 1996). Not everyone, however, benefits from a psychoanalytic approach. It would be desirable, but not at present possible, to specify criteria regarding who is most likely to benefit. This is a question that needs to be researched further.

Case example

The client

Amanda was 36 when we first met. She requested psychotherapy at the suggestion of her GP following her frequent reports of headaches and her chronically low mood. She said she felt anxious about whether she had any 'real' friends, whether she would ever have a relationship with a man, and expressed doubts about her own capabilities.

Amanda was the younger of two; her sister was three years older than her. Both her parents were still alive and working. Her parents had separated when she was six years old. She described the separation as acrimonious, reaching its peak when her mother took an overdose following the discovery of her father's infidelities. Although she maintained contact with her father throughout her childhood, she found his frequent affairs very difficult to manage. Both Amanda and her sister continued to live with her mother who remarried within two years of the divorce.

Amanda went to university where she studied economics. Although she had hopes of entering the business world, she never managed to get beyond secretarial posts in her chosen industry. It was quite apparent that she was functioning well below her intellectual capabilities and this proved to be one of the reasons for seeking therapy.

In our very first consultation Amanda expressed a longing to have a good relationship with a man. She had become aware that she was choosing relationships with men who were in some way unavailable to her and who would ultimately reject her. The desire to rescue and so become in some way indispensable to the men she was involved with was a very powerful fantasy which appeared to underlie all her relationships. In discussing her relationships with men, she revealed what she described as a kind of 'addiction to drama' which she herself linked with the highly charged, dramatic exchanges she had witnessed between her parents. Her mother had in fact been very involved in amateur dramatics throughout Amanda's life and had remarried an out-of-work actor who, though kind towards Amanda, was an alcoholic whose behaviour could be unpredictable.

Amanda's therapy lasted five years, during which time she attended on a three times weekly basis. Consequently, the account which is provided here is but a snapshot of some aspects of the work we did together and inevitably excludes the complexities and vicissitudes of what transpired over such a long period of time.

The therapy

In many respects Amanda could have been described as an accomplished psychoanalytic patient. She had read a lot about Freud before coming into therapy and took to the couch very quickly. She hardly needed any prompting from me to speak and she was very quick to comment on what was happening in our relationship. She was always very articulate and often came across as insightful. She presented her arguments clearly and these reflected the sharpness of her intellect and her knowledge of psychoanalytic jargon. She said she enjoyed talking with me and thinking about herself. This presentation was both seductive and distancing since I was at often left feeling quite redundant in the whole process.

In the first few months whenever I made an interpretation it was subjected to scrutiny and veiled criticism, thereby giving expression to what I understood to be her hostility and competitiveness in relation to me. These were the first stirrings of Amanda's negative transference. Although this was my formulation of what was happening between us I did not interpret the full extent of her negative transference at this early stage, but merely acknowledged her mixed feelings about starting therapy and seeing herself as in some way needy. I considered it far more important at this point to establish a good working alliance with the part of Amanda that clearly wanted my help.

On the whole, I remained fairly silent and unobtrusive. I viewed my role as that of facilitator of Amanda's own self-analytic capacities by using prompts and the odd interpretation to help her focus in more depth on certain aspects of what she brought to the sessions. I did not always find this more passive stance easy since at times I felt I was not doing anything. On occasions I succumbed to my own narcissistic urge to display my analytic skills, making interpretations that were either premature or that pre-empted Amanda's own interpretations in an unhelpful way. It seemed to me that I was then enacting what I came to understand to be the very competitive dynamic Amanda re-created in many of her relationships. In so doing I was also inappropriately discharging my own counter-transferential hostility towards Amanda, who was adept at delivering trenchant criticism. Since I was myself still in training when I started to see her, such criticisms touched a raw nerve.

Amanda maintained a defensive distance from everybody. This led her to feel lonely and envious of those around her when she perceived them to have what she felt she lacked. She frequently spoke of her envy of friends who had a man in their life. She felt that having reached her mid-thirties she should have met a man by now. Although her relationships with men had been very limited, she nevertheless had a very active fantasy life where she would elaborate romantic scenarios with men whom she had just seen in the street or had spoken to on the phone as part of her work. It seemed as though in fantasy she retained a measure of control and so protected herself from the reality of actually relating to a man, a prospect which filled her with anxiety and challenged her with her fear of abandonment.

Amanda chose men who were in many respects quite similar: they found commitment very difficult, they had complex psychological problems (several had a psychiatric history), they turned to her as a confidante and they all ultimately rejected her. The conflict and uncertainty which underpinned these relationships seemed important to Amanda. I sensed she was excited by the relationships although she was also clearly hurt by them and I interpreted this. Amanda appeared to derive masochistic gratification from her suffering; she said that if she did not feel pain she didn't think something was worth anything to her. Therefore, to have a relationship with a so-called 'normal' man who might want her was not at all appealing to her. She seemed to be seeking a relationship as volatile as the one her parents had experienced, full of drama and disputes, punctuated by passionate reunions. Part of the excitement stemmed from the omnipotent fantasy that she could change these men, tame them and make them love her. We came to understand this as an attempt to reverse the earlier rejection by her father and her impotence: she had not been 'enough' for her father and had been unable to reclaim the attention which she felt was wasted on the string of women whom he dated over the years. In the first year of therapy, any observations that I made about such issues were experienced by Amanda as an attempt to deprive her of her exciting and comforting fantasies.

Throughout most of the therapy we focused on Amanda's unresolved Oedipal strivings and the defences that she had erected against the anxieties generated by intimacy. This exploration involved both transference and extra-transference interpretations on my part, that is, the focus was not restricted to, or heavily biased towards, an analysis of transference phenomena, but was far broader in its range. Consequently, throughout the therapy, I made use of a range of interventions including asking questions, prompts, dream analysis, reconstructive and transference interpretations, as well as more supportive interventions. On the whole I erred on the side of remaining silent, but there were stages in the therapy where I undoubtedly became more active, for example when I felt we were becoming stuck because of a resistance.

Amanda was frequently angry and rivalrous with me and could be very contemptuous too. Towards the end of the first year I began to interpret the negative transference more explicitly. I felt that the relationship between us mirrored her highly ambivalent and competitive relationship with her mother, whom she experienced as depriving and neglectful. She was very angry with her mother for having remarried so soon and seemed to have felt somewhat excluded by her mother's narcissistic involvement with her own needs to the neglect of Amanda's. Although my understanding of Amanda's hostility was rooted in a reconstruction of her early relationship with her mother I did not, nevertheless, make any such reconstructive interpretations. My emphasis at this point was on highlighting her hostility towards me and engaging Amanda in an exploration of this dynamic as it arose in the room between us without linking it explicitly with her relationship with her mother. The here-and-now actualization of patterns of relationships provided the raw material for us to work with, in keeping with more Contemporary Freudian aims.

In the first 18 months of therapy it would be fair to say that Amanda's capacity for trust remained quite limited. I was experienced either as a depriving rival or as a parental figure whose reliability could not be depended upon. She anticipated rejection on my part, to which she responded by ensuring she would reject me first, for example by planning last-minute holidays which she only announced the day before she was about to take them. At best her attitude towards me was somewhat indifferent, as if she could really leave the therapy at any time and it would not make much difference. The quality of our initial relationship was not surprising to me, given her chaotic and unstable early environment, which had been punctuated by the comings and goings of her parents and her parents' partners.

By the end of the second year of therapy, Amanda showed greater capacity to acknowledge positive feelings towards me and felt that the therapy was helpful to her. These disclosures were, however, accompanied by considerable anxiety as she dreaded depending on me. Amanda managed this anxiety by becoming, once again, critical of the therapy generally and of myself. She became withdrawn and depressed, sometimes refusing to speak. She would then contradict her previous statements and say that she was concerned that the therapy wasn't bringing about any change in her behaviour. She thus oscillated between revealing her attachment to me and rubbishing what I offered her.

Through a process of clarification and confrontation of her defensive manoeuvres, aided by prompts and interpretations on my part, we understood these repetitive shifts in her pattern of relating to me as an expression of her fear of establishing an attachment as this placed her in a vulnerable position where she might be rejected. In addition, her oscillating commitment to the therapy appeared to be an attempt to engender in me an uncertainty about her attachment, thereby seemingly mirroring her own early experience of erratic displays of affection and attention by her parents, especially her father. The enactment of these dynamics in the context of the therapy shed light on Amanda's original complaint when she entered therapy, namely her difficulty in establishing relationships with men. Although this continued to be a concern for her she nevertheless gained insight into her tendency to choose unavailable men, like her father. She also began to recognize her withdrawal into a depressed state as a hostile gesture, intended to hurt and punish those who disappointed her.

Amanda's transference to me was quite intense and led to very explicit expressions of love as well as rage and disappointment for not being the idealized parent/partner she needed me to be. I experienced Amanda's request for undivided attention and perfect attunement as very demanding. What she perceived to be my shortcomings were, in turn, experienced by her as confirmation of her belief that she would always be let down by others and it was therefore least painful to stay on her own. This triggered an attacking, hostile, response whereby she belittled me by doubting my competence.

Well into the fourth year, the negative transference continued to characterize a large part of our exchanges and I would interpret this consistently. In turn,

Amanda referred explicitly to my interpretations as 'banal' and 'simplistic' and she questioned my ability to really understand the complexity of her problems. Her envy and competitiveness got in the way of her taking good things from me as she so much wanted to deny her dependency on me. Amanda's criticisms of me were sometimes trenchant and I did not find them easy. At times I most probably failed to understand her, but her accusations were clearly not just related to actual failures on my part. Rather, I understood them as reflecting her deep grievance towards her parents. When she was at her most enraged, I was experienced as a neglecting, overexcited parent (usually her mother) who was just interested in myself and had no time for her.

Although Amanda's sexuality had been discussed in the therapy, I had always sensed a resistance to address this issue fully. My suggestion in one session early in the fourth year that some of her difficulties with men were related to a fear of sexual intimacy sparked an enraged response. Amanda said she doubted my capacity as a therapist as she felt this was entirely my agenda. The sessions which followed over the next few months were very difficult and Amanda threatened to leave the therapy. She said she no longer trusted me and felt I was as intrusive as her mother.

Her resistance in the therapy was very powerful. However, perseverance with the theme of sexuality proved to be helpful insofar as Amanda was eventually able to talk about her disgust at her own body and her sense that she was not sexually desirable. She felt deeply ashamed about her sexual fantasies. She herself made an equation between sexual desire and incestuous feelings which inhibited her from establishing a sexual relationship with a man. Although these were difficult months, it seemed to me that we were making very good progress, since the therapy was strong enough to withstand her hostile attacks on me and her ability to think about herself was undoubtedly deepening. She reported many of her sexual dreams, which expressed clear wish-fulfilment but invariably there was an impediment to her realizing her sexual desire.

Towards the end of the fourth year of therapy and throughout much of the final year, Amanda explored more openly her dissatisfaction with her own sense of feminity and her sexuality. She felt that her mother had never given her permission to be a sexual woman in her own right and this enabled us to explore in more depth her competitiveness with her mother, especially in relation to her father. This revealed her denigration of her mother for not having been attractive enough to retain her father, whom she perceived to have been 'won' by other women. She felt that her mother had never felt herself to be an attractive woman and that she had, as it were, inherited this 'disability' from her. In an identification with her mother she felt herself unable to sustain a man's interest. For this she harboured a grievance against her mother. The anger that she felt towards her father was also displaced on to her mother, thereby allowing Amanda to protect the idealized relationship with her father, though this idealization was gradually eroded.

We understood her sense of grievance towards both parents as contributing to her feeling of stuckness. To get better seemed to be equated for Amanda as in some way letting her parents off the hook for all the terrible things she felt they had done to her. This turned out to be the focus of the final year of therapy. Getting better meant acknowledging that her parents were not wholly responsible for her predicament.

Towards the beginning of the fifth year of therapy, Amanda started to talk about wanting to end. This had been partly prompted by her desire to go travelling with a friend and to rethink her career. We therefore started to plan for the ending and I explicitly referred to it in my interventions when it seemed appropriate.

Over the last seven months of the therapy Amanda seemed to feel much more relaxed and although at times she was still hostile towards me, there was very much a sense that she could begin to acknowledge that the therapy had been of some help to her. Her embattled stance gave way to a more reflective and grateful attitude. This was mirrored in a change in her way of relating to her mother in particular whereby she seemed to feel that her mother was much more on her side rather than against her. She developed a less idealized view of her father and acknowledged that it had not just been her mother's fault but that he had been as much to blame for what had gone wrong in their relationship. During this period she also met a man, with whom she fell in love. By the time we ended the therapy she had not yet started a sexual involvement with him, but it was apparent that they both got on very well and that he did not seem to fit the profile of the men she had previously been drawn to.

Ten months after we finished working together, Amanda sent me a card to let me know that she was in fact about to move in with this man and was hopeful that the relationship would be a long-lasting one. She also informed me that she had applied for a Master's degree course.

References

SE refers to the *Standard Edition of the Complete Psychological Works of Sigmund Freud*, 24 vols (1955–74) ed. and trans. J. Strachey, London: Hogarth Press and the Institute for Psycho-Analysis.

Balint, A. and Balint, M. (1939) 'On transference and counter-transference', *International Journal of Psychoanalysis*, 20: 225–30.

Beebe, B. and Lachmann, F. (1988) 'The contribution of mother/infant mutual influence to the origins of self and object representations', *Psychoanalytic Psychology*, 5: 305–30.

Beebe, B. and Lachmann, F. (1994) 'Representation and internalization in infancy: three principles of salience', *Psychoanalytic Psychology*, 11: 127–65.

Couch, A. (1979) 'Therapeutic functions of the real relationship in psychoanalysis' (unpublished paper). Revised version of a paper on 'The role of the real relationship in analysis' given at the Scientific Meeting in the Boston Analytic Society, 10 January.

Crews, F. (1993) 'The unknown Freud', *New York Review of Books*, 18 November: 55–6.

Fenichel, O. (1946) *The Psychoanalytic Theory of Neurosis*. London: Routledge & Kegan Paul.

Ferris, P. (1997) *Dr Freud: A Life*. London: Random House.

Fonagy, P. and Target, M. (1997) 'Perspectives on the recovered memories debate', in J. Sandler and P. Fonagy (eds), *Recovered Memories of Abuse: True or False?* London: Karnac.

Fonagy, P., Steele, H., Moran, G., Steele, M. and Higgitt, A. (1993) 'Measuring the ghost in the nursery: an empirical study of the relation between parents' mental representations of childhood experiences and their infants' security of attachment', *Journal of the American Psychoanalytic Association*, 41: 957–89.

Freud, A. (1936) *The Ego and the Mechanisms of Defence*. London: Karnac.

Freud, S. (1905) *Three Essays on Sexuality*, Vol 7. London: Penguin

Freud, S. (1912) 'The dynamics of transference'. *SE12*: 99–108.

Freud, S. (1917) 'Fixation to traumas in the unconscious', Vol 1. London: Penguin.

Freud, S. (1926) 'The question of lay analysis', *SE15*. London: Penguin

Freud, S. (1938) 'An outline of psychoanalysis', Vol. 15. London: Penguin.

Greenberg, J. (1996) 'Psychoanalytic words and psychoanalytic acts', *Contemporary Psycho-analysis*, 32: 195–203.

Greenson, R. (1967) *The Technique and Practice of Psychoanalysis*. London: Hogarth Press.

Greenson, R. and Wexler, M. (1969) 'The non-transference relationship in a psychoanalytic situation', *International Journal of Psychoanalysis*, 50: 27–39.

Hamilton, V. (1996) *The Analyst's Pre-conscious*. Hilderdale, NJ: The Analytic Press.

Horvath, A. and Luborsky, L. (1993) 'The role of the therapeutic alliance in psychotherapy', *Journal of Consulting & Clinical Psychology*, 61(4): 561–73.

Kirsner, D. (1990) 'Mystics and professionals in the culture of American psychoanalysis', *Free Associations*, 20: 85–104.

Klauber, J. (1986) *Difficulties in the Analytic Encounter*. London: Free Association Books & Maresfield Library.

Krupnik, J. et al. (1996) 'The role of the therapeutic alliance in psychotherapy & pharmacotherapy outcome: findings in the NIMH Collaborative Research Programme', *Journal of Consulting & Clinical Psychology*, 64: 532–9.

Lambert, M., Shapiro, D. and Bergin, A. (1986) 'The effectiveness of psychotherapy', in S. Garfield and A. Bergin (eds), *Handbook of Psychotherapy and Behaviour Change*. New York: Wiley.

Lemma, A. (1995) *Invitation to Psychodynamic Psychology*. London: Whurr.

Malan, D. (1979) *Individual Psychotherapy and the Science of Psychodynamics*. Oxford: Butterworth Heinemann.

Milner, B., Squire, L. and Kandel, E. (1998) 'Cognitive neuroscience and the study of memory', *Neuron Review* 20: 445–68.

Morris, J., Ohman, A. and Dolan, R. (1998) 'Conscious and unconscious emotional *learning* in the human amygdala', *Nature*, 393: 467–70.

Perelberg, R. (ed.) (1999) *Psychoanalytic Understanding of Violence and Suicide*. London: Routledge.

Raphael-Leff, J. (1991) *Psychological Processes of Childbearing*. London: Chapman & Hall.

Robert, M. (1977) *From Oedipus to Moses: Freud's Jewish Identity*. London: Routledge & Kegan Paul.

Roith, E. (1987) *The Riddle of Freud*. London: Routledge & Kegan Paul.

Roth, A. and Fonagy, P. (1996) *What Works for Whom?* London: Guildford Press.

Sameroff, A. (1983) 'Developmental systems: contexts and evolution', in W. Massey (ed.), *Massey's Handbook of Child Psychology*, Vol. 1. New York: Wiley.

Sandler J. and Dreyer, A. (1996) *What Do Analysts Want?* London: Routledge.

Sandler, J. and Sandler, A.M. (1984) 'The past unconscious, the present unconscious: an interpretation of the transference', *Psychoanalytic Enquiry*, 4: 367–99.

Sandler J. and Sandler, A.M. (1997) 'A psychoanalytic theory of repression and the unconscious', in J. Sandler and P. Fonagy (eds), *Recovered Memories of Abuse* London: Karnac Books.

Sandler, J., Holden, A. and Dare, C. (1973) *The Patient and the Analyst*. London: Karnac Books.

Steiner, J. (1989) 'The aim of psychoanalysis', *Psychoanalytic Psychotherapy*, 4(2): 109–20.

Stern, D., Sander, L., Nahum, J. et al. (1998) 'Non interpretative mechanisms in psychoanalytic therapy: there's something more than interpretation', *International Journal of Psychoanalysis*, 79(5): 903–22.

Stevens, R. (1983) *Freud and Psychoanalysis*. Milton Keynes: Open University Press.

Stolorow, R. and Attwood, G. (1992) *Contexts of Being*. Hillsdale, NJ: Analytic Press.

Szasz, T. (1963) 'The concept of transference', *International Journal of Psychoanalysis*, 44: 432–43.

Szasz, T. (1978) *The Myth of Psychotherapy*. Syracuse University Press.

Zetzel, E. (1956) 'Current concepts of transference', *International Journal of Psychoanalysis*, 37: 369–76.

Suggested further reading

Bateman, A. and Holmes, J. (1995) *Introduction to Psychoanalysis*. London: Routledge.

Bettelheim, B. (1982) *Freud and Man's Soul*. New York: Fontana.

Greenson, R. (1967) *The Technique and Practice of Psychoanalysis*. London: Hogarth Press.

Lemma, A. (1995) *Invitation to Psychodynamic Psychology*. London: Whurr.

Sandler, J., Holder, A., Dare, C. and Dreher, A. (eds) (1997) *Freud's Models of the Mind: An Introduction*. London: Karnac Books.

3 Psychodynamic Therapy: The Kleinian Approach

Cassie Cooper

Historical content and development in Britain

Historical context

Melanie Klein born in Vienna (1882) was an 'unexpected' baby, the youngest of four children; her siblings were Emilie, Emanuel and Sidonie. Her father (Morris Reiz) was a highly orthodox Jew. Her mother (Libussa Deutsch) was the daughter of a local rabbi. In accordance with Jewish custom their marriage was arranged whilst her father was still a student at a local yeshiva (religion school).

Melanie's birth followed the turbulent period in European history which came after the Napoleonic Wars. This was the so called 'age of emancipation' for the Jewish community, when professional barriers and prejudices wavered at the onset of the new, radical political theories and philosophies.

Facilitated by new professional opportunities, Morris Reiz left his religious studies and attempted to read medicine. This became too difficult so he moved instead into dentistry. He was never a successful wage earner. The family had to struggle financially and Sidonie (their third child) died tragically at the age of eight. The family were traumatized.

Melanie's parents considered themselves intellectuals and pursued their interests in art and science. They expected their remaining children to do the same. Her father visibly indicated his preference for her sister Emilie, whilst Melanie, in turn, looked to her brother Emanuel for validation and affection. Emanuel, now a medical student, was supportive to Melanie and encouraged her education and ambition. She hoped to emulate him, to become a doctor, and studied hard at Latin and Greek, the necessary requirements for entry into a gymnasium (grammar school); she did well at school and was full of enthusiasm for the future.

The family continued to struggle financially. The health of her father and her brother declined. Eventually, Emanuel had to curtail his studies and take time off to recuperate. He was advised to travel to warmer climates, leaving Melanie to continue her studies alone. In 1900 her father died and Emanuel's health continued to deteriorate. She was now 18 years old.

Melanie had to reassess her future. The prospect of continuing her medical studies was not possible. Reluctantly, she reconsidered her position. Always attractive and courted by several friends of her brother who were proposing marriage, she selected Arthur Klein, an industrial chemist. This was a complete capitulation to the social and religious conventions of her day that found it more acceptable for a Jewish woman of her age and class to marry and have children. In 1902 at the age of 25 Emanuel died. Melanie was devastated. Life was bleak and comfortless. She married in 1903, but the birth of three children, Melitta (1904), Hans (1907) and Eric (1914), did little to lift the disappointment and disillusionment in her marriage. Arthur Klein was frequently unfaithful, restlessly seeking to move his business interests to Budapest. In 1911 despite a move from Vienna to Budapest his business developed severe financial problems. Melanie had begun to revive her interest in medicine and psychiatry. She read the works of Sigmund Freud and became attracted to Freudian theory. This offered ideas on personal development that resonated with her own feelings of bereavement, loss, disappointment and anger, and she was determined to pursue these interests.

Arthur Klein was spending more and more time away from home. Melanie arranged to meet Dr Sandor Ferenezi, a leading Hungarian analyst, a colleague and correspondent of Freud. She was his analytic patient between 1912 and 1919 while the First World War ravaged Europe.

Melanie's personal analysis stimulated her emerging ideas which focused on the application of psychoanalytic theory and interpretation to work with young children. Ferenezi encouraged her to develop techniques in which toys and play were used as the equivalent of the dream interpretation and free association which are part of the analytic process for adults.

Melanie was now able to embark on her own career. In the turbulent period which followed the war she began to specialize in the analysis of children and to establish a practice. In 1921 her first published paper, 'The development of a child' was read to the Hungarian Psychoanalytic Society. The paper received a mixed reception from the strictly Freudian group, whose understanding of the analysis of young children was minimally based on Freud's own work with 'Little Hans'.

With growing interest in her work, Dr Karl Abraham, President of the Berlin Psychoanalytic Society, invited Melanie to Berlin where she could devote herself to psychoanalytic practice and research. Melanie accepted, and moved the family to Berlin. This precipitated the end of her unhappy marriage. Arthur chose to stay in Sweden where he now had business interests, and they were divorced in 1924. The end was rancorous, with both parties arguing bitterly about the custody of their children.

In Berlin, Melanie returned to analysis with Karl Abraham. She was strongly influenced by his theories on infantile development. They became strongly attracted to each other and formed a deep attachment. Melanie blossomed, developing new techniques in her work with children which offered innovative ideas on the processes of child and adult analysis.

Karl Abraham was her admirer, her staunch supporter and advocate and his early death in 1925 (after a fatal illness) was a devastating blow. Following his death Melanie resorted to regular daily self-analysis, a process which Freud had initiated. All her later material was based on daily analysis of her own and her patients' behaviour compared, examined and interpreted one against the other. Melanie continued to develop new insights and interpretations about the early years of a child's life. Her contributions to the Berlin Society evoked a great deal of controversy, but in London, Ernest Jones, one of Freud's original pupils and his biographer (the doyen of psychoanalysts in Britain) gave support to Melanie's ideas. In 1925 she was invited to London to give a series of lectures to the British Society and to analyse Ernest Jones's children. In 1926, she was invited to stay and work permanently in London.

At this time, controversy still raged about the professional position of women in medicine, psychiatry and psychoanalysis. Melanie Klein was a divorced Jewish woman with three children in an increasingly hostile and anti-Semitic climate. After consideration of the options available to her in Berlin, Melanie agreed to stay and work in London. She was happy to do so: it was in London that her work flourished, and her very individual clinical and theoretical approach was emulated by leading British analysts. She continued to live in London writing, practising, teaching and arguing until the time of her death in 1960, aged 78.

Developments in Britain

Members of the British Psychoanalytic Society are often referred to as the 'English School', to differentiate the theory and practice that was developing in London (under the influence of Melanie Klein) from that of other centres of psychoanalytic learning, notably that of the so-called 'Viennese School' developed by Sigmund Freud.

These differences were accentuated by the opinion of the British (Kleinian) analysts that the relationship of mother and baby during the first few months of life is of primary importance in the development of the individual. The English School maintained that it was possible to explore and analyse the anxieties, defences and unconscious fantasies of children as young as two years of age. The transference relationship could also be interpreted using the methods of free association and play techniques. In this context, the word 'transference' is used to depict the development of an evaluative relationship between therapist and patient which is either 'positive' (good feelings) or 'negative' (rejection and hostility).

In the early 1930s, prior to the Nazi invasion of Europe, there was an exchange of lectures (Rivière unpublished, 1936; Waelder 1937), when the London, Berlin and Viennese societies were endeavouring to clarify their different stances on this and other issues. They could not agree and so agreed to differ. When the persecution of Jews became the official policy of the Nazi Party, psychoanalysis was dubbed 'The Jewish disease'. In 1938 German and Austrian analysts, knowing that they would be persecuted and unable to practise, fled to London, and to North and South America, where institutes of psychoanalytic learning had already been established.

At this point theoretical stances and points of conflict became polarized, threatening to cause a split within the established British Society. Sigmund Freud was now living and working in London accompanied by his daughter, Anna. She became fiercely antagonistic towards Melanie Klein, whose work continued to attract a large group of analysts and psychotherapists who were applying to her for training analyses and supervision. Alix Strachey, Susan Isaacs, Donald Winnicott, Paula Herman, Joan Rivière, Ernest Jones, T.E. Money-Kyrle and Hannah Segal formed part of this group, and an increasing number of students came to work with and benefit from these new ideas. Anna Freud persevered in her venomous attacks on Melanie. The British Society was shaken. Unity was preserved only by with the establishment of two separate streams for training courses within the Society: the 'Continental' School of Anna Freud and the 'English' School of Melanie Klein. Later on an independent group evolved who were able to develop their own techniques and interpretations without adherence to one school or another.

In its early days psychoanalysis was considered a 'fringe' profession which guaranteed only an uncertain income and a distinct lack of the upmarket prestige enjoyed by the predominating sphere of academic psychiatry. Most of the analysts who left Germany and Austria were attracted to the USA, where psychoanalysis is now firmly established, and they have become, financially and socially, members of the upper middle class. For many years the American School tended to be narrow and conservative in its approach to conflicting psychodynamic theories. This contrasted with the English School which in the early 1920s was substantially non-medical and contained so-called 'gifted amateurs'. It was considered to be more experimental in its approach to Freudian theories and Kleinian concepts. Psychoanalysis in England can never be regarded as intellectually complacent. This is due in part to the influence of Melanie Klein and her adherents who were able to remain constant in spite of a continuous barrage of venomous anger, humiliation, malicious gossip and rumour. Few women in the profession of psychoanalysis have aroused such ire in the male establishment.

Melanie Klein, appreciated as one of the great innovators in dynamic psychotherapy, nevertheless adhered to the concepts in psychotherapy which are basic to all psychoanalytic theories. These theories (which Farrell, 1981 simplified) were as follows:

- No item in mental life or in the way we behave is accidental. It is always the outcome of antecedent conditions.
- Mental activity and behaviour is purposeful or goal directed.
- Unconscious determinants mould and affect the way we perceive ourselves and others. These are thoughts of a primitive nature, shaped by impulses and feelings within the individual, of which they are unaware.
- Early childhood experiences are overwhelmingly important and pre-eminent over later experience.

In addition to these fundamental concepts, Melanie Klein enlarged and expanded on the hitherto unknown regions of the pre-Oedipal stage (i.e. the child's unconscious wish to be sexually united with a parent of the opposite sex, thus eliminating the other parent).

She went on to propose the following:

- that environmental factors are much less important than had previously been believed;

- that the beginnings of the superego can be identified within the first two years of life;
- that an analysis is unfinished if it fails to investigate the stages of infantile anxiety and aggressiveness in order to confront and understand them;
- that the most important drives of all are the aggressive ones.

Theoretical assumptions

Image of the person

The birth of a baby somewhere in the world will, during the next few years, signal that the population of our planet has reached 11 billion. Every minute of every day 150 babies thrust their way into life: 220,000 a day, 80 million a year, wrested supine and exhausted from the darkness of the birth canal into the glare of light. Many of these babies will go hungry and their families will starve. They will arrive unwanted, neglected, to be abandoned, abused and used. Life for them will be the days full of pain and vexation portrayed in the Bible. Life is no bowl of cherries but a series of events that have to be endured, experienced and overcome. For some it would be better not to have been born.

Kleinian theory encompasses this bleak view, but also emphasizes the fact that each human being possesses the capacity to tap into resources that rest deep in the psyche waiting to be mobilized and utilized. Kleinian theory is engaged with the primal processes of conception, pregnancy and birth, the elements of life which evolve in the foetus before it develops into a living being. Parents may bring to their newborn child their own already developed capacity for living their lives in a certain way. But the baby's persona is nebulous, split, at one moment a clear page waiting to be inscribed, at another a mass of powerful instinctual drives which focus on one aim – survival.

The foetal environment is rich in acoustic stimulation and the foetus responds to the mother's moods, her eating, drinking, breathing and heartbeats. A foetus eight weeks after conception can move its limbs and in a further eight weeks has gained sufficient strength to communicate these movements to its mother through the uterine walls. At approximately 26 weeks this tiny being can change position at will and, when poked or prodded by external examination, will attempt to avoid this contact. The baby is sensitive to pain, it winces, sometimes opening its mouth in a silent cry, responding to temperature and taste. The foetus has been observed drinking amniotic fluid and responding to its mother's food intake: sweetness which it likes and bitterness which is avoided. The foetus responds to stroking of the abdomen and gentle noise, turning its face, opening its mouth and moving its tongue. It can reach forward to obtain comfort by sucking its thumbs, fingers and toes. The ability to see, hear and feel are not senses which are magically bestowed at birth, and the foetal heartbeat resonates rapidly to the external situation of its mother. The dark encapsulated environment of the uterine world is dynamic, full of changes which respond to the outside world. The environment of the uterus changes continuously during gestation. 'Each foetus inhabits a singular world subjected to different experiences and stimulations' (Piontelli, 1992: 37).

Unlike the other mammals most closely related to our species, the human baby arrives prematurely, it is weak and helpless and seems to have poor instinctual notions of how to avoid danger or to obtain satisfaction of its vital needs. It is dependent upon others. When its caretaker (usually its mother) satisfies the baby's hunger, she is at one with it and so not experienced as a separate object. If, however, the mother is unable to satisfy the baby's needs, she (or her breast) is felt to be separate from the baby and thus becomes its first distinct psychological object. When the mother leaves the baby, two things happen. The first is that the loss or removal of the breast (or its substitute) produces anxiety in the baby. Anxiety is an affectual state that warns the baby of danger. Secondly, in order to cope with this anxiety the baby has to create a mother for itself. The feeling of satisfaction that a mother represents has to be fantasized so that the baby can conjure up in its mind the imagery and feelings of a warm breast and a good feed. These feelings when internalized become the ego, the separate area within oneself.

It seems unbelievable in the 21st century that the processes of mothering and the emphasis on early childhood experiences were of little interest to the main body of the early psychoanalysts. Today, the observations and theories of Bowlby, Winnicott and Stern are relevant to the work of every psychoanalyst.

Sigmund Freud, and those who followed him, concentrated instead upon the divisions of mind that affect the human condition. Human beings are born under one law but bound unremittingly to another. Each individual, at birth, is unique but faces a headlong incursion into a world which is an arena for the orders, wishes, desires, fantasies and commands of other people. A world which is racked by the tortured patterns of humankind's laws, prohibitions, aggression and culture.

Melanie Klein and Karl Abraham pioneered the importance of the 'pre-Oedipal' layers of personality development. The connections between the ego and the impulses, the drives and the body feelings and their relationship to the outside world (represented by the touch and feel of a parent's hands) are the two poles of Klein's basic model of the neonate. She maintained that the baby brings into the world two main conflicting impulses: love and hate. Love is the manifestation of the life drive. Hate, destructiveness and envy are the emanations of the death drive. These innate feelings are constantly at war with each other. The neonate tries to deal with these conflicts.

A tiny body struggling to cope with conflicting impulses, a body with sensations which are constantly threatened by the need to gratify overwhelming desires, and which, in a very short space of time, has to develop mature mechanisms for dealing with them. The baby meets a world which is both satisfying and frustrating. It exists from the moment it seeks and finds its mother's breast or its substitute, then gradually the world becomes more complicated as it seeks and finds again its father.

During the early months of life it must be supposed that the baby can make no distinction between itself as a personal entity and the bewildering world of light and darkness which surrounds it. At this stage the baby can only experience them as objects. Its mother's nipple, a good feed, a soft cot or the touch of a hand that gives it pleasure are experienced as good objects, while something that gives pain, like hunger, wet, cold or discomfort, can easily be converted into experiences that are bad.

To the baby, hunger is a frightening situation; it is not able to understand the meaning of time, of patience, the tolerance of frustration. It cannot appreciate that these situations are of a temporary nature, and will soon be followed by a feeling of pleasurable relief as the warm milk goes down. A small change in the immediate situation can change feelings of anger and discomfort into blissful gratification. It follows then that the baby is able to love and hate one and the same object in rapid succession. There are no qualifications. It is all or nothing at all, good or bad.

Conceptualization of psychological disturbance and health

Hanna Segal explains: 'In interpreting projection one indicates to the patient that he/she is attributing to another person a characteristic which is in fact their own' (1973: 121). The therapist is endeavouring to make the patient aware of the motives that lie behind the projection and the constricting distortions that can be conjured up, distorting one's view of the object and oneself. If one's own aggressive sexuality is projected on to the sexual activity of parents, the sexual intercourse of parental figures could then be perceived as cruel or sexually dangerous. This could inhibit the development of one's own sexuality in later life.

Introjection and projection

In a paper 'Notes on some schizoid mechanisms' (1952a), which was read to the British Society in 1946, Melanie Klein introduced the concepts of ego splitting and projective identification and later she related these concepts to the onset of psychosis. It was her view that anxiety was a predominant factor in psychosis since our earliest anxieties (in infancy) are psychotic in content. 'The normal development of infants,' she wrote, 'can be regarded as a combination of processes by which anxieties of a psychotic nature are bound, worked through and modified' (Klein, 1952a: 81). This was more complicated than the theory of projection described by Freud. An understanding of the processes of introjection and projection are of major importance since in the therapeutic process we can find parallels for all these situations. Every human being will go through phases in life in which they return to or experience relationships which were unsatisfactory in their past.

For every human being the outer world and its impact, and the kind of experiences they live through, the objects they come into contact with, are not only dealt with externally but are taken into the self to become part of their inner world, an entity inside the body. As we *introject* these new experiences into our personalities, we take on the concept that we can truly rely on ourselves. An enduring self-image and increased self-esteem can be facilitated by this form of introjection.

Where this can go awry relates to the relative strength or weakness of a person's ego and the supportive nurturing processes which do or do not accompany one throughout life. If, for example, we admire someone else to such an extent that we endow this other person with abilities and characteristics (good or bad) that we wish to emulate and identify with them to such an extent that we endeavour to live as they do, taking into ourselves the image and behaviour of another being, we fail to take responsibility for our own future development.

Projection goes on simultaneously. It is a manifestation of a person's ability to project on to other people those aggressive and envious feelings (predominantly those of aggression) which by the very nature of their 'badness' must be passed on by projection or, alternatively, carefully repressed. An example of this process is where the patient attempts to arouse in the therapist feelings that he or she finds impossible to tolerate but which the patient unconsciously wishes to express – using the therapist as a means of communication – evacuating unpleasant, dangerous and guilt-ridden thoughts and attempting to take over the mind of another.

It is important to understand that although projection is a general term used in other analytical theories, *projective identification* is a strictly Kleinian concept which is held, by Kleinian therapists, to be responsible for severe difficulties in both establishing one's identity and feeling secure enough to establish other outward-looking relationships. The term 'projective identification' covers a complex clinical event: one person who does not wish to own his or her feelings of love and hate manipulatively induces another into experiencing them; with consequent visible changes of affect in behaviour of both people concerned, bringing pressure to bear on the therapist, sometimes subtly, sometimes powerfully causing them to act out in a manner which reflects the patient's own projections.

It is a difficult and complicated concept to understand as it deals – in the main – with the subjective experience of a therapist and the use to which the therapist is put in being unwittingly drawn into the patient's fantasy world. For example, a patient may deal with the deprived part of his or her own childhood by idealizing the parenting process in therapy. This can in turn deprive the patient of future resourcefulness, but may also trigger off in the therapist a mutual longing for the closeness and dependence of parenthood. Inevitably the therapist must respond to these pressures, however imperceptibly they intrude.

This process highlights the internal world built up in the child and adult alike, which is partially a reflection of the external one. This two-way process continues throughout every stage of our lives, zigging and zagging, interacting and modifying itself in the course of maturation but never losing its importance in relation to the world around us. The judgement of reality is never quite free from the influence of the boiling mercury of our internal world.

Meltzer (1979) considers the concept of projective identification to be one of Melanie Klein's greatest contributions to psychoanalysis: 'A concrete conception of the inner world. . .a theatre where meaning can be generated'. Bion (1988) has led the way to considerable developments in techniques in distinguishing between normal and pathological projective identification. Bion's formulation of a container/contained model illustrates how projective identification can be an essential expression of the experiences that a patient cannot capture in the spoken word.

Melanie Klein did not really consider herself to be a theoretician; she saw herself as a face worker describing these phenomena as and when she observed them, with an awareness that one may get it wrong and an emphasis on the constant need for supervision to avoid the hazard of confusing one's personal feelings with that of a patient.

Basic ideas from Freud and Bion enter into Klein's theories. We can identify with our own hatred (at times) of reality and thinking, which are the precursor to the ego's loss of reality in psychosis. We can resonate to the psychotic's unmodified primitive anxieties and their use of the defences of projection and introjection in a desperate search for a cure. Bion in his 1957 paper 'The differentiation of the psychotic from the non-psychotic personality', comments:

> The differentiation of the psychotic from the non-psychotic personality depends on a minute splitting of all that part of the personality that is concerned with awareness of internal and external reality, and the expulsion of these fragments so that they enter into or engulf their objects. (Bion, 1988: 43)

Splitting

In *Our Adult World and its Roots in Infancy* Melanie Klein (1960) described the situation which arose when the projected bad objects (representations of the child's own ferocious and aggressive impulses) rebound on it. The situation of a young mother who tries to please a baby who is literally biting the hand that feeds it, is a case in point. Children may refuse food and scream even when they are desperately hungry, kick and push when they mostly long for a caress. These stages, which thankfully are largely outgrown in the process of normal development, can be identified with the delusional sense of persecution sometimes found in the paranoid adult. A residual persecutory element can always be found in the sense of guilt which is central to all civilizations. Since the infant continues to need a good mother, indeed its life depends upon it – by splitting the two aspects and clinging only to the good one like a rubber ring in a swimming pool, it has evolved for the time being a means of staying alive. Without this loving object to keep it buoyant the child would sink beneath the surface of a hostile world which would engulf it.

Melanie Klein's view was that, in the early years of life, the objects that surrounded the infant were not seen and understood in visual terms. This included a wide range of 'objects' – parents, siblings, blankets, food, bathing, cots, prams, toys, etc. These would be construed only as they were experienced as good or bad. Klein took this further and became concerned with the splitting of aspects of the ego itself into good and conversely bad parts. In later life, these split-off parts could become more obsessional, leading to a fragmentation of the self. Klein linked this fragmentation to the onset of schizophrenia. Here the patient has carried this process of splitting to the extreme, splitting each split yet further into a multifarious and bewildering group of repressions and concessions that in the end become chaos.

Greed and envy

In a paper 'Notes on some schizoid mechanisms' Klein (1952a) singled out greed and envy as two very disturbing factors, relating them first to the child's dominant relationship with the mother and later with relationships to other members of the family, and eventually she extended them to the individual's cycle of life.

Greed is exacerbated by anxiety, the anxiety of being deprived, the need to take all one can from the mother and from the family. A greedy infant may enjoy what it has for the time being, but this feeling is soon replaced by the feeling of being robbed by others of all that it needs in the way of food, love, attention or any other gratification. The baby who is greedy for love and attention is also afraid that it is unable to give these to others, and this in turn exacerbates its own situation. The baby needs everything, it can spare nothing and therefore what can it reasonably expect to receive from others? If an infant is relatively unable to tolerate frustration and anxiety on its own, serious difficulties can arise if the mother is unable, through depression or environmental problems, to provide consolation and mediation.

The infant can then experience murderous feelings towards this seemingly ungiving mother. In seeking to destroy that which is needed for its own survival, the infant is experiencing ambivalent feelings – one moment contemplating murder, the next, suicide. Caught up in a vicious cycle, the need to attack or withdraw produces panicky feelings of being trapped, unpleasant claustrophobic feelings which are replicated in later life.

Envy is a spoiling pursuit. If milk, love and attention are being withheld for one reason or another, then the loved object must be withholding it and keeping it for their own use. Suspicion is the basis of envy. If the baby cannot have what it desires there is a strong urge to spoil the very object of desire so that no one can enjoy it. This spoiling quality can result in a disturbed relationship with the mother, who cannot now supply an unspoilt satisfaction. Envious attacks give rise to greater anxiety – particularly when these attacks are directed towards the mother. It is difficult to acknowledge what has been done – the baby's fear is that it has gone too far but it is resentful of attempts which may be offered to facilitate, to make reparation. It is only when there is such a breakdown of the natural protective forces that one notices how distorted the relationship between mother and child can become, exacerbating the post-natal situation and leading to the depressive illness to which some women are liable.

Melanie Klein enlarged on these problems, stating quite firmly that the aggressive envy experienced in infancy can inhibit the development of good object relations, i.e. the child's ability to develop an intense and personal relationship with other objects (such as toys) which they may treat as alive, lovable, able to give love in return, needing sympathy or producing anger, and able to develop personalities which could be seen to be alive. This in its turn can affect the growth of the capacity to love. 'Throughout my work I have attributed fundamental importance to the infant's first object relations – the relation to the mother's breast and to the mother – and we have drawn the conclusion that, if this primal object which is introjected, takes root in the ego with relative security, the basis for a satisfactory development can be laid' (Klein, 1957: 389).

Projective identification

Projective identification illustrates most clearly the links between human instinct, fantasy, and the mechanisms of defence. Sexual desires, aggressive impulses, can be satiated by fantasy. Fantasy can be as pleasurable and as explicit as we wish to make it, and it is also a safety net – it contains and holds those bad parts of our inner self. The use of fantasy is obvious in literature, in science, in art and in all activities of everyday life.

One aspect of murderous fantasy is the rivalry which results from the male child's desire for the mother: his rivalry with his father and all the sexual fantasies that can be linked to this. The Oedipus complex, which is described in Chapter 2, on Freudian therapy, is rooted in the baby's suspicions of the father who takes the mother's love and attention away from him. The same applies to the female child, for whom the relationship to the mother and to all women is always of supreme importance.

Klein, however, placed her emphasis on earlier and more primitive stages as precursors of the Oedipus complex. She argued that these Oedipal feelings were identifiable in the baby at the age of six months and were the result of the projection of infantile fantasies of rage and aggression on to the parent. Whilst continuing to support Freud's tripartite differentiation of the psychic apparatus into ego, id and superego, she went on to claim that each of these areas of the psyche was identifiable almost from the day of birth.

The term 'projective identification' (as defined by Klein) has become one of the most popular of all her concepts. It has been accepted (albeit grudgingly) throughout the psychoanalytic world. However, there is still considerable con-troversy over its definition. The controversy focuses on the difference between projection and projective identification. To simplify matters 'projective identifica-tion' is best kept as a general concept broad enough to include both cases in which the recipients are emotionally affected and those in which they are not. The motives which lie at the root of projective identification are the wishes: to control the object, to acquire its attributes, to evacuate bad qualities, to protect good qualities and to avoid separation.

The paranoid-schizoid position

Klein's conception of the paranoid schizoid position as a constellation of anxie-ties, defences and object relationships, characteristic of infancy, has been a major source of inspiration to her colleagues. Work on the psychotic aspects of normal patients has confirmed Klein's delineation of the anxieties and defences of the

paranoid-schizoid position, especially the defences of splitting, projective identification fragmentation and idealization.

The paranoid-schizoid position is distinguished by the characteristic persecutory anxiety of threat to the individual. This is distinct from the threat to the object
(the anxiety characteristic of the depressive position). The paranoid-schizoid
position is easily identifiable in earliest infancy when at the beginning of life the
child builds up its inner world of the self and others, but it is not confined to early
childhood development and continues throughout the life of an individual,
fluctuating constantly with the depressive position.

Because of the strength of these early primitive feelings, an infant will initially
experience two separate feelings about its primary object (i.e. its mother or
caregiver). At one level there is the need to idealize this person, and this conflicts
with moments when the loved one is experienced as horrendous. The world is
experienced as light and dark, good and bad, distorted by fluctuating moods of
pleasure and pain and conflicting needs and desires.

The infant lives in a constricted world peopled by individuals who are experienced as good or bad. These are the early distortions which Klein described as the
paranoid position. It is with difficulty and depression that the infant grows,
realizing that life is a mixture of good and bad; that those we idealize are
vulnerable and can let us down. The mother we idealize as the source of comfort,
nourishment and support can at the same time be the one who is the centre of
attack and hatred by the loving and hating ego: a split in which good experiences
predominate over bad ones. In normal development, this process is a necessary
precondition for true integration in childhood, adolescence and adult life.

If, however, for any reason this process is disturbed, many pathological changes
can occur. When anxiety, hostility and envious feelings become overwhelming,
projective identification takes on another dimension. If there is no tidy split
between the good and the bad, fragmentation takes place. The object of anger is
split into tiny fragments, each one containing a small but violently hostile part of
the ego. This is damaging to the development of the ego and in its attempts to
relieve itself of the pain of disintegration a vicious circle can be established in
which the very painfulness of confronting reality brings with it increased feelings
of persecution. Reality is then distorted by bizarre objects and enormous hostility,
which frighten and threaten the depleted ego.

A successful negotiation of the paranoid-schizoid anxieties experienced in the
early months of the infant's development leads to a gradual organization of its
universe. Splitting, projection and introjection combine to help sort out perceptions and emotions and to separate the good from the bad. From the beginning
the tendency is towards integration as well as splitting. When these integrative
processes become more stable and continual, a new phase of development
occurs. This is how Klein describes the move to the depressive position.

The depressive position

The depressive position begins when the baby begins to recognize its mother. In
the early months of life the baby is concerned with the integration of the sights,

sounds and stimuli, both pleasant and unpleasant, with which it is surrounded. Out of this dreamlike world sufficient integration is achieved for the baby to experience its mother as a whole object – not a succession of parts. She is no longer breasts that can feed, hands that can hold, a voice that can soothe, facial grimaces that either please or frighten, but a complete entity on her own, separate, divided from the baby – someone who can choose to hold it close or stay away, can kiss or neglect or abuse her child. This gradual understanding of the separation process, this gradual awakening to the fact that it is one and the same person who is the container of both good and bad feelings, is then transposed internally to the baby. The infant is as separate from her as she is from it, and can both love and hate its mother.

Its previous fears of being the frail object of destruction extend subtly to an inner knowledge that it too can destroy the one person it loves and needs for survival. The anxiety has changed from a paranoid to a depressive one. In acknowledging the very existence of a separate being, the baby becomes exposed to the fear that it has made the cut. Aggression has destroyed the cord which linked the baby to the mother, leaving the child with feelings of unutterable guilt, sadness and deprivation, a hurt that can never be healed, a pain that can never be assuaged.

In the depressive situation, the baby has to deal not only with a destroyed breast and mother but also with the influx of Oedipal envy and jealousy. These processes involve intense conflict, which is associated with the work of mourning and which always results in anxiety and mental pain. In the Kleinian view, mental pain is pain: it hurts, and mere gratification does not make it go away. Separation is painful, is experienced as a kind of death, the death of that which was and can never be again.

This process of separation and the depressive anxieties that it invokes was described in a 1948 paper, 'On the theory of anxiety and guilt' (Klein, 1952b). It emphasized that depressive anxieties are a part of everyone's normal develop-ment, and that the guilt feelings which have developed are understood as part of the imagined harm done to a child's love object.

When this is facilitated it can enable reparation to commence. A child can then show subtle tenderness to those around it and the anxieties and paranoid fears of early infancy can become modified during this period, although these anxieties may be painfully reawakened in the normal mourning processes of later life. Adult depression is known to involve a reactivation of this stage of infantile depression, so Kleinian psychotherapists consider the actual mourning situation a productive period in therapy. When an adult admits to feeling menaced and persecuted, the recriminations and self-reproaches of the depressed patient are interpreted and hopefully understood as a manifestation of the early persecutory impulses which were directed so savagely at the self.

In preceding paragraphs some developmental models have been explained, in particular those of the impulses of destruction, greed and envy, illustrating how the persecutory and sadistic anxieties of early life can disturb the child's emotional balance and inhibit its ability to acquire and maintain good social relationships. Melanie Klein's understanding of what she was later to label 'the depressive position' highlighted the simple truth that human beings feel better when they are labelled as being 'good' than they do when they are made to feel bad. The world in which we now live has taken its toll of childhood. Alongside the obvious signs of materialistic success comes the urgent need to be seen to be a good and successful parent. Whatever the criteria for this measure of success and in order to make sure of being loved, the child has to go along with this fantasy. If they feel unloved, it must be their fault. They are too slow at school, too ugly, naughty, unacademic, lacking in social graces, poor at sport, should have been a boy or should have been a girl. Their self-esteem is low. Their parents have suppressed any recollection of their own innocent and painful childhood experiences. We are terrified of the possibility that hatred can overpower the love we are expected to profess.

Twenty years on from the death of Melanie Klein, Dr Alice Miller wrote:

> Almost everywhere we find the effort, marked by various degrees of intensity and by the use of coercive measures, to rid ourselves as quickly as possible of the child within us i.e. the weak, helpless, dependent creature – in order to become an independent competent adult deserving of respect. When we encounter this creature in our children we persecute it with the same measures once used on ourselves. And this is what we are accustomed to call child rearing. . . .The methods that can be used to suppress vital spontaneity in the child are: laying traps, lying, duplicity, subterfuge, manipulation, 'scare' tactics, withdrawal of love, isolation, distrust, humiliating and disgracing the child, scorn, ridicule and coercion even to the point of torture. (Miller, 1983: 105)

All human beings, wherever they live, exist only in relationship to other human beings. The physical processes of conception, pregnancy and birth are the same for us all. In the uterus all babies exist in comparative safety; it is only when the baby makes its post-natal appearance, head or feet first or precipitately by Caesarean section, that it learns about the reality of solitary existence.

Acquisition of psychological disturbance

Loss of the parent in any form – breast or hand – gives rise to a primary separation anxiety, which gives way to grief and then to the experience of mourning that which is lost. Aggression is also a major part of the mourning process.

If the normal processes of childhood are disrupted in some way, if fantasy becomes reality and the loved object dies, leaves, neglects, batters, sexually abuses, reacts too possessively, becomes obsessional, it follows that these disruptions of a normal interaction are likely to take a pathological course later in life. This leads not only to an aggressive stance towards society but to self-aggression and abuse. Dr John Bowlby gave the following examples:

> Many of those referred to psychiatrists are anxious, insecure individuals usually described as over-dependent or immature. Under stress they are apt to develop neurotic symptoms, depression or phobia. Research shows them to have been

exposed to at least one, and usually more than one, of certain typical patterns of pathogenic parenting, which include:

a) one or both parents being persistently unresponsive to the child's care-eliciting behaviour and/or actively disparaging and rejecting him;
b) discontinuities of parenting, occurring more or less frequently, including periods in hospital or institution;
c) persistent threats by parents not to love a child, used as a means of controlling him; threats by parents to abandon the family, used either as a method of disciplining the child or as a way of coercing a spouse;
d) threats by one parent either to desert or even kill the other or else to commit suicide (each of them more common than might be supposed);
e) inducing a child to feel guilt by claiming that his behaviour is or will be responsible for the parent's illness or death. (Bowlby, 1979: 136–7)

Cassie Cooper wrote:

> To be a child and especially to be a 'good' child in today's world is not to be a child at all. Instead these children of the twenty-first century, the children of projection, grow up too quickly to become in their turn mothers, friends, comforters, translators, advisers, support and sometimes lovers of their own parents. In taking care of other siblings, throwing themselves between parents in order to save a marriage, attempting to provide academic kudos, high earnings, sexual titillation and satisfaction, masochistic or sadistic gratification, the child will do anything, anyhow, for parental love and approval. (Cooper, 1988: 12–13)

It is these anxieties which are the cause, if not confronted, of both childhood psychoses and mental illness in adult life.

Perpetuation of psychological disturbance

In Kleinian theory human development is postulated as a series of events: events that have to be endured, experienced and overcome. In particular the theory aims to understand the difficulties experienced in early childhood by both parents and child. It emphasizes that loss of closeness to a parent figure gives rise within the individual to separation anxiety. This feeling of anxiety is internalized by the child and changes as time passes to the experience of bewildered mourning for that which has been lost. Aggression and self-destructiveness become a major part of this mourning process as throughout life the child tries again and again to re-enter that fantasized place of safety to become one with its mother.

We now know (and the dissolution of family life in contemporary society proves the point) that if the normal processes of separation are disrupted in any way, if fantasy becomes reality and the love objects die, leave, reject, batter, disparage, react too possessively or obsessionally, lose face, become depressed, unemployed, redundant, are forced to move home, these disruptions of a normal interaction are likely to take a pathological course later in life.

W.R. Bion postulated that when the infant was accosted by feelings that could not be managed, the fantasy developed that these feelings could be evacuated and then put on to their primary caregiver (i.e. the mother). Obviously if the mother is capable of understanding and accepting the child's anxiety and helplessness without her own balance of mind being disturbed, she can contain these feelings and comfort her child in a way that will make these feelings more acceptable. The child would then feel reassured enough to live with these feelings in a way that is manageable. However, if this process goes wrong – and it can go wrong, particularly if the mother herself is distressed and cannot take the child's projections – the child is forced to internalize these anxieties, repress and bottle them up, empty them out of mind, so that he or she does not have to bear those unpleasant feelings. If this condition persists, the child is well on the way to psychotic behaviour later in life.

There is no such thing as a person who does not have areas of psychological disturbance within their personality; equally, in every person there are areas of their personality which are neurotic and capable of forming good relationships, however ephemeral these relationships may seem to be. In psychoanalytic psychotherapy, provided this healthier part of a patient's ego is in evidence, it is possible to work with this patient with the professed aim of strengthening this healthy part and enabling it to become dominant in relation to the disturbed part of the personality.

In her work with small children, Melanie Klein was of the opinion that infantile neurosis was the structure which defends the child against primitive anxieties of a paranoid and depressive nature. She subsequently maintained that it is this form of psychotic anxiety that in later years blocks off the growth of symbol formation and the development of the ego. It is the resolution of this anxiety that is the aim of therapy, in that this frees the ego to develop and re-establish its symbolic processes.

> It is our contention that psychotic illness is rooted in the pathology of early infancy where the basic matrix of mental function is formed. . . .In psychosis it is all these functions that are disturbed or destroyed. The confusion between the external and the internal, the fragmentation of relationships and the ego, the deterioration of perception, the breakdown of symbolic processes, the disturbance of thinking: all are features of psychosis. Understanding the genesis of the development of the ego and its object relationships and the kind of disturbance that can arise in the course of that development is essential to understanding the mechanisms of the psychotic. (Segal, 1986: 153)

The ability to contain the infant's anxiety by a mother or caregiver capable of understanding is the beginning of stability. If this does not happen, the anxiety is introjected and can grow and develop into the experience of an even greater terror, a nameless fear of excessive destructive omnipotence. In the psychotherapeutic setting these intolerable feelings can be projected on to the therapist, who is capable of tolerating and understanding these terrifying projections – this can be acknowledged and understood by the patient, who feels that the situation becomes more tolerable. With careful interpretation and thought this patient can identify and allow the growth of a part of their personality – the part which is capable of real commitment, caring and understanding.

Change

Kleinian psychotherapy adheres to the common principles which underlie psychoanalytic theory: stressing the unconscious mechanisms which operate within the human psyche and which dominate the process of change for every human being. However, Klein had more to add to this original concept.

Let us take the well-used analogy that, at birth, every human being is a *tabula rasa*, a white tablet, a clean slate: the circumstances of one's life are then written on the white surface. To this end the human being learns to live with their history and the alternating vicissitudes and pleasant episodes of life. What is important here is the emphasis placed by Kleinian therapists on two factors:

1   There is no gain in life without a subsequent loss and the ambivalent feelings that temper any form of progress, i.e. the baby gains approval from its parents when it takes its first mouthful of solid food – but the breast is then lost to it for ever. The pride a baby will experience when learning to walk diminishes when it acknowledges that the intimacy of helplessness is relinquished.
2   Survival in a dangerous world depends on one's ability to reconcile oneself to the fact that every 'have' is balanced by a 'have not'.

The well-known game played by children, 'I'm the King of the Castle', is a case in point. The consciousness of the self and the feeling of enjoyment in winning are transient. As the child grows up it becomes more aware of the effect of its behaviour on other people and it learns to compromise and to understand the implications of frustration. The process of change can never be viewed as a clear and shining goal; rather it is the development of a growing sense of wise detachment towards life. Developing from this detachment comes the sense of personal identity which enables us to go through life with a tolerant irony and strengthens our resistance to the temptations of fame, wealth and self-aggrandizement and enables us to take what comes. Hinshelwood identifies the change processes within Kleinian theory as:

1   the development of the subject's awareness of psychic reality;
2   balancing the currents of love and hate which run within the self. (Hinshelwood, 1989: 19)

In our therapeutic work we may find that an adult has emerged from this therapeutic process, an adult whose ego can organize and substantiate its own defences against the anxieties that belong to primary separation and loss.

Practice

Goals of therapy

Melanie Klein never altered the technical principles which were the foundation of her early work, *The Psychoanalysis of Children* (1932). This continues to form the basis of the psychodynamic work undertaken by Kleinian psychotherapists and colours their concepts of mental functioning.

It is important to stress here that the theories of Melanie Klein have never been popular. Freudian and post-Freudian doctrines have had more appeal. It was perhaps easier to accept Oedipal conflicts and the 'tidy' process of oral, anal and later libidinal development than to take on board the confrontation with a life and death struggle which lies at the root of Kleinian thinking. To tilt at the precious idealization of the 'loving' mother and to confront instead the infantile struggle for 'survival' are unpleasant and uncomfortable. In Kleinian therapy we have to take a long, hard look at our fantasies of parental love: if these are removed, what bleak prospect of life does the therapist provide?

Patients who undertake this kind of psychotherapy are bound to come to the first session full of hopes and fears, with deep-rooted fantasies and phobias about themselves and their therapist. They present material in the very first session which concerns anxieties that are central to them at that moment. Predominantly they want to feel 'better', to obtain relief from suffering (Colby, 1951), and are seeking, like an infant, immediate gratification of their needs. Wish-fulfilment is not confined to those who seek psychotherapy. Eavesdrop on any everyday conversation and you will conclude that people always hope to get what they feel they need to make them happy and want to obtain it in the shortest possible time and with a minimum of effort: powerful wishes for a magical solution rather than facing up to the realities that underline our complex psychological make-up.

In Kleinian psychotherapy it is maintained that anxiety can act as a spur to development and personal achievement, providing this anxiety is not excessive. At the commencement of therapy it is important to work with the patient's unconscious fantasies about themselves and others, and in particular how such fantasies relate to the reality of the outside world, the way life has been experienced both in the past and in the present.

This may sound simplistic. When studying certain isolated aspects of human behaviour the reductive approach is very appealing. The plain facts are, however, that human beings are complex and that the very process of functioning as a person requires a conceptual level that does justice to what is revealed of these complex forces. Behaviour which is as thoughtless, demanding and extortionate as the infant's relationship with its mother reflects the need to exhaust and exploit the therapist and to experience yet again the feelings of guilt and anxiety which are associated with such behaviour.

A Kleinian therapist would have it that psychotherapy has more in common with an educational experience than a form of medical treatment. Successful psychotherapy should begin a process of learning and personal development which moves along at its own pace. The foundation stone of this process must be the relationship between therapist and patient. If this goal is similarly perceived and worked upon by both parties, the outcome will be the achievement of some mutual satisfaction.

Melanie Klein was quite clear about the efficiency of her method in the treatment of adults. Her primary goal was the reduction of immediate anxiety by encouraging patients to face their inhibitions and to facilitate a more positive relationship with their therapist. This in turn would enable patients to experience themselves as real people in a real world able to maintain a balance between the feelings of love and hate which alternate in every psyche.

At the end of therapy it is hoped that patients will feel able to form full and satisfactory personal relationships, and will have gained insight into their personal situation and feel released from their early fixations and repressions. They will be less inhibited and better able to enjoy the good things of life while remaining sensitive, open and capable when problems arise. They will be able to assess their internal world, possess a quiet reassurance and ego strength which stems from the knowledge that even in times of great stress they will survive and, perhaps even more importantly, that they will want to survive. The means by which true reparation (growth, in the Kleinian sense) takes place are essentially mysterious. It is something which happens when the 'mental atmosphere is conducive to objects repairing one another. The frame of mind of tolerance, of pain, of remorse over one's destructiveness' (Meltzer, 1979: 18–19). These reparative mental conditions follow when there is an understanding of one's infantile dependency upon internal objects – an idealized mother and father at the moment of one's own creation – so that one can in life accept oneself as a product of what was past and is in the future in an atmosphere of tolerance and acceptance. Melanie Klein stated:

> My criterion for termination of analysis is, therefore, as follows: have persecutory and depressive anxieties been sufficiently reduced in the course of analysis, and has the patient's relation to the external world been sufficiently strengthened to enable him to deal satisfactorily with the situation of mourning arising at this point? (Klein, 1950: 78–80)

Selection criteria

Only uncommonly aware and brave people seek to know about themselves and to face up to what psychotherapy can reveal. There are many patterns to therapy and many different approaches to the relief of psychic pain. Patients have a choice in the kind of treatment they would prefer, and can and do move from individual to group therapy, from group therapy to family therapy, if they so wish, and in whatever sequence seems beneficial to them at a particular time.

Initially the referral of a patient for psychotherapy would be made by their psychiatrist or general practitioner. With luck, the would-be patient and their doctor have discussed a preference for one modality or another. There is a need for each patient to accept responsibility for their problem and, in seeking amelioration of their situation, to actively participate in making the decision, choosing to work on a one-to-one basis in individual therapy or deciding that they would gain greater motivation and strength from the support and challenge that can be offered in a therapy group or a family group setting.

In selecting patients for individual therapy there are criteria which the Kleinian psychotherapist would seek to fulfil:

• that the patient has problems which can be clearly defined in psychodynamic terms;

- that the patient appears motivated enough for change and insight into their previous behaviour;
- that the patient has enough internal strength to cope with the demands and tensions that are to be created by the process of interpretation and confrontation;
- that the patient produces evidence that they are able to accept and sustain a long-standing relationship with the therapist and with significant others in their immediate surroundings.

Patients may arrive with little knowledge of how Kleinian therapy differs from other forms of treatment, how the procedure works, and even less knowledge about the outcome of psychotherapy. Initially the psychotherapist will indicate that therapy involves a detailed process of examining and discussing problems. Patients are told that it could be distressing and painful, that there are no guaranteed 'cures', but that they can be enabled to help themselves to identify the origin of their symptoms, the reaction to these symptoms and the ways in which these symptoms constrict their life.

The therapist has the right to decide if he or she is prepared to work with a specific patient. Personal feelings will obviously affect the outcome of an initial diagnostic interview. Conversely, the patient may decide that he or she will be unable to work with the therapist. It is essential to respect the rights of both parties in such a delicate transaction. What is important is that the relationship between therapist and patient can be one in which there is mutual respect, the respect of one human being for another and hope for the potentialities of this other person. This is termed the 'therapeutic alliance'. It is hoped that each patient has the capacity to come out of therapy with the opportunity to love well, to play well and to have some optimism for the future.

A Kleinian psychotherapist finds it most suitable to work with patients whose underlying conflicts are towards the narcissistic side, whose egos have undergone considerable deformation or weakening. Patients may come into therapy express-ing inability to love or to be loved by others, with conflicts about dealing with people in a social, sexual or work setting, general intellectual and academic underfunctioning, symptomatic phobias, anxiety states and minor perversions.

With some patients there may be a need to limit the period of treatment. It is useful anyway to indicate that the treatment will not go on indefinitely, that it will end at a certain time. A statement of this kind may not be indicated for all patients, but could be necessary in certain instances. In contrast to psycho-analysis, Kleinian psychotherapy gives a realistic indication that the treatment will terminate some day. The therapist will point out that the therapeutic relationship will come to an end. This is an important and necessary factor in working through the attachment process, a process which is repeated throughout life when some aspect of a 'good object' is given up.

Qualities of effective psychotherapists

Kleinian psychotherapists are always in short supply. As with other modalities, it is an expensive and prolonged training, in most cases a postgraduate training, and in every case a training which involves the student in an extensive commitment both of time and money over many years; they must tailor their lifestyle to personal therapy four or five times a week.

It is a training which centres on the personality of the would-be therapist, and this understanding of the self is tuned to perfect pitch like the finest violin. The therapist is encouraged to become an instrument which can interpret, colour and respond to the musical score, resonate and bend beneath the fingers of the musician, constantly changing and developing their diagnostic sensitivities in interpretation and technique. Kleinian psychotherapists will have experienced this long-term period of personal analysis, three years (minimum) of theoretical input, followed by a shorter period of training analysis at one of the formal institutes, plus ongoing supervision of their work with individual clients. In *The Psychoanalysis of Children*, Melanie Klein wrote:

> The analysis of children at puberty demands a thorough knowledge of the technique of adult analysis. I consider a regular training in the analysis of adults as a necessary foundation. . . .No one who has not gained experience adequately and done a fair amount of work on adults should enter upon the technically more difficult field of child analysis. In order to be able to preserve the fundamental principles of analytic treatment in the modified form necessitated by the child's (and the adult's) mechanisms at the various stages of development, the therapist must besides being fully versed in the technique of early analysis possess complete mastery of the technique employed in analysing adults. (Klein, 1932: 342)

It is the Kleinian view that an analyst or a psychotherapist who dogmatically believes that they and only they, plus a few other chosen spirits who adhere rationally and rigidly to their particular school and their particular form of dogmatism, will not, in Kleinian terms, have advanced beyond the paranoid-schizoid position to be capable of doubt as to whether they, or anyone else has the key to understanding the complexity of a human being. This is important since the fundamental concepts of the paranoid-schizoid and depressive positions naturally affect the ways in which the Kleinian psychotherapist will view their patients' presentations.

In dealing with the early anxieties which arise from the relationship between the baby and the breast, faced by the harsher and more persecutory anxieties which lie in the deepest strata of the mind and the primitive processes that are aroused by this process, it is vital for the Kleinian therapist to remain consistent, namely to refer the anxiety back to its source and resolve it by systemically analysing the transference situation.

The therapist will need to be sensitive to those embryonic features of emotional problems which are present in all human beings and which are clearly reflected in the patient. The therapist will be aware that possible events in one's life, both in reality and in imagination, which did occur and which could have developed, should not be denied and repressed.

The transition from childhood to adulthood requires an understanding of the fact that in every person lies the capacity to have been something and someone else. The therapist should be able to encourage the flowering of this inner self in the patient, while remaining for most of their professional life in a situation where their own self-expression is forbidden.

The steady, accepting but neutral attitude of the Kleinian psychotherapist differs from the more responsive, manipulative and role-playing attitudes advocated by certain other strategies of intervention. Power is acknowledged and interpreted but in Kleinian psychotherapy the therapist allows himself or herself to be used as an object. In this way the psychotherapist actually intrudes but does not obtrude.

Making clear the transference manifestations which develop during this process is regarded as the primary means by which the patient is helped towards better health, and able to maintain continuing psychic functioning. The personality of the therapist – calm, interested, helpful, giving full attention to each minute detail of the patient's behaviour and language – re-creates in the therapeutic alliance an opportunity to correct the infantile distorted view of object relationships that has constricted the patient's life. It provides incentive and reward in a benign relationship that encourages the patient to achieve the tasks that are imposed by the discipline of therapy and provides each patient with a model of strength and an identification with a reality: the real person of the therapist.

At times the psychotherapist, guided by the ethical goals of treatment and the understanding obtained from their own training and personal psychotherapy, must safeguard against any interference with a professional attitude to the patient based on prior knowledge of their own difficulties and the problems which stem from their own ethical values, attitudes and boundaries. For instance if the therapist is mourning the death of a parent or partner it may be difficult to work with a patient in a similar position.

Therapists are not empty husks; they have prejudices, fears, painful trigger spots. It is better for both therapist and patient to acknowledge and identify these feelings. This may mean that at times the therapist will decide not to take a particular patient into treatment. This is a serious decision for patient and therapist alike and must be handled in such a fashion that making a referral to another agency or individual does not further disturb the patient and cause more pain.

Therapeutic relationship and style

Kleinian technique is psychoanalytic and based – as are others – on classical Freudian analysis. This means that the setting for therapy is formal and the number of sessions will vary (an analysis offers five or six sessions each week), but in psychotherapy this is the exception rather than the rule. However, the session time is the same (50 minutes) and the patient can be offered a choice of either couch or chair.

The therapist uses the techniques of free association and interpretation and in all essentials, other than the frequency of sessions, psychoanalytic principles are strictly adhered to. The therapist is confined to listening and interpreting the material brought by a patient. Criticism, encouragement, reassurance and advice-giving is avoided. However, the atmosphere is relaxed and facilitative.

To understand and appreciate the difference between the Kleinian relationship in therapy with the patient and other methodologies, one must look at the nature of the interpretations given to the patient. Klein changed the emphasis in the analytic process from formal Freudian theories to aspects of material not seen before. She was impressed by the prevalence and power of the mechanisms of projection and introjection and highlighted the fact that these introjections led to the building of the inner complex being, with its projections which colour the world and our perceptions of reality. Once verbalized and 'seen', as it were, these revelations of our primitive levels of experience can be understood and detected in the material provided by our adult patients.

Kleinian therapists are aware that if a patient gains control in psychotherapy their difficulties will be perpetuated in later life. The patient will continue to live a life constricted by the paranoid-schizoid symptoms which caused them to seek therapy in the first place. It follows that however neutral and laid back the therapist may contrive to be, in successful therapy the therapist maintains control of the kind of relationship that will operate.

'In all forms of psychoanalytic psychotherapy, therapist and patient are confronted with a basic problem, the problem of object need. Every patient regards the psychotherapist as real, regards all the manifestations of the treatment situation as real and strives to regard the therapist as a real object. The therapist too wants to regard the patient as real and to respond to the patient as a real object' (Tarachow, 1970: 498–9). The primary urge in this relationship is the temptation to turn back the clock, to regress, to restore the symbiotic parental relationship that initially occurred with the mother: to lose the boundaries and fuse, to re-create the past as it was, and return to the time of ultimate dependency, replete, at one, inside the mother.

In no way should the therapist confuse the therapeutic function with the parental function. The therapist may give over part of their mind to this experience, since they come so close to the patient's life experience, but in essence the therapist must also remain detached from it, holding on to professional anonymity. The therapist will be aware of the seductive danger of imagining him/herself (even for the briefest time) as the ideal parent figure for the patient. The therapist uses these skills of awareness and identification to assess and understand the complexities of the interaction of the patient with the parent parts of the therapist.

We may be deeply affected, feel involved, but paradoxically this affection and involvement is distilled, detached, separated in a way which is impossible in the true relationship between a parent and child.

The Kleinian psychotherapist works assiduously to develop this therapeutic alliance, the intimate, real and close working together of two minds. For this to come about both the therapist and the patient undertake a controlled ego splitting (where either good or bad parts of the self are split off from the ego and projected into love or hatred of external objects: i.e. parental figures or caregivers) in the service of the treatment. The therapist and the patient work together in constructing a barrier against the need for a constricted object relationship. The therapist is not a breast, a hand or a voice, but a human being who is complete in every way. The therapist as well as the patient has to struggle constantly against the array of temptations which lead them to believe that they can allow themselves to become closer to their patient, with consequent dissolution and camouflaging of the existing ego boundaries. These temptations are further compounded because certain aspects of the therapeutic alliance are real. The therapist behaves in a caring, concerned, real and human way to the patient, and the patient is able to glean over a period of time real things about the therapist: that the therapist may be single or married, the family is away on holiday, that the therapist smokes, prefers one colour to another, that there is a secretary, a family pet, small children and that the therapist may share accommodation with other psychotherapists, etc.

These realistic aspects of the treatment relationship must be understood by a psychotherapist. Among other things they lead to identification with the reality aspects of the therapist, who uses them wordlessly to correct transference distortions and to supply the motivation necessary for the therapeutic work of transference interpretation. Close attention to what may be happening in the immediate present has many analogies with what could have been happening in the reconstructed past. What is important is the urgent need that the transference process serves in the here and now and this should not be disregarded in the therapist's search for its meaning in the past.

Every interpretation made by a therapist results in a loss or a deprivation for the patient. It can frustrate, denying the patient an opportunity to gratify their fantasy wishes, often placing them in the position of relinquishing some infantile object: 'It is a paradox that the interpretation – the act of the therapist that deprives the patient of the infantile object – also provides him with an adult object in the form of the sympathetic therapist' (Tarachow, 1970: 498–9).

Despite many changes in current practice and in how unresolved issues are being tackled by therapists, there is a strong continuity in the way in which fundamental principles have endured:

- the process – the overriding importance given to the responses to interpretation;
- the transference – the centrality of interpreting the transference; the emphasis on the patient's early childhood experiences and their level of functioning in this period;
- the belief that love and hate go side by side and that the turmoil caused by the sense of destructiveness is counterbalanced by love.

Major therapeutic strategies and techniques

The role of the psychotherapist is centred entirely on transference and its interpretation. The therapist listens intently to the patient's material, and endeavours not to be involved at all in giving practical advice, encouragement, reassurance or to offer any active participation in the life of the patient or the patient's family.

Transference interpretation

The concept of transference relates not only to an understanding of the 'here and now', the situation which is actually evolving between the psychotherapist and the patient, but to an understanding of the way facts and fantasies which relate to past relationships, especially those of internal figures from the patient's inner world, are transferred on to the therapist. The transference is expanded as a total situation which includes the functioning of the patient as well as the symbolic meanings placed on to the therapist.

This lively process takes in current problems and relationships, which are again related to the transference as it develops. The psychotherapist is aware of the transference at the very beginning of therapy, but in giving interpretations careful attention must be paid to the way they are handled, the timing, the order and the language used, and especially to the amount of interpretation.

Understanding of transference and counter-transference and their effect on therapy are the tools which are used to investigate both positive and negative feelings directed towards the therapist. Counter-transference was first seen as a neurotic disturbance in the therapist which prevented him or her from obtaining a clear and objective view of the patient, but now it is understood to be an important source of information about the patient as well as a major component in understanding the interaction of the therapist and the patient. In other words, we are deeply affected and involved but also paradoxically uninvolved with our patients. These feelings bring with them the pressure to identify with the counter-transference situation and to act it out in ways either unconsciously and subtly or obviously and aggressively.

Interpretation of these feelings should be sparse and succinct, using everyday language, avoiding technical and analytic terms which may give satisfaction to the therapist but are of little value to the patient. If your patient cannot understand you, they may as well go home. The best initial interpretations are simple restatements of the problem as presented by the client but relayed back in dynamic terms.

If it is difficult to teach psychotherapy, it is even more difficult to describe the techniques of psychotherapy. In an earlier paragraph I stressed that the Kleinian psychotherapist will have learned skills through long-term psychoanalytic psychotherapy, a process not unlike the age-old system of apprenticeship to a master or skilled craftsman of some repute and proven worth. The technique of psychotherapy is not static, and psychotherapists regularly attend case discussion groups, supervision sessions, seminars and study groups to meet and compare experiences and to learn from each other in a lively fashion.

Contemporary Kleinian technique emphasizes:

- the immediate here and now situation; all aspects of the setting – i.e. the room where therapy takes place; the importance of understanding the content of the anxiety;
- 'the consequence of interpreting the anxiety rather than the defences only (so called deep interpretation)' (Spillius, 1983: 321–2).

Winnicott humorously remarked, 'of course you can acknowledge that there is a war going on', but political statements or discussion of other issues do not belong in the consulting room. In this way the client is enabled to make contact with an expectation which relates more closely to the emotions that are experienced as a result of therapy, than they do to what is happening at that moment in the external world.

The past is connected to the present gradually. Interpretations are given in a certain sequence: preparatory interventions, interpreting resistances and defences, gauging the patient's readiness to accept the interpretation and wording it carefully. In the Kleinian model, interpretations go from the surface to the depth; from what is known or imagined to occur in the present, to what exists in the past, which is less well known or unknown, the earliest mental processes of childhood, and to the later more specialized types of mental functioning, which are the unconscious infantile archaic wishes and fantasies – those which focus on the therapist as a possible source of gratification.

The change process in therapy

Atholl Hughes, in 'Contributions of Melanie Klein to psycho-analytic technique', gives a particularly clear definition of the change process in Kleinian therapy:

> As the patient is helped to distinguish good experiences they can identify with the analyst as a person who can care for their own insight and well being and the way is open for the patient to do the same. As the patient's envy lessens it becomes possible to appreciate positive qualities in oneself and others, acknowledged along with destructive qualities. Integration of split off parts of oneself is comparable to a process in the development of the normal infant who begins, at about three months of age, to tolerate loving and hating the same object with less splitting and projection.
>
> On the basis of a repeated satisfying experience, the child is able to introject, that is to take into their own personality, ideas and feelings of a good mother with less hostility and idealisation. The child is then in a position to tolerate feelings of concern and responsibility towards the mother in whom the capacity to introject is crippled. (Hughes, 1974: 113–14)

During treatment, the patient comes to understand that feelings of aggression and love can be valuable, and so it is possible to value them. Early responses to interpretation which were felt by the patient to be prohibitive, unkind or unduly harsh, and which tended either to frustrate desire or to punish, permitting, even commanding, the patient to enter in fear and trepidation the forbidden areas of primitive and passionate feelings, these regressive infantile expectations are overcome and are replaced by a rationality that can be accepted and understood. Melanie Klein opened the door to insights which enable us at least to attempt to contend with human behaviour. We are confronted in life with a view of ourselves in a succession of social relationships which are disrupted by hatred, jealousy, rivalry, greed and other destructive feelings. The process of change in therapy enables us at least to establish more constructive relationships. It is said that as

Freud discovered the child in the adult, so Klein discovered the infant in the child.

Patients change as they become more open and free to acknowledge their constant struggle between love and hate. Facilitated by their therapy, knowledge of the destructive elements which are present in the psyche can lead to clearer judgement, increased tolerance of themselves and others, with the ability to remain in control and to be less fearful.

Change can be identified as a desire for reconciliation and reparation. The patient can begin to identify with other people in a caring and sensitive way. The patient can let go of the negative aspect of the painful frustrations and suffering of the past and believe once again in their own capacity to love and to expect to be loved in return. In making this reparation for the past the patient makes good the imagined injuries both given and received in infancy and moves on to relinquish their guilt.

Limitations of the approach

There is a proliferation of different methods of psychotherapy, some of which do not emphasize self-awareness, and which question the causation of therapeutic change. They argue that change is not engendered by the growth of self-awareness. Questions are frequently asked about the extent to which the theories and concepts of Kleinian therapy affect the technique of psychoanalysis.

Scientific examination of the causes of therapeutic change must question the examination and description of the variables which, in context, facilitate such change. Experimental methods can then be evolved to test the hypotheses which are formed. Kleinian psychotherapy, as judged by these contemporary standards, is still unable to provide the scientific evidence necessary to meet the basic criteria of disconformability. Moreover it becomes increasingly evident that it is an oversimplification to look at psychopathology as if it can be isolated from the changing attitudes of the nuclear age.

But what of the Kleinian method both as a focus of enquiry and as a therapy? Some Kleinian therapists find it difficult to acknowledge the outside environment that their patients have created and in which they function. In seeking to re-create the patient's internal and fantasized world of childhood, the Kleinian is perhaps too eager to divorce patients from their social and cultural background.

We have, after all, moved on considerably from the early 1900s and have come to realize (I hope) that our patients are a specific group of people who have reacted in a specific way to their problems and who come, specifically, to seek help from Kleinian psychotherapy. A human being cannot develop in a sterilized plastic bubble. A baby is conceived at the coming together of its parents, who contribute to this act of creation the essence of their own personalities at that given moment. The baby is born at a predicted time and season of the year, in a special place and in a particular way and significantly others become involved in its well-being. It depends throughout life on the availability and proximity of other human beings. In the wheatfields of America, a man will sow the wheat that provides bread for this child, and in the sweatshops of India another child will labour to cut its clothes.

In the heat of the moment, focusing mainly on early childhood experiences and/or recollections, the broader social context and subjective processes which brought these two human beings together can sometimes get left out of the consulting room, especially if the focus is on manoeuvrability and tactics. Psychotherapy has held the view that external events are not of primary importance, but we know that these events can exacerbate or alleviate certain aspects of the personality.

Inevitably the decision on what process to use with the patient in effecting change is shaped by one's theoretical approach. However, if the therapist practises therapy all day and every day from only one viewpoint, then there is a real danger of the Kleinian therapist becoming subsumed and consumed by their own stance. The rigorous adherence to basic psychoanalytic methods should not become rigidity. This contrasts sharply with other strategies of intervention where the emphasis has shifted from the processes within an individual to those in the context of his or her relationships with others (i.e. attachment therapy, family therapy and personal construct psychology).

B.J. Farrell (1981) criticizes the limitations imposed by strict adherence to one kind of analytic theory, and makes the point that Kleinian theory was (and still is) innovative. In continuing to extemporize and to employ new forms of psychoanalytic method, the Kleinian therapist will seek to obtain affirmation of any novel input from the patients themselves.

It was a technical invention – the technique of child analysis – which gave Melanie Klein the idea that the free play of young children can be interpreted psychoanalytically, giving access to the more primitive areas of the mind; this still provides the Kleinian therapist with a wealth of new material and has continued to provoke considerable revision of analytic theory. This technique influenced theory.

When the Kleinian therapist continues to report new case material and new findings, how is it possible to decide whether the therapist has, in fact, just misinterpreted basic Kleinian theory? If the therapist is hesitant about challenging results, does this imply that the original theory itself is 'shaky' and in need of amendment?

For every therapist the nagging doubts must persist. The crucial question remains: what effect does the use of Klein's theories have on the behaviour of this therapist? Do interpretations always dictate the therapist's goals for patients? Do Kleinian therapists only seek out what they expect to find? Do therapists, in order to fit their own expectations, distort what information patients provide? The deeper the analytic work, the more primitive the processes mobilized, the more essential it is to adhere to the boundaries of the psychodynamic model.

Therapists tend to forget that because they see their patients in such a strictly controlled analytic setting, they are immolated from a view of their patient in the external world. True, the patients report on their daily life, but these reports are highly selective and often only pertinent to the failures rather than the successes of life outside the consulting room. Anxious behaviour by one patient can be interpreted as a repression of unconscious ideas which are threatening to become conscious. The same anxious behaviour in another could be viewed externally as a way of appealing for a sympathetic approach from the therapist. These two interpretations of behaviour represent astonishingly different theoretical systems. In this way the therapist's viewpoint can be distorted.

The reader of this book will note that various theorists differ considerably on the postulation of central motives or goals for all human beings. Why do they differ so much? Is it not that the task of ferreting out the central motives of all human beings is impossible? Is it not an unattainable goal to poll every patient on their expectations of life and their private responses to the slings and arrows of outrageous fortune?

Would Kleinian psychotherapy suffer if each patient's motives were seen as unique? Psychoanalytical psychotherapy has been defined as a perspective which is essentially pre-theoretical in nature, but perspectives are often constricted by ideological underpinnings whether we are aware of them or not.

It was Huxley who wrote: 'Give me good mothers and I shall make a better world', but it is the converse which is true: 'Make me a good world and I shall give you good mothers.' It is hoped that Kleinian therapy can eventually be more explicit in stating that the amelioration of at least some areas of maternal deprivation and childhood abuse will only be possible when these intrinsic requirements can be met.

In looking forward to the future, R.D. Hinshelwood wrote:

> Increasingly throughout the 20th century human beings have been understood as psychological beings. Their difficulties have therefore been increasingly seen as psychological and less as moral. The impetus for this change has comprised many elements, but psychoanalysis has figured prominently among them. In very large measure, across the whole of our culture, the general apperception of mental illness and disturbance has been moulded by psychoanalysis itself. As psychoanalytic ideas have spread, so the presentation of psychological difficulties has become permeated by a psychoanalytic sophistication. This has created a particular situation for psychoanalysts. They face a moving target. New kinds of patients mean new ideas which in turn mean new ways of working, but they also mean patients with new ways of presenting themselves and thus a new target for the psychoanalytic probe. (Hinshelwood, 1994: 240)

Case example

The patient

Whilst many psychotherapy patients present with a sense of urgency, even of panic, initially I had no sense of this pressure from Pam. A feeling of resolve emanated from her. She knew that she had a problem. 'A deep-rooted problem' which she was determined to confront. Pam had been in therapy before, but only for one year. 'It didn't help then.' We are three years into our therapeutic relationship. Pam has agreed that her story can be told.

Our initial therapeutic contract was for two sessions per week. After one year this was reduced to once weekly. Two years on we mutually agreed to conclude. Six months later, in deep distress, Pam asked to resume therapy. We are still in weekly contact.

Of enormous help in the therapeutic process has been Pam's talent and enthusiasm for writing. To every session she brings written material, recollections from the past and insights into her present difficulties. Excerpts from this verbatim material are quoted in this case presentation: they relate significantly to a current relationship which is important and is causing much anguish.

A tall, attractive woman, naturally blonde, with dark brown eyes, trim figure, wide warm smile and air of gentle firmness, Pam at 52 has successfully completed her studies for a Diploma in Personnel Management.

Pam, was born in 1948, the younger of two children. Her brother, Brian, was 11 years old at the time of her birth. 'I grew up feeling like an only child. When I was five my brother was 16 and already thinking of work. We were a mixed up family. My mother was Welsh, father Scottish and later I married my boyfriend from Ireland.'

The family led a comfortable life. Pam's father, a skilled craftsman, worked as a typesetter for a national newspaper. Membership of a printers' union ensured that he had regular well-paid employment. Pam's mother worked briefly but serious health problems prevented her from continuing employment.

Following the birth of a son Pam's mother was told that she would be unable to conceive other children. Therefore the arrival of a daughter 11 years later shocked both parents. They behaved awkwardly, not knowing how to respond to a new baby when their elder child was already in senior school. Pam's father occasionally took her on outings but her mother's interest was limited to her little girl's outward appearance.

'I was dressed, doll-like, my hair in ringlets, wearing pretty dresses, but not allowed to compete with my mother, who always claimed the centre of attention. Mother was charming, sociable, cultivated friends whilst my father, devoted to her, remained private and unobtrusive, always working long hours.

'My brother used to take me to school, always in a hurry, other people used to take me home again. One day it was half-day finish and nobody came to collect me. I was terrified.

'At primary school I was very good, always smiling. I didn't learn very much, I was too scared of getting it wrong. School was near home and I walked there and back on my own, I was about seven. At senior school I had a friend to go with, her name was Sandra; she was big, strong and confident, we laughed so much.

'I looked around at senior school and envied the clever girls who got high marks. I couldn't do that. So I became bad. I had lots of fun, making people laugh, doing things they wouldn't dare do. When you misbehaved at senior school, you had to stand outside the headmistress's office and read the

Highway Code, for one playtime. She would ask you questions on it after-wards. I spent three months outside the head's office, reading the Highway Code. When I was 21, I passed my driving test in record time, after only a few lessons!

'My mother's rheumatoid arthritis continued to deteriorate, and became a serious problem when I was 15 and it was time to leave school. I was going to be a hairdresser. The teachers must have been pleased to see the back of me. But – I had made a decision – I really wanted to be one of the clever girls. I went, on my own, to see the headmistress, to tell her I wanted to stay at school an extra year and pass some exams. I can still remember the look on her face. Neither of my parents had ever been to the school, I can't remember them taking an interest in what I did there. A lot of the time I wasn't even there, I was off on the back of Dan's (my boyfriend's) motorbike with the wind blowing through my hair. I was very disruptive. The headmistress consulted other teachers, who looked at me in disbelief. They listed all the reasons why I should leave, but they did let me stay, and so I started a pattern collecting so many pieces of paper qualifications to wear as a suit of armour, to prove that I was one of the clever girls.

'My parents disapproved of Dan. "He's not good enough for you", they said, but I was in love with him.' While her mother grew increasingly disabled, Pam led a lonely life. Her boyfriend provided a sense of security which contrasted with the solitariness of her existence. 'Going to doctors, dentists, shopping on my own – I needed to find someone to keep me safe. My parents were never able to go to an open evening at school even though I got good exam results. When Dan came to call for me I would be straight back on his motorbike and what's more I wouldn't wear a crash helmet.'

Four years on, with Pam 18 and already pregnant, they were married. Dan was not a reliable husband. After their son arrived he took work as a long distance lorry driver and was away for many weeks. Left alone with her baby and facing the rapid deterioration in her mother's condition, depression took over. For Pam, life became a succession of hospital visits watching her mother endure painful and often demeaning forms of treatment. Pregnant once again, with little help from Dan, and with her mother desperately ill, her depression deepened – life became a nightmare. Heavily pregnant, she would push her child to and from the hospital where her mother was dying. Twenty years of life had been constricted by her mother's disfiguring illness. Tending to her, fetching, carrying, cooking, endeavouring to behave as an adult while still a child, Pam would collude in her mother's despairing attempt to remain attractive and charming whilst enduring unimaginable discomfort, bedridden, plagued by open sores.

Pam's father, at 65, retired, devoting himself to the care of his wife. After she died he sold their home and went to live in Majorca. Still abroad, one year later, he died leaving Pam abandoned, isolated, despondent and bleak. With two children, a boy and a girl, two years apart, an intransigent husband who was away for months and sending intermittent and insufficient funds to provide for the family, Pam took a succession of menial jobs, but with a biology A level she eventually found work with a bio-tech company. She is still employed.

Pam has attracted lovers and has had both short- and long-term relationships. She divorced her husband in 1979, but resisted offers of marriage, preferring to devote herself to the well-being of the children. Pam's depression remained; she did little for herself in order to be 'there' for them as they needed her. Later the children as adults went separate ways. Her son married, had two children then divorced. He has another partner. Pam's daughter has recurrent bouts of depression following the birth of a premature baby (weighing only 1 lb) and remains unmarried with two children. Pam is a supportive mother and grandmother.

Before therapy Pam had started a relationship with Tom. This was unlike any previous affair. Tom appeared seductive, difficult, challenging, intriguing and unusual – unique, in that he had been seriously injured in a car crash and was partially paralysed, but still mobile with the use of crutches and leg irons; married and divorced before his crash. Women had always found him attractive, even in his immobilized state. For Pam, Tom's immobility resonated with her mother's illness, producing feelings of passion and compassion. His very accessibility made him important in her life. He was dependent. She could be there to help this attractive man and in the throes of sexual desire, make love to him as often as possible. But he was unpredictable, moody, demanding, accepting all that Pam could give him but reticent and withdrawn at times. He would offer wine, music and food when he was affable but erratically morose and non-committent at others. Pam was distraught. She would vow never to see him again, never to phone him (especially when there were long silences and breaks in contact). Railing against him, his inconsistencies, his coolness, his hardness, Pam would implore me to take a strong line with her, forbid her to see this man again. He was dangerous, destructive, but her addiction escalated; each day she watched to see who was calling at his home.

Pam wrote:

> Went to see my therapist with a lot of sadness. I had realized from the start that my mother and Tom were linked in my mind, that I had taken Tom to my therapy because I couldn't handle him. How typical that I had put his needs before mine. . . .
>
> Felt incredibly depressed also I felt angry. I kept taking an evil demon to Cassie and somehow she diluted him and sent me home with him again. I feel like begging her to take him from me, he is going to kill me seeing that I resist the urge to kill him.

Twelve sessions later Pam's ambivalence towards her relationship with Tom took on a new meaning and she became calmer and more analytical about his behaviour, his obvious loss of affect. She could admit that this badly damaged man, physically and psychologically, was self-obsessed, unable to give her or anyone else his full attention. He could never reciprocate her 'devotion to care'.

Pam assumed an introspective view, professing to care more for herself, but who was she? A woman who loves her children too much to see their personalities destroyed by a 'crazy maker'. With faith in her kind of love she could refuse to be bullied, holding on to the power to take care of herself and her children. Why had she taken so long to recognize this power? She had 'stumbled on the right path in life by coincidence or luck. I am no longer ashamed of this lady – she is fantastic, I love her, she is coming with me forever to be thanked and appreciated. Together she and I will grow together and break this cycle of destruction. I am now concentrating on my needs. The point of this relationship has been to heal my past deprivations, to truly understand the very nature of psychotherapy, I consider this relationship a blessing. I still fear for Tom but I can't help him and I shouldn't. End of story.'

Pam left therapy at this time to concentrate on her studies, changing her telephone number and determined to change her feelings about Tom. Her son developed symptoms of rheumatoid arthritis (her mother's illness), and her daughter was again depressed, needing her support. She intended to help them, but I was convinced that this intense preoccupation with her children's welfare resembled a 'flight into health'. However, I supported her new-found confidence and optimism in her ability to survive.

Obviously the need for Tom would return. This potent mixture of past longings for a mother's attention and Tom's seductiveness was a heady combination which could not be resisted.

A year elapsed before Pam requested a further appointment. After a hysterectomy she was off work and recuperating at home. The relationship with Tom had resumed after a short break but Tom was again avoiding contact. No flowers, cards or phone calls during and after her hospitalization. A spate of frenetic writing was triggered in Pam on her return from hospital in the face of Tom's subsequent silence.

Pam was terrified, experiencing violent feelings of hate and revenge towards him and destructive feelings towards herself. Was she on the edge of madness? She was out of control, unable to sleep, conducting feverish recriminations against Tom, having conversations in her mind with Tom, the Devil, fearing his power over her and her family.

The flow of written material from Pam increased, containing insights that were remarkable. The flow of self-interpretation was impressive. Tom, the Devil incarnate, was the focus, looming large in all her thoughts: his behaviour, intentions, the malevolent influence he had on her and her family; actions and inactions which filled Pam with fear of annihilation. Pam produced more pages, writing both night and day.

Hannah Segal, in a past case presentation, once advised her audience to resist seduction and over-involvement with written material which would deflect from analaysis of events in the here and now as the primary focus of therapeutic sessions. But each piece, as submitted by Pam, was confronted and contained in an individual session. The process was free-associative, Pam had not edited her writings before sharing them. I was asked to keep the papers and I still have them. Reading aloud excerpts from the papers, Pam could own and confront her words and challenge their meaning if she wished. She wrote:

'Tom lures little girls into the pit. He offers them food/wine (sweets) tells them he will care for them and always be there for them (safety). In comfortable surroundings he lies to them with his eyes, admiring you, desiring you, accepts your good and bad and then. . .he uses your addiction to control you into giving unrealistic amounts of the above back to him. But it's never enough. How? By giving the opposite of above. Abandonment, rejection, withholding, judgmental. Then little girls crawl away in fear and want to die. They continue to look for the "good parent" who can make them feel better. They find him from time to time but they know the "bad parent" is waiting to pounce. . . .

'Cassie please take him away. I thought I could handle him, I sat with his father while he died, I didn't mind because I couldn't be with my father when he died, what's more I didn't even go to my father's funeral. But Mr Psychopathic man now won't talk to me. I feel so sad, why wouldn't he understand that I need some comfort now?

'Never mind, I hate him, he must be a Devil. Sorry Cassie, I forgot to tell you that I have grown an image of him sitting on a chair with horns and a tail swishing to and fro with anger.'

The therapy

> The experience of counter-transference appears to me to have quite a distinct quality that should enable the analyst/psychotherapist to differentiate the occasion when he is the object of a projective identification from the occasion when he is not. The therapist feels he is being manipulated so as to be playing a part, no matter how difficult to recognise in somebody else's fantasy. (Bion, 1952: 83)

All of Klein's work was initiated by the study and treatment of children. It is the basis of her emphasis on introjection and projection. Clinical material from her work with children gave her rich material to explain and develop new theories. However, theory-building was never a priority for Klein or her followers. It was used only as a means to an end, that of making better sense of the facts as they are uncovered in work with adult patients as well as children. It is true to say that Klein's most important concepts have rarely been changed or challenged even though these concepts are in everyday use.

Klein argued that the introjection of a good object (i.e. the mother's breast) was a precondition for the development of a normal child. It was a sound recipe. A form of introjective identification, coupled with a normal amount of projective identification would combine to form the foundation stones of early childhood development.

In Pam's recollections of her early childhood, her mother's ill health both before and after Pam's birth deprived her of this close connection to a mother's breast. Pam's mother had dutifully and carefully responded to her baby's material needs, but the dutiful responses to her daughter contained elements of both puzzlement and exasperation. Preoccupied as she was with the early symptoms of her impending illness and increasing disability, Pam's mother failed to understand that her baby's tears were more than just a demand for attention. An attuned mother is able to be sensitive to the anxieties with which every baby strives to cope; the anxieties which are projected into the mother with the expectation that the mother can sensitively internalize them in a balanced and empathetic way.

Feelings of relief and gratitude towards myself as therapist, a person whose close attention to detail facilitated exposure of these unmet needs in Pam, fluctuated with periods of negativity and hostility when the therapeutic process replicated for her the denial and avoidance experienced at the maternal scene. I was not Pam's mother and was experienced as resistant to the internalization of her powerful projections, feelings and frustrations which resonated with previous failures of communication in early childhood. Colluding with the powerful projective identification emanating from Pam could only result in a deterioration of her own personal development.

Pam was overwhelmed with hatred and envy at her mother's inability to shrug off her own desperate neediness for tenderness and love. Pam grew up with a mother who, preoccupied with her own battle for survival, could not tolerate her needs and a father who successfully avoided them. Both parents, unprepared for late parenthood, reacted by denial, concentrating instead on their child's external appearance. A perfect doll-like baby with golden curls and pretty clothes.

Beginning therapy, Pam's bitter recollections of early childhood were of primary importance, affording her an opportunity to express feelings of depression, loss and loneliness which had previously been withheld from her parents and her own children. The poignancy of these stressful childhood years, the pain, anger and resentment she had felt and the consciousness of her early deprivation were quickly aroused.

Pam would try to dislodge my seeming equanimity (described as her mother's 'detachment'). Detachment was experienced as hostile indifference and I was accused of being hostile, indifferent and unresponsive when Pam appealed to me to 'forbid' her tortuous relationship with Tom.

Pam's problems were twofold. She had an inborn disposition to excessive self-destructiveness and envy. These were substitutes for the mechanisms of splitting and projective identification which her mother's illness had denied her. How can you love a mother who appears to be engrossed in her own survival and hate a mother who is in constant pain and physically deteriorating before your very eyes?

She grew up preoccupied with functions, disturbances every day of a life-threatening nature, bandages, medications, bedsores, hospital visits, the pervading smell of illness and death.

Could she have investigated these feelings with a parent (either her mother or father)? Would they have had the capacity to contain them? If so, all would have been well, but it was denial of these mechanisms for understanding which characterized her early years, destroying the link between infant and breast and the ability to control emotion. Difficult enough for everyone, but intolerable for Pam.

Pam would quiver with hatred for her mother and for Tom, as representing the past denials she had experienced. She shook with rage at their seeming indifference to her pain and distress, unable to separate one projection from the other. So many patients in the course of therapy ask themselves 'why me?', but Pam gradually came to understand causation. Her current painful state of mind was exacerbated by the persistent course of action taken (in relation to Tom) which could be predicted to cause her pain. In her later written material Pam acknowledged her complicity in this process.

Pam's mother was a beautiful woman. Even during her illness she retained her attractiveness. She remained seductive, beguiling, managing to surround herself with admiring and sympathetic helpers. Her husband, when at home, made her support his priority. Pam was often ignored. She was the healthy one, part of a support system. She had chosen to replicate this system with her lover, Tom. He was partially disabled, handsome, needy, attractive to women, basking in the help and affirmation of willing others. The transference relationship was obvious. It was her expectation that this time she would get the love and attention she craved as a reward for being helpful. Pam could see that Tom and her mother were inextricably mixed. She wanted to pull back from the frustration of replicating this relationship.

Pam always came to her therapy carrying a large plastic carrier bag which she placed on the floor next to the couch. I asked her to tell me what the bag contained. She laughed and said 'I am a bag lady. My world is in this bag. Diary, work papers, lists of things to do to be helpful for other people. My "buying love" bag. In it are all the things I feel are necessary for me to be seen as a good mother, grandmother and friend.' I added, 'And patient.'

A medical condition which required surgery led to a break of several months before Pam returned to therapy. In this period she had been writing compulsively – whilst again feeling mentally unstable and again distraught over her non-relationship with Tom. They had not been in contact during this period. She was 'be-devilled and obsessed' with him and by him. Her prolific writings and the disappointments in her life railed against him and her mother. I knew they represented a catharsis – in them she had expunged so much bitterness and regret. I highlighted their value and significance. I hold Pam's writings in trust for her until she is ready to take them home. We revisit them from time to time in the months of therapy which remain.

Inevitably Pam has returned to visit Tom regularly but equally has given time and effort to reorganizing and redecorating her own home. Her son stays with her when he is at college, and her daughter has a new partner. Pam continues to see me, albeit on a monthly basis. It is experienced as a review and support session to prepare Pam for our own eventual ending.

References

Bion, W.R (1952) 'Group dynamics – a review', *International Journal of Psychoanalysis*, 33: 235–47.

Bion, W.R. (1988) 'The differentiation of the psychotic from the non-psychotic personalities' (1957), in E. Bott Spillius (ed.), *Melanie Klein Today*, Vol. I: *Mainly Theory*. London: Routledge. pp. 61–78.

Bowlby, J. (1979) *The Making and Breaking of Affectional Bonds*. London: Tavistock.

Colby, K.M. (1951) *A Primer for Psychotherapists*. New York: Ronald Press.

Cooper, C. (1988) 'The Jewish mother', in H. Cooper (ed.), *Soul Searching*. London: SCM Press.

Farrell, B.J. (1981) *The Standing of Psycho-analysis*. London: Oxford University Press.

Hinshelwood, R.D. (1989) *A Dictionary of Kleinian Thought*. London: Free Association Books.

Hinshelwood, R.D. (1994) *Clinical Klein*. London: Free Association Books.

Hughes, A. (1974) 'Contributions of Melanie Klein to psycho-analytic technique', in Y.J. Varma (ed.), *Psychotherapy Today*. London: Constable.

Klein, M. (1932) *The Psychoanalysis of Children*. London: Hogarth.

Klein, M. (1950) 'On the criteria for the termination of a psycho-analysis', *London International Journal of Psycho-analysis*.

Klein, M. (1952a) 'Notes on some schizoid mechanisms', in J. Rivière (ed.), *Developments in Psycho-analysis*. London: Hogarth.

Klein, M. (1952b) 'On the theory of anxiety and guilt', in J. Rivière (ed.), *Developments in Psycho-analysis*. London: Hogarth.

Klein, M. (1957) *Envy and Gratitude*. New York: Basic Books.

Klein, M. (1960) *Our Adult World and its Roots in Infancy*. London: Tavistock.

Meltzer, D. (1979) *The Kleinian Development*. London: The Clunie Press.

Miller, A. (1983) *For Your Own Good*. London: Virago Press.

Piontelli, A. (1992) *From Foetus to Child* (New Library of Psychoanalysis, 15). London: Routledge.

Rivière, J. (1936) Unpublished paper.

Segal, H. (1973) *Introduction to the Work of Melanie Klein*. London: Institute of Psychoanalysis/ Karnac Books.

Segal, H. (1986) *Delusion and Artistic Creativity and Other Psycho-analytic Essays*. London: Free Association Books.

Spillius, E.B. (1983) 'Some developments from the work of Melanie Klein', *International Journal of Psycho-analysis*, 64: 321–2.

Tarachow, S. (1970) *Introduction to Psychotherapy*. New York: International University Press.

Waelder, R. (1937) 'The problem of the genesis of psychical conflict in earliest infancy', *International Journal of Psycho-analysis*, 18: 406–73.

Suggested further reading

Klein, M. (1961) *Narrative of a Child Analysis*. London: Hogarth.

Likierman, M. (2001) *Melanie Klein: Her Work in Context*. London: Continuum.

Piontelli, A. (1992) *From Foetus to Child* (New Library of Psychoanalysis, 15). London: Routledge.

Quinodoz, J.M. (1992) *The Taming of Solitude* (New Library of Psychoanalysis, 20). London: Routledge.

Sayers, J. (2000) *Kleinians: Psychoanalysis Inside Out*. Oxford: Blackwell.

4 Psychodynamic Therapy: The Jungian Approach

Ann Casement

Historical context and development in Britain

Historical context

Analytical psychology is the term employed by the Swiss psychiatrist, Carl Gustav Jung (1875–1961), to depict his approach to depth psychology and psychotherapy. Though congruent with a psychodynamic perspective, Jung's approach to the human psyche and its drives displays several distinctive features, notably a marked stress on the interrelation of psyche and body.

Jung's childhood was marred by physical illness and emotional uncertainties. His relations with his pastor father and his mother were problematic (Jung, 1963). He happily asserted that his personal library and the cultural influences to which he was subjected were the formative factors in the evolution of his ideas, referring to the personal equation in saying that 'every psychology – my own included – has the character of a subjective confession' (Jung, 1961: 336).

Jung exemplified the anthropologist, Claude Lévi-Strauss's (1908–) term 'bricoleur', an intellectual handyman who finds inspiration everywhere. The quest the two men shared was for universal structures underlying the mind/psyche, which led to borrowing a metaphorical screw from here, a figurative nut from there and, from elsewhere, an imaginative bolt. This 'bricolage' reflects Jung's view of the diversity and complexity of the psyche.

The first part of this chapter will present some of the main intellectual influences on Jung's work, which stretch as far back as the pre-Socratic thinkers like Heraclitus and include Plato's ideas. The latter are the forerunners of Jung's theory of archetypes, which concerns the inherited patterns in the psychosomatic unconscious. This is Jung's way of linking two sets of opposites: psyche and soma, and instinct and image, the concept of opposites being central to his psychology.

Western philosophy, particularly German Idealism and Romanticism, has had a general impact on analytical psychology. Kant's view of the 'moral order within' is echoed everywhere in Jung's work, while some would say that his 'starry heavens above' are more evident in Jung's ideas than in his own. Herder, the father of German Expressionism, also influenced Jung's populist and pluralistic approach to the psyche.

Given that Hegel synthesized Kantian reason and morality with Herder's ideas on desire and sensibility, he is a great, though largely unacknowledged influence on Jung. This lack of acknowledgement was perhaps due to Hegel's worldliness and his writings on the state, which were not to Jung's taste. Hegelian dialectics may be compared to the coming together of psychological qualities and elements hitherto seen as opposites. In Jungian therapy, these form into a new third position and the dialectic begins again.

Other strong influences on Jung were Schelling with his view that nature is a visible spirit; Rousseau's 'voice of nature within', and, crucially, the writings of Goethe, particularly *Faust*. Jung claimed to be distantly related to Goethe and therefore felt a strong affinity with him.

The 19th-century German Romantics Schopenhauer and Nietzsche, with their idea of the Will and the Superman, also contributed to what we would now call 'Jungian' psychology. The Vitalists such as Bergson and Driesch were the inspiration for ideas of the world as process rather than a static mechanistic view of the world. In such a world view, nature is animated by spirit as opposed to being regarded as inert matter. Monists such as the 3rd-century Neoplatonist, Plotinus, contributed their theory of the oneness of all things. Jung sometimes compared his work to Gnosticism, which became the first heresy in early Christian times. One of its teachings is that initially there was a primordial oneness of all reality and existence and that there is an inherent longing for a return to this unity. The Gnostics also held that wisdom comes through direct experience leading to individual insight rather than through received dogma backed up by authority. Jung's attitude to Freud's intellectual leadership reflected these Gnostic values. Manichaeism, which has its origins in Gnosticism, held that there was an essential dualism to everything. Hence evil was not just an absence of good but a force in its own right, equal in power to good. The 'reality of evil' was a phrase Jung often used in relation to the sadistic and inhumane aspects of psyche and society alike.

Alchemy, another below-the-line phenomenon, was first brought to Jung's attention by the Sinologist, Richard Wilhelm. Knowing of Jung's long-term interest in oriental ideas, Wilhelm sent him a Chinese alchemical text, 'The Secret of the Golden Flower' (Jung, 1967). Following his study of this text, Jung joyfully announced that the alchemists – Eastern and Western – had discovered a way of exploring the path to what Jung later called individuation, meaning the realization or actualization of the potentials inherently existing in the self. The alchemical process by which base matter is transformed into gold may be compared to the corresponding 'stages' in a classical Jungian analysis in which the patient 'individuates', becoming a more or less whole person. Neurosis is transformed into selfhood. These analytical stages will be more fully described below.

At the turn of the century there was a proliferation of spiritualist groups and cultic nature movements, some of which centred around sun worship. Jung's fascination with mysticism and the occult drew him to these – and he often cites the vivid imagery, centred on the sun's phallus, of a psychotic patient of J.J. Honegger, one of his students at the Burgholzi mental hospital. Psychiatry was Jung's first profession and the major influences here were Pierre Janet, Theodore Flournoy and Eugen Bleuler.

The best-known influence of all on Jung was that of Freud, with whom Jung collaborated from 1907 to 1913. Their inherent personality, cultural and conceptual differences led to an irreparable split growing up between them. From today's standpoint, their theoretical views remain highly complementary and Jung's analytical psychology is, in part, a blend of Freud's psychoanalysis and Alfred Adler's individual psychology.

Development in Britain

A Jung club had existed in London since 1922 but the need and wish for increasing professionalization of analytical psychology led a group of analysts under the leadership of Michael Fordham to found the Society of Analytical Psychology (SAP) in 1946. This was the first Jungian training institute in the world and Jung was persuaded to be its first president in spite of the fact that he was always anti-institutional and once said: 'Thank God I am not a Jungian!'

A further development in the UK was Fordham's collaboration with Gerhard Adler, who was also a founder member of the SAP, and Sir Herbert Read to produce the English edition of Jung's *Collected Works*.

Fordham felt strongly that the split between Jung and Freud in 1913 had been a disaster and devoted himself to repairing this split. In the course of his pioneering work with infants and children, he began to bring together Jungian archetypal theory with Kleinian 'phantasies', which are the primary contents of unconscious mental processes. One of Fordham's most radical extensions of classical Jungian theory was to postulate that a 'primary self' is at work in infants from the beginning (Fordham, 1993). Instead of the psyche increasingly working towards synthesis, Fordham concluded from his work with infants and children that this 'primary self' 'de-integrates' from a state of inner wholeness to bring the infant into relation with the environment (ibid.). In this way the infant's expectation of feeding evokes the appropriate response from mother's breast in the external world. Following psychoanalytic object relations theorists, who also postulated the existence of an ego from the start, Fordham filled a gap in both classical psychoanalytic and analytical psychology theory in showing that a primary self exists from the beginning of life.

Classical theory had always seen the self (sometimes the Self) as an underlying unifying principle in the psyche–soma of the human organism which did not become directly important until the second half of life, say from a person's late thirties. 'The self is. . .as a rule in an unconscious condition to begin with. But it is a definite experience of later life, when the fact becomes conscious' (Jung, 1977: 725).

Fordham also introduced new ideas on the transference–countertransference into Jungian clinical practice. What happened in London, where analytical psychology was being blended with psychoanalytic theory and practice, came to be known as the developmental school of Jungians as it spread to other countries (see Samuels, 1985).

These and other departures from classical Jungian theory have replicated the original Jung/Freud split. Broadly speaking, there are now three groups of

Jungian analysts internationally. Andrew Samuels (ibid.) has constructed a tri-partite classification of analytical psychology into schools: the developmental school, which incorporates psychoanalytic theory and practice; the classical school, seeking to extend Jung's own ways of thinking and working; and the archetypal school, concentrating on the play of images in the psyche.

Analysts such as Gerhard Adler, the founder of the Association of Jungian Analysts, disagreed with Fordham, about the Jung/Freud split being a disaster, regarding the work of the two men as incompatible (Adler, 1979). According to Adler, Jung was essentially a *homo religiosus* for whom the meaning of anyone's life was of paramount importance. This is in direct contrast to Freud's anti-religious stance. If we compare the work of the two men, we see that Freud's system is rational, logical and limited, whereas Jung's is non-rational, religious and aims at a wide but imprecise image of wholeness.

Theoretical assumptions

Image of the person

Theory of opposites

The last paragraph of the previous section attempted to give a brief picture of the differences that exist in the Jungian community. Some practitioners would be placed firmly at the archetypal end of a spectrum of concerns, others would be called Kleinian Jungians and there are many who have a syncretistic approach to their work. The present chapter is a pluralistic attempt (Samuels, 1989a) to hold a balance between the diversity of analytical psychology today and the unity it still possesses as having been inspired by Jung's own work. It is necessary to state Jung's premises here before going on to indicate subsequent develop-ments.

The theory of psychological opposites lies at the basis of Jung's own approach to the psyche. He said, for instance, that opposites are the indispensable preconditions of all psychic life (Jung, 1955–56). To give a simple example, when someone is murderously angry with another person, their desire to destroy the other competes with its opposite – concern for other people backed up by parental and religious teachings. How it works out depends on the individual's ego holding the tension between the opposites of anger and concern – he or she may shout, or bite the bullet, or seek the intercession of another, or engage in self-reflection that undermines the 'justification' felt in relation to the anger. On a cultural level, opposites such as spirituality and sexuality also have to be recon-ciled in some way. For Jung, on both the individual and cultural levels, neurosis consists of resolution of the tension and interplay of opposites by the neurotic taking up a position aligned with one extreme or another. These days, it is widely accepted that there are usually more than three positions (the two extremes and their resolution) and 'the opposites' are usually presented as a spectrum of possibilities.

Analytical psychology itself is a synthesis of two opposites: a spiritual quest for self-knowledge with a scientific approach to the workings of the psyche. However, the spiritual and religious elements in Jung's work have made it difficult for him to be found acceptable in academic and intellectual circles, and some Jungians eschew this aspect of Jung. On the other hand, the empirical psychologist is equally a part of him, for instance in his experimental work with the word association test. This discovered the existence of feeling-toned 'complexes', which are relatively autonomous aggregates of emotions and experiences in the psyche clustered around an archetypally patterned core. This method initially attracted Freud's attention as he felt Jung was providing verification of the existence of the unconscious. However, Freud was repelled by the mystical and 'occult' Jung.

To do Jung's work full justice it is essential to maintain a balance between these two opposing forces. He pointed to the 'transcendent function' as the symbolical way of holding a balance between them and of withstanding the pull of one or the other, which would lead eventually to a rigid and rational psychology, or to its opposite: an equally rigid love of the irrational. To try to rationalize Jung by discarding the spiritual elements which speak of concerns for purpose and meaning is to reduce him to the status of a disciple of Freud. But to treat him only as a mystic leaves out the great body of work he contributed to empirical psychology.

Transcending that which presents itself to us as opposite is a chief dynamic running through Jung's work and the 'self' is a 'symbol' of this transcendence. In Jung's language, a symbol may be thought of as the intuitive way of knowing the as yet not fully knowable. 'The. . .central archetype of "self". . .seems to be the point of reference for the unconscious psyche, just as the ego is the point of reference for consciousness. The symbolism associated with this archetype expresses itself on the one hand in circular, spherical, and quaternary forms, in the "squaring of the circle"; on the other hand in the image of the supraordinate personality' (Jung, 1977: 484).

The influences from the past on Jung's theory of opposites include Heraclitus' 'enantiodromia', which encompasses the idea that sooner or later everything turns into its opposite. An abrupt change from one strongly held position to an extreme other would be an example of this and is a time of great inner conflict for an individual. This is the Jungian equivalent of the object relations theory of 'splitting'. At this point there is a concentration of 'psychic energy', Jung's more neutral term for Freud's 'libido', which Jung saw as sexually loaded, in order to resolve the conflict by seeking for a new position. This method is also directly related to Hegel's dialectical scheme of thesis/antithesis/synthesis.

The object/subject dichotomy is another aspect of opposites exemplified, for instance, in what Jung terms the 'objective psyche'. This points to the 'reality of the psyche' as both a source of objective knowledge with its own autonomous way of functioning and as a container of more than personal or subjective contents. The latter aspect of the objective psyche Jung equated with the 'collective unconscious', the locus of universal motifs shared by all humans throughout time and space. One example is that of the personal mother of an individual, which has aspects in common with the universal image of the objective mother.

'Syzygy' is a term Jung applied to any set of yoked opposites, particularly sexually based ones like male/female, masculine/feminine, and yang/yin which he took from Chinese philosophy. Jung's own terms of 'animus/anima' denote the sexually opposite inner figures of a woman (animus) and a man (anima). This dichotomy has been modified by viewing anima/animus as interchangeable and as functioning equally in men and women to produce what might be seen as creative animation in both (Clark, 1987).

As stated above, the theory of archetypes concerns inherited patterns in the psychosomatic unconscious. It is Jung's way of linking two sets of opposites: psyche and soma and instinct and image. 'Synchronistic' experiences, which Jung claimed were acausal, underwrite this continuum, as the psychic can behave like the non-psychic and vice versa.

Synthesizing opposites is central to Jung's approach. It is also evidence of his personal pathology and points to an inner split that needed healing, which he attempted to do creatively through his work. Winnicott diagnosed Jung as having had a childhood psychosis, when he reviewed Jung's autobiographical work, *Memories, Dreams, Reflections*, and saw Jung's lifelong quest as one in search of healing (Winnicott, 1964). The mercurial and paradoxical tone that runs through so much of Jung's work stems from his fascination with opposites and this is why his writings are often experienced as being elusive (as well as allusive) and difficult to pin down.

Metapsychology

As far as metapsychology is concerned, Jung owes much to Freud's model. For instance, they have in common a dynamic, economic and topographical inter-action as their centre. The dynamic and economic attributes in Jung's model are articulated by the investment of 'psychic energy' in varying degrees of equivalence amongst the topographical spheres of 'consciousness', 'personal unconscious' and 'collective unconscious'.

Consciousness has the 'ego' as its centre, this being the agent in the psyche that an individual identifies with as 'I'. 'Persona' lies also in the conscious sphere and is the mask that the individual presents to the world. The 'shadow' lies in the personal unconscious and represents all those aspects that are seen to be undesirable by the ego and which are, therefore, repressed. 'Anima' and 'animus', like all 'archetypes', originate in the 'collective unconscious' and act unconsciously through projection when activated by an outer object, for example falling in love. The 'self' as the totality of the psyche is immanent throughout and functions both as the beginning and the end of all psychic activity. It mediates the opposites of good/evil, creativity/destruction, divine/human, etc., and offers the possibility of achieving wholeness or 'individuation' through the conjunction of opposites, or 'coniunctio'. Its presence is experienced as 'numinous', i.e. mysteri-ously powerful, and this is especially prevalent when there is a great deal of archetypal activity at work in an individual as, for instance, when collective unconscious contents are beginning to push through into consciousness.

Typology

Typology, the theory of innate personality differences, is an important, if highly problematic, part of Jung's work. Some time will be spent on its definition according to the Myers-Briggs model, one of the systems used to measure these differences (Myers, 1962).

One reason for Jung's interest in typology was the break with Freud, not only his own but also Alfred Adler's. By examining these and other 'personality clashes' throughout history, Jung sought to clarify his own position by showing how people with inbuilt differences can find it difficult to understand each other. The two basic concepts here are those of orientation of attitude to the world and of ways of 'functioning' in it. Attitude is measured on a scale ranging from extraversion at one end to introversion at the other. Individuals who are extraverted tend to focus on the outer world of people and the external environment. Extraverting in this way means that the individual is energized by what goes on in the outer world and that is where energy tends to be directed. Extraverts usually prefer to communicate more by talking than by writing and need to experience the world in order to understand it and thus tend to like action.

Introverts focus more on their own inner world and while introverting, energy is invested in that direction. Introverts tend to be more interested and comfortable when their work requires a good deal of their activity to take place quietly inside their heads. They like to understand the world before experiencing it, and so often think about what they are doing before acting.

The four functions concern ways of perceiving or acquiring information: sensation, intuition, thinking and feeling. Sensing is a way of perceiving through the senses of sight, hearing, smell, touch and taste. These inform an individual of what is actually happening out there and keep one in touch with the realities of a situation. Sensing types tend to accept and work with what is given in the here-and-now, and have a realistic and practical approach to life. They are adept at working with facts.

Intuiting is the other way of perceiving and is directed to the meanings and possibilities that go beyond information given through the senses. Intuition takes in the whole picture and tries to grasp the essential patterns at work in any situation. Intuitives value imagination and inspiration and are expert at seeing new possibilities.

Once information is acquired through one of the two perceiving functions, it is necessary to make decisions or judgements about it. This is done through the two functions of thinking and feeling.

Thinking predicts the logical consequences of any particular choice or action. Decisions are made objectively on the basis of cause and effect and of analysing and weighing the evidence inherent in any situation. Individuals with a preference for thinking seek an objective standard of truth and are good at analysing what is wrong with something.

Feeling, on the other hand, considers what is important without requiring it to be logical. Values to do with the human domain are at the basis of this way of functioning and the emphasis is upon how much one cares about any situation. Individuals with a preference for feeling like dealing with people and tend to respond in a sympathetic, appreciative and tactful way to others. Feeling as used in Jung's typology is to be differentiated from actual feelings or emotions and is, instead, to do with a capacity for making judgements or decisions based on humane values.

The four functions are heavily modified by the two attitudes and an extraverted sensation type is quite different to an introverted sensation type in being orientated to the outer world. There is usually a primary and secondary way of functioning: for example an individual may have extraverted sensation as their primary function and introverted feeling as their secondary one. The two primary functions will be in the conscious part of the psyche and will be more differentiated. The two functions that are less developed will be unconscious, and when activated will bring forth unconscious material. This is why Jung stated that a great deal can be learned from the least differentiated function. This also applies to the attitudes; for instance, an extravert will have introversion in the unconscious.

The final scale that applies to all this shows how a perceiving type orientates to life in a different way to a judging one. Perceiving through sensing and intuiting will lead to a flexible, spontaneous lifestyle. Individuals with this preference seek to understand life rather than control it. They prefer to stay open to experience, enjoying and trusting in their ability to adapt to the moment.

Individuals who have a judging approach through thinking and feeling tend to live in a planned and orderly way and want to regulate and control life. Decisions are taken which lead to closure and to a passing on to something else. Individuals with a preference for judging tend to be structured and organized in their approach. It is important to differentiate 'judging' used in the above context from judgmental; any of the types may be prone to the latter.

Conceptualization of psychological disturbance and health

The psychologically healthy individual is conceptualized as one who is free to interact with a degree of autonomy, in relation both to the environment and to the inner world of the psyche. The disturbed individual, on the other hand, is conceived as being the inverse of this in finding both inner and outer worlds too persecutory to relate to freely.

In analytical psychology, the unconscious is conceptualized as consisting of two realms: the 'personal unconscious' into which unacceptable contents are repressed, and the 'collective unconscious' which is the container of mankind's psychic inheritance and potential. Psychological disturbance may be associated with both realms. For instance, too much repression of personal material that is unacceptable to the individual's conscious mind will result in neurotic symptoms.

These will also manifest if innate potential is denied existence and not integrated more consciously into the individual's life. To summarize, severe repression in relation to either of these unconscious realms will result in pathological functioning on the individual's part.

The inherent split in Jung between the empirical psychologist and his mythopoeic side are evident in his approach to psychopathology. It has already been stated that he began work as a psychiatrist. In the course of this work he was increasingly interested in schizophrenia and came to conceptualize it as a psychogenic disorder within a psychosomatic framework. This insight pointed to the possibility of using a psychological approach to the treatment of schizophrenia in particular, and psychosis in general. An example of this is given in the section below,

Practice

This was revolutionary at the time in relativizing the view that every psychosis was a purely neurological disorder. Instead, Jung suggested that schizophrenia resulted in part from the invasion of consciousness by contents from the collective unconscious, which, in turn, pointed to the possibility that there was meaning in the utterances and behaviour of schizophrenics.

However, Jung's ambivalent attitude to psychopathology can be seen in the following: 'clinical diagnoses are important, since they give the doctor a certain orientation. . .they do not help the patient. The crucial thing is the story' (Jung, 1963: 145). This has led to a concentration in treatment by some Jungian therapists on the story or myth of the individual as a way of helping an individual to achieve psychological health. 'The general ambivalence in depth psychology concerning psychopathology is to be found *par excellence* in the Jungian world' (Samuels, 1989b).

As a result, analytical psychology was greatly lacking in clinical teaching and had to borrow heavily from psychoanalysis to fill this gap. In this way, concepts such as ego defences, transference–countertransference and acting-out have been introduced into Jungian practice. This, combined with the mythopoeic stance, can produce effective results in restoring health and potency to individuals.

Acquisition of psychological disturbance

Jung questioned Freud's theory of early traumatic experience as the cause of neurosis and eventually rejected it as being too deterministic. The former said that looking for causes in an individual's past kept the person tied for ever to that past.

For Jung, on the other hand, there was an archetypal core at the centre of each neurotic symptom and he concentrated his attention on seeking this out. This is what is called the teleological approach in classical analytical psychology and is based on Aristotle's doctrine of final causes. This point of view looks at psychological phenomena to find out what they are for and where they are leading to, which, in turn, gives symptoms a purpose that results in them being experienced as not only pathological. Jung called his approach 'synthetic' in contrast to what he termed Freud's 'reductive' method. The synthetic approach puts the emphasis on what emerges from the starting point rather than on the starting point itself.

Depression seen from this viewpoint is both pathological as well as a manifestation of psychic energy being drawn from the conscious realm into the unconscious. This may arise when change is being signalled, for instance at the time of a major life event for an individual when the status quo has to be abandoned in favour of new life. If this is thwarted, the depression may well become chronic. There are many instances of this but a few will serve to illustrate the point: a young person who is unable to leave the parental home in order to take up the challenge of life; or an unhappily married person failing to deal with marital problems.

Perpetuation of psychological disturbance

A central feature for Jung in perpetuating psychological disturbance is the inability to separate from the mother, both personal and archetypal. He set out to demonstrate the failure to do so on the part of a young woman patient in his book *Symbols of Transformation* (Jung 1911–12). The patient's case history was sent to him by the psychiatrist, Flournoy and, although Jung himself never met her, he conducts a long-distance analysis from her notes, which ends with a negative prognosis of schizophrenia. However, a close reading of the book reveals that the real patient is Jung himself simultaneously working through his break with Freud and developing his own ideas through self-analysis.

The main theme of the book is to show that remaining in a state of what Jung thought of as psychological incest is a prime cause for the perpetuation of neurosis and even psychosis. This is in contrast with Freud's Oedipal theory of incest, which is a longing for actual coitus with the mother. Jung, on the other hand, splits the image of mother into a duality – the personal and the archetypal – and states that symbolic re-entry into or union with the mother is necessary in order to be reborn. Thus, the individuated person is 'twice-born', the first time physically from the personal mother and the second time symbolically from the objective mother. The book was an expression of Jung's own rebirth in his late thirties and its contents signalled the split between him and Freud.

Splitting is seen in Kleinian theory as an early defence used in controlling the object by dividing it into a good and bad part-object In the above, Jung is referring to splitting the image of the mother into personal and archetypal and into good and bad. Another similarity with psychoanalytic pathology is Jung's theory of 'participation mystique' which he took from the anthropologist, Lévy-Bruhl. This entails an identification between subject and object so that the latter is experienced as being a part of the former, e.g. a spirit or a fetish object. Looked at psychologically, this represents a neurotic dependence on another object because it is experienced as being part of the self and in this way has tremendous influence over the individual. This theory of Jung's is the equivalent of projective identification where part of the self is projected into another person and is then experienced as the projected part.

In addition, there is the psychoanalytic concept of ego defences. These act to prevent unwanted personal and archetypal unconscious contents from breaking through into consciousness through the mechanisms of repression, denial and reaction-formation.

Another neurotic defence is that of extreme introversion which manifests in narcissistic feelings of grandiosity that act to keep an individual from being involved in interpersonal relationships. There is a place for healthy introversion as described above under 'Typology', but Western culture is identified with an extraverted thinking/sensation way of functioning so that many people feel forced to comply with this. If this compliance becomes pathological, they need to be helped to achieve a better balance between introversion and extraversion. In this way, it may be said that extreme extraversion can be as neurotic as extreme introversion. Change towards a healthier way of functioning is conceptualized in the Jungian canon as leaving a collective way of being and moving towards a more highly differentiated position as an individual. This is summed up in the Jungian concept of individuating. But as Kenneth Lambert has pointed out, Jung may have overemphasized the beneficial effects of transformation 'so sharply as to suggest that normality equals false conformity' (Lambert, 1981: 33).

Although Jung tended to see individuating as relating to the Jungian path towards selfhood, Samuels states that Klein's view of healthy normality is very similar and may be summed up as 'emotional maturity, strength of character, capacity to deal with conflicting emotions, a reciprocal balance between internal and external worlds, and, finally, a welding of the parts of the personality leading to an integrated self concept' (Samuels, 1985: 132).

Certainly both Klein and Jung would agree with Freud in seeing psychic health as the outcome of the transformation of neurosis as a result of the change that occurs through the successful outcome of therapy. This change may be viewed positively by family and friends if the individual is experienced as being more flexible and spontaneous and less rigid in interacting with the environment. However, the reverse also arises, and the person may be experienced as having become more selfish and less compliant – in other words as having changed for the worse.

Practice

Goals of therapy

Goals of all kinds are of great importance in the classical Jungian approach to therapy, and its major concepts reflect this. These are based on a teleological or goal-directed view enshrined in a doctrine of final causes. This views the self as functioning essentially to push an individual towards the fulfilment of his or her destiny whether or not the ego concurs with it. This is what Jung means by the reality of the psyche. The classical approach has largely been orientated to therapy for individuals in the second half of life, i.e. in their late thirties and over, and the goal is that of individuation or attaining wholeness by the individual. This teleological view of the workings of the self points to an essentially religious attitude to life in its awareness of an immanent animated presence in all matter. Gerhard Adler's book, *The Living Symbol*, is an account of the individuating process at work in the analysis of a woman in the second half of life (Adler, 1961).

The first half of life was regarded by Jung as a period of extraversion where an individual is naturally orientated to worldly concerns such as marriage, children and career. It is in the late thirties that an individual's 'myth' challenges him or her to begin to separate from a collective worldly stance and to follow the quest for his or her own separate identity. Because of the heroic nature of this endeavour, Jung conceptualized it as a mythical confrontation with a dragon. This is, of course, a symbolic, inner dragon which is both the personal and the objective mother that seduces the individual into an attitude of inertia *vis-à-vis* life. The treasure which is hard to attain is that of the person's identity.

Both Jung's *Symbols of Transformation*, where the real 'patient' is Jung himself, and Adler's *The Living Symbol* are classical accounts about the goal of individuating in the second half of life. As previously mentioned, Fordham's reworking of the self as primary has resulted in his view that individuation as a goal is not confined to the second half of life. He cites Jung's claim that individuation is to be equated with achieving consciousness through differentiation of subject from object and shows that the child's gradual separation from the mother during its first two years of life is likewise a process of individuation (Fordham, 1976). In his synthesis of object relations theory and analytical psychology, Fordham demonstrated how, after birth, the infant's primary self deintegrates and, through increasing identification with the mother, begins to move towards early object-relating. Control over bodily functioning is increasingly mastered and the beginnings of a conscience and consciousness are set in train, which includes a synthesizing of opposites such as good/bad and from this there develops a capacity for concern. All these, combined with the start of the process of symbolization, are the prerequisites of the goal of individuation.

In this way, Fordham broadened Jung's goal-centred theory of individuation to include infancy and childhood and by doing so has established that it is a natural part of the goal of maturing rather than a work against nature, as Jung claims. The latter does allow for the fact that individuals individuate unconsciously but claims that this is not comparable with individuating through a long analysis. A further consequence of Fordham's revision of individuation is the modification of the first half/second half of life dichotomy.

Rosemary Gordon talks of a twofold goal in analysis: one is that of curing, which is to do with the expansion of ego through assimilation of contents from the personal and the collective unconscious; the other goal is that of healing, which is involved in the individuating process and the working towards a more complex wholeness of the individual (Gordon, 1979).

The above has largely concentrated on the positive aspects of the individuation process as a goal but there is a great deal of pathology involved in it as well. One danger is that of breakdown when archetypal activity is very strong and the patient may be overwhelmed with contents from the collective unconscious. Another danger is that of identifying with the mana-like power of these contents, which can lead to inflation of the ego. Jung points to Nietzsche's identification with the semi-legendary Persian prophet Zarathustra, which eventually contributed to his madness (Jarrett, 1988). Jung states that if Nietzsche had been more aware that Zarathustra was an archetypal figure calling him – Nietzsche – to explore his own inner world, he would not have seen himself as a prophet and broadcast his message of the Superman. This is an example of individuating but with a lack of the conscious integration which would have grounded Nietzsche.

Depression is another consequence of the individuating process: it becomes pathological when an individual elevates the unconscious to a position of moral supremacy over the conscious part of the personality. The latter then feels inferior and worthless and the result is that the individual becomes depressed. Nietzsche, on the other hand, identified with the mana personality and his ego became inflated (Jung, 1953).

A further complication of the goal of individuation concerns the behaviour of an individual intent on fulfilling his or her potential in respect to others. An extreme example of this would be a psychopath, but on a more mundane level every individual must to a greater or lesser extent curb potential fulfilment in relation to other people. Jung's awareness of these limitations is expressed in his saying: 'Certainly that consciousness, which would enable us to live the great Yea and Nay of our own free will and purpose, is an altogether superhuman ideal. Still, it is a goal' (Jung, 1953: 59).

To go back to Gordon's model of curing, one of the goals of Jungian therapy would be the enlargement of the ego, in other words an increase in consciousness of both outer and inner worlds. This in turn would lead to a greater balance of the two and a spontaneous flow of energy between them. In short-term therapy, the goal would be to enable an individual to reach a better-adapted relationship to problems posed by the environment through supportive work by the therapist.

Selection criteria

Jungian therapists usually refer to individuals who come into therapy as 'patients' rather than 'clients', which has to do with the concept of suffering inherent in that word, the extension of this being the fact that *every* therapist has been through his or her own painful therapy. The term also expresses the patience that will be needed in a long therapy. Lastly, 'analysis' and 'therapy' are the terms used in the treatment of 'patients' who are being seen two or more times weekly. This is a simple way of differentiating this type of therapy from 'counselling', which applies to work with 'clients' on a once-weekly basis. However, it must be stressed that these are not hard and fast definitions as a patient seeing a therapist once a week may well be in analysis rather than counselling.

The terms 'analysis' and 'psychotherapy' are difficult to clearly differentiate. One way of doing so is to view analysis as working in greater depth and for longer duration than psychotherapy. In addition, Jungian psychotherapy may be understood as a method that employs some Jungian ideas.

There are no disorders that cannot be alleviated in some way by analysis or psychotherapy, and this will be demonstrated below. But there are a few caveats which it is important to bear in mind. Any persisting physical symptom must be treated by a medical practitioner and not viewed only as psychosomatic hysterical conversion which could justify analytical treatment. Another point to bear in mind is that the analytic process is primarily a relationship between two people and that a genuine rapport is necessary between them for any creative work to be made possible. If there is no 'fit' between analyst and patient from the start, it would be unwise to begin the treatment. It would be preferable to refer the patient to another practitioner.

At this point it would be useful to give an example of how a physical symptom may be treated both organically and analytically. A woman patient started analysis with me 11 years ago and her presenting problem was the messy breakdown of her marriage, combined with an increasingly problematic relationship with her teenage son. It was soon apparent that she was caught in a negative mother complex, which dominated all her relationships in a destructive way. A few months after starting therapy, she was diagnosed as having cancer of the breast and underwent major surgery. She needed many months of supportive therapy throughout this period but when she was ready to work on herself analytically, she began to see that the physical cutting out of 'mother' had been necessary in order to give her a chance to begin to separate herself from her complex and to find her own identity quite apart from that of 'mother'.

Traditionally, Jungian practitioners, in contrast to psychoanalysts, had a tendency to take on highly disturbed patients. Freud held to the view that psychoanalysis was really only suitable as a treatment for the neuroses but he looked to Jung's work with schizophrenic patients, initially as a psychiatrist, then as an analyst, to extend the frontiers of psychoanalysis to the treatment of the psychoses.

Winnicott's claim that Jung's quest for self-healing, rather than resolution through analysis, came from the latter's psychotic illness (Winnicott, 1964), is not borne out by early psychotherapeutic work done by Jung in the treatment of schizophrenia. In a paper he wrote in 1919 (Jung, 1960), Jung explores the possibility of psychotherapy for the psychoses. Initially he summarizes the difficulties of any such endeavour, e.g. that any apparent cure would be seen only as a remission of symptoms, and admits that he is not optimistic in this regard. He stresses the importance of searching out the psychological aetiology and course of psychosis and says that this is more easily done in comparatively simple cases.

He gave the example of a young girl who suddenly became schizophrenic. She was a peasant's daughter, who had trained as a teacher and who until that time had displayed no abnormal symptoms. One night she heard the voice of God, and Jesus also appeared to her. When Jung saw her, she was calm but completely uninterested in her surroundings, and her answers to questions were given without any accompanying affect – as Jung comments, she might as well have been talking of the stove which she was standing next to, rocking gently back and forth all the while.

Jung asked her if she had kept any notes of her conversations with God and, saying yes, she handed him a piece of paper with a cross on it. Eventually, after a long period of questioning her, Jung discovered that the young woman felt herself to be in a state of sin because she had been attracted to a man she saw the day that her symptoms appeared. That night she experienced a religious conversion and God appeared to her.

Jung acknowledged that there must be a predisposition in someone who becomes schizophrenic but held that it is possible to discover the psychogenic causes of the disease and in this way to alleviate the symptoms. In Jung's view, psychosis was the result of a poorly differentiated consciousness and a sparsely stocked personal unconscious so that the subject is at risk of invasion by archetypal contents from the realm of the collective unconscious. This is why he advocated the identification of mythological motifs in the expressions of psychotics. He went on to associate psychosis with anima/animus and the neuroses with the workings of the ego (Jung, 1951).

All Jungian analysts have an internship in psychiatry as part of their training and work psychotherapeutically with psychotic and borderline patients, in circumstances where these patients are contained in a holding environment and are also on medication. Most of the work done with these patients would be psychotherapeutic rather than analytic, i.e. supportive and aimed at alleviating symptoms rather than the long and complicated inner journey that a full analysis involves. To summarize, as long as the practitioner is not over-optimistic about outcome and as long as the patient is contained in a holding environment, Jungian therapy can be applied effectively to psychosis.

Addiction is another complicated area that some Jungians have worked with therapeutically. The Italian, Luigi Zoja, has worked intensively in therapy with drug addicts and has come to see that the underlying motivation amongst young addicts is a need for the kind of initiation rituals that are so lacking in Western society (Zoja, 1985). He points to the need for treatment that is aimed at helping addicts to give up drugs and to heal damaged organs, also taking into account the underlying psychological needs that are expressed by addiction. He advocates bringing people together in a community which instils a common spirit and goal and in this way creates an atmosphere of being part of a mystical group. This gives meaning both to the addiction and to the process of treatment.

All of this echoes work done by anthropologists and sociologists; for instance the French anthropologist Arnold van Gennep, in his writing about rites of passage described every ritual as having three distinct phases (van Gennep, 1960). The first is that of separation from the profane world; the second is being contained in the sacred world that exists outside normal social intercourse; the third is reincorporation into the world but with a new identity. The present writer works with the idea that a whole analysis or therapy is a rite of passage, as well as every session, with separation, containment and reincorporation being part of the process in each case.

To elaborate further the need for meaning and containment there is also the need for 'communitas', the term Victor Turner, the anthropologist, applies to a mystical coming together for a joint purpose, in which individual identity is submerged in a meaningful way into community feeling as, for example, on a pilgrimage (Turner, 1969). The negative correlate of this is what the sociologist, Erving Goffman, calls the 'stripping process', which is to be seen at work in total institutions, e.g. the Army, prison and hospitals (Goffman, 1961). This involves stripping the person of any individual identity in a brutal fashion by making them wear a uniform, by giving them a number instead of a name, etc. Many hospitals and psychiatric wards exemplify this negative stripping process at work rather than any positive group feeling of *communitas* and asylum. It is this dimension that psychotherapy can bring to bear on psychiatry.

Phobias are also amenable to analytical insight, although the symptoms may persist, e.g. fear of flying. When a patient is able to relate this fear to the anxiety that comes from being out of control – as in the sensation of being out of touch with the earth combined with not being at the controls of the plane – then it may be possible to connect the phobia to its origins in infancy or childhood. One patient was able to recall being terrified *every* time her father threw her up in the air. Another managed to remember the fact that she had been dropped as an infant. Some behavioural therapy may also be required in working with phobic patients.

In addition, it may seem beneficial for a patient to have family or couples therapy when these sorts of problem begin to dominate the therapeutic work in each session. Another way of locating a major problem at any time is through working with dreams. These tend to throw up a constant stream of images related to a problem when it moves into the acute stage.

Where a patient is in both individual and another form of therapy at the same time, it is vital for the analyst to be aware of any signs of splitting between the two modalities, e.g. all the good being seen as belonging in one and all the bad in the other. An example of this is a patient I have who is also going to Alcoholics Anonymous, who began to split between the good analyst and the bad sponsor. By becoming aware of this in the analytic work, she was enabled to modify her projections on to both. Some analytic patients come from GPs and psychiatry and are on medication such as antidepressants or psychotropic drugs. In these cases, it is important for the therapist not to become involved in the medical treatment, although the therapist may well have to liaise with the medical practitioner involved with the patient. This must be done with the consent of the patient at all times, the only exception being when a patient may be a danger to him/herself or to others, particularly a child. Once again the therapist must be aware of possible splitting between, say, a GP and the therapist and to take steps to counteract this.

It is clear from all the above that therapy not only does not preclude treatment by other modalities but actively welcomes this as long as discrete boundaries are maintained and there is sufficient awareness of splitting and idealization.

Qualities of effective therapists

Therapy is a vocational profession and therapists may experience an inner calling which usually arises from their own deep psychic wounds. If these are left largely unhealed. there is a danger that a therapist will react to patients pathologically from neurotic counter-transference feelings, e.g. retaliating to or over-identifying with patients' disturbed behaviour. Where these wounds have been sufficiently healed, a therapist will be able to empathize with a patient's trauma and be of service. Self-awareness on the therapist's part combined with empathy are the key to effective therapeutic intervention.

Every therapist has an extensive training analysis lasting for several years. This is preceded by pre-training analysis. For the duration of training, a trainee therapist also works under supervision with two senior analysts or therapists with clinical cases. The developmental school has started to require candidates to undertake a two-year infant observation with an attendant discussion group as part of training. However, it is important to pay attention here to Daniel Stern's recent writings on the difference between the psychoanalytic infant and the observed infant (Stern, 1985).

A training candidate does not need to be medically qualified but has to have had some experience of working in a psychiatric unit. Candidates also need to have a background in the helping professions, for example as teachers, social workers or counsellors.

It was Jung who first pointed out in 1911 the necessity of a training analysis for all would-be analysts while he was President of the International Psychoanalytic Association from 1910 to 1914 (Jung, 1961). The therapist's most important tool in therapeutic work is his or her own personality and character, which needs to be married to a capacity for awareness of limitations with regard to the level of disturbance that can be tolerated from patients. This capacity for self-awareness must be combined with what Gerhard Adler called the four 'Hs': honesty, humanity, humility and humour which, in turn, need to be linked to skills acquired during a long training lasting for several years. This includes personal therapy and supervision, theoretical seminars and scientific and clinical meetings which seek to build on an inherent psychological-mindedness in the trainee therapist. Continuous professional development is needed to ensure that a practitioner stays up to date with new theoretical and clinical ideas.

Therapeutic relationship and style

Above all a therapist must to be able to combine spontaneity with an appropriate observance of boundaries. The first session is taken up with information-giving on the part of the patient and setting up of the therapeutic 'contract'. This includes agreeing between the therapist and patient the amount to be paid per session, the number of sessions that will be necessary per week across a spectrum that ranges from one session weekly to five, and whether the patient would benefit from being on the couch or in a chair. This 'contract' or therapeutic alliance is negotiated with what may be thought of as the functioning part of the patient's personality and will be needed throughout the work in relation to the more pragmatic side of analysis, as detailed above.

After establishing the contract, it is necessary to create a holding environment wherein the patient can feel safe to regress and to reflect on experiences that happen in therapy. There is no set plan for each session and this can often feel threatening for a patient, who will need to be able to endure not knowing what may happen. In order for this to happen, the therapist must communicate a feeling of security to the patient that he or she will not be let down. In this holding environment, the therapist must be sensitive to the feeling-tone of a session, for instance whether silence represents an angry withholding or resistance on the patient's part, or whether it is a creative silence which is allowing the patient to be truly in touch with his or her inner world.

The therapeutic approach is passive/receptive rather than active or directive. It is also somewhat formal and there is no physical contact between the two participants. Added to this, there is virtually no self-disclosure on the part of the majority of therapists apart from the minimum information required by the prospective patient to make an informed choice of therapist. It is always possible, even after years of experience, to be tempted into revealing personal details about oneself. In a recent session, a long-standing patient of mine recounted a dream which portrayed precisely an aspect of my personal life which she could not consciously know. I had to struggle momentarily with responding in a con-gratulatory manner about her wonderful intuition and with a desire on my part to show off, as it was a positive thing that she had intuited. Humour is a necessary quality for any therapist but so is the awareness that too much of it in a session may represent a manic defence.

In the final stages of a long therapy, a practitioner will begin to be more open in the interaction, perhaps at times admitting to liking something, or vice versa. But, on the whole, boundaries are all-important to this approach so that the analyst's stance will remain largely neutral and formal.

Major therapeutic strategies and techniques

Some Jungian analysts and therapists only use the couch, some only the chair, whereas others, like the writer, use either depending on the patient, or even both at different stages in the analytic work with the same patient. The couch is beneficial for a patient who is strongly resistant to regression, when this is necessary, to a more infantile stage. Resistance involves unconscious ego defences such as repression, denial, reaction-formation and 'acting-out' in various ways. The latter can include almost anything, but some examples would be flooding sessions with dream material, being consistently late or bringing an 'agenda' each time. The therapist needs to be sensitive to the timing of when it is safe to dismantle defences. This is most likely to be when the patient has sufficient ego strength to do so. To sum up, it may be said that the couch is appropriate to a more psychoanalytic approach.

The chair, on the other hand, is suited to the classical Jungian strategy which is based on a dialogue between therapist and patient.

Transference/countertransference, as defined by psychoanalysis, are central to a developmental therapist's approach. In Freud's words, transferences are:

> new editions or facsimiles of the impulses and phantasies which are aroused and made conscious during the progress of the analysis; but they have this peculiarity, which is characteristic for their species, that they replace some earlier person by the person of the physician. (Freud, 1912)

Countertransference applies to the therapist's unconscious reactions to the patient, particularly to the latter's transferences. Jung was alert to the utility of these reactions, referring in 1920 to countertransference as 'an important organ of information' (Jung, 1954). Freud tended to depreciate countertransference as residual neurosis on the part of the therapist but Jung's greater flexibility enabled Fordham to develop a detailed theory of there being two kinds of counter-transference. The first he calls 'syntonic', which is when an analyst may be so in tune with a patient's inner world that he finds himself feeling or behaving in a way that he comes to realize, on reflection, shows that there are aspects of his patient's inner workings projected into him (Fordham, 1957). This process puts at the disposal of the patient parts of the therapist that are spontaneously responding to the former in a way that is needed.

The other sort of countertransference Fordham hit upon when he made a recording of a session of analysis he conducted with a boy of 11 who had problems with aggressive feelings. Later, on listening to the recording of this session, Fordham discovered that his own aggression had been in evidence, in that a reactivation of a past situation from his own childhood had replaced his relation to the patient. During that time, no analysis of the patient was possible. This phenomenon Fordham termed 'illusory' countertransference.

A therapist working with these concepts of personal transference and counter-transference in mind would use interpretation both in and of the transference as a central strategy. All this is directed towards reparation of the patient's damaged inner object world and to an improved interaction with the environment. Working with the above kind of transference/countertransference represented a major change of strategy to Jung's original one, the end-goal of which is individuation.

The change process in therapy

The change process in Jungian therapy has already been signalled. Pathological symptoms are usually what bring an individual into therapy and may be seen as the opener of the way into a deeper awareness on the part of that individual. This chapter has already stated that if there are physical symptoms they need to be diagnosed by a medical practitioner in order to ascertain that medical treatment is not necessary alongside analysis. If the symptoms appear to be largely neurotic, i.e. originating in the psyche, then they can be treated analytically. In fact, symptoms may well persist as the therapy progresses.

The work of therapy, in this regard, is to identify what lies behind the symptom. For instance, repressed emotional disturbances will often manifest somatically if they are not attended to. Above all, therapy is an inner journey and the goal of this quest is the individual's true identity, which may have been hidden for a whole lifetime under a 'false self'. It is, in fact, in the patient's symptom or wound that his or her true identity lies hidden and here we see again the analogy with alchemy of the base metal being transformed into gold. Jung's depiction of an analyst as a 'wounded healer' stems from this 'telelogical' view of pathology.

Alchemy grew more important in Jung's work and he saw what he thought of as the archetypal transference/countertransference reflected in the alchemical text, *Rosarium Philosophorum* (Jung, 1954). For his own purposes he used 10 of the woodcut prints that make up the *Rosarium*. These illustrate the story of an incestuous couple, sometimes depicted as king and queen, sometimes as brother and sister, and at others as sun and moon. The human figures are fully clothed in some of the pictures and naked in others. Jung thought that these 10 pictures contained the overall structure of an in-depth analysis culminating in individuation.

These pictures are for Jung a representation of the criss-crossing of both the conscious and unconscious relationship of analyst and patient. This is multifaceted, i.e. on the personal as well as collective unconscious level, and involves the anima/animus of both individuals. As the analysis deepens beyond the persona and conventional level the couple are shown without clothes in the third picture called 'The naked truth' (Jung, 1954: Figure 3). Figure 4 shows the two still trying to hide their 'shadow' from each other: when it comes into the analysis it can lead to the termination of the work.

If the analysis survives this stage a conjunction takes place between the two protagonists, who are then joined together in working towards greater consciousness. This is depicted in 'The conjunction' (Jung, 1954: Figure 5), which shows the couple having intercourse. However, as the whole of the analytic process is an 'as if' rather than a concrete endeavour, this is a symbolic conjunction and physical gratification between the two has to be forgone. This sacrifice leads to death-like feelings, which are depicted in the next picture. The two have to endure the difficulties that ensue from this stage of the analysis and the analyst needs to withstand the temptation to 'explain' what is happening and to give reassurances to the analysand.

If the analytic container can withstand all the difficult feelings up to this point, there will come a time when the analysand begins to be aware of experiencing the beginnings of 'new life'. This is the coming into being of the capacity for symbolization and is depicted in 'The new birth' (Jung, 1954: Figure 10) as an androgynous figure symbolizing the union of opposites. Eros is central to this kind of Jungian analysis, not just that which is sexually charged but also that which is to do with soul. In both meanings of the word, psyche needs eros.

The *Rosarium*, according to Jung, depicts the structure of a classical Jungian analysis, during the course of which dream analysis takes place through 'amplification' of dream images, which connects them to mythological and cultural motifs. 'Active imagination' may also be part of the work. Jung described this as dreaming with open eyes (Jung, 1921).

The developmental approach would look at change as reparation, through work in the transference, of damaged inner objects and an increased capacity for more real interaction with the environment. Compulsive behaviour will be modified, symptoms will be recognized as having inner meaning, and the capacity for tolerating anxiety and guilt will increase.

The lack of change is usually due to fear of relinquishing old patterns of behaviour even though they cause suffering. A patient may cling to a pathological way of functioning because it maintains fantasies of omnipotence, which are dependent on the pathology being experienced as the only thing the patient has in life. In some instances, the internalized parental voice is so strong that the person cannot go against it as doing so incurs unbearable feelings of guilt about getting better.

Ambivalence is common: patients often present with a compliant conscious wish to change and an unconscious defence against doing so. A male patient brought a dream early on in the analysis which showed him coming to the defence of a weak man who was losing a fencing match against an unknown but stronger opponent. We looked at this as his strong ego defending the vulnerable parts of himself that felt under attack from me in the sessions.

Limitations of the approach

Jung was an empiricist and his metapsychology evolved out of his phenomeno-logical observations but he never aspired to be a scientist like Freud, who systematized his observations into a quasi-scientific body of knowledge. There are Jungian hypotheses which could lend themselves to even more rigorous epi-demiological research than has so far been done, e.g. the word association test and psychological types. There is much in the writings which is prospective and has potential for further elaboration.

There is also much that is faulty, as scholars are increasingly discovering. A recent example is Richard Noll's debunking of the solar phallus man alluded to above. In his book, Noll asserts that popular literature detailing myths about sun cults from antiquity was easily available at the time. This undermines Jung's claim that the patient's vision gave credence to his discovery of the 'collective uncon-scious' (Noll, 1994).

Deficiencies in Jungian clinical theory and practice were corrected by Michael Fordham's work in synthesizing analytical psychology and psychoanalysis. Apart from work in transference/countertransference, Jungians have benefited from incorporating into their ethos insights on ego defences and resistance and from using the couch, where patients may be enabled to get in touch with persecutory anxiety and envy.

In recent years there has been an increase in the serious charges levelled at Jung and, by extension, at analytical psychology. Post-Jungians are becoming more rigorous in their efforts to face honestly Jung's failings in regard to his attitudes of racism, anti-Semitism and sexism. Andrew Samuels's work in this area has demonstrated that all of these charges have some foundation in fact and need to be taken seriously (Samuels, 1993). The most damaging charge against

Jung is that of anti-Semitism, and Samuels has explored this in his usual thoughtful way. He says that the short answer to it has to be 'yes' and cites the following quotations from Jung's 1934 paper, 'The state of psychotherapy today': 'The "Aryan" unconscious has a higher potential than the Jewish.' 'The Jew, who is something of a nomad, has never yet created a cultural form of his own and as far as we can see never will, since all his instincts and talents require a more or less civilized nation to act as host for their development', and 'the Jews have this peculiarity with women; being physically weaker, they have to aim at the chinks in the armour of their adversary' (Samuels, 1993: 292–3).

There are many instances of these sentiments on Jung's part, although Geoffrey Cocks offers in his defence that 'Jung conceded more to the Nazis by his words than his actions' (Cocks, 1985: 134).

The above quotations from Jung have much in common with the ideas of Otto Weininger, expressed in his book *Sex and Charter* (1903). Women are equated with Jews in being seen as inferior to the Aryan male: they share in common, amongst other qualities, inherent amorality, irreligion and hysteria. 'The organic untruthfulness of woman' cited in the book is very close to Freud's view on the subject of the female sex.

The concepts of 'self' (supraordinate personality) and 'numinosity' have tremendous potential for healing but, conversely, can be extremely hazardous when they lead to inflation of the ego. This arises when an individual becomes identified with the archetype of the Redeemer and loses touch with his or her common humanity. The danger then is that instead of using these concepts as a psychological tool, analytical psychology can be turned into a religious cult with all that that means in the impulse to convert, proselytize and to become a closed system.

Case example

The client

The case I am presenting is a fiction as are the vignettes above because of confidentiality but it is psychologically true and is based on many years' experience of working with the kind of cases of which this is an example. As an anthropologist, my work is also greatly influenced by concepts such as rites of passage. At the start of any therapy I ask myself what rite of passage the patient/client is needing to negotiate at this particular point of their lives. For women, the major rite of passage they typically have to negotiate is that of going through the menopause and finding meaning in life both during it and when they emerge at the other end. Approaching the menopause brings with it the possible threat of a major illness and/or a series of losses to do with attractiveness, partner, children leaving home, social position and so on. All this can lead to suicidal thoughts and behaviour, depression and a feeling that any meaningful life is over. A major rite of passage may be accompanied by the activation of the archetypal shadow, which for a woman takes the form of the gorgon that can manifest as the petrifying or devouring mother. On the other hand, the successful negotiation of this particular rite of passage through the releasing of new creative psychic energy may enable her for the first time to come into her own life.

Roberta was 49 when she was referred to me for therapy. She is the elder of two children, with a sister three years younger. Her mother went through a difficult pregnancy and birth with the second child and Roberta was sent to loving grandparents when she was three for several months. She had a reasonably comfortable upbringing but felt that her relationship to her mother remained distant from the time of her sibling's birth. She turned instead to her father who was kindly but absent a great deal of the time. Roberta found an outlet in sport at which she became proficient, particularly tennis, and she was a gregarious and popular child. After leaving school, she went to a respectable redbrick university at 18, graduating with a good degree three years later. After this, she worked in public relations and married a man she met through her professional life. They have two adult daughters aged 23 and 21.

The therapy

In the first session along with setting up the contract and hearing about the presenting symptom or problem, I also take mental note of whether the client is an extravert or introvert, what her persona is like and what might be her dominant function e.g. thinking or feeling. Roberta presented as extraverted sensation which is a type that is supremely well adapted to the outside world. This made her good at her work in public relations and subsequently had helped her in her married life to create and maintain an efficient household. She was the perfect wife and mother with a well-functioning adult persona.

Roberta had decided from the first session to use the couch and seemed completely at ease on it from the start. The work has been in progress for three and a half years at a frequency of twice-weekly increasing to four-times-weekly sessions. Using the couch has enabled her to express much of herself that had remained repressed, for instance she has been able to regress to being an infant in the transference and it has become manifest that the distance between her and her mother goes right back to the beginning (she was not breast fed) and preceded the birth of her sister.

This has led to the realization that the same pattern was set up with her older daughter and that she could only be intimate with the younger one, underlined by the following dream about a pink hat. In the dream she is with her two daughters. They are all three much younger than their current ages: she is in her late twenties and the girls are aged three and five. In other words, both daughters are pre-latency and at the Oedipal stage. Roberta is holding a pink hat which she proceeds to bestow lovingly on her younger daughter's head. The older daughter goes out of focus at this point and Roberta is only aware of the warm connection between herself and the younger one.

The dream may be seen as her awarding the crowning glory of her warm feminine feelings to her younger daughter while those for her older daughter are far less clear. In exploring this dream we discovered that her younger daughter is also extraverted and already well adapted to outer world demands but the older one is much more introverted with a tendency to be a dreamer. This is the objective side both of the dream and of her relationship to the two but the dream also points to a subjective, i.e. inner, dynamic that shows up her one-sided adaptation to outer things with a corresponding neglect of her inner world. Although on the face of it this does not appear to be a particularly significant dream it drew our attention not only to the emotional distance between her older daughter and herself but also to an aspect of herself that is neglected and in need of more attention.

This seemingly simple dream had an electrifying effect on Roberta and led to a deepening awareness on her part that she had another less known part of herself to which she had never had any intimate relationship. The lack of intimacy with her mother had carried on not only to her relationship to her own daughter but also to an aspect of herself. Through active imagination (a method of raising contents immediately below the threshold of the unconscious to consciousness), Roberta began to let this shadow side of herself come more into consciousness and slowly be integrated into her own personality.

Her husband had always been more introspective than herself and the two partners in this marriage of opposites had been powerfully attracted to each other at first. The marriage was fulfilling for both in the early years as they found things in the other that were new and exciting and shared similar careers. After both children had gone to school, Roberta thought of continuing with her profession but, to her surprise, found she enjoyed domestic life and sank slowly into a round of children's activities, dinner parties and tennis on Sundays.

Three or four years before coming into analysis, she became increasingly aware that she and her husband had drifted into a routine existence with an occasional sexual encounter at the weekend but very little intimacy besides that. Her daughters were becoming independent of her and she realized that she was in danger of falling into the trap of the mid-forties woman who has nothing but late middle age to which to look forward. She began to make demands on her husband for attention to which he did not respond as he found most of his fulfilment in his work and with his colleagues.

Roberta started drinking more and more heavily at night and was often morose and depressed during the day. Her husband, Colin, began to scold her and that made her even more depressed, especially as the sexual side of their marriage now dried up altogether. She eventually went to see her GP about her heavy drinking and, being one of the more psychologically minded ones, he suggested some therapy.

Three and a half years later, Roberta has managed to control her drinking which, in any case, was more symptomatic (taking to the bottle) than real addiction, and she has reached the point of discovering an aspect of herself that she felt would enable her to embark on a more meaningful relationship to her husband. To her chagrin, he was not responsive to her attempts to have intimate discussions and she was hurt and puzzled by this.

Colin had always worked long hours and often came home late but there now seemed to be a new pattern to his long absences. Roberta decided to take up a part-time job in a friend's gallery and at a private view one day she met an older man in his late sixties. It was love at first sight and she came to her next session in a state of huge excitement to tell me what a wonderful thing had happened to her. By origin he was German Jewish and his parents had brought him to London from Germany before the war when he was an infant. They had made a success of their lives in the UK and had built up an antiques business which Lude had inherited.

Roberta's world turned upside down as she threw herself into a passionate love affair with Lude, whom she described as masterful, urbane and an intellectual. For a while they were inseparable, with Roberta only going home to keep up appearances when Lude had to be at work. He wanted her to leave Colin and live openly with him so that they could travel together for his business, and eventually she did so.

The actual living with Lude, however, brought Roberta up against the other side of his masterfulness and urbanity and she experienced him increasingly as a bullying hypochondriac who wanted to control her completely. The passion slowly deteriorated into a power struggle for domination between them and eros died to be replaced by a cold hatred. Lude became impotent but was nevertheless constantly flirting with other younger women.

Colin had tried to persuade Roberta to return to him at first but finally agreed to a divorce. Ironically, around the time of the decree nisi, she and Lude also came to the realization that their union had become so unsatisfactory that they wanted to end it. At this point, Roberta came very close to despair and lapsed into a crippling depression which a lot of the time kept her in bed, from which she would manage to crawl out to her sessions.

We increased the frequency of the therapy to four times weekly and simultaneously she started having very dark dreams in which she was often at risk. This phase of the therapy lasted about 18 months, during the course of which she went through constant negative thoughts and feelings about herself. Now she felt that she was really on the shelf, alone in the world as both daughters had disapproved of her leaving the marital home, and with no worthwhile occupation to fall back on.

This stage is what Jung calls the dark night of the soul. If it can be endured, it allows for the possibility of transformation which comes through the increasing interaction of the conscious personality and the unconscious. The Oedipal transference/countertransference becomes very intense at this time as client and therapist are interacting with each other, as well as intrapsychically, at both a conscious and an unconscious level. The archetypal Oedipal relationship that had got going between Roberta and Lude had released in her many of the unresolved Oedipal issues from her early life. As these could not be worked through and humanized in that relationship, they came into the analysis and she went through a period of huge dependence on the therapy.

The Oedipal issues that come up at this stage are both personal and archetypal and it is the latter that can endanger a woman at this time by getting her in the grip of the paralysing gorgon which leads to psychological and often physical suicide.

Roberta was very depressed and despairing and clung to the therapy as a lifeline until gradually there was a lightening of the darkness and intensity. She found a new interest in living and started to work in a more committed way at the friend's gallery and is helping to make that a success.

What Roberta had lived through was an encounter with the self that transcends ego experience: if she had taken this at an ego level only she would have blamed herself for being a bad person. In other words, if she had succumbed to the interpretation of her misfortune as being all her own fault, she would have precluded the possibility that there was a higher force at work. The result could easily have been a breakdown and the disintegration of her ego personality. Through the work in the analysis, she was able to hold fast to this experience as an authentic centre of her own being and the 'other' or self could become visibly manifest.

Therapy often leads to greater awareness of an individual's problems and an increase in autonomy but classical Jungian therapy would be seeking as its outcome an opening up of the relationship between the ego and the self and an ongoing relationship between the two. This opens the way to the capacity for symbolization and through that to the individual's own creative living.

Epilogue

I would like to end this chapter by returning to Jung and to the intellectual historian, Henri Ellenberger's account of what he calls Jung's 'creative illness' during the period 1913–19 (Ellenberger, 1970). This followed the break with Freud (who had also undergone the experience of a 'creative illness') in 1913 when Jung felt deserted by all his friends and went through an emotional illness akin to a psychotic episode. He continued his work with patients and his relations with his family but spent a great deal of time alone brooding by Lake Zurich and relating to unconscious processes through 'active imagination'. This method of dreaming while still awake involves starting from an image, word or picture and allowing fantasies associated with it to evolve. This can create a new situation which allows unconscious contents to surface (Jung, 1955–56).

Ellenberger goes on to say that a 'creative illness' remits suddenly and is followed by a short period of euphoria and increased activity. The end result is a permanent change in personality evinced by feelings of being freed from the burden of social conventions and a move towards valuing one's own subjective feelings and ideas. This helps to throw light on the ideological battles that have taken place in the analytical world since the beginning of this century and that continue to take place up to the present time.

References

CW refers to *The Collected Works of C.G. Jung*. London: Routledge & Kegan Paul.

Adler, G. (1961) *The Living Symbol*. New York: Pantheon Books.

Adler, G. (1979) *Dynamics of the Self*. London: Conventure.

Clark, G. (1987) 'Animation through the analytical relationship: the embodiment of self in the transference and countertransference', *Harvest*, 13: 104–14.

Cocks, G. (1985) *Psychotherapy in the Third Reich: The Goering Institute*. London and New York. Oxford University Press.

Ellenberger, H.F. (1970) *The Discovery of the Unconscious*. New York. Basic Books.

Fordham M. (1957) *New Developments in Analytical Psychology*. London: Routledge & Kegan Paul.

Fordham, M. (1993) *The Making of an Analyst*. London: Free Association Books.

Fordham, M. (1976) *The Self and Autism*. London: Heinemann.

Freud, S. (1912) Vol XII ed. and trans. J. Strachey. London: Hogarth Press.

Goffman, E. (1961) *Asylums*. New York: Anchor Books.

Gordon, R. (1979) 'Reflections on curing and healing', *Journal of Analytical Psychology*, 24(3).

Jarrett, L. (ed.) (1988) 'Nietzsche's Zarathustra: notes of the seminar given in 1934–39 by C.G. Jung, *Bolingen Series XCIX*. Princeton, NJ: Princeton University Press.

Jung, C.G. (1911–12) *Symbols of Transformation*, in *CW*, Vol. V.

Jung, C.G. (1921) *Psychological Types*, in *CW*, Vol. VI.

Jung, C.G. (1951) *Aion*, in *CW*, Vol. IX(2).

Jung, C.G. (1953) *Two Essays on Analytical Psychology*, in *CW*, Vol. VII.

Jung, C.G. (1954) *The Practice of Psychotherapy*, in *CW*, Vol. XVI.

Jung, C.G. (1955–56) *Mysterium Coniunctionis*, in *CW*, Vol. XIV.

Jung, C.G. (1960) *The Psychogenesis of Mental Disease*, in *CW*, Vol. III.

Jung, C.O. (1961) *Freud and Psychoanalysis*, in *CW*, Vol. IV.

Jung, C.G. (1963) *Memories, Dreams, Reflections*. London: Collins/Routledge & Kegan Paul.

Jung, C.G. (1967) *Alchemical Studies*, in *CW*, Vol. XIII.

Jung, C.G. (1977) *The Symbolic Life*, in *CW*, Vol. XVIII.

Jung, C.G. (1988) *Nietzsche's Zarathustra*, ed. James L. Jarrett. Princeton, NJ: Princeton University Press.

Lambert, K. (1981) *Analysis, Repair and Individuation*. London: Academic Press.

Myers, L. (1962) *The Myers-Briggs Type Indicator*. Palo Alto, CA: Consulting Psychologists Press.

Noll, R. (1994) *The Jung Cult*. Princeton, NJ: Princeton University Press.

Samuels, A. (1985) *Jung and the Post-Jungians*. London: Routledge & Kegan Paul.

Samuels, A. (1989a) *The Plural Psyche: Personality, Morality and the Father*. London: Routledge.

Samuels, A (1989b) *Psychopathology*. London: H. Karnac Books.

Samuels, A. (1993) *The Political Psyche*. London: Routledge.

Stern, D. (1985) *The Internal World of the Infant*. New York: Basic Books.

Turner, V. (1969) *The Ritual Process: Structure and Anti-Structure*. London: Routledge & Kegan Paul.

Van Gennep, A. (1960) *Rites of Passage*. London: Routledge & Kegan Paul.

Winnicott, D.W. (1964) 'Book review: *Memories, Dreams, Reflections*, by C.G. Jung', *International Journal of Psychoanalysis*, 45.

Zoja, L. (1985) *Drugs, Addiction and Initiation: The Modern Search for Ritual*. London: Sigo Press.

Suggested further reading

Casement, A. (2001) *Carl Gustav Jung*. London: Sage.

Hauke, C. (2000) *Jung and the Postmodern: The Interpretation of Realities*. London: Routledge.

Kirsch, T. (2000) *The Jungians: A Comparative and Historical Perspective*. London: Routledge.

Samuels, A. (2001) *Politics on the Couch: Citizenship and the Internal Life*. London: Profile Books.

Stein, M. (1998) *Jung's Map of the Soul*. Peru, IL: Open Court.

Zoja, L. (1995) *Growth & Guilt: Psychology and the Limits of Development*. London: Routledge.

5 Adlerian Therapy
Jenny Warner and Gerhard Baumer

Historical context and development in Britain

Historical context

Alfred Adler (1870-1937) was a doctor in Vienna who became interested in functional disorders (neuroses) in which physically healthy patients complained of and genuinely suffered from physical symptoms which disrupted their lives. From 1902 to 1911 Adler attended the Wednesday evening meetings of the Viennese Psychoanalytical Society at Freud's invitation. Adler was the most active member of this group and Freud held him in high esteem. Adler's book, *Study of Organ Inferiority and its Psychical Compensation: A Contribution to Clinical Medicine* (1917), first published in 1907, was well received by Freud and considered by him to complement psychoanalytical theory. In this book Adler described the relative weakness of an organ or a system in the body and the reaction of compensation either by the weak organ, another organ or the nervous system. In 1910 Adler became President and Stekel, Vice-President, of the Vienna Psychoanalytical Society; the two men were joint editors, under Freud, of their new journal, *Centralblatt*. By 1911, however, it became obvious that Adler's views differed greatly from Freud's; Adler and Stekel resigned their positions and with a few others left to form a new society, which later became the Society for Individual Psychology.

In 1912 Adler published *The Neurotic Constitution*, outlining his theory of neurosis and laying down many of the basic tenets of Individual Psychology. Adler was now specializing in treating psychiatric patients, neurotic rather than psychotic. In 1914 the *Journal for Individual Psychology* was founded and Adler's ideas spread to Europe and the USA.

Adler was mobilized into the Austrian-Hungarian Army in 1916 and worked as an army physician in a military hospital in Cracow. On returning from the war to a destitute Vienna, Adler directed his energies towards educating people about Individual Psychology. His concept of *Gemeinschaftsgefühl* or 'social interest' fitted well into the new atmosphere of rebuilding a nation. (There is no direct translation in English of *Gemeinschaftsgefühl* and Adler was said to prefer the term social interest.) As well as a welfare programme and a housing and health programme, educational reforms were taking place in Vienna. Adler held open sessions with teachers and their problem children so that as many people as possible could learn about his ideas to enable children to grow up mentally healthy. He also lectured to teachers and at the teachers' request he was appointed professor at the Pedagogical Institute of Vienna in 1924.

In 1923 Adler lectured in England for the first time, at the International Congress of Psychology in Oxford, although he spoke very little English. In 1926 he was invited back to England by a few interested medical and psychological societies and by 1927 an Individual Psychology Club was founded in Gower Street, London; this club later became political and Adler dissociated himself from it. In 1927 Adler's book *Understanding Human Nature* was published. Based on a year's lectures given at the People's Institute in Vienna, it gives a complete description of Individual Psychology and its aim is to enable people to understand themselves and one another better. From 1926 to 1934 Adler spent the academic term in the USA and June to September in Vienna with his family. He went on lecture tours all over the USA; he was appointed lecturer at Columbia University from 1929 to 1931 and in 1932 a chair of medical psychology was established for him at Long Island Medical College. In 1933 he published *Social Interest: A Challenge to Mankind*, which described the concept of *Gemein-schaftsgefühl* (social interest) and placed it at the centre of his psychological theory. By 1934 Adler had settled permanently in the USA, where he was eventually joined by his family. A year later he founded the *International Journal of Individual Psychology* in Chicago. The theory of Individual Psychology and its application in medicine and education was now spreading throughout Europe and the USA. In 1937 Adler had planned a lecture tour in Holland and England and Scotland. In Holland, he gave over 40 lectures in three weeks, but suffered severe angina before he left for Britain. He and his daughter, Dr Alexandra Adler, herself a psychiatrist, had public and private lectures as well as university vacation courses booked at Aberdeen, York, Hull, Manchester, London, Edinburgh, Liverpool and Exeter. Sadly Adler died of a heart attack on the fourth day in Aberdeen while taking an early morning walk; he was 67 years old. Alexandra Adler arrived in Britain and fulfilled most of her father's and her own lecture commitments. She and her brother Kurt, also a psychiatrist, formed an Adlerian group in New York, which is still functioning today.

During the 1920s Rudolph Dreikurs, a young doctor, had worked with Adler's followers in their child guidance clinics in Vienna. In 1937 he went to the USA and soon established an open centre for family counselling in Chicago. From 1942 to 1948 he was professor of psychiatry at the Chicago Medical School where he exposed medical students to Adler's theories of personality, behaviour and psychopathology. By 1950, he was teaching a postgraduate course in child guidance at Northwestern University. Manford Sonstegard, who attended this course, afterwards went on to develop child guidance centres and parent education in Iowa and West Virginia and on his retirement as professor in counselling he went to Britain.

Development in Britain

A new Adlerian Society had been formed in London just before Adler's death, with Adler as its president. This stopped meeting during the Second World War but afterwards was reconstituted with Dr Alexandra Adler as its president. It was and still is called the Adlerian Society of Great Britain, and was affiliated to the Individual Psychological Medical Society which had been founded in the 1930s.

Dr Joshua Bierer, who was personally trained by Adler, emigrated to Britain and founded the first self-governed social therapeutic group for acute and chronic inpatients at Runwell Hospital, Wickford, Essex. He also set up a social psychotherapy centre – now a day hospital – and clubs for outpatients and discharged patients. Group therapy and community psychiatry are legitimate offspring of Alfred Adler's thought and work, according to Ellenberger (1970).

In 1958, Rudolph Dreikurs visited England and Scotland and lectured at Edinburgh, Aberdeen, Liverpool and London Universities at Dr Joshua Bierer's invitation. Dreikurs found that Adlerian psychologists in England were engaged in private practice but were not training parents, teachers, other psychologists or psychiatrists. Adler, during the last 20 years of his life, had emphasized the need to educate teachers, who have influence over large numbers of children so that the ideas of Individual Psychology could benefit future generations and prevent mental illness. Dreikurs too concentrated his efforts on teaching parents and teachers so that children could be enabled to grow up mentally healthy and psychologically able to participate in a democratic society. In 1976 Sonstegard came to England and trained a group of health professionals in Buckinghamshire. These people joined the Adlerian Society of Great Britain, some of whose members had worked with Adler in Vienna. Sonstegard visited England annually and started to train people to do family counselling, lifestyle assessment, group counselling, self-awareness and psychotherapy. He was particularly interested in training lay counsellors and encouraging parents to form study groups and family education centres.

There are no formal Adlerian psychotherapy training courses in Britain recognized by the Institute for Individual Psychology, which is the training division of the Adlerian Society of Great Britain. In Europe Adlerian therapists undergo many years of training. British Adlerian therapists have travelled to America, Israel and Europe to continue their training as well as attending the International Committee for Adlerian Summer Schools and Institutes (ICASSI) which takes place annually in different countries.

Theoretical assumptions

Image of the person

The *holistic socio-teleological* approach of Adlerian therapy based on Adler's Individual Psychology, maintains that people should be viewed in their social contexts in order that their goals can be identified. People choose their own goals based on their subjective perceptions of themselves and their world, their bodies, minds and feelings in harmony with their consistent movement towards these goals. Adlerians consider that people are creative, responsible, self-determined and unique. The holistic socio-teleological approach can be defined as having three parts.

Holistic

The term, 'individual', of Individual Psychology was used by Adler to describe the indivisibility of a person: as such it is a holistic approach to psychotherapy. Adler wanted to stress the self-consistent unity of a person as opposed to other theories which described conflicting divisions of the personality.

Social

Human beings are socially embedded and their actions can be understood only when observed within a group.

Teleological

All behaviour has a purpose and consequently it is possible to identify people's short- and long-term goals, which are of a social nature and reveal the total personality. Individual Psychology emphasizes that people are unaware of their goals and the private logic which underpins their movement towards the goals.

People can always choose how to respond to their inherited qualities and to the environment in which they grow up. People's basic concept of themselves and of life provides a guiding line, a fixed pattern; this is called the lifestyle. The ideas and beliefs according to which a person operates are called *private logic*. They are not common sense but *biased apperception*. Common sense is shared and understood by all people; private logic is owned and understood by one individual and characterizes his or her own biased perceptions of his or her experiences. A person's private logic is created in childhood and contains generalizations and oversimplifications. Individuals create their own unique lifestyle and are therefore responsible for their own personality and behaviour; they are creative actors rather than passive reactors. The lifestyle concept, the theory of private logic and goal orientation and the idea of repeating early lifestyle patterns are psychodynamic descriptions.

People will have developed their own characteristic lifestyle by the time they are five years old, based on their own creative and unique perceptions of their situation in their family. Parents and their values and the atmosphere they create in the family will set the scene for each child to begin to make some assumptions about themselves, their world and their chosen direction of movement. Siblings and their choices of direction will have a major effect on the individual child.

The Adlerian view is that everyone is born with a desire to belong – to the family, to larger groups, to society and to the whole human race. Everyone is born in an inferior position and strives to overcome this position. If this striving for superiority takes place in the context of social interest, the whole group, all society and the future human race benefit. The feeling of belonging (or *Gemeinschaftsgefühl*) is an innate potentiality in every human being. If this potentiality develops in a person he or she feels an equal member of the human race, with a useful part to play, willing to contribute and co-operate; this potentiality can become severely limited or be non-existent when individuals feel inferior to their fellows, unsure of their place and unable to make a useful contribution.

The meaning we attribute to life will determine our behaviour so that we will behave as if our perceptions were true. Life will turn out as we expected and people will respond as we expected; this is a self-fulfilling prophecy.

Conceptualization of psychological disturbance and health

Mental health can be measured by the amount of *social interest* a person has. Mentally healthy people are assured of their place and contribute to the tasks of the groups to which they belong; they co-operate with their fellow human beings and are part of a community. The human race, when looked at from an evolutionary point of view, is always moving towards an improved position from a minus to a plus. The word *courage* is used by Adlerians to describe activity plus social interest, and a person who is said to be acting with social interest is *encouraged*. The encouraged individual has a positive attitude towards him or herself and has self-confidence and self-respect. The goal of mentally healthy people is to belong as *social equals* in the family, in larger groups and in the whole of humanity, making their unique and useful contribution to these groups. Social equality was a concept that Rudolph Dreikurs developed and wrote about: '[Social equality] implies that each individual is entitled to respect and dignity, to full and equal status, regardless of any personal quality or deficiency' (Dreikurs, 1967: 39).

A person who has social interest will feel equal to other people and will treat others as social equals. The mentally healthy person is moving on a *horizontal plane* towards others and is *task orientated*. Their behaviour is useful and is determined solely by the demands of the situation and by *common sense*. Their feeling of belonging enables them to identify with all human beings and to empathize with them.

Adler considered there were three major *life tasks* required of each member of the human race – work (or occupation), friendship and love. Dreikurs added two more – getting on with oneself and relationship to the cosmos. In Adler's time the way that people could fulfil the life tasks was seen as getting a job, having a social life and friendships, getting married and having children. Successful completion of these life tasks was seen as essential to the healthy perpetuation of the human race. More recently Adlerians have given a broader definition of the three life tasks to take account of unemployment and homosexual relationships. Of the three life tasks the intimate relationship with one partner is considered to be the most testing of a person's social interest and willingness to co-operate.

Psychological disturbance occurs when an individual *feels inferior* and unworthy of an equal place amongst his or her fellows. Social interest, which is an innate potentiality in every human being, does not grow in the presence of strong feelings of inferiority. The inferiority feelings are substituted by a *compensatory striving for personal superiority*. People who feel inferior and act superior cannot adequately fulfil the life tasks of occupation, friendship and marriage because they are concerned with preserving their own prestige rather than responding to the needs of the situation and making their contribution to these tasks. Their movement is on a vertical plane away from the group, withdrawing from some or all of the life tasks. An unrealistic, unattainable goal of personal superiority is set by the individual and in the *neurotic individual* excuses then have to be found to explain why the goal is never reached. Neurotic symptoms or behaviours serve as such excuses and the mistaken ideas and attitudes that justify the useless behaviour are called *private logic*. An example of private logic might be 'I am the best at everything I do – unfortunately, I get bad headaches when I am under stress so I am never able to perform at my best.' The goal of being best at everything is unrealistic and unattainable, and the headaches are a neurotic symptom which safeguards the individual from having to admit that he is not as superior as he thinks he is. He likes to think he is superior because he feels inferior; the reality of the situation is that he is socially equal to all human beings. If his feelings of equality and social interest could be developed, he could divert his attention from his own self-esteem, personal security and prestige and concentrate on making his contribution to the tasks of living. His private logic could then be replaced by common sense – Adler's 'ironclad logic of social living' (Terner and Pew, 1978).

Psychotic individuals in the presence of certain predisposing conditions escape totally from the logic of social living and assume a reality of delusions and hallucinations that conforms to their own private logic. *Psychopaths* openly reject common sense and, like neurotics and psychotics, are motivated only by self-interest but, unlike the other two, have no conscience; they do not need the neurotic's excuses and symptoms nor the psychotic's distorted reality.

Acquisition and perpetuation of psychological disturbance

All human problems are essentially social in nature. (Dreikurs, 1967: 104)

We do not develop neurotic symptoms or behaviour as long as we feel we can function adequately. Neurosis will develop as soon as we feel unable to fulfil our obligations in one of the life tasks – at work, in friendships, in an intimate relationship. The symptoms and behaviour will be the excuse for not fulfilling the tasks adequately, not engaging in them at all, or retreating from them. Rather than facing failure and being found to be inadequate the symptom enables the discouraged individual to hesitate or evade and yet not lose face. Neurotics may not appear to have any difficulties until they meet a crisis for which they feel unprepared. For example a crisis for one individual might be having to find a job when she feels incapable of fulfilling the demands of employment. Facing the demanding task of marriage might become a crisis situation for another individual, so forcing her to break off an engagement. Rather than developing a symptom, an individual may choose safeguarding behaviour such as being totally absorbed in one life task, so leaving no time or energy to engage in the other two life tasks in which they feel inadequate.

Individuals feel unable to find their place due to varying degrees of inferiority feelings. As children they learned to feel inferior. Their parents may have spoiled them and given in to their demands, in which case they would have developed the mistaken idea that they were very special people who should be served by others. They may have learned to use displays of emotion to get this service – temper tantrums, tears or sulks. Adler uses spoiling and pampering synonymously in his writings. Sonstegard makes a distinction between the two: spoiling is giving in to a child's demands whereas pampering is doing for the child those things that the child can do for himself. Pampering is regarded by Sonstegard as the most disabling form of parenting. Pampered children feel unable to accomplish many tasks and constantly seek help from others. They lack self-confidence when they grow into adulthood, because they have such limited experience of learning and doing for themselves. Their parents' over-protection stunts their growth, so they doubt their ability to be independent or to make choices or to take risks and face hardships. Spoilt children in adult life will still be expecting others to serve them and let them have their own way. Pampered and spoilt people feel that the world is their enemy because it does not respond in the same way as did their parents. Adler pointed out that children play an active part in enlisting help in the case of pampering, or in demanding service in the case of spoiling. Criticized children grow up afraid of taking risks and making mistakes. Neglect is far less common than papering and spoiling but was acknowledged by Adler to produce discouraged children. Dreikurs was convinced that the parenting methods and education of our competitive society did not encourage mental health. Mistake-centred education and 'you could do better' parenting discourage children.

People's perception of their position in their family constellation forms the basis of their lifestyle. The parents set family values and create a family atmosphere and the children decide their place in the family. A competitive family will produce discouragement, the children competing against each other and eventually channelling themselves into separate spheres of success. They each choose something they can be best at, even if that is being naughty. As each child strives for superiority this necessitates putting the other siblings down. An eldest child is an only child for a while, possibly the centre of attention until the second child arrives and dethrones the first child. The first child has several options, one of which is to strive to retain her superiority. The second child may want to catch up with the first child and may succeed, in which case the first child will feel discouraged. The second child may give up because the first child is too capable and too far ahead. The youngest child may remain a baby for a long time, the other children acting as pampering parents; they have a vested interest in keeping the youngest a baby, as it enhances their superiority. However, some youngest children can become the most accomplished members of their families; they are never dethroned and strive to overcome all the other children. Individual children make their choice and choose their goals supported by mistaken ideas or private logic, interpreting their position in the family constellation. Neither the child nor the adult is aware of these goals or their private logic.

Even though people may not be co-operating and may not be fulfilling all of the life tasks, as long as their lifestyle is in harmony with their environment, there will be no disturbing behaviour or distressing symptoms. An adult, spoilt as a child, may find partners, relatives, children, friends who are willing to give in to her demands. An adult, pampered as a child, may find sufficient rescuers, helpers and advisers to take over responsibility for his life. If these individuals should lose their slaves or supports a crisis would ensue and disturbing behaviour might emerge in order to attract more applicants for the vacant posts. People may consciously regret their symptoms and seek treatment for them. They may convince themselves and others of their good intentions to get rid of their symptoms or their disturbing behaviour. Their efforts to fight the symptoms merely aggravate and perpetuate them. People's private logic maintains their mistaken and unrealistic life goals. Adler referred to this as a 'yes-but' personality where the individual is aware of their social obligations (yes) – (but) due to their private logic they have to continue with their useless behaviour. The feared situation is still avoided, the task or duty is evaded and the obligations of a relationship are side-stepped. Sometimes the symptom is cured but it recurs or is replaced by another symptom if its safeguarding tendency is still needed.

Change

Any occurrence in people's lives may become an encouraging experience, so causing them to change their perceptions. New behaviours which challenge the old premisses of the lifestyle may cause a revision in social interest with a consequent decrease in inferiority feelings. The new behaviour may be embarked upon as a result of encouragement from another person or, less often, due to an independent decision on the part of the individual. Changed circumstances – e.g. leaving home, partners or parents, or being left by partners or parents, leaving school, passing exams or failing exams, getting a job or losing a job – can start the changed behaviour. If the new behaviour has encouraging results then the private logic which underpinned the old behaviour is challenged and possibly revised.

As mentioned in the previous section, people may change their overt behaviour without any change in their motivation. Adlerians would consider that a behavioural change is superficial if not accompanied by an alteration of perception and an increase in social interest. People need to gain some insight into their mistaken ideas after changing their behaviour. Substituting acceptable behaviour for unacceptable behaviour is not a change in lifestyle if people still do not feel equal to their fellows. People who feel they must always be the centre of attention, and who change from unacceptable behaviour to acceptable behaviour, are still focused on their own superiority and sense of being special; they are not concentrating on what they can contribute to the task and the needs of the situation.

Practice

Goals of therapy

Adlerian psychotherapy is a learning process where there is re-education of clients' faulty perceptions and social values, and modification of their motivation. It is intended that clients should gain insight into their mistaken ideas and unrealistic goals, both of which are a source of discouragement. After insight there is a stage of reorientation of short- and long-term goals and readjustment of personal concepts and attitudes. The clients' original feelings of inferiority are superseded by a growing social interest They feel encouraged as they recognize their equality with their fellow human beings. They concentrate on making their contribution and co-operating instead of looking at their personal status within groups.

There are four phases, each with its own goal in the Adlerian psychotherapy process:

1 establishing and maintaining a relationship with the client;
2 uncovering the dynamics of the client;
3 giving insight;
4 encouraging reorientation.

Selection criteria

There are no rigid guidelines for selecting individual therapy rather than couples therapy or group therapy. Individual choice on the part of both the therapist and the client is respected, although clients' rights to choose their kind of therapy are limited by what is available. Some therapists prefer to work with people in a group, acknowledging that each individual's problems are of a social nature, the group acting as an important agent in the psychotherapeutic process. Some therapists are reluctant to work with married individuals unless their partner is aware of the implications of psychotherapy and the changes it may encourage. When working with children, Adlerian therapists work with the whole family, parents and siblings, as they realize that if one child makes changes then the whole family will need to change too. Dreikurs, Mosak and Shulman (1952, 1982) introduced multiple psychotherapy: several therapists working with one client. This provides an ideal training opportunity. The client enjoys the attention of more than one therapist, and since the atmosphere is educational, discussion of interpretation of the clients' lifestyle, including disagreements between therapists, is enlightening and encouraging to the client. The client participates as an equal in explaining and understanding his or her private logic. It does happen that clients move from individual to group therapy or from a group to individual therapy and this move is mutually agreed between clients and therapists. Some clients receiving group therapy may have additional individual sessions from the group therapist. If a couple have a relationship problem the therapist may want to work with them as a couple; however, it may emerge that one or both partners need to do some individual work, in which case they would have some individual therapy. Clients who feel ridiculous if they share feelings and personal ideas tend to prefer individual therapy, one therapist being less threatening than a group of people.

Qualities of effective therapists

The effective Adlerian therapist feels truly equal to all human beings, and this includes clients and children. The therapist shows respect to the client, but this does not necessarily mean that the therapist is always nice and kind and accepting of all the client's behaviours. The relationship with the client is one of mutual respect, so the therapist shows herself respect by not tolerating unacceptable behaviour from the client and by giving honest feedback. The therapist shows respect towards the client by genuinely acting as if he had full responsibility for his decisions and actions. The therapist is warm and accepting of the person as he is and sincerely interested in understanding without judgement his lifestyle, his unique perception of life and his chosen life goals. The Adlerian therapist models social interest and shows herself to be a fallible human being who is making her own contribution, unafraid of making mistakes. The Adlerian approach is based on a clear philosophy of life and the therapist will espouse social values that enable all human beings to live together in harmony as equals now and in the future. The relationship with the therapist may be the first one where the client experiences a democratic, co-operative partnership between equals. The therapist needs to have the skills to win people over as well as the personal maturity to model social interest. Many clients resist entering a partnership between equals because this gives them too much responsibility. The therapist must resist the temptation to dominate, rescue, manipulate or fight with the client; all these therapist behaviours are disrespectful and belong to an authoritarian relationship rather than a democratic one.

There are many varied, creative and adaptable Adlerian therapists who use different modes of gaining insight and encouraging reorientation. Art therapy, psychodrama, non-verbal exercises, group exercises and dream analysis are some of the major approaches that Adlerian therapists use.

Therapeutic relationship and style

There is no prescribed style for Adlerian therapists but the relationship is one of equality. Initially, the therapist will respond sensitively to the client in order to quickly establish an atmosphere of trust and acceptance. The setting is usually relaxed and comfortable with the therapist and client facing each other in chairs of equal height. After the presenting problem has been briefly described by the client, some Adlerian therapists will want to move on to gathering information in order to be able to understand the client's lifestyle. The client may be surprised to be moved away from the problem and although the therapist's style is directive at this point it is respectful, so that an explanation is given as to why the therapist wishes to move on and the client's agreement is sought. Other therapists gather lifestyle information in a more informal way during the course of therapy. Both client and therapist embark upon this educational voyage of discovery actively as partners, the client providing the information and the therapist giving interpretations. The therapist's style will vary according to each client's needs, so that *empathy* is established. For instance, the therapist might use the client's vocabulary, seeking clarification if she is not sure what the client is saying; the therapist might give time and space for clients to express their feelings or might use humour during the sessions, and some therapists may self-disclose in order to give clients feedback on their behaviour in the session. Gradually the private logic will be uncovered and understood by the therapist. Interpretations need to be put to the client as they are merely hypothesized by guessing on the part of the therapist. The therapist will wish to see whether the client acknowledges if the therapist has made a true interpretation.

The whole educational process will not take place unless therapist and client are co-operating and sharing mutually agreed goals. It is in the last phase – reorientation – that it becomes clear if both therapist and client share the same therapy goals. Clients have the right to gain insight and then decide not to make any changes. If the client does wish to make some changes, the therapist is there to guide him. Task-setting and completing the assignments also require a co-operative relationship. There will be difficult times, there may be strong emotions to work through, disagreements between therapist and client, but their resilient relationship endures these tests. The time-scale for the last phase (reorientation) will vary with each client. Some clients spend useful time with their therapist when they want to make some changes; others may need to be away from the therapist, having decided to stick to old familiar patterns. The door is always open for them to return when they feel ready to work on themselves again. The therapist demonstrates complete faith in the client by giving him total responsibility for his own reorientation.

Major therapeutic strategies and techniques

Adlerian psychotherapy can be described as a co-operative educational enterprise between equals – the therapist and client. The first stage of therapy is to *establish a co-operative relationship*, recognized by the presence of mutual respect. A co-operative relationship requires mutually agreed goals. An open approach towards stating goals will prevent ineffectual therapy between a therapist and a client who have different goals. If it is not possible to find mutually agreed goals psychotherapy will be ineffectual and may as well be terminated. Mutual respect is established by the therapist showing herself respect by refusing to play any *games* with the client, by only working towards agreed therapy goals and by openly commenting about behaviour towards herself that she finds unacceptable. If transference takes place the therapist can reveal this to the client as part of the educational experience. The therapist shows respect for clients by listening and accepting and acknowledging clients' rights to make their own decisions and take responsibility for their lives. The client needs to feel that the therapist cares but will not manipulate, dominate nor rescue. Dictatorial prescription and rescuing are equally disrespectful behaviours on the part of the therapist. This democratic relationship becomes part of the client's retraining; it is an action experience.

The second stage of the therapy is to *gather information* and *understand clients' lifestyles* and then to show clients how the presenting problem fits into their overall characteristic pattern of movement. From the first minutes of meeting clients, information will be available to the therapist from non-verbal clues – how clients enter the room, where they choose to sit, their posture, how they speak, etc. Adler was reportedly very clever at picking up information from this non-verbal behaviour. Verbal information is also available in the client's short description of the presenting problem, the subjective situation. The Adlerian therapist will not want to spend too long initially on the presenting problem, as she will need to discover the client's lifestyle before the significance of the problem can be understood. The objective situation of the client is also explored as the therapist finds out how the client is functioning in the three life tasks: work, friendships and intimate relationships. Some therapists may also enquire about relationships to God and moral-ethical beliefs. If clients are complaining of symptoms then they are asked, 'the question', i.e. what would be different if you were well/if you did not have this symptom? Clients' answers will reveal the particular area of difficulty for them and their unrealistic goals.

The therapist will then move on to *lifestyle assessment*, which consists of understanding the client's family constellation and interpreting his early memories. A child creates his own unique lifestyle in the context of his family and in relation to his siblings. The therapist, therefore, asks the client to describe himself and his siblings as children. Family constellation is not just a reflection of birth order. Adlerians might describe typical eldest, second, youngest, middle and only children but as Adler said, 'Everything can also be different', and children may interpret their positions in the family constellation quite differently. An eldest child chooses how to respond to family values and to the experience of being dethroned by a younger child; all elder children experience being only children for a time. A second child chooses whether to compete with the eldest by overtaking them or by doing something or being something entirely different. A youngest may decide to remain the baby of the family or to surpass all the siblings in achievement. Family values will determine whether the competition takes place in academic achievements or in being an acceptable person or in some other realm of behaviour important to that family. Many children will decide to rebel against family values, either silently or openly. Most families are competitive; very few are democratic.

The therapist will want additional information, in order to verify the hypothesis that she is beginning to form about the client's lifestyle. Dreikurs said that you needed two points on a line before you could make a hypothesis about a person's lifestyle. The therapist asks the client for some of his early memories. Adler found that people remembered incidents, often innocuous and ordinary, that fitted in with their lifestyle. Clients are asked to think back as far as they can and tell the therapist the first thing they think of, if possible something that happened to them before they were five years old. People select, out of all their life experiences, those memories that depict a certain aspect of their lifestyle. It may be their view of themselves, their view of their world and the people in it, their view of how life should be or how they have to behave. The therapist has to interpret the early memories and align this information with that already gleaned from the description of the family constellation. The therapist wants to find out clients' life goals and their underlying mistaken assumptions, i.e. their private logic. The overall movement of the client needs to be recognized. The presenting problem and future problems will fit into this basic pattern of living.

The third phase of *interpretation* and *giving insight* is now entered. The therapist's approach is to find enough points on a line to begin to make a hypothesis. This informed guess is then put to the client, so that it can be verified. The therapist is looking for the client's recognition. Previously, clients were unaware of their goals and private logic, so this phase of the therapy is where the therapist particularly needs to demonstrate her empathy; she needs to be able to describe the client's goals and mistaken ideas in words that the client understands, recognizes and owns. This disclosure does not have to be perfect at the first attempt. The therapist shows her fallibility and encourages the client to help her shape the lifestyle summary, so that it feels right for the client. The summary usually takes the form of 'Life is. . .'; 'Others are. . .'; and 'I am. . .' themes. The therapist explains how clients choose their particular goals, so that there is no mystique in the interpretation of the lifestyle. Private logic once it is verbalized begins to lose its strength. The overgeneralizations, oversimplifications and unrealistic ideas can be challenged. 'Is it reasonable to expect. . .?' 'Is this really how people are?' 'Is it realistic for you to expect to always be. . .?'

Dreams may also be analysed. Adler said dreams were the 'factory of the emotions'; they set the mood that fuels people's actions. Remembered dreams that clients produce always fit within a person's lifestyle and never contradict it.

The therapist places the client's concerns and problems in the context of the lifestyle and shows how certain situations, relationships or demands can cause a crisis because they challenge the client's lifestyle. Neurotic symptoms can be understood as alibis which were necessary because the client was pursuing unattainable goals. Making clients aware of the purpose of their neurotic symptoms was described by Adler as 'spitting in the patient's soup'. The patient can persist with the symptoms but they will not give the same satisfaction as before.

The *reorientation phase* follows on from gaining insight. The Adlerian therapist will use a mirror technique to show clients familiar patterns of movement towards consistent goals in all their behaviour. Attainable assignments may be set for clients that challenge their private logic. If the assignments are completed successfully then there is a weakening of clients' private logic. Clients will begin to catch themselves pursuing the same goals and making the same justifications for their behaviour. Clients will catch themselves after, during, and then before they engage in the useless behaviour. Each 'aha' experience increases clients' new learning and growing understanding of their own personality. Each individual, once they have some insight, will decide whether or not to change and if to change, over how long a period. The old patterns are well tried and tested, automatic and to some extent feel comfortable. New patterns are scary. One method that Adler used when a client was fighting against a symptom or behaviour and actually increasing both was to encourage the client to increase the symptom or behaviour; this is known as paradoxical intention.

The change process in therapy

Once people's mistaken goals are revealed to them they can no longer pursue them with such conviction. Once their mistaken ideas are revealed to them they can choose to change. Gaining insight and choosing to change is one choice; gaining insight and choosing not to change is another. Insight will develop as individuals begin to recognize their patterns of behaviour. New behaviours which challenge the old assumptions are then tested out. New behaviours or assignments may be successful – the old private logic is then challenged and weakened and replaced by common sense. New behaviours may have disastrous outcomes, in which case clients may be tempted to retreat to old ways and to feel comfortable with familiar private logic. As their private logic decreases and common sense grows they will display increased social interest in all spheres of their lives and they will take on responsibility for their own life goals, perceptions and behaviours. As soon as they accept full responsibility for their own behaviour they enable themselves to make changes. Their increased sense of belonging and feeling of equal worth will be a source of encouragement to them. Inferiority feelings will diminish; their focus of interest will be on their personal contribution to the task in hand. They will feel content with themselves. Their unattainable goals will be replaced by the courage to be imperfect, an acknowledgement that all active, co-operating human beings make mistakes. The new behaviours and new goals will be followed by new assumptions. This process can be instant in a child, as when one of the Four Mistaken Goals of Misbehaviour (Dreikurs and Soltz, 1995) is revealed to them, very quick in a teenager and increasingly slower in a mature adult. It is harder for adults in established relationships to make changes as these changes will inevitably have an effect on partners in intimate relationships, and on close friends. The therapist, who has always treated the client as an equal, encourages the client to contribute as an equal. Clients may make a partial or complete change of personality, their private logic replaced by common sense, their inferiority feelings replaced by social interest and a feeling of belonging. The correction of one mistaken concept will enable growth and release further courage to tackle new behaviours and additional mistakes. The therapist will respect the client's right to choose when and how much to change. Behaviour change can occur years after initially gaining insight. It is best for the therapist not to fight with the client during times of inactivity; the therapist can be available when the client wants to make some changes but does not know how to. Each person, if they choose to change, will do so in their own unique and creative way.

Limitations of the approach

Adler's theory of personality provides Adlerian therapists with a complete understanding of all human behaviour. The practice of Adlerian therapists is very varied but always based on the foundation of a holistic socio-teleological view of people. Much of Adler's Individual Psychology has permeated other approaches in psychotherapy and counselling; many of his ideas are incorporated into other people's theories without acknowledgement. Adlerian theory appears to have widespread acceptance and relevance to students of human behaviour.

The psychotherapeutic procedures practised by Adler himself and by Rudolph Dreikurs are used today by therapists, and any technique which a therapist finds helpful is added to the basic approach. The insight and the skills are only part of Adlerian psychotherapy. Psychotherapists need to have social interest and need to use their skills 'for the purpose of establishing an ideal community' (Dreikurs, 1953: v). The Adlerian approach can give a great deal of insight; to use the insight and understanding of people with social interest is an exacting demand on every therapist. Many people, including therapists, have grown up in families where power was used either openly in the form of control by anger or disguised in the form of manipulation. Therapists have to work on understanding their own skills in the arena of power before they can work with clients in a truly equal co-operative relationship. Many clients will find the idea of being responsible for their own behaviour distasteful and unacceptable.

The client may leave therapy with insight but unwilling to change. If therapy outcomes are looked at over too short a time the long-term effects of the insight may not be recorded. Changes have been seen several years after a lifestyle assessment was done. It is always worthwhile enabling a person to gain insight. It is never worthwhile fighting with them afterwards in order to force or persuade or shame them into change.

There are limitations to using Adlerian psychotherapy only in a one-to-one situation. So much information can be gained by observing clients in groups. So much can be gained by clients when trying out new behaviours in a safe group. So much can be gained by clients experiencing equal membership of a group with a shared goal of mutual growth.

Case example

The client

Richard called me in December 1997 and we arranged an appointment. He had been given my number by a colleague of mine in Cambridge when he was visiting his children who live with his ex-wife. It took him a while before he made an appointment. We worked together for one and a half years. Richard had 27 sessions during this time. Because of time restrictions for both of us the meetings were not very regular.

On our first session he giggled, apologized for bothering me and pointed out that his German wife had strongly advised him to see a psychologist. He expected that a German therapist would be able to give him some clue about his wife's strange behaviour. He sat down, laughed and said that there was nothing wrong with him. Describing his marriage he said, 'Of course we quarrel now and then. A couple of weeks ago we had a big argument because I was angry about the way she spoils the kids. At the moment we are arguing about Christmas. I want to go out and have fun, but she wants me to stay at home and celebrate Christmas Eve with her and the boys.'

What else did I learn about Richard during the first session? He and his wife have both been married for a second time. Richard worked as a self-employed builder, did some antique trading and took all kinds of opportunities to make money. He had worked in Germany for a while after he had to fold up his business in England during the recession. He mentioned that he found it very difficult to get up in the morning, he slept badly, felt exhausted and ran out of energy, suffered from headaches, stomach ache and periodically from asthma and bronchitis. He had doubts about his future prospects, had no friends and felt a bit as though he was in a hostile world where he could not trust easily. 'I am a loner,' he said, 'always have been. The people in my village are reserved. When I open my mouth they hear my northern accent. They let me know that I am a stranger.' When I went into his actual situation in more detail he suddenly burst into tears, sobbed his heart out and became very fragile. It seemed to be a big relief and he softened and became serious. We agreed that we should continue the sessions, having five more in order to build up a relationship with me so that we could work, explore his lifestyle and decide whether he was willing to continue with me.

The therapy

During the following sessions we talked about Richard's actual problems and explored his upbringing. It was quite painful sometimes. He giggled a lot as a defence mechanism, was sometimes moved, shaken and in tears. I don't use the lifestyle assessment as a fixed structure. I go along with the client (with the flow), just asking questions, sometimes, if there is something not clear enough. In the following I will describe or use Richard's own words where useful. I cannot show the whole process that we went through during the sessions so I have selected parts which show typical Adlerian understanding and intervention.

This was Richard's family constellation. He was born and brought up in a very poor and rough area of Liverpool. His family lived in a tiny council house. His father was in the army for 15 years and worked in the docks after that. He spent a lot of time in the pub and got drunk. 'My father was aggressive and a thug. The Army educated and civilized him a bit. My mother got pregnant with me before they married. My father disliked me because of that; I think he hated me. My parents were very different.' Richard described his mother as bright and artistic but she could not stand up to his father. His parents argued a lot but then his mother gave in. She was Jewish with a German background. She didn't have very much in common with her husband, according to Richard. He had two younger brothers, one two years and one three years younger and a sister five years younger. She died when she was four. The father's favourite was Bill, the youngest son. Richard felt very neglected, for example when his father 'forgot' his birthday, which was just some days before Christmas. He argued that there was no money left because of Christmas presents. His father was very strict and punished Richard a lot. He saw him as the bad one who had ruined his life. How did Richard interpret this situation? He felt very strongly that father was unfair, life was unfair, mother (women) were sympathetic but weak and siblings are preferred. He felt dethroned and went into revenge. He began to hate his father and started to fight with his two brothers. 'I was very bossy – a tyrant. They had to obey. I never shared my things with them. I exploded when they even touched my things.' He continued that he had destroyed their toys and had been bullying and very cruel to them, which caused guilt feelings. He went into seeking negative attention, became a bed-wetter until he was nine years old and behaved very spitefully. His first early recollection was: 'I am six. All the others have gone out. I eat the chocolate my brothers have saved in a box. I know I will get punished but I have great pleasure knowing that my brothers will be disappointed when they discover that their sweets have gone.' Richard became an unhappy child and withdrew into his fantasy world. He had a lot of guilt feelings and believed that he was a very bad person.

School was terrible. Richard was frightened to death. 'The boys at school bullied me and beat me up. I was anxious and timid and hid in the cloakroom during breaks. I became the clown, the fool and laughed all the time, even when they bullied me. This helped me not to get beaten up by the other kids but made some teachers furious. I tried to be independent and got out of the house as much as possible. At 12 I had two jobs, delivering newspapers and helping in a butcher's shop. Having money became important. It meant power. I helped father out when he was broke and he showed me some respect.' After he had left school at 15, Richard trained as a butcher. He won some prizes in professional competitions. When he was 20 he decided to change his professional career. Out of the blue he trained as a builder and later he sold tyres as well. He liked to have two or more jobs and was very successful, bought property, married a bipolar depressed middle-class girl ('a real beauty') had one daughter and two sons, had problems in his marriage which ended up in power struggles, lost interest in his work, developed a drinking problem, had to sell his properties and got broke. His wife asked for a divorce. At that time his father died. They had had a long talk before the father died where he admitted that he was proud of Richard and that he liked him. When Richard talked about that in therapy he was very upset. After his father's death Richard developed psychosomatic symptoms and became depressed for a long time. It took a while for him to get back his energy and his interest in the world.

It became obvious that Richard blamed others for all his failures. He felt quite inferior and compensated by being 'better', more successful, cleverer, faster at work. He had quite a competitive tendency, looked down on others and tried to use them in order to maintain his self-esteem. He tried hard at the beginning to win me over so I could see life through his eyes. But as his trust improved he did admit that he played silly games with people like his wife. He needed secrets – for example not telling her where he was the night before; he upset her and nagged her. It became obvious in our talks that this helped to avoid closeness and that he could feel superior by putting her down. He felt empowered. It was his way to test whether she really loved him or not. After this session he began to co-operate and be more open in his relationship with her, which removed a lot of tension. He started to see and treat her more as an equal. He worked on his jealousy of the children which was behind his complaints about how she brought them up and spoiled them. He became aware that he saw them as brother substitutes and as rivals for attention and love. He saw that this was a big issue in his life and had poisoned the atmosphere in his former marriage as well.

From the 20th session on I noticed that his transference had altered. It was no longer idealizing. He compared us, and asked certain questions like, 'Can you fix things?', 'What kind of car do you drive', 'Do you think I could help people as well?' He was becoming less competitive and had a greater sense of belonging and this was improving his relationships at home and at work.

In the 27th session he mentioned a recurring dream. It was connected with his change of profession at the age of 20. At that time he and his boss went to a pig farm to fetch some animals. The farmer sold them a pig which had been used as a pet by his daughter. Richard saw her sobbing at the gate when they left. From then on he dreamt quite regularly that this pig, called Sally, came into the slaughterhouse with some others, crying. Richard became very sad at that moment. After a pause he continued: 'That's strange. I remember something I had completely forgotten. I was about nine, it was quite near to the time of my sister's death. I took her rabbit, called Hoppsy, out of her cage in our little back garden. It liked that very much. She found a tiny hole, went through the fence and was torn to pieces by a big dog shortly after. I couldn't help. I never told anybody that I had opened the cage, had terrible guilt feelings because my sister, I loved very much, felt so miserable about the loss. She died two weeks later. I thought it was my fault.' We talked about guilt feelings and it turned out that he blamed himself that father got cancer and died. 'I was so bad as a child,' he said. 'I sometimes thought it might have ruined his health.'

After that session he went abroad for three months because of a work contract. After two months I got a letter. He thanked me, told me that there were no recurring dreams and that his life was going well and he felt much better physically. 'There is a good atmosphere at work and colleagues seem to like me. Things are changing. Even my wife has changed. She is much more easygoing.'

References

Adler, A. (1912) *The Neurotic Constitution*. London: Kegan Paul, Trench, Trubner & Co.

Adler, A. (1917) *Study of Organ Inferiority and its Psychical Compensation: A Contribution to Clinical Medicine*. New York: Nervous and Mental Diseases Publishing.

Adler, A. (1933) *Social Interest: A Challenge to Mankind*. London: Faber & Faber.

Adler, A. (1992) *Understanding Human Nature* (1927), trans. Colin Brett. Oxford: Oneworld Publications.

Dreikurs, R. (1953) *Fundamentals of Adlerian Psychology*. Chicago, IL: Adler School of Professional Psychology.

Dreikurs, R. (1967) *Psychodynamics, Psychotherapy and Counselling. Collected Papers*. Chicago, IL: Adler School of Professional Psychology.

Dreikurs, R. and Soltz, V. (1995) *Happy Children* (1964). Melbourne: Australian Council for Educational Research.

Dreikurs, R., Mosak, H.H. and Shulman, B.H. (1952) 'Patient–therapist relationship in multiple psychotherapy. II: its advantages for the patient', *Psychiatric Quarterly*, 26: 590–6.

Dreikurs, R., Mosak, H.H. and Shulman, B.H. (1982) *Multiple Psychotherapy: Use of Two Therapists with One Patient*. Chicago, IL: Adler School of Professional Psychology.

Ellenberger, H.F. (1970) 'Alfred Adler and individual psychology', Ch. 8 in *The Discovery of the Unconscious*. New York: Basic Books.

Terner, J. and Pew, W.L. (1978) *The Courage to be Imperfect: The Life and Work of Rudolf Dreikurs*. New York: Hawthorn Books.

Suggested further reading

Adler, A. (1964) *Superiority and Social Interest: A Collection of Later Writings*, ed. H. L. Ansbacher and R. R. Ansbacher. New York: Norton.

Adler, A. (1992) *What Life Could Mean to You* (1931), trans. Colin Brett. Oxford: Oneworld Publications.

Ansbacher, H.L. and Ansbacher, R.R. (eds) (1967) *The Individual Psychology of Alfred Adler*. New York: Harper & Row.

Corsini, R.J. (1984) 'Adlerian psychotherapy', Ch. 3 in *Current Psychotherapies*. Itasca, IL: Peacock.

Dreikurs, R. (1971) *Social Equality: The Challenge of Today*. Chicago, IL: Henry Regnery.

6 Person-Centred Therapy
Brian Thorne

Historical context and development in Britain

Historical context

Dr Carl Rogers (1902–87), the American psychologist and founder of what has now become known as person-centred counselling or psychotherapy, always claimed to be grateful that he never had one particular mentor. He was influenced by many significant figures, often holding widely differing viewpoints, but above all he claimed to be the student of his own experience and of that of his clients and colleagues.

While accepting Rogers's undoubtedly honest claim about his primary sources of learning there is much about his thought and practice which places him within a recognizable tradition. Oatley has described this as

> the distinguished American tradition exemplified by John Dewey: the tradition of no nonsense, of vigorous self-reliance, of exposing oneself thoughtfully to experience, practical innovation, and of careful concern for others. (Oatley, 1981: 192)

In fact in 1925, while still a student at Teachers College, Columbia, New York, Rogers was directly exposed to Dewey's thought and to progressive education through his attendance at a course led by the famous William Heard Kilpatrick, a student of Dewey and himself a teacher of extraordinary magnetism. Not that Dewey and Kilpatrick formed the mainstream of the ideas to which Rogers was introduced during his professional training and early clinical experience. Indeed when he took up his first appointment in 1928 as a member of the Child Study Department of the Society for the Prevention of Cruelty to Children in Rochester, New York, he joined an institution where the three fields of psychology, psychiatry and social work were combining forces in diagnosing and treating problems. This context appealed to Rogers's essentially pragmatic temperament.

Rogers's biographer, Kirschenbaum (1979), while acknowledging the variety of influences to which Rogers was subjected at the outset of his professional career, suggests nevertheless that when Rogers went to Rochester he saw himself essentially as a diagnostician and as an interpretative therapist whose goal, very much in the analytical tradition, was to help a child or a parent gain insight into their own behaviour and motivation. Diagnosis and interpretation are far removed from the primary concerns of a contemporary person-centred therapist and in an important sense Rogers's progressive disillusionment with both these activities during his time at Rochester marks the beginning of his own unique approach. He tells the story of how, near the end of his time at Rochester, he had been working with a highly intelligent mother whose son was presenting serious behavioural problems. Rogers was convinced that the root of the trouble lay in the mother's early rejection of the boy but no amount of gentle strategy on his part could bring her to this insight. In the end he gave up and they were about to part when she asked if adults were taken for counselling on their own account. When Rogers assured her that they were she immediately requested help for herself and launched into an impassioned outpouring of her own despair, her marital difficulties and her confusion and sense of failure. Real therapy, it seems, began at that moment and was ultimately successful. Rogers commented:

> This incident was one of a number which helped me to experience the fact – only fully realised later – that it is the client who knows what hurts, what direction to go, what problems are crucial, what experiences have been deeply buried. It began to occur to me that unless I had a need to demonstrate my own cleverness and learning, I would do better to rely upon the client for the direction of movement in the process. (cited in Kirschenbaum, 1979: 89)

The essential step from diagnosis and interpretation to listening had been taken and from that point onwards Rogers was launched on his own path.

By 1940 Rogers was a professor of psychology at Ohio State University and his second book, *Counseling and Psychotherapy*, appeared two years later. From 1945 to 1957 he was professor of psychology at Chicago and executive secretary (his own term) of the university counselling centre. This was a period of intense activity, not least in the research field. Rogers's pragmatic nature has led to much research being carried out on person-centred therapy. With the publication of *Client-Centered Therapy* in 1951 Rogers became a major force in the world of psychotherapy and established his position as a practitioner, theorist and researcher who warranted respect. In an address to the American Psychological Association in 1973 Rogers maintained that during this Chicago period he was for the first time giving clear expression to an idea whose time had come. The idea was

> the gradually formed and tested hypothesis that the individual has within himself vast resources for self-understanding, for altering his self-concept, his attitudes and his self-directed behaviour – and that these resources can be tapped if only a definable climate of facilitative psychological attitudes can be provided. (Rogers, 1974: 116)

From this 'gradually formed and tested hypothesis' non-directive therapy was born as a protest against the diagnostic, prescriptive point of view prevalent at the time. Emphasis was placed on a relationship between counsellor and client based upon acceptance and clarification. This was a period, too, of excitement generated by the use of recorded interviews for research and training purposes and there was a focus on 'non-directive techniques'. Those coming for help were no longer referred to as patients but as clients, with the inference that they were self-responsible human beings, not objects for treatment. As experience grew and both theory-building and research developed, the term 'client-centred therapy' was adopted which put the emphasis on the internal world of the client and focused attention on the attitudes of therapists towards their clients rather than on particular techniques. The term 'person-centred' won Rogers's approval in the decade before his death, because it could be applied to the many fields outside therapy where his ideas were increasingly becoming accepted and valued and because in the therapy context itself it underlined the person-to-person nature of the interaction where not only the phenomenological world of the client but also the therapist's state of being are of crucial significance. This 'I–Thou' quality of the therapeutic relationship indicates a certain kinship with the existential philosophy of Kierkegaard and Buber and the stress on personal experience recalls the work of the British philosopher/scientist Michael Polanyi (whom Rogers knew and admired). In the years before his death, Rogers also reported his own deepening respect for certain aspects of Zen teaching and became fond of quoting sayings of Lao-Tse, especially those that stress the undesirability of imposing on people instead of allowing them the space in which to find themselves. The interest in Zen was also a significant indication of Rogers's late-flowering interest in the spiritual dimension of experience and its importance in the therapeutic relationship.

Since Rogers's death in 1987 the influence of his work in the United States of America has rapidly declined but in Europe person-centred therapy is strongly represented in many countries and there is continuing interest in the approach in both South America and the Far East (Thorne and Lambers, 1998). There now exists a World Association for Person-Centered and Experiential Psychotherapy and Counseling whose constitution was formally approved at an international conference in Chicago in 2000.

Development in Britain

In Britain the ideas of Carl Rogers first appeared in the context of the development of the Marriage Guidance Council (now called Relate) during the late 1950s and early 1960s. Client-centred therapy was first introduced into British universities, mainly by visiting Fulbright professors from America, in the late 1960s as part of the curriculum for those training to become counsellors in schools. The enthusiasm for humanistic psychology in general which took London by storm at the end of the 1960s resulted in the emergence of a loosely knit network of persons, mainly working in education and social work, for whom Rogers became a major source of inspiration.

The turning point came, however, in 1974 when Rogers himself had planned to come to Britain in order to attend a workshop initiated by a young psychologist from Scotland, Dave Mearns, who had studied with Rogers in California in 1971–72. In the event, the grave illness of his wife prevented Rogers from coming but the workshop went ahead and a key participant was Dr Charles (Chuck) Devonshire from the College of San Mateo in California, director of the Center for Cross-Cultural Communication and a close associate of Rogers. In the years following, the co-operative efforts of Devonshire, Mearns, Elke Lambers, a

Dutch client-centred therapist living in Scotland and myself, led to the founding of the Facilitator Development Institute which provided annual summer residential workshops for members of the helping professions who wished to learn more of person-centred theory and practice especially as it applied to small and large groups. In 1985 the Institute (afterwards renamed Person-Centred Therapy (Britain)) began to offer full-scale training for person-centred therapists. During the same period Devonshire was developing programmes throughout Europe and his Person-Centred Approach Institute International began to offer a British programme in 1987. A splinter group from Devonshire's original staff team subsequently founded the Institute for Person-Centred Learning and all three of these private institutes, which have in recent years been joined by several others, continue to offer professional training at a basic or advanced level.

Since 1990 person-centred therapy has established a firm foothold in British universities with significant centres for training and research at the Universities of Strathclyde and East Anglia where Mearns and Thorne respectively hold professorships in counselling. Another person-centred practitioner, Professor John McLeod, has established a formidable research reputation, initially at the University of Keele and more recently at Abertay University in Dundee, while at the University of East London Tony Merry provides a powerful person-centred presence in the metropolis. This significant powerbase – buttressed by a succession of influential publications (Mearns, 1994, 1997; Mearns and Thorne, 1988, 1999, 2000; Thorne, 1992, 1998, 2002; McLeod, 1994; Merry, 1995, 1999) – does much to resource the 20 or so courses currently accredited by the British Association for Counselling and Psychotherapy which identify person-centred therapy as their core theoretical model. The strength of the approach is further indicated by the existence of two strong professional associations, the British Association for the Person-Centred Approach (BAPCA) founded in 1989 and its younger sister organization the Association for Person-Centred Therapy (Scotland).

Theoretical assumptions

Image of the person

Person-centred therapists start from the assumption that both they and their clients are trustworthy. This trust resides in the belief that every organism – the human being included – has an underlying and instinctive movement towards the constructive accomplishment of its inherent potential. Rogers (1979) often recalled a boyhood memory of his parents' potato bin in which they stored the winter supply of potatoes. This bin was placed in the basement several feet below a small window, yet despite the highly unfavourable conditions the potatoes would begin to send out spindly shoots groping towards the distant light of the window. Rogers compared these pathetic potatoes in their desperate struggle to develop with clients whose lives have been warped by circumstances and experience but who continue against all the odds to strive towards growth, towards becoming. This directional, or actualizing, tendency in the human being can be trusted and the therapist's task is to help create the best possible conditions for its fulfilment.

The elevated view of human nature which person-centred therapists hold is paralleled by their insistence on individual uniqueness. They believe that no two persons are ever alike and that the human personality is so complex that no diagnostic labelling of persons can ever be fully justified. Indeed, person-centred therapists know that they cannot hope to uncover fully the subjective perceptual world of the client and that clients themselves can do this only with great effort. Furthermore clients' perceptual worlds will be determined by the experiences they have rejected or assimilated into the self-concept.

For Rogers the term 'self-concept' was equated with the term 'self'. For him this was a pragmatic decision because it rendered the notion 'self' open to investigation by research. By seeing 'self' as available to the conscious awareness of the person, Rogers placed himself firmly outside the psychoanalytic tradition with its emphasis on the importance of unconscious dimensions. In a recent extension of the theory my colleague, Dave Mearns, and I have proposed a slight modification of Rogers's concept of self to include material which is on the edge of awareness. (Rogers used the expression 'subceived' to indicate this 'almost but not quite' conscious material.) By widening the definition of self so that it = self-concept + edge of awareness material we accept the legitimacy of 'focusing' – a method developed by Eugene Gendlin for deepening inner awareness – as a dimension of person-centred therapy and we also make it possible to consider new 'configurations' of self as they emerge during therapy which alter – sometimes radically – the structure of the self-concept (Mearns and Thorne, 2000: 175).

Conceptualization of psychological disturbance and health

The self-concept is of crucial importance in person-centred therapy and needs to be contrasted with the actualizing tendency. It is the actualizing tendency which gives access to the essential resources for living and to the organismic valuing process which enables an individual to make judgements about his or her existence. The human organism can essentially be relied upon to provide trustworthy messages and this is discernible in the physiological processes of the entire body and through the process of growth by which a person's potentialities and capacities are brought to realization. As life proceeds, the actualizing tendency is informed by the promptings of social reality and the need for belonging but it never loses its capacity to provide unerring guidance to the heart of a person's unique and essential personhood. Such an organismic valuing process and its trustworthiness, even if at times it does not easily reveal its wisdom, is to be contrasted with the self-concept which is a person's conceptual construction of him or herself (however poorly articulated) and does not by any means always find itself in harmony with the promptings of the actualizing tendency and its allied organismic valuing process. On the contrary, it is possible, and not at all rare, for a self-concept to become so firmly entrenched that the actualizing tendency becomes almost totally obscured from consciousness.

The self-concept develops over time and is heavily dependent on the attitudes of those who constitute the individual's significant others. It follows that where a person is surrounded by those who are quick to condemn or punish (however subtly) the behaviour which emanates from the promptings of the actualizing tendency, he or she will become rapidly confused. The need for positive regard or approval from others is overwhelming and is present from earliest infancy. If behaviour arising from what is actually experienced by the individual fails to win approval an immediate conflict is established. A baby, for example, may gain considerable satisfaction or relief from howling full-throatedly but may then quickly learn that such behaviour is condemned or punished by the mother. At this point the need to win the mother's approval is in immediate conflict with the promptings of the actualizing tendency which engender howling. In the person-centred tradition disturbance is conceptualized in terms of the degree of success or failure experienced by the individual in resolving such conflicts. The badly disturbed person on this criterion will have lost almost complete contact with the experiencing of his or her organism, for the basic need for self-regard can in the most adverse circumstances lead to behaviour which is totally geared to the desperate search for acceptance and approval. The signals from the organismic valuing system in such cases are silenced and a self-concept is developed which bears little relationship to people's deepest yearnings, from which they are essentially cut off. Not surprisingly, perhaps, such attempts to create a self-concept which runs counter to the actualizing tendency cannot in the long run be successful.

In most cases individuals, whatever face they may present to the world, hold themselves in low esteem and a negative self-concept is usually a further sign of disturbance at some level. In those rarer instances where the self-deception is more extreme the self-concept may at a conscious level appear largely positive but it will be quickly evident to others that such self-affirmation has been won at the cost of a deliberate and sustained refusal to allow adverse judgements into awareness, whether these threaten from within or from outside sources. Disturbed people can seldom trust their own judgement and for the person-centred therapist another sure mark of disturbance is the absence of an internalized locus of evaluation. This somewhat cumbersome term describes the faculty which determines individuals' capacity to trust their own thoughts and feelings when making decisions or choosing courses of action. Disturbed people show little sign of possessing such a faculty: instead they constantly turn to external authorities or find themselves caught in a paralysis of indecision. In summary, then, disturbance may be conceptualized as a greater or lesser degree of alienation from the actualizing tendency and the organismic valuing process prompted by the fundamental need for self-regard. The resulting self-concept, usually negative and always falsely based, is linked to a defective capacity to make decisions, which in turn indicates the absence of an internalized locus of evaluation.

If individuals are unfortunate enough to be brought up amongst a number of significant others who are highly censorious or judgmental, a self-concept can develop which may serve to estrange them almost totally from their organismic experiencing. In such cases the self-concept, often developed after years of denying the promptings of the organism, becomes the fiercest enemy of the individual's true and unique identity and must undergo radical transformation if the actualizing tendency is to reassert itself.

The person-centred therapist is constantly working with clients who have all but lost touch with the actualizing tendency within themselves and who have been surrounded by others who have no confidence in the innate capacity of human beings to move towards the fulfilment of their potential. Psychologically healthy persons on the other hand are men and women who have been lucky enough to live in contexts which have been conducive to the development of self-concepts which allow them to be in touch for at least some of the time with their deepest experiences and feelings without having to censure them or distort them. Such people are well placed to achieve a level of psychological freedom which will enable them to move in the direction of becoming more fully functioning persons. 'Fully functioning' is a term used by Rogers to denote individuals who are using their talents and abilities, realizing their potential and moving towards a more complete knowledge of themselves. They are demonstrating what it means to have attained a high level of psychological health and Rogers has outlined some of the major personality characteristics which they seem to share.

The first and most striking characteristic is *openness to experience*. Individuals who are open to experience are able to listen to themselves and to others and to experience what is happening without feeling threatened. They demonstrate a high level of awareness, especially in the world of the feelings. Second, allied to this characteristic, is the *ability to live fully* in each moment of one's existence. Experience is trusted rather than feared and is the moulding force for the emerging personality rather than being twisted or manipulated to fit some preconceived structure of reality or some rigidly safeguarded self-concept. The third characteristic is the *organismic trusting* which is so clearly lacking in those who have constantly fallen victim to the adverse judgements of others. Such trusting is best displayed in the process of decision-making. Whereas many people defer continually to outside sources of influence when making decisions, fully functioning persons regard their organismic experiences as the most valid sources of information for deciding what to do in any given situation. Rogers put it succinctly when he said 'doing what "feels right" proves to be a. . .trustworthy guide to behaviour' (1961: 190).

Further characteristics of the fully functioning person are concerned with the issues of personal freedom and creativity. For Rogers a mark of psychological health is the sense of responsibility for determining one's own actions and their consequences based on a feeling of freedom and power to choose from the many options that life presents. There is no feeling within the individual of being imprisoned by circumstances, or fate or genetic inheritance, although this is not to suggest that Rogers denies the powerful influences of biological make-up, social forces or past experience. Subjectively, however, people experience themselves as free agents. Finally, the fully functioning person is typically creative in the sense that he or she can adjust to changing conditions and is likely to produce creative ideas or initiate creative projects and actions. Such people are unlikely to be conformists, although they will relate to society in a way which permits them to be fully involved without being imprisoned by convention or tradition.

Acquisition of psychological disturbance

In person-centred terminology the mother's requirement that the baby cease to howl constitutes a *condition of worth*: 'I shall love you if you do not howl.' The concept of conditions of worth bears a striking similarity to the British therapist George Lyward's notion of contractual living. Lyward believed that most of his disturbed adolescent clients had had no chance to contact their real selves because they were too busy attempting – usually in vain – to fulfil contracts, in order to win approval (Burn, 1956). Lyward used to speak of usurped lives and Rogers in similar vein sees many individuals as the victims of countless internalized conditions of worth which have almost totally estranged them from their organismic experiencing. Such people will be preoccupied with a sense of strain at having to come up to the mark or with feelings of worthlessness at having failed to do so. They will be the victims of countless introjected conditions of worth so that they no longer have any sense of their inherent value as unique persons. The proliferation of introjections is an inevitable outcome of the desperate need for positive regard. Introjection is the process whereby the beliefs, judgements, attitudes or values of another person (most often the parent) are taken into the individual and become part of his or her armamentarium for coping with experience, however alien they may have been initially. The child, it seems, will do almost anything to satisfy the need for positive regard even if this means taking on board (introjecting) attitudes and beliefs which run quite counter to its own organismic reaction to experience. Once such attitudes and beliefs have become thoroughly absorbed into the personality they are said to have become internalized. Thus it is that introjection and internalization of conditions of worth imposed by significant others whose approval is desperately desired often constitute the gloomy road to a deeply negative self-concept as individuals discover that they can never come up to the high demands and expectations which such conditions inevitably imply.

Once this negative self-concept has taken root in an individual the likelihood is that the separation from the wisdom of the organism will become increasingly complete. It is as if individuals become cut off from their own inner resources and their own sense of value and are governed by a secondary and treacherous valuing process which is based on the internalization of other people's judgements and evaluations. Once caught in this trap the person is likely to grow more disturbed, for the negative self-concept induces behaviour which reinforces the image of inadequacy and worthlessness. It is a fundamental thesis of the person-centred point of view that behaviour is not only the result of what happens to us from the external world but also a function of how we feel about ourselves on the inside. In other words, we are likely to behave in accordance with our perception of ourselves. What we do is often an accurate reflection of how we evaluate ourselves and if this evaluation is low our behaviour will be correspondingly unacceptable to ourselves and in all probability to others as well. It is likely, too, that we shall be highly conscious of a sense of inadequacy and although we may conceal this from others the awareness that all is not well will usually be with us.

The person-centred therapist recognizes, however, that psychological disturbance is not always available to awareness. It is possible for a person to establish a self-concept which, because of the overriding need to win the approval of others, cannot permit highly significant sensory or visceral (a favourite word with Rogers) experience into consciousness. Such people cannot be open to the full range of their organismic experiencing because to be so would threaten the self-concept which must be maintained in order to win continuing favour. An example of such a person might be the man who has established a picture of himself as honourable, virtuous, responsible and loving. Such a man may be progressively divorced from those feelings which would threaten to undermine such a self-concept. He may arrive at a point where he no longer knows, for example, that he is angry or hostile or sexually hungry, for to admit to such feelings would be to throw his whole picture of himself into question. Disturbed people are by no means always aware of their disturbance, nor will they necessarily be perceived as disturbed by others who may have a vested interest in maintaining what is in effect a tragic but often rigorous act of self-deception.

Perpetuation of psychological disturbance

It follows from the person-centred view of psychological disturbance that it will be perpetuated if an individual continues to be dependent to a high degree on the judgement of others for a sense of self-worth. Such persons will be at pains to preserve and defend at all costs the self-concept which wins approval and esteem and will be thrown into anxiety and confusion whenever incongruity arises between the self-concept and actual experience, an incongruity which may sometimes uncomfortably be 'subceived' below the level of conscious awareness while remaining unacknowledged in accurate symbolization. In the example above the 'virtuous' man would be fully subject to conscious feelings of threat and confusion if he directly experienced his hostility or sexual hunger, although to do so would, of course, be a first step towards the recovery of contact with the organismic valuing process. He will be likely, however, to avoid the threat and confusion by resorting to one or other of two basic mechanisms of defence – perceptual distortion or denial. In this way he avoids or stifles confusion and anxiety and thereby perpetuates his disturbance while mistakenly believing that he is maintaining his integrity.

Perceptual distortion takes place whenever an incongruent experience is allowed into conscious awareness but only in a form that is in harmony with the person's current self-concept. The virtuous man, for instance, might permit himself to experience hostility but would distort this as a justifiable reaction to wickedness in others: for him his hostility would be rationalized into righteous indignation. *Denial* is a less common defence but is in some ways the more impregnable. In this case individuals preserve their self-concept by completely avoiding any conscious recognition of experiences or feelings that threaten them. The virtuous man would therefore be totally unaware of his constantly angry attitudes in a committee meeting and might perceive himself as simply speaking with truth and sincerity. Distortion and denial can have formidable psychological consequences and can sometimes protect a person for a lifetime from the confusion and anxiety which could herald the recovery of proper contact with the actualizing tendency and the organismic valuing process.

Change

For people who are trapped by a negative self-concept and by behaviour which tends to demonstrate and even reinforce the validity of such a self-assessment, there is little hope of positive change unless there is movement in the psychological environment which surrounds them. Most commonly this will be the advent of a new person on the scene or a marked change in attitude of someone who is already closely involved. A child, for example, may be abused and ignored at home but may discover, to her initial bewilderment, that her teachers respect and like her. If she gradually acquires the courage to trust this unexpected acceptance she may be fortunate enough to gain further reassurance through the discovery that her teachers' respect for her is not dependent on her 'being a good girl'. For the young adult a love relationship can often revolutionize the self-concept. A girl who has come to think of herself as both stupid and ugly will find such a self-concept severely challenged by a young man who both enjoys her conversation and finds her physically desirable. There are, of course, dangers in this situation, for if the man's ardour rapidly cools and he abandons her the young woman's negative self-concept may be mightily reinforced by this painful episode. Where love runs deep, however, the beloved may be enabled to rediscover contact with the organismic core of her being and to experience her own essential worth. For clients beginning therapy the most important fact initially is the entry of a new person (the therapist) into their psychological environment. As we shall see, it is the quality of this new person and the nature of the relationship which the therapist offers that will ultimately determine whether or not change will ensue.

Practice

Goals of therapy

The person-centred therapist seeks to establish a relationship with a client in which the latter can gradually dare to face the anxiety and confusion which inevitably arise once the self-concept is challenged by the movement into awareness of experiences which do not fit its current configuration. If such a relationship can be achieved the client can then hope to move beyond the confusion and gradually to experience the freedom to choose a way of being which approximates more closely to his or her deepest feelings and values. The therapist will therefore focus not on problems and solutions but on communion, or on what has been described as a person-in-person relationship (Boy and Pine, 1982: 129). Person-centred therapists do not hesitate to invest themselves freely and fully in the relationship with their clients. They believe that they will gain entrance into the world of the client through an emotional commitment in which they are willing to involve themselves as people and to reveal themselves, if appropriate, with their own strengths and weaknesses. For the person-centred therapist a primary goal is to see, feel and experience the world as the client sees, feels and experiences it and this is not possible if the therapist stands aloof and maintains a psychological distance in the interests of a quasi-scientific objectivity.

The theoretical end-point of person-centred therapy must be the fully functioning person who is the embodiment of psychological health and whose primary characteristics were outlined above. It would be fairly safe to assert that no client has achieved such an end-point and that no therapist has been in a position to model such perfection. On the other hand there is abundant evidence, not only from the USA but also, for example, from the extensive research activities of Reinhard Tausch and his colleagues at Hamburg University (Tausch, 1975) and of Germain Lietaer at the University of Leuven in Belgium (e.g. Lietaer, 1984), that clients undergoing person-centred therapy frequently demonstrate similar changes. From my own experience I can readily confirm the perception of client movement that Rogers and other person-centred practitioners have repeatedly noted. A listing of these perceptions will show that for many clients the achievement of any one of the developments recorded could well constitute a 'goal' of therapy and might for the time being at least constitute a valid and satisfactory reason for terminating therapy. Clients in person-centred therapy are often perceived to move, then, in the following directions:

1   away from façades and the constant preoccupation with keeping up appearances
2   away from 'oughts' and an internalized sense of duty springing from externally imposed obligations
3   away from living up to the expectations of others
4   towards valuing honesty and 'realness' in oneself and others
5   towards valuing the capacity to direct one's own life
6   towards accepting and valuing one's self and one's feelings whether they are positive or negative
7   towards valuing the experience of the moment and the process of growth rather than continually striving for objectives
8   towards a greater respect and understanding of others
9   towards a cherishing of close relationships and a longing for more intimacy
10 towards a valuing of all forms of experience and a willingness to risk being open to all inner and outer experiences however uncongenial or unexpected. (Frick, 1971: 179)

Selection criteria

Person-centred therapy has proved its effectiveness with clients of many kinds
presenting a wide range of difficulties and concerns. Its usefulness even with
psychotics was established many years ago when Rogers and his associates
participated in an elaborate investigation of the effect of psychotherapy on
schizophrenics. More recently the innovative work of Garry Prouty (1995) has
extended the application of person-centred theory to what he calls pre-therapy
with hospitalized patients many of whom are severely dysfunctional. Rogers
himself, however, offered the opinion that psychotherapy of any kind, including
person-centred therapy, is probably the greatest help to the people who are
closest to a reasonable adjustment to life. It is my own belief that the limitations of
person-centred therapy reside not in the approach itself but in the limitations
of particular therapists and in their ability or lack of it to offer their clients the
necessary conditions for change and development. Having said this I freely admit
that in my own experience there are certain kinds of clients who are unlikely to be
much helped by the approach. Such people are usually somewhat rigid and
authoritarian in their attitude to life. They look for certainties, for secure
structures and often for experts to direct them in how they should be and what
they should do. Their craving for such direction often makes it difficult for them to
relate to the person-centred therapist in such a way that they can begin to get in
touch with their own inner resources. Overly intellectual or logically rational
people may also find it difficult to engage in the kind of relationship encouraged
by person-centred therapy, where often the greatest changes result from a
preparedness to face painful and confusing feelings which cannot initially be
clearly articulated. Clients falling into these categories often turn out to be poorly
motivated in any case and not infrequently they have been referred in desperation
by an overworked medical practitioner, priest or social worker. Inarticulacy is in
itself no barrier to effective therapeutic work, for inarticulate people are often
brimming over with unexpressed feeling which begins to pour out once a
relationship of trust has been established.

Clients who perhaps have most to gain from person-centred therapy are those
who are strongly motivated to face painful feelings and who are deeply committed
to change. They are prepared to take emotional risks and they want to trust even
if they are fearful of intimacy. In my own work I often ask myself three questions
as I consider working with a prospective client:

- Is the client really desirous of change?
- Is the client prepared to share responsibility for our work together?
- Is the client willing to get in touch with his or her feelings, however difficult that may
  be?

Reassuring answers to these three questions are usually reliable indicators that
person-centred therapy is likely to be beneficial.

The person-centred approach has made significant contributions to small group
and large group work and the person-centred therapy group (with two therapists
or 'facilitators') is a common modality. Clients who give evidence of at least some

degree of self-acceptance and whose self-concept is not entirely negative may well be encouraged (but never obliged) to join a group from the outset. More commonly, however, membership of a counselling group will occur at the point when a client in individual therapy is beginning to experience a measure of self-affirmation and is keen to take further risks in relating. At such a stage membership of a group may replace individual therapy or may be undertaken concurrently. In all cases it is the client who will decide whether to seek group membership and whether or not this should replace or complement individual therapy.

The person-centred therapist will be at pains to ensure that a client whose self-concept is very low is not plunged into a group setting prematurely. Such an experience could have the disastrous outcome of reinforcing the client's sense of worthlessness. In such cases individual therapy is almost invariably indicated.

Person-centred therapists can work successfully with couples and with family groups but in these contexts much will depend on the therapist's ability to create the environment in which the couple or the family members can interact with each other without fear. In order for this to be possible it is likely that the therapist will undertake extensive preparatory work with each individual in a one-to-one relationship. Ultimately the principal criterion for embarking on couple or family therapy (apart, of course, from the willingness of all members to participate) is the therapist's confidence in his or her own ability to relate authentically to each member. (For further discussion of this issue see Mearns, 1994: 56–60.) Such confidence is unlikely to be achieved in the absence of in-depth preliminary meetings with each person involved. Indeed, in couple therapy it is common for the therapist to agree to work for a negotiated period with each partner separately before all three come together in order to tackle the relationship directly. With a family the process is clearly more complex and the preparatory work even more time-consuming. Perhaps this is the main reason why person-centred family therapy remains comparatively rare. It may well be, however, that this situation will change in the years immediately ahead not least because a recent book has appeared devoted to person-centred work with couples and families. The author, Charlie O'Leary, provides fascinating evidence of the effectiveness of the person-centred approach in this area of practice and his passionate enthusiasm is sure to inspire others to follow his example (O'Leary, 1999).

Qualities of effective therapists

It has often been suggested that of all the various 'schools' of psychotherapy the person-centred approach makes the heaviest demands upon the therapist. Whether this is so or not I have no way of knowing. What I do know is that unless person-centred therapists can relate in such a way that their clients perceive them as trustworthy and dependable *as people*, therapy cannot take place. Person-centred therapists can have no recourse to diagnostic labelling nor can they find security in a complex and detailed theory of personality which will allow them to foster 'insight' in their clients through interpretation, however gently offered. In brief, they cannot win their clients' confidence by demonstrating their psychological expertise for to do so would be to place yet another obstacle in the way of clients' movement towards trusting their own innate resources. To be a trustworthy person is not something which can be simulated for long and in a very real sense person-centred therapists can only be as trustworthy for another as they are for themselves. Therapists' attitudes to themselves thus become of cardinal importance. If I am to be acceptant of another's feelings and experiences and to be open to the possible expression of material long since blocked off from awareness I must feel a deep level of acceptance for myself. If I cannot trust myself to acknowledge and accept my own feelings without adverse judgement or incapacitating self-recrimination it is unlikely that I shall appear sufficiently trustworthy to a client who may have much deeper cause to feel ashamed or worthless. If, too, I am in constant fear that I shall be overwhelmed by an upsurging of unacceptable data into my own awareness then I am unlikely to convey to my client that I am genuinely open to the full exploration of his or her own doubts and fears.

The ability of the therapist to be congruent, accepting and empathic (fundamental attitudes in person-centred therapy which will be explored more fully later) is not developed overnight. It is unlikely, too, that such an ability will be present in people who are not continually seeking to broaden their own life experience.

Therapists cannot confidently invite their clients to travel further than they have journeyed themselves, but for person-centred therapists the quality, depth and continuity of their own experiencing becomes the very cornerstone of the competence they bring to their professional activity. Unless I have a sense of my own continuing development as a person I shall lose faith in the process of becoming and shall be tempted to relate to my clients in a way which may well reinforce them in a past self-concept. What is more, I shall myself become stuck in a past image of myself and will no longer be in contact with the part of my organism which challenges me to go on growing as a person even if my body is beginning to show every sign of wearing out. It follows, too, that an excessive reliance on particular skills for relating or communicating can present a subtle trap because such skills may lead to a professional behavioural pattern which is itself resistant to change because it becomes set or stylized.

Therapeutic relationship and style

Person-centred therapists differ widely in therapeutic style. They have in common, however, a desire to create a relationship characterized by a climate in which clients begin to get in touch with their own wisdom and their capacity for self-understanding and for altering their self-concept and self-defeating behaviours. Person-centred therapists' ability to establish this climate is crucial to the whole therapeutic enterprise, since if they fail to do so there is no hope of forming the kind of relationship with their clients which will bring about the desired therapeutic movement. It will become apparent, however, that the way in which they attempt to create and convey the necessary climate will depend very much on the nature of their own personality.

The first element in the creation of the climate has to do with what has variously been called the therapist's *congruence*, realness, authenticity or genuineness. In essence this congruence depends on therapists' capacities for being properly in touch with the complexity of feelings, thoughts and attitudes which will be flowing through them as they seek to track their clients' thoughts and feelings. The more they can do this the more they will be perceived by their clients as people of real flesh and blood who are willing to be seen and known and not as clinical professionals intent on concealing themselves behind a metaphorical white coat. The issue of the therapist's congruence is more complex than might initially appear. Although clients need to experience their therapists' essential humanity and to feel their emotional involvement they certainly do not need to have all the therapist's feelings and thoughts thrust down their throats. Therapists must not only attempt to remain firmly in touch with the flow of their own experience but must also have the discrimination to know how and when to communicate what they are experiencing.

It is here that to the objective observer person-centred therapists might well appear to differ widely in style. In my own attempts to be congruent, for example, I find that verbally I often communicate little. I am aware, however, that my bodily posture does convey a deep willingness to be involved with my client and that my eyes are highly expressive of a wide range of feeling – often to the point of tears. It would seem that there is frequently little need for me to communicate my feelings verbally: I am transparent enough already and I know from experience that my clients are sensitive to this transparency. Another therapist might well behave in a manner far removed from mine but with the same concern to be congruent. Therapists are just as much unique human beings as their clients and the way in which they make their humanity available by following the flow of their own experiencing and communicating it when appropriate will be an expression of their own uniqueness. Whatever the precise form of their behaviour, however, person-centred therapists will be exercising their skill in order to communicate to their clients an attitude expressive of their desire to be deeply and fully involved in the relationship without pretence and without the protection of professional impersonality.

For many clients entering therapy, the second attitude of importance in creating a facilitative climate for change – *unconditional positive regard* – may seem to be the most critical. The conditions of worth which have in so many cases warped and undermined the self-concept of the client so that it bears little relation to the actualizing organism are the outcome of the judgmental and conditional attitudes of those close to the client, which have often been reinforced by societal or cultural norms. In contrast, the therapist seeks to offer the client an unconditional acceptance, a positive regard or caring, a non-possessive love. This acceptance is not of the person as she might become, a respect for her as yet unfulfilled potential, but a total and unconditional acceptance of the client as she seems to herself *in the present*. Such an attitude on the part of the therapist cannot be simulated and cannot be offered by someone who remains largely frightened or threatened by feelings in himself. Nor again can such acceptance be offered by someone who is disturbed when confronted by a person who possesses values, attitudes and feelings different from his or her own. Genuine acceptance is totally unaffected by differences of background or belief system between client and therapist, for it is in no way dependent on moral, ethical or social criteria.

As with genuineness, the attitude of acceptance requires great skill on the part of the therapist if it is to be communicated at the depth which will enable clients to feel safe to be whatever they are currently experiencing. After what may well be a lifetime of highly conditional acceptance clients will not recognize unconditionality easily. When they do they will tend to regard it as an unlikely miracle which will demand continual checking out before it can be fully trusted. The way in which a therapist conveys unconditional acceptance characterized by positive regard will again be dependent to a large extent on the nature of his or her personality. For my own part I have found increasingly that the non-verbal aspects of my responsiveness are powerfully effective. A smile can often convey more acceptance and regard than a statement which, however sensitive, may still run the risk of seeming patronizing. I have discovered, too, that the gentle pressing of the hand or the light touch on the knee will enable clients to realize that all is well and that there will be no judgement, however confused or negative they are or however silent and hostile.

The third facilitative attitude is that of *empathic understanding*. Rogers (1975) himself wrote extensively about empathy and suggested that of the three 'core conditions' (as congruence, unconditional positive regard and empathy are often known), empathy is the most trainable. The crucial importance of empathic understanding springs from the person-centred therapist's overriding concern with the client's subjective perceptual world. Only through as full an understanding as possible of the way in which clients view themselves and the world can the therapist hope to encourage the subtle changes in self-concept which make for growth. Such understanding involves on the therapist's part a willingness to enter the private perceptual world of the client and to become thoroughly conversant with it. This demands a high degree of sensitivity to the moment-to-moment experiencing of the client so that the therapist is recognized as a reliable companion even when contradictory feelings follow on each other in rapid succession. In a certain sense therapists must lay themselves aside for the time being with all their prejudices and values if they are to enter into the perceptual world of the other. Such an undertaking would be foolhardy if the therapist feels insecure in the presence of a particular client for there would be the danger of getting lost in a perhaps frightening or confusing world. The task of empathic understanding can be accomplished only by people who are secure enough in their own identity to move into another's world without the fear of being overwhelmed by it. Once there, therapists have to move around with extreme delicacy and with an utter absence of judgement. They will probably sense meanings of which the client is scarcely aware and might even become dimly aware of feelings of which there is no consciousness on the part of the client at all. Such moments call for extreme caution for there is the danger that the therapist could express understanding at too deep a level and frighten the client away from therapy altogether. Rogers, on a recording made for *Psychology Today* in the 1970s, described such a blunder as 'blitz therapy' and contrasted this with an empathic response which is constructive because it conveys an understanding of what is currently going on in the client and of meanings that are just below the level of awareness but does not slip over into unconscious motivations which frighten the client.

If the communication of congruence and unconditional positive regard presents difficulties, the communication of empathic understanding may be even more challenging. Often a client's inner world is complex and confusing as well as a source of pain and guilt. Sometimes clients have little understanding of their own feelings. Therapists often need to marshal the full range of their emotional and cognitive abilities if they are to convey their understanding thoroughly. On the other hand, if they do not succeed there is ample evidence to suggest that their very attempt to do so, however bumbling and incomplete, will be experienced by the client as supportive and validating. What is always essential is the therapist's willingness to check out the accuracy of his or her understanding. I find that my own struggles at communicating empathic understanding are littered with such questions as 'Am I getting it right? Is that what you mean?' When I do get a complex feeling right the effect is often electrifying and the sense of wonder and thankfulness in the client can be one of the most moving experiences in therapy. There can be little doubt that the rarity of empathic understanding of this kind is what endows it with such power and makes it the most reliable force for creative change in the whole of the therapeutic process.

It was Rogers's contention – and he held firm to it for over 40 years – that if the therapist proves able to offer a relationship where congruence, unconditional positive regard and empathy are all present, then therapeutic movement will almost invariably occur. Towards the end of his life, however, he pointed to another quality which he saw not as additional to the core conditions but as sometimes resulting from their consistent application. This he called 'presence' and having first called attention to it in *A Way of Being* (Rogers, 1980: 129) he returned to it in an article published shortly before his death (Rogers, 1986). He talks of 'presence' in terms which seem somewhat at variance with the pragmatic, hard-headed tone of the scientific scholar of earlier years but I have come to see this later statement as capturing the essence of the therapeutic relationship when it is functioning at its most effective level.

Rogers wrote:

When I am at my best, as a group facilitator or a therapist, I discover another characteristic. I find that when I am closest to my inner, intuitive self, when I am somehow in touch with the unknown in me, when perhaps I am in a slightly altered state of consciousness in the relationship, then whatever I do seems to be full of healing. Then simply my *presence* is releasing and helpful. There is nothing I can do to force this experience, but when I can relax and be close to the transcendental core of me, then I may behave in strange and impulsive ways in the relationship, ways which I cannot justify rationally, which have nothing to do with my thought processes. But these strange behaviours turn out to be *right*, in some odd way. At those moments it seems that my inner spirit has reached out and touched the inner spirit of the other. (Rogers, 1986: 199)

It is my own belief that the therapist's ability to be 'present' in this way is dependent on his or her capacity to be fearlessly alongside the client's experience even to the extent of being willing on occasions *not* to understand what is occurring in the client's world (Mearns, 1994: 5–9). Such a capacity is likely to develop in a relationship where counsellor and client have established a deep level of trust and where mutuality is increasingly possible (see following section). It explains, too, why the most fruitful relationships will be characterized by a developing ability on the part of both counsellor and client to move between different levels of experiencing with ease and confidence. As therapy proceeds, seriousness and humour, for example, will alternate and the pattern of inter-activity will shift frequently as client and counsellor adopt, by turns, more active or passive roles. Furthermore a therapist's way of being fully present to his or her client is again likely to be indicative of the unique personality of the therapist. I find that when I am able to be totally present in the moment this releases in me a quality which I have defined as 'tenderness' (Thorne, 1985, 1991). This in turn enables me to live with paradoxes and gives me the will to wait in hope when I am feeling powerless. With Rogers, who later in the same article acknowledges that his account 'partakes of the mystical' and goes on to speak of 'this mystical, spiritual dimension', I am persuaded that the relationship in person-centred therapy is at its most liberating and transforming when it 'transcends itself and becomes part of something larger' (Rogers, 1986: 199).

Major therapeutic strategies and techniques

There are no strategies or techniques which are integral to person-centred therapy. The approach is essentially based on the experiencing and communication of attitudes, and these attitudes cannot be packaged up in techniques. At an earlier point in the history of the approach there was an understandable emphasis on the ebb and flow of the therapeutic interview and much was gained from the microscopic study of client–therapist exchanges. To Rogers's horror, however, the tendency to focus on the therapist's responses had the effect of so debasing the approach that it became known as a technique. Even nowadays it is possible to meet people who believe that person-centred therapy is simply the technique of reflecting the client's feelings or, worse still, that it is primarily a matter of repeating the last words spoken by the client. I hope I have shown that nothing could be further from the truth. The attitudes required of the therapist demand the highest level of self-knowledge and self-acceptance and the translation of them into communicable form requires of each therapist the most delicate skill, which for the most part must spring from his or her unique personality and cannot be learned through pale imitations of Carl Rogers or anyone else.

In *Person-Centred Counselling in Action* (Mearns and Thorne, 1988, 1999) attention is drawn to the fact that the most productive outcomes seem to result from therapeutic relationships which move through three distinct phases. The first stage is characterized by the establishing of *trust* on the part of the client. This may happen very rapidly or it can take months. The second stage sees the development of *intimacy*: during this stage the client is enabled to reveal some of the deepest levels of his or her experiencing. The third stage is characterized by an increasing *mutuality* between therapist and client. When such a stage is reached it is likely that therapists will be increasingly self-disclosing and will be challenged to risk more of themselves in the relationship. When it occurs this three-stage process becomes so deeply rewarding for the therapist that a cynical critic might view it as the outcome of an unconscious strategizing on the therapist's part. So insidious is this accusation that I am now deeply concerned to monitor my own behaviour with the utmost vigilance in order to ensure that I am *not* embarked on a manipulatory plot aimed at achieving a spurious mutuality which may be deeply satisfying for me but quite irrelevant to the client's needs.

The realization that person-centred therapy at its best may give access to a quality of relating which embraces the spiritual raises important questions about the counsellor's fitness for such a task and the personal discipline that this implies (Thorne, 1994, 2002; Mearns and Thorne, 2000). In an approach which explicitly turns its back on strategies and techniques as being contrived and potentially abusive of a client's autonomy, it becomes of the utmost importance that the therapist is preserved from self-deception, not only by the challenge of rigorous supervision but also by the willing acceptance of a discipline which has as its aim the most thorough integration of belief and practice. Without such integration the person-centred therapist runs the risk of mouthing and peddling the core conditions as if they were little more than behavioural conditions to be applied mechanically by a psychological technician after a few hours' 'skills training'. Such a travesty of the approach has led in the past to the ill-informed notion that person-centred therapy is 'easy' or that it can be useful *as a technique* in the early stages of therapy before more sophisticated and effective methods are introduced (Mearns and Thorne, 1999: 5).

The change process in therapy

When person-centred therapy goes well clients will move from a position where their self-concept, typically poor at the entry into therapy and finding expression in behaviour which is reinforcing of the negative evaluation of self, will shift to a position where it more closely reflects the person's essential worth. As the self-concept moves towards a more positive view so, too, clients' behaviour begins to mirror the improvement and to enhance their perception of themselves. The therapist's ability to create a relationship in which the three facilitative attitudes are consistently present will to a large extent determine the extent to which clients are able to move towards a more positive contact with the promptings of the actualizing tendency.

If therapy has been successful clients will also have learned how to be their own therapist. It seems that when people experience the genuineness of another and a real attentive caring and valuing by that other person they begin to adopt the same attitude towards themselves. In short, a person who is cared for begins to feel at a deep level that perhaps she is after all *worth* caring for. In a similar way, the experience of being on the receiving end of the concentrated listening and the empathic understanding which characterize the therapist's response tends to develop a listening attitude in the client towards herself. It is as if she gradually becomes less afraid to get in touch with what is going on inside her and dares to listen attentively to her own feelings. With this growing attentiveness comes increased self-understanding and a tentative grasp of some of her most central personal meanings. Many clients have told me that after person-centred therapy they never lose this ability to treat themselves with respect and to take the risk of listening to what they are experiencing. If they do lose it temporarily or find themselves becoming hopelessly confused they will not hesitate to return to therapy to engage once more in a process which is in many ways an education for living.

In Rogers and Dymond (1954) one of Rogers's chapters explores in detail a client's successful process through therapy. The case of Mrs Oak has become a rich source of learning for person-centred therapists ever since, and towards the end of the chapter Rogers attempts a summary of the therapeutic process which Mrs Oak has experienced with such obvious benefits to herself. What is described there seems to me to be so characteristic of the person-centred experience of therapy that I make no apology for providing a further summary of some of Rogers's findings.

The process begins with the therapist providing an atmosphere of warm caring and acceptance which over the first few sessions is gradually experienced by the client, Mrs Oak, as genuinely *safe*. With this realization the client finds that she changes the emphasis of her sessions from dealing with reality problems to experiencing herself. The effect of this change of emphasis is that she begins to experience her feelings in the immediate present without inhibition. She can be angry, hurt, childish, joyful, self-deprecating, self-appreciative and as she allows this to occur she discovers many feelings bubbling through into awareness of which she was not previously conscious. With new feelings there come new thoughts and the admission of all this fresh material to awareness leads to a *breakdown of the previously held self-concept*. There then follows a period of disorganization and confusion although there remains a feeling that the path is the right one and that reorganization will ultimately take place. What is being learned during this process is that it pays to recognize an experience for what it is rather than denying it or distorting it. In this way the client becomes more open to experience and begins to realize that it is healthy to accept feelings whether they be positive or negative, for this permits a movement towards greater complete-ness. At this stage the client gradually comes to realize that *she can begin to define herself and does not have to accept the definition and judgements of others*. There is, too, a more conscious appreciation of the nature of the relationship with the therapist and the value of a love which is not possessive and makes no demands. At about this stage the client finds that she can make relationships outside of therapy which enable others to be self-experiencing and self-directing and she becomes progressively aware that at the core of her being she is not destructive but genuinely desires the well-being of others. Self-responsibility continues to increase to the point where the client feels able to make her own choices – although this is not always pleasant – and to trust herself in a world which, although it may often seem to be disintegrating, yet offers many opportunities for creative activity and relating (Rogers, 1954). I would add that for those clients who repeatedly experience those moments in therapy where 'inner spirit touches inner spirit' there is a strong likelihood that their sense of the numinous will be awakened or rekindled and that the search for meaning will be strengthened. Not infrequently clients towards the end of therapy report a new acknowledgement of spiritual reality which in some cases leads to a re-engagement with previously rejected religious observances or, more often, to the exploration of hitherto uncharted spiritual terrain.

Person-centred therapy is essentially an approach to the human condition based on trust. There is trust in the innate resourcefulness of human beings, given the right conditions, to find their own way through life. There is trust that the direction thus found will be positive and creative. There is trust, too, that the process of relating between counsellor and client will in itself provide the primary context of safety and nurture in which the client can face the pain of alienation from his or her own actualizing tendency and move towards a more integrated way of being. Where blocks occur in therapeutic process they can almost invariably be traced back to a lack or loss of trust on the part of client or counsellor or both in the basic premises of the approach, and more particularly in the essentially healing process of the therapeutic relationship. In many instances where the lack of trust is firmly lodged in the client, the person-centred therapist has the unenviable but clear task of learning to wait, of exercising patience while committing himself or herself to the consistent offering of the core conditions in the face of the client's fear, hostility or increasing pain.

The situation is potentially more grave when the lack of trust resides in the therapist. He or she doubts his or her capacity to offer the core conditions to this particular client and is consumed with a fear of mounting failure. In such a situation, where supervision fails to resolve the stuckness, the therapist has no option but to address the issues with the client, not knowing whether this will herald movement forward or the end of the relationship. An ebbing of trust in the relationship itself can often be guarded against by an agreement at the outset between therapist and client to review their process periodically *as a matter of course*. Such 'stocktaking' facilitates an openness between counsellor and client which ensures that difficulties and doubts are not allowed to fester but can be faced squarely and in this way serve to strengthen rather than undermine the therapeutic relationship. This practice also reinforces the essentially shared nature of the therapeutic work and makes more likely the achievement of the 'relational depth' where the most profound changes can occur (Mearns, 1996). It also offers the client the opportunity, as therapy proceeds, to invite the therapist to respond in new ways. Not infrequently, for example, clients wish to enlist the therapist's support in implementing new behaviours which are more in keeping with their changing self-concept and greater confidence. Progress can be unnecessarily impeded if in such instances clients believe that the therapist is interested solely in their state of being and is not concerned to help initiate action or to involve others in their development. Regular stocktaking will ensure that such misconceptions are rapidly dispelled. Would that such a practice was commonly adopted by married couples and others in close relationships!

Limitations of the approach

After 33 years as a person-centred therapist I am drawn to the conclusion, as I stated earlier, that the limitations of the approach are a reflection of the personal limitations of the therapist. As these will clearly vary from individual to individual and are unlikely to be constant over time I am sceptical about the usefulness of exploring the limitations of the approach in any generalized fashion. None the less I am intrigued by the question with respect to two particular issues. I believe that person-centred therapy has been in danger of selling itself short because of its traditional emphasis on the 'here and now' and because of what is seen as its heavy reliance on verbal interaction. Both these tendencies are likely to be reinforced when the therapist's congruence remains at a relatively superficial level.

In my own practice I have discovered that the more I am able to be fully present to myself in the therapeutic relationship the more likely it is that I shall come to trust the promptings of a deeper and more intuitive level within myself. Cautiously and with constant safeguards against self-deception I have come to value this intuitive part of my being and to discover its efficacy in the therapeutic relationship. What is more, when I have risked articulating a thought or feeling which emanates from this deeper level I have done so in the knowledge that it may appear unconnected to what is currently happening in the relationship or even bizarre to my client. More often than not, however, the client's response has been immediate and sometimes dramatic. It is as if the quality of the relationship which has been established, thanks to the consistent offering of the core conditions, goes a long way towards ensuring that my own intuitive promptings are deeply and immediately significant for the client. Often, too, the significance lies in the triggering of past experience for the client – not in the sense simply of locating memories of past events but in releasing a veritable flow of feeling whose origin lies in past experience which is then vividly relived. Commonly, too, the therapist's intuitive response seems to touch a part of the client's being which cannot find immediate expression in words. I am astonished how often at such moments the client reaches out for physical reassurance or plunges into deep but overflowing silence in which new movement is mysteriously generated.

There are many in the person-centred tradition whose frustration with the essentially verbal nature of the therapy has led them to supplement the approach with methods culled from other disciplines (e.g. Tausch, 1990). Rogers's own daughter, Natalie, has pioneered an approach she calls person-centred expressive therapy (Rogers, 1993) which incorporates movement, art, music, pottery and creative writing as well as other essentially non-verbal channels of expression. Eugene Gendlin, referred to earlier, has developed the method of focusing for deepening inner experience (Gendlin, 1981). Gendlin's work is particularly impressive, giving access as it does to a level of self-knowledge which is initially just outside the bounds of conscious awareness. Indeed, focusing has developed into what is now known as experiential psychotherapy but its kinship to person-centred therapy is reflected in the title of the new World Association which seeks to embrace both in the same family.

Those who would see a limitation of the approach as being its unwillingness to entertain the notion of working with the unconscious can perhaps find some reassurance in Gendlin's contribution. Focusing works on the premise that there *is* material outside of awareness and that it can profitably be tapped into and integrated into the self-concept. The same is true of the innovative work undertaken in recent times by Dave Mearns on 'configurations' within the self. Person-centred practitioners by their willingness to enter into relational depth with their clients make it safe enough for them to engage with parts or dimensions of their being which they had not previously dared fully to encounter. These 'configurations' – denoting a coherent pattern of feelings, thoughts and behavioural responses – do not constitute material derived from 'working with the unconscious' for the client remains at the centre of the therapeutic endeavour and dictates his or her own path and pace into awareness. The therapist, as always, is the faithful companion who by his or her commitment to authentic relating makes the path less frightening and the pace manageable (Mearns and Thorne, 2000: 101–43). Far from being a limitation, person-centred therapy's refusal to work directly with the unconscious can lead to a mutuality of in-depth relationship where fear can be faced and advances in awareness achieved. These do not depend on elaborated maps of the unconscious but on the therapist's willingness and ability to be fully present to him or herself as well as to the client. Rogers discovered towards the end of his life that simply his presence could be healing for others in ways he had not previously conceptualized. He found, in effect, that to be fully congruent was a constant challenge to his own integrity and trust in life. It is on the continuing response to that challenge that the further development of person-centred therapy must ultimately depend with all the existential and spiritual questionings which that will inevitably entail.

Case example

The client

Jeremy, a mature student in his early thirties, first presented himself to me early on in the academic year because he had ground to a halt in his academic work. This was particularly serious for he was a member of a prestigious creative writing course where his fellow students seemed exceptionally gifted and where it was expected that each student, by the end of the year, would have produced a substantial piece of writing worthy of publication. Jeremy was almost overwhelmed with self-doubt and was regretting that he had joined the course in the first place. He believed that he had overestimated his own ability and was somewhat disillusioned with the course tutors, whom he seemed to blame for selecting him in the first place and then for failing to provide him with a structured learning environment by which he could feel supported. He was on the point of abandoning his course but realized that if he did so he had no alternative plan and would be likely to end up in the dole queue. He felt trapped, demoralized and powerless. And he was appalled at the thought of spending yet more days staring despondently at blank paper.

The therapy

At the outset I was struck by Jeremy's powerful presence. He was a tall, handsome man and it was soon clear that he had an agile mind and an ability to express himself lucidly and expressively. It was equally apparent, however, that he was desperate and his comments were interspersed with constant references to his lack of ability and his inadequacy as a person. 'I'm about the least creative person I've met. . .I never know what to say in seminars. . .The other students think I'm a moron. . .I must come across as utterly boring. . .The women avoid me, and I don't blame them.' The first and second sessions were taken up almost entirely by a catalogue of Jeremy's short-comings as a person and as a writer with, in the background, the continuing inability to produce anything on paper.

For my part, I felt instinctively drawn to Jeremy. I enjoyed his articulacy and his use of language which was sometimes humorous and sometimes almost lyrical. I liked him and by my responses I hoped I was conveying to him my acceptance and affirmation of him as a person. I did not have to simulate my respect for him and I felt sure that if I had done so he would have been quick to spot my inauthenticity. My attempts to understand him, however, seemed initially to be woefully incompetent. As I struggled to engage with his inner world I was caught in its complexity. The inadequacy of my efforts to be empathically attuned to him was painfully apparent. Almost invariably Jeremy would refute my attempts to understand him. He would frown at my, as I thought, skilled empathic responses and was quick to correct my stumbling attempts to move into his reality. Towards the end of the second session his despair overflowed but instead of the anger which I half expected him to express at my incompetence, he turned the whole process against himself: 'You see how hopeless I am. I can't even get across to you what's going on for me and nobody could be kinder and trying harder than you are. And I'm supposed to be in the communications business. What a joke!' Although my own confidence was rapidly diminishing, I tried once more to be empathically accurate: 'You feel that you're a hopeless case because you can't commu-nicate to me what you're experiencing. And you *ought* to be able to because you're a communications specialist.' At last, Jeremy's face reflected that sense of relief which often comes when someone feels properly understood. And a moment later he burst into tears.

As is so often the case with someone who is trapped in a vicious circle of self-denigration, Jeremy was the victim of a whole array of self-imposed 'oughts' and conditions of worth. My phrase 'ought to be able to' unleashed a torrent of misery and the second session (mercifully there was no further client waiting to see me) overran by some 20 minutes. Having been accepted on such a prestigious course Jeremy believed he *ought* to be brilliant, he *ought* to be able to contribute spontaneously to seminar discussion, he *ought* to be socially polished and admired by women and, above all, he *ought* to be able to produce the kind of work which previous students on the course had done who were now household names in the literary firmament. In short, he ought to be the perfect student, the perfect person and an obvious future contender for the Booker Prize. No wonder he deemed himself such a failure and that his self-concept as a creative writer had all but collapsed.

Subsequent sessions threw many more shafts of light on Jeremy's predicament and how it was that he had landed in such a place of self-contempt. First of all it became clear that his fellow students, through their own anxiety and competitiveness, created a climate in which it was almost impossible to admit to inadequacy and self-doubt. It was, in short, a very unsafe place in which to be real. What is more, the necessity to be seen as creative and imaginatively gifted led in the group to magnificent displays of affected self-confidence which, for Jeremy, unable at that point to perceive the spuriousness of the performance, served to exacerbate his own feelings of worthlessness. He ought to be like the others, he told himself, without tumbling to the fact that for many of the others their apparently confident behaviour was the result of their own insecurity and need to keep up appearances. Much more significant, however, was what emerged about Jeremy's family background and history.

Both Jeremy's parents, he told me as he progressively relaxed into being 'real' with me, were high-flyers. His father was the managing director of a large public company and his mother was a well-known barrister. Success, high visibility, hard work and a certain ruthlessness were characteristic of the family culture. It was expected that Jeremy would manifest the same characteristics but he had failed miserably to come up to his parents' expectations. They could not conceal their disappointment and disapproval when he decided to become a schoolteacher. The fact that he obtained a first-class degree in English literature was scarcely acknowledged.

As this story unfolded, the relationship between the two of us changed markedly and it was I who nearly jeopardized the progress we were making by my own failure properly to acknowledge what was going on inside me. As I listened to Jeremy I felt more and more drawn to him. His language became increasingly rich and laden with metaphors and images which I found entrancing. I experienced a sense of intimacy with him which was startling as I became almost awe-struck at the complexity of the person who was emerging in my presence. I could see the different aspects of his being – the elusive but distinctive 'configurations' – which made it almost impossible to define him. There was the little boy desperately needing affirmation, the consummate wordsmith who revelled in language, the insecure man doubting his sexual desirability, the inept social being who feared the unpredictable encounter, the supremely confident interpreter of great literature. In the face of this kaleidoscopic personality, I panicked. I was so full of feeling that I did not know what to do with it all and I retreated into a caricature of a person-centred therapist. I mouthed empathic responses, I conveyed an anaemic acceptance, I distanced myself while maintaining what I believed to be a facilitative environment. How could I say: 'Jeremy, I am experiencing overwhelming feelings of excitement in your presence: I am amazed at the complexity of your being: I am privileged to be your companion and I think I'm worthy of that role'? I failed even to begin to be congruent and therefore it was not surprising that Jeremy did not appear for his next session.

My devastation at this non-appearance, together with the help of my ever-supportive supervisor, led to the writing of a letter to Jeremy which expressed my concern for him, my delight in the work we were doing together and my deep regard for the person he had allowed me to see. I was not unaware of the irony that I, the therapist, had been brought to the point of writing to the client who had first presented with writer's block. Jeremy returned and never commented on why he had failed to appear for the previous session. He thanked me for my letter, told me he had read most of *my* books, was glad that I believed in spiritual reality because his father was an atheist and that I would have got on well with his grandmother who had died the previous year. Many of our later sessions were taken up with Jeremy's grief for his grandmother, who had been his committed champion and supporter from his infancy. Her death, it became clear, had left Jeremy undefended against the assembled battalions of the expectations of his family, the judgements of a materialistic society, the competitive jealousies of his fellow students and the undermining voice of his own self-doubt. When he told me in his final session that I had been a pretty good grandmother it was my turn to weep a little. I doubt he will win the Booker Prize, but stranger things can happen.

References

Boy, A.V. and Pine, G.J. (1982) *Client-centered Counselling. A Renewal.* Boston, MA: Allyn & Bacon.

Burn, M. (1956) *Mr Lywards' Answer.* London: Hamish Hamilton.

Frick, W.B. (1971) *Humanistic Psychology: Interviews with Maslow, Murphy and Rogers.* Columbus, OH: Charles E. Merrill.

Gendlin, E. (1981) *Focusing.* New York: Bantam Books.

Kirschenbaum, H. (1979) *On Becoming Carl Rogers.* New York: Delacorte Press.

Lietaer, G. (1984) 'Unconditional positive regard: a controversial basic attitude in client-centered therapy', in R. Levant and J. Shlien (eds), *Client-Centered Therapy and the Person-Centered Approach.* New York: Praeger. pp. 41–58.

McLeod, J. (1994) *Doing Counselling Research.* London: Sage.

Mearns, D. (1994) *Developing Person-Centred Counselling.* London: Sage.

Mearns, D. (1996) 'Working at relational depth with clients in person-centred therapy', *Counselling,* 7(4): 306–11.

Mearns, D. (1997) *Person-Centred Counselling Training.* London: Sage.

Mearns, D. and Thorne, B.J. (1988) *Person-Centred Counselling in Action.* London: Sage.

Mearns, D. and Thorne B.J. (1999) *Person-Centred Counselling in Action,* 2nd edn. London: Sage.

Mearns, D. and Thorne, B.J. (2000) *Person-Centred Therapy Today: New Frontiers in Theory and Practice.* London: Sage.

Merry, T. (1995) *Invitation to Person-Centred Psychology.* London: Whurr.

Merry, T. (1999) *Learning and Being in Person-Centred Counselling.* Ross-on-Wye: PCCS Books.

Oatley, K. (1981) 'The self with others: the person and the interpersonal context in the approaches of C.R. Rogers and R.D. Laing', in F. Fransella (ed.), *Personality*. London: Methuen.

O'Leary, C. (1999) *Couple and Family Counselling: A Person-Centred Approach*. London: Sage.

Prouty, G.F. (1995) *Theoretical Evolutions in Person-centered/Experiential Therapy*. Westport, CT: Praeger.

Rogers, C.R. (1942) *Counseling and Psychotherapy*. Boston, MA: Houghton-Mifflin.

Rogers, C.R. (1951) *Client-Centered Therapy*. Boston, MA: Houghton-Mifflin.

Rogers, C.R. (1954) 'The case of Mrs Oak: a research analysis', in C.R. Rogers and R.F. Dymond (eds), *Psychology and Personality Change*. Chicago: University of Chicago Press.

Rogers, C.R. (1961) *On Becoming a Person*. Boston, MA: Houghton-Mifflin.

Rogers, C.R. (1974) 'In retrospect: forty-six years', *American Psychologist*, 29(2): 115–23.

Rogers, C.R. (1975) 'Empathic: an unappreciated way of being', *The Counseling Psychologist*, 2: 2–10.

Rogers, C.R. (1979) 'The foundations of the person-centered approach', unpublished manuscript. La Jolla, CA.

Rogers, C.R. (1980) *A Way of Being*. Boston, MA: Houghton-Mifflin.

Rogers, C.R. (1986) 'A client-centered/person-centered approach to therapy', in I. Kutash and A. Wolf (eds), *Psychotherapist's Casebook*. San Francisco: Jossey-Bass. pp. 197–208.

Rogers, C.R. and Dymond, R.F. (eds) (1954) *Psychology and Personality Change*. Chicago: University of Chicago Press.

Rogers, N. (1993) *The Creative Connection*. San Francisco: Science and Behavior Books.

Tausch, R. (1975) 'Ergebnisse und Prozesse der klienten-zentrierten Gesprächspsychotherapie bei 500 Klienten und 115 Psychotherapeuten. Eine Zusammenfassung des Hamburger Forschungsprojektes', *Zeitschrift für praktische Psychologie*, 13: 293–307.

Tausch, R. (1990) 'The supplementation of client-centered communication therapy with other validated therapeutic methods: a client centered necessity', in G. Lietaer, J. Rombauts and R. van Balen (eds), *Client-Centered and Experiential Psychotherapy in the Nineties*. Leuven: Leuven University Press. pp. 448–55.

Thorne, B.J. (1985) *The Quality of Tenderness*. Norwich: Norwich Centre Occasional Publications.

Thorne, B.J. (1991) *Person-centred Counselling: Therapeutic and Spiritual Dimensions*. London: Whurr.

Thorne, B.J. (1992) *Carl Rogers*. London: Sage.

Thorne, B.J. (1994) 'Developing a spiritual discipline', in D. Mearns, *Developing Person-centred Counselling*. London: Sage. pp. 44–7.

Thorne, B.J. (1998) *Person-Centred Counselling and Christian Spirituality*. London: Whurr.

Thorne, B.J. (2002) *The Mystical Power of Person-Centred Therapy*. London: Whurr.

Thorne, B.J. and Lambers, E. (eds) (1998) *Person-Centred Therapy: a European Perspective*. London: Sage.

Suggested further reading

Mearns, D. and Thorne. B.J. (1999) *Person-centred Counselling in Action*, 2nd edn. London: Sage.

Mearns, D. and Thorne B.J. (2000) *Person-Centred Therapy Today: New Frontiers in Theory and Practice*. London: Sage.

Rogers, C.R. (1951) *Client-centered Therapy*. Boston, MA: Houghton-Mifflin.

Rogers, C.R. (1961) *On Becoming a Person*. Boston, MA: Houghton-Mifflin.

Thorne, B.J. (1992) *Carl Rogers*. London: Sage.

7 **Personal Construct Therapy**
Fay Fransella and Peggy Dalton

Historical context and developments in Britain

Historical context

George A Kelly (1905–1967) was not a man of his time. He was a revolutionary thinker who had dreams of what the psychological study of human beings should be like. These dreams were in direct contrast with the current psychological ethos of behaviourism. His ideas expressed in the philosophy of *constructive alternativism* can be traced back to the dim distant past, as can those of his contemporary, Jean Piaget. It was largely the approach of these two men that has triggered off the interest, starting in the 1980s, in the philosophy of 'constructivism'.

This approach to the study of human beings is also in direct conflict with the science of the past. No longer are there facts to be found and truths to be gleaned. All we can hope to do is come to a 'best guess' that we know will be superseded by a better 'best guess' in due course. In Kelly's terms, 'there are always alternative ways of looking at any event'. We each live in our own personal world although we may, of course, share with many others our perceptions of events if we come from the same culture or the same family.

In Kelly's theory we act upon our world rather than respond to it as the behaviourists would have us do. We are actors, we create our own lives and can therefore re-create them if we find ourselves not to our own liking. We are also forms of motion. We are alive, and one aspect of living matter is that it is always on the move. What needs explaining is why we behave as we do. Here Kelly turned behaviour, described by the behaviourists as a response *to* something, into a question. That is, we make sense of our world by applying to it the personal constructs we have created in the past. These personal constructs are our mini-theories about how things are. In this way we can predict what may happen as the result of some action. Having made a prediction that, say, this client has normal hearing, we put this prediction to the test *by behaving* 'as if' this client can hear what is being said. Now, that prediction may be correct or incorrect, but the behaviour was asking the question, 'Am I right in thinking this person can hear well enough?'

Kelly received his PhD in psychology – with particular emphasis on physiology – in the early 1930s. He became professor and director of clinical psychology at Ohio State University in 1946. However, in order to gain a fuller insight into the context in which his ideas developed it is important to know something of his earlier studies: in 1926 he obtained a BA degree in physics and mathematics, later a Master's degree in educational sociology, and in 1930 a Bachelor of Education degree at Edinburgh University.

His university courses in physics and mathematics took place around the time when Einstein's ideas were shaking the world of science, as were those of quantum mechanics. With this early training, it comes as no surprise to find that Kelly's model of the person is couched in the language of science, as is his whole theory (see Fransella, 1984 and 2000 for a more detailed discussion of how training in physics and mathematics may have influenced Kelly's psychological theorizing). But Kelly's is a science based on the philosophy of constructive alternativism: a science in which there are no 'facts', only support for current hypotheses. These hypotheses may lead to other hypotheses, which encompass new events, and so on. He argues that there *is* a reality 'out there' and at some infinite moment in time we may learn all there is to know about the universe, but this is unlikely since the universe, like the person, is in a constant state of motion (see Fransella, 1995 for details of George Kelly the man and his psychology).

Development in Britain

George Kelly, an American, found receptive readers first and foremost in Britain. He believed that the attention given to his theory by British psychologists would determine whether his work would stand or fall. Only from the 1980s has there been a quickening of interest in his work in its country of origin. Neimeyer (1985a) has described its development in the context of the sociology of science. He uses Mullins's (1973) model of the sociohistorical development of new theory groups, which focuses on the changing patterns of communication.

The development of personal construct theory goes, according to Neimeyer, something like this. Before and for some time after the publication of Kelly's *magnum opus*, *The Psychology of Personal Constructs* in 1955, he and others worked largely in isolation, However, by 1966 workers in Britain had attained a cluster status; that is, local groups with a minimum of seven people had developed and there had been a publication explosion. The major force behind the development of interest in the theory in Britain was the lecturing and publications of Don Bannister.

Neimeyer finds that by 1972 the major clusters in Britain were beginning to dissolve and that personal construct theory was steadily establishing itself as a mature speciality; by contrast, America and the rest of Europe only started to enter the cluster stage of development in the 1980s.

Up to 1978 there was surprisingly little work published on the application of personal construct psychology (PCP) to psychotherapy – surprising since this is its 'focus of convenience'. But things have changed, and the quantity of publications in the therapy field is now considerable. Interest in Kelly's theory and philosophy is worldwide. Fay Fransella convened the first international congress in Oxford, UK in 1977 and since then they have taken place *every* two years in different countries around the world. Continental conferences also take place in the intervening years in Australia, the United States, and Europe. In 1981, Fay Fransella founded the first centre devoted solely to the teaching and applications of personal construct in London.

Theoretical assumptions

Image of the person

Kelly suggests we might look at the person 'as if' you and I were scientists. By this he means that we could all be seen as doing the same sorts of things that scientists traditionally do. We have theories about why things happen; erect hypotheses derived from these theories; and put these hypotheses to the test to see whether the predictions arising from them are validated or invalidated. We test our predictions by behaving. Viewing all behaviour 'as if' it were an experiment is one of Kelly's unique contributions to our understanding of the person.

We approach the world not as it *is* but as it appears to us to be; we gaze at our world through our construing *goggles*. We make predictions about events constantly and continually – there is no let-up. We are active beings, 'forms of motion'.

He suggests that we might come to understand ourselves and others in psychological terms by studying the personal constructs we have each evolved to discriminate between events and to help us predict other events in the future. Construing is not all going on in the head, though; we construe just as much with our bodies as with our minds. Kelly gives as an example our digestive system. Our stomach anticipates food, secretes gastric juices, behaves towards what it receives in an accepting manner if the food is in line with expectation, or rejects the food if it is not up to expectation and so forth. Kelly considers dualistic thinking a hindrance to our understanding of the person. At any given moment it is just as appropriate to ask what a person is feeling as what he is thinking, for many of our constructs (discriminations between events) were formed either before we had created the words to express them or else those discriminations have never acquired verbal labels. Personal construct theory is thus very much a theory of human experiencing.

For example, a young child may discriminate between types of voice: a harsh, grating voice and a soft, smooth one. The harsh, grating voice is related to feelings of reassurance, a large body to snuggle up to, and is there before the child goes to bed. The soft, smooth one gives conflicting messages: sometimes it is comforting like the harsh, grating one, but at other times – often when it is particularly soft and smooth – there are feelings of unease, of all not being well. Later, as an adult, that person may never be able to put into words exactly why he cannot abide women who have soft, smooth voices and why he himself has developed a harsh, grating one. His pre-verbal construing is being applied in adult life.

Conceptualization of psychological disturbance and health

Kelly argues fiercely against the use of the medical model in the field of psychological disorder. Like many others, he believes that those with psychological problems are not 'ill' and therefore should not be 'treated' by medical doctors. He argues further that the use of the medical model hampers our attempts to understand people and to help them deal with whatever it is that is troubling them. If there is no 'illness' there can be no 'health'. For Kelly, all personal constructs are bipolar.

Instead, he suggests that we might use the concept of functioning (e.g. Kelly, 1980). A person who is functioning fully is one who is able to construe the world in such a way that predictions are, for the most part, validated. When invalidation does occur, the person deals with it by reconstruing. For example, you are at a party and go up to a stranger whom you construe as likely to be friendly. You start a general conversation and, before a few moments have passed, that 'friendly' person is arguing fiercely with you and being quite unpleasant. He is certainly not being 'friendly'. You have been invalidated in your prediction that this was a 'friendly' person. If you are a well-functioning person, you will accept this invalidation and reconstrue the person, perhaps as someone who has a very deceptive façade and that you were stupid not to have seen through the veneer. You leave the incident behind you and put it down to experience.

But someone else, who is incapable of dealing with such invalidation, may not come out so unscathed. She may become more and more embarrassed, flustered and bereft of words. She would then become increasingly anxious since she has been confronted by an event which she now has difficulty in construing at all. Not only is she unable to predict the outcome of this event, but she finds she is increasingly unable to predict herself. The situation is a traumatic one. Hopefully, either someone will soon come to her rescue, or the stranger will move off. The person who experiences a considerable number of such predictive failures will often consider herself to 'have a problem'.

Another way of dealing with invalidation is to 'make' things work out the way we have predicted. When we do this we are being 'hostile' (we are extorting validational evidence for a social prediction that we have already seen to be a failure). For example, having construed the stranger as friendly, you might behave as if you were going to faint. He then puts his arm under your elbow to support you and guides you towards a chair. Now you can say to yourself: 'There you are! I knew he was really a friendly person!' Such hostility as this is well known in counselling and therapy. Yet there is nothing essentially 'bad' about hostility; it is a way of dealing with events when our construing lets us down.

Nevertheless, the person who functions reasonably well is one who does not use too much hostility to deal with invalidation and does not find himself too often confronted by events he cannot construe (and thus be overwhelmed with anxiety). The well-functioning person has been able to 'update' those potentially troublesome pre-verbal constructs. That is, he has been able to explore, at some level of awareness, those early childhood discriminations. For instance, is it valid, in adult life, to take an instant dislike to people who have soft, smooth voices? Perhaps the construction does not now lead to useful predictions.

Acquisition of psychological disturbance

It makes no theoretical sense to ask how a disturbance in construing is acquired. Personal construct theory takes the position that we act upon the world and construe (predict) events in the world, we cannot 'acquire' something as if we were buying it in a shop or having it imposed upon us, like measles.

A client may construe his incapacitating headaches as a 'bodily symptom' which he 'acquired' as a result of some stressful psychological event. It is the client's construing that the therapist has to understand. However, to the therapist, the headaches are as much to do with construing as is the way the client describes them. *There is no body/mind dichotomy in Kelly's theory.* As the therapist examines the client's construing system (in verbal and non-verbal terms) she may examine the context within which the headaches arose. She will be asking herself such questions as: 'What experiment is my client conducting when he has these headaches?' 'What answers is he seeking from himself or others around him by behaving in that way?'

It is important always to remember that behaviour is the experiment. So we look at the event as if the child's first headache (or the way the client remembers it) was his way of asking a question of his world. It may have gone something like this: 'My mother does not cuddle me as much as I need. But when I have a headache she does. She is ignoring me again now. I feel a headache coming on. Yes, she is coming towards me.' Has he 'acquired a disturbance'? We think not. He has tried an experiment which, according to the way in which he construes the world, works. He gets his love.

We need to stress that, although we have spelled out a possible process in words, this does not mean that the thought goes consciously through the child's head in this way. A great deal of our experimenting goes on at a non-verbal level.

Perpetuation of psychological disturbance

The headaches are perpetuated because 'they work'. The child's predictions are validated. He may have started the process whereby whenever he feels unloved, he gets stressed and develops headaches.

Invalidation of our important notions of our selves comes most often, of course, from other people in our lives. Our experiments in life succeed or fail in relation to our understanding of others' understandings of us. But it can also come from within. Problems may persist until the person is able to find acceptable alternative ways of dealing with the world. Many long-standing problems, such as stuttering, become enmeshed in the person's core-role construing. The person comes to see himself as 'a stutterer', 'a headache sufferer', 'an unlovable person'.

The reasons for problems persisting must be sought within a person's constru-ing of himself and his world. He behaves in a particular way because that is most meaningful to him; it is in that way he is able to achieve maximal control over events – and over himself. The problem becomes enmeshed in his core-role superordinate construing system. The longer the problem persists, the more difficulty the person is likely to have in changing – to change the construing of one's self is no easy undertaking.

Change

Since part of the model of the person in personal construct psychology is that we are a form of motion, the process of change is built into the theory. Kelly wrote his theory at two levels. There is the structure in the form of postulate, corollaries and other theoretical constructs. There is also the theory of human experiencing in the form of cycles of movement and transitions.

The *fundamental postulate* states that 'a person's processes are psycho-logically channelized by the ways in which he anticipates events'. Three of the elaborative corollaries are specifically concerned with change.

The *experience corollary* states that 'a person's construction system varies as he successively construes the replication of events'. Merely being in a situation does not, of itself, mean that one has had experience. An agoraphobic woman placed in a situation at some point in her behaviour therapy hierarchy will only have experience of that situation if her construing of the world is in some way different after it from what it was before. Kelly equates experience with learn-ing:

> The burden of our assumption is that learning is not a special class of psychological process; it is synonymous with any and all psychological processes. It is not something that happens to a person on occasion; it is what makes him a person in the first place. (Kelly, 1991, Vol I: 53)

The *choice corollary* states that 'a person chooses for himself that alternative in a dichotomized construct through which he anticipates the greater possibility for extension and definition of his system'. This is a basic motivation construct. As living beings we strive to make our world a more predictable and personally meaningful place. We may not like the world in which we are living, but it is preferable to live in it than to launch ourselves into a vast sea of uncertainty.

In a certain sense, the client is 'choosing' to remain as he is rather than change. The person who has stuttered since early childhood sees no alternative but to continue stuttering in adulthood; that is the way he can make sense of himself interpersonally. If he were to suddenly become a fluent speaker, he would be launched into chaos (Fransella, 1972). In much the same way, smoking becomes personally meaningful for the smoker, obesity for the obese and depression for the depressed.

A personal construct approach involves helping the client construe what he or she is going to become and not simply eliminating the undesired behaviour.

The *modulation corollary* discusses a third aspect of change. It states that any variation within a construing system 'is limited by the permeability of the constructs within whose range of convenience the variants lie'. Construing new events is difficult if many of a person's constructs are not open to receive them; they are pumice stone rather than sponge. Someone who stutters and knows too precisely how people respond to his attempts at communication will find it difficult to employ new constructions of those interactions. He will not 'see' different responses.

While the corollaries of personal construct theory describe the theoretical structure underpinning change, the cycles of movement describe the change process. These are the cycles of experience, creativity and decision-making (CPC cycle).

The cycle of experience is about the process of reconstruing itself. The whole of psychotherapy therefore is seen in terms of human experiencing rather than as treatment. Kelly puts it like this:

> Psychotherapy needs to be understood as an experience, and experience, in turn, understood as a process that reflects human vitality. Thus to define psychotherapy as a form of treatment – something that one person does to another – is misleading. (Kelly, 1980: 21)

In the first place we have to have anticipation. Behaving is our experimentation to test out our anticipations about what confronts us. But we also have to be committed to these anticipations. We have to care about what happens. We have to invest something of ourselves in our experiments. The problem with problems is that we continue to conduct the same old experiments again and again without adding the final, essential component – reconstruing. As reconstruing completes one cycle of experience, so others start.

The *creativity cycle* starts with loosening up our construing of events and then tightening them again, hopefully in a different pattern. We have a problem in life. We go for a long walk and 'mull it over'. We allow ideas to come and go as they please (we are construing loosely). Then we suddenly have a flash of inspiration. Quickly, before it can slip away, we tighten things up again so we can look to see whether or not we have indeed found a solution. This cycle of creativity, like that of experience, repeats itself again and again. Kelly puts it like this:

> The loosening releases facts, long taken as self-evident, from their rigid conceptual moorings. Once so freed, they may be seen in new aspects hitherto unsuspected, and the creativity cycle may get under way. (Kelly, 1991, Vol. II: 301)

The ability to loosen the construing of events is often one of the first lessons the client has to be taught. Problems very often result in our tightening our construing so as to make it more manageable, more predictable. It can therefore be quite threatening to a client to be asked to let go the anchors that hold the construing together – even for a short time. Tightened construing was a problem with Mandy (who will be discussed later).

The *decision-making or CPC cycle* is independent of tightening or loosening construing. We have a decision to make. First of all we look at the alternatives available to us (we Circumspect). Eventually we focus on the way that makes the most sense (we Pre-empt the issue). Now we are in a position to make a Choice and so are precipitated into action.

Practice

Goals of therapy

The person with a psychological problem is seen as being 'stuck' – she keeps repeating her behavioural experiments over and over again. Since personal construct psychology views the person (amongst other things) as a form of motion, enabling the person to 'get on the move again' becomes the goal of therapy. As Kelly puts it:

> The task of psychotherapy is to get the human process going again so that life may go on and on from where psychotherapy left off. There is no particular kind of psychotherapeutic relationship – no particular kind of feelings – no particular kind of interaction that is in itself a psychotherapeutic panacea. (Kelly, 1969: 223)

Selection criteria

Since everyone is seen as a construing process, no one person would be deemed unsuitable for personal construct psychotherapy. What usually provides the limiting factor is the context in which the therapy will take place. Not all places can deal with the overactive, the catatonic, the violent. There is also another limiting factor, but one less easy to define – the psychotherapist him or herself. There are very few therapists who would wish to say they are equally successful with any client with any type of problem. The limitations are thus in the physical therapy context and in the therapist, and not in the client.

There are a few criteria which help the therapist decide whether or not the client is likely to benefit from personal construct psychotherapy. But none would automatically lead to a rejection of the client. One is that the client should be willing to go along with the idea that the therapist does not have the answers – the client does. All the therapist has is a theory about how people may go about the business of making sense of themselves and the world around them. If the client is basically looking for psychological 'pills', then they are not likely to take to the idea that psychotherapy means work.

A good prognostic sign is that the client has some existing construct to do with psychological change. Not only that it is possible to change, but that they, themselves, may find it possible to change.

In choosing whether the client is most likely to be able to contemplate change in the one-to-one situation or in the presence of others, a number of factors have to be considered. For instance, a very withdrawn adult would rarely be seen without any contact being made with those caring for that person. The choice is then between only seeing the client in the company of one or two relatives;

seeing client and relatives on different occasions; or seeing the client alone for part of the session with the relative(s) joining later. The choice will depend on the problem as seen by all parties. If the problem seems to be very definitely one that focuses on interactions and the withdrawn client not seeming to want to communicate more, then the emphasis would probably be on seeing client and relative(s) together. If the client is clearly withdrawn and experiencing some internal turmoil, most work would be done with the client alone.

However, the die is not cast for ever. As the withdrawn client becomes less so, the relatives may increasingly be brought into the sessions; as they come to understand what their interactions with their client are all about *from the client's point of view*, and vice versa, the client may well increasingly be seen alone.

Clients are referred for group therapy if their problem is clearly related to interpersonal issues: for instance, if they feel poorly understood by others or that others are something of a mystery to them. It is of interest to note that for Kelly group work was the preferred method, certainly within a hospital setting.

It is not uncommon for a client to be seen both individually and in a group. Here it is important that the same therapist is not involved in both. The client needs to be able to separate out the two experiences. There are experiments which the client may wish to conduct with or upon the therapist individually which would not be appropriate in a group. This requires very close collaboration between the therapists, for it is they who must ensure that the client moves along a single path toward reconstruing and does not get mixed messages. For instance, it would be counter-therapeutic for one therapist to be working with the client on the basis that the client needs to be helped to 'tighten' aspects of their construing while the other therapist is focusing on 'loosening'.

Qualities of effective therapists

Establishing the qualities of personal construct therapists more likely to lead to success or failure with clients is proving a very difficult and complex task (for details see Winter, 1992). However, Kelly specifies a number of skills he believes they need to acquire. These are outlined below.

A subsuming system of constructs

Above all, therapists must have a 'subsuming construct system' and be skilled in its use. Every therapist needs a set of professional constructs within which to subsume the client's own personal system of constructs. For the analyst, it is spelt out in psychoanalytic terms; for the cognitive therapist, in cognitive terms; for the personal construct therapist it is spelt out in terms of the theoretical constructs stated in the psychology of personal constructs. Kelly describes it thus:

> Since all clients have their own personal systems my system should be a system of approach by means of which I can quickly come to understand and subsume the widely varying systems which my clients can be expected to present. (Kelly, 1991, Vol. II: 28)

A therapist should be able to specify precisely what constructs are being used whenever a therapeutic decision is made. For example, if he systematically uses the writing of a self-characterization (see p. 173) with clients, he should be able to state precisely what this procedure is designed to do.

In personal construct therapy, the subsuming system is that which defines the theory itself. Those constructs most commonly used in psychotherapy are referred to as 'professional constructs'. One already mentioned is *loose* versus *tight*: is the client using constructs in a way that leads to varying predictions (loosened construing) or to predictions which state that events will definitely be one way or another (unvarying or tight construing)? Bannister (1962) based his theory of the origins and maintenance of schizophrenic thought disorder on this construct.

To be effective the personal construct therapist must be able to 'work within' a client's construing system whether it be overly tight or overly loose. She has to understand these process differences both experientially and theoretically. Therapists who lack an adequate knowledge of the professional constructs or who lack the skill of suspending their own value system in order to subsume that of the client, may fail to help a client change. Once the therapist allows his own construing to intervene between himself and the client, he not only fails to be of use to the client but may also find himself being used by that client and have difficulty extricating himself. Peggy Dalton refers to her own difficulty in suspending her own construing in the case study.

Creativity, versatility and aggression

Given the focus on the client and therapist as personal scientists, the therapist needs to be creative, versatile and aggressive. Kelly comments that 'Every case a psychotherapist handles requires him to devise techniques and formulate constructs he has never used before.' Such creativity means the readiness to try out unverbalized hunches, and a willingness to look at things in new ways:

> Creation is therefore an act of daring, an act of daring through which the creator abandons those literal defences behind which he might hide if his act is questioned or its results proven invalid. The psychotherapist who dares not try anything he cannot verbally defend is likely to be sterile in a psychotherapeutic relationship. (Kelly, 1991, Vol. II: 32)

To be creative the therapist must be able to adopt a variety of roles and be aggressive in testing out hypotheses (personal construct aggression being the active elaboration of one's construing). In psychotherapy, both client and therapist must be prepared to be aggressive and to take risks.

It must be borne in mind that an unwritten basic tenet of personal construct psychology is that we have created ourselves and can therefore re-create ourselves if we so wish.

Verbal ability

The therapist must be skilled both verbally and in observation. A therapist must be able to speak the client's language in addition to having a wide-ranging vocabulary. By understanding the meanings that word-symbols have for the client the therapist can minimize the risk of misunderstandings.

Therapeutic relationship and style

The personal construct therapist's relationship and style can best be understood by looking once again at the model of the 'person as scientist'. Client and therapist are partners in the struggle to understand and so find a solution to the same problem. The therapist, like a research supervisor, knows something about designing experiments, has experience of some of the pitfalls involved in any type of research and knows that, ultimately, only the research student can carry out the research.

This supervisor/research student model may sound cold and calculating, but it is not. Anyone who has ever been in one or both of those positions know only too well how totally involving and challenging is the task. One important aspect of such a relationship is that both client and therapist must have a personal commitment to solving the problem and to the necessary work and experimentation that this involves.

A central feature of the therapeutic relationship is spelled out in the *sociality corollary*. This says that we may be seen as playing a role in relation to another if we try to see the world through the *eyes* of the other. The personal construct therapist, above all else, is struggling to see things as the client sees them. Only by being successful in this can any meaningful therapeutic strategy be undertaken.

To start with the therapist adopts the *credulous approach*; all personal evaluation is suspended; there are no judgements. Everything the client says is accepted as 'true'. This cannot, of course, go on, but it is essential to the establishment of the initial role relationship. As the therapist gains increasing access to the client's world and begins to formulate hypotheses about the nature of the problem, the therapist begins to put these to the test. However, being active in therapy does not mean that the therapist necessarily adopts a directive role; she may, in fact, be very quiet and give the client absolute freedom to do, say or think whatever he wishes. Nevertheless, the role is decided on by the therapist. Her construing of the client's constructions leads her to consider that this 'quiet' role is something the client can use *at this stage of the therapy*.

This all means that the personal construct therapist will change style according to what is most likely to help the client's reconstruing process. A therapist may be humorous at one time and serious at another; active and then passive, or formal and then informal. Self-disclosure, as with all these other styles, will only be used if the client can make use of the disclosure, otherwise it is self-indulgence on the part of the therapist. The personal construct therapist, therefore, is a *validator or invalidator of the client's construing*.

One implication of construing the therapist as validator of the client's construing, is that she uses the relationship as another valuable 'tool' for helping the client's reconstructions. For instance, 'transference' or 'dependency' is not a general problem to be 'dealt with'. At a particular stage in therapy it may be useful to use the construct of 'dependency', such as when the client attempts to verbalize pre-verbal constructs; at another time or with other clients, dependence on the therapist may prevent the client from conducting useful experiments outside the therapy consulting room.

The therapeutic style is thus dictated by the ways in which the therapist construes the needs of the client, always remembering that client and therapist are both in the experimenting and reconstruing business and work as partners.

Major therapeutic strategies and techniques

The therapist hopes that all interactions with the client will aid the client in reconstruing. The therapist's principal goal is to help the client find alternative ways of looking at himself, life, and the problem. But before the therapist can be reasonably sure about these possible alternative ways, she has to have a moderately clear idea of what it is that is holding the client back from doing this on his own.

Most of the techniques stemming directly from personal construct psychology are concerned with providing the therapist as well as the client with information on how the client views the world at the present time. In that sense the methods can be called 'diagnostic'. Only fixed role therapy is a therapeutic tool in its own right – designed specifically to bring about reconstruing (alternative constructions). However, the diagnostic techniques do themselves bring about reconstruing in many instances, although this is not their prime aim.

Kelly talks about techniques thus:

> Personal construct psychotherapy is a way of getting on with the human enterprise and it may embody and mobilize all of the techniques for doing this that man has yet devised. Certainly there is no one psychotherapeutic technique and certainly no one kind of inter-personal compatibility between psychotherapist and client. The techniques employed are the techniques for living and the task of the skilful psychotherapist is the proper orchestration of all of these varieties of techniques. Hence one may find a personal construct psychotherapist employing a huge variety of procedures – not helter-skelter, but always as part of a plan for helping himself and his client get on with the job of human exploration and checking out the appropriateness of the constructions they have devised for placing upon the world around them. (Kelly, 1969: 221–2)

A few specific methods that have arisen from Kelly's work are outlined below.

Repertory grid technique

This technique has been modified a number of times since Kelly first described it in 1955 (see Fransella and Bannister, 1977). Its uses are many and, although the raw data can give rise to many useful insights, there are a variety of methods of statistical analysis. It is basically a technique which enables the therapist to obtain some degree of quantification of the relationships between constructs and how these relate to individuals who are being construed, as can be seen with Mandy in the case study. Many different types of grid have been designed for specific purposes. For instance, Neimeyer describes a 'biographical grid' in which the client construes elements that are important events in his or her life (Neimeyer, 1985b) and Ravenette (1999) a 'self-description grid' for use with children.

Though grids have a place in the psychotherapy setting, they are not essential to it. A grid is only useful if the therapist sees it as such. It can be used to validate therapists' hunches, for monitoring change over time, or in helping clients explore their construing of events more fully. In all cases grids are a part of the therapy as the results are fed back to the client.

Laddering, pyramiding and the ABC model

These are all methods for exploring construct relationships without getting into the complexities of statistical analyses that are often necessary with repertory grids.

Laddering helps the client explore the relationships between constructs at more and more abstract levels (Hinkle, 1965). For instance, if the client uses the construct 'dominant' versus 'submissive', the client would be asked which he would prefer to be. If the answer was submissive, the therapist would ask 'Why do you prefer to be that? What are the advantages of being a submissive rather than a dominant person?' The client might answer that submissive people do not get attacked, whereas dominant people do. The client is again asked why he prefers not to be attacked. The reply might be that he would not know how to respond if he were attacked, he would not know what to do. And so the questioning goes on, until the construing has reached such a superordinate level that it has nowhere else go to (in this example, it might be something to do with self-preservation).

Laddering is not easy to learn. It can go round in circles or produce answers that block all further enquiry. But having learned how to make it work, most people find it an invaluable tool for gaining insight very quickly into the most important values the client holds about himself and others. Not only does it enable the therapist to learn about the client, but frequently it also enables the client to gain considerable insight into his own construing.

Pyramiding (Landfield, 1971) aims at identifying the more concrete levels of the construing system of the client. Instead of asking 'Why?', the client is asked: 'What?' or 'How?': 'What sort of person is a submissive person?' 'How would you know that a person is being submissive?' This method can be very useful when planning behavioural experiments.

The ABC model involves finding out the advantages and disadvantages to the client of each pole of a construct (Tschudi, 1977). This can be used to advantage with constructs connected with 'the problem'. A woman whose 'problem' is being overweight might be asked for an advantage of being the desired weight (perhaps she would be able to wear nice clothes); then for a disadvantage of being overweight (perhaps she gets out of breath when going upstairs). Next, she is asked for a disadvantage of being the normal weight (perhaps she would find there was too much choice around and so get confused), and finally for an advantage of being overweight (perhaps men do not bother her). These answers are regarded not as 'truths' but as guidelines for understanding and further exploration.

The self-characterization

Kelly says that if he were to be remembered for one thing only, he would like it to be his first principle: 'If you do not know what is wrong with a person, ask him, he may tell you' (Kelly, 1991, Vol. I: 241). A working model for this is the self-characterization he described. The instructions are carefully worded as follows:

> I want you to write a character sketch of (e.g. Harry Brown) just as if he were the principal character in a play. Write it as it might be written by a friend who knew him very intimately and very sympathetically, perhaps better than anyone ever really could know him. Be sure to write it in the third person. For example, start out by saying 'Harry Brown is. . .' (Kelly, 1991, Vol. I: 242)

There is no formal method of analysis. However, one might look at the first sentence as if it were a statement of where the person is now and at the last as a statement of where the person is going. One might look for themes running through the whole piece. What one tries to do is go beyond the words and glimpse inside where the person lives. These character sketches can be written from a variety of standpoints: 'Harry as he will be in ten years' time', '. . .as he will be when his problem has disappeared', or any other form which seems to offer the person a way of exploring and communicating his constructions of the world. An example of the use of the self-characterization as the main therapeutic instrument can be found in Fransella (1981). Jackson (1988) has developed ways of using the self-characterization with children and adolescents. It also plays an important part in the case study at the end of this chapter.

Fixed role therapy

This is the only method that is offered by Kelly as a therapeutic tool in its own right. He gave it as an example of the theory in action and based it on the self-characterization. In his description of fixed role therapy, he also gives an implicit account of the way we invent and create ourselves. Kelly acknowledges his indebtedness to Moreno (1964) and his methods of psychodrama here.

The therapist writes a second version of the client's original self-characterization. This is not a replica of the first, since that would only lead back to where the client is now; nor should it be a complete opposite, since no one will readily turn his life on its head. Instead, the client's fixed role sketch is written so as to be 'orthogonal' to the first. For instance, if the client is using the construct 'aggressive' versus 'submissive' in relation to his boss, the sketch might talk of being respectful.

When the sketch has been written, client and therapist pore over it together. They modify it until it describes a person the client feels it would be possible for him to be. The client now lives the life of that person for a few weeks: he eats what his new person eats, dresses as he would dress and relates to others as this person would relate. During this period of fixed role enactment the therapist has to see the client fairly frequently. The sessions focus on what the client sees as going on, which ventures were successful and which were not, what messages he is getting from others and so forth.

The purpose of this fixed role enactment is to get over the idea that we can, indeed, change ourselves; that even the client can change, though he seems so stuck at the moment. He learns about self-inventiveness; he learns what happens when he alters a particular item of behaviour, and whether it is useful to explore this line of enquiry further or whether he should try something else. He discovers how the way we construe others and behave towards them influences how they behave towards us. He learns to read new messages from others. This is particularly important since the person we have invented is, in large part, the result of the way we have construed the reactions of others to us.

Fixed role therapy is certainly not suitable for everyone, but it can be very useful in modified form. For instance, the client and the therapist may choose to work out just one experiment for the former to carry out during the period before the next appointment. This might be to experiment with being respectful to his boss on just one occasion and see what difference it makes to how the boss reacts, and to how the client feels about himself. These 'mini' fixed roles need to be worked out carefully with the client, but can give useful insights into the direction in which both client and therapist think he might profitably travel. This procedure was used with the client discussed at the end of this chapter.

Techniques from other therapies

The choice of technique is always determined by the current formulation of the problem, which is couched in the language of the professional theoretical constructs. Personal construct therapists find the use of dream material, guided fantasy, systematic desensitization and many other techniques of great value for specific purposes, but it must be emphasized that the choice of technique is guided by theory.

The change process in therapy

There are no clear stages in the change process that are applicable to all clients. We have to ask questions derived from the theory. How permeable is the client's construing in the problem area? What is at stake for him if he were to contemplate changing in some radical way? How loosely or tightly knit is his construing in areas relating to anticipated change? And so on. In other words, the change process will be determined by the 'diagnosis' the therapist makes of why the client is unable to move forward on her own.

Diagnosis is the planning stage of treatment for the therapist. This does *not* imply that the therapist is placing the client in some medical pigeonhole such as 'depression', 'schizophrenia' or 'psychopathy'. Personal construct diagnosis does not imply any illness or disturbance on the part of the client. It is couched in the language of the theory to provide guidance for the therapist as to a possible way forward for the client. There is no one way forward for all-comers.

There are some specific factors that may impede the reconstruction process by the client. These factors are often to be found in the constructs to do with transition. The change process can involve anxiety, threat or hostility. All can impede movement if not dealt with sensitively by the therapist.

Any change is accompanied by anxiety as we move into areas we find it difficult or impossible to construe for a while. But this is rarely a problem if the client moves forward in moderate steps. Threat can bring the client up short as she perceives that, if things go on as they are at the moment, she will have to change how she construes some essential aspect of her 'self'. As one client put it after writing a self-characterization:

> Writing the self characterisation focused on something which I suppose has been associated with panic – although not consciously associated with panic – the feeling that I was going to have to change more drastically – in a sense either remain more or less the same or the change would have to be more drastic than I had thought. Writing the self characterisation focused my attention on not wanting to change. Not wanting to change because I felt that if I was going to have to change as dramatically as I was feeling was necessary, I'd lose 'me'. (Fransella, 1981: 228)

If a client is able to put the threat into words like that, it is usually possible to move on forward from there. The client had to elaborate precisely what the 'me' was that was in danger of being lost and whether, on close examination, that was necessarily true. But some clients are not able to put the threat into words. Often the client realizes, at some level of awareness, that these radical changes are just too much to be contemplated. She relapses. She has made a positive choice – in her terms – and has signalled that an alternative therapeutic strategy is required. Relapse is not a negative event, but the client's safety-net. This might have happened with Mandy in the case study, but did not.

The problem becomes particularly difficult if the client defends her position by becoming hostile: that is, by extorting evidence to prove that she really should be the sort of person she always knew herself to be. She can 'make' the therapy fail. It is really the therapist's fault not the client's. She can produce evidence that there has really been no great change at all by pointing out that the experience indicating psychological movement to the therapist was really 'a chance event – that combination of circumstances will never happen again!'

Hostility is dealt with by discovering, on the one hand, what it is that is so important for the client to retain and on the other hand, exploring areas of construing that will help elaborate the sort of self the client wants to become. Exploration with the client just mentioned revealed that the 'me' he was afraid of losing was 'the child me'. This was to do with a rich fantasy life and a world of deep experiencing. He evolved for himself a way in which he could change to becoming 'an adult' and yet retain areas of living in which he could still experience the valued childlike qualities.

Limitations of the approach

A major undeveloped area for personal construct therapy is group work. Although Kelly advocated its use and devoted a chapter to working with groups of people, little use has been made of it. Its focus has nearly always been on the one-to-one situation. One exception has been Landfield's Interpersonal Transaction (IT) groups (see Neimeyer, 1988).

Apart from this, limitations lie with the therapist rather than with personal construct therapy. The therapist finds it easier if she has the full co-operation of the client – at least implicitly. She finds it easier to work with those who are verbally fluent – but that is not essential. She finds it easier to work with those from a culture similar to her own but, again, this is by no means essential. If all human beings are seen as experiencing, construing beings, then personal construct therapy should be able to be used by all.

Case example

The client

Mandy had contacted me on the suggestion of a friend, with whom I [P.D.] had worked a few years previously. She was very tense and distressed and wept several times during the first session. Over the past six months or so she had spent £15,000 on clothes. And it wasn't her money. During the absence of the head of the design firm for whom she worked she had access to a credit card, which she had started to use for herself on small things and then got 'carried away'. He had recently returned earlier than expected and discovered the loss immediately.

When I asked her whether she had not anticipated this she said that, to begin with, she had intended to pay back what was to be a small amount and then it just 'escalated'. She had told her husband, who was very supportive and had arranged to pay off the debt over time. She seemed most upset about the reaction of her boss's wife, who was a friend, as well as other people in the firm whose opinion she valued. She expressed no concern about her boss, Alan, and at no point showed any remorse for what she had done – only the fear of the loss of friendship and regard. She felt she had to go on working for him. She was apparently a vital member of a small team. She was angry that Alan referred to the money in front of others.

In order to put all this into context I asked her about her life generally, and her focus was very much on relationships. She was very close to her mother, who denied her nothing, it seemed, but had difficulty with her stepfather. She had been to child guidance at the age of nine when her mother remarried. Her husband, Jeremy, she described as very loving and generous, incapable of getting angry with her, whatever she did. Just like her mother. They had been trying for a child for some years (she was now 38) and were shortly to embark on a second attempt at infertility treatment. Her circle of friends was very important to her and she obviously went to a great deal of trouble to care for them and seemed to be the one to whom everyone poured out their problems.

The impression I had after that first session was of someone who was warm and impulsive, cared passionately for other people, needed them to care for her; who loved the good things of life, but wanted to share them with others; worked hard, played hard and generally lived very intensely. She could not bear to be thwarted when she wanted something, whether it was for herself or someone she loved.

What for the moment seemed an anomaly was her behaviour over spending someone else's money and her apparent freedom from guilt about it. (She experienced shame at others knowing what she had done, rather than any dislodgement of her sense of self, as Kelly defines guilt.) Reflecting on this I realized that I personally had some very important constructs around taking something that was not mine, which I had to suspend in order to subsume her construing.

The possibility of there being some kind of transference of her feelings about her stepfather on to Alan naturally occurred to me. Also the likelihood of fragmentation as an explanation of her being at once caring of others and so careless of the effect on Alan. I wondered what part the stress of trying for a baby played in it all. But I needed to understand a great deal more about her construing before I attempted any coherent 'diagnosis'. We agreed on four sessions to clarify what was needed.

Exploring the problems

To elicit her general view of herself I asked her to write a self-characterization and she completed a rated grid. Both were enlightening. In the first she speaks of being 'devoted to family and friends'. She is 'quite controlling', 'impatient and impulsive and sometimes regrets decisions or actions that are taken when acting on impulse'. She 'does not find it easy to face up to her own problems and has trouble seeing that she has done anything wrong in her life'. She is clearly aware that something does not make sense.

This was borne out when, setting up the grid, she chose 'Me the Aberration' as one of her self-elements. It is as if her adult self is commenting on a separate, wayward self. She saw 'As I would like to be' as very closely related to her mother and her husband; and her stepfather and Alan were rated as very much alike.

Diagnosis

Her construing of people was quite tight – they were either 'goodies' or 'baddies'. Being unable to put herself in Alan's shoes or differentiate very much between him and her stepfather, she clearly lacked sociality, the ability to construe the construing of others. The splitting off of 'Me the Aberration' from the rest of her suggested awareness of an aspect of herself which was incompatible with herself as a whole. Kelly describes this phenomenon in his fragmentation corollary.

One area of threat that I felt it important to be aware of was the sudden realization of the implications of what she had done. She rated 'Me Now' on her grid as 'honest with self' and 'genuine' and 'Me the Aberration' as 'hiding from self' and 'false'. How could she accept responsibility for what had happened without plunging into intolerable guilt?

Goals of therapy

When Mandy first came I asked her what it was she wanted me to help her with. Then she said, 'Just to be in less of a state all the time.' But by now we were able to clarify a number of things. She was determined not to spend any more money in that way and felt that the shock of discovery had 'cured' her. She wanted her friends to remain important to her but not to be so reliant on having their 'constant positive feedback'. She needed to work out how to be towards Alan, and to be less of a burden to Jeremy and her mother. She was looking for quite major changes, many of them around the issue of dependency. She said she was happy to go on.

The therapy

Bearing in mind the need for her to relate the different aspects of herself without being unbearably threatened, I decided to use the ideas developed in Miller Mair's 'The community of self' (1977). Here the person is asked to look at themselves as if the different aspects of them were 'selves' which came to the fore in different situations. Mandy liked this idea and was able to delineate 'Mandy the friend', 'Mandy the daughter', 'Mandy the businesswoman' and so on. Her 'Me Now' was 'the grown-up', who was clearly someone who was able to reflect on the nature of 'Me the Aberration', a difficult child. There was also a child in her whom she liked: 'Mandy the fun person'. She acknowledged that too often the difficult child was in charge and set about establishing communication between her and the other selves. Mandy began by attacking this child but when we thought about how she might negotiate with a difficult child of her own in the future, she became more sympathetic. In this way she gradually took responsibility for her aberrant self and had more control over her.

This approach also helped with the problem of how to relate to Alan at work. For some time she found it unbearable and quite often was 'off sick'. But after a while she was able to set herself to be 'the businesswoman' and was better able to remain in professional mode, letting most of Alan's references to the money 'wash over her'. It also seemed important for her to construe him more as a whole, rather than as the source of her discomfort. She needed to develop more sociality with regard to him. I asked her to tell me about him in more detail and a complex picture emerged. Although he was 'the boss', a brilliant businessman and authoritarian, he needed the support of those who worked for him as he was in many ways unsure of himself. He had been on drugs at one time and Mandy suspected that this might have recurred. What did he want from her? 'Just to get on with things,' she thought. She acknowledged that it had not really occurred to her before that he was vulnerable.

She had been struck by the similarity between Alan and her stepfather and I asked her to elaborate on how she saw the latter, to see whether, here too, she could develop greater sociality. Her stepfather was really quite generous but it had been a shock to her as a child when he said 'no' to many of her demands and was critical of her. So unlike her mother. She had felt unloved by him but was not so sure now. He showed great concern over her distress about having a baby and had offered to pay for the infertility treatment. So she was able to loosen her construing of him.

She continually came back to her worries about what Jane, Alan's wife, thought about her and had been unable to meet her since she learned about the credit card. When I asked her why Jane was so important to her it emerged that she saw her in many ways as a mother-figure. She desperately wanted her good opinion, and to be rejected by her would be like being cast off by her mother, whom she had not dared to tell about the problem. I then asked her to try to put herself in Jane's shoes. What must it be like if Alan were taking drugs again? Wouldn't Jane be more concerned about this than Mandy's trouble? Why not focus on that now? Although she cancelled arrangements with Jane several times, she found when at last she met her for a drink that she *was* more worried about Alan than reproachful of her. And Mandy was able to take one remark about her own behaviour's 'not being much help' without running away.

By now Mandy felt 'more in control' and had begun to find ways of helping to pay back the money, rather than leave it to Jeremy. She had expressed a wish to be less dependent on him and her mother and was making a start, but it seemed to me that it would take a great deal of work and time to change in this core area. She was very soon to start the fertility treatment and decided to have a break before embarking on a new phase of therapy. She had managed to establish communication between different aspects of herself and to construe some other people more differentially, through the development of greater sociality. We had worked together for 10 months. During the last session she reflected on whether she would be 'a good mother' and realized that she would have to create yet another Self.

References

Bannister, D. (1962) 'The nature and measurement of schizophrenic thought disorder', *Journal of Mental Science*, 108: 825–42.

Fransella, F. (1972) *Personal Change and Reconstruction: Research on a Treatment of Stuttering*. London: Academic Press.

Fransella, F. (1981) 'Nature babbling to herself: the self characterization as a therapeutic tool', in H. Bonarius, R. Holland and S. Rosenberg (eds), *Personal Construct Psychology: Recent Advances in Theory and Practice*. London: Macmillan.

Fransella, F. (1984) 'What sort of scientist is the person-as-scientist?', in J.R. Adams-Webber and J.C. Mancuso (eds), *Applications of Personal Construct Theory*. Ontario: Academic Press.

Fransella, F. (1995) *George Kelly*. London: Sage.

Fransella, F. (2000) 'George Kelly and mathematics', in J.W. Scheer (ed.), *The Person in Society: Challenges to a Constructivist Theory*. Giessen: Psychosozial-Verlag.

Fransella, F. and Bannister, D. (1977) *A Manual for Repertory Grid Technique*. London: Academic Press.

Hinkle, D. (1965) 'The change of personal constructs from the viewpoint of a theory of construct implications'. Unpublished PhD thesis, Ohio State University.

Jackson, S. (1988) 'A self-characterization: development and deviance in adolescent construing', in P. Maitland and D. Brennan (eds), *Personal Construct Theory: Deviancy and Social Work*. London: Inner London Probation Service and Centre for Personal Construct Psychology.

Kelly, G.A. (1969) 'The psychotherapeutic relationship', in B. Maher, (ed.), *Clinical Psychology and Personality: The Selected Papers of George Kelly*. New York: Krieger.

Kelly, G.A. (1980) 'A psychology of optimal man', in A.W. Landfield and L.M. Leitner (eds), *Personal Construct Psychology: Psychotherapy and Personality*. New York: Wiley.

Kelly, G.A. (1991) *The Psychology of Personal Constructs* (1955), Vols I and II. London: Routledge.

Landfield, A.W. (1971) *Personal Construct Systems in Psychotherapy*. New York: Rand McNally.

Mair, J.M.M. (1977) 'The community of self', in D. Bannister (ed.), *New Perspectives in Personal Construct Theory*. London: Academic Press.

Moreno, J.L. (1964) *Psychodrama* Vol. I. New York: Beacon.

Mullins, N. (1973) *Theories and Theory Groups in Contemporary American Sociology*. New York: Harper & Row.

Neimeyer, R.A. (1985a) *The Development of Personal Construct Psychology*. Lincoln, NE: University of Nebraska Press.

Neimeyer, R.A. (1985b) 'Personal constructs in clinical practice', in P.C. Kendall (ed.), *Advances in Cognitive Behavioral Research and Therapy*. San Diego, CA: Academic Press

Neimeyer, R.A. (1988) 'Clinical Guidelines for conducting interpersonal transaction groups', *International Journal of Personal Construct Psychology*, I, 181–90.

Ravenette, A.T. (1999) 'Personal construct psychology in the practice of an educational psychologist', in *Personal Construct Theory in Educational Psychology: a Practitioner's View*. London: Whurr.

Tschudi, F. (1977) 'Loaded and honest questions', in D. Bannister (ed.), *New Perspectives in Personal Construct Theory*. London: Academic Press.

Winter, D. (1992) *Personal Construct Psychology in Clinical Practice: Theory, Research and Applications*. London: Routledge.

Suggested further reading

Button, E. (ed.) (1985) *Personal Construct Theory & Mental Health*. London: Croom Helm.

Dalton, P. and Dunnett, G. (1999) *A Psychology for Living*. Farnborough: EPCA Publications.

Dunnett, G (ed.) (1988) *Working with People: Clinical Uses of Personal Construct Psychology*. London: Routledge.

Fransella, F. (1995) *George Kelly*. London: Sage.

Fransella, F. and Dalton, P. (2000) *Personal Construct Counselling in Action*, 2nd edn. London: Sage.

8 Existential Therapy
Emmy van Deurzen

Historical context and development in Britain

Historical context

The existential approach is first and foremost philosophical. It is concerned with the understanding of people's position in the world and with the clarification of what it means to them to be alive. It is also committed to exploring these questions with a receptive attitude, rather than with a dogmatic one. The aim is to search for truth with an open mind and an attitude of wonder rather than to fit the client into pre-established frameworks of interpretation.

The historical background to this approach is that of 3,000 years of philosophy. Throughout the history of humankind people have tried to make sense of human existence in general and of their personal predicaments in particular. Much of the philosophical tradition is relevant and can help us to understand an individual's position in the world. The philosophers who are especially pertinent are those whose work is directly aimed at making sense of human existence. But the philosophical movements that are of most importance and that have been directly responsible for the generation of existential therapy are phenomenology and existential philosophy.

The starting point of existential philosophy (see Warnock, 1970; Macquarrie, 1972; Mace, 1999) can be traced back to the last century and the work of Kierkegaard and Nietzsche. Both were in conflict with the predominant ideologies of their time and committed to the exploration of reality as it can be experienced in a passionate and personal manner.

Kierkegaard (1813–55) protested vigorously against Christian dogma and the so-called 'objectivity' of science (Kierkegaard, 1941, 1944). He thought that both were ways of avoiding the anxiety inherent in human existence. He had great contempt for the way in which life was being lived by those around him and believed that truth could ultimately only be discovered subjectively by the individual in action. What was most lacking was people's courage to take the leap of faith and live with passion and commitment from the inward depth of existence. This involved a constant struggle between the finite and infinite aspects of our nature as part of the difficult task of creating a self and finding meaning. As Kierkegaard lived by his own word he was lonely and much ridiculed during his lifetime.

Nietzsche (1844–1900) took this philosophy of life a step further. His starting point was the notion that God was dead (Nietzsche, 1961, 1974, 1986) and that it is up to us to re-evaluate existence in light of this. He invited people to shake off the shackles of moral constraint and to discover their free will in order to soar to unknown heights and learn to live with new intensity. He encouraged people not to remain part of the herd, but to dare stand out. The important existential themes of freedom, choice, responsibility and courage are introduced for the first time.

Husserl (1859–1938). While Kierkegaard and Nietzsche drew attention to the human issues that needed to be addressed, Husserl's phenomenology (Husserl, 1960, 1962; Moran, 2000) provided the method to address them in a rigorous manner. He contended that natural sciences are based on the assumption that subject and object are separate and that this kind of dualism can only lead to error. He proposed a whole new mode of investigation and understanding of the world and our experience of it. Prejudice has to be put aside or 'bracketed', in order for us to meet the world afresh and discover what is absolutely fundamental and only directly available to us through intuition. If we want to grasp the essence of things, instead of explaining and analysing them we have to learn to describe and understand them.

Heidegger (1889–1976) applied the phenomenological method to understanding the meaning of being (Heidegger, 1962, 1968). He argued that poetry and deep philosophical thinking can bring greater insight into what it means to be in the world than can be achieved through scientific knowledge. He explored human being in the world in a manner that revolutionizes classical ideas about the self and psychology. He also favoured hermeneutics, an old philosophical method of investigation, which is the art of interpretation. Unlike interpretation as practised in psychoanalysis (which consists of referring a person's experience to a pre-established theoretical framework) this kind of interpretation seeks to understand how the person herself subjectively experiences something.

Sartre (1905–80) contributed many other strands of existential exploration, particularly in terms of emotions, imagination, and the person's insertion into a social and political world. He became the father of existentialism, which was a philosophical trend with a limited life span. The philosophy of existence on the contrary is carried by a wide-ranging literature, which includes many other authors than the ones mentioned above. There is much to be learned from existential authors such as Jaspers (1951, 1963), Tillich and Gadamer within the Germanic tradition and Camus, Marcel, Ricoeur, Merleau-Ponty and Levinas within the French tradition (see for instance Spiegelberg, 1972, Kearney, 1986 or van Deurzen-Smith, 1997). Few psychotherapists are aware of this literature, or interested in making use of it. Psychotherapy has traditionally grown within a medical rather than a philosophical milieu and to a large extent has yet to discover the possibility of a radical philosophical approach.

From the beginning of this century some psychotherapists were, however, inspired by phenomenology and its possibilities for working with people. Binswanger, in Switzerland, was the first to attempt to bring existential insights to his work with patients, in the Kreuzlingen sanatorium where he was a psychiatrist. Much of his work was translated into English during the 1940s and 1950s and, together with the immigration to the USA of Tillich (Tillich, 1952) and others, this had a considerable impact on the popularization of existential ideas as a basis for therapy (Valle and King, 1978). Rollo May played an important role in this, and his writing (1969, 1983; May et al., 1958) kept the existential influence alive in America, leading eventually to a specific formulation of therapy (May and Yalom, 1985; Yalom, 1980). Humanistic psychology was directly influenced by these ideas, but it invariably diluted and sometimes distorted their original meanings.

In Europe existential ideas were combined with some psychoanalytic principles and a method of existential analysis was developed by Boss (1957a, 1957b, 1979) in close co-operation with Heidegger. In Austria Frankl developed an existential therapy called logotherapy (Frankl, 1964, 1967), which focused particularly on finding meaning. In France the ideas of Sartre (1956, 1962) and Merleau-Ponty (1962) and of a number of practitioners (Minkowski, 1970) were important and influential but no specific therapeutic method was developed from them.

Development in Britain

Britain became a fertile ground for the further development of the existential approach when Laing and Cooper took Sartre's existential ideas as the basis for their work (Laing, 1960, 1961; Cooper, 1967; Laing and Cooper, 1964). Without developing a concrete method of therapy they critically reconsidered the notion of mental illness and its treatment. In the late 1960s they established an experimental therapeutic community at Kingsley Hall in the East End of London, where people could come to live through their madness without the usual medical treatment. They also founded the Philadelphia Association, an organization providing alternative living, therapy and therapeutic training from this perspective. The Philadelphia Association is still in existence today and is now committed to the exploration of the works of philosophers such as Wittgenstein, Derrida, Levinas and Foucault as well as the work of the French psychoanalyst Lacan. It also runs a number of small therapeutic households along these lines. The Arbours Association is another group that grew out of the Kingsley Hall experiment. Founded by Berke and Schatzman in the 1970s, it now runs a training programme in psychotherapy, a crisis centre and several therapeutic communities. The existential input in the Arbours has gradually been replaced with a more neo-Kleinian emphasis.

The impetus for further development of the existential approach in Britain has largely come from the development of a number of existentially based courses in academic institutions. This started with the programmes created by van Deurzen, initially at Antioch University in London and subsequently at Regent's College, London and since then at the New School of Psychotherapy and Counselling, also in London. The latter is a purely existentially based training institute, which offers postgraduate degrees validated by the University of Sheffield. In the last decades the existential approach has spread rapidly and has become a welcome alternative to established methods. There are now a number of other, mostly academic, centres in Britain that provide training in existential counselling and psychotherapy and a rapidly growing interest in the approach in the voluntary sector and in the National Health Service.

British publications dealing with existential therapy include contributions by Jenner (de Koning and Jenner, 1982), Heaton (1988, 1994), Cohn (1994, 1997), Spinelli (1997), Cooper (1989), Eleftheriadou (1994), Lemma-Wright (1994), Du Plock (1997), Strasser and Strasser (1997) and van Deurzen-Smith (1997, 1998, 2002). Other writers such as Lomas (1981) and Smail (1978, 1987, 1993) have published work relevant to the approach although not explicitly 'existential' in orientation. The journal of the British Society for Phenomenology regularly publishes work on existential and phenomenological psychotherapy. An important development was that of the founding of the Society for Existential Analysis in 1988, initiated by van Deurzen. This society brings together psychotherapists, psychologists, psychiatrists, counsellors and philosophers working from an existential perspective. It offers regular fora for discussion and debate as well as major annual conferences. It publishes the *Journal of the Society for Existential Analysis* twice a year. It is also a member of the International Federation for Daseinsanalysis, which stimulates international exchange between representatives of the approach from around the world.

Theoretical assumptions

Image of the person

The existential approach considers human nature to be open-minded, flexible and capable of an enormous range of experience. The person is in a constant process of becoming. I create myself as I exist and have to reinvent myself daily. There is no essential self, as I define my personality and abilities in action and in relation to my environment. This impermanence and uncertainty give rise to a deep sense of anxiety (Angst), in response to the realization of one's insignificance, and simultaneous responsibility to have to create something in place of the emptiness we often experience. Everything passes and nothing lasts. We are never able to hold on to the present. We are always no longer or not yet what we would like to be. We find ourselves somewhere in the middle of the passing of time, grappling with the givens of the past and the possibilities of the future, without any sure knowledge of what it all means.

Existential thinkers seek to avoid restrictive models that categorize or label people. Instead they look for the universals that can be observed cross-culturally. There is no existential personality theory which divides humanity into types or reduces people to part components. Instead there is a description of the different levels of experience and existence with which people are inevitably confronted.

The way in which a person is in the world at a particular stage can be charted on this general map of human existence (Binswanger, 1963; Yalom, 1980; van Deurzen-Smith, 1984). One can distinguish four basic dimensions of human existence: the physical, the social, the psychological and the spiritual. On each of these dimensions people encounter the world and shape their attitude out of their particular take on their experience. Our orientation towards the world defines our reality. The four dimensions are obviously interwoven and provide a complex four-dimensional force field for our existence. We are stretched between a positive pole of what we aspire to on each dimension and a negative pole of what we fear.

Physical dimension

On the physical dimension (*Umwelt*) we relate to our environment and to the givens of the natural world around us. This includes our attitude to the body we have, to the concrete surroundings we find ourselves in, to the climate and the weather, to objects and material possessions, to the bodies of other people, our own bodily needs, to health and illness and to our own mortality. The struggle on this dimension is, in general terms, between the search for domination over the elements and natural law (as in technology, or in sports) and the need to accept the limitations of natural boundaries (as in ecology or old age). While people generally aim for security on this dimension (through health and wealth), much of life brings a gradual disillusionment and realization that such security can only be temporary. Recognizing limitations can bring great release of tension.

Social dimension

On the social dimension (*Mitwelt*) we relate to others as we interact with the public world around us. This dimension includes our response to the culture we live in, as well as to the class and race we belong to (and also those we do not belong to). Attitudes here range from love to hate and from co-operation to competition. The dynamic contradictions can be understood in terms of acceptance versus rejection or belonging versus isolation. Some people prefer to withdraw from the world of others as much as possible. Others blindly chase public acceptance by going along with the rules and fashions of the moment. Otherwise they try to rise above these by becoming trendsetters themselves. By acquiring fame or other forms of power, we can attain dominance over others temporarily. Sooner or later we are, however, all confronted with both failure and aloneness.

Psychological dimension

On the psychological dimension (*Eigenwelt*) we relate to ourselves and in this way create a personal world. This dimension includes views about our character, our past experience and our future possibilities. Contradictions here are often experienced in terms of personal strengths and weaknesses. People search for a sense of identity, a feeling of being substantial and having a self. But inevitably many events will confront us with evidence to the contrary and plunge us into a state of confusion or disintegration. Activity and passivity are an important polarity here. Self-affirmation and resolution go with the former and surrender and yielding with the latter. Facing the final dissolution of self that comes with loss and the facing of death might bring anxiety and confusion to many who have not yet given up their sense of self-importance.

Spiritual dimension

On the spiritual dimension (*Überwelt*) (van Deurzen-Smith, 1984) we relate to the unknown and thus create a sense of an ideal world, an ideology and a philosophical outlook. It is here that we find meaning by putting all the pieces of the puzzle together for ourselves. For some people this is done by adhering to the dogma of a religion or some other prescriptive world view, for others it is about discovering or attributing meaning in a more secular or personal way. The contradictions that have to be faced on this dimension are often related to the tension between purpose and absurdity, hope and despair. People create their values in search of something that matters enough to live or die for, something that may even have ultimate and universal validity. Usually the aim is the conquest of a soul, or something that will substantially surpass human mortality (as for instance in having contributed something valuable to humankind). Facing the void and the possibility of nothingness are the indispensable counterparts of this quest for the eternal.

Conceptualization of psychological disturbance and health

Disturbance and health are two sides of the same coin. Living creatively means welcoming both. Well-being coincides with the ability to be transparent and open to what life can bring: both good and bad. In trying to evade the negative side of existence we get stuck as surely as we do when we cannot see the positive side. It is only in facing both positive and negative poles of existence that we generate the necessary power to move ahead. Thus well-being is not the naive enjoyment of a state of total balance given to one by Mother Nature and perfect parents. It can only be negotiated gradually by coming to terms with life, the world and oneself. It doesn't require a clean record of childhood experience, or a total devotion to the cult of body and mind. It simply requires openness to being and to increasing understanding of what the business of living is all about. From an existential perspective psychological well-being is seen to be synonymous with wisdom. This results from being equal to the task of life when it is faced honestly and squarely. Psychological disturbance is seen as a consequence of either avoidance of truth or an inability to cope with it. Discontent is generated for many people through self-deception in a blind following of popular opinions, habits, beliefs, rules and reasons. Others are at a loss to make sense of the paradoxes of life that they are forcefully confronted with and that overwhelm them.

To be authentic is to be true to oneself and one's innermost possibilities and limitations. Finding one's own authority and learning to create an increasingly comfortable space inside and around oneself, no matter what the circumstances, is a considerable challenge. As the self is defined by its vital links to the world around it, being true to oneself has to be understood as being true to life. This is not about setting one's own rules or living without regard for others. It is about recognizing the necessities, givens and limitations of the human condition as much as about affirming freedom and insisting on one's basic rights. Many people avoid authentic living, because it is terrifying to face the reality of the constant challenges, failures, crises and doubts that existence exposes us to. Living authentically begins with the recognition of one's personal vulnerability and mortality and with the acknowledgement of the ultimate uncertainty of all that is known. It is superficially far more rewarding to play at being certain, role-defined and self-important. Even the self-image of sickness or madness can seem more attractive than having to struggle with yourself and face your vulnerability in an uncertain world.

Ultimately it is the essential human longing for truth that redeems. We are reminded of truth by the pangs of conscience, which may expose our evasion of reality. A sense of courage and possibility can be found by stopping the dialogue with the internal voices of other people's laws and expectations. In the quietude of being with myself I can sense where truth lies and where lies have obscured the truth. The call of conscience reaches me through a feeling of guilt, that is, existential guilt, which tells me that something is lacking, something is being owed to life by me: I am in debt to myself.

The call of conscience comes through an attitude of openness to possibilities and limitations. This openness leads to Angst as it exposes me to my responsibilities and possible failure, but when I accept this anxiety it becomes the source of energy that allows me to be ready for whatever the future holds in store. And so, in facing the worst, I prepare myself for the best. I can live resolutely only when I can also surrender and release myself. I can be free only when I know what is necessary. I can be fully alive only when I face up to the possibility of my death.

Acquisition of psychological disturbance

When well-being is defined as the ability to face up to the disturbing facts of life, the notion of disturbance takes on a whole new meaning. Problems and obstacles are not necessarily an impediment to living well, for any potentially distressing situation can be seen as a challenge that can be faced. Problems are first of all problems in living and will occur at any stage in human development. In fact the only thing you can be sure of is that life will inevitably confront you with new situations that are a challenge to your established ways and evasions of the human paradox. When people are shocked out of their ordinary routine into a sudden awareness of their inability to face the realities of living, the clouds start to gather. Even though we may think of ourselves as well-adjusted people who have had a moderately acceptable upbringing, unexpected events, such as the death of a loved one, the loss of a job or another significant sudden exposure of our vulnerability, may still trigger a sense of failure, despair or extreme anxiety. Everything around us suddenly seems absurd or impossible and our own and other people's motives are questioned. The value of what used to be taken for granted becomes uncertain and life loses its appeal. The basic vulnerability of being human has emerged from behind the well-guarded self-deception of social adaptation. Sometimes a similar disenchantment and profound disturbance arise not out of an external catastrophe but out of a sense of the futility of everyday routines. Boredom can be just as important a factor in generating disturbance as losses or other forms of crisis.

No matter how securely a person is established in the world some events will shake the foundations of that security and transform the appearance of existence. For some people, however, such false security is not at first available. They never achieve 'ontological security' (Laing, 1960), which consists of having a firm sense of one's own and other people's reality and identity. Genetic predisposition obviously makes some of us capable of greater sensory awareness and psychological susceptibility than others. People who have such extraordinary sensitivity may easily get caught up in the conflicts that others are trying to avoid. If they are exposed to particularly intense contradictions (as in certain family conflicts) they may fall into a state of extreme confusion and despair and withdraw into the relative security of a world of their own creation. Both the ontologically secure person who is disturbed by a crisis (or boredom) and the ontologically insecure person who is overwhelmed by the less pleasant sides of ordinary human existence are struggling with an absence of the usual protective armour of self-deception. Life is suddenly seen in all its harshness and paradoxical reality. Without the redeeming factor of some of the more positive aspects of life such realism can be distressing.

This does not mean that this kind of crisis or generation of anxiety should be avoided. It can be faced and integrated by making sense of it. The existential view of disturbance is that it is an inevitable and even welcome event that everyone will sooner or later encounter. The question is not how to avoid it but on the contrary how to approach it with determination and curiosity.

Perpetuation of psychological disturbance

Problems start to become more serious when the challenge of disturbance is not faced but evaded. Then a self-perpetuating negative spiralling downward can happen which leads to confusion and chaos. This is most likely to occur if we are not linked to a vital support system. As long as our family or other intimate networks of reference are strong and open enough to absorb the contradictions in which we get caught up, distress can be eased and overcome: the balance can be redressed. But if we find ourselves in isolation, without the understanding and challenge of a relative, a partner or a close friend, it is easy to get lost in our problems. Society's rituals for safeguarding the individual are these days less and less powerful and secure. Few people gain a sense of ultimate meaning or direction from their relationship to God or from other essential beliefs. Many feel at the mercy of temporary, ever-changing but incessant demands, needs and desires. In time of distress there seems all too often to be nowhere to turn. Relatives and friends, who themselves are barely holding their heads above water, may be unavailable. If they are available, they may want to soothe distress instead of tackling it at the root. Spiritual authority has gradually been eroded and has been replaced with scientific authority, which is unable to address moral or spiritual dilemmas. It is hardly surprising that people turn increasingly to psycho-therapists or counsellors. Unfortunately, there is little evidence that psychotherapy and counselling are able to lessen distress. To some extent a reliance on therapeutic cure may present another perpetuation of disturbance, as long as the basic existential issues are not dealt with and the client is kept in a passive role.

Paradoxically, the institutions in our society often seem to encourage the very opposite of what they are supposed to be about. When the family becomes a place of loneliness and alienation instead of one that fosters togetherness and intimacy, when schools become places of boredom and reluctance instead of inspiring curiosity and learning and when doctors' surgeries become places of dependence and addiction instead of centres of healing and renewal of strength, it is time for essentials to be reconsidered. Much disturbance is not only generated but also maintained by a society that is out of touch with the essential principles of life. Often it is in the distress of those who face a crisis that the disturbance of society is expressed. It is therefore hardly surprising that we are inclined to want to obliterate this reminder of failings at the heart of our own existence. If we are willing to attend to the message of such distress we give ourselves a chance to be reminded of the ways in which we perpetuate our own misunderstanding and avoidance of life.

Change

Life is one long process of change and transformation. Although people often think they want to change, more often than not their lives reflect their attempts at maintaining the status quo. As a person becomes convinced of the inevitability of change she may also become aware of the many ways in which she has kept such change at bay. Almost every minute of the day people make small choices that together determine the direction of their life. Often that direction is embarked upon passively: people just conform to their own negative or mediocre predictions of the future. But once insight is gained into the possibility of reinterpreting a situation and opting for more constructive predictions a change for the better may come about. This requires the person to learn to live deliberately instead of by default, and it can only be achieved by first becoming aware of how one's daily attitude and frame of mind is set to a form of automatic functioning that keeps one repeating the same mistakes.

It is not easy to break the force of habit, but there are always times when habits are broken by force. Crises are times when old patterns have to be revised and when changes for the better can be initiated. This is why existential therapists talk about a breakdown as a possible breakthrough and why people often note with astonishment that the disaster they tried so hard to avoid was a blessing in disguise. In times of crisis the attention is refocused on where priorities lie so that choices can be made with more understanding than previously.

Whether such an event is self-imposed (as in emigration or marriage) or not (as in natural disasters or bereavement) it has the effect of removing previously taken for granted securities. When this happens it becomes more difficult for us to obscure the aspects of existence that we would rather not think about, and we are compelled to reassess our own attitudes and values. In the ensuing chaos we must make choices about how to proceed and how to bring new order into our lives. If we can tolerate the uncertainty of such situations instead of fleeing towards a new routine, such times can be an opportunity for rectifying life's direction.

Once a crisis has been faced in such a constructive manner it becomes easier to be open to change at other times as well. People can learn to re-evaluate their values and reassess their priorities continually, thus achieving a flexibility and vitality that allows them to make the most of life's naturally transformative character. Many people dread change and hide from it but they have to face it at a time of crisis. Existential therapy can be particularly helpful in those circumstances.

Practice

Goals of therapy

The goals of existential therapy are to enable people to:

- successfully negotiate and come to terms with past, present and future crises;
- become more truthful with themselves;
- widen their perspective on themselves and the world around them;
- find clarity on what their purpose in life is and how they can learn from the past to create something valuable and meaningful to live for;
- understand themselves and others better and find ways of effectively communicating with others.

The word 'authenticity' is often used to indicate the goal of becoming true to oneself and therefore more real. This is a much-abused term, which misleadingly suggests that there is a true self; whereas the existential view is that self is relationship and process – not an entity or substance. Authenticity can also become an excuse for people who want to have their cake and eat it. Under the aegis of authenticity anything can be licensed: crude egoism may very well be the consequence. In fact, authenticity can never be fully achieved. It is a gradual process of self-understanding, but of the self as it is created in one's relationships to the world on all levels. Helping people to become authentic therefore means assisting them in gaining a greater understanding of the human condition, so that they can respond to it with a sense of mastery, instead of being at its mercy. To be authentic means to face one's human limitations and possibilities.

The task of the therapist is to have attained sufficient clarity and openness to be able to venture along with any client into murky waters and explore (without getting lost) how this person's experience fits into a wider map of existence. Clients are guided through the disturbances in which they are caught and are helped to examine their assumptions, values and aspirations, so that a new direction can be taken. The therapist is fully available to this exploration and will often be changed in the process. The poignancy of each new adventure over the dangerous ground of life requires the therapist to become aware of previously unrecognized aspects of life. Therapy is a journey that client and therapist embark upon together. Both will be transformed, as they let themselves be touched by life.

Selection criteria

Clients who come specifically for existential therapy usually already have the idea that their problems are about living, and are not a form of pathology. This basic assumption must be acceptable to clients if they are to benefit from the approach. A genuine commitment to an intense and very personal philosophical investigation is therefore a requirement. A critical mind and a desire to think for oneself are an advantage. People who want another's opinion on what ails them and who would prefer symptom relief to a search for meaning might be better referred to other forms of therapy.

The approach is especially suitable for people who feel alienated from the expectations of society or for those seeking to clarify their personal ideology. The approach is relevant to people living in a foreign culture, class or race, as it does not dictate a specific way of looking at reality. It also works well with people confronting adversity in their lives or who are trying to cope with changes of personal circumstances (or want to bring those about). Bereavement, job loss or biological changes (in adolescence, middle age or old age) are a prime time for the reconsideration of the rules and values one has hitherto lived by. Generally speaking the existential approach is more helpful to those who question the state of affairs in the world, than to those who prefer the status quo. This approach seems to be most right for those at the edge of existence: people who are dying or contemplating suicide, people who are just starting on a new phase of life, people in crisis, or people who feel they no longer belong in their surroundings. It is less relevant for people who do not want to examine their assumptions and who would rather not explore the foundation of human existence.

Even though existential work consists in gaining understanding through talking, the client's level of verbal ability is not important. Very young children or people who speak a foreign language will often find that the simpler their way of expressing things, the easier it becomes to grasp the essence of their world view and experience. The approach is not about intellectualizing, but about verbalizing the basic impressions, ideas, intuitions and feelings a person has about life.

The existential approach can be applied in many different settings: individual, couple, family or group. When it involves more than one person at a time, the emphasis will be on clarifying the participants' perceptions of the world and their place in it, in order to encourage communication and mutual understanding. The focus is always on the individual's experiences and relationships. A dimension of existential exploration can easily be added to almost any other approach to psychotherapy, but it will soon be found that this makes a re-evaluation of one's method necessary. Many of the more directive and manipulative forms of therapy are in flagrant contradiction of existential principles. Interpretative methods such as psychoanalysis or analytical psychology betray the existential rule of openness to the different meanings that emerge for individuals. In the final analysis existential work requires a commitment to a philosophical investigation, which necessitates its own guidelines and parameters.

Qualities of effective therapists

Good existential therapists combine personal qualities with accomplishment in method, but on balance it is more important that they have strength of character as people than that they have a high level of skill. Qualities can be described as falling into four categories: (a) life experience, (b) attitude and personality, (c) theoretical knowledge, (d) professional training.

Life experience

The existential therapist will be psychologically and emotionally mature as a human being. This maturity will manifest itself in an ability to make room in oneself for all sorts of, even contradictory, opinions, attitudes, feelings, thoughts and experiences. They will be open-minded about the many different facets of human living. Rather than clinging to one point of view, existential therapists will be capable of overseeing reality from a wide range of perspectives. They will also be able to tolerate the tension that such awareness of contradictions generates. There are a number of life experiences that appear to be particularly helpful in preparing people for such maturation and broad-mindedness. Cross-cultural experience is an excellent way to stretch the mind and one's views on what it means to be human. People who have permanently had to adjust their whole way of perceiving and dealing with the world (especially when this includes a change of language) have had the all-important experience of questioning previous assumptions and opening up to a new culture and perspective.

Raising a family, or caring for dependants in a close relationship, is another invaluable source of life experience relevant to creating an open attitude. Many women have great practical experience in this area. Their life experience can become one of the building blocks of the kind of maturity needed to become an existential therapist.

The experience of having been immersed in society from several angles, in different jobs, different academic studies, different social classes and so on, is a definite advantage. The existential therapist is likely to be someone who has lived seriously and intensely in a number of ways and not just through the caring professions. People opting for psychotherapy as a second career are often especially suitable. Finally, the *sine qua non* of becoming an existential therapist is to have negotiated a number of significant crossroads in one's personal life. Existential therapists will have had their share of existential crises. Of course they will also have had to develop their ability to deal with these satisfactorily, so that their own lives were enriched rather than impoverished by the experience. Although all this maturity conjures up the image of someone advanced in age, it must be noted that maturity is not always commensurate with years. Some young people may have weathered greater storms than their elders and, what is more, may have lived their relatively shorter lives with greater intensity, maturing into fuller human beings.

Attitude and personality

Existential therapists should be capable of critical consideration of situations, people and ideas. They are serious, but not heavy-handed, downtrodden or cynical. They can be light-hearted, hopeful and humorous about the human condition, whilst intensely aware of the tragic poignancy of much of existence. They should be capable of self-reflection, recognizing the manner in which they themselves represent the paradoxes, ups and downs, strengths and weaknesses that people are capable of. They should have a genuine sense of curiosity and a strong urge to find out what it means to be human. They should be capable of sustaining an attitude of wonder. Existential therapists will now and then abandon psychological theory altogether and reach for poetry, art or religion instead. They will tend to be quite personal in their way of working. Before anything else they must demonstrate their ability to tolerate experiences of anxiety and despair without faltering and without succumbing.

Theoretical knowledge

A basic working knowledge of philosophy, that is of the controversies and perspectives that the human race has produced over the centuries, is more useful to this approach than any other kind of knowledge. Included in this would be a familiarity with the history of psychology and psychoanalysis and a wide study of the many different approaches to psychotherapy that have been developed over the years. This will provide a map of different views on human nature, health and illness, happiness and unhappiness, which again will train and broaden the mind and personal outlook of the therapist. In addition a practical knowledge of human interaction and the dynamics of the therapeutic relationship is essential.

Professional training

The existential therapist needs the kind of training that an eclectic therapist needs: a generic one. But instead of borrowing bits and pieces of technique from each to produce a complex amalgam, essentials are distilled and applied within a consistent philosophical framework. Specific skills of dialectical interaction can then be developed. Training should consist of a significant amount of therapeutic work under supervision and of self-reflection and analysis. Here again it is the quality that will be judged instead of the quantity. Numbers of hours of individual and group therapy are irrelevant. Some people will not reach the necessary perspective and depth with any amount of therapy. Others will be well ahead by having engaged in a discipline of self-reflection for years. The degree of readiness usually becomes obvious in supervision sessions, for one's response to other people's troubles is an excellent test of one's own attitude to life and level of self-knowledge. Existential training will enable therapists to think creatively about complex human dilemmas.

Therapeutic relationship and style

It is important for the existential therapist to have a flexible attitude towards therapeutic style. Not only do different therapists interpret the approach in diverse ways, but clients also have their own individual requirements, which may vary over time. The existential therapist is ready and willing to shift her stance when the situation requires this. In a sense this variability is characteristic of the existential therapeutic style.

There are, of course, common features running through all of this. All existential therapists, for example, strive to recognize and question their pre-conceptions and prejudices as much as possible in their work. There is also a consistent appreciation of the unique situation of the client. The existential therapist strives to take the dilemmas of the client seriously – eschewing recourse to diagnoses and solutions. This seriousness includes openness and wonder as essential attributes of the existential attitude and does not preclude humour when appropriate.

Existential therapists are fundamentally concerned with what matters most to the client. He or she avoids making normative judgements, and renounces any ambition to, even implicitly, push the client in any particular direction. The attitude is non-directive, but not directionless. The client is assisted in finding his or her own perspective and position in the world in relation to the parameters and limits of human existence. At times the therapist might facilitate the client's investigations through an attitude of relative passivity and silent intervention. At other times active dialogue and debate are required. On such occasions the therapist intervenes to point out contradictions in or implications of the client's avowed point of view. The use of confrontation to offer opinions or moral evaluations of the client is not consistent with the existential attitude.

The existential therapist resists the temptation to try and change the client. The therapy is an opportunity for the client to take stock of her life and ways of being in the world. Nothing is gained from interfering with these. The client is simply given the space, time and understanding to help her come to terms with what is true for her. What she wants to do with this afterwards is up to her. The therapist does not teach or preach about how life should be lived, but lets the client's personal taste in the art of living evolve naturally within the context of existential and social constructions.

The only times when the therapist does follow a didactic line is when she reminds the client of aspects of a problem that have been overlooked. She gently encourages the client to notice a lack of perspective, think through consequences and struggle with contradictions. She puts forward missing links and underlying principles. The therapist never does the work for the client but makes sure that the work gets done. The client's inevitable attempts to shirk and flee from the task in hand are reflected on and used as concrete evidence of the client's attitude to life. The same can be said of the actual encounter between the client and the therapist, which is also reflected on and seen as evidence of the client's usual ways of relating.

Generally speaking the therapeutic style follows a conversational pattern. Issues are considered and explored in dialogue. The rhythm of the sessions will follow that of the client's preoccupations – faster when emotions are expressed and slower when complex ideas are disentangled. Existential therapists need to learn to allow clients to take the amount of space and time in this conversation that they need in order to proceed at their own pace. Existential therapists create sufficient room for the client to feel that it is possible to unfold their troubles.

Existential sessions are usually quite intense, since deep and significant issues often emerge. Moreover, the therapist is personally engaged with the work and is willing to be touched and moved by the client's conflicts and questions. The human dilemmas expressed in the therapeutic encounter have as much relevance to the therapist as to the client. This commonality of experience makes it possible for client and therapist to work together as a team, in a co-operative effort to throw light on human existence. Every new challenge in the client's experience is grist for the mill. The therapeutic relationship itself brings many opportunities to grasp something of the nature of human interaction. The therapist, in principle, is ready to consider any past, present or future matter that is relevant to the client. The therapist is constantly aware of her own bias in approaching the client's difficulties and aims to recognize it sufficiently for it not to interfere with the work on the client's bias.

Major therapeutic strategies and techniques

The existential approach is well known for its anti-technique orientation. It prefers description, understanding and exploration of reality to diagnosis, treatment and prognosis. Existential therapists will not generally use particular techniques, strategies or skills, but they will follow a specific philosophical method of enquiry, which requires a consistent professional attitude. This method and attitude may be interpreted in various ways, but it usually includes some or all of the following ingredients.

Cultivating a naive attitude

By consistently meeting the client with an open mind and in the spirit of exploration and discovery a fresh perspective on the world will emerge. This requires a great deal of intellectual discipline on the part of the therapist, who continuously has to observe and question her own prejudice and bias.

Themes: clear themes will run through the apparently confused discourse of the client. The therapist listens for the unspoken links that are implicit in what is said. When the theme is obvious and has been confirmed several times, the client's attention can be drawn to it. Personal myths and stories are recognized and beliefs and fantasies about the world unveiled. Existential work enables people to create more satisfactory life narratives.

Assumptions: much of what the client says will be based on a number of basic assumptions about the world. Generally people are unaware of these. Clarifying implicit assumptions can be very revealing and may throw new light on a dilemma. Every statement we make reveals our assumptions, and therapists need to make sure these become explicit.

Vicious circles: many people are caught up in self-fulfilling prophecies of doom and destruction without realizing that they set their own low standards and goals. Making such vicious circles explicit can be a crucial step forward. Self-fulfilling prophecies can become positive instead of negative.

Meaning: often people assume that they know what they mean when they talk about something. But the words they use can hide, even from themselves, the significance of what they mean. By questioning the superficial meaning of the client's words and asking her to think again of what she wants to express, a new awareness may be brought about.

Values: people live their lives by standards and principles that establish values which they often take for granted and of which they are only dimly aware. Getting clarity about what makes life worth living and which aspects of life are most important and deserve making sacrifices for is a key step towards finding one's sense of direction and purpose.

Facing limitations

As the existential approach is essentially concerned with the need to face the limitations of the human condition, the therapist will be alert for opportunities to help the client identify these. This means facing up to ultimate concerns, such as death, guilt, freedom, isolation, meaninglessness, etc.

Self-deception: much of the time we pretend that life has determined our situation and character so much that we have no choices left. Crises may provide us with proof to the contrary. The safe crisis of the therapeutic interaction is a suitable place for rediscovering opportunities and challenges that had been forgotten.

Existential anxiety: the anxiety that indicates one's awareness of inevitable limitations and death is also a dizziness in the face of freedom and a summoning of life energy. Existential anxiety is the *sine qua non* of individual awareness and full aliveness. Some people have dulled their sensitivity so as to avoid the basic challenges of life, others are overwhelmed by them and yet others have found ways of disguising them. Optimal use of anxiety is one of the goals of existential work. The therapist will recognize the client's existential anxiety and will assist in finding ways of living with it constructively.

Existential guilt: the sense of being in debt to life and owing it to oneself to do or not do something is another source of insight into one's limitations and priorities. Therapists watch for existential guilt hidden in various disguises (such as anxiety, boredom, depression or even apparent self-confidence).

Consequences: clients are sometimes challenged to think through the consequences of choices, both past and future. In facing the implications of one's actions it becomes necessary to recognize limitations as well as possibilities. Some choices become easier to make; others become less attractive. Existential therapy does not condone the clients' tendency to want only support and acceptance and wallow in a sense of their own suffering; it encourages clients to confront their own responsibilities in relation to the world, other people and themselves.

Paradoxes: in helping the client to become more authentic the concept of paradox can be of great help. If clients are inclined to evade the basic human dilemma of life and death and contradictions that flow from it, their self-affirmation may look more like egocentricity. Checking that a person is aware of her capacity for both life and death, success and failure, freedom and necessity, certainty and doubts, allows one to remain in touch with a fundamental search for truth.

Exploring personal world view

The existential approach is open to all of life's dimensions, tasks and problems, and the therapist will in principle explore together with the client all information that the latter brings along. It is essential to follow the client's lead and understand her particular take on the world.

The fourfold world: using the model of four dimensions of existence discussed earlier it becomes possible to listen to the client's account of herself as revealing her preoccupations with particular levels of her existence. A systematic analysis of how the client expresses her relationship to the physical, social, psychological and spiritual dimensions of her world can provide much insight into imbalance, priorities and impasses. An impression can be formed of where on the whole territory of human existence the client is struggling for clarity. Intuitions, feelings, thoughts, sensations, dreams and fantasies are all grist for the mill

Dreams: listening to dreams with this model in mind can be extremely enlightening. The dream is seen as a message of the dreamer to herself. The dream experience reflects the dreamer's attitudes on the various dimensions of existence and the client's dream existence and world relations in it are considered as concrete as those of waking life.

Of course the same applies to the fantasies or stories that the client reports. Each of these is a miniature picture of the way in which she relates to the world and much can be learned from examining them carefully.

Questioning: exploring the client's world view is an ongoing enterprise and it is best done with an observation-orientated attitude. Questions are often asked in order to check whether a certain event or situation is seen in a particular light. Existential therapists will often make observations and inferences and elicit further material that will either confirm or disconfirm hypotheses. The therapist draws the client's attention to what seems to be the case. Sometimes an enquiry might be made in order to clarify a perception, along the lines of an exploration: 'What makes this so important to you?', or 'What is this like for you?', or 'What does it mean to you?' The question never suggests a solution or judges right or wrong, but investigates the client's personal opinion and inclination. Initial explanations will almost always be questioned and explored in greater depth.

Enquiring into meaning

All investigations eventually lead to a greater understanding of what makes the world meaningful to the client. The idea is to assist the client in finding purpose and motivation, direction and vitality. In the process a number of irrelevant and misleading motivations may be encountered and eliminated. Quite often new interpretations of past or present events are arrived at, altering the client's orientation to life and the future.

Emotions: feelings are of great help in this process. Understanding the meaning of one's emotions and moods and the message they contain in terms of what one aspires to or is afraid to lose is of crucial help in finding the pattern of purpose currently at work. Each emotion has its own significance (van Deurzen, 2002) and the whole range of the emotional spectrum can be used as a compass in indicating one's direction in life. Emotions like shame, envy and hope are indicators of values that are still missing but implicitly longed for. Love, joy and pride are within the range of emotions that indicate a sense of ownership of what is valued. Whereas jealousy and anger express an active response to the threat that what is valued may be lost, fear and sorrow come with the giving up and eventual loss of what really mattered.

Beliefs: all observations on the client's preoccupations lead to a picture of her opinions, beliefs and values. It is important to extract these respectfully. Nothing can be gained from opposing the client's values with an alternative set of values. It is the client's conscience that has to be uncovered and revitalized. If deeply held values are contested or criticized conformity will be encouraged rather than reliance on an inner sense of purpose. Light is thrown on the ways in which personal beliefs may fail to take into account wider implications for others. This will expand the system of beliefs into something that can encompass the facts of life and a broader frame of reference.

Talents: many talents, abilities and assets will have been hidden by the client's preoccupation with what is wrong with her. The therapist will attend to these and strive to draw attention to the wisdom and strength that are lying fallow. Often it is useful for the therapist to build on the example of the client's abilities as they come to the fore and use them as the point of reference for further understanding.

Recollection: memories will be seen as malleable and open to new interpretation. While clients often set out with fixed views of their past they discover the possibility of reconsidering the same events and experiences in different ways. It is essential to encourage clients to discover how they influence their future with their own version of the past and how it is within their power to re-collect themselves in new ways, thereby opening new vistas. When the client realizes that she is the ultimate source of the meaning of her life, past, present and future, living is experienced as an art rather than a duty.

The change process in therapy

The aim of existential therapy is not to change people but to help them to come to terms with the transformative process of life. The assumption is that when people do face reality they are likely to find a satisfactory way forward. People are often hurried and under the impression that they can speed life up and force great rewards out of it with relatively little effort. One of the aims of existential therapy is to enable people to stop deceiving themselves about both their lack of responsibility for what is happening to them and their excessive demands on life and themselves. Learning to measure one's distress by the standards of the human condition relieves pressure and at the same time provides a clearer ideological basis for making sense of personal preoccupations and aspirations. Clients change through existential therapy by gradually taking more and more of life's ups and downs in their stride. They can become more steadfast in facing death, crises, personal shortcomings, losses and failures if they accept the reality of constant transformation that we are all part of. They can find ways of tuning into these changes, instead of fighting them or trying to speed them up.

In other words they can acquire a measure of wisdom in learning to distinguish between the things they can change and those they cannot change. They can come to terms with the givens and find the courage to tackle the uncertainties. They can find out what matters enough to them to be committed to it, live for it and ultimately perhaps even die for it.

As they are constantly reminded to do their own thinking on these issues, people can learn to monitor their own actions, attitudes and moods. The therapy gives clients an opportunity to rediscover the importance of relating to themselves and taking time for contemplation and recreation. Existential therapy teaches a discipline for living which consists of a frequent process of checking what one's attitude, inclination, mood and frame of mind are, bringing them back in line with reality and personal aspirations.

Change is initiated in the sessions, but not accomplished in them. The process of transformation takes place in between the sessions and after therapy has terminated. The therapeutic hour itself can never be more than a small contribution to a person's renewed engagement with life. It is only a kind of rehearsal for life. The change process is never-ending. As long as there is life there will be change. There is no place for complacency or a self-congratulatory belief in cure.

As existential therapy has no criterion for cure, it could in theory be an endless process. To make sure it does not become this, the criterion for finishing a series of sessions is simply to stop when the client feels ready to manage on her own again. To encourage such self-reliance, relatively short-term therapy is encouraged (three months to two years), though sometimes the process will take a little longer.

Limitations of the approach

The emphasis that the existential approach places on self-reflection and under-standing can lead to certain limitations. The approach often attracts clients who feel disinclined to trust other human beings because they perceive the existential approach as leaving them in total control. This limitation can only be overcome by a therapist who neither fights the need nor leaves it unchallenged, but who assists the client in turning such self-reliance to a positive end.

The approach is also often misconstrued as 'intellectual'. Some existential therapists tend to emphasize the cognitive aspect of their clients' preoccupations and some clients are attracted to the approach with the hope of avoiding senses, feeling and intuition. A good existential therapist would heed all these different levels of experience, as full self-understanding can be achieved only through openness to all different aspects of being. Nevertheless the emphasis on self-reflection remains central and the criticism is therefore a valid one to some degree.

The practical limitations of the approach have already been referred to in the section on selection criteria. As the approach does not stress the illness–health dimension, people who directly want to relieve specific symptoms will generally find the existential approach unhelpful.

The existential therapist neither encourages the client to regress to a deep level of dependency nor seeks to become a significant other in the client's life and nurture the client back to health. The therapist is a consultant who can provide the client with a method for and systematic support in facing the truth, and in this sense is there to allow the client to relate to herself more than to the therapist. This might be considered a limitation of the approach by clients who wish to regress and rely on the therapist as a substitute parental figure. Good existential therapists obviously enable the client to confront that issue just as bravely as any other issue and come through with greater self-understanding.

Perhaps the most absolute limitation is that of the level of maturity, life experience and intensive training that is required of practitioners in this field. It should be clear from the above that existential therapists are required to be wise and capable of profound and wide-ranging understanding of what it means to be human. The criteria of what makes for a good existential therapist are so high that the chances of finding bad existential therapists must be considerable.

One can imagine the danger of therapists pretending to be capable of this kind of wisdom without actual substance or inner authority. Little would be gained by replacing technological or medical models of therapy, which can be con-cretely learned and applied by practitioners, with a range of would-be existential advisers who are incapable of facing life's problems with dignity and creativity themselves. The only way around this is to create training organizations that select candidates extremely carefully on personal qualities and experience before putting them through a thorough training and a long period of intensively supervised work.

Case example

The client

Rita is a young woman of 33, who is referred to me by her GP for depression. She has had 12 sessions of counselling in the GP practice but it is clear that this will not be sufficient. Rita looks very striking, dressed all in black, with long dark hair, olive skin, and deep worry lines that give her a worn-out, intense look. She wears baggy clothes that hide her emaciated body and she obviously uses no make-up. Her hair is pulled tightly back in a ponytail, but she has a heavy grown-out fringe that shades her eyes effectively. She averts her gaze most of the time in the initial interview, but when she looks up, invariably there are tears rolling down her cheeks and dripping off her chin, without her seeming to notice, as she soundlessly weeps. Her voice does not betray these tears and she speaks in a monotone, frequently supporting her head with her hands.

Rita has been severely depressed for nearly a year since the accidental death of her husband and five-year-old son in a car crash. She is currently living with her mother- and father-in-law and does not find this arrangement particularly satisfactory. She says that she does little else but sit and watch television. She considers the atmosphere to be gloomy, which is not surprising since her in-laws have, like her, suffered a severe bereavement losing their son and grandson. Although Rita does not really like staying with them she appreciates them looking after her and protecting her from herself. She has made a number of half-hearted suicide attempts, which her in-laws have been able to abort. She cannot face going back to the flat where she lived with Steven (her husband) and Ralph (her son) before the tragedy and she has left the place more or less as it was when she was first told of their deaths.

Her own parents live abroad and she is a foreign national by birth, but has British nationality by virtue of her marriage to Steven. She does not consider going back to her birth country an option: her parents would not understand her situation and she would feel as if she had abandoned Steven and Ralph. Her parents, for business reasons, did not even come to England for the funerals. She is fairly dismissive of them, as she is of most other potential sources of help. She is not sure what she wants from therapy. She doubts whether it will make any difference and she does not want to be made to do any more 'grief work'. She sounds quite vehement when she objects to the idea of going back to her country of origin and when she ridicules her GP counsellor's obsession with 'grieving'. She comes across initially as a very wilful and dynamic person who has clear views and strong opinions of her own, but quickly goes back to the monotone detachment afterwards.

When we explore her resentments a little further we discover that she does not want to be made to let go of Steven and Ralph, who mean everything to her. Grieving is synonymous with giving them up and she does not want to do that. She perceives people who want her to grieve as wanting to force her to let go of those she loves so much. Although she is aware that the arrangement with her in-laws is not good for her, she prefers to stay with them out of a sense of commitment to her dead husband and child. She still senses Steven and Ralph's presence very acutely and talks to them when she is on her own. She has been on antidepressants and sleeping tablets for nearly a year and although she could not envisage doing without the medication she feels very dull and out of touch with herself. She is unmotivated to make any changes in her life, including changing her medication or putting energy into psycho-therapy.

Rita describes herself as pretty desperate and wryly remarks that she has heard that I am supposed to be a last-resort therapist. There seems to be a kind of challenge in this and I ask her whether this is the case. She acknowledges that deep down she would like to think it would be possible to find a way to enjoy life again, but she cannot imagine how it could be done. She feels it isn't really safe or right for her to even think about enjoyment. Somehow that would mean a betrayal of Steven and Ralph. I note that she views the challenge as her own rather than as mine and that for now it might be sufficient to do some work together to find out whether or not she can take up this challenge without hurting or betraying Steven and Ralph. She agrees readily to work with me to this effect and to explore ways of doing right by them that are not hurtful to her and perhaps even find a way to do right by herself that is not hurtful to Steven and Ralph. We agree to aim for her to bear or endure her grief and learn to live with it rather than to overcome it. This modest goal seems to give her some confidence and we agree to work for a couple of months and then decide whether the process is worth her while. In the event we end up working together for two and a half years on a once a week basis, with a short period of twice-weekly sessions from month two to month five.

The therapy

First few sessions

In the first session after the initial interview Rita seems desperate to get her story off her chest. In the intervening week she has come to realize that it is a matter of life or death for her to sort herself out and talk about her pain. This is quite a switch from her previous reserve and scepticism. She has thought a lot about me saying that she needs to find a way to look after Steven and Ralph that is not at her own expense and has realized that if she is to survive her tragedy, she will have to make a real effort to sort herself out. She has also concluded that when she went to see the counsellor before she was not really ready to talk yet: it was too soon after the accident for her to comprehend what had happened and she could only sit and sob for much of the hour. Since then she has basically tried to keep her pain at bay. This week has clarified things for her and she sees that she needs to take stock of her situation, as

I had apparently said to her in the initial interview. She then tells me her story, without much prompting on my part.

She describes herself as an intelligent and capable person who has lost all her self-determination and zest since losing her husband and child. Yet, she volunteers, she knows that if she is honest about the situation there was already something of this in the air before the accident happened. She had stopped working as a senior bank clerk when she got pregnant and had stayed at home to look after Ralph, but had become rather frustrated after Ralph went to nursery school. In fact she had missed being a career woman from the moment she gave up work and she had, sort of, resented this, without ever mentioning it to Steven, for fear of seeming ungrateful.

Ralph had just started primary school when the accident happened. She had been so proud of him. She sobs for a long time when she tries to describe how grown up and radiant Ralph had looked when he went to big school on his first day, only months before the tragic event. Her pain is raw and unremitting. It is hard to watch her being so wretched without becoming tearful. She is glad of my strength when I encourage her to talk about how Ralph is there with her now. She has a box full of his drawings and Lego constructions in the flat, but cannot manage to look at any of these yet. This is one of the reasons she stays with her in-laws: the flat is haunted with memories. She also cannot bear to be in touch with any of the other parents in Ralph's school. She has once or twice had the misfortune of meeting one of them in a shop. She froze inside when seeing their children, now six and so much more grown up than Ralph when he died. It all just seems too much to bear.

She talks a lot about the unfairness of life and wonders why this has hit her rather than anyone else. She has begun to try to understand, but cannot. She realizes that her avoidance of confrontation with reality is a problem and wants to break out of the shell she has been hiding in while she was in shock. She is desperately trying to keep the threads that attach her to Steven, and especially to Ralph, intact: her entire identity is based on her connection to them. She feels she cannot unravel her attachment to them unless she is prepared to give up her own existence. It seems to her that she has a choice between holding on to them and keep herself alive or let them go and die with them. I remark that at the moment she seems to have kind of opted for letting herself die with them by devoting herself so totally to their memory. She cries softly, but audibly, for the first time and keeps nodding her agreement with that statement. I point out that these are tears for herself rather than for her family and that she is finally beginning to care for herself again. She seems to gain some relief from being given encouragement to be concerned for her own well-being, and over the next weeks begins to balance her preoccupation with the death of Steven and Ralph with a growing interest in understanding her life experience.

Rita came to this country ten years previously on a foreign exchange programme with the bank she was employed by. She had fallen in love at first sight with Steven, her senior in the bank she was working in. He courted her with great enthusiasm and she felt quite rushed off her feet when they got married within a year of her moving to the UK. Steven was besotted with her and he wanted them to marry quickly so that she could stay here when her work permit ran out. It did mean leaving her family and friends behind 'at home'. I notice that this first reference to home is reserved for her home country, not for the flat she lived in with Steven and Ralph, which she refers to as 'the flat', and not to the place she lives now, which she tends to call 'at my in-laws'. She tells me that this is true: she somehow lost her home when she decided to stay in England. She also lost her parents, who did come over for the wedding, but spent most of their time touring the country and warned her that they would not be able to afford to visit again. She had wept for hours after the wedding, knowing that she was giving up so much. She had felt as if she might perhaps never see her parents again. I point out that this too had been a kind of bereavement: it had certainly involved a great sense of loss. This makes her cry uncontrollably and she sobs audibly for quite a while. When I gently ask her to put some words to the tears, she mentions a sense of guilt over that loss, which she felt was self-inflicted. We come back to this guilt over the next weeks, until at last she dares to connect it to the guilt she feels currently over the fatal accident.

Crisis

It is in month two of the therapy that Rita appears one day, determined to tell me about the worst of her grief. She warns me that she has not mentioned this to anyone before and she is still hesitant to talk about it to me as well, but she feels as if there is a big shadow hanging over her sorrow, which she has somehow to bring into the picture she has thus far painted for me. I encourage her to speak her fears and bring the horror out in the open rather than let it haunt her in silence and solitude. The story of her guilt on the day of the accident now comes out.

She and Steven had a row on the morning of his death. It was a row about control, she says, one of many over recent years. She goes on a side track, telling me about their disagreements over how often they should visit Steven's parents and over whether or not they should have another child. She feels guilty because she generally tried to stop Steven seeing his parents whenever she could. She can see that this probably had something to do with her resenting him living so near his parents whilst she has lost her own, who are so many miles away. She realizes also that her trying to stop having another baby, whilst Steven was always keen to have another child, was something to do with her wanting not to feel so stuck on her own at the flat any more, wanting to recover her freedom to work once Ralph went to school. She had in fact started making enquiries into possible job opportunities when Ralph had started school a few months before the accident. Even Steven had not known about this. Somehow she felt he would not have liked it.

We do a little work around all these fears and hidden guilt feelings and take some of the pressure off this background atmosphere of imagined wrong-doing. Rita eases into a sense of greater security and agrees that it is understandable that she should resent Steven's parents if she can't have access to her own and that not working was a major obstacle to her getting to feel at home in the UK; that somehow she needed to give birth to herself before she could give birth to another child. It all feels like real work and progress and yet in the background there is a sense of working at the surface and a feeling that something is still not being addressed. I voice my sense that there is something bigger that triggers guilt in her about her loss. She responds by very calmly telling me that on the day of the accident the row she and Steven had was about driving to his parents'. Rita had refused to go because of the thick fog and ice on the roads and Steven had gone off with Ralph, angry with her for failing him once again. The last thing he had said as he left was something like: 'You will use any excuse not to let Ralph see his grandparents. That fog is nothing at all. Ralph and I are not afraid of a bit of ice, are we, Ralph?' She had felt very angry about his manipulation of her son and had shouted something like – and here her voice falters and comes to a halt, until she finally whispers – 'I actually said', and she sobs for minutes before finally, nearly choking on it, admitting, 'I said to them: "Go then and I hope you slip on the ice" '. This is precisely what did happen, or rather it was another driver whose car careered into them after slipping on the ice, taking both cars into a spin and down a fairly steep bank.

Not only is Rita stone cold as she tells me this but I feel a sense of awe and terror in the face of her horrific experience. She has removed all feeling from herself at this moment and she sits very still as if she might bring about another misfortune by moving a muscle. She waits for my judgement. We sit together in silence for a while until the silence becomes a little softer and warmer and perhaps until I find a place of composure and comfort from which to help her face the horror. Then I venture gently: 'So it seems to you as if the accident is your fault.' It is not a question. It is what she has just told me and she nods imperceptibly in agreement. 'Your sense of guilt is what makes the grief so unbearable, isn't it?' Again she nods and the tears begin to flow, first very quietly and then building into a loud sobbing and wailing, which continues for perhaps 10, perhaps more like 20 minutes. It is as if time is standing still. Her sorrow is finally exploding instead of imploding inside of her. I almost experience relief in her ability to express her pain visibly and audibly: it is much more concrete than the tension and terror she was previously cloaked in. Yet, I am also aware that she is at the limit of her ability to endure and that she feels very overwhelmed by this sudden outburst.

As she howls and wrings her hands, she cries that she will never be able to pay enough for wasting their lives. Now I intervene forcefully in order to set some boundaries to the uncontainable sorrow and help her to begin to find her way through this massive mountain of pain. I tell her that she is beginning to face the reality that she has run away from for so long and that she will discover that it is not quite as nasty as she is experiencing it just at the minute.

Now that she is allowing herself to confront her experience, she will be able to gain some perspective and find out for herself what is actually the case. She may be guilty of all sorts of things, but not of killing Steven and Ralph, nor of wasting their lives. She can easily agree with the voice of reason, even though her fear still tells her she is guilty and she asks if we can meet again that week to continue the process of uncovering that she now feels may lead to her recovery if she can get help. The time is ripe to start unravelling and disentangling the mess in her heart and mind. She comes twice weekly for the next few weeks.

The process of uncovering

The work continues apace during this period and every session sees the repetition of a cycle of reluctance and restraint followed by growing emotional expression, weeping and working through Rita's worst worries and fears. There are torrents of tears and oceans of regret to be expressed and collected. We work on her relationship with Steven, real and imagined, as if it were still current, since for Rita at this moment it is current. Gradually she is better able to address the disagreements between her and Steven and stops idealizing him or taking all the blame on her self. It is sometimes as if we are doing posthumous couple therapy. In fact Rita has started to begin running things by Steven in her mind. She argues with him in the sessions sometimes and I help her hear a more positive response from him as she begins to realize that he would have been able to help her address her frustrations and solitude, her sense of homelessness and uselessness if they had had the time to discover about all these things together.

It is a terrible tragedy when people die before the promise of a relationship can be realized or its challenges confronted, but there is no reason why those who are left behind should suffer unnecessarily for the failure of time to provide opportunities to work things out. Just because Steven has died does not mean that Rita's experience of herself in the relationship has to remain frozen in the fearful state of guilt and shortcoming. She owes it to herself and to Steven as well as to Ralph to come to terms with what has been and might have been and to find a place of peace for her love for them both.

Over the weeks she discovers so many things about herself, her marriage, her motherhood, her relationship to her in-laws, to her own parents, to her career and to her aspirations for herself that the focus gradually, imperceptibly, shifts away from grieving for what has been taken from her to an exploration of what is still possible for her. Then as she becomes better able to face all that she feels went wrong between her and Steven and work out how it might have happened and where she might go from here, her sorrow over Ralph's death comes more to the fore. Her sadness in relation to Ralph is much softer and open than her grief for Steven. There is a wistfulness and devotion in her when she speaks of her little boy that carries her forwards in spite of herself. She learns to relish remembering a lot of the good things she shared with Ralph and she talks of him with tenderness and with a kind of bittersweet joy. She tells me the words he favoured, the games they played, the grimaces he made, the ways in which he could be naughty, all the things that she feared she had lost when she lost him and which she dares to bring back to life again now that she is determined to live on. She harvests all that was precious in those five years of his life and she allows herself to treasure it. She is bitter about giving up on the fantasies she had about his teenage years, his adulthood. Losing his future seems like a loss of her own future self. But these unravelling threads connect up with her own thwarted plans to reclaim a professional future and slowly, but surely, she begins to think about the life that she has nearly lost herself and how she wants to live it now for Steven's and Ralph's sake, as a sort of memorial to them. I am not sure that I like her sacrificing herself so much to their memory, but if this is her way to rebuild her life, then so be it. Seeing her beginning to weave the old strands of her life back into a new pattern of future is a pleasure and a half.

Recovery

Rita continues bravely onwards with her work to reclaim her life. There are so many ramifications in her story and the way in which she experiences her sudden losses, that it would take many long pages to do it any real justice. Every session is like a hero's journey; every discovery made reveals new ground to uncover and then dig over. Rita takes much heart from my repeated confirmation of her courage to do this work and she becomes increasingly steady in her explorations. The sobbing returns every so often when she bridges a new gap and suddenly finds herself with the realization of some other thing that has been lost for ever. She has a rapidly growing under-standing of the inner strength that her battles with misfortune have brought her. In every sorrow she feels she learns to look for a kernel of truth about life and about herself. She accepts that she has to make her tragedy into a meaningful event and that the best way to safeguard Steven and Ralph is to do justice to her relationship with them by making it real and by learning from it.

Rita learns to go through various rituals of her own making to move forwards through her grief. On the second anniversary of the accident she is able for the first time to start facing her desire to embrace life without Steven and Ralph. She no longer feels that she has to protect them as much as feeling that she can claim her right to feel protected by them. It is quite a miracle for her to find that now that she has made peace with the past she can face Steven and Ralph's ghosts without feeling afraid or guilty. They become like good friends to her in the subsequent months and she feels more peaceful in a sense of their benevolent wish for her to do well. There are many practical steps that aid her progress. Leaving her in-laws and giving up the wish to make up to them for stopping Steven visiting them is an important step. Going back to the flat and starting to sort out her husband and son's belongings are landmarks on the long road of recovery. We often discuss the concrete steps she is able to take and sometimes slow things down when it is all going too fast.

Sometimes the progress suddenly seems to be in jeopardy when new events occur that temporarily interfere with her carefully managed process of recovery. There are confrontations with her in-laws that start out as possible catastrophes and setbacks but with a little assistance turn out to be boosts to her growing self-esteem. At this point she claims back her right to look after Steven's estate, of which she is the executor, but which her in-laws have thus far managed. Rita needs a little help in remembering her own financial skills but when she does remember she thrives on the rediscovery of her efficiency and begins to flourish as a person again. Before too long Rita decides to find a job, even though Steven's death has left her fairly comfortably off. She is reluctant to claim the benefits that are now coming to her, but finds that she can think of Steven as standing by her and encouraging her to get her life together for his sake as well as hers. He would, indeed, not like seeing her so sad and wasting her life. Her tender remembrance of Ralph teaches her that her maternal feelings should not be wasted either and she eventually admits to wanting to become a mother again one day.

Two years after the beginning of the therapy Rita has reclaimed a life of her own. She has started a new professional training, which will lead to a much more senior position in finance and she has redecorated the flat and claimed it as 'her home'. There is still a room for Steven and Ralph in it, but all the rest she now considers hers. Her work brings her in contact with lots of concrete human relations and everyday concerns which are troublesome and which increasingly take up the space of the sessions. She is, in other words, learning to live again instead of hiding in grief-stricken terror. Hesitantly, she starts a warm friendship with a male friend in the final months of our work together and she spends a lot of time trying to be more honest in this relationship than she was ever able to be with Steven. She begins a correspondence with her parents to try and work out with them some of the things she has come to understand about the problems that happened between her and them. Her new boyfriend is very helpful to her in relation to this and they decide to travel to her home country together to meet them. Upon her return there is much to process, but she is now determined to do all this mostly with her new friend. They decide to move in together and she wants the therapy to end at this point, since she feels she has made the transition and that she needs to stop talking to me about Steven and Ralph behind her new partner's back. She is full of energy and quite a different person than the Rita I first met two years previously. She has a clear sense of what she wants and a much stronger image of herself than she has ever had before. She realizes that the tragedy will always be a part of her and that Steven and Ralph will always have a place in her heart, but she does not want them to overshadow the rest of her life. She wants to opt for life, not for death, and she believes that she has been blessed to overcome something that she thought was impossible to over-come. She now thinks that what has happened to her has wounded her and in this way opened her up to herself and made her come to life. I cannot resist the temptation to say that it is death that has taught her about life, and she smiles in agreement. Although our regular sessions stop at this point, Rita comes back for a couple of later sessions to renew her sense of direction, but also, as it transpires, to purge a remaining sense of occasional guilt towards her new partner, for still thinking so much about Steven and Ralph.

References

Binswanger, L. (1963) *Being-in-the-World*, trans. J. Needleman. New York: Basic Books.

Boss, M. (1957a) *Psychoanalysis and Daseinsanalysis*, trans. L.B. Lefebre. New York: Basic Books.

Boss, M. (1957b) *The Analysis of Dreams*. London: Rider.

Boss, M. (1979) *Existential Foundations of Medicine and Psychology*. New York: Jason Aronson.

Cohn, H.W. (1994) 'What is existential psychotherapy?', *British Journal of Psychiatry*, 165(8): 669–701.

Cohn, H.W. (1997) *Existential Thought and Therapeutic Practice*. London: Sage.

Cooper, D. (1967) *Psychiatry and Anti-psychiatry*. New York: Barnes & Noble.

Cooper, R. (ed.) (1989) *Thresholds between Philosophy and Psycho-analysis*. London: Free Association Books.

De Koning, A.J.J. and Jenner, F.A. (1982) *Phenomenology and Psychiatry*. New York: Academic Press.

Deurzen-Smith, E. van (1984) 'Existential therapy', in W. Dryden (ed.), *Individual Therapy in Britain*. London: Harper & Row.

Deurzen-Smith, E. van (1997) *Everyday Mysteries: Existential Dimensions of Psychotherapy*. London: Routledge.

Deurzen, E. van (1998) *Paradox and Passion in Psychotherapy*. Chichester: Wiley & Sons.

Deurzen, E. van (2002) *Existential Counselling and Psychotherapy in Practice*, 2nd edn. London: Sage.

Du Plock, S. (1997) *Case Studies in Existential Psychotherapy*. Chichester: Wiley & Sons.

Eleftheriadou, Z. (1994) *Transcultural Counselling*. London: Central Book Publishing.

Frankl, V.E. (1964) *Man's Search for Meaning*. London: Hodder & Stoughton.

Frankl, V.E. (1967) *Psychotherapy and Existentialism*. Harmondsworth: Penguin.

Heaton, L.M. (1988) *The Provocation of Levinas*. London: Routledge.

Heaton, L.M. (1994) *Wittgenstein for Beginners*. Cambridge: Icon.

Heidegger, M. (1962) *Being and Time*, trans. J. Macquarrie and E.S. Robinson. New York: Harper & Row.

Heidegger, M. (1968) *What is Called Thinking?* New York: Harper & Row.

Husserl, E. (1960) *Cartesian Meditations*. The Hague: Nijhoff.

Husserl, E. (1962) *Ideas*. New York: Collier.

Jaspers, K. (1951) *The Way to Wisdom*, trans. R. Manhneim. New Haven and London: Yale University Press.

Jaspers, K. (1963) *General Psychopathology*. Chicago: University of Chicago Press.

Kearney, R. (1986) *Modern Movements in European Philosophy*. Manchester: Manchester University Press.

Kierkegaard, S. (1941) *Concluding Unscientific Postscript*, trans. D.F. Swenson and W. Lowrie. Princeton, NJ: Princeton University Press.

Kierkegaard, S. (1944) *The Concept of Dread*, trans. W. Lowrie. Princeton, NJ: Princeton University Press.

Laing, R.D. (1960) *The Divided Self*. Harmondsworth: Penguin.

Laing, R.D. (1961) *Self and Others*. Harmondsworth: Penguin.

Laing, R.D. and Cooper, D. (1964) *Reason and Violence*. London: Tavistock.

Lemma-Wright, A. (1994) *Starving to Live. The Paradox of Anorexia Nervosa*. London: Central Book Publishing.

Lomas, P. (1981) *The Case for a Personal Psychotherapy*. Oxford: Oxford University Press.

Mace, C. (ed.) (1999) *Heart and Soul: The Therapeutic Face of Philosophy*. London: Routledge.

Macquarrie, J. (1972) *Existentialism: an Introduction, Guide and Assessment*. Harmondsworth: Penguin.

May, R. (1969) *Love and Will*. New York: Norton.

May, R. (1983) *The Discovery of Being*. New York: Norton.

May, R. and Yalom, L. (1985) 'Existential psychotherapy', in R. S. Corsini (ed.), *Current Psychotherapies*. Itasca, IL: Peacock.

May, R., Angel, E. and Ellenberger, H.F. (1958) *Existence*. New York: Basic Books.

Merleau-Ponty, M. (1962) *Phenomenology of Perception*, trans. C. Smith. London: Routledge & Kegan Paul.

Minkowski, E. (1970) *Lived Time*. Evanston, IL: Northwestern University Press.

Moran, D. (2000) *Introduction to Phenomenology*. London: Routledge.

Nietzsche, F. (1961) *Thus Spoke Zarathustra*, trans. R.J. Hollingdale. Harmondsworth: Penguin.

Nietzsche, F. (1974) *The Gay Science*, trans. W. Kaufmann. New York: Random House.

Nietzsche, F. (1986) *Human, All Too Human: A Book for Free Spirits*, trans. R.J. Hollingdale. Cambridge: Cambridge University Press.

Sartre, J.P. (1956) *Being and Nothingness: An Essay on Phenomenological Ontology*, trans. H. Barnes. New York: New York Philosophical Library.

Sartre, J.P. (1962) *Sketch for a Theory of the Emotions*. London: Methuen.

Smail, D.J. (1978) *Psychotherapy, a Personal Approach*. London: Dent.

Smail, D.J. (1987) *Taking Care*. London: Dent

Smail, D.J. (1993) *The Origins of Unhappiness: A New Understanding of Personal Distress*. London: HarperCollins.

Spiegelberg, H. (1972) *Phenomenology in Psychology and Psychiatry*. Evanston, IL: Northwestern University Press.

Spinelli, E. (1997) *Tales of Unknowing*. London: Duckworth.

Strasser, F. and Strasser, A. (1997) *Existential Time Limited Therapy*. Chichester: Wiley & Sons.

Tillich, P. (1952) *The Courage to Be*. Harmondsworth: Penguin.

Valle, R.S. and King, M. (1978) *Existential Phenomenological Alternatives for Psychology*. New York: Oxford University Press.

Warnock, M. (1970) *Existentialism*. Oxford: Oxford University Press.

Yalom, I. (1980) *Existential Psychotherapy*. New York: Basic Books.

Suggested further reading

Deurzen, E. van (1998) *Paradox and Passion in Psychotherapy*. Chichester: Wiley & Sons.

Deurzen, E. van (2002) *Existential Counselling and Psychotherapy in Practice*, 2nd edn. London: Sage.

Macquarrie, J. (1972) *Existentialism: an Introduction, Guide and Assessment*. Harmondsworth: Penguin.

Warnock, M. (1970) *Existentialism*. Oxford: Oxford University Press.

Yalom, I. (1980) *Existential Psychotherapy*. New York: Basic Books.

9 Gestalt Therapy
Malcolm Parlett and Judith Hemming

Historical context and development in Britain

Historical context

Gestalt therapy did not appear in a flash. As is usual with any movement, there were preceding ideas forming a fertile substratum, out of which grew this radical revision of psychoanalysis.

The two primary founders of the approach were Frederick (Fritz) Perls (1893–1970) and his wife and collaborator, Laura Perls (1905–92). The pre-history of Gestalt therapy begins in Germany, where they were born and educated and where, throughout the 1920s, they were exposed to the ideas and experimental culture that flowered at that time. Philosophy, education, the arts, politics and psychology were all in creative upheaval. The young couple were of the radical avant-garde.

Fritz Perls, after active service in the First World War, trained and practised as a neuropsychiatrist and had analysis with several orthodox Freudians and then with Wilhelm Reich. Laura Perls was taught by leading members of the then popular Gestalt school of psychology. An accomplished musician, she also studied with Paul Tillich and Martin Buber. Some of the 'ancestors' of Gestalt therapy can be identified: Freud, with his instinct theories; Reich, with his emphasis on the body; Buber, with his passionate views on the need for human 'meeting'; the Gestalt psychologists (Wertheimer, Kohler, Koffka and Lewin), with their criticism of reductionist psychology and their view of perception and thinking being organized in coherent patterns, or *gestalts*.

Before their analytic trainings, Laura and Fritz had met at the neurological institute directed by Kurt Goldstein, whose views of 'self-actualization' and 'organismic self-regulation' (he coined the terms) also fed into the eventual synthesis. This was their first experience of holistic thinking. The Perls were also exposed to the radical philosophy of existentialism and phenomenology, both of which became major foundations of the Gestalt approach. Fritz was involved in theatre with the director Max Reinhardt – his love of dramatization was later reflected in his training workshops; Laura was involved in dance, movement, and Eastern philosophy.

This extraordinary cultural epoch did not, of course, survive. By 1933, Fritz and Laura Perls were on the Nazi blacklist as left-wing radicals. They fled to Holland, and then to South Africa, where they remained working as psycho-analysts till 1946. They continued to lap up other ideas and influences, for example holism, as first written about by Smuts, the South African philosopher and prime minister. Perls's first major statement, *Ego, Hunger and Aggression* (Perls, 1969a but first published in 1942) criticized psychoanalysis and suggested a new approach to therapy. After the war they emigrated to the USA.

Post-war New York was another place and time marked by great cultural ferment. The Perls became a focus for a group of writers, political activists and therapists, including the poet, educator and social critic Paul Goodman, who was to write a major part of the 'founding book': *Gestalt Therapy* (Perls et al., 1951). The first Institute of Gestalt Therapy was set up in New York in 1952 and Laura Perls continued to be a key figure until her death in 1992. In contrast, Fritz Perls began moving restlessly between different locations. He was not successful until he turned up at the famed Esalen Institute in California. Then, at the height of the 1960s counterculture, he became widely known. At this time Gestalt therapy became linked to the human potential movement, encounter, and the development of humanistic psychology generally.

Numerous stereotypes and misconceptions about Gestalt stem from this period. Many would-be Gestalt practitioners imitated Perls and his personal style of work, taking the techniques he was experimenting with to be the essence of the whole approach. For many, Gestalt became equated with what Fritz Perls did, and the full depth and substance of the Gestalt philosophy and practice was not communicated. The history of Gestalt therapy since that time has included returning to European philosophical roots, and building on other founding influences and teachers. The depth and effectiveness of the approach has been reaffirmed, and many of the original ideas have been developed greatly (Wheeler, 1991).

Occasionally, however, misinformation still surfaces – e.g. that Gestalt is confrontational, has little theory, and has to do with specific techniques that any therapist can use without Gestalt training. Such notions are finally giving way to appreciation of Gestalt therapy more for its practical philosophy, its roots in psychoanalysis, and its compatibility with holistic, relativistic and postmodern trends of thought (see Wheeler, 1991; Mackewn, 1997). It has matured in its methods. There is more focus than in the early days on longer-term individual work, greater acknowledgement of group process in group therapy settings, and more appreciation of its rich intellectual heritage. Along with many other therapeutic approaches, there is ever greater recognition that the work calls for intensive training, professionalism and scrupulous attention to ethical matters.

Development in Britain

There have been three distinct phases of Gestalt activity in Britain. In the 1970s there were two growth centres in London, Quaesitor and Community, which offered Gestalt workshops along with other kinds of humanistic and alternative approaches. Gestalt therapy was an import from the US (despite its original European roots) and a succession of American visitors presented weekends and therapy 'marathons'. Gestalt training was offered by Owen and Joan O'Leary, Roger Dalton, Ischa Bloomberg, and others.

The second phase, from 1981 to 1992, was a period of expansion. Landmarks included the founding of the Gestalt Centre, London by Ursula Fausset, and the setting up of the Gestalt Psychotherapy and Training Institute (GPTI). The Metanoia Institute, Gestalt SouthWest, Cambridge GATE, the Sherwood Institute, Manchester Gestalt Centre, and centres in Edinburgh and elsewhere, all began training courses specifically in Gestalt therapy.

The third phase, growing from the second, has involved greater professionalization, national and international contacts, with well-attended British Gestalt conferences, and increased attention to accreditation. GPTI and the Gestalt Centre, London became founding member organizations of the UK Council for Psychotherapy. The third phase has been marked by a steady flow of new British publications (e.g. Houston, 1993; Mackewn, 1997; Philippson, 2002). Another major development was the publication of the *British Gestalt Journal* from 1991, now an acclaimed international professional journal.

Alongside the setting up of organizations and systems of accreditation, there has been an undertow of disquiet. Gestalt began as a questioning approach, radical and innovative, with an anti-establishment ethos. Some now believe that the pendulum has swung too far – that the sparkle of Gestalt has been dulled by respectability. Others say it has matured and consolidated and is a strong candidate for being the focal point for a more integrated psychotherapy in the future (Resnick, 1995).

Theoretical assumptions

Image of the person

Gestalt therapy, a powerful synthesis of differing ideas and outlooks, has a central idea that human beings are in constant development. The person is regarded as an exploring, adapting, self-reflecting being, in a process of continuous change. We are constantly making and remaking ourselves throughout life. Gestalt therapy focuses on the process of experiencing this unfolding life.

Such change comes about naturally and inevitably through our constantly interacting with others and dealing with life's challenges, opportunities, possibilities and problems. This leads to another central assumption, namely that human beings should not be theorized about as if they have some isolated, independent existence (and psychology). Realistically, the individual has to be seen as always being 'in relation' – as one pole within a constantly changing 'field' (Parlett, 1991; Yontef, 1993) encompassing both the individual and her/his milieu. 'Inner' and 'outer' realms of existence cannot be separated. Thus, family, colleagues, work, organizational, communal and national life, as well as being 'other', are also so much part of the actual experience of life and living that they are, in effect, 'part of oneself'.

The lack of a hard and fast cut-off point between person and the physical and social world is evident at every level. Breathing and the presence of air are so interlinked that to separate them is an academic abstraction. In a similar way, lovers require a beloved, a person is not an 'employer' without others who are employed, people can only be 'therapy clients' because therapy and therapists exist. Neither pole exists without its accompaniment. The whole of life involves such interdependent relationship. Thus, human beings are communal animals, each 'carrying' the language and values of their cultural heritage and embodying attitudes and behaviours derived from family and society, work, home and the media.

The Gestalt perspective on the image of the person is therefore a holistic one, in contrast to a dualistic or compartmentalized one. The outlook is manifest, too, in viewing the individual as a complex biological organism. Just as a child without a 'growing up context' is inconceivable, so is a mind or soul without a body. Human beings have inbuilt physiological patterns of reacting (for instance to shock), physical needs which dictate a lot of daily life, and muscular involvement and a phenomenological 'felt sense' that accompanies every thought and action taken. All experience is embodied and the process of living involves immersion in the physical realities of feeling states, the emotions, and in the life of our bodies – e.g. our state of health, fluctuations of energy, ageing, sensual satisfactions, pain, and the quality of sleep.

Gestalt therapists believe that enquiring into the *actually lived experience* of the person leads inevitably to a holistic, rather than reductionistic, perspective. Human life and experience cannot be divided into parts. Our lived existence is grounded both in the social and familial realities of our present world – its technologies, its economics, its pressures – *and* in the 'experience of our body [which is] experience of our self, just as our thinking, imagery, and ideas are part of our self' (Kepner, 1987: 10).

Creative adjustment

The Gestalt approach emphasizes that each person is actively 'self-organizing'. At every level we are managing the conditions and possibilities of life, minimizing discomfort, seeking to meet our needs (with or without awareness), dealing with the demands and obligations of the systems that are part of our field or life space. Much of life relates to preserving ourselves in equilibrium. Thus, we 'self-regulate' ourselves at an organismic level – e.g. sleeping when tired, crying when in grief, eating when hungry. Biologically, these capabilities allow the person to live in a state of health. At the same time, obviously, we also choose sometimes intention-ally to disturb our equilibrium – extending ourselves in order to meet some broader need for, say, stimulation at a party or to serve others through self-sacrifice. So the ways we self-organize are many and complex.

Existence as a whole calls for continuous 'creative adjustment' (Perls et al., 1951). Adjustment is not only reactive but also proactive – a process of 'approach-ing, laying hold of, and altering old structures' (ibid.: 9) within the field. Thus, the person both adapts to, and seeks to modify, obstacles, habits, traditions and systems within the field in ways that meet needs, improve conditions, or sustain life through assimilation and learning. These modifications might take the form of destroying part of 'what is other' (as in eating or throwing away old papers), or 'aggressing upon it' (as in editing someone's writing, or questioning authority), or 'deconstructing' it (such as altering the shape of a garden or the nature of a relationship). Again, the idea that we are changers and makers of our life and reality as well as adapting to it underlines the participatory or 'co-created' nature of our lived existence.

Altogether, then, the person is viewed in a more fluid, continuously interactive way than is perhaps common in psychology and in conventional ways of thinking about the person. The self is not regarded as a 'thing-like mental entity', but as 'the process of experiencing' (Wolfert, 2000). As a process, 'selfing' is an activity, 'a dynamic relation which is ever-moving, ever-changing – an organisation shaped by and shaping experiences in the play of the forces in the field' (ibid.: 77). The theory which goes with this view is radical: the self is variable, and at times of maximum intensity and involvement there is greater 'self' than at times when energy is low and the person feels directionless or unfocused.

The view of the self espoused in the Gestalt approach fits with many present-day notions of what it means to be human. In a postmodernist time, and with the new discoveries of physics and the changing cosmology of our time, we have become used to abandoning fixed structures, categories and mechanisms – the static framework for thinking about human being – in favour of a more dynamic, relativistic, fluid picture of what it means to be human. Gestalt therapy and theory is in tune with these developments. It emphasizes processes – continuous development, ever-changing responses to evolving conditions, and shifting perspectives – rather than mechanisms, causes and effects, diagnostic categories and fixed treatment plans.

The bias towards acknowledging fluidity and change does not mean that the opposites are ignored; 'stuckness', fixity and resistance to change are also part of what Gestalt therapists attend to. There are patterned sequences and continuities, habits of thought and body structures, as well as social, family, economic, cultural and organizational structures that provide the necessary counterpoint influences of stability in a person's lived existence. In other words, although life is continuously forming and re-forming, and the self and field are always in flux, there are also consistent patterns to self-organizing. It is to these habitual responses and patterns of responding that we turn next.

Conceptualization of psychological disturbance and health

Given what has been said so far, it is not surprising that Gestalt therapists are wary of language and assumptions that seem to 'fix' a person or pattern of experience as 'disturbed'. They argue that we are all 'disturbed' at times. The incidence of mental ill health, of depression and anxiety in particular, in present-day society suggests that we are talking of wide-scale phenomena that, in certain cases and at certain times, become acute and debilitating. Given adverse enough circumstances, any human being may come to operate in a way that can be seen as disturbed. The overwhelming sense of how human beings operate, however, is that they organize themselves and their lives as well as they can, even if their life skills and human abilities are not always well developed (Parlett, 2000).

Disturbance is therefore not conceived as some kind of personal dysfunction that is attributable to an individual's psychological history or character. Rather it is seen in a wider, 'whole field' way which takes into account the family, work, and societal pressures that are acting in the person's life space – pressures that many have to cope with, and which 'reach breaking point' in certain individual lives at certain times.

A definition of health

Many approaches avoid defining health, by referring to it as 'absence of disturbance or illness'. In Gestalt therapy we suggest that health is a living expression of a person's present field relationships: whether their lives feel integrated (or 'together'); the extent to which they are creatively adjusting to present challenges and opportunities; and whether they feel 'in balance' physically and energetically.

The notion of health derives from regarding human experience as being most rewarding when we feel most alive and are well supported. As energized, embodied, focused centres of consciousness, human beings are able to engage fully with whatever life situation they are presently encountering. At such moments (or periods of time), they are able to apply their life knowledge freely – that is, without self-consciousness, loss of focus, inhibitions or intellectualizations.

Existence calls for versatility, a capacity to learn from experience and self-orienting principles by which to live and to exercise choice and self-responsibility. Obviously for most people in a broad range of circumstances the same impulse is there: to improve on one's life or to evolve. Even in unfavourable conditions (e.g. as hostages or in situations of grinding poverty) people can often retain a capacity to operate creatively. They make choices and are not overwhelmed, whereas for others there is insufficient support in the field at that time for them to adjust creatively in the face of obstacles. Such individuals, at least at that time, require more benign and supportive circumstances before they can act with dignity or elegance, or 'with good form' (Zinker, 1994). The Gestalt approach rests on the belief that anyone can, if they want to and have sufficient support (incentives, back-up, urgency of need), learn how to function in life with greater skill and satisfaction.

Disturbance

To be disturbed at times, then, is to be expected. The individual is responding to the whole field, and the field may be in chaos or crisis, which impacts those within it. However, there are sometimes individual patterns of repeated confusion and distress. Human beings are creatures of habit. In situations where we are not comfortable and are not managing, we are likely to fall back on repertoires and responses that were once adequate solutions (or creative adjustments) but that do not 'work' in present circumstances. In 'healthy' modes we are capable of the necessary involvement with what is actually in front of us; in 'disturbed' modes we can seem fixated in inappropriate habitual patterns of thinking, feeling and reacting in ways that interfere with functioning in the circumstances being encountered in the present. Life calls for us continuously to extend our abilities to maintain ourselves in changing conditions, rather than perpetuating obsolete responses, or 'fixed gestalts', which are self-limiting. In times of personal or collective chaos, graceful and creative qualities are often among the first casualties.

The exact ways in which individuals act stereotypically, do not 'flow', and experience themselves as adrift become the foci for Gestalt investigation (as do their creative opposites).

The management of 'gestalts'

Gestalt therapists are interested in how people organize their experience. Human beings are preoccupied with differing things at different times, and with various degrees of intensity. For example, if I meet an old friend in the street, how exactly I relate to him will be a function of the field conditions as a whole. Thus, I may be pleased to see him but I may also have a critically important appointment in a few minutes' time. Alternatively, I may have a longing for human contact and bumping into him is particularly welcome. The total situation or field includes constraints (e.g. the lack of privacy or time available); needs (e.g. to quell a sense of loneliness, or not to be late); and ongoing structures (e.g. assumptions about the social 'etiquette' of meeting old friends and the physical arrangement of the street).

Life is full of these processes – these temporary configurations of a person's experience, the patterns or *gestalts* of a life, which form and, when completed, dissolve. When a person becomes more interested in something (whatever it happens to be), attention becomes more focused, and the field is reorganized. The matter in hand becomes more *figural*, giving competing interests and concerns lower priority. What is not attended to becomes correspondingly dimmer, vaguer or more distant-seeming (becomes part of the *ground*).

As we continue to focus on a particular figure, coming more and more in contact with this 'other' (e.g. a mathematical problem, a lover, a conversation), we eventually reach a point where the sense of difference between the problem (or lover, etc.) and 'me' lessens. The 'contact boundary', at the point of fullest contact between self and other, dissolves altogether, and the field of one's experience is momentarily full and unified. Such a state alters again, as we lose interest following completion of the task (the problem is solved, the lovemaking complete), and 'we come back to ourselves' with a renewed sense of 'self' and 'other'.

This model of involvement (Perls et al., 1951) highlights that our attention and interest varies, along with our sense of energetic engagement or contact, and also our sense of self. Our conscious experience is forever changing. We may be acutely interested in the whereabouts and relative qualities of restaurants before lunch, but do not notice them after lunch. Another matter of persistent interest arises in its stead – for example, the meeting we are going to.

When adjusting in a creative and effective way to circumstances arising in life, the configurations of existence (that we call gestalts) tend to be well formed, graceful and fulfilling, and when complete or finished they disappear into the background. However, when gestalts are left *unfinished* (e.g. a conversation is interrupted) they tend to continue to occupy some of our attention intermittently. Some gestalts are *not well-formed* in the first place (e.g. the meeting starts off 'on the wrong foot'), or are short of energy (e.g. the participants in a project are half-hearted in their enthusiasm), and these do not satisfy us. The Gestalt therapist attends to the quality of a person's experiences: disturbance is manifested in the very processes of gestalt formation and destruction.

Of course, it is not just small life-episodes that interest us. While some gestalts are short-lived, many are of long duration. Many different gestalts operate in someone's life at any one time. Our creative adjustment involves seeking overall balance within our experiential field or life space. Some *interrupted* gestalts have a huge effect on the course of a person's life (as for instance when a young person's studying stops, through having to take over the family business); and some *fixed* gestalts dominate everyday life (such as addiction to alcohol).

Often, gestalts have a life-cycle. Whether it is with a street encounter, or having a baby, or taking an exam or completing a major life project, there are discernible phases in how the cycle unfolds; and they relate to both energy and time. Typically, there is a build-up of interest and vital energy as we become more focused and more involved – say, in preparing for an exam. There is usually a discernible high point in the cycle, when 'something happens' which is significant (in this case, writing the exam paper), and thereafter the energy slowly or rapidly dissipates: the examinee becomes less involved and more easily distracted by other priorities (new needs emerging). The arising and receding of different gestalts is a continuous process. If interrupted, a gestalt may not complete its life-cycle. (If the exam were cancelled, the examinee might be 'left hanging'.) A state of feeling unfulfilled results from such interruptions, many of which are self-induced and repetitive. For some, the satisfaction of completing gestalts and moving on is rarely achievable.

Some interruptions to the natural flow of experience are environmental (e.g. someone arrives as I am about to say goodnight to my child). Other interruptions are consciously chosen, and wisely so – if I have an urge to assault a traffic warden, interrupting that particular gestalt is a wise and mature choice. More often, however, interruptions are self-constructed (e.g. 'people are not interested in what I have to say'); and involve lack of awareness, (e.g. I do not register my dissatisfaction with a conversation till it is over).

Present-centred awareness

The abilities of self-organizing are enhanced by having an awareness of present, ongoing experience. Being unable to 'tune in' to what is actually arising in one's experience, or to notice what one is doing in the moment, is a major impediment in coping with the world as it is encountered. Awareness includes noticing, recognizing, being in touch with. . . .Its opposites include being distracted, oblivious, desensitized or out of touch. Part of being aware relates to the five senses and the capacity to take in information from our surroundings. It also involves recognizing feeling states and bodily sensations. By attuning to reality, whether internal or external (and the field perspective of Gestalt therapy suggests there is no cut-off point between the two), the individual can orientate him/herself with more flexibility and choice.

Awareness of self and of the world involves direct experience, not merely talked-about or conceptualized versions of it. We all engage in self-talk – e.g. planning, remembering, futurizing and arguing with oneself – and these are essential for human living; but they can displace our capacity to hear, see, smell, and to tune into bodily reactions and emotional feelings. The person with a rich, sensation-filled somatic and emotional life feels generally more alive than someone who identifies him/herself only with what is going on 'in the mind'.

The issues are philosophically difficult, but there is, in Gestalt therapy, a conviction that despite the importance of thinking and rationality, a person is limited if s/he is out of touch with his or her primary experience. Knowing what one feels 'in one's bones', or recognizing one's 'heart's desire', is essential for the refining of values. To know that something does not 'feel right' is a human sensibility that collectively and individually needs cultivating if we are to assume full personal responsibility. In Gestalt therapy the body is regarded as a source of wisdom, a provider of organismic truth; and client perception as a more reliable guide than applying a concept or principle.

Contact styles

Gestalt therapists also attend to the 'contact boundary', the relationship between person and situation, noticing the exact patterns of how people connect (or fail to connect) to their surroundings and circumstances. Particular attention has been given in Gestalt therapy to four kinds of transaction at the contact boundary (Mackewn, 1997).

The first relates to the way in which the contact boundary is subjected to overload or potential invasion from the outside. For instance, suppose an employee receives a repeated message from his boss (e.g. that he is 'careless'). The man may take on the message without question, as an automatic given, so that it becomes a part of his outlook. He has *introjected* it. Alternatively, the man may incline to the opposite response and reject utterly any message from 'authority'.

If he is adjusting creatively – i.e. responding flexibly and appropriately – there will be times when he introjects to good effect (introjecting instructions in an emergency might be life-saving); and other times when he sensibly rejects, say a gratuitous insult, out of hand. The contact boundary here operates like a membrane with different degrees of permeability – sometimes letting information in, sometimes keeping it out. The more situations that evoke disturbed reactions, the less likely he/she is to operate flexibly: a fixed pattern of managing contact at the boundary results. And always (or never) rejecting what is said to one would represent a self-defeating contact style. In most circumstances, operating 'semi-permeably' allows us to be influenced to a degree by what impinges on us, neither 'swallowing it whole' nor 'spitting it out', but instead 'chewing it over' before assimilating and digesting it.

A second kind of contact boundary transaction relates to containment or expression of feelings, responses or energy. Again a failure of adaptability is evident if, say, a man has grown into adulthood rarely able to contain his angry feelings, so he flies into uncontrollable rages when frustrated. Another may have the opposite tendency, repeatedly to hold in or hold back – or *retroflect* – all his angry feelings, so that he becomes held in muscularly, in his voice, and with some possible accompanying somatic problems. A profoundly unbalanced life could follow from either habitual submergence of angry energy or from its repeated expression.

Again, most situations call for some combination of expression and control, with the contact boundary operating flexibly. We recognize that in some contexts release and full-bodied expression of feelings, or of our opinions, is appropriate and safe, whilst in other settings the consequences of expressing them might be serious. If, however, we are 'stuck' in either habitually retroflecting or alternatively expressing ourselves in extreme fashion, irrespective of the circumstances, we are likely to suffer unpleasant consequences of one kind or another.

A third contact boundary disturbance of particular interest in Gestalt therapy is where 'what belongs to self' is located as 'belonging to the environment'. Thus, a woman who is not owning her intelligence may be delighted by how intelligent her colleague seems. She *projects* her own qualities on to the other. When she learns to acknowledge that she herself is intelligent, the fascination with the other person's qualities may be less.

Projection is present universally, and is by no means always dysfunctional. Indeed, empathy and identifying with others' experience depend upon it, and in certain situations the complete absence of an ability to project would suggest a profoundly insensitive or even psychopathic response. Much projection, however, is limiting and the basis for much intractable human conflict in relationships and communities (e.g. two sides of a conflict regarding each other as aggressive and unreasonable).

A fourth focus of particular interest in contact styles relates to the extent to which the contact boundary separates 'self' from 'other'. If a boy joins a gang and his identity is altogether submerged, his separateness is temporarily put aside: he has become *confluent* with his environment. If, by contrast, he cannot fit in, feels altogether different and regards the situation as completely alien, he leans in the opposite direction of extreme differentiation or isolation.

If the contact boundary is operating flexibly, we can experience times both of 'losing ourselves in' and 'of not going along with' something in our environment. Both are functional. If, however, we habitually and without awareness lean towards one or the other pole, regardless of circumstances, then there are bound to be occasions when the result interrupts creative living.

There are a number of other contact transactions which form part of what Gestalt therapists notice, e.g. relating to how attention is sustained or deflected; and the degree to which individuals 'watch themselves' as they engage in an activity or, alternatively, 'surrender' to the experience (Clarkson, 1989). Since the Gestalt therapist is focusing on the ongoing act of living, the focus on contact styles is inevitably central. (Fuller descriptions are available elsewhere, e.g. Polster and Polster, 1973; Mackewn, 1997).

Acquisition of psychological disturbance

Gestalt therapists think of traumas and setbacks – such as disappointments, humiliations, being terrorized, rejections – as times when a person's field or life space is disrupted, perhaps massively or repeatedly. They endorse the widespread view that such emotional injuries are likely to be more disruptive the earlier in life that they occur. Research into post-traumatic stress reactions (Yule, 1999) reveals that experiences of terror, pain or other acute distress have long-term effects for those who have experienced them. These include dissociation and desensitization (both interruptions of present awareness), relational problems (including extreme contact styles of the kind described above), and damage to the sense of self.

While abuse or other severe traumas have received attention, as defined and recognized points where development was set back or psychological harm was done, Gestalt therapists go further. They are more inclined to approach human distress with an 'injury' model in mind rather than one implying 'illness'.

When a person experiences herself, say, as deeply misunderstood by a teacher, there is a 'rupture in the relational field' (Wheeler, 1995). She may feel awkward or embarrassed (which are varieties of the experience of shame) and – not feeling supported or 'met' by the environment – she adapts as resourcefully as she can. This may mean retroflecting or holding back her tears, recognizing that she may be further shamed if she cries; and/or she may decide to conform exactly to the teacher's wishes. Her spontaneous response is thereby partly or wholly replaced with a newly learned deliberate response. The episode, while over, has not as a gestalt been satisfactorily resolved. Her learning has taken a certain path, away from being a 'natural' or organismic reaction involving all of her. While the response in the short term is a creative adjustment to this particular field, the learning that has taken place could well limit her responses in other situations. At the moment of trauma – when feeling secure is suddenly lost – certain feeling states, body positions, thoughts, sensory experiences and biochemical secretions arise and occur together, and the situation is seen as dangerous or distressing. These holistic reactions form a specific gestalt which, if appropriate support were promptly reinstated, might well 'run their course'. Thus, were the traumatized child physically held by someone she trusted, the trauma might be short-lived and recovery swift. When, however, the loss of support is perpetuated, this gestalt remains unresolved as a *fixed gestalt*, frozen in time, and the adaptive responses become a fixed part of the repertoire of responses available to the child.

What happens is that this painful, perhaps consciously forgotten, traumatic time can be easily restimulated subsequently, with a concurrent re-emergence of the field conditions (including feelings or thoughts) which constituted aspects of the frozen or unresolved gestalt. When this occurs, the immediate response is to avoid further re-entry to this state of being. The learned adaptive response (e.g. the conformity to the powerful other) then appears as the known way to avoid its being reawakened, and is replayed.

To fall back on previously established habits of perceiving, feeling, thinking and acting is another way of saying that the person is no longer reacting experimentally and creatively to a newly emerging unique situation, but responding with an obsolete response to a different (past) situation. Instead of responding to the actual circumstances of here and now existence, the person is projecting the past into the present, and responding with yesterday's attempted solution. Obviously, the more that a person does this, the more 'out of touch' he or she will be. Behaviour, thinking and feeling will become stereotypic, and adaptability to real-life circumstances becomes more and more difficult. Further shaming experiences can follow (because the person is now behaving 'oddly'), and also changes in self-image. Emotionally injured people begin to suppress (or even blot out) feelings; they stop discriminating between their own needs and what they are expected to do (or feel); and they learn to function 'intentionally' and require – in order to act spontaneously and autonomously – more favourable and supportive conditions than before. Inevitably, their capacity to make and complete gestalts – wholes of experience – has been eroded. This in turn limits their capacity to self-manage and live experimentally. Their habitual contact styles are essentially adaptive and self-protective for the time being, but as they get older and move to new environments, these styles are not related at all to the actual situations they encounter. Yet they remain as hangovers from the past, played out in the present.

There are obviously many degrees of emotional injury. Life invariably has setbacks and problems, even for the most privileged. For some, who have been persistently abused or traumatized at an early age, their whole way of self-organizing and adjusting to life may have become dislocated, such that most contact with others and their ability to self-manage in a complex society has become affected. Such inability may be perceptual, in not taking in information but relying on fantasy (or in being hyper-vigilant, or both); or physically, in that the person may have little sensitivity (or alternatively may be 'allergic' to the slightest touch). Sometimes the person may be thought-disordered (or take refuge in logical intellectualizing). In some cases people begin to operate and relate in ways that strike others as bizarre or 'sick'. Tracing the origins, however, reveals that usually there is some particular set of field circumstances which were themselves strange or horrifying, and that the individual 'adjusted' to these conditions by adopting a particular style of being.

Perpetuation of psychological disturbance

It is central to Gestalt thinking that even though a person's pattern of disturbed functioning may have originated in the past, the manifestation of the disturbance is played out and witnessed in the present, and can only be undone (decon-structed) in the present. Individuals' fixed patterns (of adapting, getting by, manipulating, etc.) are often so habitual and taken for granted that they are not easily accessible to the person's present awareness. Indeed, he or she may not realize at all how much he/she is 'operating on automatic', and that alternative choices might be possible that would be more life-enhancing or creative.

As we have seen, these automatic patterns of thinking, moving and feeling arise as a result of some form of re-enactment of a previously unresolved, frozen or fixed gestalt. Suppose, for instance, that someone has to confront an angry person in a work setting. This evokes or triggers the memory (in or out of awareness) of an earlier traumatic situation (like being shouted at by an angry teacher). Then the old reactions, feeling state and sense of powerlessness are likely to be at least partially reawakened. An up-to-date, more mature or 'healthy' response may be possible, provided that the individual has enough self-support (a feeling of inner strength) and environmental support (in the form, say, of an assertive colleague being present when she confronts the angry person). How-ever, if the present total situation is no more supportive than at the time of the original trauma, then the old response is likely to be experienced similarly to how it was in the past.

The undoing or deconstructing of a fixed gestalt requires experimenting with a novel solution, usually experienced as a dangerous enterprise. Feeling unable to deal 'healthily' with the present situation may well lead to anxiety, a sense of confusion, and experiences of shame – which include 'feeling awkward', embar-rassed or shy. To change, and to update oneself, requires existentially entering the unknown. Catastrophizing is common – e.g. 'If I allow myself to feel sad, I'll fall apart altogether', or 'If I say "no" to him, he will walk out.' Only by changing the balance of forces, as it were, so there is sufficient backing and encourage-ment, will the person be able to take the risk of doing something new. The provision of adequate support is therefore crucial.

Given that it is so unsettling to deconstruct a fixed way of being – even if the person recognizes that the pattern is self-damaging or self-limiting – it is not surprising that disturbed patterns of behaviour and feeling are very difficult to shift. Moreover, in cases of more severe disturbance there often has to be extensive initial work of becoming more aware and finding ways to access available support in the field, before these experiments can be countenanced. So the familiar, if unwelcome, patterns are unlikely to alter for some time, even after therapy is under way.

Two further factors help to keep the fixed gestalt intact. The version of the self, which forms a part of that gestalt (e.g. my 'frightened self'), is only one of many selves. Another may be the 'self-critical self' (Polster, 1995). What often happens is that when one self appears the other soon follows, and an internal debate is set up between different selves. The individual recognizes that 'part of me wants to do X, but another part of me knows that it will be hopeless if I try'. This is a very frequent kind of confusion. So part of how 'disturbance' is maintained is by the endless circulating through these contradictory versions of self, without integra-tion or their 'working together'.

Secondly, the person, existing in a relational world, does not create a version of himself in isolation, but always with a 'self–other' referent (Beaumont, 1993). If he creates himself as 'a failure' he is probably creating others in his field as 'condemning of his failure' or as 'successful', and then he acts towards these imagined versions of the other as if these fantasies were true. Such expectations are well known to be often self-fulfilling. For instance, a man who was abused by a woman as a child, may believe that 'no women are trustworthy'. He therefore breaks eye contact, disregards evidence (that others may see) that the woman in front of him is kindly looking and 'safe', and seizes on the slightest evidence to confirm his view that she is unsafe. Finding confirmation of belief systems leads often to unaware manipulation of other people or of groups, and is a major way in which disturbed approaches to living are maintained.

Change

Gestalt therapy can be thought of as a potent means for speeding up the evolution of a person, yet development occurs anyway. People 'grow up', 'take on a new lease of life', 'come to their senses', or 'are forced to come to terms with things', as a result of changes in their life situation – like promotion at work, meeting a new partner, coping with illness, becoming a grandparent, or redundancy.

A person fixed in their relating to human situations has a reduced capacity for dealing with novel or stressful situations. Yet Gestalt therapists operate with the belief that the human being has an inbuilt urge to complete situations and to find an inner sense of balance and good form. They see themselves as assisting a natural life process of human creativity, potential resourcefulness and a desire to grow. A man, say, has a pattern of retreating from social contacts; it does not mean he will retain this as a fixed personal characteristic throughout life. He may find himself in a new work group where he is stimulated and encouraged to break his habit of withdrawal, and then finds that he 'is taken out of himself'. The next time he may be a little less reluctant to take part. Such growth experiences occur for all of us, throughout life, and many people change, mature and mellow as a result of unlearning patterns of avoidance and stereotyped reactions they acquired earlier in life. Some make these changes through therapy, others through life experience or a combination of both.

Gestalt therapy is based on a model of the change process that builds on these normal ways in which people develop and mature, and extends them. In offering a supportive relationship and context Gestalt therapists provide opportunities for personal exploration of how the client flourishes in the world and how he/she concurrently limits and distorts life experience in certain ways. The process of therapy becomes itself one of life's new situations: it offers an opportunity to experience life differently and to extend the range of ways in which a person can operate in the world with greater satisfaction.

Incremental change through assimilating new life (or therapy-generated) experiences is quite different from intentional self-reform or 'improvement' according to rules (as in diets or some religious teachings). This difference is reflected in Gestalt therapy in what is called the 'paradoxical theory of change' (Beisser, 1970). This says that change occurs when a person 'becomes what he is, not when he tries to become what he is not'. In other words, deliberate attempts to change by conscious control or acts of will are usually doomed: they set up an unconscious conflict between the will of the person and the unconscious 'saboteur' or 'underdog'. Instead, for individuals to 'move on' in life they need to begin with accepting what they are already doing. They may realize how they have left gestalts incomplete (e.g. by mourning a loss or expressing a resentment) and risk trying a new adaptation or response. Ordinary life situations call for these personal innovations, which are usually accompanied by fear reactions (from 'stage fright' to intense anxiety) but which, once achieved and practised, become part of the person's natural repertoire.

Practice

Goals of therapy

The work of therapy is to foster conditions in which individuals, at whatever level of awareness they start from, become active participants in developing *awareness, self-support, integration* and *the ability to interact authentically with others*. Building awareness is one key task. Much psychotherapy, deliberately or unwittingly, subscribes to a model in which the expertise of the specialist helper fosters dependency in the patient. The emphasis of Gestalt therapy is on encouraging the person, through developing greater self-awareness, to recognize his or her own expert status.

Developing the realization that ultimately we are the authors of our own lives (our own 'authority') may take time. At the beginning of therapy the person may be unable to assimilate this, in which case empowerment will be one focus of therapy. The goal is to promote self-support sufficient for the person to live a life of freedom and choice (thus increasing his or her 'response-ability'), so that he or she is not automatically dependent on favourable aspects of the environment in order to function creatively.

Integrating new ways of living and relating is not a one-off process – it continues throughout life. As Perls noted: 'there is always the possibility of richer maturation – of taking more and more responsibility for yourself' (1969b: 65). The therapeutic journey, as conceived in Gestalt therapy, is therefore potentially lifelong and for many people can turn into a meditative discipline or path (Parlett, 2001). Of course, not everyone engaged in Gestalt therapy whether as a client, trainee or therapist, goes this far; many will stop when they have restored, or learned, more satisfying ways of functioning in the world.

Gestalt therapy values individuals finding unique solutions to unique situations, recognizing the special nature of each person's history, circumstances, values, needs and preferences. The emphasis is on people finding their own goals and discovering their potential to meet these goals. Given that there are many aspects of our culture that do not support human well-being (e.g. overworking), the client may develop ways which run counter to normative expectations. Gestalt therapy has never been an 'adjustment' therapy (Perls et al., 1951)

Selection criteria

The Gestalt therapy approach orientates the work of its practitioners, but each therapist applies Gestalt principles in individual ways and uses different methods according to her/his training, professional background and personal style.

It follows from this that each therapist–client pairing is also individual and that to argue that certain persons are 'suitable' for Gestalt therapy as such, while others are unsuitable, does not make sense. A clinical psychologist working, say, in a hospital setting and from a Gestalt therapy base, may work therapeutically with severely fragmented and disoriented individuals, applying Gestalt principles appropriately and effectively. A school counsellor, on the other hand, though trained in Gestalt, would almost certainly not work with such individuals, although she might be well qualified to apply Gestalt thinking and practice to working with the children referred to her.

The most likely course of action for a practitioner, faced with an enquirer, will be to have an introductory meeting in order to assess what the individual might benefit from most – perhaps once- or twice-weekly individual sessions, joining an ongoing therapy group, or participating in a weekend workshop.

Practitioners of Gestalt therapy give emphasis to the unique nature of each person's therapeutic needs. Suppose, for instance, that the extent of disturbance is such that a client has little stability, and has been labelled 'psychotic' or 'borderline'. A high degree of environmental support and time, commitment and attention on the part of the therapist may be called for. This could entail residential care, with the therapist seeing the client *every* day for a specified period of time. Such conditions, even in hospital settings, are often not available, and it would be irresponsible to engage such a client in intensive exploration without sufficient environmental support.

Obviously, then, initial meetings and contacts are very significant. The person's presenting problem may indicate one form of intervention rather than another – a relationship problem might best be explored with the partner in couples therapy; someone cut off and lonely might benefit from a group. But the stress is on the special nature of each enquiry, not on any rule.

In weighing up what the person might benefit from most, the Gestalt therapist does not ignore the usual psychiatric diagnostic categories (Melnick and Nevis, 1992). However, she will want most to observe how aware the person is of his own process – i.e. of the current direction of his interest, bodily state, physical and social needs, feeling sense, and how capable he is of articulating his inner experience as it unfolds, i.e. in the 'here and now'. She will also note how he communicates with her (the client's contact style or functions), how he interrupts or blocks the flow of his experiencing himself, and how aware he is of doing so. The therapist may also think in terms of polarities, and be influenced by what strikes her as 'missing' with this person: e.g. he may manifest no assertiveness or, though married, fail to mention his wife or children. All of this may suggest to the therapist the appropriateness of a specific course of action. At this stage, one-to-one therapy might be suggested for someone who was unaware of, or unable to externalize, his inner experience. Joining a group might be thought desirable at a later stage, when the person has become more familiar with the Gestalt method – i.e. has acquired facility with its self-investigative procedures (which constitute both a demand for, as well as a means to, greater awareness).

Qualities of effective therapists

Basic to all training of Gestalt psychotherapists is that all trainees have prolonged individual and group therapy themselves. Gestalt therapy is an approach which is based on developing a full sensory awareness of self and others, and has to be learned by active participation. It decidedly cannot be learned from books and lectures. The approach has to be known from the inside, experienced as a powerful means of self-enquiry and progressively incorporated into one's own personal life and work as a therapist.

Effective Gestalt therapists, aside from having an adequate level of integration themselves, vary greatly in their personal and professional qualities. However, they are expected to manifest authenticity and openness about their feelings and reactions; as well as (hopefully) being skilful in handling a broad spectrum of interpersonal transactions (including intimacy, conflict, appropriate physical contact, emotional expression, separation and endings, and maintaining clear boundaries). In addition, they need to have acquired the ability to recognize their own preoccupations and problems and to deal with them in such a way as to be fully present and available for the client. On occasions when they are unable to do this they need to acknowledge that they are not competent to practise for the time being. They need to have a strong ethical base in other ways as well, and to be non-exploitative, having a fundamental respect for the integrity of the therapy process.

Therapeutic relationship and style

Although there are wide differences between Gestalt therapists, most would conceptualize what they do along the following (or similar) lines.

They aim to provide a relationship and setting which supports and provokes the person's exploring her 'here and now' experience – that is, what she is aware of in the actual, present context of being in the therapy room, relating to the therapist (or, in a group, with the other members). A further aim is to explore how the patterns that emerge in the therapy room or relationship may relate to the patterns that occur in the rest of the client's life – and especially the patterns that have brought him to therapy.

The emphasis given to exploring present reality in Gestalt therapy can easily be misunderstood: it does not mean that references to past and future are banned – that would be absurd. But when dwelling on past or future events, what the person is currently and actually doing is *remembering* or *anticipating*, both of which involve constructing an imagined reality in the present. Exactly *how* the person reconstructs her past, or formulates a vision of the future, is part of what she is doing at the moment. It is an essential part of the investigation of what the person actually does in the present, which is often more significant than what she says or reports about another time or place.

The emphasis on working with present experience as it arises in the consciousness of the client, moment by moment, places Gestalt broadly in the tradition of phenomenology (Spinelli, 1989). The Gestalt therapist is interested in first, rather than second thoughts; in the immediacy of images, however fleeting, and in passing ideas about himself rather than lengthy self-descriptions. The therapist may interrupt long discourses, inviting the client instead to notice what is happening now, in their immediate experience.

For the kind of exploratory work favoured by Gestalt therapists, a strong and supportive therapeutic relationship is necessary. The therapist's personal presence, interest in the client's life, and her commitment to the client's well-being, are taken for granted as being necessary foundations. A strong and loving connection supports the work of open-ended enquiry, the focus on the immediacy of exploring live experience in the therapy room, and on experimental action rather than on merely gaining insight. These can flourish only within a relationship where each party meets the other as a person, not as a role. The two parties engage in dialogue, not in one-way communication (Yontef, 1993; Jacobs, 2000). Gestalt therapists let themselves be themselves and encourage those they work with to do the same. Sometimes they may communicate (selectively) some of their own life experience, or express their own feelings. Obviously, this needs to be done with respect and a sense of timing, honouring the validity of the other's reality and not imposing their own views and values. Relating dialogically also calls for the therapist to 'show his caring by his honesty more than by his constant softness' (Yontef, 1984: 47). The major emphasis on the 'dialogic relationship' in present-day Gestalt therapy was inspired by the work of Martin Buber (1970), with his views of the healing power of meeting another person in an authentic way.

In addition to offering the possibility of a person-to-person relationship, and the focus on present experience and its direct investigation, Gestalt therapists also emphasize experimentation ('try it rather than talk about it': Zinker, 1977). 'All therapy is play,' said Fritz Perls, and the effective Gestalt therapist is skilled in creating experimental situations and methods to provide learning experiences which extend a person's repertoire. Experimenting enables the therapist and client, working together, to create (or re-create) conditions of the person's life space or field that can provide 'rehearsal space' for the development of new strategies, behaviour, or non-habitual modes of relating, moving, sensing, etc.

When it comes to the individual style it is difficult to generalize. The competent Gestalt therapist employs different styles according to person, situation and stage of therapy. His choices are based on skills and experience; his response to a particular instance depends on his creativeness (e.g. in finding ways to heighten the person's awareness of their surroundings). The therapist may at times be challenging, pointing out how he feels manipulated by a certain response of the client; at another time he may extend a hand, literally, to establish a channel of support when the client momentarily falters before taking a risk. He may listen intently and sympathetically to an emotionally laden account of an early trauma now being recounted for the first time. In contrast, with another person at another time, he may report his sense of being bored by the repeated recital of well-known facts. He is, after all, attending to individuals' unfolding realities, to their unique experiences; and this demands authentic, spontaneous and creative responses – not rehearsed reactions and 'therapy techniques', which demean the relationship.

Each Gestalt therapist is enjoined to find his or her own way of integrating and applying the philosophy and methodology of Gestalt therapy in a creative, intelligent, sensitive and ethical fashion that does justice to their talents, personality and background (Parlett, 2001). Each is encouraged to continue to develop their own ways of working skilfully.

Major therapeutic strategies and techniques

The exact way in which a Gestalt therapist will work varies from person to person and occasion to occasion. However, Resnick (1995) has suggested that (1) *attention to phenomenology*, (2) *dialogue in the relationship,* and (3) *holding a field perspective* all need to be present, for the therapy to be described as Gestalt therapy. The three are closely related. For instance, in building a therapy relationship based on dialogue and trust, the co-created field of 'therapist and client' and how the therapy fits within the person's wider life, are central and significant; and the exploration proceeds via investigating the 'live experience' of both the client and the therapist – i.e. their phenomenological realities. Within these broad parameters, there are also areas of concentration.

Support

The establishment of a sufficiently supportive context for therapy is perhaps the most important single feature of the approach in practical terms. Successful Gestalt therapy requires achieving a 'subject–subject' relationship between therapist and client, rather than one that is 'subject–object' (Wheeler, 1995). We exist, and grow, in relationship. Establishing the relationship as a real one based on a level of respectfulness equivalent to love is healing in itself (Latner, 1995). Inauthenticity or lack of being fully present can be deleterious to establishing a degree of openness and sense of security, which are necessary for risky life changes to be attempted.

Providing the right kind and level of support is a crucial skill. What is supportive – i.e. assists the process of enquiry and the client's 'flow' – has to be discovered in each case. Automatically handing a weeping client a box of tissues may be highly supportive for some, but for others who, when young, had parents who forbade their crying, the box of tissues arriving could be seen as a covert demand that they come out of the experience. (Of course, if the therapist makes a 'mistake' about such matters, it can be itself informative; if the therapist goes on to apologize for the 'rupture', it can sometimes be a therapeutic turning point: Jacobs, 2000.)

Almost intrinsic to therapy are shame reactions of various kinds. The client may be bringing issues that are intimate, difficult to talk about, and embarrassing. Some feel huge degrees of shame about aspects of their life, or about being in therapy at all. The therapist needs to be acutely aware of the possibility of heightening feelings of exposure, embarrassment or shame, often inadvertently or without recognizing that he or she is doing so. For some clients, even asking questions or making statements that are felt as 'personal' can be shaming. Taking 'a professional stance', including the making of interpretations by the therapist, can be subtly diminishing of the client from being 'subject' to 'object', and can be shaming.

Some degree of experienced shame is usually inevitable, given the nature of the therapeutic process and the broad intention of experimenting with novel behaviour. It is important that the experience of feeling ashamed is seen as a normal reaction to the feeling of being unsupported by others (Lee and Wheeler, 1996) and that clients discover they do not need to feel 'ashamed of their shame'. Ultimately, learning to tolerate the experience of shame is more useful to the client than trying to avoid it completely. Working with shame issues requires a particularly supportive setting: developing a therapy relationship where shame reactions can be safely addressed is of the first importance.

Awareness training

An important priority in Gestalt therapy is the focus on awareness training. The approach offers an equivalent (some say) to Zen training or other forms of meditation. Awareness is the key to personal experiment and change. If a man has suppressed his feelings, say, of love for his father, the process of becoming aware of *how* and *what* he suppresses is the first and necessary stage. He may simply wake up to what he is doing, or practise allowing the feelings to be expressed and even communicated to his father in person.

Awareness work involves practising attending to the bodily 'felt sense'. Through education in heightened awareness, individuals are effectively acquiring a 'biofeedback'system. By more accurately attuning themselves to their actual physical and emotional experience, moment by moment, they can recognize more accurately when they are tensing up, withdrawing, suppressing a feeling and, with this additional information, can choose to relax, breathe differently, speak out or withdraw, or whatever they need to do in order to feel more balanced or satisfied. The greater awareness of her process a person has, the more she can influence her life choices and destiny.

Working with polarities

The Gestalt therapist not only reacts to what is presented – the client's behaviour and experience in the session itself – but is also interested in 'what is missing'. It is a central tenet of Gestalt therapy that all of us have within us the potential for acting and experiencing differently from how we usually do. Each time someone identifies strongly with a particular 'quality' the more likely he is to have 'alienated' (Perls et al., 1994/1951) or rejected its polar opposite. Thus, if a man is always tidy and organized, he may be losing out on the experience of letting a little disorder and unpredictability into his life. He may represent the latter to himself as 'chaos and catastrophe'.

Gestalt therapy involves attending to such polarities, often renaming them in less pejorative language, exploring the associated feeling reactions to them, and uncovering gently the potentialities latent in the hitherto rejected behaviours and experiences.

Recognizing interruptions and avoidances

Human beings stop the flow of their naturally unfolding experience in numerous different ways. We may attempt to avoid painful or unpleasant memories, or certain emotions, or uncomfortable realizations. We interrupt awareness or restrict feelings by holding the breath, at the same time as tensing the musculature in certain parts of the body. Inhibition (wholesale avoidance of certain impulses), intellectualizing (often in the form of 'explaining away'), and displacement (e.g. instead of dealing with his wife he takes it out on his employee), are among other common patterns of avoidance.

By 'tracking' – or following closely what is happening for a person who is attending to and reporting his moment-by-moment thoughts, percepts, and feelings – the therapist is able to spot points of 'interruption of flow' in the ongoing process: e.g. shifts in vitality, changes in eye contact, movements in body position, a sentence left unfinished. All may indicate something withheld, glossed over, blotted out or diverged from. The therapist may sometimes draw attention frequently to such interruptions. At other times she may not intervene for long periods, perhaps letting the person tell his story (Polster, 1987) or leaving him to struggle to articulate some hitherto undefinable feeling. All depends on the total situation and the moment. Becoming aware of interrupted gestalts and avoidances in contact with others is the first step to relearning.

Working with the theme

Identifying a theme of a specific session, usually based on identifying something which *energizes* the client in the moment (not necessarily what they have planned to bring to therapy to discuss) permits the session to have a form – a gestalt in itself. Often it helps to clarify the theme, including a statement of something the individual *needs* (wants, craves, is determined to have) and pointing out how the person is *resisting* getting what she wants (holding back through fear of retribution, an imagined rejection, etc.). The therapist signals that she has no investment in a particular outcome, but is interested in the client exploring equally both the desire and the reluctance, the need and resistance.

It is easy to fall into imagining that if a client refuses a suggestion the therapist makes, he is 'resistant'. Yet resistance (rather like the French Resistance) can be celebrated as fighting spirit or sensible reluctance. In the field in which, say, 'holding back' was learned as a pattern, the choice then made (to hold back) was the best creative adjustment of which the client-as-child was then capable. In exploring the theme in the present, a realignment becomes possible, provided there is enough support in the present 'field of forces', which includes the presence and sensitivity of the therapist.

Working with transference

Transference reactions inevitably arise in the therapeutic relationship. However, in building the relationship, Gestalt therapists are continuously seeking a real rather than a transferential relationship. The therapist respectfully invites clients to use their eyes and ears to see and listen to the actual person behind their projections. The process of dissolving the transference is probably never fully completed but the whole tenor of the work is to acknowledge, investigate, and then move on from the imaginings a client may have, not to allow them to continue uninvestigated. Being able to maintain an 'adult to adult' relationship in parallel with episodes and periods of regression is a necessary part of integrating the therapy experience into the wider field of a person's present life. Important as is visiting the 'past-that-arises-in-the-present', Gestalt therapy is primarily about living present life, which includes in therapy a real relationship with a real human being.

Experimentation and techniques

Gestalt therapy provides experiential learning and the experiment is central: 'It transforms talking about doing into doing, stale reminiscing and theorizing into being fully here with all one's imagination, energy and excitement' (Zinker, 1977). It is the pursuit of greater awareness through active behavioural expression, entailing senses, skeletal muscles and full bodily and emotional involvement.

Experiments grow out of themes emerging during the tracking of ongoing awareness and are ways of 'thinking out loud (concretizing) one's imagination' (Zinker, 1977). There are no set structures or techniques, though necessary preconditions for a successful experiment include ensuring that the person is 'grounded' and has sufficient self-support; that the experiment is pitched at the right level of risk for the individual at the time; and that he understands what he is doing and has agreed to it. It also needs to incorporate the person's own language and images. The therapist's creativity in expanding on these ideas is also important.

Experiments can be simply minor additions to 'tracking' – i.e. following the awareness reporting of the client. Thus, a man reporting that he is 'fed up with working' may be hunching his shoulders as he says it. The therapist might invite him to exaggerate the posture of his body, or to stay in the hunched position to explore what it may represent. Alternatively the experiment might be exploring an 'opposite' body position. All of these would be designed to fill out the experience – always more than a verbal description.

Other experiments may involve deliberately rearranging the field to provide for a risky-seeming 'first try' at a new behaviour which the client wishes to explore – perhaps asking fellow members of a group for feedback about her appearance. The task of the therapist is to help design and focus the experiment, checking that there is sufficient support in the field (e.g. enough encouragement, time, freedom from interruptions) to enable the person to try out what she wants. The conditions should not be so safe that the client finds the experiment 'too easy' with no extending of her experience.

Experimentation can employ any of a whole variety of media, from dramatizations, dance or other physical movement, to dialogues between parts of the self, sculpting, artwork, working with dreams, fantasy trips, trying out specific language or behavioural changes. Often the therapist will encourage metaphorical and intuitive thinking, which in the majority of people is less developed than their capacity to be verbal and explanatory.

Some experiments have become classics – for instance the 'empty chair', in which a person speaks to someone with whom she has unfinished business, or to another part of herself, a polar opposite (the 'weak' side may speak to the her 'strong' side). She may then move to the other chair and react from that position – either being the other person or the other aspect of self.

'Two-chair work' has been widely copied and used by therapists from other schools, so we shall say more about it. As a means of exploring communication between different selves (or between 'self' and 'other'), physical shifts – such as moving from seat to seat – can assist in symbolizing profound changes in field conditions, i.e. how a life scene is seen from one position or from another. However, many Gestalt therapists use other ways of differentiating the field, perhaps by inviting the client to take two particular body positions or turning the lights down or up, and do not rely on chairs. If they do set up this particular experiment they are likely to adapt it according to circumstances – which can never be anticipated. What is important is to attend to what is needed at the time: perhaps turning the experiment into moving between three places, or the therapist taking one of the parts herself, or upturning or reversing or elevating one chair to make a point. The precise 'technique' is irrelevant, because the focus is actually upon, say, heightening differentiation and exploring possible integration of selves, and there are any number of ways in which this can be done, once the principle has been understood.

Gestalt therapy experimentation needs to be perpetually innovative to accord with exactly what is required in a unique situation. Although Gestalt techniques have been widely copied, their use in isolation from the rest of the Gestalt therapy system is highly questionable. They are not recipes. As Yontef has remarked: 'There is no Gestalt therapy cookbook. . .therapy is an art [requiring] all of the therapist's creativity and love' (1988: 32).

The change process in therapy

Work with awareness lies at the heart of Gestalt therapy: attending to present experience, noticing what the person is doing, and recognizing her processes of contact and avoidance. Yontef (1988) has suggested a developmental sequence within therapy in which initially the client may talk about her problem but may have little awareness of what she is actually doing. In the course of therapy she recognizes how unaware she was previously; she begins to notice her character-istic style of avoidance. In time, she learns to recognize the ways she has been interrupting the natural process of gestalt formation and completion. She becomes aware of being aware and (paradoxically) of being unaware. The next stage is when the person 'becomes aware of [her] overall character structure', her general patterns and the conditions which give rise to her being less aware. Finally, the high level of awareness reached in therapy 'permeates the person's ordinary life' (Yontef, 1988).

Another way that Gestalt therapists think of change is in terms of figure formation and completion of gestalts. Movement in therapy is signalled by the person being more skilful in completing unfinished situations from the past and also with new gestalts arising in the present. He learns to avoid his avoidance; he interrupts more of his interruptions as they happen. In the process he acquires greater facility in forming and completing gestalts, and experiences more fulfil-ment and less dissatisfaction.

Limitations of the approach

The major limitation of Gestalt therapy is the reverse side of one of its strengths. Because it requires a high level of therapeutic participation and creativity, and an ability to work in numerous different ways, there are real difficulties in teaching the approach, in communicating its essence to those who have not directly experienced it, and in codifying its methods and concepts in ways that are helpful to practitioners and trainees while not oversimplifying it.

Additionally, there is wide acknowledgement that until recently Gestalt ther-apists have paid little attention to infant development. Developmental theories have tended to be borrowed from psychoanalytic sources. Daniel Stern's (1985) book presents a model of infant development which is congruent with Gestalt theory and the development of the self (Gillie, 1999).

More generally, certain criticisms of therapy (see, for instance, Hillman and Ventura, 1992) strike home hard for Gestalt therapists. Acknowledging the environment or situation as a major co-determinant of the person's mental health means there is an obvious responsibility for linking therapy with activity directed at social, community-orientated or political change (Parlett, 2000). Yet by and large Gestalt therapists have done little in this regard, working with individuals and couple systems without attending to the wider field of society and the times we live in. They are not alone in this among therapists, but the model of Gestalt therapy offers no comfortable justification for avoiding such involvement.

Case study

The client

Frankie came to see me for three years. She had joined AA the week before, having been on a major drinking binge again after a period of abstinence. She had major reservations about going into therapy, having worked for many years as the administrator of a therapy centre. As a result of this exposure she knew quite a lot about that kind of therapeutic style of intervention, one that happened to emphasize expression and catharsis. This 'insider' knowledge fuelled her cynicism and fear and nearly paralysed her.

Almost as soon as she had sat down, she thrust a large envelope into my hands, looking terrified, mumbling that she was a drunk, a failure, and had been sexually abused as a child. These notions, of confession, expression and release, were what she thought she needed, like a dreadful purgative. I could see that Frankie was pushing herself without regard for the supports that were not yet in place, so I concentrated on her sense of personal safety. I asked her what she would lose if she gave me her story in this fashion. Without hesitation she answered, 'My privacy.' I told her that I had the impression that it might still be needed. Why, at this early stage, would she yet want to trust me? I asked her if she would be willing to keep her papers until she had something other than privacy to support her. I did very little else at that first meeting except make space to listen. She said later that my lack of reactivity was crucial. It set the tone of her being in charge, of her feeling that the *whole of her*, rather than her abuse and alcoholism alone, were what mattered; and that I was already different enough from the therapists whose approach had frightened her.

We are writing here of field conditions, those all-important features of the entire situation that frame and support the therapeutic process. There were others. At this first meeting Frankie met my cat. Since her only intimate relationship was with her own cat (who was at that time very sick with a terminal illness), this common aspect of our lives created a crucial bridge between us, as the first few months of our working together centred on this. Even though my cat had an entirely different meaning in my life than did Frankie's in hers, it provided an opportunity for me to see what she projected of her own lost self on to them.

My first impression of Frankie was of a *large* woman in her forties who didn't seem connected to her body, for which she had an unselfconscious disregard – often sprawling like an un-jointed wooden puppet at rest. Her nails were chewed down to the quick. She seemed completely non-sexual. Indeed, even the matter of her sexual orientation was something that we did not explore for a long while, being nearly as much a mystery to her as to me.

In the first few months I began to piece together the story of Frankie's life, alongside the unfolding drama of the illness and the death of her cat which occurred after some weeks. The loss of this familiar means of support was a huge shift in her life space. It triggered a deluge of grief. I had told Frankie that she should feel free to call me. This level of availability is certainly not standard practice, but I knew that Frankie was learning to lean on another for the very first time in her life, so I wanted to be available, even at some cost to me. I knew she would not misuse this loosening of boundaries. She fell into my arms as she poured out her grief. My willingness to hold Frankie was not something automatic but arose out of the specific field conditions of our relationship. She would not, I judged, feel my touch as abusive or seductive, but as comforting. She rightly saw the gesture as a human sharing of grief, rather than the opening up of a transferential need. It was a source of pride to her that she could let herself be comforted, to put her needs above what she imagined mine to be, just for once.

Frankie was born the youngest child to a highly placed academic family. It was a privileged life, though full of restrictive family rules. Her mother was loving, but in practice more devoted to making sure that nothing disturbed the genius of her husband than noticing the personal needs of her children. So by the age of 11, it was part of Frankie's way of experiencing herself to feel somewhat left out. This had made her decide, one day, to disobey her mother's words of warning and go with a group of older children to an unsupervised place where she was sexually abused by several boys. Knowing that she had already broken the rules by going with them, and believing that she would be treated with anger rather than concern, she tried to manage her terror and shame alone. She turned that anger against herself and held it in for the next 35 years.

After this episode, Frankie could not really continue to develop. She was suspended in an 11-year-old's mind and body. Instead of ending up at university like her brilliant siblings, she veered off and went to live abroad, gradually developing the lifestyle of an alcoholic. She had so much fear around sex that her rare moments of possible intimacy ended disastrously as soon as they began. On returning to this country she slid further into difficulties, losing her financial security and the patience of her family. By making a huge effort, she managed to substitute work for drink, although overwork eventually made her ill – she lost weight and eventually succumbed again to drink.

The therapy

Employers saw in her a capacity to do things formidably well. But she could not use this power wisely, on her own behalf. Instead she projected it, on two of her great loves. Music was the first, and the voice and presence of Jessye Norman in particular. Like Frankie, Jessye Norman was a large woman, but unlike her, Jessye was not afraid of the glare of publicity, or of being brilliant. The second love was flying. Frankie adored being a passenger in planes. She experienced flight as pure freedom and loved the marvel of feeling the huge power of the engines, although her nightlife was peppered by nightmares about planes crashing.

So the question for me as her therapist was, *what might help Frankie have these powers for herself?* Given her particular history, what should we attend to?

Frankie generally did things well. Coming from a scientific background she was methodical and practical. Allowing herself to de-focus, to make interpretive leaps, to enter into the experience of others – all those abilities seemed less developed. Although she had tried hard to forget about her difficulties, certain memories continued to surface – mostly in her nightmares. She had desensitized herself especially by alcohol. She was almost permanently critical, even enraged, but accustomed to being isolated and to dealing with the ferocious and cruel voices of her family introjects by silent submission.

I therefore wanted, initially, to concentrate on being the 'missing' listener. I encouraged her to recount her entire story in considerable detail, which she did – except the abuse and her relationship with her mother. In helping her develop a sense of dialogue and mutuality, I encouraged her to take pauses and let herself take in the impact of her story on me – to see my admiration, my distress for her, my engagement, my lack of judgement. But I did not intervene more actively. Occasionally she needed help to lower the intensity of her experience.

After some months, she was ready to talk about the trauma of her mother's death. I heard Frankie's detailed narrative, and then invited her to imagine her mother present in the room with us, so she could tell her everything she had never spoken of. This brought forth a massive release of tension and grief and of the surfacing of many profound and unanswered questions, which took place over many sessions. Gradually, she came into contact with a fuller sense of her mother, of both her strengths and her limitations. However, she continued to avoid mentioning anything about either her sexuality or the abuse.

Frankie had been attending AA meetings several times a week since our first meeting, and what she could share with me she gradually took out into that community and begin to share with her fellow members of AA. I considered this 'layered' therapy extremely beneficial. After me came AA, and after that she was able to start talking to her siblings and friends.

There came a session after about 18 months when Frankie was wanting to go beyond storytelling. She spoke despairingly of her heart as being locked inside many boxes, wondering if she would ever come to meet it. So I invited her to travel through to her heart in fantasy, encouraging her to unlock door after door and find out. She did this as an internal exercise, her eyes closed, with me just making quiet suggestions as she sat opposite me. The impact of this exercise was enormous. For the first time in her adult life she felt wide open, very soft, and, at least in my presence, extraordinarily safe. However, once she left the room, she was terrified, believing that her heart's vulnerability could not cope with the buffeting of everyday life. She asked for an extra session where I showed her how to close the doors again in her imagination so that she could choose the level of vulnerability that felt safe.

Frankie saw those 'locked doors' as guardians of deep hurts from the abuse which she would not be able to open safely until she had found some kind of healing. She was very frightened and veered off the topic, session after session. I let her, telling her that she would know the right moment to begin. She would often panic and retreat. I showed her how to manage the panic, how to breathe, ground and soothe herself. I normalized this crisis until eventually, by the end of our second year together, she was able to break through the appalling silence enveloping the event. I was greatly moved by the simplicity and truthfulness of her telling. Every detail of what happened was etched deep in her child-body memory. During the many sessions that it took to tell me what happened there were times when she couldn't breathe, look me in the eye or speak. She spent sleepless nights remembering, reliving the terror. I reminded her to use her capacity to dissociate on her own behalf, to put distance between herself and the events so that she was not so over-whelmed. Gradually, as she unpacked the story with more and more feeling and detail, she drew close enough to feel her bewildered terror, grief, fury and despair, her shame and hatred and, gradually, her compassion.

This was a long process. It was important that she could see I was affected, over and over, by her suffering, and yet remain separate. I knew these violent waves of feeling would pass, and they did, though there were moments when I would have loved to relieve her of the savagery of the self-hatred that sometimes erupted in her.

There came a time, however, when this was no longer the sole focus of our meetings. As the abuse began to lose its power she could turn her attention to other matters. Our sessions became times for assimilating the impact of the contact she was having outside the therapy room with the people who really mattered to her. When Frankie was blunt and opinionated, or deeply uncertain, I often took the missing tack, providing ballast for her more extreme positions. She became less extreme, less impatient and judgmental, and her natural funniness emerged more often. We were making up for the missing years. I interrupted more often, disagreed, extended and reformulated, suggested, challenged, and lingered.

It was through AA that Frankie met her first intimate lover. Halfway through the third year with me she fell ecstatically in love, with a woman. She did not tell me immediately but I could sense that something had changed. Whatever ordinary difficulties now lay ahead for Frankie it was wonderful to see her experiencing an intimate friendship with another person. The need for me fell away sharply, although she stayed for a few months just to get used to her new status as a loved woman.

Soon after Frankie left therapy, she sent me a copy of a certificate she had gained, of her first pilot's flight. She now was literally in charge of that engine of power, and she adored it as much as she had always imagined she would. The dreams of crashing had faded. After a while, I also heard that she went on to do distinguished work in her field, earning respect from people as prestig-ious as her family.

Frankie had given me tapes of Jessye Norman's concerts at various times during our meetings. I enjoyed listening to them and learning more about her particular fascination. But as she was leaving, she also bought an extra ticket to a live Jessye Norman concert and asked me to come. I spent a long time puzzling out with her the importance of my being present. What might it mean to her for me to agree to step outside the specific field of our relationship into the 'outside world', a place where symbol and reality might truly meet? The more I pressed her, the clearer she was that she wanted me to *share* her enormous pleasure in the music, nothing more. In her private and fiercely guarded inner world she had never truly wanted to share anything precious before. Sharing involved loss of control (what if Jessye Norman was having an 'off' night?), and this she wished to experience in reality, not just in the therapy room. She knew I enjoyed the music; she was not foisting something on me I would not have accepted with pleasure in another setting.

Therapists are assumed to be givers to, rather than receivers from, their clients. They take payment, and satisfaction, so that give and take remain balanced. Here I was being asked to be another kind of receiver: a fellow concert-goer, and also a person to be acknowledged. Accepting this invitation would require of me that I put down some of the established culture's expectation (as well as my own) of being a 'detached' professional. Yet, within the practice of Gestalt is a much stronger requirement: that of the healing potential of genuine contact. I decided to accept the invitation, and enjoyed the concert, though I felt 'strange'. Paradoxically, Frankie told me later that she had gradually become less enthralled by Jessye Norman as that great sense of power was now her own.

Acknowledgements

We would like to thank Joel Latner and Jenny Mackewn for their helpful comments on an earlier draft.

References

Beaumont, H. (1993) 'Martin Buber's "I–Thou" and fragile self-organization: Gestalt couples therapy', *British Gestalt Journal*, 2(2): 85–95.

Beisser, A. (1970) 'The paradoxical theory of change', in J. Fagan and I. Shepherd (eds), *Gestalt Therapy Now*. New York: Harper & Row.

Buber, M. (1970) *I and Thou*. New York: Scribner's.

Clarkson, P. (1989) *Gestalt Counselling in Action*, 2nd edn. London: Sage.

Gillie, M. (1999) 'Daniel Stern: a developing theory for Gestalt?' *British Gestalt Journal*, 8(2): 107–17.

Hillman, L. and Ventura, M. (1992) *We've Had a Hundred Years of Psychotherapy and the World's Getting Worse*. New York: Harper.

Houston, G. (1993) *Being and Belonging*. Chichester: John Wiley.

Jacobs, L. (2000) Interview 'Respectful dialogues' with J. Mackewn, *British Gestalt Journal*, 9 (2): 105–16.

Kepner, J. (1987) *Body Process. A Gestalt Approach to Working with the Body in Psychotherapy*. New York: Gardner Press (Gestalt Institute of Cleveland Press).

Latner, L. (1995) Letter to the Editor, *British Gestalt Journal,* 4(1): 49–50.

Lee, R. and Wheeler, G. (eds). (1996) *The Voice of Shame*. Cleveland: GIC Press.

Mackewn, J. (1997) *Developing Gestalt Counselling*. London: Sage.

Melnick J. and Nevis, S. (1992) 'Diagnosis; the struggle for a meaningful paradigm', in *Gestalt Therapy – Perspectives and Applications*. New York: Gardner Press (Gestalt Institute of Cleveland Press).

Parlett, M. (1991) 'Reflections on field theory', *British Gestalt Journal*, 1(2): 69–81.

Parlett, M (2000) 'Creative adjustment and the global field', *British Gestalt Journal,* 9(1): 15–27.

Parlett, M (2001) 'Being present at one's own life', in *Embodied Theory*. London: Continuum.

Perls, F.S. (1969a) *Ego, Hunger and Aggression: The Beginning of Gestalt Therapy* (1942). New York: Vintage Books.

Perls, F.S. (1969b) *Gestalt Therapy Verbatim*. Moab, UT: Real People Press.

Perls, F.S., Hefferline, R.F. and Goodman, P. (1994) *Gestalt Therapy: Excitement and Growth in Human Personality* (1951). Highland, NY: Gestalt Journal Press.

Philippson, P. (2002) *Self in Relation*. Highland, NY: Gestalt Journal Press.

Polster, E. (1987) *Every Person's Life is Worth a Novel*. New York: Norton.

Polster, E. (1995) *A Population of Selves*. San Francisco: Jossey-Bass.

Polster, E. and Polster, M. (1973) *Gestalt Therapy Integrated*. New York: Brunner Mazel.

Resnick, R. (1995) Interview 'Gestalt therapy: principles, prisms and perspectives' with M. Parlett, *British Gestalt Journal*, 4(1): 3–13.

Spinelli, E. (1989) *The Interpreted World*. London: Sage.

Stern, D.N. (1985) *The Interpersonal World of the Infant*. New York: Basic Books.

Wheeler, G. (1991) *Gestalt Reconsidered: A New Approach to Contact and Resistance*. New York: Gardner Press.

Wheeler, G. (1995) 'Shame in two paradigms of therapy', *British Gestalt Journal*, 4(2).

Wolfert, R. (2000) 'Self in experience, Gestalt therapy, science and Buddhism', *British Gestalt Journal*, 9(2): 77–86.

Yontef, G.L. (1984) 'Modes of thinking in Gestalt therapy', *The Gestalt Journal*, 7(1): 33–74.

Yontef, G.L. (1988) 'Assimilating diagnostic and psychoanalytical perspectives into Gestalt therapy', *The Gestalt Journal,* 11(1): 5–32.

Yontef, G.L. (1993) *Awareness, Dialogue and Process*. New York: The Gestalt Journal Press.

Yule, W. (ed.) (1999) *Post-Traumatic Stress Disorders*. Chichester: Wiley.

Zinker, J. (1977) *Creative Process in Gestalt Therapy*. New York: Brunner Mazel.

Zinker, J. (1994) *In Search of Good Form*. San Francisco: Jossey-Bass.

Suggested further reading

Clarkson, P. and Mackewn, J. (1993) *Fritz Perls*. London: Sage.

Mackewn, J. (1997) *Developing Gestalt Counselling*. London: Sage.

Polster, E. and Polster, M. (1973) *Gestalt Therapy Integrated*. New York: Brunner Mazel.

Yontef, G.L. (1993) *Awareness, Dialogue and Process*. New York: The Gestalt Journal Press.

Zinker, J. (1977) Creative Process in Gestalt Therapy. New York: Brunner Mazel.

10 Transactional Analysis
Keith Tudor and Robin Hobbes

Historical context and development in Britain

Historical context

Transactional analysis (TA) was founded by Eric Berne (1910–70), a Canadian psychiatrist who originally trained as a psychoanalyst. Its theories of personality, child development and psychopathology offer a comprehensive theory of therapy, whilst its theory of communication, applied to social (*inter*-personal, *extra*-psychic) as well as psychological (*intra*-personal, *intra*-psychic) systems, offers a framework for understanding and analysing groups and organizations (see Berne, 1963, 1966). Historically, its philosophical and intellectual roots lie in empiricism, phenomenology, existentialism and humanism, roots nourished by the political radicalism of aspects of American and, specifically, Californian culture in the 1960s and 1970s.

The history of TA is well documented – see, for instance, James (1977), as well as previous editions of this handbook (Collinson, 1984; Clarkson and Gilbert, 1990; Clarkson et al., 1996). Here, we are concerned to identify the historical context and development of TA in terms of the influences on Berne, both personally and philosophically.

Two major influences on Berne were Paul Federn (1870–1950) and Eric Erikson (1902–94), with both of whom he was in analysis and from whom he derived and developed key ideas in TA:

- an interest in ego psychology (Federn, 1952) – which was seminal in Berne's later development of the ego state model of personality (see below, pp. 244–5);
- a concern in working with severely disturbed patients in the context of psychiatric hospitals (again from Federn) – which informed Berne's development of TA as a model for understanding and working with disordered thinking (contamination) and regressiveness (exclusion) (see below, p. 246);
- the structured and sequential view of human development (Erikson, 1951) – which has informed TA's theory of 'life script' (although more recent studies in child development have questioned this linear view, a critique which has been taken up within TA, see Cornell, 1987);
- the view that personality can only be understood in a psycho-*social* context (Erikson, 1951, 1968) – a perspective which is echoed in Berne's (1975a) view of TA as a 'social psychiatry' and, fundamentally, a *group* psychotherapy.

As we have indicated, four major philosophical influences may be discerned in the history and development of TA.

Empiricism

Whilst Berne was clearly influenced by psychoanalysis, he was critical of its overtheorizing and of its elitism. This led him to construct a theory, which, although psychodynamic in concept, could be checked out directly against observations. For Berne, (visual) observation 'is the basis of all good clinical work' (1966: 65–6) and, ideally, the therapist should use all five senses in diagnosis, assessment and treatment planning. This emphasis has led to a strong cognitive-behavioural strand to TA (see, for instance, Mothersole, 2001). The requirements for a valid therapeutic contract in TA – that it is behavioural, observable and finishable (as well as bilateral) – clearly reflects empiricism. Stewart suggests that observability is important in Berne's theory for three reasons:

1 It means that TA is effective as a social psychology.
2 It makes TA practice relatively easy to replicate, and therefore relatively straightforward to teach.
3 It renders the theory of TA testable (1992: 18).

Phenomenology

The view that we can best understand the world by direct personal experience finds its expression in TA in one of the (four) requirements for ego state diagnosis which is only validated 'if the individual can finally re-experience in full intensity, with little weathering, the moment or epoch when he assimilated [in this case] the parental ego state' (Berne, 1975a: 76). Indeed, with its structural analysis of ego states, Berne viewed TA as a 'systemic phenomenology' which (then) filled a gap in psychological theory.

Existentialism

There are many different views of existentialism and differences of emphasis, especially between American and European traditions. Berne (1971b: 8), who was a dedicated poker player, used this to describe what he meant by existentialism:

> poker is one of the few really existential situations left in the world. . .everybody's on their own. Nobody's going to feel sorry for you. You're fully responsible for everything you do. Once you've put the money in the pot, you've put it in the pot. You can't blame anybody else. You have to take the consequences of that.

TA's three basic philosophical tenets – that people are OK, that everyone has the capacity to think, and that people decide their own destiny (and that these decisions can be changed) – are generally viewed as reflecting existential thinking. C. Sills (personal communication, May 2001), however, suggests that the true existential position is 'I am, You are' and that the attributed value of OKness is a humanistic influence. Nevertheless, Berne's 'I'm OK, You're OK' (I + U +) life position was a significant addition to the previous Kleinian 'positions': paranoid (I + U –), depressive (I – U +) and schizoid (I – U –). In his last work *What Do You Say After You Say Hello* Berne (1975b) extended these four two-handed positions to include third parties thus: I + U + They + – a significant development, the importance of which for human conduct is, in our view, underestimated both within and outside TA (see Tudor, 1999b).

Humanism

A number of TA's theoretical strands and principles derive from humanism and, historically, both drew on the (then) emerging 'third force' humanistic psychology and contributed to its development:

- TA's therapeutic slogans (Berne, 1966): Above all do no harm; (a belief in) the curative power of nature; and the notion that 'I treat, God cures'.
- TA's therapeutic attitudes (Berne, 1966), including the importance of the therapist's authenticity. This is echoed in the importance of mutuality in TA, as represented, for example, in the bilaterality of the therapeutic method and, specifically, therapeutic contracts.
- Open communication and accessibility. Berne once said that 'anything that can't be said in front of the patient isn't worth saying' and he was one of the first psychiatrists to develop staff–patient case conferences (see Berne, 1968b). Berne's insistence on accessibility extended to theory. The translation of complex ideas – Freud's 'repetition compulsion' becomes 'psychological games' – has been one of the great contributions of TA to psychology and psychotherapy in general, and, at the same time, has laid it open to accusations of 'pop psychology', charges not helped by the misrepresentation of TA theory from both outside and, at times, within TA.

TA's humanistic roots, identity and location are the subject of some debate amongst both generic writers and within TA: Stewart (1992), for instance, places TA within the psychodynamic stream and Moiso and Novellino (2000: 186) argue vociferously for TA as 'the most promising form of neo-psychoanalytic psychotherapy'. Whilst clearly drawing on elements from the other two 'forces' in psychology – indeed, humanistic psychology itself is, as Maslow acknowledged, an *epi*-psychology (epi = 'building upon') – we consider TA to be essentially (i.e. ontologically), epistemologically and methodologically a humanistic psychotherapy (see Tudor, 1996) and as consistent with core beliefs of humanistic psychology theory and practice (see AHPP, 1998).

Now, 50 years on from Berne's early writings, TA has developed both theoretically and organizationally (for details of which see the *International Transactional Analysis Association [ITAA* website]; Stewart and Joines, 1987; Clarkson et al., 1996). This is supported by a number of publications: the international quarterly *Transactional Analysis Journal* and monthly newsletter *The Script*, both produced by the ITAA, and, in Britain, the journal *TA UK*, produced by the Institute of Transactional Analysis (ITA). TA's developing theory and practice is also well represented in publications of the last four years (see especially Midgeley, 1999; Hargaden and Sills, 2002; Joines and Stewart, 2002;

Lister-Ford, 2002; Sills and Hargaden, in press; Tudor, 2002). In addition to the clinical field which encompasses psychotherapy and counselling, TA has recognized applications in educational and organizational fields. Reflecting the diversity of thinking and practice within the field of psychotherapy in general, there are a number of distinct strands or 'Schools' within TA (see p. 243).

Development in Britain

The beginnings of TA in Britain have been recorded by Allaway (1983) and Collinson (1983) and summarized in previous editions. Collinson describes three broad and overlapping stages to the development of TA in Britain, beginning in 1962 with the first TA classes run by John Allaway and Joe Richards at the University of Leicester. The second stage was marked in April 1972 by the establishment of a TA discussion group in London initiated by Lawrence Collinson and David Porter, and in November 1972 by the first official '101' introductory course in Sheffield, organized by Alan Byron and run by Warren Cheney, a psychotherapist and teaching member of the ITAA. The third stage began in 1973 with the establishment of TA groups and workshops with the authorization of the ITAA. Here, in the spirit of the narrative turn of psychotherapy, we invite Michael Reddy, one of the people most associated with the development of TA in Britain in its early days, and the first British teaching member of the ITAA, to take up its story.

> 1973 was a watershed year for TA in the UK. I was back in London after six years abroad mostly in the USA. A diffident young man called David Porter tracked me down via ITAA and introduced me to a TA study group which met somewhere in Hampstead or Highgate. David later became the first Editor of ITA's tiny *Bulletin*. Margaret Turpin was a member of that group. She and I were the only professionals involved (from medicine and psychology, respectively) and it was not long before we found four others keenly interested in TA: two doctors, David Connell from London and Alan Byron from Sheffield, Emeritus Professor John Allaway from Nottingham, and Paul Brown a London-based psychologist. We six formed a Steering Group which I chaired, most of our meetings taking place at 39 Fitzjohns Avenue, Hampstead. We produced a Constitution and became the founders of the Institute of Transactional Analysis, doing all the things a professional body does: running approved courses, setting training standards, mounting conferences and seminars, and producing a house journal. We would have called it 'The British Association for Transaction Analysis' but the use of 'British' had (then) been recently banned so we chose 'Institute' as best expressing the professional standing for which we were aiming.
>
> By now TA in the UK was growing rapidly. ITA conferences were well attended, membership grew, and standards were being developed, though I have to admit my own clinical member (CM) exam would scarcely have passed muster today! The core of the exam was Jack Dusay (a psychiatrist and successor to Eric Berne as ITAA President) role-playing a florid paranoid schizophrenic in a café on the Boulevard St Germain in Paris. My strongest recollection is of the place emptying rather quickly!
>
> Alan Byron remained active for quite some time and to some extent David Connell, but it is Margaret Turpin who has devoted half a lifetime to TA. I went on to chair the

Steering Group for the European Association for Transactional Analysis (EATA), following an inspired initiative in 1974 by Bob Goulding when an amazing number of people turned up for the first European Congress at Villars in Switzerland. Most of the prominent Americans were there but what surprised us was the large number of practitioners from every corner of Europe. Konstanz Robertson-Rose (Switzerland), Arnold Van Westering (Netherlands) and I put our heads together, held an inaugural meeting on the spot and EATA was born. I stayed with EATA as Chair and then first President.

Theoretical assumptions

As we have indicated, there are a number of different traditions or 'Schools' within TA,[1] drawing on a broad range of influences:

- *Classical TA (psychodynamic)*, drawing on Berne's early work, developed most recently by Carlo Moiso and Michele Novellino (see Moiso, 1985) and influenced by object relations theory;
- *Classical TA (cognitive-behaviourist)*, also drawing on Berne's work (for a recent contribution to which see Mothersole, 2001), a tradition which has also been influenced by methods from neurolinguistic programming (see Stewart, 1996);
- *Redecision School*, founded by Mary and Robert Goulding (see Goulding and Goulding, 1979) and influenced by Fritz Perls and Gestalt therapy;
- *Cathexis School*, founded by Jacqui Schiff (see Schiff et al., 1975) and developed from Jacqui and Mo Schiff's experience of working with severely disturbed and psychotic clients;
- *Radical or Social Psychiatry* (in many ways, the 'lost tradition' of TA), originally promoted by Claude Steiner and others (see Agel, 1971; Wyckoff, 1976), based on a theory of alienation and influenced by radical politics (for a more recent summary of which see Steiner, 2000);
- *Integrative TA*, influenced by Gestalt conceptualizations of the ego and self-psychology (see Erskine and Moursund, 1988; Clarkson, 1992);
- *Narrative TA*, influenced by field theory, social constructivism and dialogic psychotherapy (see Allen and Allen, 1995, 1997; Summers and Tudor, 2000).

Of course each tradition, drawing on and emphasizing different theory and models, carries different and, at times, differing underlying theoretical assumptions. In this section (and, indeed, in the chapter as a whole) we aim to represent TA whilst acknowledging and in part reflecting the complexity and diversity of contemporary TA theory and practice. We will summarize the key elements of TA theory, introduce relevant concepts with examples and offer our own view of more recent and critical developments in TA theory.

Image of the person

TA is based on three basic philosophical propositions, all of which centre on the innate capacities of the person:

1   that people are OK, having intrinsic worth, the capacity to relate and to resolve problems;
2   that people can think;
3   that people make decisions and decide their own destiny – and that these decisions can be changed (hence 'redecisions').

Berne (1971a: 98) also talked about the force of Nature or *physis* 'which eternally strives to make things grow and to make growing things more perfect' and whose existence made it easier to understand the human being, which he described as:

> a colourful energy system, full of dynamic strivings. . .continually trying to reach a state of tranquillity. . .whose tensions give rise to wishes which it is his task to gratify without getting into trouble with himself, with other people, or with the world around him. (1971a: 65–6).

This describes the aspirational and transformative quality of human beings or persons – *and* reflects Berne's own conservatism and conformity: a dynamic and tension which we see manifested in the theory, practice and organization of TA in a number of ways.

The central concept in TA regarding the image of person is that of ego states. Drawing on research on memory and the brain (notably Penfield, 1952), Berne described an ego state as follows: 'phenomenologically as a coherent set of feelings related to a given subject, and operationally as a set of coherent behavior patterns; or pragmatically, as a system of feelings which motivated a related set of behavior patterns' (1961/1975a: 17). From Weiss (1950) and Federn (1952), Berne drew on the notion of an ego state:

1   as actually experienced reality;
2   as retained in potential existence within the personality;
3   as, under special conditions being 're-cathected' or re-energized (Berne originally cited hypnosis, dreams and psychosis as such conditions).

Berne (1975a) identified three systems or organizations of the ego which he referred to as psychic organs: a system aimed at organizing introjected psychic material (*exteropsyche*); an elaborative system connected to the mental/emotional analysis of the here-and-now (*neopsyche*); and a system linked to the organization of instinctual drives, basic needs and primary emotional experiences (*archeopsyche*) which he termed, respectively: Adult, Parent and Child (see Figure 10.1).

Following Lapworth, Sills and Fish (1993) we prefer a further clarification of: Introjected Parent, Integrated (or *Integrating*) Adult and Archaic Child. Whilst Berne implied correspondence between psychic organs and three ego states, he himself and other TA writers and clinicians since have proposed a number of ego states especially within the Parent and Child. It is thus more accurate and consistent to think in terms of three psychic organs but many ego states (see Jacobs, 2000; Tudor, in press).

In the 40 years since Berne's original formulation, ego state theory has been the subject of much debate within TA (for summaries of which see Friedlander,

Figure 10.1   Psychic organs and corresponding ego states (Berne, 1975a)

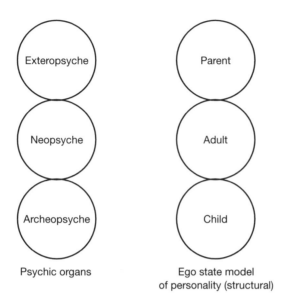

Psychic organs

Ego state model
of personality (structural)

1988; Clarkson, 1992; Midgeley, 1999). Our own view is a constructivist one which is, broadly, that ego states are ways of describing intrapsychic and interpersonal *processes* with regard to personality. They are constructed, deconstructed and reconstructed in an ongoing, interpersonal process, based on dialogue, i.e. transactions: 'this perspective shifts the therapeutic emphasis away from the treatment of ego-state structures and toward an exploration of how relational possibilities are cocreated on a moment-to-moment basis' (Summers and Tudor, 2000: 36).

Conceptualisation of psychological disturbance and health

TA's conceptualization of health and disturbance is reflected in its four theoretical foundations: ego states, transactions, scripts and games. Like many other approaches to psychotherapy, TA has, in our view, overemphasized disturbance and pathology at the expense of health. As Cornell observes: 'like many clinicians, Berne became possessed by the effort to understand pathology. He lost track of health' (1987: 32). With some others, we believe that, alongside its detailed theory of psychopathology, TA also offers a psychology of health, albeit one which needs further development. Thus, psychological health may be conceived, in terms of *ego states*, as being a state of flexibility and one which emphasizes the here-and-now, present-centred Integrating Adult. Similarly, *transactions*, which in themselves are also neutral, may be viewed as representing and supporting healthy interactions comprising stimuli and responses. Berne's classification of *scripts* includes a 'winning' script, defining a 'winner' as 'someone who accomplishes his declared purpose', to which Bob Goulding added 'and makes the world a better place as a result' (cited in Stewart and Joines, 1987). Berne's (1968a: 44) definition of a *game* as 'an ongoing series of complementary ulterior transactions progressing to a well-defined, predictable outcome' offers a non-pathologizing view of a 'game' as a confirmation of a transactional or relational pattern. Acknowledging TA as a health psychology and following Summers and Tudor (2000), we consider transactions as co-creative relationships, ego states as co-creative personalities in process, script as co-creative identity, and games as co-creative 'confirmations'.

This said, we turn our attention to the conceptualization of disturbance in terms of ego states, scripts and games. Whilst a number of transactions contribute towards the acquisition and maintenance of psychopathology, we do not think of transactions themselves in terms of 'disturbance' (see next section pp. 247–9).

Ego states

In terms of ego states psychological health is conceived as being a state of flexibility; and disturbance, inflexibility. There are three primary inflexible states:

1 *Excluding ego states* in which one ego state excludes awareness of the other two. Paranoid states can be understood as states where a Parent ego state excludes awareness of Child and Adult material, whilst hallucinatory states can be conceived as excluding Child ego states in which the Child excludes awareness of Parent and Adult functioning.
2 *Contaminating ego states* refers to disturbance that is specifically related to discrete experiences such as prejudice (Parent contaminating Adult) or phobias (Child contaminating Adult). In contrast to exclusions, contaminations are much less pervasive and tend to result in inflexibility only in specific situations such as a perceived threat or the presence of spiders.
3 *Symbiotic ego states* refers to a type of relational dependency in which two people rely very heavily on each other, leading to the development of dependent personalities: they sense that they can only exist relationally if they only have three ego states between them. This is often perceived and presented as when one person in the relationship cathects Parent and Adult ego states whilst the other occupies the Child position.

Scripts

Transactional analysts conceive of script as an ongoing psychological process in which meaning is given to life experiences. As Stewart (1992) points out, similar concepts may be found in the work of Otto Rank, Carl Jung, Eric Erikson and, particularly, Alfred Adler and his concept of 'life goal', on whose work Berne drew. In TA, life script is essentially thought of as a decisional process which takes place from the cradle to the grave and is an essential component of the life process that influences the course of action somebody will take throughout their life. Whilst a healthy script is conceived as a 'winning script', there are two types of unhealthy script:

- *losing or harmartic script* in which the meanings and actions arising from those meanings are such that the person turns away from life, either ending up dead or in an institution unable to care for themselves;
- *a non-winning or banal script* in which the meanings and actions arising from those meanings are such that the person never fully engages in life and fails to reach their full potential.

Again, over the years, the concept of script has developed. Berne himself refined his definition over 17 years (Berne, 1958, 1975b) and others such as Steiner (1966, 1974) have also developed the concept and analysis of script (for a summary of which see Müller and Tudor, 2002).

Games and rackets

Games and rackets refer to relational and emotional patterns that people create to maintain the script decisions they have taken. Here, transactional analysts identify relational disturbance. This disturbance is found to lie in the relational patterns people develop to maintain the sense of identity they have established through their script. Essentially these patterns are another way to understand transference phenomena in which the projections that people make on to each other are acted out with each other, and these 'dramas' are often repeated. Karpman (1968) famously applied role theory to the drama in a game. He identified three roles, Rescuer, Persecutor and Victim, and suggested that in a game each person adopts one of these roles and then (as in all good drama) switches roles, say, from Persecutor to Rescuer. A 'racket' refers to emotional patterns people develop that, again, result in an emotional inflexibility. English (1976) considered the main feature of a racket was that it was a substitute feeling; thus, a depressed person may substitute depressive feelings for angry feelings.

Acquisition of psychological disturbance

Much of the discussion in the previous section explains the conceptualization TA has of psychological disturbance as well as its acquisition. Nevertheless, there are a number of ways in which TA conceptualizes the acquisition of disturbance, one of which is the script system (Erskine and Moursund, 1988). Based on some original work by Erskine and Zalcman (1979), the script system is one in which the various components of script are categorized. The script system is described by Erskine and Moursund (1988: 38) as a collection of beliefs, current behaviours, memories and fantasies that 'serve as a defense against awareness of childhood experiences, needs, and related emotions while simultaneously being a repetition of the past'. Table 10.1 shows the script system of the client whose work is discussed below (pp. 258–62).

Of course, it is the daily transactions – stimuli and responses – which maintain and confirm or question and challenge the script. Unsurprisingly, TA – the

Table 10.1   Peter's script system

Script beliefs	Script displays	Reinforcing experiences
Self: I shouldn't be here	**Observable behaviours:** 'Pushy' voice Losing track	**Current events:** Socially isolated Let down by others
Others: They are never available when you need them	Mumbling 'I don't know' **Reported internal experiences:**	**Old emotional memories:** Fighting with father Being teased by father
Quality of life: There's nothing in life		Mother pleading for him to stay off school
(Intrapsychic processes)	**Fantasies:**	**Memories of the fantasies**

**Repressed needs and
feelings:**
To be protected by stable
  other
Anger and grief
	I am made of glass
	Important people are letting
	  me down
		as real:
		Father making promises and
		  not keeping them
		Mother not being around
		  when needed

Source: based on Erskine and Moursund, 1988

analysis of transactions – has developed a sophisticated language for describing various types of transactions, e.g. complementary, crossed and ulterior (for explanations of which see Stewart and Joines, 1987) which Berne (1975a) linked to three rules of communication. Other types of transaction include redefining transactions which discount either the stimulus, the response or both.

Perpetuation of psychological disturbance

Building on the notion that it is the transactions people engage in (or do not) that stimulate the acquisition of psychological disturbance, it is primarily the psychological games people play in order to reinforce their script that perpetuate their distress or disturbance. In this statement, of course, is embedded the humanistic slogan that 'defences are for protection': so-called 'games' may perpetuate something which we (as therapists) may regard as unhealthy; they may also help the person to protect themselves against greater disturbance and survive. Indeed, if we conceptualize games as an example of transference phenomena in which early relationships are replayed by people who fit the early figure – for example, a woman who had a distant and remote father is drawn to distant and remote men – it is easy to see how embedded in the game will be a wish that this time maybe things will turn out differently. E. Ruppert (personal communication, 1982) has gone further, suggesting that Berne failed to realize the full implications of his own theory, as games can be understood as only being resolved by a movement into intimacy and are thus an attempt to enter intimacy rather than to avoid it. One positive aspect of game analysis is its emphasis on the relational: it takes two to tango and (at least) two to play a game. TA therapists may take this as a modern-day Zen koan through which to study humility, or as a challenge to be mindful of 'Ah-ha' moments and certainties, and as a way of avoiding such consulting room games as identified by Berne (1968a) such as 'I'm only trying to help you' or 'Psychiatry'.

Change

There are two views of change in transactional analysis psychotherapy. One emphasizes the notion of cure, the other that the process of change is given. The first, somewhat medical model view of cure derives from Berne (1975b) who identifies four goals and stages of cure whereby clients achieve: *social control* over their symptoms or dysfunctional behaviours; *symptomatic relief* from the subjective discomfort of the dysfunction; *transference cure* (defined as staying out of script but only by substituting the therapist); and *script cure*. Traditionally, this is effected through identifiable and observable (usually behavioural) changes, through contractual psychotherapy. The other stream emphasizes the existential truism that, as organisms, human beings and persons, we are in a constant process of change and development, a drive or 'force for Nature' which Berne (1963, 1971a, 1975b), drawing on ancient writings, referred to as 'physis'. In response to this, the psychotherapist's role is to help the client to harness this developmental drive.

Whilst the focus of the first two stages of cure is on behavioural change, in both views of change the therapeutic relationship is the medium for change. This is borne out by psychotherapy research and is increasingly stressed in TA, despite the differences between 'Schools' and practitioners regarding the use of transference (see Tudor, 1999a). From a constructivist and co-creative TA perspective, therapist and client share the responsibility to create, explore and learn from the process of establishing, contracting about, working through and ending the therapeutic relationship. In this sense, just as there has been a movement from cure to change, there may be a further movement in emphasis from change to *learning* as defining the process and focus of TA psychotherapy (G. Summers, personal communication, May 2001).

Practice

Goals of therapy

Transactional analysis psychotherapy has as its primary goal the creation and development of a meaningful relationship within which transformation and development can occur. The therapist will pay a lot of attention to the development of a working alliance in which goals are mutually arrived at and agreed. Therapists differ in their attention to therapeutic goals, this difference being reflected in the multiplicity of orientations TA therapists take. On one end of the continuum TA practitioners will take a cognitive/behavioural approach devising behavioural goals the attainment of which is the focus of their therapy; at the other end of the continuum practitioners will take an approach which sees the developing relationship as primary and in which a multiplicity of developments will occur as a healing relationship is established. In this, the therapist refrains from emphasizing behavioural goals so as to minimize overadaptation.

Generally the goal of TA therapy is autonomy. The TA therapist understands autonomy to consist of three dimensions: awareness, spontaneity and intimacy (Berne, 1968a). Awareness is where the client knows both experientially and cognitively those parts of their experience that are regressive (i.e. that reside in the Child ego state), those parts that are introjected (Parent ego state), and those parts of experience that are directly related to the here-and-now (Adult ego state). Therefore awareness is knowing the self. Spontaneity, the second component of autonomy, refers to the client recovering freedom to express this growing awareness without censorship. The third component of autonomy is intimacy, which is the capacity to be aware and spontaneous with someone else in a way that accounts for both people. An example of this process is a client who, in the course of his therapy, develops from being depressed into some sense of inner and outer contentment. This is achieved in many dimensions but includes development of the awareness of angry feelings. The awareness may be that the client's father expressed uncontrolled anger in a violent way (internalized in the client's Introjected Parent) and that the client adapted to that experience by deciding to inhibit his experiencing of that feeling in case he himself became violent (Archaic Child). As the therapy develops, spontaneity of expression of angry feelings evolves while at the same time the capacity to express those feelings with others (intimacy) is frequently explored. This involves questions like: 'Who can I be angry with?' 'How can I express my anger?' 'When can I express my anger?' This movement through awareness, spontaneity and intimacy occurs multidimensionally in TA therapy, resulting in the attainment of autonomy.

Selection criteria

Berne was very concerned to avoid selection criteria for suitability for therapy based on a diagnostic category. He thought such selection processes were arbitrary and would result in ineffectual, elitist therapy: 'the real issue. . .is not the one commonly debated, "What are the criteria for the selection of patients?", but the underlying, usually unstated assumption "Criteria for selection are good" ' (Berne, 1966: 5). There is also another assumption embedded in the concept of selection that 'People are usefully categorized in terms of "client groups" '. As we have already said, TA was devised as a method of psychotherapy that could be applied to those 'groups' that previously had been debarred from psychotherapeutic (and psychiatric) interventions because they were deemed 'too disturbed' to be able to tolerate the experience of therapy. This is topical as regards current debates about the 'treatability' of people diagnosed as having personality disorders. The TA practitioner working with individual clients then does not select clients based on diagnostic categories or 'client population groups', believing that everyone has the potential to benefit from TA therapy.

Nevertheless, a TA therapist will be *selective*, according to the criteria for making a contract, originally identified by Steiner (1971a) and based on the requirements for legal contracts i.e. *mutual consent, valid consideration, competency* and *lawful object*. Informed *mutual consent* means that the client and therapist freely choose to be in therapy together. The therapist will expect the client to be intelligently involved in his or her own therapy. As TA takes the approach that theory used by the therapist is put on the table between therapist and client, the client is involved in his or her own treatment planning and there are no case conference secrets. If a client has been sent to therapy or has not chosen to work with the particular therapist or is not willing to be involved in his or her own assessment and the planning of therapy, then they are unlikely to be selected. TA therapists expect some *valid consideration* or exchange to occur between therapist and client, believing that an exchange of services equalizes the relationship and encourages the realization of autonomy. This can range from being paid for the therapy to the client demonstrating equality of involvement in the psychotherapeutic process. A high proportion of TA therapists are in private practice and this may be because of this basic belief. To decide *competency* the therapist needs to find out if they have the resources and expertise to help this particular client with the particular development that the client wants to make. This often involves the therapist in making a time-specific agreement to work with a client to assess her or his own competency. The therapist will question their own competency for a number of reasons: if the therapist considers themselves insufficiently experienced to work with the client or does not have the resources that the client needs for effective psychotherapy to take place, such as being unable to meet a twice-weekly appointment commitment. If the therapist considers that they cannot develop sufficient flexibility to engage the client effectively because of, say, boundary issues, for example the client is in a training group that the therapist was once in, then the therapist is unlikely to agree to work with the client. Finally the TA practitioner will want to be clear that the request for psychotherapeutic involvement and the desired outcome of the therapy is *lawful*. The practitioner is unlikely to agree to help someone develop inner security in their chosen career of bank robbery! These requirements have informed the ITAA's (1989) statement of ethics and the EATA's (1993) ethics guidelines as well as the clinical, organizational and educational applications of TA. Updating Steiner's requirements in terms of British contract law, three elements create a legal, written contract: valid consideration, dates and signatures.

Having ascertained if a client's request for therapy meets these criteria the therapist is likely to offer different modes of therapy. One mode will be individual therapy, usually weekly or fortnightly. (The other mode will be weekly group therapy. TA was originally a group psychotherapy and this tradition is still very strong in the TA community. Trainee transactional analysts are required to have group work experience and demonstrate it to an exam board before they can be accredited.) There is a variety of criteria applied to whether individual or group psychotherapy is recommended. The establishment of a therapeutic alliance is usually seen as a precursor to group work, although Tudor (1999a) questions the assumption that individual therapy is the default setting for the therapy of choice.

Nevertheless, the therapeutic goals of the client influence the decision for group work. If the client wishes to focus on developing relationship skills then often a group, with its variety of potential relationships, is chosen. As ever, in terms of the emphasis on mutuality, the mode of psychotherapy needs to be the choice of the client as well as the psychotherapist – and this is still, most often, individual therapy.

Qualities of effective therapists

From TA's basic philosophy and Berne's (1966) therapeutic attitudes and slogans, it is clear that the qualities of an effective TA therapist must include: respect for self and others; a belief in self-responsibility and autonomy; a factual (not false) humility; and authenticity as a therapist (see Tudor, 1999a). In discussing the requirements of the (group) therapist, Berne cites the ability 'to use all five senses in making a diagnosis, assessing the situation, and planning the treatment' (1966: 65) – and, indeed, some of the practical qualities and skills of well-trained and effective TA therapists are: fine observation skills, phenomenological awareness, and an ability to analyse transactions. Other qualities which are required for certification as a certified transactional analyst include the:

- ability to describe their own ideological beliefs and to relate them to the philosophical assumptions of TA, including the implications of cultural, racial and social identities and their significance;
- capacity to conceptualize psychotherapy in terms of TA;
- ability to integrate theory and practice;
- ability to demonstrate creativity and effectiveness, including discussing interventions within the context of the relationship;
- capacity for self-reflection (see EATA, 2001).

Finally, in our view, two further qualities define effective therapists (derived, respectively, from psychoanalysis and the person-centred approach): that of therapeutic neutrality and independence, and non-defensiveness.

Therapeutic relationship and style

Whilst there is increasing emphasis on and understanding of the therapeutic relationship in TA (for discussions of which see Clarkson, 1992; Clarkson et al., 1996; Tudor, 1999a), there is great richness and diversity of styles embodied by transactional analysts. Underpinning therapeutic 'style' is the requirement for the therapist to be authentic. Working with the philosophical principle of mutual OKness ('I'm OK, You're OK'), the TA therapist takes as their starting point that all psychological problems are potentially solvable, given sufficient resources and enough expertise. The practice of psychotherapy is thus essentially a collaborative one, in which both client and therapist are actively and intelligently involved. The requirement for authenticity, together with the requirement to be therapeutic and relational and to promote the client's innate and/or desired development, results in the TA therapist using a wide variety of styles of communication: interruptive, directive, requestive, nurturative and emotive – styles which Kahler (1979) defines as the five communication channels.

This range of styles used can be illustrated by examining the various approaches a transactional analyst might use to understand and work with ego states. To assess or diagnose ego states the therapist will both observe the client and pay close attention to their own experiences which are emerging as the therapeutic relationship develops. The therapist will draw tentative hypotheses as to the ego state structure of the client, based both on the observations they are making (behavioural diagnosis) and on the internal responses they are experiencing in being with the client (social diagnosis). Thus we could say that self-experiencing, or the phenomenology of the psychotherapist, has a strong influence on the style the psychotherapist uses. To confirm their provisional diagnosis, the therapist may enquire about the client's experience (historical and phenomenological diagnoses). In order to do this, the therapist may adopt an empathic approach, attuning to the perceived inner experience of the client, or they may become more purposefully active, involving themselves through sharing their own experience of being with the client. In order to help the client in recognizing and distinguishing between ego states, the practitioner remains receptive to pre-conscious and unconscious processes, again both through the observation of transactions and through self-observation. The therapist's awareness is then available to the client. This process becomes a kind of relational dance between psychotherapist and client in which these three primary styles of enquiry, attunement and involvement weave a complex matrix of relational development (Erskine and Trautmann, 1996).

As ego states are recognized, the psychotherapist has a variety of stylistic responses available to her or him. An interruptive response in which the therapist adopts a commanding and directional manner such as 'Breathe, look at me, notice what you can smell and hear' tends to be used to direct clients to a body-based awareness when the client needs to integrate thinking and feeling with bodily responses. 'Tell me what you are thinking' utilizes a directive channel in which the therapist encourages the client to strengthen ego state boundaries through cognitive work. Straightforward, cognitive transactions such as 'What do you want to focus on today?' are requestive. Empathic transactions in which the therapist shares her or his here-and-now experience such as 'I feel sad as you talk' are predominantly emotive. Finally, a practitioner may seek to contain or hold the client within the relationship by establishing and maintaining contact, by noticing relational needs as they emerge and responding to them by using a nurturative channel of communication. As an example, Simon starts his therapy session in an agitated state. The therapist interrupts the agitation by saying, 'Simon, calm down, look at me, breathe and notice your breath' (interrruptive channel). The therapist goes on to say, 'When you get excited like that, what are you thinking?' (directive). The therapist then says, 'What do you want to work on?' (requestive). Simon then focuses on how he finds fear hard to contain. The therapist responds in a caring manner: 'Maybe you need to know I am here when you feel frightened' (nurturative) and 'I feel sad when you say you were left all alone to look after yourself' (emotive channel).

Major therapeutic strategies and techniques

Traditionally, from Berne onwards, transactional analysts have adopted a strategic view of the progress of psychotherapy. Stewart suggests that there is always 'a three-way interplay between. . .choice of interventions, the treatment contract . . .and diagnosis of the client' (1989: 9) – a perspective which has led to the concept of the *treatment triangle* (in which these three elements are represented as diagnosis, contract and treatment planning, or treatment direction (see Stewart, 1996). For us, this model, based in the medical tradition, overemphasises diagnosis and the external authority of the psychotherapist/diagnostician. It is mediated, however, by TA's emphasis on the contractual method and the more recent emphasis within TA on *process* (e.g. Kahler, 1979; Lee, 1997) which contributes to our understanding of all three elements of the treatment triangle, and on the *therapeutic relationship* (e.g. Hargaden and Sills, 2002). Traditionally, TA has been viewed (from both within and without) as a 'technical' therapy and, indeed, it has developed a number of techniques to facilitate therapeutic change. Berne (1966) himself defined eight, sequential 'therapeutic operations': interrogation, specification, confrontation, explanation, illustration, confirmation, interpretation and crystallization which he defines precisely, and TA psychotherapists are trained in their use and application. For further elaboration and discussion of these see Müller and Tudor (2001) and Hargaden and Sills (2002). Nevertheless, as Berne himself put it: 'observation is the basis of all good clinical work, *and takes precedence even over technique'* (1966: 65–6, our emphasis). Indeed, detailed observation and (literally) the analysis of transactions may be viewed as the most desirable and effective quality of the transactional analyst as well as their most effective 'technique'. Other key therapeutic strategies and techniques include:

- the *decontamination* and strengthening of the Adult ego state (from the intrusion of archaic material), often effected by means of Berne's therapeutic operations;
- the *deconfusion* of the Child ego state whereby unmet archaic needs and feelings are identified and expressed. This may be through catharsis or by means of parenting and reparenting techniques (see James, 1974, 1981; Osnes, 1974; Schiff et al., 1975);
- the resolution of different degrees of *impasse* based on early script decisions, often through use of two-chair work – a theory and practice particularly developed in redecision therapy (see Goulding and Goulding, 1979; Mellor, 1980);
- much of the above also applies to *therapeutic work with the Parent ego state* which, as this comprises introjected or incorporated parental figures, may take the form of therapeutic 'interviews' with a psychic entity whose origins lie in a historical figure, personal to the client (see Dashiell, 1978; Mellor and Andrewartha, 1980).

For further details of these techniques see Stewart and Joines (1987), Stewart (1989, 1996) and Clarkson et al. (1996).

Whether actionistic and directive (in its traditional form) or more reflective and relational, TA is an interactive psychotherapy in which strategies and techniques are continually evolving within the psychotherapeutic space which both client and therapist are uniquely creating. Some contemporary views of TA eschew defined, prescribed procedures in favour of more focus on the process, co-creation and narrative of the therapeutic relationship.

The change process in therapy

Traditionally, the process of change in TA psychotherapy has focused on and emphasized *cure* (see p. 249), the journey to which may be more or less structured, depending on the client, the nature of the issue or problem and on the person of the therapist. Berne's (1975b) original 'treatment planning' sequence – i.e. establishing a working alliance, decontamination, deconfusion and relearning – has (in our view) suffered from over-elaboration (see Woollams and Brown, 1978; Clarkson, 1992 and summarized in Clarkson et al., 1996). For us, change or learning takes place in a complex interactional and relational process between client and therapist, through which the client makes sense of and integrates past experiences into an expanded and expanding Adult ego state (see Tudor, in press). This process of integration allows for the development of a flexible, autonomous person who can be freely active and engaged in their world. Having largely eschewed technique, strategy and sequence, we view the change process in TA psychotherapy as comprising three overlapping processes: *building the working alliance, restructuring* and *reorganization* (Clark, 1991).

Building the working alliance

As much research in the field has now shown, the single most important factor in determining the effectiveness of psychotherapy is the impact of the therapeutic relationship: the relationship *is* the therapy. Thus, as with many colleagues of different therapeutic orientations, the TA psychotherapist (of whatever 'School') focuses on the establishment, maintenance, development and ending of the therapeutic relationship. Although there is some debate about the relation between the therapeutic relationship and the working alliance (see, for instance, Barrett-Lennard, 1985), we view both as important and as ongoing. As Bordin (1975) conceptualizes it, the working alliance comprises: the establishment of *an emotional bond*, and *an agreement* – or, in TA terms, a *contract* – about the goals and tasks of therapy. The TA practitioner seeks to establish contact with the client and often uses an initial period to make an assessment and provisional diagnosis, and to agree a contract which, in turn, traditionally informs their treatment planning and direction. Such 'treatment' is, nevertheless, subject to the contractual method and, therefore, agreed, bilateral, specific – and changeable.

In the early days of working with a client, many TA therapists also want to ensure that the client has closed their self-harming 'escape hatches' (see Holloway, 1973). An escape hatch is a term for destructive behaviours: self-harm or suicide, hurting others or going crazy. Transactional analysts have tended to view serious failure of self-care, suicide, homicide and madness as ways in which clients flee from problem-solving and the promotion of their own development. It is considered a way clients enter into *not* solving their problems, and the self-limiting behaviours that reinforce the script decisions they have taken. The procedure for 'closing escape hatches' is one of asking clients to make a commitment to themselves to stay alive, to stay sane, to take care of themselves, and to respect the lives of others, *no matter what experiences they have.* Formerly this technique was used rather ritualistically, with the resulting consequences that existential issues such as questioning the meaning and purpose of life were shelved by clients who, consciously or unconsciously, perceived the therapist as communicating a 'no go area' for these issues. Over the past five years, this practice has been questioned (see, for instance, Mothersole, 1996, 1997) and a much more flexible approach has emerged in the practice of TA by which the technique of escape hatch closure is applied appropriately and sensitively only to those clients who are seriously at risk of a lack of self-care, of ending their own lives, of killing someone, or of ending up in a psychiatric hospital.

Restructuring

The restructuring of the personality occurs as the client develops awareness. Awareness requires clients being able to understand their own experiences and responses to others in terms of ego states, that is, that they become aware which experiences and responses are borrowed from significant others (Parent), which are old, regressive patterns of thinking, feeling and behaving (Child), and which are a direct response to the here-and-now (Adult). Whether adopting a traditional cognitive-behavioural or a more relational TA approach at this stage, the strategy is to promote awareness so that the client develops symptom or social control and symptomatic relief – the first two of Berne's (1975b) four stages of cure (see p. 249). As the client develops insight into the courses of action they have chosen for their unfolding life, so they can exercise greater control and autonomy.

The approaches used by the TA psychotherapist relate to ego state awareness and the awareness of how the client embodies ego states with others (i.e. transactions). Hence the transactional analyst might teach the client key concepts from TA so that the client becomes intelligently involved in their own decontamination. The client will develop awareness of her or his own games, rackets and scripts. The TA practitioner may use actionistic techniques borrowed from Gestalt therapy (such as two-chair work) to encourage awareness of internal ego state dialogues. S/he will also use enquiry to facilitate the decontamination process. This process as a whole is referred to as restructuring and is often understood and encapsulated in such expressions 'I now know why I do/think or feel that. . .'.

Reorganization

Reorganisation refers to the more emotionally intense, regressive processes that occur in psychotherapy in which clients develop and change their internal responses to stressful situations. Essentially they reorganize themselves and develop autonomy. The 'strategy' of this stage of psychotherapy is to facilitate this reorganization, especially through deconfusion. Reorganization occurs through the client integrating Parent and Child ego state material into their Adult ego state. Integration only occurs through the client fully identifying with expressing the ego state, that is, by experiencing and expressing it physiologically.

Transactional analysts take two approaches to this stage in therapy. This may involve an actionistic approach to the Child and Parent ego state material that emerges. This can include setting up early scenes in which the client replays key early experiences in their past in which they externalize their inner ego state dialogues, or the psychotherapist may directly address either the Child or Parent ego states. Addressing the Child, the client identifies a parenting response that was missing and devises with the therapist a way for that parenting to be provided now. Addressing the Parent, the client cathects their relevant Parent ego state and the TA psychotherapist in effect conducts a therapy session with the client's 'mother', 'father' or significant parental figure.

The second approach the transactional analyst may adopt is to focus on the developing relationship in order to provide a space for holding and containing the intensity that emerges in the deconfusion stage. The TA practitioner attunes to and involves themselves with their client's process, paying particular attention to the presence of relational needs. The transactional analyst will notice the transactions taking place between herself and her client and through enquiry, attunement and involvement facilitate a process of integration (Erskine and Trautmann, 1996). As the therapeutic relationship develops the practitioner will notice the presence of relational needs, for example the need for recognition by a stable significant other. She will notice how the client has defended against the experience of the failure of this need as a child. She will encourage the client to dissolve those defences and to find more satisfying ways to relate to people when the client experiences that need. The techniques emphasized in this approach are less actionistic and require more rhythmic, receptive and empathic responses.

Limitations of the Approach

The limitations of any approach are in the eye of the beholder. As we value the contribution TA as a form of social psychiatry makes in encouraging both practitioners and clients to be interested in the social dimension of their own and each other's psychology, so we are concerned about any theory, practice and organization in TA which limits open communication, autonomy, mutuality and co-creativity. Here we mention three areas of limitation. (The common accusation that TA is superficial is itself somewhat superficial and is well rebutted by Stewart, 1992.)

Motivation

In TA, motivation is often explained and understood in terms of social reward or punishment, often described as the client establishing a system for recognition in their early life in which they seek positive or negative strokes and establish a pattern for human contact. This pattern is considered to be the primary motivation for human interaction. This is too limiting an explanation for why people do things and why they relate to others in specific ways. In this, no account is given of the biological and spiritual drives that influence human interaction. This means that the TA practitioner has to broaden their outlook to accommodate these wider understandings into their work as a therapist. It may mean, for example, that practitioners miss the important dimension of the need and yearning for spiritual fulfilment and mistake it for the effect of a social experience such as an unavailable mother. With few, rare exceptions, the lack of a coherent spiritual dimension to the main body of TA theory and method means that this is a fertile field for development (see Midgeley, 1999).

Pathology

TA (along with most other psychotherapies) overly emphasizes the psychopathology of the client at the expense of their health, and erroneously places that pathology in the nuclear family. In this case an entire course of therapeutic exchanges may take place which are more the result of practitioners following expectations arising from their theory than the result of careful observation and mutual consideration with the client. As discussed, constructivist approach within TA is offering new possibilities to TA in this respect.

Conservatism

Despite its radical roots and its contribution to the development of radical psychiatry, TA today appears very traditional. The influence of the medical model, especially on notions of 'cure' and (ironically) adaptation to social norms; the predominance of the nuclear family as the basic social and theoretical unit; the largely uncritical acceptance (with the exception of Steiner, 1971b) of diagnosis and diagnostic formulations; and the hierarchical and hegemonic nature of its organization: all give TA a flavour of being part of the social and psychotherapeutic establishment. This is also offered as a criticism by both Yalom (1970) and Kovel (1976) – and whilst these criticisms which are largely rebutted by Stewart (1992), this is no basis for complacency in TA which, in our view, needs to revisit its radical roots.

Case example (RH)

The client

Peter telephoned me one evening. He said he was looking for a therapist and had heard my name. He wanted to meet up and I agreed. His voice had this strange 'push' in it. I felt mildly coerced by him. When he arrived at my office

I was surprised by how young he was. He was 20 years old. He had had therapy in early adolescence, which he had found rewarding, but felt he 'really needed somebody to talk to'. I tried to gather a standard social history, with limited success. He would quickly lose track of what he was talking about, change the subject, or go into a dazed place mumbling, 'I don't know'.

I later found out that he had an older brother. He had been parented in a chaotic and neglectful way. His father was the chaotic one, engaging in frequent violent fights over control issues with Peter's brother and relentlessly teasing Peter until he showed tears, then laughing at his expression of vulnerability. This process of excitement and feeling scolded for being excited was often to repeat itself in our work. His mother was neglectful in protecting Peter and overly anxious about any separations: 'My mum needed me around. She didn't want me to go to school and would often want me to stay home'. Peter remembered his first day at school as traumatic. He was not prepared for the separation and found the whole experience highly distressing.

His schooldays were punctuated by frequent absences. He had a whole series of hospital admissions following accidents. He left school at 18 having not completed his exams and was currently living alone in a youth hostel with little social contact. He had never had a sexual relationship. As far as I could tell, Peter spent much of his time alone in his one room. He had developed an interest in meditation and would spend many hours meditating. He had read a book on transactional analysis and sensed that TA psychotherapy could help him.

The therapy

In writing this case study I describe a linear pattern. This is really for ease of reading and writing. In fact the three strands of my TA psychotherapy practice – building the working alliance, restructuring and reorganization – follow a more spiral structure in which the client and I move from alliance to restructuring to reorganization and then back to alliance-building and then through the sequence again. Indeed at one point in this therapy we kept returning to the alliance, with Peter questioning the value and purpose of psychotherapy, then moving into some reorganization work around needing others, and then back again to testing and continuing to develop the working alliance.

Establishing and building the therapeutic/working alliance

To begin with, Peter was well motivated to do therapy but this quickly faded as his Child ego state started to exclude his Adult ego state. Within two or three weeks of therapy he was having great difficulty maintaining Adult awareness. He explained later that he was starting to hear voices that were commenting on me (as therapist). He was convinced that I was communicating secret messages to him and that I had direct access to his mind. I wasn't aware of any of this. To me he appeared to be acting in a dissociated way. Essentially the longer we worked together the more dysfunctional he was getting. It seemed that the psychotherapy was resulting in him experiencing an acute prolonged persecutory inner Parent/Child dialogue. For six months of therapy I experienced being involved in a chaotic, directionless encounter that was highly charged. I found myself thinking about Peter in an obsessive way. This seemed to me to be an attempt by me to contain the high level of anxiety we were both experiencing when we were together. I was uncertain if I was having a healthy impact on Peter, and unsure if Peter had the internal resources to handle outpatient therapy. He was getting more and more dysfunctional: not eating, spending days alone and gradually declining into a zombie-like state.

I realized that I had to develop a more purposeful therapeutic structure and that with this structure he might start to strengthen his ego state boundaries and be able to control his regressive tendencies. I decided to temporarily increase my contact with him. We would meet every day for 10 minutes. I also insisted that, if he wanted therapy from me, he would have to put more structure into his life. He agreed to make regular contact with people and to enrol on a couple of further education courses. He started to deliver his side of the contract. The working alliance had been established.

Restructuring

It was now important for Peter to make two developments: first, he had to strengthen his ego state boundaries so that he could control his impulses to move into Child ego state; and, secondly, he had to develop a way of integrating some of the transcendental experiences he had. Peter developed the capacity to control his regressive impulses by learning and practising 'grounding' or sensory-based techniques: essentially he became able to place all experience (cognitive, emotional and spiritual) into a physical, body-based context. I contributed to this in a rather painstaking fashion by encouraging him to locate the physical dimension of any experience he was having with me. In time Peter was able to develop the capacity to put and maintain energy into his Adult ego state when he felt strong regressive impulses: he was able to *think about* what he was *feeling*. Secondly, Peter needed to integrate the transcendental aspects of his experience into his Adult ego state. He had learned from an early age to seek refuge in 'higher' spiritual states. He would spend long amounts of time in a meditative state, dissociating from his surroundings, while at the same time experiencing a profound sense of inner peace. The difficulty for Peter was that he had taken a decision to learn to be in the world and these transcendental moments belonged, to him, outside 'the world': 'I live within glass. No one is there.' Again I took an approach to facilitate the incorporation of bodily awareness while he was in these states.

Our relationship veered between calm and appreciative, and conflictual and controlling. At times I would directly experience Peter's own ego state structure, in particular the Parent structure he had introjected from his father. I would sense and occasionally act on the impulse to push him into excited states and then be critical of him getting excited. This mostly played itself out over his meditation practice and spiritual development in which I encouraged him; at other times, however, I challenged his pushing himself into meditational situations which he did not have the internal resources to handle. Nevertheless, at this time, Peter was pulling his life together, establishing a social network, moving into a house with friends, and starting to return and complete his education.

Reorganization

Peter started to work on the experiences he was having within the therapeutic relationship. He entered into this domain of relatedness gradually as he developed more internal resources to self-support. Three main processes emerged during this phase of treatment.

First, Peter was hankering after the experience of a stable and protective other being, able to contain the extraordinarily high level of anxiety he experienced and to protect him from his persecutory Parent. About two years into the therapy I found myself spending long periods being very inactive. The experience was literally like holding someone in my gaze and symbolically providing a containing environment. The result of this rather quiet period of therapy was that Peter would start to feel a boundary around himself and would then start to allow strong emotions to rise in him, especially anger. This containment allowed him to express and integrate the Child ego state material into his Adult ego state.

Secondly, we explored Peter's experience of separation from me, in particular when I was away on holidays. Initially he would react to my absences *after* I had returned. His reaction would be to retreat into a place of angry passivity and take a strong position that my absence was having no impact on him. At this point, I thought in terms of games, with Peter initially taking a Victim position and then moving into the Persecutory position on the drama triangle (Karpman, 1968). However, he would act out his anger outside of the therapy session by failing to care for himself. It was as if he wanted to demonstrate to me that the therapy was failing by returning to old patterns of social isolation and lack of self-care. Eventually he was able to bring these hostile feelings he had into the therapy room. At this point, in terms of time structuring, Peter had moved from the game position into increased intimacy.

This brought us to the third and final part of the restructuring phase, which was characterized by Peter entering a grief process that involved him dissolving his defensive processes around loss in relationship and the integration of ego state material, thereby achieving a state of autonomy. I was both containing and responsive to his angry disappointment in me. At this point in our work we returned to alliance-building in which, for Peter, therapy had become not only a fascinating and valuable healing process but also, at its centre, a deeply flawed, hypocritical process in which the therapist's (my) involvement was temporary and not 'real'. To Peter 'real' involvement meant a much more enduring commitment somewhat akin to a 'good parent' who is continually available. My absences, coupled with my openness about the level of involvement and commitment I was willing to provide, resulted in us going through a tempestuous period. This time, however, Peter was able to move beyond his previous defences and reveal his anxieties, disappointments and rage in the relationship with me.

When Peter had gone through this process I suggested that now was the time to leave therapy and to 'get a life'. He punched the air, saying 'Yeesss!' Now (some time after the therapy ended), I hear that he is studying for a professional qualification and has a number of long-lasting friends.

Note

[1] Historically, within TA, three 'schools' have been recognized: the Classical School, the Redecision School and the Cathexis School and until this year was a requirement for qualification and accreditation that all TA practitioners were familiar with the theory and practice of these three Schools. Woollams and Brown (1978) expanded the list; and, more recently, 'Integrative TA' has become viewed as a possible 'fourth school'. We consider the present categorization as most accurately representing the current strands of thinking and practice within TA. Most recently, Lee (2001) identifies 10 distinct approaches within TA.

References

Agel, J. (ed.) (1971) *The Radical Therapist*. New York: Ballantine.

AHPP: Association of Humanistic Psychology Practitioners (1998) 'The AHPP statement of core beliefs', *Self & Society*, 26(3): 3–6.

Allaway, J. (1983) 'Transactional analysis in Britain: the beginnings', *Transactions: Journal of the Institute of Transactional Analysis*, 1: 5–10.

Allen, J.R. and Allen, B.A. (1995) 'Narrative theory, redecision therapy, and postmodernism', *Transactional Analysis Journal*, 25(4): 327–34.

Allen, J.R. and Allen, B.A. (1997) 'A new type of transactional analysis and one version of script work with a constructivist sensibility', *Transactional Analysis Journal*, 27(2): 89–98.

Barrett-Lennard, G. (1985) 'The helping relationship: crisis and advance in theory and research', *The Counseling Psychologist*, 13(2): 279–94.

Berne, E. (1958) 'Transactional analysis: a new and effective method of group therapy', *American Journal of Psychotherapy*, 11, 293–309.

Berne, E. (1963) *The Structure and Dynamics of Organizations and Groups*. New York: Grove Press.

Berne, E. (1966) *Principles of Group Treatment*. New York: Grove Press.

Berne, E. (1968a) *Games People Play* (1964). Harmondsworth: Penguin.

Berne, E. (1968b) 'Staff–patient staff conferences', *American Journal of Psychiatry*, 123(3): 286–93.

Berne, E. (1971a) *A Layman's Guide to Psychiatry and Psychoanalysis*. Harmondsworth: Penguin.

Berne, E. (1971b) 'Away from a theory of the impact of interpersonal interaction on non-verbal participation', *Transactional Analysis Journal*, 1(1): 6–13.

Berne, E. (1975a) *Transactional Analysis in Psychotherapy* (1961). London: Souvenir Press.

Berne, E. (1975b) *What Do You Say After You Say Hello?* (1972). London: Corgi.

Bordin, E.S. (1975) 'The generalizability of the psychoanalytic concept of the working alliance', *Psychotherapy: Theory, Research and Practice*, 16: 252–60.

Clark, B.D. (1991) 'Empathic transactions in the deconfusion of ego states', *Transactional Analysis Journal*, 21(2): 92–8.

Clarkson, P. (1992) *Transactional Analysis Psychotherapy: An Integrated Approach*. London: Routledge.

Clarkson, P. and Gilbert, M. (1990) 'Transactional analysis', in W. Dryden (ed.), *Individual Therapy: A Handbook*. Buckingham: Open University Press.

Clarkson, P., Gilbert, M. and Tudor, K. (1996) 'Transactional analysis', in W. Dryden (ed.), *Handbook of Individual Therapy*. London: Sage. pp. 219–53.

Collinson, L. (1983) 'Autonomy soon? A brief history of transactional analysis in Britain', *Transactions: Journal of the Institute of Transactional Analysis*, 1: 11–12.

Collinson, L. (1984) 'Transactional analysis', in W. Dryden (ed.), *Individual Therapy: A Handbook*. London: Harper Row Press. pp. 205–34.

Cornell, W.F. (1987) 'Life script theory: a critical review from a developmental perspective', *Transactional Analysis Journal*, 18(4): 270–82.

Dashiell, S.R. (1978) 'The Parent resolution process: reprogramming psychic incorporations in the Parent', *Transactional Analysis Journal*, 8(4): 289–95.

EATA: European Association for Transactional Analysis (1993) 'Ethics guidelines', in *Training and Examination Handbook*. Nottingham: EATA.

EATA: European Association for Transactional Analysis Professional Standards and Training Committee (2001) *PTSC Telegram No.15*. Aix-en-Provence: EATA.

English, F. (1976) 'Racketeering', *Transactional Analysis Journal*, 6(1), 78–81.

Erikson, E. (1951) *Childhood and Society*. New York: W.W. Norton.

Erikson, E. (1968) *Identity, Youth and Crisis*. New York: W.W. Norton.

Erskine, R. and Moursund, J. (1988) *Integrative Psychotherapy in Action*. Newbury Park, CA: Sage.

Erskine, R. and Trautmann, R. (1996) 'Methods of an integrative psychotherapy', *Transactional Analysis Journal*, 26(4), 316–28.

Erskine, R. and Zalcman, M.J. (1979) 'The racket system: a model for racket analysis', *Transactional Analysis Journal*, 9(1), 51–9.

Federn, P. (1952) *Ego Psychology and the Psychoses*. New York: Basic Books.

Friedlander, M.G (ed.) (1988) 'Ego states'. Special issue of *Transactional Analysis Journal*, 18(1).

Goulding, M. and Goulding, R. (1979) *Changing Lives through Redecision Therapy*. New York: Brunner-Mazel.

Hargaden, H. and Sills, C. (2002) *Transactional Analysis – A Relational Perspective*. London: Brunner-Routledge.

Holloway, W. (1973) Shut the Escape Hatch. Monograph IV in *The Monograph Series I–X*. Medina, OH: Midwest Institute of Human Understanding. pp. 15–18.

International Transactional Analysis Association (1989) *Statement of ethics*. Available from 436 14th Street, Suite 1301, Oakland, California CA94612–2710, USA.

International Transactional Analysis Association. *website*: http://www.itaa-net.org/

Jacobs, A. (2000) 'Psychic organs, ego states, and visual metaphors: speculation on Berne's integration of ego states'. *Transactional Analysis Journal*, 30(1): 10–22.

James, M. (1974) 'Self-reparenting: theory and process', *Transactional Analysis Journal*, 4(3): 32–9.

James, M. (1977) 'Eric Berne, the development of TA and the ITAA', in M. James (ed.), *Techniques in Transactional Analysis for Psychotherapists and Counsellors*. Reading, MA: Addison-Wesley.

James, M. (1981) *Breaking Free: Self-reparenting for a New Life*. Reading, MA: Addison-Wesley.

Joines, V. and Stewart, I. (2002) *Personality Adaptations*. Nottingham: Lifespace Publishing.

Kahler, T. (1979) *Process Therapy in Brief*. Little Rock, AR: Human Development Publications.

Karpman, S. (1968) 'Fairy tales and script drama analysis', *Transactional Analysis Bulletin*, 7(26): 44.

Kovel, J. (1976) *A Complete Guide to Therapy*. Harmondsworth: Penguin.

Lapworth, P., Sills, C. and Fish, S. (1993) *Transactional Analysis Counselling*. Bicester: Winslow.

Lee, A. (1997) 'Process contracts', in C. Sills (ed.), *Contracts in Counselling*. London: Sage. pp.94–112.

Lee, A. (2001) 'The schools of change'. Workshop presentation. The Berne Institute, Kegworth (June).

Lister-Ford, C. (2002) *Skills in Transactional Analysis Counselling & Psychotherapy*. London: Sage.

Mellor, K. (1980) 'Impasses: a developmental and structural understanding', *Transactional Analysis Journal*, 10(3): 213–20.

Mellor, K. and Andrewatha, G. (1980) 'Reparenting the Parent in support of redecisions', *Transactional Analysis Journal*, 10(3): 197–203.

Midgeley, D. (1999) *New Directions in Transactional Analysis Counselling*. London: Free Association Books.

Moiso, C. (1985) 'Ego states and transference', *Transactional Analysis Journal*, 15(3): 194–201.

Moiso, C. and Novellino, M. (2000) 'An overview of the psychodynamic school of transactional analysis', *Transactional Analysis Journal*, 30(3): 182–7.

Mothersole, G. (1996) 'Existential realities and no-suicide contracts', *Transactional Analysis Journal*, 26(2): 151–60.

Mothersole, G. (1997) 'Contracts and harmful behaviour', in C. Sills (ed.), *Contracts in Counselling*. London: Sage. pp. 113–24.

Mothersole, G. (2001) 'TA as short-term cognitive therapy', in K. Tudor (ed.), *Transactional Analysis Approaches to Brief Therapy*. London: Sage. pp. 64–82.

Müller, U. and Tudor, K. (2002) 'Transactional analysis as brief therapy', in K. Tudor (ed.), *Transactional Analysis Approaches to Brief Therapy*. London: Sage. pp. 19–44.

Osnes, R.E. (1974) 'Spot reparenting', *Transactional Analysis Journal*, 4(3): 40–6.

Penfield, W. (1952) 'Memory mechanisms', *Archives of Neurology and Psychiatry*, 67: 178–98.

Schiff, J.L., Schiff, A.W., Mellor, K., Schiff, E., Schiff, S., Richman, D., Fishman, J., Wolz, L., Fishman, C. and Momb, D. (1975) *Cathexis Reader: Transactional Analysis Treatment of Psychosis*. New York: Harper & Row.

Sills, C. and Hargaden, H. (eds) (in press) *Ego States*. London: Worth Reading.

Steiner, C. (1966) 'Script and counterscript', *Transactional Analysis Bulletin*, 5(18): 133–5.

Steiner, C. (1971a) *Games Alcoholics Play*. New York: Grove Press.

Steiner, C. (1971b) 'Radical psychiatry: principles', in J. Agel (ed.), *The Radical Therapist*. New York: Ballantine. pp. 3–7.

Steiner, C. (1974) *Scripts People Live*. New York: Bantam.

Steiner, C. (2000) 'Radical psychiatry', in R.J. Corsini (ed.), *Handbook of Innovative Therapy*. Chichester: Wiley. pp. 578–86.

Stewart, I. (1989) *Transactional Analysis Counselling in Action*. London: Sage.

Stewart, I. (1992) *Eric Berne*. London: Sage.

Stewart, I. (1996) *Developing Transactional Analysis Counselling*. London: Sage.

Stewart, I. and Joines, V. (1987) *TA Today*. Nottingham: Lifespace Publishing.

Summers, G. and Tudor, K. (2000) 'Cocreative transactional analysis', *Transactional Analysis Journal*, 30(1): 23–40.

Tudor, K. (1996) 'Transactional Analysis *intra*gration: a metatheoretical analysis for practice', *Transactional Analysis Journal*, 26: 329–40.

Tudor, K. (1999a) *Group Counselling*. London: Sage.

Tudor, K. (1999b) 'I'm OK, You're OK – and They're OK: therapeutic relationships in Transactional Analysis', in C. Feltham (ed.), *Understanding the Counselling Relationship*. London: Sage. pp. 90–119.

Tudor, K. (ed.) (2002) *Transactional Approaches to Brief Therapy or What Do You Say between Saying Hello and Goodbye?* London: Sage.

Tudor, K. (in press) 'The neopsyche: the integrating Adult ego state', in C. Sills and H. Hargaden (eds), *Ego States*. London: Worth Reading.

Weiss, E. (1950) *Principles of Psychodynamics*. New York: Grune & Startton.

Woollams, S. and Brown, M. (1978) *Transactional Analysis*. Dexter, MI: Huron Valley Institute.

Wyckoff, H. (ed.) (1976) *Love, Therapy and Politics: Issues in Radical Therapy – The First Year.* New York: Grove Press.
Yalom, I.D. (1970) *The Theory and Practice of Group Psychotherapy.* New York: Basic Books.

Suggested further reading

Berne, E. (1975) *Transactional Analysis in Psychotherapy* (1961). London: Souvenir Press.
Clarkson, P. (1992) *Transactional Analysis Psychotherapy: An Integrated Approach.* London: Routledge.
Erskine, R. and Trautmann, R. (1999) *Beyond Empathy: A Therapy of Contact-in-Relationship.* New York: Brunner/Mazel.
Hargaden, H. and Sills, C. (2002) *Transactional Analysis – A Relational Perspective.* London: Brunner-Routledge.
Steiner, C. (1974) *Scripts People Live.* New York: Bantam.
Stewart, I. (1992) *Eric Berne.* London: Sage.

11 Cognitive Analytic Therapy
Mark Dunn

Historical context and development in Britain

Historical context

CAT was developed by Dr Anthony Ryle, consultant psychotherapist, over a period of 25 years commencing around 1975. It was his intention to develop an integrative therapy which would make use of the theoretical insights of cognitive-behavioural therapy and the object relations theorists of the British School, hence the therapy's name. The urge towards integration came partly from frustration with the divided nature of psychotherapy practice in the UK, partly from intellectual frustration with the philosophical positions adopted by some main-stream theorists and partly from the urge to give access to psychotherapeutic help to those most often excluded by reason of poor health service provision or through a perception of their insufficient intellectual development. In a nutshell he is against the 'balkanization' of psychotherapy and its resulting tower of psycho-babel (sic), and in favour of pragmatics and public usability.

The integrative theory of CAT was developed to provide an accessible model of mental functioning and a time-limited and focused practice for both the staff and patients of the NHS. It is essentially a constructivist model of how the mind works and how it interacts with other minds; it is based in the language of cognitive psychology which is seen as the most accessible language for describing mental processes; it seeks to build bridges to all theories from a notional starting point, acknowledging that the truth of the how the mind works is unlikely ever to be fully known and even less likely to be encompassed by any one theory; it proposes that the more theoretical and practical tools there can be integrated in the psycho-therapist's tool box the better.

CAT's historical roots lie in both the European tradition of psychoanalytic thinking and the North American tradition of cognitive psychology. In CAT these ideas are seen as being like flour and yeast in the making of bread and not, as is sometimes suggested, the oil and vinegar in salad dressing which may be shaken together but in reality do not mix. CAT holds that, while the unleavened bread of CBT has nutritional value and the yeast of psychoanalysis has flavour (perhaps an acquired taste like Marmite), needed together in CAT they are more palatable and satisfying. However, not everything can be translated; CAT tends to see the dynamic unconscious as an unnecessary construction and the information-processing models of cognitive theory to be inhuman. The water in the bread would be the semiotic understanding of the social construction of the mind in the intersubjective field and how this is expressed in voice, language and the body – gesture.

Development in Britain

Ryle started his career after the Second World War as a GP and became interested in counselling patients with common psychiatric and neurotic problems. He moved to Sussex University health service to provide psychoanalytic-type individual and group therapy to students. He developed research into neurosis based on Kelly's (1955) essentially cognitive repertory grid technique attempting to describe psychoanalytic formulations in cognitive-behavioural language (Ryle, 1975). He found that 'descriptions of patients' problems based on repertory grid testing produced more precise, acceptable and useful descriptions of the patients' difficulties than did those based on hypotheses based on psychoanalytic theory' (Ryle 1990, Ch. 1: 2). These researches led to an interest in the possibility of integrating psychotherapy theories by way of a common language, using cognitive language to translate psychoanalytic theory (Ryle, 1978) and the naming of three common types of neurotic problem understood in this way, as Traps, Dilemmas and Snags (Ryle, 1979).

In 1982 Ryle was appointed to the post of consultant psychotherapist at St Thomas's and Guy's Hospitals in London and commenced to develop CAT as a brief, focused, integrative, individual psychotherapy treatment for NHS patients. He published many papers and two main books developing the core integrative theory of the Procedural Sequence Object Relations Model (PSORM) (Ryle, 1982, 1985, 1990). During this period Ryle was also experimenting with practical innovations that would facilitate brief treatment by concentrating on target problems including the use of questionnaires such as the CAT Psychotherapy File, prose reformulation letters to the patient summarizing understandings, the use of flow chart style diagrams as well as techniques from cognitive-behavioural therapy (CBT) such as diary-keeping and rating sheets. In keeping with the integrative ethos Ryle would exclude nothing that might support and motivate both the client and the therapist and empower them to make changes.

In the 1990s Ryle continued to pursue the integration of theory and the establishment of CAT in his writings (Ryle, 1994a 1994b, 1995a; Ryle et al., 1992). He extended the theory and practice to understand personality disorders, particularly borderlines (Ryle, 1995b, 1997a, 1997b; Ryle and Beard, 1993; Ryle and Marlowe, 1995; Ryle and Golynkina, 1999) and conducted debate with Kleinian and other psychoanalytic writers (Ryle, 1992, 1993, 1995c, 1996, 1998; Ryle and Fonagy, 1995). In collaboration with Finnish psychologist Mikael Leiman he extended CAT theory to integrate the activity theory of Russian psychologist Vygotsky and the semiotic theory of Bakhtin (Ryle, 1991; Leiman, 1992, 1994, 1995, 1997). Psychotherapists who have trained in CAT have published research and practical papers describing its application in different settings: eating disorders (Treasure et al., 1995, 1997a, 1997b; Bell, 1996), deliberate self-harm (Cowmeadow, 1994; Sheard et al., 2000), survivors of sexual abuse (Clarke and Llewelyn, 1994), non-compliant diabetics (Fosbury et al., 1996, 1997), forensic offenders (Pollock, 1996, 1997; Pollock and Kear-Colwell, 1994), group CAT treatment (Mitzman and Duignan, 1993, 1994), organizational environments and systems (Walsh, 1996; Kerr, 1999), and the treatment of alcoholics (Leighton, 1995, 1997).

Ryle retired from the NHS in 1995 but continues to write, research and teach part time as Emeritus consultant psychotherapist at Guy's Hospital. His special interest is in researching the treatment of borderline and other personality disorders. His early students formed the Association for Cognitive Analytic Therapy (ACAT) in 1990 to promote research and training and to represent and develop the membership. CAT has been taken up mainly within the NHS (for which it was designed) and there are training courses throughout the UK.

Theoretical assumptions

Image of the person

In CAT a person is seen as inseparable from their social environment and culture and the person's personality is understood to be a social construction of their environment and culture. From the moment of birth (or even from the moment of conception) a baby is a set of biological and psychological processes in continuous motion sensitive to and adapting to the environment. This process continues in various complex ways until death. In early childhood the important social environment is the parents. Later on, peers, teachers and others are added; in adult life peer groups, work groups and close partnerships dominate but the media also have a large shaping effect. The adaptability of a person throughout life depends on the qualities of their early adaptive experiences.

Understanding the early development of the baby is essential to the understanding of the person. The baby's psychological processes are pre-set to detect and react to pattern and relationship in the physical and social environment. These are given meaning by the psychological and verbal responses of the parents, meanings which the baby cannot *not* acquire. Baby's actions, including random actions, are responded to as signs, as if carrying meaning and intention, and in this way the baby's mind is shaped to the meanings and intentions of the family and culture. The baby's activity meshes with and is mediated by the parent's activity and is treated meaningfully (Vygotsky, 1978; Leiman, 1992). This joint activity is described as *procedures*, simple at first but building up over time into complex interactions. An example of a simple procedure would be: baby scanning the world perceives the pattern of mother's face and smiles in recognition, mother perceives baby's smile and responds with a smile whereby both feel connected (the meaning of the interaction). This 'smile-recognition' procedure reaches completion through mother's mirroring response (though it may continue in an escalating repetition of happy arousal). This procedure is but a small bit-part of what develops into the more complex range of procedures of a mother–child relationship (and, of course, we never outgrow that particularly useful procedure).

CAT's essentially Vygotskian view of early development acknowledges several psychoanalytic writers: Bowlby's patterns of attachment are interpreted as interpersonal procedures (Bowlby, 1969), Fairbairn's interpersonal object relations are reinterpreted as reciprocal roles (Fairbairn, 1952) while Winnicott's transitional objects mediating interpersonal experience are reinterpreted as signs mediating interpersonal process (Winnicott, 1970).

As the range of interpersonal interactions grows between parents and baby, the acquisition of jointly mediated signs results in the acquisition of language, first between mother and baby, secondly as baby's self-talk and then as language 'goes underground' as an *intra*personal procedure called thinking. As this develops complexity and becomes decontextualized, self-reflective thought becomes possible and self-consciousness emerges. In response to self-consciousness the good parent aims to jointly mediate the procedures of self-reflection by helping the child reflect on her thoughts, her feelings and the consequences of her actions in relation to herself and to others, thereby helping develop a moral sense of what in the social environment must be adapted to and what may be resisted and changed.

Mother as mediator of the world and its meanings reduces in importance as the child becomes increasingly shaped by dialogue with peers, teachers and culture through books, television, travel, etc. The quality of the early relationship with parents, however, is seen as the major factor in the ability to go on adapting to the wider world and as the source of psychological disturbance. Any restrictions on early relating are unavoidably maintained in adult life by re-enactment in relation to others and also in the self-to-self relationship.

A person who has had a good enough childhood is therefore able to participate in social culture both at work and in relationships and to dialogue with others. She can adapt to hostile environments to survive and can also refuse to adapt and take necessary action to change the environment. She has a sense of her own flexibility and adaptiveness. She can live with the consequences of what cannot be changed in a creative rather than a defeated way.

Conceptualization of psychological disturbance and health

Psychological health and disturbance is conceptualized through the *Procedural Sequence Object Relations Model (PSORM)*. This models how the person expresses her intentions as actions in relation to the other in repetitive, sequential ways and how responses are elicited from the other. The mind is understood to be a continuous process of the following activities: perceiving the thoughts and feelings of the self or the intentions of the other, appraising these in relation to memory and belief systems, pursuing intentions through planning, enacting plans and appraising feedback from the results of actions.

These repetitive sequences of thinking, feeling and acting (called procedures) are aim or goal oriented. Procedures can be enacted

- towards other people in an interpersonal way (e.g. asking someone to pass the salt);
- towards the self in an intrapersonal way (e.g. reminding oneself not to use so much salt);
- towards inanimate object-others such as food and drink or machines (e.g. putting salt on one's chips and eating them);
- towards the other as group (e.g. putting salt on one's chips because everyone is having salt);
- towards the other as culture (e.g. throwing salt over one's shoulder to ward off the evil eye).

Procedures enacted towards other people, whether individuals or groups, usually seek corresponding sequences in reply from the other. So a procedure whereby you smile at someone and ask them to pass the salt will be completed when they smile in return and pass the salt. However, sequences can proceed in many directions: they may reply with a request that you pass the vegetables, they may scowl and refuse to pass the salt or they may ignore your request and praise your shirt, etc. The theory implies that intentions usually carry a clear indication of the reciprocation required and that if we can get the reciprocations we need throughout the range of our activities and relationships, we feel OK. We are perhaps not OK when we are, for example, too anxious to smile and ask for the salt or too aggressive in asking, or when the other doesn't respond as we would wish.

The theory of *reciprocal relating* is derived from object relations theory. CAT theory prefers to describe self and other as processes in action rather than objects in relation. The positions from which intentions are enacted towards the other are described as *roles*. These positions are learned from earliest childhood onwards as the result of mother taking up the positions in relation to baby and requiring or shaping particular responses from the baby. If m/other enacts a flexible and playful process with the baby then the baby will grow up with the ability to enact a flexible and playful process with the other, a process which allows the self to move easily through different role positions (linked in CAT theory to the development of the key meta-role of self-reflection). If mother enacts a rigid and strict process, the baby will grow up with a rigid and strict process encompassing few roles enacted inflexibly. The latter case results in the kinds of problems that require psychotherapeutic intervention.

The notion of the *role* in this model is understood to be the position from which *procedural sequences* are enacted. However, a role also carries an agenda, i.e. its *intention* (in the same way that an actor will ask, 'What's my motivation?'). This is also linked to analytic theory as the intention is linked to (a) the pursuit of what is wanted or desired, (b) the avoidance of what is unwanted or feared (often the desires of others), and (c) the acquiescing (or adapting) to what is required by belonging to culture and group (the demands and responsibilities of duty). The intentions of the self are always potentially in tension with and possibly in conflict with the intentions of the other and with the demands of culture to adapt and the fears and desires of other parts of the self (intrapersonal conflict). These tensions and conflicts may be avoided by becoming skilled at negotiation and management both of the self and of the other, including, when necessary, withdrawal from the other.

Roles are also inextricably linked to the notion of activity (cf. Vygotsky's activity theory: Ryle, 1990). Activity is simply what you are doing when you are going about your life. All activity is seen to be procedural and driven by agendas (or intentions). Procedures describe the steps of the activity; the agenda describes the meaning of the activity, for example what is reinforced, maintained or reduced by the activity. Self and other may agree or may have different views of the meaning of any activity, leading to conflict. Agendas can be overt but also covert: e.g. the activity of cooking a meal for another

1   may maintain the caring and nurturing aspect of the self's role while also maintaining the cared-for and dependent aspect of the other's;
2   may reduce the anxiety of the self by pleasing the other;
3   may reinforce the dominance of the self over the submissive other who is forced to eat the unpalatable;
4   may be a sadistic act of the self toward the humiliated and poisoned other

– and so on.

Psychological health can then be defined as repertoires of roles and procedures which result in mutual benefit and a sense of well-being. Psychological disturbance can be defined as roles and procedures which are not mutual, which may benefit one but oppress or harm the other, including those that restrict or harm the self. Disorders of personality are understood to reflect a failure to integrate roles and procedures resulting in disruptions in relating, intense affect and harmful coping procedures towards self and other to deal with intense affect. Psychological health can be further defined as the ability to constantly revise roles and procedures appropriately.

Psychological health is also defined in relation to cultural norms. In Western liberal culture a person is generally expected to achieve psychological flexibility and autonomy, reflected in an ability to relate to self and other with high levels of communication and awareness. In other cultures a tight repertoire of roles and procedures may be expected, reflected in inflexible and dependent relating with strict role assignment. Many problems are generated by the mixing and confusion of differential cultural demands.

Acquisition of psychological disturbance

Psychological disturbance is related to a fixed or inflexible early social environment. This can also be described as a less than adequate attunement of the parents to the child's psychological state. The child cannot help but adapt to what is. For example parents who adopt fixed role positionings and rigid responses will develop a child that expects those intentions from all others and shapes towards them so as to elicit those responses. In turn the child learns she can enact those role positions towards others reciprocally. The child adapts but at the cost of frustration of her natural intentions with a resulting affect (e.g. anger or fear) described in CAT as *core pain*. The initially playful child who is required to excessively control herself by strict parents and is punished for being out of control will adapt and learn to control herself but at the cost of frustrated and ultimately lost playfulness, as well as awkwardness and frustration around playful others, and severe internal self-control. In adult life this may appear as a variety of disturbances such as anorexia, social isolation, restricted sexual performance as well as being overcontrolling and punitive towards her own children and also eliciting strict control from her partner. In CAT these reciprocal roles could be described as 'controlling and criticized to controlled, crushed and angry'.

CAT describes three categories of disturbance:

1 *Neurotic parenting*: typically of four sorts: (a) overly conditional, demanding, critical, bullying or guilt/shame inducing; (b) overly caring, controlling, smothering or discouraging; (c) under-demanding, controlling, spoiling or giving in to the child; (d) weak or overdependent parents who create an overly responsible 'parental-child' (often due to mental or physical illness or other preoccupation in the parent).
2 *Abusive parenting*: typically of four sorts: (a) overt rejection and/or repeated abandonment; (b) physical violence or punishment, psychological cruelty or terrorism; (c) sexual abuse leading to confusion around care, intimacy and abuse; (d) physical and emotional deprivation.
3 *Narcissistic parenting*: typically of two sorts: (a) too much attention, either excessive admiration leading to arrogance, or invasion of privacy leading to shaming; (b) too little attention, leading to feeling overlooked, worthless, rejected, unpraised and a desperate need to be noticed and to please others.

In addition psychological disturbance is seen as arising in associated parenting styles and other conditions of childhood which, with abusive parenting, disrupt the ability to be in the right role at the right time in relation to others. James Low (2000) writes:

> When the child is responding to an environment whose overpowering intensity endures for a long period of time the range of possible responses is experientially reduced. This leads to a felt enclosure within one reciprocal role formation so that other options become invisible. Thus repeated abuse can result in a person feeling hurt, lost, anxious, mistrustful – and thereby unable to shift to a different mode of relating. In extreme cases the person can develop a very limited repertoire of R-R [reciprocal roles] each of which operates as a quasi-autonomous self-state separated by dissociation leading to a very fragmented experience of being in the world.

These kinds of experience are seen as the origins of personality disorder.
Parenting styles and associated conditions would include:

* repeated unassimilated losses (deaths of parents, siblings, relatives, always moving home, etc.);
* unpredictable parenting, leading to confusion and anxiety (parents with radically different parenting styles, schizophrenic parents, multiple chaotic parents);
* threatening parenting, leading to general high anxiety;
* thinking dominant parenting, leading to an emotionally deprived child;
* emotion dominant parenting, leading to a thinking deprived child;

- unreflecting parenting, leading to an unreflecting child that cannot assimilate or integrate childhood experience;
- parenting with no notion of ZPD (zone of proximal development: Vygotsky, 1978) resulting in the child having to do things that are beyond its grasp and ending up feeling defeated or becoming bored by being restricted to easy tasks and, by extension, having to be either too grown up (parent's confidante or sib) or too regressed (parent's pet or doll).

Perpetuation of psychological disturbance

CAT describes disturbance as being maintained first by distortions and restrictions of the procedural and role repertoire (Level 1), secondly by distortion and restriction of higher order or meta-procedures (Level 2) for the organizing and connecting of Level 1 procedures and thirdly by restrictions on self-consciousness and self-reflection disabling any problem-solving ability (Level 3). Problematic procedures persist because all procedures are understood to be self-reinforcing. Interpersonal role procedures seek a particular reciprocating response from others which is also reinforcing when received and maintains stability; at the same time disruptions or coercions from the other will be disallowed or avoided unless they fit with the repertoire.

All of these patterns acquired in early life are stored as procedural memory: this is not directly or easily accessible to introspection which, with constant reinforcement, makes them resistant to revision. In more disturbed individuals the meta-procedures normally responsible for mobilizing role procedures appropriately in relation to context and for connecting and integrating the repertoire of roles (Level 2) may be disrupted, leading to dissociation and the repertoire being divided up into relatively disconnected *self-states*.

CAT recognizes three typical patterns of procedural restriction (Ryle, 1979): Traps, Dilemmas and Snags. *Traps* are vicious circles of thinking, feeling and acting, the results of which confirm the negative assumption driving them: e.g. a Placation Trap: 'feeling inadequate and scared and believing others to be aggressive bullies (because my father was an aggressive bully) I try to please them by giving them what they seem to want, they take advantage and abuse me, confirming and reinforcing my beliefs and feelings about them'. *Dilemmas* are falsely dichotomized choices of thinking, feeling and acting, neither of which work: e.g. Bottling up or Explode Dilemma: 'feeling angry but believing that I will be rejected if I express my feelings (as tended to happen when I was a child) I bottle them up and feel frustrated and ignored; eventually I cannot contain my resentment any longer and give vent to an angry outburst which results in me being rejected, confirming and reinforcing that bottling up anger is the thing to do'. *Snags* describes the sabotaging of appropriate intentions due to negative beliefs about self and other often outside of consciousness: e.g. 'Feeling plain and wanting to look smart I try to buy nice clothes but find I cannot go through with it and put them back at the last minute feeling relieved but miserable (because of what my envious and competitive stepmother would say/used to say when I was a child).'

Restrictions on self-reflection and resulting restrictions on self-management take two main forms: either restricted or distorted self-consciousness or restricted self-consciousness in the service of avoiding awareness and unmanageable emotion (see Ryle, 1994b). Of the first sort:

a) *restricted self-reflection*, parents who do not offer the child any reflection on experience produce an inability in the child to reflect on her experience and the discounting of personal needs or feelings;

b) *disjointed self-reflection*, inconsistent or contradictory parenting accompanied by incoherent or distorted accounts of what is going on leave the child incapable of integrating contradictions, resulting in the persistence of dissociated sub-personalities of limited awareness;

c) Errors of attribution – for some children reasonable procedural aims are treated as dangerous or forbidden and become associated with symptomatic, avoidant or submissive procedures instead. The true aims and (adult) causes are never tested out or understood and the (child's) feelings about the feared consequences are not distinguished from the intention itself, leading to irrational guilt.

Of the second sort:

a) Unmanageable experiences are often traumatic and overwhelm the ability to think, feel, act or remember, with the result that procedures become organized to keep certain feelings and memories out of consciousness and avoid activities or experiences that will bring them to mind;

b) Silencing – when the child's abusive experiences are accompanied by denying accounts from adults often linked to dire consequences if mentioned, this results in these experiences being unspeakable and unrecallable though the evidence may be obvious in the pattern of abusive relationships in adult life;

c) Defensive anxiety reduction – where the child's natural aims or desires have been overly criticized or prohibited, the possibility of expressing those aims or desires becomes associated with intense anxiety, leading to avoiding or denying the aim or desire.

Change

In CAT change comes from accurate agreed *descriptions* of the problems and procedures, constructed collaboratively by the client and the therapist; from the client and therapist's practice of *recognition* of roles and procedures in action through increased self-reflection, leading to *revision* by the client resisting or stopping old roles and procedures and practising new ones. The therapist will use a variety of techniques in support of these tasks.

Most of the work of change consists of the therapist deconstructing the client's roles and procedures by reflecting on their origins in the past and the present, reflecting on causes and effects, reallocating responsibilities for causes and effects, identifying emotions, describing and linking them and encouraging authentic expression and reflecting on consequences – losses, gains, secondary gains and unseen negative consequences. Attention is paid to the operation of these in relation to Malan's triangle (Malan, 1976) of how procedures operated in the past, in the present and in the therapeutic relationship. In the last of these it is essential that the therapist resist colluding with the client's enaction of their unhelpful roles and procedures towards the therapist. Described in psychoanalytic therapy as transference and projective identification, these enactments are subject to the same process of accurate description, recognition and revision.

Deconstruction with the aid of the client's descriptions and recognitions implies and leads to the construction of new procedures towards the achievement of appropriate, negotiated aims and outcomes (from dissolution to resolution to solution). Care is taken not to undermine a client's coping procedures even when they may be less than effective until better alternatives have been described and tested. Using Kelly's metaphor, the ship must be rebuilt at sea without sinking.

Most important and often most difficult is helping the client desist from self-harming behaviours or mood-altering procedures (with drink, drugs, food, etc.) because such procedures are almost 100 per cent effective though damaging. A useful strategy is to combine (a) avoiding conflicts that result in a need to shift mood with (b) witnessed and managed expression of the intense affect that drives the shift with (c) the substitution of less harmful but affective alternative procedures, all linked to a map, called an SDR (sequential diagrammatic reformulation).

For many neurotic clients change stems directly and quickly from the process of description in the reformulation of the client's story. The new perspective allows swift and decisive movement towards new ways of relating and acting. In more difficult cases the therapist is much more involved, modulating her interventions to provide and encourage manageable steps towards change, acting as mentor to the client's attempts at recognition and revision and handing over the tasks as the client's awareness and skills increase. With the most difficult cases, such as borderline personality disorders, the therapist's main task is to take up the position of the calm central point (psychologically) around which the client whirls, describing and mapping from that point while refusing to be either provoked into hostile retaliation or rejection and abandonment, or seduced into being abusive or overly caring, protective or controlling. In most cases the client can eventually join the therapist in the calm centre and begin to use the map to control their behaviour, resulting in often remarkable changes.

Practice

Goals of therapy

The main goal of the CAT approach is to help the client recognize how repetitive use of a limited range of roles and procedures results in their endlessly reinforced problems and to help them stop and revise their procedures as well as to broaden their role repertoire. To this end the therapy is an active, focused, contracted collaboration.

The first subsidiary aim is to teach the client self-reflection so as to increase self-management skills. A client who can reflect on the interactions in her life and has the ability to recognize her own patterns of thinking, feeling and acting, and those of others, has the capacity to predict the outcome of interactions more successfully and thereby has a greater degree of control and choice. She is no longer stuck in repetitive circular patterns and can maintain revision independent of a therapist. The second subsidiary aim supports the first and is to help the client learn to use the specific tools of self-reflection and self-management. The goals of therapy are tailored to the needs of the client. Clients with personality disorders will need more work in developing self-reflection in service of integration before moving on to specific changes.

The results of therapy may be symptom relief, life change, personality change, self-actualization, a sense of freedom or any other concept. CAT sees no reason to define that meaning for the client. The theory does imply that since the mind is a socially constructed phenomenon, to be increasingly cut off from social discourse is to become increasingly disordered. Therefore good enough psychological functioning is related to effective social functioning and the ability to engage in dialogue with others flexibly from appropriate role positionings.

Selection criteria

Individual CAT is seen as a safe first intervention for most clients seeking therapy. The therapy is designed to be brief, collaborative and active with a negotiated and agreed target problem focus. Therapists conduct an initial assessment to ascertain the nature of the problem, personal, psychiatric and therapy histories, and the client's motivation and alignment to the ethos of the therapy. Initial therapy contracts are for 8 or 16 sessions followed by a 2–3 month break and then a follow-up evaluation session at which problem resolution or further treatment can be discussed.

CAT, being pragmatic, does not generally attempt to treat clients with no motivation or alignment to the ethos. This generally excludes active substance abusers and those with uncontrolled psychotic episodes. CAT by the same token does not generally attempt to treat those who would be more effectively treated by other well-recognized forms of therapy, for example those with phobias, OCD, generalized anxiety, sexual problems with CBT; grief reactions and more everyday worries may be better treated by generic counselling. Clients who, for whatever reason, are unable to engage with a brief, active, focused approach are usually advised to seek a more slowly opening therapy.

CAT therapists take the view that following a brief therapy in which a client has (hopefully) taken two steps forward it is not unusual that they will take one step back, so a brief therapy that only takes one step forward is logically a waste of time. If the first episode of therapy only achieves description, a second episode will be required to pursue recognition and revision. Similarly a first episode that only achieves description and recognition is likely to be followed by a second pursuing revision. Some clients can achieve all three steps in one therapy. Again some clients once they have achieved recognition can pursue changes independently of the therapist. Personality-disordered patients are often offered longer initial contracts of 24 sessions, recognizing the intense nature of the transference enactments and role switches which prevent or delay the development of a collaborative working alliance and often disrupt it during the therapy.

Following an initial brief CAT contract the post-therapy evaluation may result in referral on to a longer-term group therapy where what has been learned can be practised in a contained environment. A client negotiating further CAT may choose either another brief contract or a longer-term or open-ended CAT contract. With relationship problems a CAT couple therapy may be indicated.

Qualities of effective therapists

It is perhaps not too difficult to be an effective CAT therapist as the structure of the therapy and the core model makes the task of therapy clear and comprehensible. CAT was designed for use in the NHS by available mental health staff and has been successfully taken up by nurses, occupational therapists, social workers and counsellors as well as by psychologists, psychiatrists and psychotherapists working with some of the most difficult-to-treat clients.

Effective personal qualities are:

- the ability to develop a relationship with the a wide range of clients;
- an empathic ability to tune in to a client's emotional state;
- a developed sense of self-awareness, thoughtful self-reflection and a lively mind;
- a calm, unflappableness and sense of humour under fire/stress – what might be called 'maturity'.

Effective skill factors are:

- the basic counselling competencies: e.g. careful listening, accurate feeding back of what has been heard, open-mindedness, lack of prejudice, open questioning;
- an ability to recognize and describe repeating patterns in the stories told by clients;
- an ability to précis client history and describe repeating patterns in prose and diagrams;
- an ability to negotiate in a collaborative way with the client re target problems, goals, homework, etc.;
- an ability to recognize and resist invitations to collude with the client's roles and procedures and to name and challenge them (e.g. abuse of the therapist, or sympathizing with or rescuing the victim).

Personal qualities are understood to be a mixture of temperament and what is developed through ongoing life experiences in the 'growing-up' process enhanced by personal therapy. CAT skills may be learned in the classroom or in the course of clinical supervision but paramount is a developed cognitive ability as this is the channel through which most of the work is done.

Therapeutic relationship and style

CAT proposes a collaborative approach grounded in a contractually defined working alliance. As contracts are usually of brief duration it is important that the therapist and client are both active in pursuit of change. To be effective the activity has to be collaborative, 'doing with' rather than 'doing to' or 'being with'. The therapist has to be skilled in recruiting the client to the tasks of the therapy and explains these expectations at the beginning of therapy, usually not taking on a client who has little or no motivation. The therapist attunes carefully to the client's temperament and style of interacting and will adjust the collaboration accordingly following Vygotsky's theory of the zone of proximal development (Vygotsky, 1978), suggesting tasks that the client can manage and be stretched by but not be defeated by (tasks which can be broken down into steps of an appropriate size), modulating the degree of challenge and support, as well as supplying key concepts and jointly created tools at the appropriate moment.

Collaboration is understood as working in partnership. Therapist and client pursue an overt agenda based upon mutually agreed descriptions of the client's problems. Denial of problems, submission or resistance to the therapist have to be understood before therapy can go forward. The skill differential in the partnership is skewed. The therapist is understood to have highly developed skills of description, recognition and revision as well as a highly developed relational ability (to establish, maintain, repair and close the therapeutic relationship). The client is also understood to have abilities which they bring to the encounter and the skilled therapist works at developing the client's abilities (perhaps in the manner of a driving instructor) as the aim of therapy is that the client should no longer need therapy because they can solve their own problems. Though the therapist has a range of developed skills this does not make her an expert and she should be relaxed enough to use the mistakes she will inevitably make as grist to the mill of the therapy.

The therapist will vary the style of relating strategically, depending on the client's problem procedures. On a dimension of active–passive, for example with a controlling workaholic, the therapist may take up a more passive approach in order to examine the feelings that this arouses in the client, and vice versa with a patient who feels paralysed or unmotivated. Inevitably resistance is encountered and the therapist will work to understand, describe and unblock it or work around it.

The therapist will set a contract with formal boundaries around appointment times, session length and out of session contact. These are seen as diagnostic, and transgression of boundaries will be discussed with the client and understood in terms of their roles and procedures. In the same way agreements to undertake tasks and experiments in the therapy are treated as boundaries. Boundaries may be transgressed by agreement in pursuit of change (longer sessions, home visits, accompanying out of session experiments), but such acts are discussed in supervision first and must be clearly in pursuit of change. By the same token there is usually no therapist self-disclosure unless in the service of recognition and revision, for example discussing counter-transference feelings.

The emotional tone of the therapy will usually be businesslike and serious as the therapist is working to understand and describe the client's core painful beliefs and feelings underlying their problems. This requires an authentic attitude based on honesty and respect for feelings, motivations and intentions, which allows the therapist to challenge destructive thoughts and actions. In a good therapeutic alliance humour will naturally arise, often through irony about repetitive problems and procedures (the 'I've done it again!' response), but a therapy in which therapist and client are enjoying themselves is usually a collusive therapy which is avoiding tackling difficulties.

Major therapeutic strategies and techniques

As described above, the major therapeutic strategies of CAT are *description*, *recognition* and *revision*. These three strategies relate to the four phases of the standard treatment: *information-gathering*, *reformulation*, *working with aims and exits* and *ending therapy*.

Description

The aim is to arrive at a collaboratively produced account of the client's problems, the roles and procedures that maintain them and the historical events from which the roles and procedures arose. The account has to be agreed with the client or there is no basis from which to proceed. The account is not *the truth* but a working hypothesis based upon available information which may change as things proceed and new insights are gained. It can be seen as a reworking of a life story from a fresh perspective.

Techniques of description include the following:

Information-gathering: A wide variety of methods are used to gather information. Standard therapeutic interviewing gives descriptions of presenting problems, varieties of histories and some role and procedural insights through the client's theories about their problems. To augment and speed up the gathering of information the client is asked to complete tasks between the sessions including autobiography, family trees, diary-keeping, recording dreams, filling out questionnaires and repertory grids (Kelly, 1955). The therapist collates and synthesizes the information outside of the sessions and in the sessions attempts to make connections and put together the jigsaw pieces.

CAT psychotherapy file: This document is given to the client to read and fill out at home and to bring back to the therapy as a way of starting the conversation. It lists common, generic procedures and roles under their type headings of Traps, Dilemmas and Snags and invites the client to tick the ones that ring a bell for them. It also lists unstable states of mind and extreme ways of feeling that are common to those who would be diagnosed as suffering from personality disorder. The file is a bit like 'off the peg tailoring', allowing the therapist to find quick and reasonable fit descriptions which can then be adjusted by hand rather than go through the lengthy business of 'bespoke tailoring'. The file is not just a cognitive tool; much can be learned from the way it is treated by the client (obsessively filled in, ignored or forgotten, contemptuously rejected, etc.).

Reformulation: prose accounts: The name reflects the idea that the therapist is reworking the client's own formulation of their problems. A reformulation is the therapist's written prose account of what she has heard and gathered, a drawing together of ideas, hypotheses and insights into a coherent narrative. Importantly, the presenting problems will be re-presented following discussion as *Target Problems (TPs)* and the underlying procedures maintaining them will be named. The reformulation is written between sessions and read out to the client. If it has depth, balance and empathy and adequately names both the client's core pain and the way they cause pain to others, then the verbal giving can produce a powerful cathartic effect on the client who, often for the first time, has the feeling of being deeply understood. The therapeutic alliance is usually strengthened. The client is invited to make changes and reflect on the account so that it can be agreed, being the foundation on which change is built. The reformulation is usually written in the second person ('. . .when *you* were a child. . .') but the therapist may, for strategic reasons, write in either the first or third person, to bring the client closer to or to distance them from the material respectively ('. . .*I* was abandoned by my father. . .'; '. . .*he* was a sensitive boy whom everybody ignored. . .').

Reformulation: diagrammatic accounts: Following Horowitz's mapping of mental states (Horowitz, 1979) Ryle started mapping problems, roles and procedures as flow charts. This supervisory practice was then developed into a collaborative in-session technique where client and therapist sit side by side with blank paper and draw out sequences of thinking, feeling and acting. The therapist again outside the session collates and synthesizes these sketches into a more complete map called an *SDR (Sequential Diagrammatic Reformulation)* which is shared, agreed and then used to guide the therapy. The SDR and the prose reformulation will describe the same material but in a different form.

The SDR is seen as an essential tool of change as it functions as a literally portable tool for self-reflection enabling the client to understand where they are and predict what will happen next, thereby creating the possibility of choice of action. Like an A–Z map-book the SDR shows the one way streets and dead ends of the client's usual relating and as the therapy develops, new routes and exits are added to the map. The SDR also has the invaluable function of being open for reference on the table in the session, which helps the therapist understand and reflect on the client's weekly material, allowing therapist and client to think together, speculate and pre-empt, but also enabling role transference and disruptive procedures to be immediately reflected on and defused before they can disrupt the therapeutic alliance. The SDR is used in the same way in supervision, particularly to understand transference and counter-transference feelings.

Recognition

A typical reformulation will result in an agreed list of two or three salient problems linked to the roles and procedures maintaining them which are targeted for change. The origins of these problematic roles and procedures in the client's early life will have been understood as far as possible. The strategy now (from around session 5) is to aid the client to recognize these roles and procedures in action in their day to day living and to see how they maintain the problems. Recognition must come before revision, it being axiomatic that you can't change what you can't recognize. Recognition is worked on in the weekly sessions but is also the central homework task for the client.

For example a depressed client complains of being overwhelmed at work. The client and therapist agree a Target Problem description: 'I don't know how to manage my workload.' They are able to describe a placation trap where the client feels she must please her boss when he gives her overwhelming amounts of work for fear that if she protests she will be sacked. The therapist identifies the client's early family situation as the origin of the placation trap, where her mother's love was conditional on her looking after the house and her sibs and her protests were met with criticism and rejection. The procedure is identified as operating both at home and at work. The client's task is to recognize when she placates and accepts burdens. Initially this may take discussion at each therapy session to recognize the repeating pattern. With the aid of a diary focused on this pattern the time elapsed between an act of placation and the 'A-ha! I've done it again' of recognition decreases until recognition occurs at and then just before the act. The client is then ready to attempt revision of the procedure. The more places where recognition occurs, the quicker the procedure can be moved to revision: at work, at home with the children, with the partner, with friends, with the therapist, and so on.

Techniques of description include the following:

Problem focused diary keeping and rating sheets: the client is invited to keep a daily diary focused on the agreed Target Problems and Target Problem procedures and roles. The diary reminds the client of the problem and is a place to record instances of recognition and the time delay as well as any new insights about triggers, repetitions, feelings, associations, etc. The diary is brought to the session for discussion. As time is limited the therapist will ask the client to read out the most relevant, successful or distressing bits only. Recognition and revision of Target Problems and problematic roles and procedures can be briefly rated each session on graph paper as a means of discussing progress and maintaining the focus and motivation.

Using the SDR: the client is invited to carry and regularly refer to the SDR as an aid to developing reliable recognition of the repeating patterns ('I did it again, I'm here again.'). The SDR is brought to the session for discussion, development and annotation. As recognition improves, new insights are possible and these need to be accommodated on the map. Occasionally the whole map may need redrawing when an unintegrated part of the self is revealed.

The SDR is the main tool for working with personality-disordered clients. When the meta-procedures for mobilizing roles in relation to contexts and for connecting the repertoire of roles together are underdeveloped then dissociation results and the client's roles are divided into a number of disconnected self-states. The client is experienced as shifting rapidly from one state to another with sudden changes of affect, tone of voice and posture and discontinuities of cognition and memory. It is often as if different voices with different agendas are speaking. The whole task of therapy here is recognition of the self-states and voices, and the SDR is the best tool for this.

In-session enactments, transference and counter-transference: in the sessions the therapist maintains her focus on the targeted problems and procedures and attempts to avoid being distracted or blown off course. The therapist helps the client recognize enactions of the problems and procedures in the room towards the therapist (in the example above, helping the client recognize how she is placating the therapist by suggesting lots of things she herself can do to change), then names them on the SDR and discusses them as transference and counter-transference phenomena.

Revision

Revision of roles and procedures should logically result in the disappearance or amelioration of problems. Revision is pursued through the definition and operationalization of new *aims and exits*. Once recognition is reliable then possible aims and exits can be outlined and discussed and plans made for out of session experiments, the results of which, both successes and failures, are discussed at the next session. Aims are general how things could be changed for the better is negotiated with the client. Exits are the particular plans and tactics that operationalize the aim. Continuing the example above, the aim might be defined as 'Saying no to the excessive demands of others'. Exits are then proposed for each life situation: politely refusing extra typing at work, asking partner to wash up at home, limiting best friend's demands to babysit, negotiating homework with therapist. The least threatening situation is tackled first so as to provide likely success and an increase in confidence before moving on to more difficult situations.

Revision is inevitably difficult as it means disturbing the complex mesh of the client's procedures/roles with those of others in her life. Much time is spent in therapy looking at the possible consequences of revision and planning aims and exits accordingly. Typically, improving one situation will only make another situation worse, for example the client's job may be precarious and saying 'no' may result in redundancy, or the partner may get aggressive or threaten to leave when asked to help around the house. The therapist and client will then discuss whether even greater changes are called for or whether a way to tolerate the situation can be found.

Areas of revision are as follows:

Revising thinking: similarly to CBT, CAT is concerned to revise dysfunctional thinking as expressed in roles and procedures. This includes circular negative thinking, woolly or illogical thinking, obsessive, ruminatory or unproductive thinking, lack of thinking, overly solution focused thinking and using thinking on impossible targets (such as panicky thinking about whether there is life after death). Following description and recognition, revision is in the direction of good enough thinking integrated with feeling and action where thinking is appropriately applied, logical and clear.

Revising feeling: in the same way CAT is concerned to revise dysfunctional feeling. This can include too much affect (overwhelmed), too little affect (cut-off), underexpressed and overcontrolled (bottled up), overexpressed and out of control (exploding or flooding), failing to identify affects correctly (discrimination), failing to name affects correctly (lack of vocabulary), expressing feelings to the wrong target (leakage or displacement). Revision is in the direction of appropriate affect integrated with thinking and action, identified, understood, and expressed to the degree necessary to the situation in which it arises.

Revising roles and procedures: revision of roles and procedures is usually implicit in the description. For example a client who always takes up a 'caring for others but feeling needy and neglected' role will be invited to experiment with toning down the quality and quantity of her caring and to try expressing her own needs by asking for specific acts of care from others. Clearly the revision process requires the solid foundation of the description of the early life situation where the role arose and acknowledgement and expression of the core painful feelings of anger and loss the client is carrying in relation to their childhood neglect as well as the fears of what may happen if she expresses her needs. If this work has been done then the client should be able to undertake appropriate revision experiments working towards a satisfactory new role of mutual care and the ability to make appropriate demands without guilt or fear.

Revising self-destructive procedures: clients who harm themselves through poisoning, cutting, burning and so on or with drink, drugs, or other addictive practices have the clear revision-goal of stopping what they are doing. Stopping is possible only when the client has some idea of why they are doing it in the first place, hence the power of accurate description, particularly of the core painful issue lying at the heart of things (usually physical or sexual abuse, mental cruelty or sudden losses or abandonments).

Revising split roles: clients who have a borderline or narcissistic personality structure are understood to oscillate between idealizing roles (perfectly caring, completely understanding, totally accepting, fusing with, admiring) and denigrating roles (abusing, ignoring, rejecting, abandoning, rubbishing). Relationships inevitably collapse under the burden of such extreme idealizing into denigration and conflict, leading to the seeking of a new relationship or to self-harm. Recognition of the oscillating cycle allows revision of controlling the urge to idealize or denigrate and practising staying with a good enough relationship while processing anger at past denigrations of self, grief for the loss of early ideals, and shame and regret for denigrations inflicted on others.

Technical flexibility

CAT is an integrative model both in terms of theory and in terms of technique. The principle here is to have as many tools in the therapist's toolbox as possible and to not restrict the client's or therapist's potential and creativity. CAT therapists may use dreamwork, active and passive imagination exercises, Gestalt techniques, role-play and empty-chair work, art therapy exercises, body shape, voice and gesture work, active emotional expression (e.g. anger work), ritual enactments, *in vivo* CBT exercises, word association and Rorschach, story/myth telling and poetry. For example a client who is emotionally and cognitively blocked may be invited to lie down quietly and attempt to free-associate. Whatever is attempted must be in service of description, recognition and revision and be properly worked through in the therapy.

Ending therapy and following up the client's progress

Because CAT is usually practised in brief contracts of 16–24 sessions, the closing phase of the therapy is very important and ending is discussed from the very first session. A follow-up session 2–3 months after the last session is part of the contract. The period from the end to the follow-up is where the client has to 'fly solo' and try to put into practice what they have learned in the therapy, reporting back their success or failure at the follow-up. Another aspect of collaborative working is that the client is discouraged from regressing into a passive, dependent attachment on the therapist; in effect the client has to 'get down from mother's lap and explore the world', mitigating the pain of ending.

Inevitably the ending of therapy recapitulates to some degree the client's early losses; the therapist will be concerned to have discussed these and worked with the pain involved. If this work is not done it is likely that the client will avoid the pain of ending by not turning up or by sabotaging or rejecting what has been gained from the work.

The last four sessions of the therapy are given to this agenda and to writing goodbye letters. The therapist writes a prose summary of what has been worked on, what has been recognized and revised and what needs further work, including comment on the course of the therapeutic relationship and likely sabotage of gains. The client is invited to write their own view of the therapy. This provides an opportunity to share their feelings of gratitude, frustration or disappointment.

The follow-up session provides reflection and perspective on the therapy and closes the episode of treatment. It is the time and place for discussion of further treatment options, whether more CAT or a different form of treatment.

The change process in therapy

The change process in CAT is clearly defined, task focused and based on the assumption that change occurs through increased awareness.

Description and targeting

The first task then is to construct as accurately as possible, with the client's collaboration, a description of *what* the client is doing that results in problems being maintained and patterns of interaction being repeated and reinforced. Descriptions are constructed from situations in the past, the present and in the consulting room. Information is gathered from many different sources. Therapist and client negotiate the Target Problem focus for the therapy.

Reformulation

Inextricably linked to this is the construction of a plausible hypothesis of *why* the client is doing what they are doing: what it means and where it originates in early adaptations to environment. Part of this process is the redistributing of responsibility for trauma and suffering to where it most reasonably belongs, identifying and challenging distorted beliefs and thinking, and identifying appropriate affects and their expression. The therapist writes and reads out in the session a prose account in the form of a letter to the client giving them back their story in its newly understood form and a diagrammatic map of the territory is constructed and shared.

Recognition

Having arrived at a jointly agreed description of how things stand the therapy turns to the pursuit of recognition in action. The task is now to develop awareness through use of the map in life and in the session, with the client practising self-reflection with the therapist to refine the map and reflect on changes as well as attempting to connect up dissociated self-states.

Revision and resistance

The achievement of consistent recognition in action moves the task on to revision, the development of changes through the practice of aware experimentation in life and in the session with the therapist. The result of successful experiments is new learning which can be generalized to other situations and the disappearance of the Target Problems. Metaphorically speaking, the logs of present experience become jammed on the rocks of early experience, blocking the flow of the river of adaptability; the therapy unjams the logs, freeing up the flow. However, it is also true that in times of stress (lots of logs coming down the river at the same time) the client may revert to their old map (the rocks in the river haven't moved and the logs jam up again). More therapy may be needed at that point.

Resistance is nearly always encountered and must be understood and worked through. Ruptures to the therapeutic alliance must be repaired and can be helpfully understood. Inevitably the client will enact problematic roles towards the therapist. CAT recognizes two types of *transference*: *identifying* transference and *reciprocating* transference (Ryle, 1998). In the former the client seeks to deny differences and to take on the therapist's role and characteristics; in the latter the client seeks from the therapist a reciprocation of one of her problematic roles. The therapist's task is to challenge the identification, resist reciprocating and to invite recognition of the transference. In terms of the thoughts and feelings evoked by the client, *counter-transference*, CAT again recognizes identifying and reciprocating types. In the former the client induces in the therapist feelings associated with one or other of the client's roles, particularly where the affective component of the role may not be openly expressed (e.g. bland tales of horror); in the latter the client induces in the therapist feelings associated with the role reciprocal to the client's role and is a key way for the therapist to identify the client's role. As before, the therapist's task is to recognize to which role the feelings belong, not to dance to the client's tune, and to invite the client's recognition of what is occurring. Transference is not gathered in the psychoanalytic sense but the CAT therapist will usually check out her feelings in supervision before attempting recognition in session with the client.

Ending

Goodbye letters summarizing the experience and what has been achieved are exchanged by client and therapist. A brief contracted therapy usually ends before everything has been resolved so there is a temptation to work to the last minute. At the same time early losses in the client's life coupled with a helpful therapeutic relationship indicate that the ending should be handled sensitively. If it is, then the client sabotaging what she has gained or the therapist repeating traumatic losses is avoided. The client takes responsibility for unresolved or partially resolved problems during the period between ending and follow-up. Decisions about further treatment of unresolved problems are deferred until follow-up.

Limitations of the approach

There are very few clients for whom CAT is unsuitable (as described on pp. 276–7 above). The therapy currently limits itself to working conversationally with intra- and interpersonal problems and patterns and does not yet theorize the transpersonal, the dynamic or collective unconscious or the body.

There are many recognized ways in which the therapy can be frustrated. Here are four.

Failures of description: the therapist can get the description wrong due to partial information sometimes resulting from denial (e.g. of being an abuser), dissociation (e.g. of being abused) or where the 'false self'/adapted structure is seen to be all there is, or by not developing it jointly with the patient. Often descriptions can be disagreeable or un-agreeable due to shadow feelings such as envy or shame being named.

Failure to handle parentally derived roles: most clients have intrapersonal conflict between enacting parentally derived roles and child-adapted roles e.g. 'harshly critical and demanding of oneself' to 'a response of crushed but striving'. The client usually seeks help because of the miseries of the child-adapted role but at the same time the power of the parentally derived role in the psyche can feel threatened by the therapist's help. Empathizing with the child-adapted role without naming and challenging the parentally derived role maintains the conflict and defeats change. Recognition and revision of both roles is needed.

Failure to name secondary gains: narcissists often defeat therapists because the secondary gain of the therapist's attention is more satisfying than the primary gain of becoming an ordinary, good enough person (defined from the therapist's point of view). Similarly, clients stuck in the abused victim role often prefer the secondary gain of the therapist's empathy rather than the primary gain of the self-esteem derived from standing up to abuse.

Failure to understand resistance to demands: clients who have been bullied or oppressed in childhood display a range of typical responses to any kind of demand, particularly from perceived authority figures (including therapists): gloomy, depressed submission; passive resistance (must–won't); sabotaging resistance; or active and often destructive rebellion (must not–will). This needs to be described and recognized via a discussion of reasonable versus unreasonable demands before any therapeutic alliance can be achieved.

Case example

The client

Peter, a 30-year-old single man was referred for psychotherapy following appearance at an NHS A&E department feeling suicidal. He gave a history of a disrupted early life, childhood sexual abuse, anxiety, depression and difficulties in finding and sustaining relationships. He had pursued education throughout his twenties and was now attempting to complete a doctorate. He came from a white, working-class background. He presented for therapy because he had assaulted his girlfriend, who had called the police and had him charged. He had left his girlfriend's flat and moved back in with his mother and stepfather, which was causing further problems. He was keen to understand why his relationships always ended in the same way.

The therapy

A contract for 16 sessions was made and the therapist started to gather information and understand the client's story. He gave the following reasons for seeking therapy:

- rage towards his parents, stepfather and grandfather, fantasies of killing his stepfather, angry blaming of his mother, being verbally and physically abusive towards his girlfriends;
- feeling alienated, alone, never heard, negative, whingeing and depressed;
- unable to commit, claustrophobic and paranoid in intimate relationships;
- defensive around men, fearing assault;
- perfectionism and workaholism re academic work, fear of failing and being unemployable.

In the CAT Psychotherapy File he ticked (1) negative thinking, placation, social isolation, avoidance and low self-esteem traps, (2) dilemmas around perfect performance and order vs chaos and mess, brute or martyr, involved and engulfed vs distant, safe and lonely, admiration or contempt, (3) unstable states of intense, extreme and uncontrollable emotion, lack of trust and unreasonable anger, clinging, fearing abandonment and frenetic activity. These responses indicated a diagnosis of borderline personality disorder.

The client brought a comprehensive autobiography and was from the beginning actively involved and collaborative in the therapy, desperate for therapy to bring relief and understanding to him.

At session 5 the therapist offered the following reformulation:

Dear Peter,

You have come to therapy seeking help in understanding the intense feelings of anger you carry towards your family and how these are upsetting your relationships. You are anxious about the future whether you will be able to work and sustain relationships and depressed about events in the past which you feel have damaged you beyond repair. This letter aims to offer an understanding of how these feelings came about and how they are maintained in your life. By recognizing the patterns of what is happening it should be possible to start to make changes for the better.

You were born into a shaky family situation. Your parents were very young and unable to cope. You were left with your grandmother when your mother went back to work in pubs and your father left for good when you were two. When you were six your mother remarried and left you with your grandparents. Your grandfather was strict and depriving but you found you could bully your grandmother. Whenever you saw your father he was an emotional mess and leant on you, crying about his messy relationships. You stayed weekends with your mother and were sexually abused by her boyfriend's son. Eventually aged 11 and against your choice you were taken away from your grandparents to live with your mother and stepfather when they married. You coped by focusing on work at school and did well getting into college. You tried to re-create a close relationship with your mother but found your jealous stepfather in the way. However, when at college, following rejection by your first girlfriend, you felt unsupported and rejected by your mother and stepfather as if you were a nuisance and unwanted since you were born which led to conflict and angry blaming. Your stepfather attacked you with an iron bar and threw you out. You had to make your own way in the world. In adult life your perfectionist striving has resulted in success in education but the family pattern of conflict has emerged in your relationships, particularly with your recent girlfriend and again with your mother and stepfather now that you are living at home.

The Target Problem can be described as: 'I don't know how to have satisfactory relationships'. The underlying pattern seems to be as follows:

Seeking closeness (or 'hot-relating') you get into a relationship. There is a choice of roles: 1) either you are the powerful rescuer of the other, which feels good because they won't reject you, you feel safe, but become bored and eventually reject them or 2) you are rescued by an idealized other, which feels good for a while ('Wonder-land') but you don't feel safe and can feel smothered and controlled leading to conflict about control; 3) the conflict escalates into abuse and violence in which there has to be a winner and a loser ('the Battlefield'); 4) it is as if the only alternative is to stay out of relationships, feeling lonely, desperate and alienated ('the Desert').

The therapy should focus on recognizing this pattern in action both in your life and possibly in therapy so that you can make changes that will lead to more satisfying relationships in future.

An SDR was developed (Figure 11.1).

The next few sessions of therapy were spent dealing with the feelings evoked in the client by being convicted of assault and sentenced to community service. Feelings of guilt at being an abuser and identifying with those who had abused him conflicted with feelings of rage about the provocations of his girlfriend's lies and being the victim of her betrayals. The therapist linked these feelings to his feelings about his mother's and father's abandonments and betrayals and how he was treated as an object of no consequence to be messed about and lied to and how he bullied his grandmother in the past and his mother in the present while living in her house. During these sessions the client had one drinking binge with suicidal threats that resulted in an ambulance being called as well as several run-ins with his stepfather and his girlfriend.

The therapy had three focuses. First the client's core painful feelings around abuse and abandonment were focused on and the client was encouraged to express these feelings on paper directly to their source in 'no-send' letters. Secondly the client was helped to recognize invitations and provocations that would lead to 'hot-relating' and conflict and practised not responding. He and his girlfriend did get sexually involved again briefly, despite a court order on him to stay away, but this helped him to see that there was no future in the relationship. Thirdly the client learned some anger management techniques to control his temper.

The client was able to shift his attitude of blaming towards his mother, stepfather and father by understanding their limitations as abused and abandoned people themselves. He was able to accept that he would not get the apologies and hugs he sought from his mother but could value the intent behind the money she gave him; he was able to accept that his stepfather would never like him (as he was the living truth that his own son was an abuser) but he could value the intent behind the help he got from him to mend his car; he was able to accept that his father would always be weak and he (the client) could give up the counselling role he took up towards him as a way of staying in touch.

As therapy drew to a close the client was much calmer and able to recognize his pattern somewhat. He had, however, retreated into a more narcissistic position of seeing others as contemptible and feeling hopeless about ever managing himself in a relationship. He had had no further episodes of violence or binge drinking and was progressing slowly on his academic work. At follow-up he had maintained his gains but his continuing anxiety and depression about the future resulted in the offer of another episode of CAT.

Figure 11.1 Client's Sequential Diagrammatic Reformulation (SDR)

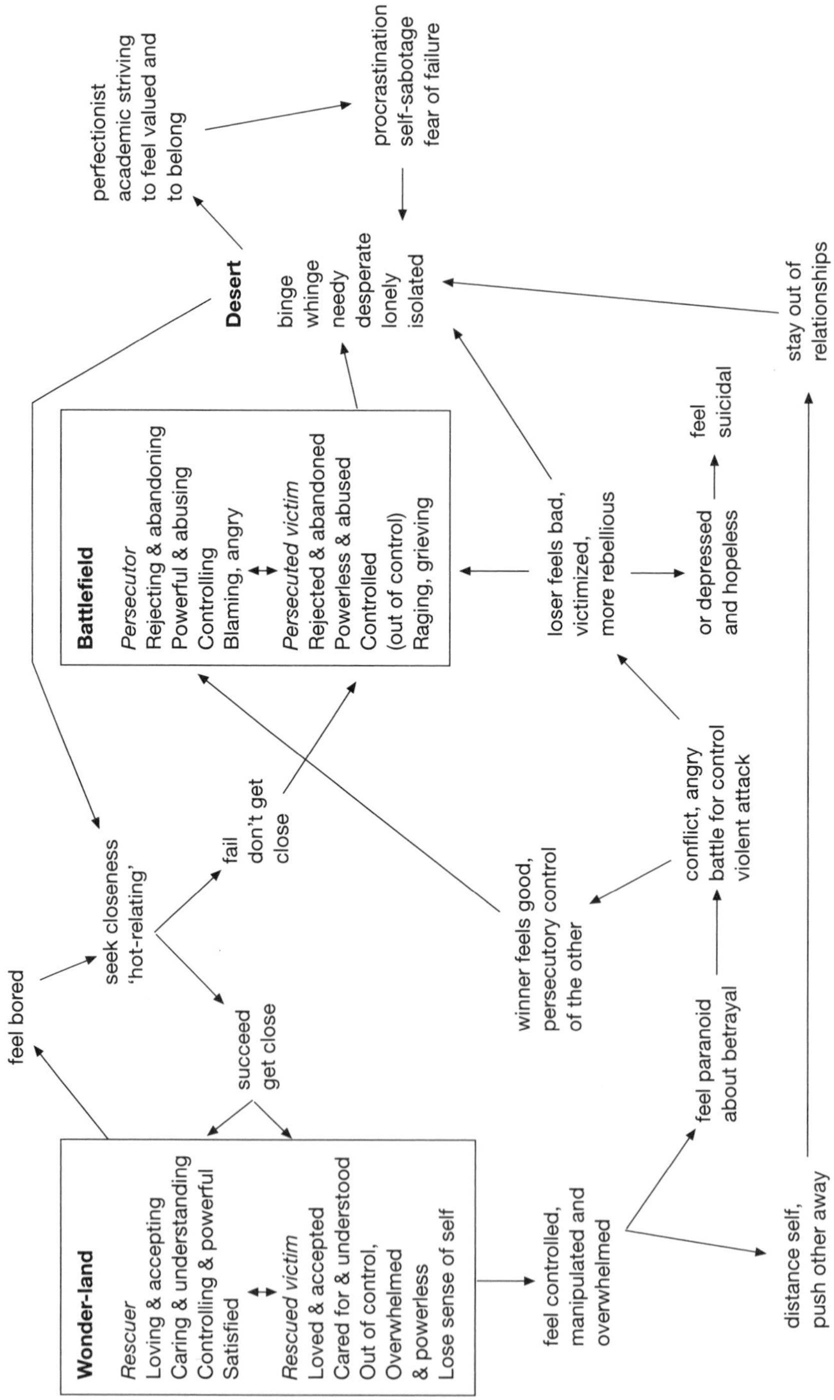

The first CAT can be seen as having tackled the acute problems, leaving the more chronic problems revealed and available for work.

References

Bell, L. (1996) 'CAT: its value in the treatment of people with eating disorders', *Clinical Psychology Forum*, 92: 5–10.

Bowlby, J.A. (1969) *Attachment and Loss*: Vol I: *Attachment*. New York: Basic Books.

Clarke, S. and Llewelyn, S. (1994) 'Personal constructs of survivors of childhood sexual abuse receiving cognitive analytic therapy', *British Journal of Medical Psychology*, 67: 273–89.

Cowmeadow, P. (1994) 'Deliberate self-harm and cognitive analytic therapy', *International Journal of Short-term Psychotherapy*, 9(2/3): 135–50.

Fairbairn, B.D. (1952) *Psychoanalytic Studies of the Personality*. London: Tavistock.

Fosbury, J. (1996) 'Psychological treatment (CAT) with poorly-controlled diabetic patients', *Practical Diabetes International*, 13(5): 158–62.

Fosbury, J. et al. (1996) 'Psychological issues in the diabetes clinic', *Practical Diabetes International*, 13(3): 92–3.

Fosbury, J. et al. (1997) 'A trial of cognitive analytic therapy in poorly controlled Type I patients', *Diabetes Care*, 20(6): 959–64.

Horowitz, M. (1979) *States of Mind: Analysis of Change in Psychotherapy*. New York: Plenum Press.

Kelly, G. (1955) *The Psychology of Personal Constructs*. New York: Norton.

Kerr, I. (1999) 'Cognitive analytic therapy for borderline personality disorder in the context of a community mental health team', *British Journal of Psychotherapy*, 15(4): 425–38.

Leighton, T. (1995) 'A cognitive analytic understanding of "Twelve Step" treatment', *New Directions in the Study of Alcohol Groups*, 20, November.

Leighton, T. (1997) 'Borderline personality disorder and substance abuse problems', in A. Ryle (ed.), *Cognitive Analytic Therapy and Borderline Personality Disorder: The Model and the Method*. Chichester: John Wiley.

Leiman, M. (1992) 'The concept of sign in the work of Vygotsky, Winnicott and Bakhtin: further integration of object relations theory and activity theory', *British Journal of Medical Psychology*, 65: 209–21.

Leiman, M. (1994) 'Projective identification as early joint action sequences: a Vygotskian addendum to the Procedural Sequence Object Relations Model', *British Journal of Medical Psychology*, 67: 97–106.

Leiman, M. (1995) 'Early development', in A. Ryle (ed.), *Cognitive Analytic Therapy: Developments in Theory and Practice*. Chichester: John Wiley.

Leiman, M. (1997) 'Procedures as dialogical sequences: a revised version of the fundamental concept in CAT', *British Journal of Medical Psychology*, 70(2): 193–207.

Low, J. (2000) 'CAT', in C. Feltham and I. Horton (eds), *Handbook of Counselling & Psychotherapy*. London: Sage. pp. 371–7.

Malan, D.H. (1976) *The Frontiers of Brief Psychotherapy*. London: Hutchinson.

Mitzman, S. and Duignan, I. (1993) 'One man's group: brief CAT group therapy and the use of SDR', *Counselling Psychology Quarterly*, 6(3): 183–92.

Mitzman, S. and Duignan, I. (1994) 'Change in patients receiving time limited cognitive analytic group therapy', *International Journal of Short-Term Psychotherapy*, 9(2/3): 151–60.

Pollock, P.H. (1996) 'Clinical issues in the CAT of sexually abused women who commit violent offences against their partners', *British Journal of Medical Psychology*, 69: 117–27.

Pollock, P.H. (1997) 'CAT of an offender with borderline personality', in A. Ryle (ed.), *Cognitive Analytic Therapy and Borderline Personality Disorder: The Model and the Method*. Chichester: John Wiley.

Pollock, P.H. and Kear-Colwell, J. J. (1994) 'Women who stab: a personal construct analysis of sexual victimisation and offending behaviour', *British Journal of Medical Psychology*, 67: 13–22.

Ryle, A. (1975) *Frames and Cages*. London: Chatto & Windus.

Ryle, A. (1978) 'A common language for the psychotherapies', *British Journal of Psychiatry*, 132: 585–94.

Ryle, A. (1979) 'The focus in brief interpretive psychotherapy: dilemmas, traps and snags as target problems', *British Journal of Psychiatry*, 134: 46–54.

Ryle, A. (1982) *Psychotherapy: A Cognitive Integration of Theory and Practice*. London: Academic Press.

Ryle, A. (1985) 'Cognitive theory, object relations and the self', *British Journal of Medical Psychology*, 58: 1–7.

Ryle, A. (1990) *Cognitive Analytic Therapy: Active Participation in Change*. Chichester and New York: John Wiley.

Ryle, A. (1991) 'Object relations theory and activity theory: a proposed link by way of the procedural sequence model', *British Journal of Medical Psychology*, 64: 307–16.

Ryle, A. (1992) 'Critique of a Kleinian case presentation', *British Journal of Medical Psychology*, 65: 309–17.

Ryle, A. (1993) 'Addiction to the death instinct? A critical review of Joseph's paper "Addiction to near death"', *British Journal of Psychotherapy*, 10: 88–92.

Ryle, A. (1994a) 'Projective identification: a particular form of reciprocal role procedure', *British Journal of Medical Psychology*, 67: 107–14.

Ryle, A. (1994b) 'Consciousness and psychotherapy', *British Journal of Medical Psychology*, 67: 115–23.

Ryle, A. (1995a) *Cognitive Analytic Therapy: Developments in Theory and Practice*. Chichester: John Wiley.

Ryle, A. (1995b) 'Transference and counter-transference variations in the course of cognitive analytic therapy of two borderline patients: the relation to the diagrammatic reformulation of self-states', *British Journal of Medical Psychology*, 68: 109–24.

Ryle, A. (1995c) 'Defensive organisations or collusive interpretations? A further critique of Kleinian theory and practice', *British Journal of Psychotherapy* 12(1): 60–6.

Ryle, A. (1996) 'Ogden's autistic-contiguous position and the role of interpretation in psychoanalytic theory building', *British Journal of Medical Psychology*, 69: 129–38.

Ryle, A. (1997a) 'The structure and development of borderline personality disorder: a proposed model', *British Journal of Psychiatry*, 170: 82–7.

Ryle, A (1997b) *Cognitive Analytic Therapy and Borderline Personality Disorder: The Model and the Method*. Chichester: John Wiley.

Ryle, A. (1998) 'Transferences and countertransferences: the cognitive analytic therapy perspective', *British Journal of Psychotherapy*, 14(3): 303–9.

Ryle, A. and Beard, H. (1993) 'The integrative effect of reformulation: cognitive analytic therapy in a patient with borderline personality disorder', *British Journal of Medical Psychology*, 66: 249–58.

Ryle, A. and Fonagy, P. (1995) *British Journal of Psychotherapy* Annual Lecture 1994: 'Psychoanalysis, cognitive analytic therapy, mind and self', *British Journal of Psychotherapy*, 11(4): 567–74.

Ryle, A. and Golynkina, K. (1999) 'Time-limited cognitive analytic therapy of borderline personality disorder: factors associated with outcome', *British Journal of Medical Psychology*. 73(2): 197–210.

Ryle, A. and Marlowe, M. (1995) 'Cognitive analytic therapy of borderline personality disorder: theory and practice and the clinical and research uses of the self states sequential diagram', *International Journal of Short-Term Psychotherapy*, 10: 21–34.

Ryle, A., Spencer, J. and Yawetz, C. (1992) 'When less is more or at least enough', *British Journal of Psychotherapy*, 8: 401–12.

Sheard, T. et al. (2000) 'A CAT-derived one to three session intervention for deliberate self-harm: a description of the model an initial experience of trainee psychiatrists in using it', *British Journal of Medical Psychology*, 73(2): 179–96.

Stern, D.N. (1985) *The Interpersonal World of the Infant*. New York: Basic Books.

Treasure, J. et al. (1995) 'A pilot study of a randomized trial of cognitive analytic therapy vs educational behaviour therapy for adult anorexia nervosa', *Behaviour Research and Therapy*, 33(4): 363–7.

Treasure, J. et al. (1997a) 'Behavioural therapy, cognitive behavioural therapy and cognitive analytic methods in the treatment of anorexia', *Psychotherapy, Psychosomatic Medical Psychology*, 47(9–10): 316–21.

Treasure, J. et al. (1997b) 'Cognitive analytic therapy in the treatment of anorexia nervosa', *Clinical Psychology and Psychotherapy*, 4: 62–71.

Vygotsky, L.S. (1978) *Mind in Society*. Cambridge, MA: Harvard University Press.

Walsh, S. (1996) 'Adapting cognitive analytic therapy to make sense of psychologically harmful work environments', *British Journal of Medical Psychology*, 69: 3–20.

Winnicott, D.W. (1970) *Playing and Reality*. London: Tavistock.

Suggested further reading

McCormick, E.W. (1996) *Change for the Better: Self Help through Practical Psychotherapy*. London: Cassell.

Pollock, P.H. (2001) *Cognitive Analytic Therapy for Adult Survivors of Abuse*. Chichester: John Wiley.

Ryle, A. (1995) *Cognitive Analytic Therapy: New Developments in Theory and Practice*. Chichester: John Wiley.

Ryle, A. (1997) *Cognitive Analytic Therapy and Borderline Personality Disorder*. Chichester: John Wiley.

Ryle, A. and Kerr, I. (2001) *A New Introduction to Cognitive Analytic Therapy: Principles and Practice*. Chichester: John Wiley.

12 Cognitive Therapy
Stirling Moorey

Historical context and development in Britain

Historical context

During the middle years of this century psychology was dominated by the twin edifices of behaviourism and psychoanalysis. For one the individual's internal world was unimportant and his or her actions were determined by environmental events. For the other the internal world was all important, but its workings were unconscious and accessible only with the help of a trained guide. The thoughts which most people regarded as central to their experience of everyday life were seen by both schools as peripheral. There were, however, some lone voices which defended the individual as a conscious agent. Kelly (1955) emphasized the way in which the person seeks to give meaning to the world, and suggested that each of us constructs our own view of reality through a process of experimentation. Ellis (1962) drew attention to the role of irrational beliefs in neurotic disorders, and developed rational-emotive therapy (RET) to change these beliefs systematically. The study of the mental processes which intervene between stimulus and response is termed 'cognitive psychology'. This includes a wide range of activities such as thinking, remembering and perceiving. It was not until the 1970s that psychology began to undergo a 'cognitive revolution' (Mahoney and Arnkoff, 1978) which led to a greater interest in the relevance of cognitive processes to therapy. This revolution came in part from within behaviourism. Starting from a learning theory perspective, some behavioural psychologists began to investigate how cognitions could be treated as behaviours in their own right, and so might be conditioned or deconditioned (Cautela, 1973). Others considered the person's contribution to the management of his or her own behaviour (Kanfer and Karoly, 1972); this led to a theory of self-regulation known as self-control theory.

Cognitive theory started to break away from Skinnerian and Pavlovian learning theory with the work of Bandura. He showed that it was possible to understand the phenomenon of modelling from a cognitive rather than strictly behaviourist perspective (Bandura, 1977; Rosenthal and Bandura, 1978). An even more radical step was taken when Mahoney drew attention to the significance of cognitive processes such as expectation and attribution in conditioning (Mahoney and Arnkoff, 1978).

This increasing interest in cognition led to the development of various cognitive-behavioural therapies. Although they all have slightly different theoretical perspectives they share common assumptions and it is often difficult to distinguish them in terms of the techniques used in clinical practice. Of these the most influential have been Ellis's rational-emotive therapy (now known as rational emotive behaviour therapy – see Chapter 14), Meichenbaum's cognitive-behaviour modification and Beck's cognitive therapy. Ellis aims through therapy to make the client aware of his or her irrational beliefs and the way in which they lead to maladaptive emotional states. His emphasis is on cognitive processes that are evaluative rather than inferential. If, for example, a client reported that she felt depressed when a friend ignored her in the street, rather than asking her if there were any alternative explanation (e.g. her friend was preoccupied and did not notice her) Ellis would home in immediately on the evaluative belief underlying her reaction 'I must be liked by people'. Meichenbaum differs from Ellis in the emphasis he places on the role of cognitive processes in coping. Meichenbaum (1985) studied the use of self-instructions as a means of coping with stressful situations and this led to the development of 'Stress Inoculation Training'. This model has had considerable influence on cognitive-behaviour therapy in general and on stress management in particular, but few therapists in Britain would use Meichenbaum's approach exclusively.

There are, however, a larger number of clinicians in Britain who would say that they practise Beck's cognitive therapy. This is certainly the form of cognitive-behaviour therapy which has been most intensively researched (Salkovskis, 1996; Clark and Fairburn, 1997). Beck, like Ellis, was originally an analyst who became disillusioned with the orthodox Freudian tradition of the 1950s. His research into depression led him to believe that this condition was associated with a form of 'thought disorder' (Beck, 1963, 1964), in which the depressed person distorted incoming information in a negative way. The therapy that arose from Beck's cognitive model focused on teaching patients to learn to identify and modify their dysfunctional thought processes. Underlying these negative thoughts are beliefs or assumptions which need to be restructured to prevent further depression. In 1977 Beck's group published the first outcome study comparing cognitive therapy with pharmacotherapy in depressed patients (Rush et al., 1977). This generated great interest, first, because previous studies had shown psycho-therapy to be less effective than drug treatment with this group of patients, and secondly, because psychologists were already becoming interested in cognitive approaches.

From its origins in the USA cognitive therapy has become increasingly popular in Europe, especially in Britain and Scandinavia. The approaches of Beck and Ellis could be described as 'rationalist' since they assume that psychological disturbance results from irrational or biased ways of seeing the world. Con-structivist cognitive therapies (Guidano and Liotti, 1983; Mahoney, 1995) on the other hand stress the person's active role in constructing reality, and is in a sense 'relativist': we each construct our own world. Therapy then becomes a journey that therapist and client embark on together, neither sure of where they will finally disembark. This form of cognitive therapy, which emphasizes developmental issues more strongly than Beck or Ellis, has become influential in Italy and other parts of Europe.

Development in Britain

Cognitive therapy first came to the attention of British psychologists and psychiatrists through the pioneering work of British researchers who sought to evaluate the efficacy of Beck's treatment for depression. Dr Ivy Blackburn carried out an outcome study in Edinburgh (Blackburn et al., 1981), while Dr John Teasdale and Dr Melanie Fennell carried out similar work in Oxford (Teasdale et al., 1984). These studies showed cognitive therapy to be as effective as antidepressants with depressed patients, and also proved that the treatment could be applied outside American private practice in a National Health Service setting. In keeping with the empirical nature of the therapy British cognitive therapists have always been committed to research. Many theoretical and clinical contributions have come from the United Kingdom, but it is probably in the areas of anxiety disorders and psychosis that Britain has been most innovative. Starting in the mid-1980s David Clark and his colleagues at Oxford have identified specific cognitive models for panic disorder (Clark, 1986), obsessive compulsive disorder (Salkovskis, 1985), hypochondriasis (Salkovskis and Warwick, 1986), social phobia (Clark and Wells, 1995) and post-traumatic stress disorder (Ehlers and Clark, 2000). Using these conceptualizations as a framework they have developed and tested focused therapies which target the core cognitive and behavioural elements of each disorder. This team has recently moved to the Institute of Psychiatry where they will be evaluating the effectiveness of their treatments when they are delivered by non-specialist health service workers as opposed to the highly trained therapists usually used in randomized controlled trials. The Institute of Psychiatry has also been at the forefront of training in cognitive therapy since it set up the first training scheme in the UK.

Cognitive therapy is now a major component of clinical psychology courses and psychiatrists in training are also expected to have some experience of this form of therapy. Until recently, psychotic patients were thought to be beyond the reach of psychotherapy, but researchers in several British universities have been developing cognitive behavioural therapies for delusions and hallucinations (Chadwick and Lowe, 1991; Birchwood and Tarrier, 1992; Kingdon and Turkington, 1994; Fowler et al., 1995).

Theoretical assumptions

Image of the person

This chapter will concern itself with Beck's cognitive therapy, but many of the theoretical and clinical points described are shared with other forms of cognitive-behaviour therapy. Cognitive therapy makes a number of assumptions about the nature of the human individual:

1   The person is an active agent who interacts with his or her world.

2   This interaction takes place through the interpretations and evaluations the person makes about his or her environment.
3   The results of the 'cognitive' processes are thought to be accessible to consciousness in the form of thoughts and images, and so the person has the potential to change them.

Emotions and behaviour are mediated by cognitive processes. This distinguishes cognitive therapy from the extreme forms of behaviour therapy which see the organism as a black box: what goes on inside the box is of little consequence. It also distinguishes it from psychoanalysis, which gives prime importance to unconscious rather than conscious meanings. According to Beck:

> The specific content of the interpretation of an event leads to a specific emotional response. . .depending on the kind of interpretation a person makes, he will feel glad, sad, scared, or angry – or he may have no particular emotional reaction at all. (Beck, 1976: 51–2)

The behavioural response will also depend upon the interpretation made: if a situation is perceived as threatening the person may try to escape, if it is perceived as an insult the person may take aggressive action, if it is perceived as a loss he may give up. An important concept in Beck's view of normal and abnormal behaviour is the idea of the 'personal domain'. The personal domain is the conglomeration of real and abstract things which are important to us: our family, possessions, health, status, values and goals. Each of us has a different set of items in our personal domain; the more an event impinges on our domain the stronger our emotional reaction is likely to be.

The meaning we give to a situation will be determined by the mental set we bring to it. Life is too short to work out what each event means to us afresh. We need rules or guidelines to allow us to make educated guesses about what is likely to happen next. If we did not have an internalized rule that we should stop at red traffic lights, our insurance bills would be considerably higher. Some of these assumptions about the world are shared, but others are intensely personal and idiosyncratic. Cognitive theorists call the hypothetical cognitive structures which guide and direct our thought processes 'schemata'. A schema is like a template which allows us to filter out unwanted information, attend to important aspects of the environment and relate new information to previous knowledge and memories (Kovacs and Beck, 1978). In areas we know well we have well-developed schemata (e.g. schemata for driving a car, or how to behave at a social gathering), whereas in new situations schemata will be less well developed.

Conceptualization of psychological disturbance and health

In psychological health our schemata are sufficiently consistent to allow us to predict likely occurrences, but also flexible enough to allow changes on the basis of new information. Most of the time we are capable of processing information in an accurate or even a slightly positively biased fashion (as evidenced by studies demonstrating that non-depressed subjects make internal attributions for success but external attributions for failure: Alloy and Ahrens, 1987; Bradley, 1978). In emotional disturbance information-processing is biased, usually in a negative distorted way.

Beck suggests that we are all capable of functioning as rational problem-solvers at least some of the time. Psychological health requires us to be able to use the skills of reality-testing to solve personal problems as they occur. For instance, an adaptive way of dealing with a failure experience such as being turned down for a job would involve thinking about the interview, assessing one's performance, taking responsibility for any faults or weaknesses that might have contributed to the failure and looking for ways to prevent it happening in the future. In psychological disturbance people revert to more primitive thinking which prevents them functioning as effective problem-solvers (Beck et al., 1979: 15). This thinking tends to be global, absolute and judgmental. So a depressed person who is not successful at a job interview would label herself as a total failure, would conclude that it was entirely her own fault that she did not get the job, and would ruminate about the interview, focusing on all the things that went wrong without thinking about any of the positive factors.

Faulty and adaptive information-processing

When this primitive thinking is in operation information-processing is biased or distorted. Beck (1976) identifies 'logical errors' which characterize the thinking in psychological disorders. Table 12.1 summarizes some of the common logical errors. The tendency to distort information repeatedly in a maladaptive way is one of the factors which distinguishes psychologically healthy from psychologically disturbed individuals. Psychological health is seen as a state where the individual is able to make relatively accurate interpretations and evaluations of

Table 12.1   Cognitive distortions

1   *Arbitrary inference* refers to the process of drawing a specific conclusion in the absence of evidence to support the conclusion or when the evidence is contrary to the conclusion.
2   *Selective abstraction* consists of focusing on a detail taken out of context, ignoring other more salient features of the situation and conceptualizing the whole experience on the basis of this fragment.
3   *Overgeneralization* refers to the pattern of drawing a general rule or conclusion on the basis of one or more isolated incidents and applying the concept across the board to related and unrelated situations.
4   *Magnification and minimization* are reflected in errors in evaluating the significance or magnitude of an event that are so gross as to constitute a distortion.
5   *Personalization* refers to the patient's proclivity to relate external events to himself when there is no basis for making such a connection.
6   *Absolutistic, dichotomous thinking* is manifested in the tendency to place all experiences in one of two opposite categories; i.e. flawless or defective, immaculate or filthy, saint or sinner. In describing himself, the patient selects the extreme negative categorization.

Source: Beck et al., 1979

events, but this does not imply that psychologically healthy people will always think and act rationally.

Taylor and Brown (1988) argue persuasively from research evidence that a degree of self-deception may be necessary for mental health. There is no clear definition of mental health in the cognitive model because it was developed to explain emotional disorder and so an absolute definition of adaptive information-processing is not possible. In fact, one strand that runs through many of the cognitive explanations of psychological problems is the assumption that the patient has much more in common with healthy individuals than he thinks. The cognitive therapist is usually able to see how the person's behaviour is not abnormal when the basic premises of his or her belief system becomes clear. Thus, for someone with obsessive-compulsive disorder (OCD), it is not the experience of intrusive thoughts that is the problem (obsessional thoughts are not uncommon in the general population and are indistinguishable from those experienced by people with OCD; Rachman and de Silva, 1978; Salkovskis and Harrison, 1984) but the interpretations that are made of them (Salkovskis, 1985). Instead of accepting that an urge to blaspheme in church is an odd but harmless intrusion, the person with OCD will believe it indicates some deep, dark impulsiveness in their nature which must be controlled at all costs. It is the consequent attempts to supress and neutralize these normal intrusions that gives rise to rituals and compulsive behaviours. Beck and other cognitive therapists have adopted the standard psychiatric classifications of mental disorders (*DSM IV*). A distinction is made between 'Axis I' disorders such as anxiety, depression, anorexia, etc. and 'Axis II' disorders, which are essentially disorders of personality. Beck has always stressed the importance of having a good theory to describe the condition you are studying or treating. Starting with his pioneering work on depression, cognitive therapists have been mapping the cognitive abnormalities seen in the various psychiatric disorders. Beck (1976) suggests that in depression there is a negative view of the self, the world and the future. In anxiety the cognitive distortions involve an overestimation of major physical or social threat together with an underestimation of the individual's ability to cope with the threat. There is evidence that anxious patients selectively attend to cues which represent threat.

Clark and Steer (1996) describe some of the tests of cognitive models of emotional disorders. More specific models of certain types of anxiety disorder have been proposed. Clark (1986) presented a cognitive model of panic, which emphasizes the way in which catastrophic misinterpretations of bodily symptoms create a vicious circle of anxiety leading to more bodily sensations and more panic. Salkovskis and Warwick (1986) adapted this model for hypochondriasis: the hypochondriac misinterprets innocuous bodily sensations such as headache, twinges, etc. as signs of chronic life-threatening illness. Each of these diagnostic groups therefore filters information in a slightly different way. In panic and health anxiety the focus of attention is usually on bodily symptoms, but in generalized anxiety disorder it is worry which is the cause of distress. According to Wells (1997), any negative events can set off worry (e.g. unpleasant news material, intrusive thoughts). Worry is then chosen as a coping strategy (often because of beliefs that it helps problem-solving or prevents bad things happening), but once this happens negative beliefs about worry (e.g. that worry can cause stress or that the person will lose control of their thinking) set in and a vicious cycle is set up, perpetuating the anxiety. Clark (for a summary see Clark, 1996) has carried out a number of compelling experiments specifically designed to test his model of panic. More limited evidence is available so far for the other anxiety models (Wells, 1997).

Negative automatic thoughts

People with psychological disorders differ from the non-distressed in the content as well as the form of their thinking. They are prone to frequent, disruptive thoughts known as 'negative automatic thoughts'. These are spontaneous thoughts or images which are plausible when the patient experiences them, but are in fact unrealistic. For instance, an anxious person may repeatedly think, 'I can't cope. There's nothing I can do about my problems. Something terrible is going to happen. What if I'm going mad?' and may have images of collapsing, or going berserk. A depressed person may ruminate about his failures, thinking, 'I'm useless, I never do anything right, I'm just a fraud.' We all experience these thoughts at times, but they are much more frequent and distressing in people with emotional disorders.

Maintaining behaviours

Cognitive therapists assume that the person's behaviour will be consistent with these thoughts processes. So in depression, the person who believes he will always fail, doesn't try anything, and the result is a confirmation of the negative belief. In panic disorder, a belief that you are about to die from a heart attack might make you sit down to take the strain off your heart. The role of these behaviours in the maintenance of psychological disturbance is described below.

Cognitive schemata

We have already seen how cognitive schemata are necessary for effective functioning in the world. Healthy schemata are reasonably flexible whereas unhealthy ones tend to be more rigid, absolute and overgeneralized. For instance, a belief that 'I must always be nice to everyone' is inflexible and irrationally universal. A more healthy rule might be 'It is generally better to be pleasant to people, but in certain circumstances it is OK to be unpleasant.' The person with the more rigid rule will tend to criticize themselves heavily if they fall short of their excessively high standard. Schemata may vary in the extent to which they are active at a given time. When they are latent they are not involved in information-processing, but when activated they channel all stages of processing (Beck et al., 1990). In a psychological disorder like depression, the negative schemata tend to become more active. Beliefs such as 'If you are not successful you are worthless' seem more plausible if you are depressed, and unconditional beliefs like 'I am stupid and unlovable' may generate negative self-referent thoughts.

Some cognitive therapists distinguish between core beliefs and conditional beliefs (Beck, 1995). A core belief is an unconditional, axiomatic assumption about the self, the world or other people. In anxiety and depression these core beliefs may be inactive until a critical incident brings them to life. In personality disorders schemata may be active more pervasively. Someone with a dependent personality disorder may believe they are helpless and unable to survive alone even when they are not depressed. The core belief 'I am helpless' is associated with various conditional beliefs like 'If I find someone to rely on I can survive', and with behavioural strategies consistent with the schema (i.e. finding and cultivating relationships where a strong person will look after you). Just as cognitive therapy has identified cognitive disturbances for emotional disorders, the different personality disorders have their own cognitive styles. The paranoid person believes that anyone is a potential enemy and so acts with suspicion and wariness; the narcissistic person believes that he is very special and so acts in a grandiose fashion (Beck et al., 1990). These schemata are more difficult to shift than in disorders such as depression because they are so pervasive and deeply embedded in the individual's belief system.

Acquisition of psychological disturbance

Beck considers that there are many factors which predispose an individual to emotional disturbance. He has considered these factors in relation to various conditions, including depression (Beck, 1987), anxiety (Beck and Emery, 1985) and personality disorders (Beck et al., 1990). He attempts to integrate cognitive factors with other factors to develop a multifactorial theory of psychological disorder. Table 12.2 shows some of the long-term (predisposing) and short-term

Table 12.2   Long-term and short-term vulnerability factors

Predisposing factors
1   Genetic predisposition.
2   Physical disease (e.g. hypothyroidism and depression, hypothyroidism and anxiety).
3   Developmental traumas which lead to specific vulnerabilities (e.g. loss of a parent in childhood may be associated with depression in adult life).
4   Personal experiences too inadequate to provide adequate coping mechanisms (e.g. parents who provide poor models of how to cope with rejection).
5   Counterproductive cognitive patterns, unrealistic goals, unreasonable values and assumptions learned from significant others.

Precipitating factors
1   Physical disease.
2   Severe external stress (e.g. exposure to physical danger may precipitate anxiety, loss of a partner may induce depression).
3   Chronic insidious external stress (e.g. continuous subtle disapproval from significant others).
4   Specific external stress (which acts on a psychological vulnerability).

Source: Adapted from Beck and Emery, 1985: 83

(precipitating) factors which may be associated with anxiety or depression in adult life.

This suggests a much more complex aetiology for emotional disorders than the simplistic notion that cognitions cause emotions. Beck very clearly asserts that

> the primary pathology or dysfunction during a depression or an anxiety disorder is in the cognitive apparatus. However, it is quite different from the notion that cognition causes these syndromes – a notion that is just as illogical as an assertion that hallucinations cause schizophrenia. (Beck and Emery, 1985: 85)

The aetiological factors described above can all be seen as operating on the 'cognitive apparatus' in one way or another.

Schemata as vulnerability factors

We have already begun to consider the vital role that schemata play in psychological health and disturbance. Early learning experiences, traumas and chronic stresses can all lead to idiosyncratic beliefs and attitudes which make a person vulnerable to psychological disturbance. For instance, someone who endures long periods of illness as a child and is overprotected by his parents may develop a core belief that he is frail and vulnerable and needs to be supported by others in order to survive. Someone who is continually criticized for making even small mistakes may elaborate the belief that she must get everything she does completely right. Continuing our view of the person as an active construing agent, we can conceptualize these beliefs as a way the person makes sense of the world by developing ideas about how the world does, or should, operate. The more rigid, judgmental and absolute these beliefs become, the more likely they are to cause problems. Examples of beliefs which predispose to anxiety include the following:

- 'Any strange situation should be regarded as dangerous.'
- 'My safety depends on always being prepared for possible danger.'
- 'I have to be in control of myself at all times.'

Examples of beliefs which predispose to depression include the following:

- 'I can only be happy if I am totally successful.'
- 'I need to be loved in order to be happy.'
- 'I must never make a mistake.'

One of the features of cognitive therapy in recent years has been an interest in developmental factors. Young (1990; Young and Klosko, 1994) has mapped out various ways in which family experiences can create maladaptive schemata. These assumptions may remain relatively quiescent until an event occurs which is of particular relevance to them. This causes them to be activated and to become the primary mode for construing situations. For instance, because of early childhood experiences a woman may believe that she needs to be loved in order to survive. While she is in a relationship this belief will not be salient, unless she thinks that she might lose the love of the person concerned. But if she is rejected by her lover it is likely to be activated. It acts as a premiss to a syllogism:

- 'I need to be loved in order to survive.'
- 'X has left me.'
- 'Therefore I cannot survive.'

These underlying assumptions become less obvious again when the person recovers from the depression. But they remain dormant as a potential source of vulnerability. Cognitive therapy aims not only to correct faulty information-processing but also to modify assumptions and so reduce vulnerability to further psychological disturbance.

Perpetuation of psychological disturbance

The concept of biased information-processing readily explains how information which is contrary to the client's cognitive schema is filtered out or manipulated in such a way that it is made consistent with her belief system. This is commonly seen in depression, where positive information (e.g. past achievement) is repeatedly disqualified. The depressed person will say that past successes do not count because they were due to luck, or to people helping. As Beck remarks, 'even though the depressive may be reasonably accurate in a cognitive appraisal (for example, "They seem to like me"), the overall meaning is still a negative one: "If they knew how worthless I was, they would not like me"' (Beck, 1987: 12).

Behaving in a manner that is consistent with dysfunctional beliefs can also help to maintain negative emotions. A simple example of this can be seen in a phobia, like a dog phobia, where *avoidance* of a feared stimulus (dogs) prevents the person from acquiring information that contradicts the negative belief (that dogs are dangerous). A more subtle form of avoidance is seen in panic disorder. A patient who fears she will collapse while having a panic attack because she feels dizzy may hold on to chairs or railings to keep herself from falling. This *safety behaviour* prevents the patient from discovering that she will not collapse.

In personality disorders *schema maintenance* (Young, 1990; McGinn and Young, 1996) takes place when cognitive distortions or behavioural strategies lead the individual to think or act in ways that perpetuate the problem. Someone with an abandonment schema believes that she is doomed to be rejected in any close relationship (often as the result of key experiences of rejection, loss or separation in childhood). If her partner is late for a meeting or rings up to cancel, her automatic thought is 'It's happening again. He's just like all the rest. He'll leave me soon.' She may try to prevent rejection by constantly looking for reassurance from her partner and this clinging behaviour may actually have the effect of alienating him and bringing about the very abandonment she fears. An alternative strategy which many people who fear abandonment employ is to keep away from relationships altogether and so escape the pain of rejection. This strategy has been termed 'schema avoidance' (Young, 1990; McGinn and Young, 1996).

External factors can also help to perpetuate psychological disturbance. Real-life problems such as unemployment or bereavement make it difficult for depressed people to believe that there is a future, or to believe that they are of value. Similarly, chronic stress or social rejection can contribute to the continuation of anxiety states. The influence of close personal relationships can be very important in this respect. Hooley et al. (1986) have shown that a relationship in which the partner makes frequent negative comments predicts relapse in depression. The more negative the external environment, the more difficult it is to challenge negative thinking.

Change

The cognitive model assumes that emotional and behavioural change is mediated by changes in beliefs and interpretations. In therapy this is achieved through systematic testing of these thoughts and beliefs, but the same process occurs naturally when we are exposed to situations which do not fit our assumptions about the world. If information is not consistent with our schema then we either find ways to incorporate the new information into our existing belief system, or we have to change our belief. Positive life events can therefore lift people out of depression. If your negative thoughts revolve around the idea that you are unloveable, then making a new friend can make you reconsider this. If you think you are a failure, passing an exam you expected to fail can improve your sense of competence. It is often a combination of various external events that leads to natural schema change, but it is by no means clear what allows some people to reconstrue their world in a more positive way while others interpret the new events as evidence that still supports their old beliefs – it is still possible for people to decide that their new friend is just a misfit like them, or that passing the exam was a fluke. Because many of our beliefs are tacit rules, these natural changes often occur gradually and may not be noticed. For instance, someone who has been abused in childhood may not trust anyone, but over time repeated experience of certain people being reliable and honest may lead to revision of this mistrust. Although it does not happen as a conscious re-evaluation, there is a radical change in beliefs about other people. Change in therapy probably occurs through a mixture of learning new coping strategies and modification of schemas.

Goals of therapy

Cognitive therapy has three main goals:

1 to relieve symptoms and to resolve problems;
2 to help the client to acquire coping strategies;
3 to help the client to modify underlying cognitive structures in order to prevent relapse.

Unlike other forms of psychotherapy which sometimes lose sight of the patient's presenting complaint, cognitive therapy is problem oriented. Whether the complaints are symptoms of psychiatric illness like anxiety and depression, behavioural problems like addiction or bulimia, or interpersonal ones like social anxiety, the primary goal is always to help clients solve the problems which they have targeted for change. In the first session the therapist helps to clarify the problems as the patient sees them and to establish priorities. The therapist tries to target symptoms or problems which are both important to the client and amenable to therapeutic intervention.

The whole course of cognitive therapy can be seen as a learning exercise in which the client acquires and practises coping skills. The aim is to teach skills which can be used to deal with the current episode of distress, but can also be employed if problems recur. Many clients find that the methods of cognitive therapy can be generalized to other situations beyond the initial focus of therapy. This goal of therapy is 'to help patients uncover their dysfunctional and irrational thinking, reality test their thinking and behaviour, and build more adaptive and functional techniques for responding both inter- and intrapersonally' (Freeman, 1983: 2). While cognitive therapy seeks to relieve distress it does not set out to change the personality completely. Learning how to navigate the squalls of life in our own battered vessel is often a more realistic objective than trying to rebuild it to someone else's specification as an ocean liner.

The final goal of therapy is the modification of maladaptive schemata. The intention is not to restructure all of a person's irrational beliefs, but only those which are causing problems. Beliefs that are rigid, global and self-referent (e.g. I can be happy only if I'm successful at everything I do; I need a close relationship to survive) predispose the individual to future emotional disturbance. If these beliefs can be made more flexible, specific vulnerability to psychological disturbance will be reduced.

Selection criteria

Which patients?

Psychotherapy research is showing that a variety of therapies are effective with people in emotional distress but has not conclusively determined which clients respond best to which type of treatment. As with other therapies (including drug treatment) severity and chronicity are associated with poor outcome in the treatment of depression. The quality of therapeutic alliance has also been associated with outcome in CBT for depression, but there is some evidence that the alliance builds as a result of the client making some initial improvements as a result of intervention, rather than the alliance acting as the sole vehicle for change. This is supported by evidence that early improvement is associated with better post-therapy outcome in CBT for bulimia nervosa (Agras et al., 2000). Another factor which seems to affect outcome is the extent to which the client understands and accepts the cognitive model. Fennell and Teasdale (1987) found that those who accept the rationale for therapy and find their first homework assignment a success are more likely to do well. For depression particularly, it may be the case that people who can easily engage in problem-solving might benefit more from CBT (Moorey et al., 2001).The implications are that if the clients do not respond to the idea that their thoughts might have some relevance to the problem during the initial sessions then cognitive therapy may not be the right approach. There are some people who are just not 'psychologically minded', and who find it extremely difficult to introspect even to the extent that cognitive therapy requires.

These factors are usually taken into account when considering patients for cognitive therapy, and a clinician will often test clients' suitability by assessing their acceptance of the cognitive model and their response to cognitive restructuring. Safran and Segal's Suitability for Short Term Cognitive Therapy Scale gives a more systematic method for assessing suitability for short-term CBT (Safran et al., 1993). Scores on this predict the outcome of short-term cognitive therapy on multiple dependent measures. As might be predicted, clients with personality disorders tend to score lower on alliance potential, security operations, chronicity, personal responsibility for change, and compatibility with the cognitive therapy rationale when this scale is applied (Vallis et al., 2000), which may indicate longer-term therapy for these clients.

Individual or group therapy?

Although most cognitive therapists would say that group therapy is less effective than individual therapy, results from controlled trials are contradictory. For depression Rush and Watkins (1981) found group therapy to be as effective as individual, but the effects were not as strong, but Scott and Stradling (1990) and Zettle et al. (1992) found the two modalities were equally effective. The advantages of group cognitive therapy in a busy health service are obvious and it can be a very cost-effective approach. Gould et al. (1995) carried out a meta-analysis of treatment outcomes for panic disorder and found that group CBT was half the cost of individual CBT.

Some services offer group cognitive therapy as the first intervention for all clients, and only those who do not make significant gains are then given individual therapy. In other circumstances clients may be offered a group because there are specific advantages over individual therapy. There are two main reasons for this decision:

1 If the client's problems are predominantly interpersonal, e.g. social anxiety;
2 if there will be major advantages in the client being able to see and learn from others with similar problems, e.g. group CBT for people with cancer.

Some patients may initially require individual therapy when they are most distressed but can then go on to a group as their mood improves. This can be especially helpful if interpersonal factors (e.g. lack of assertiveness or fear of disapproval) are considered to be relevant to future relapse. Young (1990) describes a combination of group and individual therapy in the treatment of patients with personality disorders. The group provides a 'laboratory' where the client can test out maladaptive beliefs in relative safety.

Qualities of effective therapists

First and foremost, cognitive therapists need to have good general interpersonal skills. Although the therapy sometimes appears to place a strong emphasis on cognitive and behavioural techniques these are deemed to be effective only if they are used within the context of a good therapeutic relationship. Warmth, genuineness and empathy are vital components of this relationship:

> We believe that these characteristics in themselves are necessary but not sufficient to produce an optimum therapeutic effect. However, to the degree that the therapist is able to demonstrate these qualities, he is helping to develop a milieu in which the specific cognitive change techniques can be applied most efficiently. (Beck et al., 1979: 45–6)

Cognitive therapists need to have good listening skills, to be able to reflect accurately the cognitive and emotional components of the client's communication, and to demonstrate an active and warm interest in the client. If this is not done there is a real danger that attempts to challenge distorted thinking will be perceived by the client as insensitive or even persecutory. Good therapists seem to be able to get inside the client's cognitive world and empathize while at the same time retaining objectivity.

Many would see the qualities described above as essential to any form of psychotherapy. It is more difficult to specify qualities which make someone a good cognitive therapist rather than a good psychotherapist in general. Perhaps one of the most important factors is the extent to which the therapist can accept the cognitive model. The therapist has to be prepared to work in a problem-oriented way without continually looking for unconscious motives in the patient's self-defeating thinking and behaviour. He or she must be able to blend the interpersonal skills described in the last paragraph with a directive approach which involves a great deal of structure and focus. While specific cognitive therapy skills can be learned, the therapist still needs to accept the basic rationale for doing therapy in this way.

No published data exist on factors which predict how well someone will function as a cognitive therapist, although it has been shown that competence in the therapy improves with training (Shaw, 1984). The impression from my own experience of training cognitive therapists is that people with more clinical experience do better than those without, people with a background in behaviour therapy do better than those with a psychodynamic background, and people who take to the model enthusiastically do better than those who are less committed.

Therapeutic relationship and style

The aim of cognitive therapy is to teach the client to monitor thought processes and to reality-test them. Rather than assume that the client's view of the situation is distorted or correct, the cognitive therapist treats *every* statement about the problem as a hypothesis. Therapy is empirical in the sense that it is continually setting up and testing out hypotheses. Client and therapist collaborate like scientists testing a theory. For instance, a depressed person may believe that there is no point in doing anything because there is no pleasure in life any more.

> *Hypothesis*
> If I visit my friend tomorrow I will get no pleasure from it.
> *Experiment*
> Arrange to visit from 3 p.m. to 4 p.m., and immediately afterwards rate the amount of pleasure I get on a 0–10 scale. Most depressed people find they get at least some enjoyment out of activities they used to find pleasurable.

Experiments like this can gradually erode the belief that it is not worth doing anything by providing evidence that there is still pleasure open to them and so increase the person's motivation.

Teaching the client to be a 'personal scientist' is done through collaboration rather than prescription. Wherever possible the therapist will encourage the client to choose problems, set priorities and think of experiments. This collaboration is the hallmark of cognitive therapy and there are a number of reasons for including the client in the problem-solving process as much as possible.

- Collaboration gives the client a say in the therapy process and so reduces conflict.
- Collaboration fosters a sense of self-efficacy by giving the client an active role. Collaboration encourages the learning of self-help techniques which can be continued when therapy is ended.
- Collaboration allows an active input from the person who knows most about the problem.

Collaboration also serves to reduce the sorts of misinterpretation that can sometimes affect the therapeutic relationship. In non-directive therapies, the impassive stance of the therapist means that the patient has to construct an image of the therapist based on her own predictions and rules about people. The resulting misinterpretation (transference) can be used therapeutically. Cognitive therapy wants to reduce this and does not use the relationship as the focus of therapy. It sees the therapist and client as partners in the process of problem-solving. This does not prevent the therapist being very active and directive at times, but it always gives space for the client to contribute and give feedback on what the therapist is doing. With more severely depressed clients there is often a need for a lot of direction at first, but as the mood improves and the client learns the principles of cognitive therapy the relationship becomes more collaborative. Ideally by the end of therapy the client is doing most of the work and thinking up his or her own strategies for change. When the therapist is most directive at the beginning of treatment he or she must also be most empathic in order to establish rapport.

In this type of therapeutic relationship the client and therapist are co-investigators trying to uncover the interpretations and evaluations that might be contributing to the client's problems. This is an inductive process of guided discovery. Wherever possible the therapist asks questions to elicit the idiosyncratic meanings which give rise to the client's distress and to look for the evidence supporting or refuting the client's beliefs. This use of questioning to reveal the self-defeating nature of the client's automatic thoughts has been termed *Socratic questioning*.

Another characteristic feature of cognitive therapy is the way in which the session is structured. At the beginning of each session an agenda is set, with both client and therapist contributing to this. Usually the agenda will include a brief review of the last session, developments in the last week and the results of homework assignments. The work then goes on to the major topic for the session. Anyone listening to a cognitive therapy session will also be struck by two further features: the use of summaries and feedback. Two or three times during a session the client or therapist will summarize what has been going on so far. This helps to keep the client on track, which is particularly important if anxiety or depression impairs concentration. Asking the client to summarize also reveals whether or not the therapist has got a point across clearly. The therapist regularly asks for feedback about his or her behaviour, the effects of cognitive interventions, and so on.

Major therapeutic strategies and techniques

Emery (in Beck and Emery, 1985) describes a four-step process of problem-solving in cognitive therapy:

1 Conceptualize the patient's problems.
2 Choose a strategy.
3 Choose a tactic or technique.
4 Assess the effectiveness of the technique.

1 Conceptualization

Cognitive therapy is based on a coherent theory of emotional disturbance, and this theory can be used to conceptualize the patient's problems. The clearer the conceptualization, the easier it becomes to develop strategies (i.e. general methods for solving the patient's problems) and techniques (specific interventions). For instance, a woman presented with complaints of fatigue and memory problems, but did not have any physical cause for these symptoms. The initial formulation was that the symptoms were stress related, and over the course of two assessment interviews the therapist was able to construct a clearer picture of the problem using the cognitive model. The client had a very poor self-image and was in a difficult marriage where her husband was very critical. She described a constant stream of thoughts criticizing herself which occurred whenever she needed to make decisions. She was also able to identify negative thoughts about the marriage ('It's hopeless, I'm trapped'). The cognitive formulation explained her memory problems as a natural result of only partly attending to anything: she was distracted by the running commentary she gave on her actions. Her fatigue probably resulted from the frequent negative thoughts she was having about herself and her marriage.

Because she had a belief that there was nothing she could do about her marital problems she tended to put these thoughts to the back of her mind using 'cognitive avoidance', and selectively focused on the physical symptoms. This in turn led to a further set of negative thoughts – 'Is there something wrong with my brain? Am I going senile?' This formulation allowed the therapist to develop a comprehensive treatment strategy.

2   Therapeutic strategies

Each therapist has a particular way of formulating a case, and strategies are tailored to the individual personality of the client. The following list tries to cover the strategies most commonly used in cognitive therapy.

Distancing and distraction: These strategies are aimed at helping the client to get some distance from the constant flow of maladaptive thinking. Distancing the client from the automatic thoughts helps to reduce the strength of the negative emotional response. Techniques that help the client to act as a more objective observer of his or her own thoughts are usually helpful here. Counting negative thoughts, explaining the rationale and defining problems all help to achieve some distance and perspective. Distraction reduces the frequency of automatic thoughts. This can be done by getting the client to engage in mental or physical activity which moves the attention from the negative thoughts to something else.

Challenging automatic thoughts: This strategy aims to change the client's thinking by challenging the validity of the cognitions. Techniques can be behavioural, e.g. setting up an experiment, or cognitive, e.g. looking for the evidence in favour, and against a maladaptive belief.

Challenging underlying assumptions: This strategy challenges the rules that guide the client's maladaptive behaviour. A broad range of cognitive and behavioural techniques are needed to achieve this. For instance, the advantages and disadvantages of an assumption can be explored, reasoning used to challenge the assumption and a behavioural experiment arranged to test it out.

Building skills: Not all problems are caused by inappropriate thoughts. Some of the difficulties the client experiences will be due to real problems, and cognitive therapy then employs problem-solving techniques. This often requires the teaching of specific skills, e.g. through assertiveness training, social skills training and time management.

3   Major cognitive techniques

In this section I will describe some of the cognitive and behavioural techniques that are commonly used in cognitive therapy. There is considerable overlap between all of these methods and the distinctions made here are somewhat arbitrary. In challenging a particular cognition a therapist might employ several cognitive and behavioural techniques.

Identifying negative automatic thoughts: The therapist teaches the client to observe and record negative automatic thoughts. Initially the concept of an automatic thought is explained: it is a thought or image that comes to mind automatically and seems plausible, but on inspection is often distorted or unrealistic. Thoughts the client has during the session can be used to illustrate this, e.g. in the first session a depressed client may be thinking 'I don't know why I've come, there's nothing anyone can do for me.' Written material such as the leaflet *Coping with Depression* (Beck and Greenberg, 1974) is also used to explain the basic features of therapy. The client is then given the homework task of collecting and recording negative automatic thoughts. The exact format of this will depend on the problem. A depressed client will be asked to monitor depressed mood, recording the situation which triggered a worsening of depression, and the thoughts associated with it. Someone with an alcohol problem would monitor cravings for drink, and again record the situations in which they occurred and the thoughts that precipitated them. This phase of identifying thoughts help clients to start making the link:

Event → negative automatic thought → disturbed emotion or behaviour

Identifying thoughts may also be therapeutic in its own right, since just recording negative thoughts sometimes reduces their frequency. Clients should try to record their thoughts as soon after the stressful event as possible, when it is fresh in their mind.

Modifying negative automatic thoughts: When the client has learned to identify the maladaptive thinking the next step is to learn how to challenge the negative thoughts. Through Socratic questioning the therapist shows the client how to change his or her thinking. This cognitive restructuring by the therapist usually brings relief in the session, but it takes longer for the client to practise challenging thoughts outside the therapy session, which becomes a situation where the therapist models the process of cognitive restructuring and gives the client feedback on his or her success at the task. Clients are encouraged to use a form to record and challenge their automatic thoughts (see p. 318) to help them internalize the process of identifying and modifying negative automatic thoughts.

There is a number of methods the therapist can use to help a client modify negative thinking:

Reality testing: This is probably the most common method of cognitive restructuring. The client is taught to question the evidence for the automatic thoughts. For example, you hear that your five-year-old son has hit another child at school. You immediately think 'He's a bully. I'm a useless parent', and feel depressed. What is the evidence that your son is a bully? Has he done this sort of thing before? Is this unusual behaviour for a five-year-old child? Bullying implies an unprovoked attack. Could he have been provoked? What is the evidence that you are a useless parent? Have you been told by anyone in your family that you are doing a bad job? Is a single instance of bad behaviour in a five-year-old child proof that you are a bad parent?

Looking for alternatives: People who are in emotional crisis, especially if they are depressed, find it difficult to examine the options that are open to them. They get into a blinkered view of their situation. Looking for alternatives is a way of helping them out of this mental set. The therapist gently asks for alternative explanations or solutions and continues until as many as possible are generated. At first these will probably all be negative but after a while the client will start to come up with more constructive alternatives.

Reattribution: A more specialized form of the search for alternatives involves reattributing the cause of, or responsibility for, an event. A client who experiences panic attacks may believe that the physical sensations of dizziness and a pounding heart are signs of an impending heart attack. The therapist, through education, questioning and experimentation, helps the client to reattribute the cause of these experiences to the natural bodily sensations of extreme anxiety. For example, the client who attributes her son's behaviour to her failure as a mother can be taught to change the focus of responsibility; many factors contribute to a child's behaviour, and a parent does not have control of all of them.

Decatastrophizing: This has been termed the 'What if' technique (Freeman, 1987). The client is taught to ask what would be the worst thing that could happen. In many cases when the fear is confronted it becomes clear that it is not so terrible after all. For example, you are preparing to visit a friend for the weekend and do not have much time to pack. You think, 'I can't decide what to pack. I mustn't forget anything.' You get into more and more of a panic trying to remember everything in time. Why would it be so awful if you did forget something? Would it be the end of the world if you turned up without a toothbrush?

Advantages and disadvantages: This is a very helpful technique to enable clients to get things into perspective. If a difficult decision has to be made or if it seems difficult to give up a habitual maladaptive behaviour, the client can list the advantages and disadvantages of a certain course of action.

Behavioural techniques

Freeman (1987) considers the behavioural techniques in cognitive therapy to serve two purposes: they work to change behaviour through a broad range of methods; and they serve as short-term interventions in the service of longer-term cognitive change. This second goal differentiates the behavioural tasks used in cognitive therapy from those used in more conventional behaviour therapy. These tasks are set within a cognitive conceptualization of the problem and are used to produce cognitive change. Seen in its simplest form, behavioural work changes cognitions by distracting clients from automatic thoughts; and challenging maladaptive beliefs through experimentation.

Behavioural methods are often used at the beginning of therapy when the client is most distressed and so less able to use cognitive techniques.

Activity scheduling
This is a technique which is particularly useful with depressed clients but can be applied with other problems too. The rationale for scheduling time centres on the

proposition that when they are depressed, clients reduce their level of activity and spend more time ruminating on negative thoughts. The schedule is an hour-by-hour plan of what the client will do. As with all the procedures in cognitive therapy, this needs to be explained in some detail and a clear rationale given. It is often set up as an experiment to see if certain activities will improve mood. The therapist stresses that few people accomplish everything they plan, and the aim is not to get all the items done but to find out if planning and structuring time can be helpful. Initially the aim may just be to monitor tasks together with the thoughts and feelings that accompany them. The emphasis is usually on engaging in specific behaviours during a certain period rather than the amount achieved. For instance, a client would be encouraged to decide to do some decorating between 10 a.m. and 11 a.m. on a certain day, rather than plan to decorate a whole room over a weekend. These tasks are set up as homework assignments and the results discussed at the beginning of the next session.

Mastery and pleasure ratings
This technique can be used in conjunction with activity scheduling. Clients rate how much mastery (feelings of success, achievement or control) or pleasure they get out of a task (on a 0–10 scale). Since depressed clients often avoid engaging in pleasant activities, this method allows the therapist to establish which activities might be enjoyable for clients and to encourage them to engage in them with greater frequency. It also challenges all-or-nothing thinking, by showing that there is a continuum of pleasure and mastery rather than experiences which (1) are totally enjoyable or unenjoyable and (2) yield complete success or failure.

Graded task assignments
All-or-nothing thinking can also be challenged using graded task assignments. Many clients think, 'I have to be able to do everything I set myself, or I have failed.' The therapist begins by setting small homework tasks which gradually build up in complexity and difficulty. The client is encouraged to set goals that can realistically be achieved, so that he or she completes a series of successful assignments.

Behavioural experiments
We have already seen how behavioural experiments are an important component of cognitive therapy. Hypotheses are continually generated and put to the test. This usually involves a negative prediction of some form. For instance, an anxious client may state that he is too anxious even to read. An experiment can be set up in the therapy session where the client reads a short paragraph from a newspaper, thus disproving the absolutism of this statement. The client can then go on to read articles of increasing length over the following week. Experiments are often set as homework. For instance, a depressed client who firmly believes that she is unable to go shopping could be asked to go shopping with her husband. Even if the client is not able to carry out the assignment the experiment is not a failure because it provides valuable information about what might be the blocks to the activity.

Other behavioural techniques

Cognitive therapy employs a variety of other behavioural techniques where appropriate. Cognitive and behavioural rehearsal is frequently used during the session in preparation for a difficult homework assignment. Role-play can be a very effective cognitive change technique. When clients have practical problems that need to be solved, behavioural techniques based on a skills training model are especially useful. This will usually involve forms of assertiveness training or social skills training for people who have deficits in interpersonal skills.

Schema change methods

All the techniques described so far can be applied to help elicit and change underlying beliefs. In addition some techniques may be specifically applied to change deeply held core beliefs or schemas. *The Historical Review of Schemas* involves testing the evidence for and against the belief across the individual's life span. While many clients will find evidence for their belief that they are inadequate or doomed to being abandoned from their recent experience, it is more difficult for them to bias information from early childhood in the same way. *The Continuum Technique* is a method where all-or-nothing thinking is challenged by plotting it on a continuum and the *Positive Data Log* involves collecting daily instances which discount the client's core beliefs. For information on how these techniques are applied the reader is directed to Beck (1995), Padesky (1994) and Persons, Davidson and Tompkins (2001).

Treating patients with personality disorders

There is not room in this chapter to describe the treatment of personality disorders in detail (see Beck et al., 1990; Young, 1990; Linehan, 1993 for useful guidelines). The schema change techniques just mentioned play an important role in working with this client group. Because it can be difficult to establish a therapeutic alliance, and because of the strength with which the dysfunctional beliefs are held, treatment is usually longer than with emotional disorders. Clients often find it difficult to identify automatic thoughts and so much of the work has to be done at the schematic level. Repeated recognition of core beliefs and the behavioural strategies stemming from them is often necessary before change can occur, and sometimes a much more confrontational style is needed to overcome schema avoidance (Young, 1990). This can include the use of emotive techniques to activate schemas. For instance, a schema may be activated by reconstructing a traumatic scene from childhood in role-play. This is often associated with powerful feelings of fear, hurt and anger. Initially the client is unable to think rationally and is overwhelmed by the feelings, but a skilful therapist can help the client get some distance from the affect without getting caught up in it. Cognitive restructuring can then be used to challenge guilt or blame the person feels for the trauma or abuse, and to challenge beliefs that the past must always poison the present. More active techniques like imagery rescripting can help to change the sense of powerlessness which is often part of the memory. The conceptualization is even more important in this work than in standard cognitive therapy. To guide the interventions the therapist needs a clear picture of how core beliefs were developed as a result of childhood experiences, how compensatory beliefs and coping strategies emerged, and how these schemata operate in the clients' present to maintain the maladaptive interpersonal patterns. Sharing this conceptualization with the client can help give meaning to a seemingly chaotic and meaningless present.

The change process in therapy

It is difficult to summarize a typical course of cognitive therapy since strategy and technique depend on the individual client and the problems being treated. There is, however, generally a progression through therapy. At the beginning of therapy the emphasis is on conceptualizing the client's problems, teaching the cognitive model and producing early symptom relief. Techniques aimed at symptom relief in the early stages of therapy tend to be more behavioural. As therapy progresses the client learns to monitor and challenge automatic thoughts and this forms the major focus in therapy. As the client's problems reach some resolution the emphasis shifts to identifying and challenging underlying assumptions, and to work on relapse prevention. There is still debate about which components of cognitive therapy are most important in bringing about change. Is it the learning of new ways of dealing with negative thoughts, or the modification of underlying schemata? The process of change is not always smooth. The client may come with very different expectations of treatment than the therapist. For instance, a client with a hypochondriacal preoccupation will believe that there is a physical cause for his or her problems and will be reluctant to accept the cognitive model. In the early sessions with this type of client the therapist tries to engage the client in the therapy, perhaps examining the evidence for the client's explanation of the symptoms, and getting his or her agreement to try the new approach on an experimental basis. For people who find it difficult to understand the concept of negative automatic thoughts it may take longer to explain and demonstrate their nature. Others are frightened to record such thoughts because they make them feel worse.

This may require that more time be spent in examining possible gains from exposing themselves to short-term distress in order to achieve long-term benefit. With clients who have personality problems, maladaptive patterns of relating to others will be brought into the session and these need to be addressed as part of therapy: for example dependent clients may fail to carry out homework assignments because they hope that the therapist will support and help them without the difficult learning of self-reliance. These patterns often act as blocks to therapy and must be openly discussed with the client.

Limitations of the approach

Many of the limitations of cognitive therapy are the same as those that apply to any form of psychotherapy. People with very severe mental disturbances are not readily treated with talking treatments. This applies particularly to those who suffer from delusions and hallucinations, although experimental cognitive approaches may have something to offer even these clients (Birchwood and Tarrier, 1992; Kingdon and Turkington, 1994). Motivation to change is an important construct that is not always assessable until therapy is under way. The emphasis placed on homework and self-help can be a limitation for some clients. One study of cognitive therapy for depression found that people who endorsed ideas about self-control did well with cognitive therapy, whereas those who did not responded better to drugs (Simons et al., 1986). Subsequent studies have not all supported this finding. As we have seen, the question of acceptance of the theoretical model, and the ability and willingness to carry out self-help assignments, must be taken into account when considering clients for therapy. The more clearly difficulties can be defined as problems the easier it is to do cognitive therapy. With vague characterological flaws which manifest themselves as problems in interpersonal relationships it is sometimes very hard to find a focus. With such clients the form of therapy described here may not be adequate. One major advantage that cognitive therapy has over some forms of therapy is its commitment to the scientific method. It is being applied to a widening field of disorders, and as long as its practitioners continue to evaluate its efficacy the next 10 years should provide answers to the question: what are the areas of application and the limits of this approach?

Case example

The client

Mary was a 42-year-old university senior lecturer who had been troubled by recurrent depression for the last nine years. The first episode of depression had begun with the birth of her second child and she had had three serious episodes since then. Although she had not been hospitalized, she had needed two or three months off work to recover from each episode. Her most recent depression seemed to have been precipitated by a failure to get a job she applied for at another university. Mary had made some response to anti-depressant medication prescribed by her psychiatrist, but she remained depressed. Her score on the Beck Depression Inventory was 27.

Mary described a happy childhood, where she had always felt loved and valued as the only child in the family. However, both her parents were high achievers who were respected academics, and she felt an unspoken expectation that she had to do well 'for everybody's sake'. She said her father was somewhat melancholic, but her mother was full of energy and enthusiasm for life. Her mother's competence and confidence made her feel in her shadow. She was quite a shy child, feeling lonely and awkward at school but did well academically, which seemed to make up for her difficulties in making friends. She studied social sciences at university. She enjoyed university life and felt she came out of herself more, though she still worked hard to achieve a first-class honours degree and stayed on to do a PhD. She had worked as a member of staff in the same department ever since.

She met her husband Phil at university. He now worked as a managing director of a company. She thought of him as a good man, but someone who was emotionally quite distant. Although they had a good relationship, he sometimes found it difficult to understand her depression. They had two daughters aged 9 and 12.

The therapy

The main aims of therapy were to improve Mary's depressive symptoms and to prevent relapse. She identified two main problems:

* Coping with all the demands of work and home
* Putting herself down

The first five sessions focused on activity scheduling and recording and challenging negative automatic thoughts. Mary kept a diary of what she did each day and rated the activities for pleasure and mastery. She had just returned to work part time, so the activity schedule was mainly used to help her get a balance in her daily routine. Her diary showed that she was trying to cram in as much as possible at work and at home. The result was that she would collapse exhausted and have hours at a time where she did nothing constructive. This made her fear that she was in danger of relapsing and also led to self-critical thoughts about failing to perform in any of her roles.

She agreed to approach her work in a graded way. There were not, in fact, any strong expectations from her department that she take on as much as she expected herself to do. She had a limited number of tutorials and lectures, but no one was expecting her to come to all the committees she usually sat on. Taking a more balanced approach to her timetable, rather than expecting herself to do everything as well as she used to, allowed her to take some of the pressure off herself. Her mood and her performance both improved accordingly. She challenged her negative thoughts about not doing everything as well as before by reminding herself that she had been very depressed and that this return to work was a period of rehabilitation. In fact, her GP had not expected her to go back so soon.

Another set of negative thoughts reflected her fear that the improvement in her mood would not persist. Making her timetable more manageable reduced the episodes of physical and mental collapse so she began to experiment with the possibility of allowing herself to feel good and optimistic that she might be on the road to recovery. Table 12.3 gives an example of a Thought Record which Mary used to capture and challenge her negative thoughts about the depression still being close to dragging her down again.

Sessions 5 to 10 continued the cognitive and behavioural work to counter depressive symptoms. Mary used the thought record to deal with her self-

Table 12.3 Dysfunctional thought record

Situation	Automatic thoughts	Emotion(s)	Adaptive response	Outcome
Feeling awful. Not able to do half the things I had planned today.	I can't cope. If I go on like this I'm going to get depressed again. The depression is still just below the surface. I'm not really any better.	Tired. Depressed. Hopeless. Dejected. (80%)	This is still early days, but I've made a lot of progress. My depression score is down. I'm sleeping better. I've managed two weeks at work.	Depressed (30%) Belief in automatic thought (25%) Belief in adaptive response (65%)
	Hot thought: **The depression is still just below the surface. I'm not really any better. (90%)**		My therapist says I may be pushing myself too hard. If I'm trying too hard, perhaps I'm exhausting myself so it might be this that's making me feel bad, not the depression.	**Action plan:** **Try to push myself less and see if the tiredness lessens.**

Questions to help compose an alternative response: (1) What is the evidence that the automatic thought is true? Not true? (2) Is there an alternative explanation? (3) What's the worst that could happen? Could I live through it? What's the best that could happen? What's the most realistic outcome? (4) What's the effect of my believing the automatic thought? What could be the effect of changing my thinking? (5) What should I do about it? (6) If [friend's name] was in the situation and had this thought, what would I tell him/her?

Source: Adapted from Beck, (1995)

criticism. She was functioning better at work and had by session 7 returned to work full time, but she now berated herself for not keeping the house tidy enough. She would alternate between getting angry with herself for failing as a housewife and getting angry with her husband for not helping enough. She discussed this with her husband, who was prepared to do more around the house but had not really known what Mary wanted from him, since when she was not depressed she insisted on doing everything herself because she felt it was quicker and more efficient. She gradually accepted that it was all right for her to give herself some time each day just for herself, rather than fill her evening with nothing but chores. As a behavioural experiment she scheduled some time each evening for things for herself – reading a novel, taking a relaxing bath, or just going to bed early. To her surprise she found that this made her feel less tired and allowed her to do her chores more effectively.

The theme of perfectionism had become very clear over the course of therapy. Mary believed that if she did not 'get it right' she was hopeless, so she felt she should always do everything right all the time. Mary had learned enough about how thinking could be distorted to recognize that her assumptions were too generalized, too 'all or nothing' and too extreme. These rules had been applied without ever being questioned.

Table 12.4   Cost–benefit analysis of perfectionism

Benefits	Costs
I produce good results	Takes lots of time and effort
I avoid criticism	I expect too much of other people and feel intolerant
	I feel tense and anxious in case what I did wasn't good enough
	Makes me critical and self-critical
	It reduces my enjoyment of things

When they were written in black and white – 'If I don't get it right, I'm hopeless', 'I must always do everything right all the time' – she saw them as ridiculous.

Mary talked about how as a child she had seen both her parents working hard and had concluded that success was very important. She got praise and attention when she did well at school, and just assumed that this was the way things ought to be. Her mother was quite obsessional about neatness and tidiness and could be critical if Mary made even small mistakes. Mary felt somewhat in awe of her mother and this may have led Mary to fear that her own success was quite fragile and she was something of a fraud. The therapist built on these insights by asking Mary to list the benefits and costs of her perfectionistic belief (Table 12.4).

She then read the chapter 'Dare to be average' in the self-help book *Feeling Good: The New Mood Therapy* (Burns, 1980) and found this extremely helpful. Mary was able to see how much of what had already worked for her in therapy had involved lowering the unrelentingly high standards she applied to herself. She was now starting to see that she applied the same standards to others too. Her irritation with her husband for not helping with the housework had been based on the expectation that he should know that she needed help even though she never asked for it, and that he should have the same high standards for tidiness that she did. Mary created an alternative, positive belief to replace the old one. The new rule stated that a compassionate attitude to herself and others would allow her to live life well.

Sessions 11 to 16 saw Mary working hard at living with her new rule. She deliberately tried to do things less than perfectly, while she also tried to apply the new rule in various situations, focusing on being kind to herself and others instead of expecting the impossible. Her mood was now considerably improved. The last sessions were aimed at relapse prevention. Mary identified the situations which might make her prone to depression in the future and prepared a relapse prevention plan (Table 12.5). By the end of therapy her BDI score had reduced to 7. She maintained her gains at three-month and six-month follow-up, but felt that although she was much better able to care for herself and had less harsh expectations of other people, she still found herself taking on more than was good for her. She recognized this as something that might make her vulnerable to relapse but felt able to work on this herself outside therapy.

Table 12.5   Mary's relapse prevention plan

What I have learned from therapy:
I don't have to be perfect!
If I am compassionate to myself and others, I can get the important things done and still have fun along the way.

Techniques which have been most helpful:
1   Thought records
2   Activity schedules – balancing overactivity and underactivity
3   Being a compassionate friend to myself
4   Positive Data Logs
5   Reading:
     Feeling Good: the New Mood Therapy

What I have to look out for:
1   Taking on too much and not allowing time for myself!
2   Expecting too much of myself.
3   Expecting too much of Phil, and not telling him what I am thinking (don't expect him to mind-read).
4   Life events that might make me feel a failure because I haven't been a total success.
5   All-or-nothing thinking.

Relapse prevention:
1   Have a therapy session with myself once a month. Give myself an hour to review how I'm doing.
2   If I start feeling low, don't catastrophize.
3   When I'm feeling low, tell Phil.
4   If my low mood persists for more than a week, see my GP. Don't try to cope by taking on more to prove I'm OK.

Finding a Therapist

Cognitive Therapy is available on the National Health Service, but waiting lists are often long. Most therapy is carried out by clinical psychologists, or nurse therapists. Your General Practitioner should know what is available locally and be able to make a referral to the appropriate service. Private therapy is not as much part of the culture of cognitive therapy as it is for other therapies. The organization to which most CBT therapists (working privately and in the NHS) belong in Britain is the British Association for Behavioural and Cognitive Psychotherapies. A Directory of Members is posted on their website (www. babcp.com).

Training as a Cognitive Therapist

Most cognitive therapists have a basic training as a mental health professional (Clinical Psychology, Nursing, Psychiatry or Counselling) and for this reason most of the courses are postgraduate courses which assume this professional background. A small number of courses will take trainees who do not have a previous mental health training. A list of courses can be found at the BABCP website (www.babcp.com).

References

Agras, W.S., Crow, S.J., Halmi, K.A., Mitchell, J.E., Wilson, G.T. and Kraemer, H.C. (2000) 'Outcome predictors for the cognitive behavior treatment of bulimia nervosa: data from a multisite study', *American Journal of Psychiatry*, 157: 1302–8.

Alloy, L.B. and Ahrens, A.H. (1987) 'Depression and pessimism for the future: biased use of statistically relevant information in predictions for self versus others', *Journal of Personality and Social Psychology*, 53: 366–78.

Bandura, A. (1977) *Social Learning Theory*. Englewood Cliffs, NJ: Prentice-Hall.

Beck, A.T. (1963) 'Thinking and depression: 1. Idiosyncratic content and cognitive distortions', *Archives of General Psychiatry*, 9: 324–33.

Beck, A.T. (1964) 'Thinking and depression: 2. Theory and therapy', *Archives of General Psychiatry*, 10: 561–71.

Beck, A.T. (1976) *Cognitive Therapy and the Emotional Disorders*. New York. International Universities Press.

Beck, A.T. (1987) 'Cognitive models of depression', *Journal of Cognitive Psychotherapy: An International Quarterly*, 1: 5–39.

Beck, A.T. and Emery, G. with Greenberg, R.L. (1985) *Anxiety Disorders and Phobias: A Cognitive Perspective*. New York: Basic Books.

Beck, A.T. and Greenberg, R.L. (1974) *Coping with Depression*. New York: Institute for Rational Living.

Beck, A.T., Rush, J.L., Shaw, B.E. and Emery, G. (1979) *The Cognitive Therapy of Depression*. New York: Guilford Press.

Beck, A.T., Freeman, A. and Associates (1990) *Cognitive Therapy of Personality Disorders*. New York: Guilford Press.

Beck, J.S. (1995) *Cognitive Therapy. Basics and Beyond*. New York: Guilford Press.

Birchwood, M. and Tarrier, N. (1992) *Innovations in the Psychological Management of Schizophrenia*. Chichester: John Wiley.

Blackburn, I.M., Bishop, S., Glen, A.I.M., Whalley, L.J. and Christie, L.E. (1981) 'The efficacy of cognitive therapy in depression: a treatment trial using cognitive therapy and pharmacotherapy, each alone and in combination', *British Journal of Psychiatry*, 139: 181–9.

Bradley, G.W. (1978) 'Self-serving biases in the attribution process: a re-examination of the fact or fiction question', *Journal of Personality and Social Psychology*, 36: 56–71.

Burns, D.D. (1980) *Feeling Good: The New Mood Therapy*. New York: William Morrow.

Cautela, L.R. (1973) 'Covert processes and behaviour modification', *Journal of Nervous and Mental Diseases*, 157: 27–36.

Chadwick, P.D.J. and Lowe, C.F. (1991) 'Measurement and modification of delusional beliefs', *Journal of Consulting and Clinical Psychology*, 58: 225–32.

Clark, D.A. and Steer, R.A. (1996) 'Empirical status of the cognitive model of anxiety and depression', in P.M. Salkovskis (ed.), *Frontiers of Cognitive Therapy*. New York: Guilford Press.

Clark, D.M. (1986) 'A cognitive approach to panic', *Behaviour Research and Therapy*, 24: 461–70.

Clark, D.M. (1996) 'Panic disorder: from theory to therapy', in P.M. Salkovskis (ed.), *Frontiers of Cognitive Therapy*. New York: Guilford Press.

Clark, D.M. and Fairburn, C.G. (1997) *Science and Practice of Cognitive Behaviour Therapy*. Oxford: Oxford University Press.

Clark, D.M. and Wells, A. (1995) 'A cognitive model of social phobia', in R. Heimberg, M. Liebowitz, D.A. Hope and F.R. Schneier (eds), *Social Phobia: Diagnosis, Assessment and Treatment*. New York: Guilford Press.

Ehlers, A. and Clark, D.M. (2000) 'A cognitive model of posttraumatic stress disorder', *Behaviour Research & Therapy*, 38: 319–45.

Ellis, A. (1962) *Reason and Emotion in Psychotherapy*. Secaucus, NJ: Lyle Stuart.

Fennell, M.J.V. and Teasdale, L.D. (1987) 'Cognitive therapy for depression: individual differences and the process of change', *Cognitive Therapy and Research*, 11: 253–71.

Fowler, D., Garety, P. and Kuipers, E. (1995) *Cognitive Behaviour Therapy for Psychosis: Theory and Practice*. Chichester: Wiley.

Freeman, A. (1983) 'Cognitive therapy: an overview', in A. Freeman (ed.), *Cognitive Therapy with Couples and Groups*. New York: Plenum Press.

Freeman, A. (1987) 'Cognitive therapy: an overview', in A. Freeman and V. Greenwood (eds), *Cognitive Therapy: Application in Psychiatric and Medical Settings*. New York: Human Sciences Press.

Gould, R.A., Otto, M.W. and Pollack, M.H. (1995) 'A meta-analysis of treatment outcome for panic disorder', *Clinical Psychology Review*, 15, 819–44.

Guidano, V.F. and Liotti, G. (1983) *Cognitive Processes and Emotional Disorders. A Structural Approach to Psychotherapy*. New York: Guilford.

Hooley, L.M., Orley, L. and Teasdale, J.D. (1986) 'Levels of expressed emotion and relapse in depressed patients', *British Journal of Psychiatry*, 148: 642–7.

Kanfer, F.H. and Karoly, P. (1972) 'Self-control: a behaviouristic excursion into the lion's den', *Behaviour Therapy*, 3: 378–416.

Kelly, G. (1955) *The Psychology of Personal Constructs*, Vols I and II. New York: Norton.

Kingdon, D.G. and Turkington, D. (1994) *Cognitive Behaviour Therapy of Schizophrenia?* Lawrence Erlbaum Associates.

Kovacs, M. and Beck, A.T. (1978) 'Maladaptive cognitive structures in depressions', *American Journal of Psychiatry*, 135: 525–7.

Linehan, M.M. (1993) *Cognitive-behavioural Treatment of Borderline Personality Disorder*. London: Guilford Press.

Mahoney, M.J. (ed.) (1995) *Cognitive and Constructive Psychotherapies*. New York: Springer.

Mahoney, M.J. and Arnkoff, D.B. (1978) 'Cognitive and self-control therapies', in S.L. Garfield and A.E. Bergin (eds), *Handbook of Psychotherapy and Behaviour Change*, 2nd edn. New York: Wiley.

McGinn, L.K. and Young, J.E. (1996) 'Schema-focused therapy', in P. Salkovskis (ed.), *Frontiers of Cognitive Therapy*. New York: Guilford Press. pp. 182–207.

Meichenbaum, D. (1985) *Stress Inoculation Training*. New York: Pergamon Press.

Moorey, S., Holting, C., Hughes, P., Knynenberg, P. and Michael, A. (2001) 'Does problem solving ability predict outcome in a clinical setting?', *Behavioural and Cognitive Psychotherapy*, 29: 485–95.

Padesky, C.A. (1994) 'Schema change processes in cognitive therapy', *Clinical Psychology and Psychotherapy*, 1: 267–78.

Persons, J.B., Davidson, J. and Tompkins, M.A. (2001) *Essential Components of Cognitive-Behavior Therapy for Depression*. Washington, DC: American Psychological Association.

Rachman, S.J. and deSilva, P. (1978) 'Abnormal and normal obsessions', *Behaviour Research and Therapy*, 16, 233–8.

Rosenthal, T.L. and Bandura, A. (1978) 'Psychological modelling: theory and practice', in S.L. Garfield and A.E. Bergin (eds), *Handbook of Psychotherapy and Behaviour Change*, 2nd edn. New York: Wiley.

Rush, A.J. and Watkins, L.T. (1981) 'Group versus individual cognitive therapy: a pilot study', *Cognitive Therapy and Research*, 5: 95–103.

Rush, A.J., Beck, A.T., Kovacs, M. and Hollon, S. (1977) 'Comparative efficacy of cognitive therapy and imipramine in the treatment of depressed outpatients', *Cognitive Therapy and Research*, 1: 17–37.

Safran, J.D., Segal, Z.V., Vallis, T.M., Shaw, B.F. et al. (1993) 'Assessing patient suitability for short-term cognitive therapy with an interpersonal focus', *Cognitive Therapy & Research*, 17: 23–38.

Salkovskis, P.M. (1985) 'Obsessive-compulsive problems: a cognitive-behavioural analysis', *Behaviour Research and Therapy*, 23: 571–83.

Salkovskis, P.M. (ed.) (1996) *Frontiers of Cognitive Therapy*. New York: Guilford Press.

Salkovskis, P.M. and Harrison, J. (1984) 'Abnormal and normal obsessions: a replication', *Behaviour Research and Therapy*, 22: 549–52.

Salkovskis, P.M. and Warwick, N.M.C. (1986) 'Morbid preoccupations, health anxiety and reassurance: a cognitive-behavioural approach to hypochondriasis', *Behaviour Research and Therapy*, 24: 597–602.

Scott, M.J. and Stradling, S.C. (1990) 'Group cognitive therapy for depression produces clinically significant reliable change in community-based settings', *Behavioural Psychotherapy*, 18: 1–19.

Shaw, B.F. (1984) 'Specification of the training and evaluation of cognitive therapists for outcome studies', in L. Williams and R.L. Spitzer (eds), *Psychotherapy Research: Where Are We and Where Should We Go?* New York: Guilford Press.

Simons, A.D., Murphy, G.E., Levine, L.L. and Wetzel, R.D. (1986) 'Cognitive therapy and pharmacotherapy for depression', *Archives of General Psychiatry*, 43: 43–8.

Taylor, S.E. and Brown, I.D. (1988) 'Illusion and well-being: a social psychological perspective on mental health', *Psychological Bulletin*, 103: 193–210.

Teasdale, L.D., Fennell, M.J.V., Hibbert, G.A. and Amies, P.L. (1984) 'Cognitive therapy for major depressive disorder in primary care', *British Journal of Psychiatry*, 144: 400–6.

Vallis, T.M., Howes, J.L. and Standage, K. (2000) 'Is cognitive therapy suitable for treating individuals with personality dysfunction?', *Cognitive Therapy & Research*, 24: 595–606.

Wells, A. (1997) *Cognitive Therapy of Anxiety Disorders*. New York: Wiley.

Young, L.E. (1990) *Cognitive Therapy for Personality Disorders. A Schema-focused Approach*. Sarasota: Professional Resource Exchange.

Young, L.E. and Klosko, L.S. (1994) *Reinventing Your Life*. New York: Plume Books.

Zettle, R.D., Haflich, J.L. and Reynolds, R.A. (1992) 'Responsivity to cognitive therapy as a function of treatment format and client personality dimensions', *Journal of Consulting and Clinical Psychology*, 48: 787–97.

Suggested further reading

Beck, A.T. (1976) *Cognitive Therapy and the Emotional Disorders*. New York: International Universities Press.

Beck, J.S. (1995) *Cognitive Therapy. Basics and Beyond*. New York: Guilford Press.

Clark, D.M. and Fairburn, C.G. (1997) *Science and Practice of Cognitive Behaviour Therapy*. Oxford: Oxford University Press.

Hawton, K., Salkovskis, P.M., Kirk, L. and Clarke, D.M. (eds) (1989) *Cognitive Behaviour Therapy for Psychiatric Problems*. Oxford: Oxford Medical Publications.

Young, L.E. and Klosko, L.S. (1994) *Reinventing Your Life*. New York: Plume Books.

13 Behaviour Therapy
David Richards

Historical context and developments in Britain

Historical context

The traditional view of behaviour therapy is that it is the practical and clinical manifestation of laboratory-based research work, which itself developed from theories of human behaviour dating from the early part of the 20th century. Central to these theories is 'learning theory', the science of understanding how living beings learn. In particular, classical and operant conditioning models were developed and tested, which went some way to explaining human behaviour.

During the latter part of the century, however, behaviour therapy as a term came to be used more loosely to describe a range of techniques that often relied less on learning theory and more on data from empirical research trials which have demonstrated clinical efficacy. What was more important to many practitioners was that, in contrast to other psychotherapies developed solely from *theoretical* models that stressed past developmental conflicts as the source of psychological distress, a new range of *evidence-based* therapeutic techniques was becoming available. Such techniques attracted the name 'behavioural psychotherapy', the preferred term to describe the clinical techniques described in the rest of this chapter. Behavioural psychotherapy has thus developed via a potent mix of evidence from both basic science and clinical trials. It cannot be stressed too much at the beginning of this chapter that, for many clinicians, the theories of learning most often associated with behavioural psychotherapy matter far less than evidence-based technical eclecticism – i.e. what works for patients.

There have been many historical references to techniques that we would now refer to as behavioural. There is an oft-quoted 17th-century reference whereby the principles of graded exposure were outlined for those who had a fearful child:

> if your child shrieks and runs away at the sight of a frog, let another catch it and lay it down at a good distance from him; at first accustom him to look upon it; when he can do that to come nearer to it and see it leap without emotion; then to touch it lightly, when it is held fast in another's hand; and so on until he can come to handle it as confidently as a butterfly or sparrow. (Locke, 1693)

Buddhist writings, reviewed in detail by Padmal de Silva (1984) refer much to behavioural approaches, particularly relaxation, imaginal and real life exposure. Even Freud noted the efficacy of behavioural approaches when he wrote:

> One can hardly master a phobia if one waits until the patient lets the analysis influence him to give it up. . . .One succeeds only when one can induce them by the

influence of the analysis to go and to struggle with the anxiety while they make the attempts. (Freud, 1919)

At this point it is usual to describe the development of those two planks of behavioural thinking – classical and operant conditioning. Unfortunately, the term 'conditioning' is actually a mistranslation from Russian (since Pavlov and others were working in relative isolation from the West it took some time before their ideas were passed on) and it also implies something that one imposes on another. 'Learning' is a better term. Another problem with traditional explanations is that they appear highly mechanistic (as indeed they are) and have produced much disapproval from those that value a sense of choice and self-determination in human behaviour. Although classical and operant learning, as described below, are distinct processes they are laboratory derived and even here require a huge amount of ingenuity to produce a situation where only one is operating at a time. In real life, a complex mixture of reinforcements is acting on an organism and any attempt to explain emotional responding using only one process will be unsatisfactory. Although these terms will be elaborated below, it is important to recognize that their description does not imply adherence to principles of Social Darwinism. Classical and operant learning take place in a sophisticated and complex manner in the real world.

Learning theory got off to a systematic start with the work of Pavlov (1927) on classical learning and others such as Thorndike (1911), Jones (1924) and Skinner (1953) for operant learning. It was shown that reliable and reproducible effects could be demonstrated from the pairing of unconditioned stimuli (i.e. environmental cues which produce an innate physiological or behavioural response in all cases; for example, the blink of an eye in response to a puff of air or salivation in response to food) with previously innocuous cues (for example, a coloured light or a bell). After a number of pairings, living beings come to associate the new, previously innocuous cue with the effects of the unconditioned stimuli and, if presented with the new cue on its own, behave as if it were the unconditioned stimuli. Thus, a coloured light might invoke an involuntary blink, whilst a bell might induce salivation. Such reactions are termed conditioned responses, the new cues are known as conditioned stimuli and the process by which conditioned responses are acquired is called classical learning.

The second plank – operant learning – is basically the assertion that the probability of a behaviour being repeated is determined by its consequences. If the consequences are beneficial the behaviour is more likely to be repeated. If they are harmful the behaviour will be reduced. Consequences which are beneficial are called reinforcers, come in two types (positive and negative reinforcement) and always increase the probability of a behaviour occurring. A positive reinforcement is something that increases the behaviour because it is a pleasant experience, for example a child receiving a chocolate as praise for clearing their toys away. Negative reinforcement also increases behaviour, although in this case it is by the removal of something aversive. For example, if a person feels highly anxious in the presence of a dog and by running away feels a reduction in their anxiety, they will be more likely to repeat the exercise next time they see a dog. Two other types of consequence will reduce rather than increase the probability of behaviours occurring. Behaviours which are punished – associated with aversive events – will reduce, as will behaviours in situations where an expected reward is omitted, a situation called frustrative non-reward.

Few behavioural psychotherapists in current practice spend much of their day reflecting on such definitions. This can be clearly illustrated by the fate of the first theoretically driven behavioural treatment – systematic desensitization. Developed by Wolpe, systematic desensitization was based on classical learning principles. By pairing a pleasant stimulus with a conditioned aversive one, Wolpe was able to demonstrate a change in fear and arousal levels in the face of the aversive stimulus, which gradually lost its power to disturb. Of clear utility for treating phobias, relaxation was used by Wolpe as the inhibitory stimulus; he called his procedure 'psychotherapy by reciprocal inhibition' (Wolpe, 1958). Although it was effective for up to 80 per cent of people with phobias, Wolpe required patients to develop a highly complex hierarchy, work up it very gradually, keeping levels of anxiety always at an absolute minimum, and conducted the treatment using visual imagery techniques. The next decade saw empirical trials which demonstrated that none of these elements was required. Complex imaginal hierarchies and competing relaxation techniques were all proved to be redundant as the singularly most effective psychotherapeutic technique of modern times was developed: graded exposure *in vivo*. Therefore, whereas Wolpe (1976) favoured a strong theory base others (e.g. Marks, 1982a) argued for empirical pragmatism.

This work was accompanied by a general dissatisfaction with traditional psychoanalytical techniques. Eysenck (1952, 1985) was instrumental in drawing attention to the many flaws and irrelevancies in such work. Key was the discovery that improvements attributed to psychoanalysis could be easily explained by spontaneous remission rates. At this time a massive research effort began to take shape in order to develop effective psychotherapy for all. In amongst this effort arose one element of laboratory theory which many therapists regard as crucial to their understanding of emotion: Lang's three systems theory of emotion (Lang, 1979). In this theory, emotional responses can be conveniently defined as physiological (autonomic responses), behavioural (responses controlled by the individual) and cognitive (internal events such as thoughts and images). The three systems are linked together but often change at different rates during therapy. This analysis of emotion has had an enormous influence on the way behavioural psychotherapists organize their assessment and treatment techniques.

The development of cognitive therapy has added to the early work on behavioural psychotherapy. With the understanding of emotion that came from Lang's 'three systems' model, behavioural psychotherapy and cognitive therapy came together as 'cognitive behavioural therapy' (CBT). Behavioural psychotherapy, CBT and cognitive therapy now lie on both a theoretical and a practical continuum, where the two schools of thought borrow from each other's theoretical, empirical and clinical knowledge bases. Behavioural and cognitive therapists generally adopt a position somewhere along this continuum, which they then use to describe their theoretical rationale and clinical practice. However, there tends to be more debate and difference around theory than one can observe reflected in clinical practice. Furthermore, the empirical evidence base does not support the primacy of behavioural, cognitive or cognitive-behavioural techniques. Studies, reviewed by Lovell and Richards (2000), repeatedly demonstrate that behavioural, cognitive or mixed approaches achieve the same level of satisfactory outcomes for equivalent numbers of patients. More complex, multi-strand combined cognitive and behavioural approaches do not appear to deliver improved outcomes for the majority of clients.

Development in Britain

Britain developed a unique approach to behavioural psychotherapy which can be traced to its publicly funded system of 'socialized medicine', the National Health Service (NHS). One of the characteristics of behavioural psychotherapy in Britain is its multiprofessional practitioner base, a situation rare elsewhere. Psychologists, doctors and nurses are all major professional groups practising behavioural psychotherapy and increasingly it is becoming possible for other health workers such as counsellors to become trained as behavioural or cognitive-behavioural therapists. This healthy multiprofessionalism is due to three reasons.

First, the presence of a group of doctors and psychologists working at the Institute of Psychiatry, Maudsley Hospital, London during the 1960s and 1970s led to a huge surge in collaborative research work. It was during this time that some of the empirical foundations were laid for key techniques such as exposure and response prevention.

Secondly, part of the reason for the vibrant mix of therapists can be ascribed to the establishment in 1972 of the British Association for Behavioural Psychotherapy (BABP), now the British Association for Behavioural and Cognitive Psychotherapy (BABCP). Set up as an interest group, based around the Maudsley group and a few other British collaborators, the BABCP reflected the pioneering spirit of the times and did not restrict its membership to specific professions. Because the BABCP was not a professional body and did not embark on its practitioner registration scheme until much more recently, it was open to anyone with an interest in behavioural psychotherapy. As such, as well as psychiatrists and psychologists, nurses, social workers, teachers, general practitioners and many more joined.

The third reason for the vibrant mix of professions was the pioneering work of the psychiatrist Isaac Marks, a renowned empirical scientist and part of the Maudsley group. In the mid-1970s Marks was so concerned to spread the availability of the newly developed behavioural psychotherapy, that he conducted a government-funded trial of nurse-delivered behavioural psychotherapy. This first trial of specialist nurse practitioners in mental health proved that they could deliver behavioural psychotherapy as effectively as medical practitioners and others and was so successful that it led to the development of an 18-month post-registration course in behavioural psychotherapy. This course has trained over 250 nurse behavioural psychotherapists who themselves have gone on to disseminate behavioural psychotherapy via local innovative training programmes.

From this secure professional and empirical evidence base, nurses in the UK are now firmly accepted as part of the multiprofessional body of workers who can deliver and develop behavioural psychotherapy. In Britain, unlike some other countries, there have been no sterile debates about who 'owns' behavioural psychotherapy. Behavioural psychotherapy is now owned quite properly by those who have the skills to deliver it effectively.

Theoretical assumptions

Image of the person

Behaviourists view a person as a physiological being who under the influence of the environment and genetic predispositions will behave in a particular manner. Behaviourists reject the mind–body dualism prevalent in Western thought and regard concepts such as mind and ego as unscientific and unhelpful since they are explanatory fictions. Because one cannot observe such concepts directly – only infer them by observing behaviour – they do not help explain the human condition. Such non-explanations are termed examples of mentalism. Rejection of mentalism does not exclude consideration of thinking and sensory experiences since these phenomena can be seen as private behaviours (i.e. experienced by one person only) which share all the properties of public behaviours (i.e. experienced by many people). Behaviourists strongly believe that any natural event arises only from other natural events, not from mysterious notions of personality or ego, for example. These are merely explanatory constructions which ultimately impede scientific enquiry. If we are tempted to describe a person as having a depressive personality it is because we are observing certain depressed behaviours such as withdrawal, sleeplessness or tearfulness. We are not able to observe the personality directly.

Behaviourists view a person's past history as extremely important because of the wealth of learning or conditioning events within it. Analogous to evolutionary explanations of species behaviour, an individual's past experiences will have an effect on their current behaviour, even if that experience is some considerable time in the past. In some ways, the concept of natural selection for a species is an identical idea to the learning history of an individual, as both provide explanations for behaviours in the present. They are also similar in that both ideas are more appropriate explanations than a retreat into beliefs about enigmatic internal or external forces directing either behaviour or evolution.

Conceptualization of psychological disturbance and health

Psychological disturbance is considered to be expressed as behaviours which cause the individual problems in their interactions with the environment. Societal norms allow individuals to operate within an envelope of acceptable behaviours.

A 'healthy' individual is one who is able to interact with others and the environment in such a way as to derive high rates of positive reinforcement. Mastery and control are usually cited as positive elements of an individual's relationship with the environment. However, all individuals are genetically 'set' at a specific autonomic level – one only has to parent two or more children to appreciate this particular truth. As a consequence the impact of social and other environmental stimuli on two children will vary enormously. As a result, words such as stoicism and nervousness are used to describe individuals at different ends of a genetically determined arousal spectrum. The complex interplay of genetic predispositions and environmental stimuli produces our own uniqueness.

A range of thinkers have coined terms to describe the results of this interplay. Particularly dominant have been the theories of self-efficacy (Bandura, 1977) and learned helplessness (Seligman, 1975). These related ideas concern the ability of an individual to cope with whatever the world throws at them. Coping is often divided into practical, emotional and avoidant categories. Individuals use these strategies to different degrees depending on the situations they face and on their individual abilities and range of personal skills. Women are traditionally seen as more competent in emotional coping – listening, empathizing, etc. – whereas men use more practical coping strategies – doing things to alter the situation – although there is, of course, huge individual variation. Avoidant coping is generally seen as maladaptive given that it may lead to a perpetuation of unhelpful learned helplessness. However, where environmental stimuli are potentially overwhelming, avoidant coping may be extremely effective, at least in the short term.

Acquisition of psychological disturbance

The earlier observations on classical and operant learning are pertinent here. It has been reliably demonstrated that fears can be learned through a process of pairing real aversive stimuli with initially innocuous stimuli and that these stimuli, once established, are extremely difficult to eradicate. A famous example of this is the well-known experience of the poor unfortunate 'Little Albert' who at the tender age of 11 months was conditioned to be afraid of white rats by their pairing with a loud noise (Watson and Rayner, 1920). This effect even extended to other similarly looking stimuli such as the scientist's white hair. However, this simple phenomenon does not explain why humans are apparently more prone to some types of fear than others. Although not unheard of, it is extremely rare for someone to complain of fearing tweed trousers (rather than appropriately merely abhorring them) whereas fears of spiders, snakes, heights and the sight of blood are extremely common. This selectivity in fear acquisition is a central pillar of the argument for genetic evolutionary preparedness in the acquisition of psychological disturbance. However, the term 'innateness' is now used since preparedness assumes that the predisposition must be paired with an aversive experience for it to become activated. For example, preparedness does not explain why in many countries large numbers of people are afraid of snakes despite the fact that the chances of coming across one are infinitesimally small and it is unlikely that anybody will have experienced a conditioning event involving snakes.

The types of innate feared stimuli are many. Isaac Marks (1987) sums this up by reference to the evolutionary merit in the selection of individuals whose make-up is innately programmed to avoid certain stimuli which herald objective danger. Fear is generally brought on by 'stimuli which are abrupt, intense, irregular, and rapidly increasing' (Marks, 1987: 52). Heights, too much or too little space around us, newness, loudness, being looked at, the sight of one of our fellows being injured – all provoke fear even where we have no previous direct experience of an aversive consequence associated with the specific stimulus.

Clearly, not all psychological disorders can be explained by this innateness. Social experience also has a role to play. As discussed earlier, variation across individuals is enormous. There is also variation across gender. For example, the prevalence of agoraphobia is between a 1:2 and 1:3 male to female ratio. Many explanations have been advanced, including the greater ability of women in Western cultures to express their fears or the feminist view that women are sex-stereotyped in a patriarchal society into promoting the display of fear. Potentially, men are enabled to overcome their innate fears by social pressures to go forth into the world and prosper – a process not unlike the clinical procedure of graded exposure *in vivo*.

The impact of environmental experience is most clearly seen in traumatically induced disorders such as post-traumatic stress disorder (PTSD). Commonly, people with PTSD describe no previous experience of pathological psychological disturbance. As a consequence of an encounter with some incident such as an accident or an assault, a severe anxiety disorder can result which the individual experiences as a series of severe autonomic, behavioural and cognitive symptoms. Here, the inducting stimuli may not be of the innate variety and the fearful reaction of people with PTSD to ordinarily innocuous stimuli is a particular feature. This leads us on to the next section – the perpetuation of psychological disturbance.

Perpetuation of psychological disturbance

Most people would be extremely sympathetic towards someone who had just experienced an assault or an accident which involved a real or potential threat to life, even if they had merely witnessed such an event. We would expect them to be in a state of 'shock' – experiencing a range of autonomic symptoms and possessed of a strong desire to talk repeatedly about their experience. However, despite our initial sympathy we would also expect them to recover. Indeed, given time, this is what happens to most of us who are unfortunate to endure a traumatic event. For some, however, recovery does not occur. The mechanisms behind this maintenance of fearful reactions is central to behavioural understandings of both psychological disturbance and, more importantly, their treatment.

In order to advance some understanding of the concept of fear maintenance it is necessary to return to the principles of operant learning. Mowrer (1950) described the deficiencies of psychopathological models based on classical learning alone and integrated them with operant paradigms. Essentially, if a fearful organism engages in behaviours which reduce their anxiety, such as escape or avoidance, the resultant negative reinforcement strengthens the probability of the escape and avoidance still further. This 'two process' theory has been extremely influential. Much behavioural psychotherapy is directed towards assisting clients to modify the operant reinforcers or 'maintenance factors' for their problematic behaviours. This approach has yielded much greater therapeutic fruit than the unproductive attempts at uncovering and modifying postulated early experiences engaged in by many other schools of psychotherapy. Breaking the cycle of fear and avoidance is a central goal of much behavioural psychotherapy.

One important concept in fear maintenance is the failure of a person's fear to 'habituate' in the face of noxious stimuli. Ordinarily, if a person is repeatedly presented with a feared stimulus, provided it is not contiguous with real pain or permanent discomfort, the arousal experienced in the face of this stimulus reduces over time. The person becomes more confident and can face the previously feared situation. This most often happens when faced with novel situations. Initially timid, the person eventually habituates and grows more confident. Someone with agoraphobia, however, has not experienced this natural arousal reduction and continues to be distressed and consequently avoidant in the face of crowds, enclosed spaces, etc.

Explanations involving the psycho-biological processes involved are necessary to shed light on the above phenomenon. When faced with a stimulus which is innately fear inducing, all organisms, from the highest to the lowest, find that their ordinary behaviours are inhibited, selective attention is paid to the new stimulus and they become highly aroused. This 'behavioural inhibition' allows organisms to appraise the potential threat and prepare for subsequent action – fight or flight – without distraction from other competing stimuli. If the organism decides to run, it gives itself no opportunity to ascertain the true threat involved. This is essentially what happens with the maintenance of fear. The person with agoraphobia does not stay with the anxiety-provoking stimulus for a sufficiently long time or frequently enough to lead to this behavioural inhibition system becoming habituated. The phenomenon of habituation can be observed in ordinary life many times, for example in the case of someone living with a loudly ticking clock. Over time they will cease to notice it, although an occasional visitor will find the noise intrusive, at least for a time. Repetition and duration are key principles in effective treatments for fear reduction.

One final principle needs to be explained: that of sensitization. Sensitization refers to the increasing levels of arousal experienced by people when confronted by short, intense exposures to fear-provoking stimuli. Erratic and involuntary contact with previously feared or innately fearful stimuli is most likely to lead to increasing sensitization. Therefore, not only does running away or escape from a feared situation prevent habituation, it may also lead to a net increase in fear via sensitization.

Change

Mental health waxes and wanes in all individuals in response to the complex interplay of biological arousability and environmental pressure. The behavioural view of change is that organisms will be motivated by responding to reinforcers. Rewards, whether in the form of negative or positive reinforcement, will lead to increases in behaviour. Punishment or frustrative non-reward will lead to behavioural reductions. The propensity of individuals to respond to these environmental stimuli varies according to their genetic set. As behavioural changes occur, the autonomic and cognitive systems also move – not always at the same pace – until the three systems of physical arousal, behaviour and cognitions achieve equilibrium again. Further, as individuals learn new and more complex skills, for example by watching others, they may learn how to become more assertive and can exert more choice in their behavioural repertoires. This enables them to employ more diverse responses to the problems and stresses of everyday life.

Practice

Goals of therapy

In all instances, the goals of behavioural psychotherapy are arrived at in a collaborative process of negotiation between therapist and client. Different clients will have different objectives. In general, the goal of most programmes of behavioural psychotherapy will be to assist a client reduce the intensity of their problems such that their difficulties impact less upon their activities of daily living. For some clients an appropriate goal will be the complete eradication of all symptoms, most commonly achieved in specific phobias and PTSD. In other cases clients will seek a reduction in the impact of their difficulties sufficient to allow them to engage in normal activities again – an end-point which sufferers of obsessive-compulsive disorder strive for. Whilst empowerment and personal growth is often a product of behavioural psychotherapy's fundamental principle that clients should be enabled to address their problems using their own resources, therapy is not framed as a search for personal enlightenment.

Therapists seek to use behavioural activities as a way of entering and modifying the three emotional response systems (autonomic, behavioural and cognitive). When the client is assisted to change one of these systems (behaviour) directly, the autonomic and cognitive systems also change, although there is often a lag or de-synchrony between systems. The behaviours targeted for change are those that are implicated in the antecedent/behaviour/consequence sequence of triggers and reinforcement.

Importantly, behaviour therapists do not believe that they are missing some mysterious unacknowledged personal conflict from either the past or present when they target current behavioural symptoms for change. This is because as well as the theoretical rejection of mentalist thought, a key principle is that techniques must be based on the best empirical research evidence available. Research does not support a search for mentalist solutions. Quite the reverse: previous theoretical assumptions of other schools of psychological therapy have proved to be unfounded. Arguments such as 'symptom substitution' have floundered on empirical demonstrations of success in behavioural psychotherapy whilst the maintenance of behavioural treatment gains has been demonstrated with very long follow-up studies. It is a key element of the BABCP's code of practice that therapists should only utilize techniques with such a sound evidence base. The goal of behavioural psychotherapy is, therefore, to deliver the best evidence-based therapy, focusing on the 'here and now', which is action orientated, collaborative and aimed at relieving current distress and disability caused by acute or chronic psychological disturbance.

Selection criteria

The principle of an evidence base is applied right at the start of definitions of suitability for behavioural psychotherapy. Where there is clear evidence that behavioural methods can improve a client's condition the client must be initially considered as suitable for therapy. Such evidence is most believable if it comes from a systematic review, at least one randomized controlled trial or, if these are not available, from other empirical evidence from less robust study designs. As more clinical problems are being researched the list of suitable conditions is growing; it currently comprises all the anxiety disorders including obsessive-compulsive disorder and PTSD, depression, some somatizing disorders such as chronic fatigue, sexual difficulties, habit disorders, eating problems particularly bulimia, nightmares and morbid grief. Recently, in combination with some cognitive techniques, behavioural methods have been shown to be effective with psychosis (Slade and Haddock, 1996).

However, all clients are individuals and each individual will present with a unique constellation of symptoms. Once it has been established that a client has a general type of problem for which there is evidence that behavioural psychotherapy can help, there are several criteria which should be applied (Richards and McDonald, 1990). First, the client's problem should be expressed as observable behaviour. Behavioural psychotherapy is most likely to be useful if a person is complaining of a handicapping excess or deficit of behaviour, such as avoidance or excessive cleaning or waking in the night after frequent nightmares. This does not exclude symptoms such as intrusive images or obsessive ruminations. These are regarded as private behaviours and have been shown to be just as amenable to change as public behaviours.

Secondly, the client's difficulties must be current and predictable. Behavioural psychotherapy techniques usually require the client to address their difficulties regularly and repeatedly. Clients should be able to predict a reasonably consistent degree of handicap in particular situations. This is not to say that their problems cannot vary in intensity or severity from time to time, but the problem should manifest itself by and large in a predictable fashion. It is perfectly possible that a problem's origins may lie in the past – morbid grief would be an example here –

however, it should be manifesting itself as a current difficulty to render it suitable for treatment using behavioural psychotherapy.

A third suitability principle is that client and therapist should be able to define and agree on specific goals for therapy. Purposeful and participatory, behavioural psychotherapy cannot work unless client and therapist work together towards achieving clearly defined end-points and intermediary goals, usually expressed as behavioural targets. Fourthly, and in line with the third principle, clients should understand and agree to the type of treatment being offered. Once again, the participatory criterion is being invoked here. Behavioural techniques do not 'do things to people'; rather, people 'do things with behavioural techniques'.

The final criterion should be that there are no contra-indications for behavioural treatment. There are many and varied reasons why a client may present with an apparent psychological problem when in reality there is an underlying physical cause for their distress, for example hyperthyroidism and anxiety or diabetes and impotence. Other contra-indications are very severe depression which might pose a risk to the individual through suicide, self-harm or self-neglect; excessive use of anxiolytic medications such as benzodiazepines; or severe problem illegal drug and alcohol use. These conditions must be treated separately. In the case of depression, antidepressants do not interfere with the psychological processes harnessed in behavioural psychotherapy so treatment can be concurrent.

Qualities of effective therapists

Behavioural psychotherapists display a set of behaviours with their clients which are the outward manifestation of assumptions they make about people who seek help for psychological problems. Chief amongst these are:

- This person is responsive.
- This person is honest.
- This person is trying to cope.

Behavioural psychotherapists believe that these assumptions will drive client responses. If a therapist approaches a clinical situation with negative attitudes it will quickly become apparent to the client, the client will behave in response to these negative assumptions and very little effective work will be undertaken. The reverse, the set of assumptions listed above, will be more likely to elicit a positive response from the client. Belief in client *responsivity* is a prerequisite for collaborative working. The second assumption, *honesty*, reflects the principle of behavioural psychotherapists' valuing the client as a true partner in therapy. Change can only be achieved if clients and therapists know what the client is experiencing. Generally, this must be ascertained through client self-report. A positive assumption must be that the client will report these experiences honestly for progress to be validly monitored. Finally, the principle of *coping* is essential. However different from the norm is the behaviour that is causing the client their life problems, it has to be understood in terms of an attempt to cope with emotional arousal. Avoidances, rituals, excesses and deficits in behaviour are all seen as attempts to cope rather than as discrete pathological processes.

In addition to these essential positive assumptions, behavioural psychotherapists must be able to interview effectively. Patient-centred interviewing is the essential method of information-gathering, treatment planning, review and evaluation. At all times the therapist is interested in the 'here and now', not the client's past history except where it has a direct and crucial bearing on the present. To this end, therapists use an interview process which is free-flowing, has a progressive focus and elicits client-centred information. Typically, therapists start with a general open question then, guided by the client's responses, move to specific open questions and finally ask closed questions to arrive at a mutually agreed accurate problem definition (Richards and McDonald, 1990). Within this structure information on triggers, the three systems of emotion, consequences, frequency, duration and intensity of symptoms is all gathered. The same patient-centred interview process is utilized in subsequent therapy sessions where the therapist will use information from the client to review progress. Many authors regard this whole process and way of working as an essential ethical dimension to behavioural psychotherapy (Fox and Conroy, 2000; Newell, 1994; Newell and Gournay, 2000).

Other qualities of effective behavioural psychotherapists are the ability to tolerate and handle expressed emotion, to be able to plan coherent treatment programmes, to be able to use clinical measures accurately, to be comfortable with 'selling' clinical strategies and to display behaviours consistent with the 'scientist practitioner'. Behavioural psychotherapists must use information from the scientific evidence base, plan personal experiments with clients to test individual hypotheses and report their results in the wider public domain.

Therapeutic relationship and style

The therapeutic style of a behavioural psychotherapist is best described as purposeful and participatory. The aim of the therapist is to assist the client to address their problems and move towards a position of greater health and reduced handicap. The therapist enables the client to make this change through the provision of information and participatory shaping of therapeutic activities. The relationship between client and therapist is not, therefore, developed for its own sake. Indeed, there is much evidence that behavioural psychotherapy can be delivered very effectively without the presence of a human therapist (e.g. Greist et al., 1998). The therapeutic relationship is merely one of a range of potential delivery systems including books, computers, interactive telephone systems for behavioural psychotherapy.

Where face-to-face individual therapy is selected as the delivery mode, the quality of the therapeutic relationship is vital since the therapist may have to assist the client to engage in some therapeutic behavioural activities which might at first appear aversive. The therapeutic relationship is enhanced in the following manner. Attention and continuity are demonstrated by nods, facial expression, eye contact and the setting of the environment to avoid interruptions. Non-intrusive note-taking is also utilized to aid the flow of therapy sessions. Rapport and partnership are established through the totality of the client-centred interviewing process including mutual comments on the progress of the session. Where the therapist has to assist the client to manage emotion, empathy rather than sympathy is used, as is very limited self-disclosure (usually restricted to factually accurate statements to establish a therapist's relevant expertise). Reassurance is also limited to truthful, preferably conservative, predictions about events which are under the therapist's control. In behavioural psychotherapy, therapists do not use interpretation, excessive reassurance, inappropriate probing or evaluative statements.

The techniques described in the previous paragraph are not unique to behavioural psychotherapy. They are used in many individual therapies to develop warm and trusting relationships between helper and the person seeking help. In behavioural psychotherapy, however, the relationship is not an end in itself. Both each session and the treatment programme itself are prefaced by a clear agreement between client and therapist on session time limits and goals. The quality of the relationship should assist both partners in utilizing evidence-based interventions in order to meet these goals. Therapy is a partnership, initially and mutually unequal in that the therapist has more knowledge and professional expertise whereas the client has more personal understanding of their particular circumstances and problems. By the end of therapy the relationship should have become more equal.

Major therapeutic strategies and techniques

Given that they target the behavioural emotional response system, behavioural techniques appear deceptively simple. However, they are extremely subtle and sophisticated in application. The use of a behavioural treatment such as exposure, with its explicit goal of promoting habituation to feared stimuli, requires an understanding of psychobiological mechanisms and the nature of the environmental and personal characteristics necessary to make the most effective use of the techniques. The deceptive simplicity of behavioural techniques can lead unwary therapists into designing poorly understood and ultimately ineffective programmes.

The current view, supported by a considerable evidence base, is that in the application of almost all behavioural techniques it is what the client does between sessions that is the crucial determinant of therapeutic success or failure. In the past, therapists spent a great deal of time 'walking the streets' accompanying clients with agoraphobia. We know now that this is both unnecessary and potentially harmful in that it may lead to client dependence on the therapist. Inter-session 'homework' is the most important part of any programme. The nature of this homework will be determined by the client's problems and the selection of the appropriate evidence-based intervention. The most robust and common of these is prolonged exposure.

Exposure

This is defined as the therapeutic confrontation with a feared stimulus until the physical, behavioural and cognitive responses to that stimulus have habituated (become reduced). In order to facilitate this psychobiological process, key principles have to be observed. First, exposure must be prolonged. Fear does not habituate unless one confronts it for a sufficient length of time. Figure 13.1 details this effect by comparing a typical fear/avoidance response to a feared stimulus, contrasted with a response to the same stimulus in an exposure paradigm. If the person remains in contact with the feared stimulus (exposure 1) prolonged exposure will lead to a gradual reduction in fear over time. This contrasts with the fear/avoidance response where the person escapes from the stimulus as soon as it reaches its peak, experiencing temporary reduction in fear but no long-term improvement. Each subsequent contact with the feared stimulus produces exactly the same fear and avoidance response. In the same time frame, where the exposure paradigm produces a reduction in anxiety over time, the approach/ avoidance paradigm leads to a continuation of the same level of fear.

The figure also illustrates the second principle of exposure: exposure must be repeated. Subsequent confrontation with the feared stimuli leads both to less initial fear and to a more rapid reduction (habituation) of the fear response. This is shown clearly by the line 'Exposure 5', a hypothetical fifth exposure session for someone undergoing an exposure treatment programme. The number of

Figure 13.1   Fear and avoidance (the solid line) versus exposure (the broken lines): the effect on anxiety over time

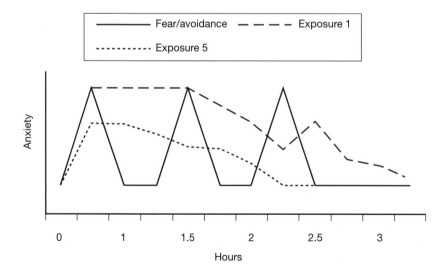

repeated exposure sessions depends on the individual's response and is ultimately determined by the levels of intra- and inter-session habituation.

A third principle of exposure is that it should be graded. People who fear situations or objects can usually place their fears in a hierarchy. They can then work up this hierarchy, from least to worst feared, moving up as they habituate to lower items via prolonged and repeated exposures.

Most of this happens between sessions as homework. In order for client and therapist to decide together on suitable exposure targets and the speed of progress, the client monitors their levels of anxiety using a simple scale (e.g. 0–8; 0–100). Behavioural psychotherapists use special self-monitoring diary sheets where the client rates their anxiety before, during (every 15 minutes) and after each exposure exercise, particularly those done as homework. Review of these diaries forms a key part of each therapy session.

The stimuli used in exposure exercises are those that the client has selected as most appropriate and are usually those which cause them most anxiety. In general, real-life situations and objects are chosen and are regarded as the most effective. Occasionally it may not be possible to have access to real-life examples of feared stimuli and in these circumstances imaginal exposure may be used (e.g. Richards, 1988). Imaginal exposure is particularly useful in the treatment of PTSD. Here individuals fear memories of their trauma and spend considerable energy avoiding thinking about it. As well as the many theoretical and ethical objections to real-life exposure to situations associated with the trauma, in many cases it is impossible to re-create the trauma situation. Imaginal exposure not only gives access to the evoking stimuli but also enables the feared stimuli to be reproduced so that it resembles as closely as possible the real event, maximizing the effectiveness of exposure. Imaginal exposure is also used with obsessive-compulsive disorder (OCD). OCD often involves covert ritualizing so imaginal exposure to anxiety-provoking cognitive ruminations can be used to promote habituation.

One further type of stimulus useful for exposure is interoceptive cue exposure. People who are hypersensitive to changes in their body often get labelled as 'hypochondriacs'. Exposure to these cues either in imagination or in real life can lead to habituation and reduced sensitivity. An example of interoceptive cue exposure would be the client with an inappropriate fear of having a heart attack brought on whenever s/he experienced a faster pulse rate. In this case, exposure would take the form of a graded exercise regime to produce sustained periods of faster heart rate.

Response prevention

This is an adjunctive technique used with exposure for people who are suffering problems with OCD. As well as fearing and avoiding stimuli which provoke anxiety (for example various 'contaminants') people with OCD also engage in excessive behaviours such as cleaning and checking. These serve to reduce or neutralize the anxiety provoked by confrontation with their feared stimuli, and are rather like the avoidance behaviour undertaken by our hypothetical client in Figure 13.1. Clearly, if exposure is to be effective in OCD, clients also have to desist from their neutralizing behaviours while in contact with the fear-producing situation or object. Response prevention refers to the voluntary cessation of these behaviours during prolonged exposure. The principle of response prevention is also applied to requests from clients with OCD for 'reassurance' which can become extremely excessive and once again are concerned with escape from anxiety (for example, repeated requests from a client with OCD to a partner to confirm that the client has locked the front door on leaving the house). Involving partners and family members in rehearing consensual response prevention statements such as, 'Your therapist has informed me that I cannot answer that question' may be necessary to facilitate prolonged exposure without neutralizing. Again, for imaginal exposure to obsessive ruminations to be successful, it must also be accompanied by response prevention of the neutralizing thoughts and covert rituals.

Other techniques

Generally subsumed under the pragmatic envelope of behavioural psychotherapy are techniques to reduce appetitive behaviours and to learn new behavioural skills. Appetitive reduction techniques are often used when clients have difficulty controlling behaviours which they regard as excessive. Self-monitoring (like the diary-keeping in exposure) is a highly effective technique in its own right but is more often used to chart the effectiveness of some other technique. These include stimulus control procedures, most often used in disorders where control is poor such as bulimia and alcohol misuse. Identification of individual 'danger' signals and pre-control of stimuli to reduce the incidence of these signals assists clients to control situations: confining eating to certain times and places, only having certain foods in the house, etc. Although behavioural techniques such as meal scheduling are extremely useful in disorders such as bulimia they are usually accompanied by cognitive strategies to assist the client to address the core assumptions which are driving their behaviour (Schmidt and Treasure, 1994).

Less often used are techniques regarded as aversive in that they utilize punishment or frustrative non-reward. Currently, covert sensitization is the only technique in widespread use and is an imaginal procedure for reducing the potency of unacceptable sexual fantasies. The behavioural literature does contain many references to other procedures such as 'response cost' but these are now rarely employed.

Certain training and learning procedures are used, however, to assist clients develop new skills – assertiveness or job skills for example. Social skills training is often conducted in groups so that socially isolated and unskilled individuals can practise in a safe environment. Micro skills such as maintaining eye contact can be practised via role-play, modelling and ultimately real-life practice.

Behavioural activation

This technique is used with people who are depressed. In line with Lang's (1979) conceptualization of emotion as a combination of physical, behavioural and cognitive elements, behavioural activation targets the behavioural system for therapy. Change in this system improves all elements of the affective response and is achieved through identification of behaviours which the client used to do or would like to do but currently is not engaging in as a consequence of their depression. Engaging in pleasant, reinforcing activities (Lewinsohn, 1974) is a means to increase the positive reinforcers in a person's life and tries to redress the sense of 'learned helplessness' (Seligman, 1975) referred to earlier. Behavioural activation has been shown to be as effective as other more complex cognitive therapies in the treatment of depression (Jacobson et al., 1996).

Self-help techniques

These are not strictly separate from those listed above but have come to increased prominence since the early 1990s. With the definition and isolation of the effective elements of behavioural psychotherapy has come a movement to make such techniques more widely available. There will never be sufficient therapists to meet the massive mental health needs of the population. Further, the emphasis within behavioural psychotherapy on patient empowerment leads one naturally to the ultimate self-reliance strategy – self-care. Given sufficient instruction and explanation there is no reason why many people could not utilize these techniques successfully without a therapist. A recent systematic review of such approaches in primary care (Bower et al., 2001) revealed a considerable evidence base with some indication that self-help applications of behavioural techniques (usually via bibliotherapy) were at least as effective as standard care and might even be more effective. Computer (Ghosh and Marks, 1987) and interactive touch-tone phone systems (Greist et al., 1998) delivering self-care have already been shown to be effective for a number of anxiety disorders and are likely to be increasingly employed.

These studies also show that equivalent outcomes can be achieved with no loss of client satisfaction; in fact there is some indication that clients find it easier to disclose personal information to a computer than to a therapist (Greist et al., 1998). A final route of access for self-care is through service user groups such as Triumph over Phobia (TOPS) who run self-care groups for people with anxiety disorders using behavioural techniques. As described by Lovell and Richards (2000), these routes to behavioural psychotherapy are likely to assume greater importance as demand for effective psychotherapy increases.

The change process in therapy

The change process in behavioural psychotherapy goes through several stages. Initially, client and therapist must come to some mutual understanding of the client's problems and agree both a problem formulation and a series of goals to be worked towards during therapy. The client must fully understand what is being suggested by the therapist and agree to implement the therapeutic techniques advised. If the problem is one of anxiety the next stage will be to identify the first exposure exercise in the client's hierarchy and embark on a programme of prolonged and repeated therapeutic exposure, coupled with response prevention if this is necessary. Habituation is measured via the client's self-report of discomfort in the face of their feared stimuli and progress will be monitored by sessional review of their homework diary sheets and anxiety ratings. Habituation is observed through reductions in both peak anxiety levels and duration of symptoms in the face of anxiety-provoking stimuli. Successful habituation will occur most rapidly with specific phobias and least quickly with OCD (Marks, 1987). In general, however, within-session habituation should begin in the first hour of exposure and progress rapidly during the second hour. Changes are most likely to be observed first in the behavioural system (i.e. an increase in approach behaviours rather than the avoidance or escape seen pre-treatment), followed by the autonomic system (i.e. reduction in physical anxiety symptoms) and finally the cognitive system (replacement of fearful thoughts with less fearful ones).

Traditionally, behavioural psychotherapy treatment programmes are scheduled to last for between eight and ten weeks. In practice, this is often much less. Certainly, if progress is not being achieved after three active therapy sessions the therapist should search for potential problems such as distraction during exposure which would render exposure ineffective. If there are no problems, over time, client and therapist should observe a reduction in fear which should begin to generalize to other situations. Successful clients are able to apply the principles of behavioural psychotherapy to new situations and will make rapid progress. Where this does not occur, therapists may occasionally need to accompany clients and observe where things may be going wrong. In OCD in particular, therapists may need to search carefully for micro examples of clients' feared consequences and ensure that exposure addresses these effectively.

Finally, on discharge clients should have a maintenance plan so that gains they have made in therapy do not decay over time. Relapse prevention plans similar in principle to those developed for clients with alcohol and problem drug use (Marlatt and Gordon, 1985) ensure that clients can recognize the triggers which indicate their problems may be relapsing. They then have a series of exercises that can be used immediately to prevent any recurrence of their problems. Such plans are very effective in appetitive disorders associated with eating and drug/alcohol use. In particular, the concept of 'lapse' rather than 'relapse' allows clients to suffer a temporary recurrence of their symptoms without a complete collapse in treatment gains.

Other disorders amenable to behavioural psychotherapy described earlier usually progress along similar lines. Whether it is the learning of new skills or starting to take pleasure in previously enjoyed activities, therapy initially addresses very specific, targeted behaviours with the expectation that improvement will spread out to other situations. As this happens, changes in autonomic and cognitive responses occur, albeit at different rates for different disorders and clients. Maintenance of gains is through planned strategies to identify and nip in the bud any signs of relapse.

Limitations of the approach

Twenty years ago behavioural psychotherapy was limited to approximately 25 per cent of clients with 'neurotic' disorders and 10 per cent of the adult population (Marks, 1982b). However, with behavioural treatments increasingly being used within a cognitive-behavioural therapy (CBT) paradigm, these proportions are increasing all the time. In particular, the development of CBT for psychosis is broadening the population of clients for whom behavioural psychotherapy is now considered useful and for which there is evidence of effectiveness.

Behavioural psychotherapy requires the active participation of the client and as such is limited to those clients that are prepared to engage in purposeful activity. Therapy is not suited to individuals who are embarking on a quest for understanding of personal existential conflicts. As in other therapies, even drug therapies such as antidepressants, approximately 25 per cent of clients either refuse or drop out of therapy in the early stages. This is a phenomenon common to all psychotherapies and only partly accounted for by exposure being an initially discomforting experience. Clients do need to remain anxious until the effects of habituation reduce arousal and this can lead to some clients dropping out of therapy. With these clients, therapists will find mere knowledge of technique insufficient. The engagement and rationale-giving techniques referred to earlier are essential to enable some clients to proceed with therapy.

In very few disorders can one talk about complete cure. An exception might be PTSD, where complete resolution of all symptoms is frequently possible. In most other anxiety disorders no more than a minority of clients are wholly rid of their symptoms. It is much more common for clients to have greatly reduced symptoms but some residual anxiety, hence the discussion of relapse prevention strategies above. This is of little consequence for many clients in that therapy can progress to a sufficient extent to allow them to live a normal life, free from the crippling handicaps and disabilities they previously laboured under. Therapy cannot change the biological set of the individual, merely the impact of the combination of this set, their behaviours and their cognitions on their lives.

Behavioural psychotherapy is not a panacea for all ills. Some clients do not respond to treatment despite client and therapist exploring the details of their problems, searching for specific environmental cues and devising ingenious therapy programmes. Such clients are often resistant to other approaches too and these people have frequently been identified as an urgent priority for research (e.g. Foa and Emmelkamp, 1983). More effort needs to be made to understand the reasons for non-responding and to develop programmes for these clients.

Case example

The client

Ellen, 27, had been concerned about cleanliness since her late teens. Since that time in her life she had had to wash very carefully whenever she touched something she thought might be 'contaminated'. There were no specific fears associated with 'catching' a particular disease, merely a general sense of extreme unease and discomfort provoked even by occasionally brushing against something she thought might be 'dirty'. This had led her to avoid going out to strange and unfamiliar places unless strictly necessary and to use an excessive amount of cleaning products. Notwithstanding this, she had maintained a long-term relationship with her partner, Andrew, since they were both 19. She also worked full time in a solicitor's office as a typist and clerk. Both she and her partner had adapted to her preoccupations, for example by each keeping a set of 'inside' clothes in their utility room, into which they changed on coming home from work.

Whenever Ellen felt that she had become contaminated, she would immediately wash herself. This washing took the form of an elaborate ritual. First she would turn the taps on and rinse her hands, Then she would take some liquid soap from a dispenser, pushing the dispenser down with the heel of her left hand (she was right handed). Next she would rub the soap into her hands in a regular motion, ensuring that she soaped all parts of her hands, including her wrists. After she had done this for approximately two minutes, she would rinse her hands thoroughly and then repeat the whole process. Frequently, she would have to repeat this more than twice until she was satisfied she was free of 'contamination'. The ritual would last for 10 minutes at least.

She also spent a large amount of time cleaning the house, often staying up late each evening to finish the task until she was satisfied. This urge to clean the house was always made worse when she or her partner had been out somewhere strange and when she thought she had been touched by someone 'unclean' whilst out. If they had had visitors, even the electricity meter man, she had to clean the house from top to bottom to erase any possibility that he had brought contamination into their home.

The motivation for seeking therapy came from Ellen and Andrew's desire to start a family. They both knew that having a baby would put an incredible strain on Ellen's capacity to manage her obsessions and compulsions. They felt that Ellen's health and their relationship would be unable to adapt and yet they were desperate to have children. They wanted to cope with Ellen's fear that a baby would bring an unacceptable amount of contamination into their lives and to be able to manage this without increased cleaning. Ellen also recognized that she would not be able to find time to look after a child if she continued to clean and ritualize at her current rate.

The therapy

Ellen and Andrew attended the initial therapy sessions together. They acknowledged the scale of their problems and after a discussion accepted and understood the behavioural approach/avoidance rationale for Ellen's fears and rituals. Ellen's first task was to make a list of her feared contaminants and place these in a hierarchical order, the worst at the top of the list, the easiest at the bottom. She then devised an exercise in which she used the least difficult contaminant to 'dirty' herself and not wash afterwards. In Ellen's case her first contaminant was her own clothes after she had worn them for a day. For the next week, as soon as she got up and after her shower, Ellen touched the clothes she had worn on the previous day, making sure she first contaminated her hands and then touched herself all over, including her hair and her clean clothes. As well as this exposure element to therapy she also refrained from washing after this exercise – response prevention. In order to prolong and repeat the exposure, she carried an item of 'dirty' clothing with her during the day. As soon as she washed her hands for whatever reason, she re-contaminated herself by touching this item again. Initially she experienced significant anxiety (rated by Ellen as 90/100) but within a week this had dropped to 30/100. She was pleased with her success.

Next Ellen used the same contaminated stimulus to spread the 'dirt' around her and Andrew's home. She agreed to contaminate herself as before and then touch as many areas of her home as possible so that she could not avoid becoming contaminated. She also agreed to reduce her cleaning to twice a week. Further, after each cleaning session she had to re-contaminate the cleaned areas. Once again, Ellen experienced considerable success very quickly. However, it became apparent in discussion with herself and Andrew that this apparent dramatic improvement was in part due to the fact that she was avoiding contaminating certain areas. Their house was being divided up into 'clean' and 'dirty' areas. The bathroom was particularly difficult. After two weeks without further success, the therapist went with Ellen to her house and they did an exercise together. After selecting a jumper which Ellen had worn the previous day, Ellen took it into the bathroom and contaminated all the surfaces, taps, etc. Her anxiety was significantly raised (95/100) during this exercise and she experienced a strong urge to clean the bathroom after this. However, with help from the therapist and Andrew she resisted the urge to clean and the next day even had a shower in the 'contaminated' bathroom, re-contaminating the area after she had finished. Over the next week she was able to successfully contaminate her whole house.

Progress was now rapid. Ellen chose other sources of contamination from her hierarchy and spread contamination from sources such as tissues, work clothes and shoes around her house. A further set of exercises was instigated to reduce the intensity of her hand-washing, although this had already reduced considerably because her exercises always required her to re-contaminate herself after washing anyway. At first she timed herself in order to gradually reduce the time of each hand-wash. After a while she began to experience a reduction in the desire to wash both frequently and intensely as her fears of contaminants reduced. Hand-washing reduced greatly.

After eight sessions of therapy Ellen and Andrew reported a 65 per cent improvement. She still had bad days and some lapses. She had yet to reach the top of her contamination hierarchy but felt able to progress without further therapist assistance. Her relationship with Andrew was stronger and he felt he was in a position to assist if she slipped back.

Unfortunately, six months later, Ellen contacted the therapist reporting a relapse in her problems. This was precipitated by an incident one day when she had been approached by a person begging in the street who had become aggressive and grabbed her coat. She had had to throw the coat away and had become so disturbed by the incident that she had started to wash excessively and avoid going out. Luckily she recognized what was happening and contacted the therapist within a few days of her relapse. She and Andrew were encouraged to develop a programme of exposure and response prevention to address her newly resurrected fears. The therapist used this experience as an opportunity for Ellen and Andrew to learn how to cope with future problems and the programme they developed together was successful within a few weeks. These strategies were incorporated into Ellen's relapse prevention plan. Ellen reported being 75 per cent better than when she had sought help initially. Two years later, Ellen contacted the therapist to say she remained OK and had coped with the birth of their son nine months earlier. Despite occasional desires to wash and avoid she remained much improved and with the help of her relapse prevention plan was able to resist any tendency to revert to her previous behaviours.

References

Bandura, A. (1977) 'Self-efficacy: toward a unifying theory of behavioural change', *Psychological Review*, 84: 191–215.

Bower, P., Richards, D.A. and Lovell, K. (2001). 'The clinical and cost-effectiveness of self-help treatments for anxiety and depressive disorders in primary care: a systematic review', *British Journal of General Practice*, 51: 838–45.

De Silva, P. (1984) 'Buddhism and behaviour modification', *Behaviour Research and Therapy*, 22: 661–78.

Eysenck, H.J. (1952) 'The effects of psychotherapy: an evaluation', *Journal of Consulting Psychology*, 16: 319–24.

Eysenck, H.J. (1985) *Decline and Fall of the Freudian Empire*. London: Penguin.

Foa, E.B. and Emmelkamp, P.M.G. (1983) *Failures in Behaviour Therapy*. New York: Wiley.

Fox, J. and Conroy, P. (2000) 'Assessing clients' needs: the semi-structured interview', in C. Gamble and G. Brennan (eds), *Working with Serious Mental Illness: A Manual for Clinical Practice*. London: Ballière Tindall.

Freud, S. (1919) 'Turning in the ways of psychoanalytic therapy', in *Collected Papers*, Vol. II. London: Hogarth Press/Institute of Psycho-analysis.

Ghosh, A. and Marks, I. (1987) 'Self-treatment of agoraphobia by exposure', *Behaviour Therapy*, 18: 3–16.

Greist, J.H., Marks, I.M., Baer, L., Parkin, J.R., Manzo, P.A., Mantle, J.M., Wenzel, K.W., Spierings, C.J., Kobak, K.A., Dottl, S.L., Bailey, T.M. and Forman, L. (1998) 'Self-treatment for obsessive compulsive disorder using a manual and a computerized telephone interview: a US–UK study', *M.D. Computing*, 15(3): 149–57.

Jacobson, N.S., Dobson, K.S., Traux, P.A., Addis, M.E., Koerner, K., Gollan, J.K., Gortner, E. and Prince, S.E. (1996) 'A component analysis of cognitive-behavioural treatment of depression', *Journal of Consulting and Clinical Psychology*, 64: 295–304.

Jones, M.C. (1924) 'A laboratory study of fear', *Pedagogical Seminary*, **31:** 308–315.

Lang, P. (1979). 'A bioinformational theory of emotional imagery', *Psychophysiology*, 16: 495–512.

Lewinsohn, P.M. (1974) 'A behavioural approach to depression', in R.M. Friedman and M.M. Katz (eds), *Psychology of Depression: Contemporary Theory and Research*. New York: Wiley.

Locke, J. (1693) *Some Thoughts Concerning Education*. London: Ward Lock.

Lovell, K. and Richards, D.A. (2000) 'Multiple access points and levels of entry (MAPLE): ensuring choice, accessibility and equity for CBT services', *Behavioural and Cognitive Psychotherapy*, 28: 379–91.

Marks, I.M. (1982a) 'Is conditioning relevant to behaviour therapy?' in J. Boulougouris (ed.), *Learning Theory Approaches to Psychiatry*, New York: Wiley.

Marks, I.M. (1982b) *Cure and Care of Neuroses: Theory and Practice of Behavioural Psychotherapy*. New York: Wiley.

Marks, I.M. (1987) *Fears, Phobias and Rituals*. Oxford: Oxford University Press.

Marlatt, G.A. and Gordon, J.R. (1985) *Relapse Prevention: Maintenance Strategies in Addictive Behaviour Change*. New York: Guildford.

Mowrer, O.H. (1950) *Learning Theory and Personality Dynamics*. New York: Arnold.

Newell, R. (1994) *Interviewing Skills for Nurses: A Structured Approach*. London: Routledge.

Newell, R. and Gournay, K. (2000) *Mental Health Nursing: An Evidence Based Approach*. London: Churchill Livingstone.

Pavlov, I.P. (1927) *Conditional Reflexes*. London: Oxford University Press.

Richards, D.A. (1988) 'The treatment of a snake phobia by imaginal exposure', *Behavioural Psychotherapy*, 16: 207–16.

Richards, D. and McDonald, B. (1990) *Behavioural Psychotherapy: A Handbook for Nurses*. Oxford: Heinemann.

Schmidt, U. and Treasure, J. (1994) *Getting Better Bit(e) by Bit(e): A Survival Kit for Sufferers of Bulimia Nervosa and Binge Eating Disorders*. Hove: Lawrence Erlbaum Associates.

Seligman, M.E.P. (1975) *Helplessness*. San Francisco: Freeman.

Skinner, B.F. (1953) *Science and Human Behaviour*. New York: Macmillan.

Slade, P.D. and Haddock, G. (1996) *Cognitive-behavioural Interventions for Psychotic Disorders*. London: Routledge.

Thorndike, E.L. (1911) *Animal Intelligence*. New York: Macmillan.

Watson, J.B. and Rayner, R. (1920) 'Conditioned emotional reactions', *Journal of Experimental Psychology*, 3: 1–14.

Wolpe, J. (1958) *Psychotherapy by Reciprocal Inhibition*. Stanford, CA: Stanford University Press.

Wolpe, J. (1976) 'Behaviour therapy and its malcontents', *Journal of Behaviour Therapy and Experimental Psychiatry*, 7: 109–16.

Suggested further reading

Baum, W.M. (1994) *Understanding Behaviourism: Science, Behaviour and Culture*. London: HarperCollins.

Gamble, C. and Brennan, G. (eds) (2000) *Working with Serious Mental Illness: A Manual for Clinical Practice*. London: Ballière Tindall.

Hawton, K., Salkovskis, P.M., Kirk, J. and Clark, D.M. (2000) *Cognitive Behaviour Therapy For Psychiatric Problems*, 2nd edn. Oxford: Oxford Medical Publications.

Marks, I.M. (1987) *Fears, Phobias and Rituals*. Oxford: Oxford University Press.

Parry, G. and Watts, F.N. (eds) (1996) *Behavioural and Mental Health Research: A Handbook of Skills and Methods*, 2nd edn. Hove: Erlbaum.

14 Rational Emotive Behaviour Therapy

Windy Dryden

Historical context and development in Britain

Historical context

Rational emotive behaviour therapy (REBT) was established in 1955 by Albert Ellis, a clinical psychologist in New York, who originally called the approach rational therapy. Ellis received his original training in psychotherapy in the 1940s in the field of marriage, family and sex counselling. In the course of his practice he realized that this kind of counselling was limited because 'disturbed marriages (or premarital relationships) were a product of disturbed spouses; and that if people were truly to be helped to live happily with each other they would first have to be shown how they could live peacefully with themselves' (Ellis, 1962: 3). He thus embarked on a course of intensive psychoanalytic training and received his training analysis from a training analyst of the Karen Horney group whose technique was primarily Freudian. In 1949 Ellis began to practise orthodox psychoanalysis with his patients, but was disappointed with the results he obtained. His patients appeared to improve, claimed to feel better, but Ellis could see that their improvement was not necessarily sustained. He then began to experiment with various forms of face-to-face, psychoanalytically oriented psychotherapy. Although he claimed that these methods brought better results and within a shorter period of time than orthodox psychoanalysis, he was still dissatisfied with the outcome of the treatment. In 1953 he began to research a monograph and a long article on new techniques in psychotherapy (Ellis, 1955a, 1955b) which influenced him to practise a unique brand of psychoanalytic-eclectic therapy; still, Ellis remained dissatisfied.

Throughout his career as a psychoanalytically oriented therapist from the late 1940s and 1955, Ellis had become increasingly disenchanted with psychoanalytic theory, claiming that it tended to be unscientific, devout and dogmatic. He had always maintained his early interest in philosophy and enjoyed thinking about how this field could be applied to the realm of psychotherapy. He used his knowledge of philosophy to help him answer his most puzzling question: 'Why do highly intelligent human beings, including those with considerable psychological insight, desperately hold on to their irrational ideas about themselves and others?' (Ellis, 1962: 14). The writings of Greek and Roman Stoic philosophers (especially Epictetus and Marcus Aurelius) were particularly influential in this respect. These philosophers stressed that people are disturbed not by things but by their view of things. Ellis began to realize that he had 'made the error of stressing a psychodynamic causation of psychological problems' (namely that we are disturbed as a result of what happens to us in our early childhood); instead, he started to emphasize the philosophic causation of psychological problems (namely that we remain disturbed because we actively and in the present reindoctrinate ourselves with our disturbance-creating philosophies).

From this point he began to stress the importance that thoughts and philosophies (cognition) have in creating and maintaining psychological disturbance. In his early presentations and writings on what has become known as rational emotive behaviour therapy, Ellis (1958) tended to overemphasize the role that cognitive factors play in human disturbance and consequently de-emphasized the place of emotive and behavioural factors. This was reflected in the original name that he gave to his approach: rational psychotherapy. In 1962 Ellis published his pioneering volume, *Reason and Emotion in Psychotherapy*. In this he stressed two important points: that cognitions, emotions and behaviours are interactive and often overlapping processes; and that 'human thinking and emotions are, in some of their essences, the same thing, and that by changing the former one does change the latter' (Ellis, 1962: 122). He concluded that the label rational-emotive therapy (RET) more accurately described his therapeutic approach. In 1993, Ellis decided to change the name of the therapy once more to rational emotive behaviour therapy (REBT). This was in response to critics who claimed that RET neglected behaviour and was purely cognitive and emotive in nature.

As noted above, the theory of rational emotive behaviour therapy has from its inception stressed the importance of the interaction of cognitive, emotive and behavioural factors both in human functioning and dysfunctioning and in the practice of psychotherapy. Ellis has acknowledged, in particular, his debts to theorists and practitioners who have advocated the role of action in helping clients to overcome their problems (Herzberg, 1945; Salter, 1949; Wolpe, 1958). Indeed, Ellis employed a number of *in vivo* behavioural methods to overcome his own fears of speaking in public and approaching women (Ellis, 1973).

Initially, rational emotive behaviour therapy received unfavourable and even hostile responses from the field of American psychotherapy. Despite this, Ellis persisted in his efforts to make his ideas more widely known; and as a result REBT is now flourishing. Its popularity in the United States increased markedly in the 1970s, when behaviour therapists became interested in cognitive factors, and the present impact of cognitive-behaviour therapy has helped REBT to become more widely known there. Currently, REBT is practised by literally thousands of mental health professionals in North America and it is taught and practised throughout the world.

Development in Britain

Until the early 1990s, training in REBT was available on an *ad hoc* basis from myself or Dr A.I. Raitt. Since training opportunities in REBT were limited, there were few therapists properly trained in REBT. Then, under the auspices of the

Centre for Stress Management in Blackheath, London, I began a programme of certificate, diploma and advanced diploma courses in REBT. These courses, which are now run under the auspices of the Centre for Rational Emotive Behaviour Therapy, attracted and continue to attract people from a range of helping professions, and the number of REBT therapists increased to the extent that an Association of Rational Emotive Behaviour Therapists was formed in 1993. The association, which publishes twice a year a journal entitled the *Rational Emotive Behaviour Therapist* was in 2001 accepted to join the Behavioural and Cognitive Section of the United Kingdom Council for Psychotherapy (UKCP).

In September 1995, I established an MSc. in Rational Emotive Behaviour Therapy at Goldsmiths College, University of London. This course is the first Master's course in REBT to be established in Europe and is now the only one in the world.

Theoretical assumptions

Image of the person

Rational emotive behaviour therapy holds that humans are essentially hedonistic (Ellis, 1976): their major goals are to stay alive and to pursue happiness efficiently, that is, in a non-compulsive but self-interested manner enlightened by the fact that they live in a social world. It is stressed that people differ enormously in terms of what will bring them happiness, so rational emotive behaviour therapists show clients not what will lead to their happiness but how they prevent themselves from pursuing it and how they can overcome these obstacles. Other basic concepts implicit in REBT's image of the person include those listed below.

Rationality

In REBT, 'rational' means primarily that which helps people to achieve their basic goals and purposes; 'irrational' means primarily that which prevents them from achieving these goals and purposes. However, 'rational' also means that which is flexible, logical and consistent with reality, whereas 'irrational' also means that which is rigid, illogical and inconsistent with reality.

Human fallibility

Humans are deemed to be by nature fallible and not perfectible. They naturally make errors and defeat themselves in the pursuit of their basic goals and purposes.

Human complexity and fluidity

Humans are seen as enormously complex organisms constantly in flux, and are encouraged to view themselves as such.

Biological emphasis

Ellis (1976) argues that humans have two basic biological tendencies. First, they have a tendency towards irrationality; they naturally tend to make themselves disturbed. Ellis (1976) makes a number of points in support of his 'biological hypothesis'. These include the following:

(a) Virtually all humans show evidence of major human irrationalities.
(b) Many human irrationalities actually go counter to the teachings of parents, peers and the mass media (for example, people are rarely taught that it is good to procrastinate, yet countless do so).
(c) Humans often adopt other irrationalities after giving up former ones.
(d) Humans often go back to irrational activity even though they may have worked hard to overcome it. (Ellis, 1976)

Secondly, and more optimistically, humans are considered to have great potential to work to change their biologically based irrationalities.

Human activity

Humans can best achieve their basic goals by pursuing them actively. They are less likely to be successful if they are passive or half-hearted in their endeavours.

Cognitive emphasis

Although emotions overlap with other psychological processes such as cognitions, sensations and behaviours, cognitions are given special emphasis in REBT theory. The most efficient way of effecting lasting emotional and behaviour change is for humans to change their philosophies. Two types of cognition are distinguished in Ellis's (1962) ABC model of the emotional/behavioural episode. The first type refers to the person's inferences about events and includes such cognitive activities as making forecasts, guessing the intentions of others and assessing the implications of one's behaviour for self and others. Inferences are hunches about reality and need to be tested out. As such they may be accurate or inaccurate. They are placed under 'A' of the ABC of REBT[1] since they do not fully account for the person's emotions and/or behaviours at C. The second type of cognition – beliefs – is evaluative in nature and indicates the personal significance of the event for the person concerned; such cognitions, which are placed under 'B' of the ABC of REBT, do account for the person's emotions and/or behaviours at C.

Constructivistic focus

(Ellis, 1994) has argued that REBT is best seen as one of the constructivistic cognitive therapies. In REBT, the constructivistic focus is seen in the emphasis that REBT places on the active role that humans play in constructing their irrational beliefs and the distorted inferences which they frequently bring to emotional episodes.

Concepts of psychological disturbance and health

Rational and irrational beliefs

Ellis (1962) has distinguished between two types of belief: rational and irrational. Rational beliefs are evaluations of personal significance which are non-absolute in nature, logical, consistent with reality and self- and other-enhancing. They indicate desires, preferences and wishes and they negate absolutes such as musts, absolute shoulds and oughts (e.g. 'I want to do well in my forthcoming exam, but sadly I don't have to do so'). Feelings of pleasure result when humans get what they desire, whereas feelings of displeasure (sadness, healthy anger or annoyance, concern and remorse) result when they fail to get what they want. Such negative emotions are deemed to be healthy responses to negative events since they do not significantly interfere with the pursuit of established or new goals.

Irrational beliefs are evaluations of personal significance stated in absolute terms such as 'must', 'should', 'ought' and 'have to'. They are rigid, illogical, inconsistent with reality and self- and other-defeating. It is noted that people often change their desires into demands: negative emotions such as depression, unhealthy anger, anxiety and guilt occur when people make demands on themselves, on other people and/or the world. Ellis (1994) regards these negative emotions as unhealthy responses to negative events since they generally impede the pursuit of established or new goals. Ellis (1982) claims that rational beliefs underlie functional behaviours, whereas irrational beliefs underpin dysfunctional behaviours such as withdrawal, procrastination, alcoholism, substance abuse and so on.

The process of making absolute demands on reality is called *musturbation*. It is linked to a process called *awfulizing*. 'Awfulizing' is the process of making grossly exaggerated negative conclusions when one does not get what one 'must' or when one gets what one 'must not'. Ellis considers awful to mean 'more than 100% bad!' and to stem from the demand, 'It absolutely should not be as bad as it is.'

Self-depreciation vs self-acceptance

Self-depreciation occurs when I either fail to do what I must, or do what I must not. It involves: (a) the process of giving my 'self' a global negative rating; and (b) 'devil-ifying' myself as being bad or less worthy. This second process rests on a theological concept, and implies either that I am undeserving of pleasure on earth or that I should rot in hell as a subhuman (devil). The REBT alternative to global negative self-rating and self-depreciation is unconditional self-acceptance: unconditional acceptance of oneself as a fallible human being who is constantly in flux and too complex to be given a single legitimate rating. REBT theory advocates that it is legitimate, and often helpful, to rate one's traits, behaviours, etc., but that it is not legitimate to rate one's self at all, even in a global positive manner, since positive self-rating tends to be conditional on doing good things, being loved and approved, and so on.

Discomfort disturbance vs discomfort tolerance

According to REBT there are two types of fundamental human disturbance. These are ego disturbance (as outlined in the previous section) where demands are made on one's self, and discomfort disturbance, which stems from the irrational belief. 'I must feel comfortable and have comfortable life conditions.' Conclusions that stem from this premiss are (a) 'It's awful' and (b) 'I can't stand it when these life conditions do not exist.' Discomfort disturbance occurs in different forms and is central to a full understanding of a number of emotional and behavioural disturbances such as unhealthy anger, agoraphobia, depression, procrastination and alcoholism. Demands made on other people either involve ego disturbance (for example 'You must approve of me and if you don't it proves that I am less worthy') or discomfort disturbance ('You must approve of me and give me what I must have and if you don't I can't bear it'), and thus do not represent a fundamental human disturbance, since they include one or other of the two fundamental disturbances.

Discomfort disturbance usually impedes people from working persistently hard to effect productive psychological change. The ability to tolerate discomfort and frustration, not for its own sake but in order to facilitate constructive psychological change, is a primary criterion of psychological health in REBT theory. It forms the basis of a philosophy of long-range hedonism: the pursuit of meaningful long-term goals while tolerating the deprivation of attractive short-term goals which are self-defeating in the longer term.

Psychological health

Ellis (1983a) shows how 'musturbation' is involved in dogmatism, devout belief (religious and secular) and religiosity, since these are all based on absolute demands on reality. He equates much emotional disturbance with these processes, advocating a scepticism which is based on a non-absolute view of reality as the emotionally healthy alternative. Non-absolutism is at the core of the REBT view of psychological health, as can be seen in the following list of criteria of positive mental health outlined by Ellis (1979b): self-interest; social interest; self-direction; tolerance; acceptance of ambiguity and uncertainty; flexibility; and scientific thinking (employing the rules of logic and scientific analysis in solving emotional and behavioural problems). In this respect, psychologically healthy people are not cold and detached, as those with a scientific approach to life are commonly but erroneously assumed to be; indeed, they experience the full range of healthy emotions, positive and negative. Other criteria of psychological health emphasized in REBT include commitment, calculated risk-taking, self-acceptance and acceptance of reality (or anti-awfulizing).

Acquisition of psychological disturbance

Rational emotive behaviour therapy does not posit an elaborate theory concerning how psychological disturbance is acquired. This follows logically from Ellis's (1976, 1979b) hypothesis that humans have a strong biological tendency to think and act irrationally. While Ellis is clear that humans' tendency to make absolute commands and demands on themselves, others and the world is biologically rooted, he does acknowledge that environmental factors contribute to emotional disturbance and thus encourage humans to make their biologically based demands (Ellis, 1979a). He argues that because humans are particularly open to influence as young children they tend to let themselves be over-influenced by societal teachings such as those offered by parents, peers, teachers and the mass media (Ellis, 1979b). One major reason why environmental control continues to wield a powerful influence over most people most of the time is because they tend not to be critical of the socialization messages they receive. Individual differences play a part here also. Humans vary in their suggestibility: while some humans emerge relatively unscathed emotionally from harsh and severe childhood regimes, others emerge emotionally damaged from more benign regimes (Werner and Smith, 1982). Ellis strongly believes that we, as humans, are not disturbed simply by our experiences; rather, we bring our ability to disturb ourselves to our experiences.

In doing this we can be said to play a large role in constructing our disturbances (as noted on p. 351). We construct our demands out of our strong preferences and from these demands we construct our overly distorted negative inferences about reality. Having constructed such inferences we then focus on them and construct a further set of demands: that these inferred A's absolutely should not be as bad as they are, for example. As a result we deepen the intensity of our already constructed disturbance. As will be seen, this is a far cry from models of psychotherapy which place negative life events at the centre of an explanation of how psychological disturbance is acquired.

Perpetuation of psychological disturbance

While REBT does not put forward elaborate theories to explain the acquisition of psychological disturbance, it does deal more extensively with how such disturbance is perpetuated. First, most people perpetuate their psychological disturbance precisely because of their own theories concerning the 'cause' of their problems. They do not have what Ellis (1979b) calls 'REBT Insight 1': that psychological disturbance is largely determined by the irrational beliefs that people hold about the negative events in their lives. They tend to attribute the 'cause' of their problems to situations, rather than to their beliefs about these situations. Lacking 'Insight 1', people are ignorant of the major determinants of their disturbance; consequently they do not know what to change in order to overcome their difficulties. Even when individuals see clearly that their beliefs determine their disturbance, they may lack 'REBT Insight 2': that they remain upset by reindoctrinating themselves in the present with these beliefs. People who do see that their irrational beliefs largely determine their disturbance tend to perpetuate such disturbance by devoting their energy to attempting to find out why and how they first adopted such beliefs instead of using such energy to change the currently held irrational beliefs. Some people who have both insights still perpetuate their disturbance because they lack 'REBT Insight 3': only if we consistently work and practise in the present as well as in the future to think, feel and act against these irrational beliefs are we likely to surrender them and make ourselves significantly less disturbed (Ellis, 1979b). People who have all three insights see clearly that just acknowledging that a belief is irrational is insufficient for change to take place.

Ellis (1979b) stresses that the major reason why people fail to change is due to their philosophy of 'low frustration tolerance' (LFT). By believing that they must be comfortable, people will tend to avoid the discomfort that working to effect psychological change very often involves, even though facing and enduring such short-term discomfort will probably result in long-term benefit. As Wessler (1978) has noted, such people are operating hedonistically from within their own frames of reference. They evaluate the tasks associated with change as 'too uncomfortable to bear' – certainly more painful than the psychological disturbance to which they have achieved a fair measure of habituation. They prefer to opt for the comfortable but disturbance-perpetuating discomfort of their problems rather than face the 'change-related' discomfort which they rate as 'dire'. Clearly, therapists have to intervene in this closed system of beliefs if psychological change is to be effected. This philosophy of low frustration tolerance which impedes change can take many different forms. One prevalent form of LFT is 'anxiety about anxiety'. Here, individuals may not expose themselves to anxiety-provoking situations because they are afraid that they might become anxious if they did so: a prospect which they would rate as 'terrible' because they believe 'I must not be anxious'.

'Anxiety about anxiety' is an example of a phenomenon that explains further why people perpetuate their psychological disturbances. Ellis (1979b) has noted that people often make themselves disturbed about their disturbances; thus they block themselves from working to overcome their original psychological disturbance because they upset themselves about having the original disturbance. Humans are often inventive in this respect – they can make themselves anxious about their anxiety, depressed about being depressed, guilty concerning their anger, and so on. Consequently, people often have to overcome their meta-emotional problems (as these secondary disturbances are now called) before embarking on effecting change in their original problems.

Ellis (1979b) has observed that people sometimes experience some kind of perceived pay-off for their psychological disturbance other than the gaining of immediate obvious ease. Here such disturbance may be perpetuated until the perceived pay-off is dealt with, in order to minimize its impact. For example, a woman who claims to want to lose weight may not take the necessary steps because she fears that losing weight would make her more attractive to men: a situation which she would view as 'awful'. Remaining fat protects her (in her mind) from a 'terrible' state of affairs. It is to be emphasized that the REBT therapists stress the phenomenological nature of these pay-offs: in other words, it is the person's view of the pay-off that is important in determining its impact, not the events delineated in the person's description.

A final major way that people tend to perpetuate their psychological disturbance is explained by the 'self-fulfilling prophecy' phenomenon (Jones, 1977; Wachtel, 1977): by acting according to their predictions, people often elicit from themselves or from others reactions which they then interpret in such a way as to confirm their initial self-defeating forecasts. In conclusion, Ellis (1979c) believes that humans tend naturally to perpetuate their problems and have a strong innate tendency to cling to self-defeating, habitual patterns, thereby resisting basic change.

Change

REBT theory argues that humans can and do change without psychotherapy. First people can change their disturbance-creating philosophies by reading rational self-help material or talking to people who teach them sound rational principles. I personally derived much benefit in the 1970s from reading and acting on the principles described in Ellis and Harper's *A Guide to Rational Living* and helped myself to overcome feelings of inferiority which I experienced from my early teens. Well before that time, I heard Michael Bentine talk on the radio about how he overcame his fear of talking in public due in large part to his stammer. He said that he helped himself by telling himself, 'If I stammer, I stammer. Too bad.' I thought this was excellent advice and because I was scared in my teens to speak in public because I had a stammer, I undertook a similar programme of speaking in public (behavioural exposure) while telling myself. 'If I stammer, I stammer. Fuck it!' (cognitive restructuring). The conjoint use of behavioural and cognitive techniques is frequently the hallmark of change when people (whether they are in therapy or not) alter their disturbance-creating philosophies.

People can help themselves overcome or gain relief from their problems in a number of ways other than changing the philosophies that underpin their psychological problems. They may succeed in changing their distorted inferences about negative events at A or they may put their situation into a more positive frame. They may help themselves by learning new skills like assertion or study skills and thereby improve their relationships with people and their performance at college. They may leave a situation in which they experience their psychological problems and find a new, much more favourable situation. Similarly, they may find a job or a relationship which may help them to transform their problems into strengths. Thus, a very obsessive person may flourish in a job environment that values his obsessiveness.

Finally, people may help themselves by telling themselves obvious irrationalities. I might help myself enormously if I tell myself and believe that I have a fairy godmother who will protect me from trouble and strife or if I think that I am a wonderful person because I write books and articles on rational emotive behaviour therapy!

As this chapter shows, the most enduring psychological changes are deemed to occur when someone changes their irrational beliefs to rational beliefs. All the other changes mentioned tend to be more transient and dependent on the existence of favourable life conditions.

Practice

Goals of therapy

In trying to help clients to overcome their emotional difficulties and achieve their self-enhancing goals, rational emotive behaviour therapists have clear and well-defined aims.

In this discussion it is important to distinguish between outcome goals and process goals. Outcome goals are those benefits which clients hope to derive from the therapeutic process. Ideally, rational emotive behaviour therapists try to assist clients to make profound philosophic changes. These would involve clients (a) giving up their demands on themselves, others and the world, while sticking with their preferences; (b) refusing to rate themselves, a process which would help them to accept themselves unconditionally; (c) refusing to rate anything as 'awful'; and (d) increasing their tolerance of frustration while striving to achieve their basic goals and purposes. If therapists are successful in this basic objective, clients will be minimally prone to future ego disturbance or discomfort disturbance. They will still experience healthy negative emotions such as sadness, healthy anger, concern and disappointment, since they would clearly retain their desires, wishes and wants; however, they will rarely experience unhealthy negative emotions such as depression, unhealthy anger, anxiety and guilt since they would have largely surrendered the absolutistic 'musts' 'shoulds' and 'oughts' which underlie such dysfunctional emotional experiences. In achieving such profound philosophic changes, clients would clearly score highly on the 11 criteria of positive mental health mentioned earlier (see pp. 352–3). If such ideal client goals are not possible, rational emotive behaviour therapists settle for less pervasive changes in their clients. Here clients may well achieve considerable symptomatic relief and overcome the psychological disturbance that brought them to therapy, but will not have achieved such profound philosophic changes as to prevent the development of future psychological disturbance. In this case, clients benefit from therapy either (a) by making productive behavioural changes which lead to improved environmental circumstances at A in Ellis's ABC model; or (b) by correcting distorted inferences at A. In reality most clients achieve some measure of philosophic change, while only a few achieve a profound philosophic change.

Process goals involve therapists engaging clients effectively in the process of therapy so that they can be helped to achieve their outcome goals. Here Bordin's (1979) concept of the therapeutic alliance is helpful. There are three major components of the therapeutic alliance: bonds, goals and tasks.

Effective bonds

These refer to the quality of the relationship between therapist and client that is necessary to help clients achieve their outcome goals. Rational emotive behaviour therapists consider that there is no one way of developing effective bonds with clients: flexibility is the key concept here.

Agreement on goals

Effective REBT is usually characterized by therapists and clients working together towards clients' realistic and self-enhancing outcome goals. The role of therapists in this process is to help clients distinguish between (a) realistic and unrealistic goals; and (b) self-enhancing and self-defeating goals. Moreover, REBT therapists help clients see that they can usually achieve their ultimate outcome goals only by means of reaching a series of mediating goals. In addition, some REBT therapists like to set goals for each therapy session, although Ellis (1989) is against this practice because, he argues, it forces clients to identify goals that they do not really have. Client goals can be negotiated at three levels: ultimate outcome goals, mediating goals, and session goals. Effective REBT therapists help their clients explicitly to see the links between these different goals and thus help to demystify the process of therapy.

Agreement on tasks

REBT is most effective when therapist and client clearly acknowledge that each has tasks to carry out in the process of therapy, clearly understand the nature of these tasks and agree to execute their own tasks. The major tasks of rational emotive behaviour therapy are: (a) to help clients see that their emotional and behavioural problems have cognitive antecedents; (b) to train clients to identify and change their irrational beliefs and distorted inferences; and (c) to teach clients that such change is best effected by the persistent application of cognitive, imagery, emotive and behavioural methods. The major tasks of clients are: (a) to observe their emotional and behavioural disturbances; (b) to relate these to their cognitive determinants; and (c) to work continually at changing their irrational beliefs and distorted inferences by employing cognitive, imagery, emotive and behavioural methods.

Selection criteria

In response to a question that I once asked Albert Ellis concerning selection criteria, he said the following:

> In regard to your question about placing people in individual, marital, family, or group therapy, I usually let them select the form of therapy they personally want to begin with. If one tries to push clients into a form of therapy they do not want or are afraid of, this frequently will not work out. So I generally start them where they want to start. If they begin in individual therapy and they are the kind of individuals who I think would benefit from group, I recommend this either quickly after we begin or sometime later. People who benefit most from group are generally those who are shy, retiring, and afraid to take risks. And if I can induce them to go into a group, they will likely benefit more from that than the less risky situation of individual therapy. On the other hand, a few people who want to start with group but seem to be too disorganized or too disruptive, are recommended for individual sessions until they become sufficiently organized to benefit from a group.
>
> Most people who come for marital or family therapy actually come alone and I frequently have a few sessions with them and then strongly recommend their mates also be included. On the other hand, some people who come together are not able to benefit from joint sessions, since they mainly argue during these sessions and we get nowhere. Therefore sometimes I recommend that they have individual sessions in addition to or instead of the conjoint sessions. There are many factors, some of them unique, which would induce me to recommend that people have individual rather than joint sessions. For example, one of the partners in a marriage may seem to be having an affair on the side and will not be able to talk about this in conjoint sessions and therefore I would try and see this partner individually. Or one of the partners may very much want to continue with the marriage while the other very much wants to stop it. Again, I would then recommend they be seen individually. I usually try to see the people I see in conjoint sessions at least for one or a few individual sessions to discover if there are things they will say during the individual sessions that they would refuse to bring out during the conjoint sessions.
>
> On the whole, however, I am usually able to go along with the basic desire of any clients who want individual, marital, family or group psychotherapy. It is only in relatively few cases that I talk them into taking a form of therapy they are at first loath to try. (Ellis in Dryden, 1984: 14–15).

While I cannot say whether or not other REBT therapists would agree with Ellis on these points, his views do indicate the importance that REBT theory places on individual choice.

Within individual therapy, it is important to distinguish between those who may benefit from brief REBT and those who may require a longer period of therapy. In 1995, I published an 11-session protocol for the practice of brief REBT (Dryden, 1995a). In it I outline the following seven indications that a person seeking help might benefit from brief REBT:

1 The person is able and willing to present her problems in a specific form and set goals that are concrete and achievable.
2 The person's problems are of the type that can be dealt with in 11 sessions.

3   The person is able and willing to target two problems that she wants to work on during therapy.
4   The person has understood the ABCDEs[2] of REBT and has indicated that this way of conceptualizing and dealing with her problems makes sense and is potentially helpful to her.
5   The person has understood the therapist's tasks and her own tasks in brief REBT, has indicated that REBT seems potentially useful to her and is willing to carry out her tasks.
6   The person's level of functioning in her everyday life is sufficiently high to enable her to carry out her tasks both inside and outside therapy sessions.
7   There is early evidence that a good working bond can be developed between the therapist and the person seeking help.

The more a person meets such inclusive criteria, the more suitable she is for brief REBT.

On the other hand if one or more of the following six contra-indications for brief REBT are present, it should not be offered as a treatment modality:

1   The person is antagonistic to the REBT view of psychological disturbance and its remediation.
2   The person disagrees with the therapeutic tasks that REBT outlines for both therapist and client.
    [These two points are contra-indications for REBT (whether brief or longer term) as a treatment modality and the person should be referred to a different therapeutic approach that matches her views on these two issues.]
3   The person is unable to carry out the tasks of a client in brief REBT.
4   The person is at present seriously disturbed and has a long history of such disturbance.
    [The above two points do not mean that the person is not a good candidate for longer-term REBT.]
5   The person seeking help and the therapist are clearly a poor therapeutic match.
    [In this case referral to a different REBT therapist is in order. Brief REBT cannot yet be ruled out.]
6   The person's problems are vague and cannot be specified even with therapist's help.
    [While in this case the person is clearly not suitable for brief REBT, she may be suitable for longer-term REBT if she can be helped to be more concrete. If she cannot, then REBT may not be helpful for her.]

It should be stressed that Ellis's and my views on selection criteria are only suggestions and need to be tested empirically before firm guidelines can be issued on selection criteria for REBT in general and as an approach to individual therapy in particular.

Qualities of effective therapists

Unfortunately, no research studies have been carried out to determine the personal qualities of effective rational emotive behaviour therapists. REBT theory does, however, put forward a number of hypotheses on this topic (Ellis, 1978), but it is important to regard these as both tentative and awaiting empirical study.

Since REBT is a fairly structured form of therapy, its effective practitioners are usually comfortable with structure, but flexible enough to work in a less structured manner when the situation arises.

REBT practitioners tend to be intellectually, cognitively or philosophically inclined and are attracted to REBT because the approach provides them with opportunities to fully express this tendency.

Ellis argues that REBT should often be conducted in a strong active-directive manner; thus, effective REBT practitioners are usually comfortable operating in this mode. Nevertheless, they have the flexibility to modify their interpersonal style with clients so that they provide the optimum conditions to facilitate client change.

REBT emphasizes that it is important for clients to put their therapy-derived insights into practice in their everyday lives. As a result, effective practitioners of REBT are usually comfortable with behavioural instruction and teaching and with providing the active prompting that clients often require if they are to follow through on homework assignments.

Effective rational emotive behaviour therapists tend to have little fear of failure themselves. Their personal worth is not invested in their clients' improvement. They do not need their clients' love and/or approval and are so not afraid of taking calculated risks if therapeutic impasses occur. They tend to accept both themselves and their clients as fallible human beings and are tolerant of their own mistakes and the irresponsible acts of their clients. They tend to have, or persistently work towards acquiring, a philosophy of high frustration tolerance, and do not get discouraged when clients improve at a slower rate than they desire. Effective practitioners tend to score highly on most of the criteria of positive mental health outlined earlier in this chapter and serve as healthy role models for their clients.

REBT strives to be scientific, empirical, anti-absolutistic and undevout in its approach to people's selecting and achieving their own goals (Ellis, 1978). Effective practitioners of REBT tend to show similar traits and are definitely not mystical, anti-intellectual and magical in their beliefs.

REBT advocates the use of techniques in a number of different modalities (cognitive, imagery, emotive, behavioural and interpersonal). Its effective practitioners are comfortable with a multi-modal approach to treatment and tend not to be people who like to stick rigidly to any one modality.

Finally, Ellis (1978) notes that some rational emotive behaviour therapists often modify the preferred practice of REBT according to their own natural personality characteristics. For example, some practise REBT in a slow-moving passive manner, do little disputing and focus therapy on the relationship between them and their clients. Whether such modification of the preferred practice of REBT is effective is a question awaiting empirical enquiry.

Therapeutic relationship and style

Taking their lead from Ellis (1979d), most rational emotive therapists tend to adopt an active-directive style in therapy. They are active in directing their clients' attention to the cognitive determinants of their emotional and behavioural problems. While they often adopt a collaborative style of interaction with clients who are relatively non-disturbed and non-resistant to the therapeutic process, Ellis (personal communication) argues that they ought to be forceful and persuasive with more disturbed and highly resistant clients. Whichever style they adopt, they strive to show that they unconditionally accept their clients as fallible human beings and to be empathic and genuine in the therapeutic encounter.

They strive to establish the same 'core conditions' as their person-centred colleagues, albeit in a different style (see Chapter 6, by Thorne). They, however, do not regard such 'core conditions' as necessary and sufficient for therapeutic change to occur. Rather, they regard them as often desirable for the presence of such change. While research in the more relationship-oriented aspects of REBT is sparse, DiGiuseppe et al. (1993) did find in one study that REBT therapists were rated highly on the core conditions by their clients.

Ellis (in Dryden, 1985) has argued that it is important for REBT therapists not to be unduly warm towards their clients, since he believes that this is counter-productive from a long-term perspective, in that it may inappropriately reinforce clients' approval and dependency needs. However, other REBT therapists do try to develop a warm relationship with their clients. Consistent with this, DiGiuseppe et al. (1993) found that Ellis was rated as being less warm than other REBT therapists in their study.

While an active-directive style of interaction is often preferred, this is not absolutely favoured (Eschenroeder, 1979). What is important is for therapists to convey to clients that they are trustworthy and knowledgeable individuals who are prepared to commit themselves fully to the task of helping clients reach their goals. Therapists must develop the kind of relationship with clients that the latter will, according to their idiosyncratic positions, find helpful. This might mean that, with some clients, therapists emphasize their expertise and portray themselves as well-qualified individuals whose knowledge and expertise form the basis of what social psychologists call communicator credibility. Such credibility is important to the extent that certain clients will be more likely to listen to therapists if they stress these characteristics. Other clients, however, will be more likely to listen to therapists who portray themselves as likeable individuals. In such cases, therapists might de-emphasize their expertise but emphasize their humanity by being prepared to disclose certain aspects of their lives which are both relevant to clients' problems and which stress liking as a powerful source of communicator credibility.

Many years ago, I saw two clients on the same day with whom I emphasized different aspects of communicator credibility. I decided to interact with Jim, a 30-year-old bricklayer, in a casual, 'laid-back' style. I encouraged him to use my first name and was prepared to disclose some personal details because I believed, from what he had told me in an assessment interview, that he strongly disliked 'stuffy mind doctors who treat me as another case rather than as a human being'. However, in the next hour with Jane, a 42-year-old unmarried fashion editor, I portrayed myself as 'Dr Dryden' and stressed my long training and qualifications because she had indicated, again in an assessment interview, that she strongly disliked therapists who were too warm and friendly towards her; she wanted a therapist who 'knew what he was doing'. REBT therapists should ideally be flexible with regard to changing their style of interaction with different clients. They should preferably come to a therapeutic decision about what style of interaction is going to be helpful in both the short and long term with a particular client. Furthermore, they need to recognize that the style of interaction that they adopt may in fact be counterproductive (Beutler, 1979); for instance, they should be wary of adopting an overly friendly style of interaction with 'histrionic' clients, or an overly directive style with clients whose sense of autonomy is easily threatened. No matter what style of interaction REBT therapists may adopt with individual clients, the former should be concerned, genuine and empathic in the therapeutic encounter.

Major therapeutic strategies and techniques

The primary purpose of the major therapeutic strategies and techniques of REBT is to help clients give up their absolute philosophies and adhere to more relative ones. However, before change procedures can be used, REBT therapists need to make an adequate assessment of clients' problems.

Assessment of client problems

Clients often begin to talk in therapy about the troublesome events in their lives (A) or their dysfunctional emotional and/or behavioural reactions (C) to these events. Rational emotive behaviour therapists use concrete examples of A and C to help clients identify their irrational beliefs at B in the ABC model. In the assessment stage, therapists particularly look to assess whether clients are making themselves disturbed about their original disturbances, as described earlier in this chapter.

Cognitive change techniques

Here both verbal and imagery methods are used to dispute clients' irrational beliefs. Verbal disputing involves three sub-categories. First, therapists can help clients to *discriminate* clearly between their rational and irrational beliefs. Then, while *debating*, therapists can ask clients a number of Socratic-type questions about their irrational beliefs: for example, 'Where is the evidence that you must. . .?' Finally, *defining* helps clients to make increasingly accurate definitions in their private and public language. These verbal disputing methods can also be used to help correct their faulty inferences (Beck et al., 1979).

To reinforce the rational philosophy clients can be given books to read (bibliotherapy); self-help books often used in conjunction with REBT include *A Guide to Rational Living* by Ellis and Harper (1997); *Ten Steps to Positive Living* (Dryden, 1994) and *Overcoming Anger* (Dryden, 1996). They can also employ written rational self-statements which they can refer to at various times;

and they can use REBT with others – a technique which gives clients practice at thinking through arguments in favour of rational beliefs.

Written homework, in forms such as those presented in Dryden (1995a; 1995b), is another major cognitive technique used in REBT, as is rational emotive imagery (REI). REI is the major imagery technique used in REBT. Here clients get practice at changing their unhealthy negative emotions to healthy ones (C) while keenly imagining the negative event at A; what they are in fact doing is getting practice at changing their underlying philosophy at B. Some cognitive techniques (like REI) are particularly designed to help clients move from 'intellectual' insight (i.e. a weak conviction that their irrational beliefs are irrational and their rational beliefs are rational) to 'emotional' insight (a strong conviction in those same points) (Ellis, 1963). Others included in this category are a range of rational/ irrational dialogue techniques described in Dryden, 1995a.

Emotive-evocative change techniques

Such techniques are quite vivid and evocative in nature, but are still designed to dispute clients' irrational beliefs. Rational emotive behaviour therapists uncondi-tionally accept their clients as fallible human beings even when they act poorly or obnoxiously: they thus act as a good role model for clients. In this they judiciously employ self-disclosure, openly admitting that they make errors, act badly, etc., but that they can nevertheless accept themselves. Therapists employ humour at times in the therapeutic process, believing that clients can be helped by not taking themselves and their problems too seriously; such humour is directed at aspects of clients' behaviour, never at clients themselves.

Clients are often encouraged to do shame-attacking exercises in which they practise their new philosophies of discomfort tolerance and self-acceptance while doing something 'shameful' but not harmful to themselves or others: examples might include asking for chocolate in a hardware shop, and wearing odd shoes for a day. Repeating rational self-statements in a passionate manner is often employed in conjunction with shame-attacking exercises, and also at other times.

Behaviour change techniques

Rational emotive behaviour therapists can employ the whole range of currently used behavioural techniques (see Chapter 13); however, they prefer *in vivo* (in the situation) rather than imaginal desensitization. Ellis (1979d) favours the use of *in vivo* desensitization in its 'full exposure' rather than its gradual form, because it offers clients greater opportunities to change profoundly their ego and discomfort disturbance-creating philosophies. This highlights the fact that behavioural methods are used primarily to effect cognitive changes. Careful negotiation concerning homework assignments, where clients aim to put into practice what they have learned in therapy, is advocated, and it should be realized that clients will not always opt for full-exposure, *in vivo* homework. Other behavioural methods often used in REBT include: (a) 'stay-in-there' activities (Grieger and Boyd, 1980) which help clients to remain in an uncomfortable situation for a period while tolerating feelings of chronic discomfort; (b) anti-procrastination exercises which are designed to help clients start tasks earlier rather than later, thus behaviourally disputing their dire need for comfort; (c) skill-training methods, which equip clients with certain key skills in which they are lacking (social skills and assertiveness training are often employed, but usually after important cognitive changes have been effected); (d) self-reward and self-penalization (but not, of course, self-depreciation!) which can also be used to encourage clients to use behaviour change methods.

These are the major treatment techniques, but rational emotive behaviour therapists are flexible and creative in the methods they employ, tailoring therapy to meet the client's idiosyncratic position. A fuller description of these and other REBT treatment techniques is to be found in Dryden and Neenan (1995).

The change process in therapy

Rational emotive behaviour therapists are quite ambitious in setting as their major therapeutic goal helping clients to effect what Ellis often calls a 'profound philosophic change'. This primarily involves clients surrendering their 'demanding' philosophy and replacing it with a 'desiring' philosophy. In striving to achieve these changes in philosophy, such clients are helped in therapy to:

(a) adhere to the idea that they manufacture and continue to manufacture their own psychological disturbance;
(b) acknowledge fully that they have the ability to change such disturbance to a significant degree;
(c) understand that their psychological disturbance is determined mainly by irrational beliefs;
(d) identify such irrational beliefs when they disturb themselves and distinguish these from rational beliefs;
(e) dispute such beliefs using the logico-empirical methods of science and replace these with their rational alternatives (more specifically, such clients work towards unconditional self-acceptance and raising their frustration tolerance);
(f) reinforce such cognitive learning by persistently working hard in employing emotive and behavioural methods. Such clients choose to tolerate the discomfort that this may well involve because they recognize that without acting on newly acquired insights, change will probably not be maintained;
(g) acknowledge that as humans they will probably have difficulty in effecting a profound philosophic change and will tend to backslide. Taking such factors into account, such clients re-employ and continually practise REBT's multi-modal methods for the rest of their lives. In doing so, they learn to experiment and find the methods that work especially well for them. They specifically recognize that forceful and dramatic methods are powerful ways of facilitating philosophic change and readily implement these, particularly at times when they experience difficulty in changing. (Ellis, 1979e)

In helping clients achieve such profound change, effective REBT therapists are unswerving in their unconditional acceptance of their clients. They realize that the achievement of profound philosophic change is an extraordinarily difficult task, and one which frequently involves many setbacks. Consequently, while tolerating their own feelings of discomfort they dedicate themselves to becoming a persistent and effective change agent. They (a) identify and work to overcome their clients' resistances (Ellis, 1985); (b) interpret and challenge the many defences that their clients erect against such change; (c) continually encourage, persuade and cajole their clients to keep persisting at the hard work of changing themselves; and (d) generally experiment with a wide variety of methods and styles to determine which work best for individual clients.

Rational emotive behaviour therapists acknowledge that not all clients can achieve such far-reaching philosophic change. This knowledge is usually gained from clients' responses to the therapeutic process. When deciding to settle for less ambitious outcome goals, REBT practitioners limit themselves to help clients effect situationally based philosophic change; correct distorted inferences (Beck et al., 1979); and effect behavioural changes so that they can improve negatively perceived life events. Profound philosophic change would, of course, incorporate these three modes of change.

Limitations of the approach

I have been practising REBT now for almost 25 years in a variety of settings and I have seen a wide range of moderately to severely disturbed individuals who were deemed to be able to benefit from weekly counselling or psychotherapy. While I do not have any hard data to substantiate the point, I have found rational emotive behaviour therapy to be a highly effective method of individual psychotherapy with a wide range of client problems.

However, I have of course had my therapeutic failures, and I would like to outline some of the factors that in my opinion have accounted for these. I will use Bordin's (1979) useful concept of the therapeutic working alliance as a framework.

Goals

I have generally been unsuccessful with clients who have devoutly clung to goals where changes in other people were desired. (I have also failed to involve these others in therapy.) I have not been able to show or to persuade these clients that they make themselves emotionally disturbed and that they are advised to work to change themselves before attempting to negotiate changes in their relationships with others. It is the devoutness of their beliefs which seems to me to be the problem here.

Bonds

Unlike the majority of therapists of my acquaintance, I do not regard the relationship between therapist and client to be the *sine qua non* of effective therapy. I strive to accept my clients as fallible human beings and am prepared to work concertedly to help them overcome their problems, but do not endeavour to form very close, warm relationships with them. In the main, my clients do not appear to want such a relationship with me (preferring to become close and intimate with their significant others). However, occasionally I get clients who do wish to become (non-sexually) intimate with me. Some of these clients (who devoutly believe they need my love) leave therapy disappointed after I have failed either to get them to give up their dire need for love or to give them what they think they need.

Tasks

As Bordin (1979) has noted, every therapeutic method requires clients to fulfil various tasks if therapy is to be successful. I outlined what these tasks are with respect to REBT earlier in this chapter. In my experience, clients who are diligent in performing these tasks generally have a positive therapeutic outcome with REBT, while those who steadfastly refuse to work towards helping themselves outside therapy generally do less well or are therapeutic failures.

It may of course be that I am practising REBT ineptly and that these failures are due to my poor skills rather than any other factor. Ellis (1983b), however, has published some interesting data which tend to corroborate my own therapeutic experiences. He chose 50 of his clients who were seen in individual and/or group REBT and were rated by him, and where appropriate by his associate group therapist, as 'failures'. In some ways, this group consisted of fairly ideal REBT clients in that they were individuals of

> [1] above average or of superior intelligence (in my judgement and that of their other group therapist); (2) who seemed really to understand RET and who were often effective (especially in group therapy) in helping others to learn and use it; (3) who in some ways made therapeutic progress and felt that they benefited by having RET but who still retained one or more serious presenting symptoms, such as severe depression, acute anxiety, overwhelming hostility, or extreme lack of self-discipline; and (4) who had at least one year of individual and/or group RET sessions, and sometimes considerably more. (Ellis, 1983b: 160)

This group was compared to clients who were selected on the same four criteria but who seemed to benefit greatly from REBT. While a complete account of this study – which, of course, has its methodological flaws – can be found in Ellis (1983b), the following results are most pertinent:

> 1. In its cognitive aspects, RET. . .emphasizes the persistent use of reason, logic, and the scientific method to uproot clients' irrational beliefs. Consequently, it ideally requires intelligence, concentration, and high-level, consistent cognitive self-disputation and self-persuasion. These therapeutic behaviours would tend to be disrupted or blocked by extreme disturbance, by lack of organization, by grandiosity, by organic disruption, and by refusal to do RET-type disputing or irrational ideas. All these characteristics proved to be present in significantly more failures than in those clients who responded favourably to RET.

2. RET also, to be quite successful, involves clients' forcefully and emotively changing their beliefs and actions, and their being stubbornly determined to accept responsibility for their own inappropriate feelings and to vigorously work at changing these feelings (Ellis and Abrahms, 1978). But the failure clients in this study were significantly more angry than those who responded well to RET; more of them were severely depressed and inactive, they were more often grandiose, and they were more frequently stubbornly resistant and rebellious. All these characteristics would presumably tend to interfere with the kind of emotive processes and changes that RET espouses.

3. RET strongly advocates that clients, in order to improve, do in vivo activity homework assignments, deliberately force themselves to engage in many painful activities until they become familiar and unpainful, and notably work and practice its multimodal techniques. But the group of clients who signally failed in this study showed abysmally low frustration tolerance, had serious behavioral addictions, led disorganized lives, refrained from doing their activity homework assignments, were more frequently psychotic and generally refused to work at therapy. All these characteristics, which were found significantly more frequently than were found in the clients who responded quite well to RET, would tend to interfere with the behavioural methods of RET. (Ellis, 1983b: 165)

It appears from the above analysis that the old adage of psychotherapy applies to REBT: that clients who could most use therapy are precisely those individuals whose disturbance interferes with their benefiting from it. At present, it is not known whether clients who 'fail' with REBT are likely to benefit more from other therapies. Finally, as discussed by other contributors to this book, the practice of REBT is limited by the poor skills of the REBT practitioner.

As I have often said: 'REBT is easy to practise poorly.' There is no substitute, then, for proper training and supervision in the approach.

Case example

The client

Janice is a 36-year-old single woman who works as a health professional. She was referred to me by her GP whom she had consulted about feelings of depression. She had become depressed after the end of a two-year love relationship ('I was dumped unceremoniously without warning') and not getting a promised promotion at work.

Janice is the only child of two 'loving' parents, who are both alive. Her mother is well, but her father has muscular sclerosis and is wheelchair bound. Janice lives alone in a flat. She sees her parents three times a week to help her mother care for her father. She is very close to her parents. Janice says that she has always had a tendency towards depression, for which she sought counselling unsuccessfully three years earlier. She is adamant that she won't take drugs. She always, she says, 'gets dumped' two or three years into a relationship and has come to believe that she will never marry although she wants to. Consequently, she has put more of her energies into her job which she loves and says that she felt 'devastated' when she was passed over for promotion after 'virtually being promised it' by her supervisor.

The therapy

In the first session, I did the following:

1 I allowed Janice an opportunity to talk about her problems in her own way and responded to her so that she could see that I understood her from her frame of reference.
2 I gave Janice a brief outline about REBT, what she could expect from me and what I expected from her. In this regard I made clear that like other cognitive-behaviour therapies, clients get the most from REBT when they commit themselves to a regular and extended period of self-help between sessions. Janice was particularly interested in this aspect of REBT since her major criticism of her previous counselling was that the counsellor was too passive and didn't suggest anything practical she could do to help herself.
3 I then helped Janice to specify her problems and asked her to set goals for each of these problems.

Her problem/goal list consisted of two items:

- *Problem 1*: When a love partner ends our relationship, I become depressed. To compensate for these feelings I overeat and smoke too much.
- *Goal 1*: When a love partner ends our relationship I want to be appropriately sad rather than depressed and deal with this loss without relying on food and cigarettes to cope.
- *Problem 2*: When I think I have been let down, I feel very hurt and either attack the person angrily or I sulk.
- *Goal 2*: When I think that I have been let down, I want to feel appropriately sorrowful or disappointed rather than hurt. I also want to communicate my feelings to the other person in a firm and assertive manner rather than angrily attacking them or sulking.

Based on these goals and my view that Janice would work quite hard in therapy, I suggested that we meet for 11 sessions in total. In short, I was offering her my standard 11-session brief therapy contract since Janice met the criteria for brief individual REBT listed on pp. 358–9 (see Dryden, 1995a for a thorough exposition of brief REBT with individuals).

Conceptualization of Janice's problems

In REBT, we construct an understanding of a client's problems by assessing specific examples of them. In the beginning phase of REBT with Janice I did this, and the following irrational beliefs were revealed as they related to her target unhealthy negative emotions:

Depression
- 'My boyfriend must not leave me and if he does, this proves that I am not good enough' (ego disturbance).
  [This irrational belief led not only to Janice feeling depressed but also to clinging, jealousy-related behaviour which resulted in her boyfriend of the moment distancing himself from her and eventually ending the relationship.]
- 'I must have a man in my life and if I don't then I am worthless and life has no meaning' (ego and discomfort disturbance).
  [This irrational belief led not only to Janice feeling depressed but also to her desperately seeking a new boyfriend, often choosing men who make unsuitable partners.]

Hurt
- 'My boyfriend of the moment must treat me as if I am special and if he doesn't, it's terrible and I can't bear it' (discomfort disturbance).
  [This irrational belief led Janice to feel hurt and either attacking her partner aggressively or withdrawing from him sulkily.]
- 'People must keep their promises to me and it's terrible when they don't. I don't deserve to be treated so shabbily. Poor me!' [discomfort disturbance]
  [This irrational belief led to Janice feeling self-pity/hurt and complaining endlessly about such injustices to her long-suffering and diminishing group of friends.]

Goals of therapy

My basic therapeutic goal was to help Janice achieve her goals, as stated above. In order to achieve this primary goal, I also set myself several secondary or mediating goals:

(a) To teach Janice REBT's ABC model and to apply it to specific examples of her problems.
(b) To help Janice to see the connection between her unhealthy negative emotions of hurt and depression, the self-defeating behaviour that was associated with these feelings and the irrational beliefs that underpinned her feelings and behaviour.
(c) To help her dispute these irrational beliefs and to replace them with a set of healthy rational beliefs.
(d) To encourage Janice to practise these rational beliefs while acting in self-enhancing ways.
(e) To identify and troubleshoot any obstacles to Janice achieving her goals along the way.

Therapeutic relationship and style

REBT therapists strive to accept their clients as fallible human beings while focusing on the latter's problems in an active-directive manner. This characterized my therapeutic style with Janice. Furthermore, my early interactions with her suggested that she would respond better to a formal therapeutic style than to an informal one. Our relationship could be described as businesslike and formal where humour and counsellor self-disclosure were kept to a minimum. As it transpired, we had no reason to focus on our relationship as a microcosm of Janice's problems and, indeed, our relationship was never a subject for direct therapeutic exploration.

Major therapeutic strategies and techniques

During therapy I used most of REBT's major treatment techniques. For example, I made heavy use of bibliotherapy and particularly my client work-book, *Reason to Change* (Dryden, 2001), in which I teach clients the skills of REBT so that they can use them for themselves. This emphasis on self-help particularly suited Janice and I quickly adopted the role of consultant, going over her written homework and suggesting modifications where necessary. Janice benefited especially from my various zigzag techniques where she stated her rational beliefs, attacked these with irrational arguments and forcefully responded to these attacks on paper and on audiotape (see Dryden, 2001). She was also quite adept at developing assertive responses to people with whom she would have sulked or whom she would have verbally attacked. Janice was fond of role-play so we role-played relevant scenarios from her past so that she could re-live them with a more constructive ending.

The change process

My therapy with Janice got off to a good start because REBT seemed to fit quite well with her expectations for a therapy where her counsellor actively interacted with her and suggested practical things that she could do between sessions. Janice was something of a model REBT client. She assiduously did her homework and sometimes had to be restrained from working 'too hard' on her therapy.

She was keen to use her newly developed skills and successfully confronted her supervisor, with the result that she got a pay increase (but not the promotion, which went to another candidate). She was unable during therapy to use her REBT skills in a love relationship because she was being more discriminating about who she went out with. She said she no longer needed a relationship in order to be happy.

We finished therapy after 9 rather than 11 sessions since Janice considered that she was well on the way to meeting her therapeutic goals and wanted to see how she would manage on her own. I was not surprised by this since Janice showed strong autonomous traits where self-help is seen as a veritable virtue. I agreed with this and reminded Janice that she could always return for an extra 'consultation' session should she want one.

I telephoned Janice six months after our last session because I wanted to report on her progress for this write-up. She said that she has had no periods of depression and while she still makes herself feel hurt when others in her opinion treat her badly, she quickly rehearses her rational belief and asserts herself on such occasions. She said that she has just started going out with a 'nice guy' and was using the audiotape zigzag method to strengthen her rational beliefs about not being treated as special should that happen.

She is more optimistic about her chances of finding love and having a family. Time will tell, but she knows that she can come back for booster sessions should she request them.

Notes

1 Where A stands for Activating event, B for Belief and C for the emotional/behavioural Consequences of holding that belief.
2 Where A stands for Activating event, B for Belief, C for the emotional/behavioural Consequences of holding that belief, D for Disputing irrational beliefs and E for the Effects of disputing.

References

Beck, A.T., Rush, A.J., Shaw, B.F. and Emery, G. (1979) *Cognitive Therapy of Depression*. New York: Guilford Press.
Beutler, L.E. (1979) 'Towards specific psychological therapies for specific conditions', *Journal of Consulting and Clinical Psychology*, 47: 882–97.
Bordin, E.S. (1979) 'The generalizability of the psychoanalytic concept of the working alliance', *Psychotherapy. Theory, Research and Practice*, 16: 252–60.
DiGiuseppe, R., Leaf, R. and Lipscott, L (1993) 'The therapeutic relationship in rational-emotive therapy: some preliminary data', *Journal of Rational-Emotive and Cognitive-Behavior Therapy*, 11(4): 223–33.
Dryden, W. (ed.) (1984) *Individual Therapy in Britain*. London. Harper & Row.
Dryden, W. (1985) *Therapists' Dilemmas*. London: Harper & Row.
Dryden, W. (1994) *Ten Steps to Positive Living*. London: Sheldon.
Dryden, W. (1995a) *Brief Rational Emotive Behaviour Therapy*. Chichester: John Wiley.
Dryden, W. (1995b) *Preparing for Client Change in Rational Emotive Behaviour Therapy*. London: Whurr.
Dryden, W. (1996) *Overcoming Anger: When Anger Helps and When it Hurts*. London: Sheldon Press.
Dryden, W. (2001) *Reason to Change: A Rational Emotive Behaviour Therapy (REBT) Workbook*. London: Brunner-Routledge.
Dryden, W. and Neenan, M. (1995) *Dictionary of Rational Emotive Behaviour Therapy*. London: Whurr.
Ellis, A. (1955a) 'New approaches to psychotherapy techniques', *Journal of Clinical Psychology* (Brandon, Vermont).
Ellis, A. (1955b) 'Psychotherapy techniques for use with psychotics', *American Journal of Psychotherapy*, 9: 425–76.
Ellis, A. (1958) 'Rational psychotherapy', *Journal of General Psychology*, 59: 35–49.
Ellis, A. (1962) *Reason and Emotion in Psychotherapy*. Secaucus, NJ: Lyle Stuart.
Ellis, A. (1963) 'Toward a more precise definition of "emotional" and "intellectual" insight', *Psychological Reports*, 13: 125–6.
Ellis, A. (1973) 'Psychotherapy without tears', in A. Burton and Associates, *Twelve Therapists: How They Live and Actualize Themselves*. San Francisco: Jossey-Bass.
Ellis, A. (1976) 'The biological basis of human irrationality', *Journal of Individual Psychology*, 32: 145–68.
Ellis, A. (1978) 'Personality characteristics of rational-emotive therapists and other kinds of therapists', *Psychotherapy. Theory, Research and Practice*, 15: 329–32.
Ellis, A. (1979a) 'Toward a new theory of personality', in A. Ellis and J.M. Whiteley (eds), *Theoretical and Empirical Foundations of Rational-Emotive Therapy*. Monterey, CA. Brooks/Cole.

Ellis, A. (1979b) 'The theory of rational-emotive therapy', in A. Ellis and J.M. Whiteley (eds), *Theoretical and Empirical Foundations of Rational-Emotive Therapy*. Monterey, CA: Brooks/ Cole.

Ellis, A. (1979c) 'The rational-emotive approach to counseling', in H.M. Burks Jr and B. Stefflre (eds), *Theories of Counseling*. New York: McGraw-Hill.

Ellis, A. (1979d) 'The practice of rational-emotive therapy', in A. Ellis and J.M. Whiteley (eds), *Theoretical and Empirical Foundations of Rational-Emotive Therapy*. Monterey, CA: Brooks/ Cole.

Ellis, A. (1979e) 'The issue of force and energy in behavioral change', *Journal of Contemporary Psychotherapy*, 10(4): 83–97.

Ellis, A (1982) 'The treatment of alcohol and drug abuse: a rational-emotive approach', *Rational Living*, 17(2): 15–24.

Ellis, A. (1983a) *The Case against Religiosity*. New York: Albert Ellis Institute for Rational Emotive Behavior Therapy.

Ellis, A. (1983b) 'Failures in rational-emotive therapy', in E.B. Foa and P.M.G. Emmelkamp (eds), *Failures in Behavior Therapy*. New York: Wiley.

Ellis, A. (1985) *Overcoming Resistance*. New York: Springer.

Ellis, A. (1989) 'Ineffective consumerism in the cognitive-behavioural therapies and in general psychotherapy', in W. Dryden and P. Trower (eds), *Cognitive Psychotherapy: Stasis and Change*. London: Cassell.

Ellis, A. (1994) *Reason and Emotion in Psychotherapy*, revised and updated edition. New York: Birch Lane Press.

Ellis, A. and Abrahms, E. (1978) *Brief Psychotherapy in Medical and Health Practice*. New York: Springer.

Ellis, A. and Harper, R.A. (1997) *A Guide to Rational Living*, 3rd edn. North Hollywood, CA: Wilshire.

Eschenroeder, C. (1979) 'Different therapeutic styles in rational-emotive therapy', *Rational Living*, 14(1): 3–7.

Grieger, R. and Boyd, J. (1980) *Rational-Emotive Therapy: A Skills-Based Approach*. New York: Van Nostrand Reinhold.

Herzberg, A. (1945) *Active Psychotherapy*. New York: Grune & Stratton.

Jones, R.A. (1977) *Self-Fulfilling Prophecies: Social, Psychological and Physiological Effects of Expectancies*. Hillsdale, NJ: Lawrence Erlbaum.

Salter, A. (1949) *Conditioned Reflex Therapy*. New York: Creative Age.

Wachtel, P.L. (1977) *Psychoanalysis and Behavior Therapy. Toward an Integration*. New York: Basic Books.

Werner, E.E. and Smith, R.S. (1982) *Vulnerable but Invincible: A Study of Resilient Children*. New York: McGraw-Hill.

Wessler, R.A. (1978) 'The neurotic paradox: a rational-emotive view', *Rational Living*, 13(1): 9–12.

Wolpe, J. (1958) *Psychotherapy by Reciprocal Inhibition*. Stanford, CA: Stanford University Press.

Suggested further reading

Dryden, W. (2001) *Reason to Change: A Rational Emotive Behaviour Therapy (REBT) Workbook*. London: Brunner-Routledge.

Dryden, W. and Neenan, M. (1995) *Dictionary of Rational Emotive Behaviour Therapy*. London: Whurr.

Ellis, A. (1994) *Reason and Emotion in Psychotherapy*, revised and updated edition. New York: Birch Lane Press.

Walen, S., DiGiuseppe, R. and Dryden, W. (1992) *A Practitioner's Guide to Rational-Emotive Therapy*, 2nd edn. New York: Oxford University Press.

Yankura, J. and Dryden, W. (1994) *Albert Ellis*. London: Sage.

15 Methods, Outcomes and Processes in the Psychological Therapies across Four Successive Research Generations

Michael Barkham

The preceding chapters have documented a wide range of theoretical approaches to the practice of individual psychotherapy. Whilst interest in psychotherapy as a profession has never been greater, there exists a considerable gap between practice and research which is long-standing and has been repeatedly documented in the psychotherapy literature (e.g., Barlow et al.,1984; Talley et al., 1994). Frustration at this gap arises because one of the central roles of psychotherapy research is to inform practice. However, it has tended to be the case that clinical insights have guided research. This situation is largely attributable to researchers and clinicians having different priorities and different paradigms within which they work. Research, as reported in the major international journals, tends to employ large-scale studies and focus on differences between group means representing the 'average' client. In contrast, practitioners work with individual clients and it is often difficult for practitioners to see the relevance of research findings to the clients seen in their practices. Hence, researchers and practitioners carry out their respective functions using different paradigms which, in themselves, define different approaches or methods to investigate the subject matter.

Set against this context of differing methods are the two broad domains or categories covered by psychotherapy research activity: outcome and process. Outcome research comprises making evaluative statements about the efficacy or effectiveness of particular interventions. Process research comprises attempts to explain why improvement or deterioration occurs. The knowledge that a particular therapy is effective together with an understanding of what makes it effective can then inform practitioners' decisions ranging from planning and implementing an effective psychotherapy service delivery system to informing the moment-to-moment interventions by therapists with individual clients. Attempts have been made to identify the practical implications of findings from psychotherapy research in the domains of outcome research (e.g. Whiston and Sexton, 1993) and process research (e.g. Dryden, 1996).

It is important at the outset to appreciate that, much like psychotherapeutic practice, the quality of process and outcome research varies considerably. In the same way that practitioners aim to learn and integrate into their practice those ingredients which enhance the effectiveness of psychotherapy (i.e. 'good practice'), so researchers seek to adopt those methods and procedures which lead to good research. Increasingly, guidelines are being disseminated which aim to enhance the implementation and reporting of research activity (e.g. Oxman and Guyatt, 1988; Elliott et al., 1999). However, the foundations for high-quality psychotherapy research rests upon 'method'. The skill of the psychotherapy researcher can be summarized by a five-stage model using the acronym DIARY: design, implementation, analysis, reporting, and yield. *Design* requires a substantive knowledge base of the range of possible designs and being able to select or generate one that is best suited to address the question being asked. *Implementation* requires the ability and resources to carry out the selected design. *Analysis* requires considerable knowledge and understanding of the multiple ways in which data can be analysed and, importantly, selecting procedures appropriate to the adopted design. *Reporting* – which also includes interpretation – focuses on conveying the results in a fair way and identifying the strengths and limitations of the work. *Yield* focuses on the utility of the research – how the findings inform practice. All these skills and activities make up the activity of research. Accordingly, it is not the result of any study *per se* which is important but the foundations upon which any research is built.

Texts which incorporate methodological issues include Bergin and Garfield's *Handbook of Psychotherapy and Behavior Change* (4th edition, 1994b) which, in addition to reviewing specific content domains, contains chapters on methodology (Kazdin, 1994) and process and outcome measurement (Lambert and Hill, 1994). Kendall and colleagues (1999a) also provide a useful chapter on therapy outcome research methods. Lambert's *Handbook of Psychotherapy and Behavior Change* (5th edition, in press) contains chapters on process and outcome measurement (Lambert and Hill, in press), outcomes (Lambert and Ogles, in press) and process (Orlinsky, in press). Greenberg and Pinsoff (1986) have produced a text on process research and, in addition, Hill (1991) has summarized a range of methodological issues relating to process research as well as a collection of work on methods and findings relating to process research (Hill, 2001). A key text emanating from Britain is Roth and Fonagy's *What Works for Whom? A Critical Review of Psychotherapy Research* (1996, in press). In terms of designing and implementing research activity there is Aveline and Shapiro's *Research Foundations for Psychotherapy Practice* (1995) together with two excellent and complementary texts on research methods: Barker, Pistrang and Elliott's *Research Methods in Clinical and Counselling Psychology* (1996, in press) and McLeod's *Doing Counselling Research* (1994, in press).

Against this background, the purpose of this chapter is twofold. First, to provide an overview of current international research on the psychological therapies focusing on one-to-one settings (i.e. individual therapy), and secondly, to provide a similar overview of research carried out in Britain. The framework for presenting this research is via successive research generations, each driven by a particular thematic question and each adopting different and developing research methods to address the questions. In so doing, this chapter charts the key questions that have been raised about the psychological therapies and the research yield arising from the subsequent effort over a period of half a century – 1950 to 2000.

Focusing on the time frame from 1950 to 2000 is not meant to imply that there was no research activity prior to this time. Indeed, the equivalent time span from 1900 to 1950 saw considerable activity focusing on laying down the foundations for the empirical investigation of psychotherapy and this can be termed the 'pioneering generation'. During these years, a wealth of case material was documented. For example, Freud published many accounts of psychoanalytic therapy (e.g., the 'Rat Man', 1909: Freud, 1979) using qualitative and case study methods – methods which have once again come to the fore of psychotherapy research in recent years. Increasingly, research was influenced by developing ideas about science, in particular the notions of logical positivism (testing propositions against real world observations) and operationalism (defining how a concept is to be measured). In addition, developments in the domain of technology (e.g. audio-recordings) and further refinements in issues of design and analysis (e.g. null hypothesis) paved the way for the setting up of research programmes investigating the process of psychotherapy. The work of Rogers (1942), Porter (1943a, 1943b) and Robinson (1950) all used response mode codings (i.e. coding speech into a series of intentions – question, reflection, interpretation) to carry out investigations into the process of change. Similarly, there are early reports of work into psychotherapy outcomes. For example, Huddleson (1927) provided an account of psychoneurosis in war veterans suggesting that approaching 20 per cent of patients in his sample were either 'recovered' or 'much improved' at discharge and approaching 50 per cent at follow-up (albeit some time later). Thus, both outcome and process research were actively being carried out prior to the 1950s. However, there was no clear agenda to drive research activity. By contrast, the research from the 1950s onwards progressed in response to a range of issues driven by academia, government policies, economics and demand.

Part I: Methods, outcomes and processes – international findings

The first part of this chapter presents findings from the international scientific community as a series of four successive but overlapping research generations initiated by Eysenck's (1952) landmark critique of psychotherapy. These research generations are set out briefly here and then explicated in greater detail throughout the chapter. However, although electronic searches have been used to identify relevant work, space does not permit comprehensive coverage.

Generation I research spans the period 1950s to 1970s and addresses the outcome question 'Is psychotherapy efficacious?' and the process question 'Are there objective methods for evaluating process?' Generation II research spans the period 1960s to 1980s and utilizes scientific rigour to address the outcome question 'Which psychotherapy is more effective?' and the process question 'What components are related to outcome?' Generation III research spans the period 1970s to the present and addresses the outcome question 'How can we make treatments more cost-effective?' and the process question 'How does change occur?' Generation IV research can be seen as originating in the mid-1980s and addresses the question 'How can we make outcome and process research clinically relevant to clients, practitioners and services?' The research generations as defined here should not, however, be seen to be carved in stone. Other writers have used slightly different time frames and emphases (e.g. see Russell and Orlinsky, 1996). Research addressing outcome and process domains is addressed under separate subheadings within each generation. More specific accounts of process and outcome research can be found in a number of texts: psychotherapy process research (e.g. Llewelyn and Hardy, 2001); efficacy and effectiveness in outcome research (e.g. Nathan et al., 2000); review of process and outcome issues (e.g. Kopta et al., 1999).

An outline of the research generations is presented in Table 15.1. This identifies the research questions relating to outcome and process work together with some of the key issues addressed and the methods used to investigate these issues. In addition, Table 15.1 sets out landmark texts which are associated with each generation. The term 'landmark' is not being used as synonymous with 'classic'. It is more that these texts define a particular time rather than that they are timeless.

Generation I

Efficacy of psychotherapy

Although psychotherapy research was being carried out well before the 1950s (see Orlinsky and Russell, 1994), it was the publication of Eysenck's (1952) critique of the effectiveness of psychotherapy which marshalled activity leading to a generation of research focusing on the issue of the efficacy of psychotherapy. As such, the overarching theme of this generation is one of 'justification' for psychotherapy, with the central question 'Is psychotherapy efficacious?' and subsequently 'If so, how efficacious is it?' Eysenck (1952) claimed that approximately two-thirds of clients presenting with neurotic problems who received non-behavioural psychotherapy improved substantially within two years and that an equal proportion of people presenting with similar problems who had not received treatment also improved within the same time period. Bergin and Lambert (1978) made a number of observations about the way Eysenck had analysed his data. For example, they noted that the most stringent improvement percentage was used for psychotherapy while the most generous was used for calculating spontaneous remission rates. Also, differing rates could be deduced depending on the criterion used. In general, their view was that conclusions drawn from the studies used by Eysenck were suspect due to their inherent limitations (not surprising given the date when the data was collected). In looking at subsequent data, Bergin and Lambert (1978) found the rate for spontaneous remission to be 43 per cent rather than 67 per cent. Importantly, these authors also noted the finding from outcome studies that substantial change generally

Table 15.1 Summary of research generations

Research generations

	I 1950s–70s onwards Justification	II 1960s–80s onwards Specificity	III 1970s–2000 onwards Efficacy/cost-effectiveness	IV 1984–present Effectiveness/clinical significance
OUTCOME				
Time frame Theme				
Thematic question	Is psychotherapy effective?	Which psychotherapy is more effective?	How can treatments be made more (cost) effective?	How can the quality of treatment delivery be improved?
Methodologies	Control group comparisons; effect sizes; meta-analysis	Randomized control trial; factorial design; placebo group	Probit analysis; growth curves; structural modelling	Clinical significance; patient-focused research
Key issues	Efficacy; spontaneous remission	What treatment, by whom, is most effective for this individual with that specific problem, and under which set of circumstances?	Dose-response; medical offset; health economics; evidence-based medicine; empirically validated treatments; practice guidelines	User perspectives; evidence-based practice; outcomes monitoring
Landmark texts	Eysenck (1952); Bergin & Garfield (1971); Sloane et al. (1975); Waskow & Parloff (1975); Smith & Glass (1977; Smith et al., 1980)	Paul (1967); Gurman & Razin (1977); Garfield & Bergin (1978); Stiles, Shapiro & Elliott (1986); Elkin et al. (1989)	Howard et al. (1986); Garfield & Bergin (1986); Bergin & Garfield (1994b); Roth & Fonagy (1996); Department of Health (2001)	Jacobson et al. (1984); *Consumer Reports* (1995); Howard et al. (1996); Strupp et al. (1997); National Advisory Mental Health Council (1999)
PROCESS				
Thematic question	Are there objective methods for evaluating process?	What components are related to outcome?	How does change occur (via a quantitative approach)?	How does change occur (via a qualitative approach)?
Methodologies	Random sampling of sections of therapy; 'uniformity myth' assumed	Single-case methodologies; sampling 5-minute sections of therapy	Taxonomies; linking process to outcomes	Qualitative methods; narrative approach; discourse analysis; descriptive studies; theory development
Key issues	Verbal & speech behaviours	Rogerian facilitative conditions (e.g. empathy)	Therapeutic alliance; verbal response modes	Events paradigm; single case approach; qualitative methods
Landmark texts	Rogers & Dymond (1954); Whitehorn & Betz (1954); Rogers et al. (1967)	Frank (1971); Bordin (1979); Strupp (1980a–d)	Russell & Stiles (1979); Greenberg & Pinsoff (1986); Orlinsky et al. (1994)	Rice & Greenberg (1984); Hill et al., (1997); Stiles et al., (1998); Elliott et al. (1999)

occurred within the initial 8–10 sessions, considerably quicker than the two-year time frame of spontaneous remission.

The response of researchers to Eysenck's critique was to incorporate a no-treatment control group into the research design and one exemplar design of Generation I is the study by Sloane, Staples, Cristol, Yorkston and Whipple (1975). They contrasted psychodynamic with behavioural treatments, each with an average 14-session duration of treatment, with a wait-list control group. The total sample size used for the analysis was 90 clients, with 30 clients randomly assigned to each of the three treatment conditions. The setting was a university psychiatric outpatient centre in which 54 per cent of the clients were students. The design used three experienced therapists in each of the two psychotherapy treatment conditions. The results used interview-based measures and showed improvement in all three conditions but with the two active treatments being broadly similar and both superior to the wait-list condition. These gains were maintained at various follow-up intervals.

The findings from the Sloane et al. (1975) study were 'confirmed' later by the publication of the original meta-analytic study of psychotherapy carried out by Smith and Glass (1977) and elaborated upon in their book *The Benefits of Psychotherapy* (Smith et al., 1980). The book provides a considered way through the claims and counterclaims of various researchers. Smith and Glass (1977) collated 475 controlled studies across 18 differing therapy types (including placebo treatment and undifferentiated counselling). The average effect size (ES) across all studies was 0.85, indicative of a large effect for psychotherapy over no psychotherapy, indicating that the average treated person was better off than 80 per cent of non-treated people. The effect sizes ranged from small (0.14 for reality therapy) to large (2.38 for cognitive therapies other than rational-emotive therapy). The authors found little evidence for negative effects, with only 9 per cent of the measures being negative (i.e. control groups were better than treated groups). In terms of overall effectiveness, the subsequent refinements of meta-analytic procedures and greater specificity, as well as the inclusion of more recent and more accomplished studies, have not delivered substantially different results, with the ESs remaining relatively stable. A guide for interpreting between-group effect sizes is presented in Table 15.2 in which an ES of 0.2 is deemed to be small, 0.5 is medium, and 0.8 or above is large (Cohen, 1977).

In subsequent years, beyond the time frame of Generation I, many further studies have been included in meta-analytic reviews addressing the issue of the efficacy of psychotherapy. Lambert and Bergin (1994: 144) have stated: 'There is now little doubt that psychological treatments are, overall and in general, beneficial, although it remains equally true that not everyone benefits to a satisfactory degree'. Meta-analytic studies provide the most concise summary of outcome findings. For example, in the area of depression, the number of studies (N) included in the meta-analysis and the effect sizes (ES) for three major meta-analytic reports are as follows: Nietzel, Russell, Hemmings and Gretter (1987), N = 28, ES = 0.71; Robinson, Berman and Neimeyer (1990), N = 29, ES = 0.84; and Steinbrueck, Maxwell and Howard (1983), N = 56, ES = 1.22. In terms of more diverse presenting problems, Lambert and Bergin (1994) have provided a

Table 15.2   Guide to interpreting between-group effect sizes

Cohen's guidelines for interpreting effect sizes	Effect size (d)	Proportion of people in control condition who are below the mean of people in the treated condition
No effect	0.0	0.50
Small effect	0.1	0.54
	0.2	0.58
	0.3	0.62
	0.4	0.66
Medium effect	0.5	0.69
	0.6	0.73
	0.7	0.76
	0.8	0.79
Large effect	0.9	0.82
	1.0	0.84

summary table of 30 meta-analytic reviews covering a range of presenting problems and psychological interventions. Five studies (including that of Smith and Glass) are defined as 'mixed' and result in a large average ES of 0.90. The range of other studies is so diverse as not to warrant categorization. However, they show the smallest and largest ESs (excluding control conditions) to range from 0.00 (schizophrenia; Quality Assurance Project, 1984) to 1.30 (stuttering; Andrews et al., 1980). Using only those studies (N = 25) which report effect sizes, the median ES was 0.76, which is approaching a large ES. In terms of comparisons, an ES of 0.67 is obtained from nine months of instruction in reading, while the ESs for antidepressants range from 0.40 to 0.81. Thus, as Lambert and Bergin (1994) argue, there appears to be evidence that psychological interventions are as effective, if not more effective, as medication. Apparently contrary to these substantial effects, it has been claimed that psychotherapy accounts for only 10 per cent of the outcome variance. This might appear small. However, it needs to be realized that 10 per cent variance arises from a correlation of 0.32 between psychotherapy and outcome. This is appreciably greater than other established correlations in the field: for example, correlations of 0.03 for the effect of aspirin on heart attacks, and 0.07 for service in Vietnam and alcohol consumption.

In relation to the psychodynamic therapies, randomized controlled trials are more rare. However, Shefler, Dasberg and Ben-Shakhar (1995) report on a randomized controlled trial of Mann's time-limited psychotherapy (TLP) in which 33 patients were randomly assigned to one of two conditions: three-months of TLP immediately (experimental group), or delay for three months and then receive TLP (control group). Whilst the study reflects the increased wisdom acquired over time of carrying out RCTs, this design essentially belongs to Generation I research in that it is comparing an active treatment against a wait-list control. No alternative therapy was involved in order to advance arguments of specificity, although measures of specific effects which would be predicted from the model of therapy were administered. Results showed the group receiving TLP immediately to have improved significantly more at end of treatment than the control group after the same elapsed time. The effect size for the treatment vs no-treatment comparison (i.e. prior to the control group receiving therapy) was 0.99, which would be defined as a large effect size and is what would be expected when comparing an active treatment with a no-treatment condition.

An additional question which has been raised is whether psychotherapy is more efficacious than a placebo. In response, a critical point, well summarized by Lambert and Bergin, is worthy of reiteration: 'In interpreting this [placebo] research, it is important to keep in mind that failure to find incremental effects (effects beyond those attributable to common factors) for a specific therapy does not mean that psychotherapy is ineffective. Rather it means that no effect has been demonstrated beyond the effects of the common factors' (1994: 149). Lambert and Bergin provide a useful summary table of 15 meta-analytic studies whereby three two-way comparisons are made: psychotherapy vs no-treatment; placebo vs no-treatment; and psychotherapy vs placebo. The first of these comparisons produced a mean/median ES of 0.82 (very similar to that stated previously). The placebo vs no-treatment comparison produced a mean/median ES of 0.42, while the placebo vs psychotherapy comparison produced a mean/median ES of 0.48. By way of comment on the use of placebo controls, Lambert and Bergin summarize: '. . .we have concluded that the typical placebo controls used in outcome studies are so conceptually and procedurally flawed that they have essentially failed in their purpose of helping to isolate the active therapeutic ingredients. It is time to discontinue placebo controls and design studies with more meaningful comparison groups' (1994: 152).

Measuring the process of therapy

Within the domain of psychotherapy process, the major thrust of this generation focused on the question 'Can the therapy process (e.g. facilitative conditions) be measured?' The influence of Rogers was profound in Generation I's development of objective procedures for measuring events of recorded therapy sessions. His influence has been noted as deriving from his 'respect for the scientific method and dedication to the objective study of the efficacy of his methods' (Hill and Corbett, 1993: 5). Although there was a great surge of activity in pursuit of establishing the effectiveness of psychotherapy, it was largely Rogers and his students who pursued research on the process of therapy. While the earlier process work had focused on verbal response modes as indicators of therapist techniques, process measures turned to the evaluation of Rogers's facilitative conditions.

Examples of research in this early phase include the work of Rogers and Dymond (1954) who found evidence supporting the view that good outcome was associated with improvements in self-perceptions. Other research drew on the work of Whitehorn and Betz (e.g. 1954) who found, via a retrospective study of psychiatrists, that those who were successful in working with schizophrenic patients were warm and communicated with their patients in a personal manner.

Similar findings arose from the various reports of the classic study of the therapeutic conditions with a group of schizophrenic patients carried out at the University of Wisconsin (e.g. Rogers et al., 1967). This study arose following publication of Rogers's (1957) paper on the necessary and sufficient conditions for change. The Wisconsin project was a major empirical investigation undertaken with schizophrenic clients (Rogers et al., 1967). However, Truax and Mitchell (1971: 300), in a review of therapist variables, stated: 'it quickly became apparent to us that we were assuming that such variables are unitary when, in fact, they are not'. They went on: 'just as therapists are not unitary, neither are specific therapist variables'. They concluded: 'Therefore, in our opinion, most if not all the research dealing with therapist characteristics needs to be re-done.' This was the call for specificity.

Overall, Generation I research established the scientific foundations and methods for determining the efficacy of psychotherapy and delivered strong evidence that psychotherapy was efficacious. Similarly, the scientific foundations for process research were established although this line of research was not directly linked to the need to justify the activity of psychotherapy research. The procedures and techniques developed or espoused in this research generation (e.g. meta-analysis in outcome research and audio-recordings in process research) have become integral to subsequent research activities.

Generation II

Specificity in outcome research

Research characterizing Generation II began in large part as a search for greater specificity in response to what became known as the 'uniformity myth'. This myth reflected the held view that clients were thought to respond similarly to particular interventions. In other words, little attention had been paid to differences across clients, therapists, therapies, or across the course of therapy itself. In response to this situation, the archetypal question of Generation II research became encapsulated in Paul's litany: 'What treatment, by whom, is most effective for this individual with that specific problem, and under which set of circumstances?' (1967: 111). Clearly this was an important and logical step in research as it sought to address the issue of what was the most effective treatment. The question of whether psychotherapy was efficacious was seen as simplistic (Krumboltz, 1966) while process and outcome were increasingly viewed as differing across clients, therapists and therapies (Kiesler, 1966). Once the general theme of determining the overall efficacy of psychotherapy was instigated, Paul's matrix of specifying the various components led researchers to focus more on the differing types of intervention (e.g. Luborsky et al., 1975). In addition, the 1960s saw the rapid development of behaviour therapy within the domain of clinical psychology. The combination of seeking greater specifity together with the availability of contrasting treatments led researchers to question whether these newer therapies (or other brands of therapy) were more effective than, for example, the verbal (e.g. dynamically oriented) therapies.

Generation II research is best characterized by the randomized control trial (RCT). The most influential RCT to date has been the National Institute of Mental Health Treatment of Depression Collaborative Research Program (NIMH TDCRP; Elkin,1994; Elkin et al., 1989). The design comprised three research sites in which 250 clients were randomly assigned to one of four treatment conditions. The four treatment conditions comprised the two psychotherapies which were of major interest, namely, cognitive-behaviour therapy (CBT) and interpersonal psychotherapy (IPT). In order to provide a standard reference condition, the third condition comprised imipramine plus clinical management (IMI-CM). Finally, a placebo condition (PLA-CM) was used primarily as a control for the drug condition and also as an imperfect control for the two psycho-therapies. Among the features of the design, expert therapists were used in the two differing psychotherapies, and the particular treatments were documented in training manuals and the delivery of the treatments was investigated to check on therapists' adherence to the treatment protocols. Findings showed that clients in the IMI-CM condition improved most, clients in the PLA-CM condition improved least, and clients in the two psychotherapy conditions fared in between but were generally closer to the IMI-CM condition. However, differences were not large. Indeed, there were no significant differences between the two psychotherapies or between either of them and the IMI-CM. Differences between the psycho-therapies and the placebo condition showed only one instance of a trend towards lower scores for clients in the IPT condition as compared with PLA-CM and no significant or trend advantage to CBT compared with PLA-CM.

A meta-analysis of 28 RCTs (US DHHS, 1993) found improvement rates for individual and group treatments for depression to be comparable: 50 per cent for cognitive therapy, 52 per cent for interpersonal therapy, and 55 per cent for behavioural therapy but 35 per cent for brief dynamic psychotherapy. However, the latter group may have been adversely affected by the proportionally higher number of studies investigating group rather than individual psychotherapy. Overall, these findings have confirmed the view that technically different therapies result in broadly similar outcomes, a conclusion referred to as the 'equivalence paradox' (Stiles et al., 1986). It is not disputed that there is often a reported advantage to one particular method of therapy (invariably cognitive-behavioural), but what is important is that the size of this advantage is relatively small. How such a small advantage translates into clinical status or psychological health is unclear. The most recent meta-analysis carried out by Wampold and colleagues (1997) reaffirmed the equivalence finding. Their study found that under the most liberal assumptions, the largest extent of any true difference in effect size was in the region of 0.20, which is viewed as a 'small' effect. One important point to keep in mind is that such a finding arose from applying more rigorous procedures than previously employed. For example, it only included studies making a direct within-study comparison between contrasting treatments and therapies that were deemed 'bona fide' (i.e. treatments had to be both credible and therapeutic).

The theme of Generation II's research is being extended in terms of evaluating therapies for more challenging patients. For example, recent research on psychotherapy with borderline personality disorders has focused on the efficacy of dialectical behaviour therapy (DBT) and psychodynamic psychotherapy (Koenigsberg, 1995). The former is associated with the work of Linehan (1993) who found DBT to be superior to treatment in the community in a randomized trial over one year as defined by having fewer days in hospital and fewer and less lethal parasuicidal acts (Linehan et al., 1991). These results were largely maintained one year after treatment although there was no difference in patients' levels of general satisfaction, hence suggesting that the effects of DBT are quite specific and do not address non-behavioural symptoms or overall personality functioning (Linehan et al., 1993). An interesting note has been made regarding the discrepancy between the high level of interest from clinicians and the still relatively small amount of research evidence regarding DBT (Scheel, 2000). However, a standard RCT may not necessarily be the most appropriate research design for this particular patient population. Research on psychodynamic psychotherapy for borderlines has been carried out mainly on Kernberg's model (see Clarkin et al., 1992).

A review of the effectiveness of psychotherapy for personality disorders has been published (Perry et al., 1999). The review comprised 15 studies (although nine of these were uncontrolled observational studies). All studies showed improvements in personality disorders across a range of interventions (e.g. psychodynamic/interpersonal, cognitive-behavioural, and supportive therapies). The within-group ESs (i.e. pre-post change) were 1.11 for self-report measures and 1.29 for observational measures. Although the size of these changes may appear 'large', this within-condition ES is considerably more liberal than the traditional between-condition effect size reported in the literature (i.e. when an active treatment is compared with a control or comparison condition). The authors found evidence to suggest that psychotherapy for personality disorders may yield a recovery rate seven times faster than the natural history of borderline personality disorders. In addition to personality disorders, Generation II research is also being applied to the study of child and adolescent psychotherapy; for example, the special section in *Journal of Consulting and Clinical Psychology* (1995) on efficacy and effectiveness in studies of child and adolescent psychotherapy.

Generation II studies can be summarized by referring to Bergin and Garfield (1994a: 822) who stated: 'We have to face the fact that in a majority of studies, different approaches to the same symptoms, (e.g. depression) show little difference in efficacy'. This is the view summarized by Stiles, Shapiro and Elliott (1986) in their question 'Are all psychotherapies equivalent?' They posited three ways of understanding the supposed equivalence of outcomes. The first was methodological in that equivalence could be achieved through lack of stringency in research methodology. The second argument concerned the possibility that differing therapies may be broadly equivalent due to the overriding effects of common factors. The third argument revolved around the implementation of new research strategies to detect differences. However, the one area where there has accumulated increasing evidence of non-equivalent treatment effects are the anxiety disorders. Here, the treatment of choice is cognitive therapy.

Specificity in process research

Process research built its base on the 'recorded' therapy session and in Generation II was dominated by the work carried out to investigate the 'facilitative' conditions (i.e. empathy, warmth and genuineness). This was a logical step deriving from a theoretical basis and employing observational and self-report measures. The core period for Generation II process research was the 1970s and there is a noticeable difference between Truax and Mitchell's review from the *Handbook of Psychotherapy and Behavior Change* (1971) reported above and the Mitchell, Bozarth, and Krauft's chapter published in *Effective Psychotherapy: A Handbook of Research* (1977). The authors of the latter text acknowledged that the former had focused too much on gross outcome and not sufficiently on the potential correlates between, for example, empathy and outcome. Hence, they stated, that 'demographic and process studies were ignored which might have answered the question: "Which therapists, under what conditions, with which clients in what kinds of specific predicaments, need to reach what levels of these interpersonal skills to effect what kinds of client changes?"' (1977: 482).

In contrast to the 1971 review which implied that the facilitative conditions were both necessary and sufficient, and that they were relatively invariant, Mitchell et al. stated that 'the mass of data neither supports nor rejects the overriding influence of such variables as empathy' (1977: 483). They went on: 'their [the facilitative conditions] potency and generalizability are not as great as once thought' (p. 483). Hence, while the authors reported some studies which supported to varying degrees the positive role of the facilitative conditions, the majority of studies they reported showed little or no direct relationship between the facilitative conditions and outcome (e.g. Sloane et al., 1975).

While process research focused largely on the facilitative conditions, which in itself became the basis for subsequent research on the therapeutic alliance, it was, as Orlinsky and Russell (1994) observe, 'peculiarly flawed' to the extent that it virtually ceased by the late 1970s. The 'conceptual critique', specifically in relation to the facilitative conditions, combined with the increasing search for psychologically appropriate methods for investigating aspects of the therapeutic process, led to the demise of research in this area. In historical terms, the absence of a research centre linked to Rogers assisted the demise. More generally, there was probably a move away from investigating 'common' factors towards determining the more specific components of individual orientations. In addition, there was an increasing move towards a re-evaluation of the clinical utility of the single-case study (e.g. Strupp, 1980a, 1980b, 1980c, 1980d).

Overall, Generation II research moved the agenda on from general issues towards greater specificity in terms of one therapeutic approach versus another and in terms of the contribution of the facilitative conditions. Interestingly, although the call for specificity was a logical one, the general finding of outcome equivalence across different treatment approaches was somewhat problematic for the field. Similarly, the yield arising from the facilitative conditions fell short of expectations. However, specificity has become a major driver in both outcome and process research and set the foundations for the moves towards evidence-based practice.

Generation III

Cost-effectiveness and service delivery

The research included in Generation III spans the period from the 1970s through to the 1990s and incorporates what appear to be two quite diverse focuses: cost-effectiveness and change mechanisms. However, these two areas can be seen to be natural developments arising from the previous two generations of research. Cost-effectiveness has become a central concern, partly driven by research interest but also by the interest of a variety of stakeholders. As such, it is a natural extension of the outcome research carried out in Generation I. The focus on change mechanisms reflects an extension to the issue of 'specificity' which was a feature of Generation II process research, although it might equally be construed as a reaction to it. It is an extension in that it retains specificity as a hallmark but a reaction in terms of redirecting research on to the process of change. The focus on cost and economic aspects of psychotherapy has been reviewed by Gabbard, Lazar, Hornberger and Spiegel (1997). These authors reviewed a total of 18 studies published between 1984 and 1994 and concentrated on the impact of administering psychotherapy on the costs of care. Using actual cost accounting or data on medical care utilization or functioning at work, the data strongly indicated that psychotherapy reduces total costs. The main reductions in costs arose from decreases in work impairment.

Information on service delivery systems has been derived from the 1987 National Medical Expenditures Survey (Olfson and Pincus, 1994a, 1994b) which has provided comprehensive data on the use of services by over 38,000 individuals in the United States. The results (usefully summarized by Docherty and Streeter, 1995) suggest that 79.5 million outpatient psychotherapy visits were made by 7.3 million people (representing 3.1 per cent of the US population). Women used the service at 1.44 times the rate of men. In terms of patient characteristics, 90 per cent of patients were white with the majority being either separated or divorced, aged between 35 and 49, and having more than 16 years of education. Two-thirds of psychotherapy visits were made for a mental health reason (mainly depression, anxiety disorders and adjustment disorders). Out-patient psychotherapy accounted for 8 per cent of all expenditure on outpatient health care. The percentage of patients attending for specified numbers of sessions was as follows: 1–2 sessions, 33.9 per cent; 3–10 sessions, 37.0 per cent; 11–20 sessions, 13.4 per cent; and > 20 sessions, 15.7 per cent. This latter group accounted for 63 per cent of psychotherapy outcome expenditure. The issue of the cost-effectiveness of psychotherapy has been addressed by

Krupnick and Pincus (1992), who have provided a strategy for including this aspect into research studies.

The debate concerning length of treatment ('How much is enough?') has come to the fore in Generation III research. The major finding relating to the dose-effect literature derives from a study carried out by Howard, Kopta, Krause and Orlinsky (1986) which combined 15 outcome studies over a period of 30 years. These authors found that the percentage of clients showing measurable improvement following specified numbers of sessions was as follows: 24 per cent after a single session, 30 per cent after two sessions, 41 per cent after 4 sessions, 53 per cent after 8 sessions, 62 per cent after 13 sessions, 74 per cent after 26 sessions, 83 per cent after 52 sessions, and 90 per cent after 104 sessions. This relationship between the number of sessions received by clients and the percentage of clients showing measurable improvement was best represented by a negatively accelerating curve. This means that while the curve 'accelerates' (i.e. the percentage of clients improving gets higher as a result of more sessions), it does so 'negatively' in that the greatest improvement occurs early in therapy and there are diminishing returns thereafter such that smaller and smaller gains are made later on in therapy in response to the provision of more sessions. However, it is worth noting that almost half of the studies reported by Howard et al. (i.e. seven) had a median of 15 or more sessions, considerably more than the often-quoted averages for attendance in service delivery systems (Taube et al., 1984). Further, the data set did not comprise cognitive-behavioural, behavioural or cognitive therapy orientations. The findings from Howard et al.'s (1986) work are interesting in terms of how they have been used by people espousing differing viewpoints. Howard et al. (1986) obtained two dose-effect curves: one based on therapist ratings and one on client ratings. Defence of longer-term therapy has utilized the former curve, which suggests that diminishing returns only occur after about six months of therapy. In contrast, data from the client ratings suggest that greatest improvements are derived from the initial 8–10 sessions. More recently, the dose-effect findings have given rise to a three-phase model of psychotherapy (Howard et al., 1993). This model proposes that the first few sessions of therapy are characterized by *remoralization*, which then leads on to a phase of *remediation* of symptoms occurring upwards of about the fifth session, which then leads on in later sessions to *rehabilitation* (i.e. improvement in life functioning).

Generation III outcome research has been marked by an increase in research on brief therapies which has been summarized by Koss and Shiang (1994). However, while findings indicate that for many clients the greater impact of counselling or therapy occurs during the initial time frame, with subsequent gains requiring more time, for many clients, especially those who have been severely damaged, effective therapeutic work may not be possible until considerable work has been carried out in establishing, for example, the therapeutic alliance. What this means is that there are clients for whom briefer therapies are appropriate and clients for whom longer therapies are appropriate. The issue is to determine what is best for each client. It is not necessarily true that more therapy is always the preferred option. Given limited resources, it is important to ensure that longer-term interventions are appropriately used and that they are evaluated in order to provide supporting evidence for their use.

The focus on brief therapies has continued, with researchers investigating and reviewing the components that make brief therapies effective. Messer (2001) has reviewed components that contribute to making brief psychodynamic therapy time efficient while McGinn and Sanderson (2001) have done likewise for cognitive behavioural therapy. Of particular note is a review by Elliott (2001) of brief experiential therapy. What is of interest is that this review attempts to re-establish the research base for experiential therapies. Elliott (2001) identified a sample of 28 studies comprising both controlled and comparative studies. The pre-post change effect size (i.e. within group) was in the order of 1.1 with the effects consistent across the three main types of problems studied: neurotic problems (ES = 1.02), depression (ES = 1.61) and anxiety (ES = 1.16). When comparisons were made between treated and untreated clients, there was a large effect size difference (ES = 1.14). Comparisons between experiential and non-experiential therapies showed very little difference (ES = −0.04). These findings suggest there is increasing evidence for the efficacy of brief experiential therapies, which has particular significance in that the outcomes work on experiential therapies is closely linked with many of the principal process researchers emanating from Generation IV.

The culmination of Generations I, II and III can be seen in the activities centring around the broad development of the 'evidence-based practice' (EBP) paradigm. This movement grew in the early 1980s at McMasters University and arose from attempts to help readers appraise the existing research literature in medicine. This movement rapidly expanded to other disciplines such that texts can now be found on 'evidence-based psychotherapy' (e.g. Parry, 2000). The gold standard in terms of evidence within this paradigm consists of the randomized control trial and meta-analytic studies. This is the rationale for why the EBP movement is being placed in Generation III even though much of its impact is only becoming apparent in the 2000s. The critical point here is that the underlying themes (i.e. specificity, cost-effectiveness) and the methods (RCTs) are those of Generations II and III.

The EBP paradigm has also underpinned the identification and validation of what have been called 'empirically supported treatments' (ESTs; for a review see Chambless and Ollendick, 2001; DeRubeis and Crit-Christoph, 1998). The concerns within the US about the number of psychological treatments on offer led to initiatives to marshal the levels of existing evidence for particular therapies. Three levels of criteria were set by Division 12 (Clinical Psychology) Task Force: well-established treatments, probably efficacious treatments, and experimental treatments. These are set out below.

- *Well-established treatments*: At least two good between-group design experiments must demonstrate efficacy via superiority to pill or psychotherapy placebo (or to other treatment) or equivalence to already established treatment with adequate sample sizes. Or a large series of single-case design experiments must demonstrate efficacy with use of good experimental design and comparison of intervention to another treatment. Experiments must be conducted with treatment manuals or equivalent clear description of treatment. Characteristics of samples must be specified and effects must be demonstrated by at least two different investigators or teams.

- *Probably efficacious treatments*: Two experiments must show that the treatment is superior to waiting-list control group, or one or more experiments must meet well-established criteria. Or a small series of single-case design experiments must meet well-established-treatment criteria.
- *Experimental treatments*: Treatment not yet tested in trials meeting task force criteria for methodology.

However, a raft of criticisms have been levelled at the concept of ESTs (e.g. Wampold, 1997, 2001). These include the wholesale adoption of a 'medicalization' of psychotherapy, omitting quasi-experimental studies (which are more representative of psychotherapy as practised in routine settings), and premised on DSM-IV diagnostic categories. In terms of ecological validity, one dilemma is that many of the therapies used in routine clinical settings do not meet the EST criteria (e.g. eclectic therapy, long-term psychodynamic therapy). The concept and research evidence for ESTs build on the combined and developmental research traditions from Generations I, II and III and provide the most fully developed response to Eysenck's (1952) original critique of psychotherapy. Equally, they serve to draw a transition line between Generations I–III and Generation IV.

Change pathways

The review of process and outcome in psychotherapy by Orlinsky, Grawe and Parks (1994) summarized a wealth of material relating to possible effective pathways. They identified stability of treatment arrangements and counsellor adherence to a treatment model as showing promise. They identified 'patient suitability' and 'therapist skill' as particularly robust with over two-thirds of studies in each of these areas reporting significant findings. In terms of therapeutic operations, the authors summarised three areas: problem presentation; expert understanding; and therapist intervention. With regard to problem presentation, the cognitive and behavioural processes within the client's problem presentation are related to outcome. Findings on 'expert understanding' target client problems and client affective responses during sessions. In terms of therapist interventions, there appears to be substantial evidence supporting experiential confrontation as well as interpretations. In addition, paradoxical intention appears to show a consistent relationship with outcome. In terms of the therapeutic bond, this showed strong associations with outcome, especially when assessed from the client's perspective.

Specific techniques
The use of verbal response modes (VRMs) in various research studies has shown that therapists use responses which are consistent with their theoretical orientation (Elliott et al., 1987). Relating VRMs to immediate outcomes (i.e. in-session), a range of studies have identified 'interpretation' (or responses closely allied to it) as being 'effective'. For example, O'Farrell, Hill and Patton (1986) found

interpretation to be related to a decrease in client problem description and an increase in experiencing and insight. However, the role of therapist 'intentions' is just as important. Horvath, Marx and Kamann (1990) found clients' ability to identify the intention of the counsellor depended, in addition to other factors, upon the stage of therapy, with understanding increasing from initial to mid-therapy and then decreasing. Factors accounting for this may involve the intentions becoming more complex or tacit as therapy develops. The complex relationship between these factors (e.g. response modes and intentions) is summarized by Sexton and Whiston:

> Based on a variety of complex factors (experience, training, client behavior), counselors develop intentions or goals that guide their choices of intentions or response modes. After each counselor response, the client reacts (decodes, interprets, and experiences) and responds. In response, the counselor develops an adjusted intention and subsequent response mode. Over time these patterns become stabilized in client and counselor expectations. (1994: 21)

However, it has been found that response modes account for very little of the outcome variance, even for immediate outcome. Hill reports that 'therapist intentions and client experiencing in the turn preceding the therapist intervention each contributed more to the variance than did response modes' (1990: 289). She cites her intensive analyses of eight single cases (Hill, 1989) in which she found that 'client personality, therapist orientation and personality, and adequate therapeutic relationship, and events external to therapy all influenced whether or not clients incorporated changes begun in therapy' (1990: 289).

Research into the effectiveness of interpretations has been summarized by Orlinsky et al. (1994). These authors cited a total of 38 findings from 16 studies, of which 24 findings were positively related to overall outcome, 11 showed no association, and 3 showed negative associations. Hence, while two-thirds of the findings showed a positive association between interpretations and outcome, inspection of their data (Orlinsky et al., 1994: 303) in which 11 studies yielded sufficient information for the reviewers to determine effect sizes, showed the average size of this effect to be small (ES = 0.21). Garfield (1990), albeit basing his views on a previous review (Orlinsky and Howard, 1986), when only half of the reported findings supported the link with a positive outcome, was also somewhat sceptical. Research into the accuracy of therapist interpretations has been carried out by Crits-Christoph, Cooper and Luborsky (1988) who found that accuracy of interpretation was the best predictor of outcome. However, rather surprisingly, it was not related to improvements in the therapeutic alliance. A useful summary of important domains related to change in psychotherapy is included in a special section of the *Journal of Consulting and Clinical Psychology* (1993) which is devoted to curative factors in dynamic psychotherapy. Areas include interpersonal problems and attachment styles, the therapeutic alliance, psychodynamic formulations, transference interpretations, and patients' representations of psychotherapy.

Generation III process research has combined much of the more 'technical' and quantitative research efforts. However, difficulties undoubtedly occur when evaluating specific techniques and many researchers within this domain have contrasting views. For example, Garfield has stated that there is 'no truly strong support for the accuracy of interpretation as a process variable of importance. . .the interpretation of explanation that is accepted by the patient is the one that may have some positive therapeutic impact' (1990: 276). Others, for example Silberschatz and Curtis (1986), have argued that the interpretations which are important are those which are consistent with the client's unconscious plan for therapy rather than those relating, for example, to the transference.

The role of specific techniques in CBT has also been investigated. For example, patient change in the later stages of therapy has been linked specifically to the procedure of cognitive restructuring (DeRubeis et al., 1990). Further, evidence suggests certain cognitive techniques (e.g. logical analysis and hypothesis testing) are linked with amelioration of symptoms in the mid-to-later phases of therapy (Jarrett and Nelson, 1987). In addition, the potential prophylactic effect of CBT has been suggested by results showing that patients who have received CBT are less likely to relapse than patients receiving medication (Evans et al., 1992). Hence, patients who have learned cognitive techniques appear to be offered a degree of protection against subsequent depressive experiences by applying the learned techniques. These findings are congruent with the 'compensatory skills' model of change which suggests that CBT offers a set of effective coping strategies (i.e. compensatory skills) which are implemented by patients. This model appears to be more consistent with research evidence than that which suggests that CBT results in any permanent change in patients' schema. A review by Iliardi and Craighead (1994) suggested that non-specific factors may play a significant role in the early part of CBT. This suggestion arose from an analysis of a set of studies which showed that early response to CBT (i.e. symptomatic improvement) occurred prior to the formal introduction of cognitive restructuring techniques. The authors suggested that these findings are consistent with the three-phase model of therapy (see Howard et al., 1993) in which the early phase is characterized by remoralization (i.e. non-specific effects of expectancy and hope).

Common factors

Process research has often been viewed as a dichotomy comprising common factors and specific techniques. As indicated above, research interest has moved from the facilitative conditions to investigating the therapeutic alliance. While the facilitative conditions have been viewed as a possible mechanism of change, the therapeutic alliance is best viewed as a mechanism which enables the client to remain in and comply with treatment (Bordin, 1979). Sexton and Whiston (1994) reviewed the research literature on the client–therapist relationship since 1985 using three domains: the 'real' relationship, the transference, and the working alliance. Findings summarized here focus on the last of these: the working alliance. A meta-analytic review of 24 studies (Horvath and Symonds, 1991) found that the working alliance was positively related to outcome and that client and observer ratings were better predictors of outcome than therapist ratings. However, the overall effect only approached medium size and it appears that findings from individual studies are affected by such factors as when the alliance was assessed and the particular outcome index used. Overall though, from the available evidence, it appears the therapeutic alliance might account for upwards of 45 per cent of outcome variance (Horvath and Greenberg, 1989).

The perspective taken by the rater influences the results and it is invariably the client's rating of the alliance that is most predictive of outcome. Further, if client change is the criterion for measuring outcome, then client ratings of process are the best judges. There is also evidence that clients have predispositions to the quality of the alliance they might develop. Horvath and Greenberg (1994) cite work suggesting that clients who have difficulty in maintaining their social relationships or have experienced relatively poor family relationships prior to therapy are less likely to develop strong alliances. However, severity of presenting symptoms did not appear to impact on the quality of the alliance. In terms of the temporal nature of the therapeutic alliance, research findings are equivocal with some researchers (e.g. Eaton et al., 1988) finding that it is constant while others (e.g. Klee et al., 1990) have suggested the opposite. This is an area requiring further research as it relates to the development and maintenance of the client–therapist relationship. While there has been considerable effort in the development of measures of the therapeutic alliance, there has been 'greater emphasis on interrater reliability and predictive validity and less emphasis on issues of dimensionality and convergent and discriminate validity' (Marmar, 1990). Thus, it is not clear that equivalent emphasis has been placed on furthering our understanding of what are the actual components of this 'umbrella' concept.

Nevertheless, it is clear that 'umbrella' or overarching models can be helpful in providing a framework for increasing our understanding of therapeutic processes. In an attempt to provide an overarching model for understanding the process of change through therapy, Stiles, Elliott, Llewelyn, Firth-Cozens, Margison, Shapiro and Hardy (1990) developed the assimilation model. This model presents change along a continuum comprising eight stages from 'warded off', through 'unwanted thoughts' and 'emerging awareness' and on to 'problem clarification' and 'insight/understanding'. Thereafter come the stages of 'application/working through', 'problem solution' and 'mastery'. The model focuses on problematic experiences such that different problems can progress at a different pace. Evidence is encouraging (e.g. Stiles, in press; Stiles et al., 1994) and further refinements have been made. The model requires considerably more rigorous testing, but it does have a high face validity upon which to hang research questions.

The debate concerning the respective roles and contributions of specific and common factors is still as much an issue as ever and has been referred to as 'the great psychotherapy debate' (see Wampold, 2001). Ahn and Wampold (2001) carried out a meta-analytic study to determine the extent to which proven psychological therapies (i.e. those that had shown themselves to be efficacious) produce client change via specific mechanisms as opposed to common factors.

Importantly, the studies used were 'component' studies which involved comparisons between the treatment package and the treatment package without a theoretically important component. A total of 27 studies met the criterion for inclusion in the study and the results showed that the effect size for the difference between the two conditions (with component versus without the component) was not significantly different from zero. Further, the authors suggested that because there was very little variance in the effect sizes, it was unlikely that important variables were moderating the effect sizes.

Overall, Generation III outcome research has built on the basis of Generation II research but advanced it by setting it in the context of service settings and costs. Hence, it can be viewed as an extension of Generation II research. The moves towards taking account of real world situations set the agenda for prioritizing the needs of clinicians and practitioners in routine service settings. Meanwhile, research on process issues built up a huge research base but was unable to resolve the debate on the contributions of specific and common factors in psychotherapy.

Generation IV

Towards a paradigm of clinically meaningful outcome research

Generation IV outcome research has developed both 'from' and 'in reaction to' the previous research generations. In the broadest sense, what is 'new' in Generation IV is the central focus on the user perspective and on prioritizing the external validity derived from studying routine settings. In terms of the former, a landmark but controversial study of psychotherapy even at the time of its publication was the Consumer Report Survey (*Consumer Reports*, 1995). *Consumer Reports* – the equivalent of *Which?* magazine in the UK – carried out a survey of its readers who had experienced stress or other emotional problems at any time during the previous three years for which they had sought help from a range of support systems. Seligman (1995) reported the following key findings: (1) treatment by a health professional usually worked; (2) long-term therapy produced more improvement than short-term therapy; (3) there were no differences between psychotherapy alone and psychotherapy plus medication for any disorder; and (4) no specific modality of psychotherapy did any better than any other for any problem. His conclusions were that the findings confirmed the overall effectiveness of psychotherapy. However, there was widespread criticism of the Consumer Report because of the small sample who actually responded to the mental health questions (around 4 per cent of the original sample), lack of a control group, paucity of information on a range of client, therapist and treatment variables, and lack of a reliable metric for summarizing therapeutic change. Seligman viewed most of the criticisms as focusing on what the CR might have done rather than what it actually did within the financial and time constraints and stated that 'this was first-rate journalism and credible science as well' (1995: 1086). Yet some commentators have noted that the criticisms of the design noted above suggest that the CR survey is more akin to a consumer satisfaction survey and should not be held up as an exemplar of effectiveness research (Nathan et al., 2000).

Within mainstream outcome research, the momentum towards seeking a new paradigm has been driven by general disquiet at the ability of the research paradigms used in Generations I, II and III to increase our understanding of psychotherapy outcomes. For example, recent meta-analyses continue to report broadly similar outcomes for different therapies (Grissom, 1996; Wampold et al., 1997). However, as Kopta et al. state: 'It seems clear though that no one believes all psychotherapies are equally effective for all disorders' (1999: 444). One way forward suggested by Elliott, Stiles and Shapiro (1993) is that researchers should focus on the specific effects of specific psychotherapies on specific types of patients. At one level such an argument appears to hark back to the theme of Generation II research, but there is greater sophistication about this call which recognizes the considerable variation in the effect sizes obtained in earlier meta-analyses (e.g. the standard deviation of the 0.85 effect size was 1.25). The need to consider therapist effects is crucial as well as taking into account possible unwitting biases due to researcher allegiance. There is also the need to consider what criteria must be satisfied in order for two or more treatments to be deemed as having a differential impact.

In relation to this issue, a principal driver for Generation IV research has been the central issue of whether outcomes are meaningful. Jacobson and colleagues (1984, 1986, 1991) devised a heuristic to address two key questions: (1) Is the extent of client change reliable given the change measure used?, and (2) What is the end state of the client in relation to any given population? Jacobson and Truax (1991) have summarized this work on determining reliable and clinically significant change and have provided three methods for calculating this index. The principle they use is movement by the client from one population (i.e. dysfunctional) to another population (e.g. general population, or non-distressed population). Of course, it is only possible to determine membership of the 'normal' population when normative data are available. In the absence of such data, movement to two standard deviations below the intake mean would signify 'clinical' change (i.e. belonging to a different population, although not necessarily a non-distressed population). This approach enables clinicians to identify individual clients who have met a specified criterion of improvement (e.g. Kendall et al., 1999b; Kendall and Sheldrick, 2000). A review of the history, definitions and applications of clinical significance is provided by Ogles, Lunnen and Bonesteel (2001).

Generation IV research has built on these methodological developments which have provided the means to achieve better outcomes monitoring in practice settings. One component to this has been the recognition of an agreed core outcome battery – that is, an attempt to standardize the selection of outcome measures in order to facilitate increased comparisons across treatments, settings and services (Strupp et al., 1997). Lest it be thought that this was a new development, the idea of a 'core outcome battery' was first developed at a landmark conference in the 1970s (see Waskow and Parloff, 1975). But whatever measure is selected, there is a considerable problem in collecting Time 2 data – that is, data at termination or discharge. Many clients terminate therapy unilaterally and it is difficult to obtain post-therapy data. Accordingly, monitoring outcomes is most likely to inform practice through the application of session-by-session tracking of individual patients in the context of empirically derived parameters that determine the range of response to particular interventions for particular diagnoses (e.g. Lutz et al., 1999). This 'patient-focused' outcome paradigm can provide individual dose response curves to help inform individual case management and support clinical decision-making in service of enhanced quality (e.g. Howard et al., 1996; Lambert et al., 2001a; Lueger et al., 2001). Systems have also been developed and validated for the early identification of 'signal' cases (e.g. Kordy et al., 2001). Evidence that outcomes monitoring enhances clients' outcomes has been shown in a study evaluating the effects of providing practitioners with feedback on their clients' progress (Lambert et al., 2001b). Clients who were deemed not to be 'on track' in terms of expected outcomes trajectories and whose therapists were provided with outcomes feedback yielded a treatment effect size advantage of 0.44 over an equivalent 'not on track' group whose therapists were not provided with outcome feedback. Although these results should be treated with caution – the authors note that the confidence intervals for the size of treatment effect ranged from 'just above zero to more than 0.80' – there is a clear indication of the potential for a direct impact on clinical practice.

A key concern for Generation IV research has been the clinical relevance of the body of efficacy research. Shadish and colleagues (1997, 2000) addressed the key question of whether the findings from psychotherapy outcome studies were different as a function of their clinical representativeness. That is, are there outcome differences from studies spanning the continuum from efficacy to effectiveness? If no substantive differences are found, then this might help to allay concerns that efficacy results are not transportable to routine clinical practice. And indeed, the findings reported by Shadish (Shadish et al., 1997, 2000) provide support for this argument. Effect sizes from 56 studies were categorized into three stages that increasingly represented routine clinical practice. There were no substantive differences in effect size as a function of clinical representativeness. This finding was replicated in a refinement of the earlier study (Shadish et al., 2000). Hence, this programme of work suggests that the concern about applying efficacy results to routine practice may be more apparent than real.

However, even if actual outcome results are similar, it still leaves the outcomes of routine settings as being determined by the results from efficacy studies. It is simply impossible for the efficacy paradigm to address the many questions that need to be asked and to deliver answers quickly enough in order to meet the needs of services and patients. Other outcome paradigms are needed regardless of the transportability of efficacy results. Indeed, there have been recent calls for some radical reappraisals of how outcome research is carried out. In response, the NIMH has been proposed an integration initiative in an attempt to bridge the gap between efficacy and effectiveness research (NAMHC, 1999; Norquist et al., 1999). In effect, a new paradigm is proposed that would be inclusive of both experimental and observational data and that would require development of existing methods and new statistical techniques.

Towards a paradigm of clinically meaningful process research

In the same way that the method of investigating reliable and clinically meaningful change employed a rigorous but clinically useful approach applicable to outcome research, so there is a range of methods adopted in psychotherapy process research which are rigorous but remain sufficiently close to the clinical material that they are seen to be clinically relevant to practitioners. The traditional model of investigating process–outcome correlations has been challenged (Stiles and Shapiro, 1989) and there has been a movement towards the adoption of newer styles of research aimed at focusing on the 'change process' (Greenberg, 1986, 1994). In this paradigm, 'the process of therapy can. . .be seen as a chain of patient states or suboutcomes that are linked together on a pathway toward ultimate outcome' (Safran et al., 1988). A hallmark of qualitative research is that the data comprise 'vivid, dense, and full descriptions in natural language of the phenomenon under study' (Polkinghorne, 1994).

Akin to the desire to make research relevant to the practitioner, process researchers adopted a particular paradigm – the events paradigm – to investigate the mechanisms of change. The logic was that in therapy, 'significant events' occur which initiate the change process. The logic of the events paradigm was to capture and study such events rather than using other sampling techniques. Hence, the 'events' paradigm assumes that the intensive study of significant moments occurring during therapy is more informative than aggregating within and across sessions whereby considerable 'noise' is included in the data. It is a substantially better informed strategy than sampling random segments of therapy sessions. The events paradigm emphasizes the experiences and perceptions of participating patients and therapists by focusing on a particular class of events (e.g. moments of perceived empathy, or insight). The events are usually derived from a variant of a procedure called interpersonal process recall (IPR; Elliott, 1984) which requires the patient, following a therapy session, to identify with an assessor a significant event that occurred during the session. This event then becomes the focus of subsequent intensive analysis. In order to make IPR less labour intensive, a brief format has been devised (see Elliott and Shapiro, 1988). The events paradigm aims to investigate change episodes in therapy and to develop 'micro-theories' to explain how change takes place. The focus is on 'providing causal explanations of therapeutic change and on making explanation rather than prediction the primary goal of psychotherapy research' (Greenberg, 1994: 115).

A related procedure, called task analysis, is uniquely suited to the analysis of the psychotherapeutic change process. It attempts to explicate a model of the information-processing activities which the patient and therapist perform across time which leads to the resolution of particular cognitive-affective tasks. The preliminary model, termed the rational model, can be developed by theoretical speculations and then its 'goodness of fit' verified against empirical examples of change processes occurring in psychotherapy. The result is a synthesis of the rational model and empirical examples termed the performance model. The rational model is then constantly revised in an iterative process between theoretical and performance models. The resulting model will potentially provide clinicians with information about the type of patient operations necessary for a therapeutic intervention to be effective or for a good outcome to be achieved. Further, such models have clear implications for training and the manualization of therapies. This overall research approach requires the intensive analysis of concrete change performances via two methods: first, the intensive observation and measurement of in-session behaviour, and secondly, accessing practitioner and client subjective recall of their experience (Greenberg , 1999).

A further initiative within Generation IV research has been the development of the concept of responsiveness. This initiative has been driven by the failure of previous research methods to confirm the importance of process variables that are self-evidently central to practitioners – and thereby perpetuating the divide between research and practice. The approach of responsiveness has been summarized as follows: 'We use the term *responsiveness* to describe behavior that is affected by emerging context, including emerging perceptions of others' characteristics and behavior. Insofar as therapist and client respond to each other, responsiveness implies a dynamic relationship between variables, involving bidirectional causation and feedback loops' (Stiles et al., 1998: 439). This approach is based on clinical experience which has assumed that it is not only an issue of *what* intervention a therapist makes but also a matter of *when* and *how* to offer an intervention. Accordingly, the therapist needs to be responsive to the individual client's needs at any given time in treatment within the broader context of the client's history and therapeutic progress. Hence, offering an interpretation may be helpful, but only in certain situations (influenced by history and progress). The concept of responsiveness has crucial methodological implications because it lays the basis for explanations as to why the research literature has failed to yield stable associations between outcome and apparently important process variables.

A key feature of Generation IV process research has been the investment in developing and disseminating qualitative methodologies that would underpin and serve the development of a knowledge base. Hill and colleagues have explicated the components, procedures and evaluation criteria for consensual qualitative research (CQR; Hill et al., 1997). They list the components as comprising the use of open-ended questions to collect data and using words to describe phenomena (i.e. as opposed to diagnostic labels). The approach invests in studying a small number of cases intensively and with an emphasis on the contribution of context. Decisions are made via consensus within a team and auditors are used to 'check' decisions which are verified against the raw data. The procedures comprise the developing and coding domains, constructing central themes, and then developing categories to reflect consistencies across cases. The results are evaluated against a range of criteria including the trustworthiness of the method, the coherence of results, representativeness of the results in relation to the sample, the utility of the results and their replicability across differing samples. Similarly, Elliott and colleagues have produced 'evolving guidelines' for the publication of qualitative research studies in psychology which are highly applicable to psycho-therapy research (Elliott *et al.*, 1999). A central aim of their work has been to legitimize qualitative research and generate more appropriate reviews of qual-itative research and increase aspects of quality control.

Overall, Generation IV has moved outcome and process research in the direction of the practitioner and attempted to combine process and outcome work into a single activity. In this way, change is seen as the process of achieving small outcomes that in turn become processes working towards further outcomes. The process methods used to achieve this are increasingly drawing on qualitative approaches while outcomes work has prioritized the individual in the context of social norms.

Part II: Methods, outcomes and processes – research in Britain

It is clear from the work reported above that a considerable proportion of research has derived from the United States. In addition, there has always been a strong research tradition in continental Europe although it is only recently that this is becoming accessible through publications in the English language (see the journal *Psychotherapy Research*). Although it might be thought that research in Britain would be very much a poor relation, there is a wealth of high-quality research which has been, and currently is being, carried out. The aim of the second part of this chapter is to provide an overview of past and present work on individual psychotherapy research in Britain employing the same structure as in the first part of this chapter.

Generation I

Initial response to Eysenck

Generation I research began in Britain, as elsewhere, with Eysenck's (1952) critique of the effectiveness of psychotherapy. The response in Britain came from work by Malan and his colleagues based at the Tavistock Clinic who investigated rates of spontaneous remission in 45 cases of untreated people presenting with neurotic symptoms (Malan et al., 1968, 1975). Malan and his colleagues found that while 49 per cent of clients had improved using symptomatic criteria, only 24 per cent had done so when using dynamic criteria. However, the general-izability of these findings is compromised by the highly selective nature of the sample. Malan also carried out two series of studies on analytic psychotherapy (Malan, 1963, 1976). In the first of these, Malan (1963) investigated a sample of patients in which psychodynamic formulations were devised for all clients based on disturbances in their social relationships which required a resolution between the id and the superego. Malan assessed therapy according to whether patients improved in their social relations consequent on their symptom improvement. Of the 21 patients in the sample, five met the criterion for substantial improvement. In the second series of studies, Malan (1976) studied the outcome of a further 30 clients and found significant improvement in five. In particular, he found a significant association between outcome and interpretations linking transference with patient or sibling. In reality, the value of these two studies lies more in their attempt to study the material of psychotherapy by keeping closely to the clinical material rather than as definitive studies of the effectiveness of psychoanalytic therapy. Ironically, therefore, they might almost be seen to have come full circle and sit within Generation IV research.

The advent of meta-analytic techniques provided the field with a much-needed procedure for summarizing findings in a quantitative and replicable fashion. Following Smith and Glass's (1977) meta-analytic publication, Shapiro and Shapiro (1982) replicated and refined the analysis. They analysed the effects of 143 outcome studies in which two or more treatments were compared with a control group. The mean effect size for treated versus untreated groups approached one standard deviation unit (slightly higher than the 0.85 effect size obtained by Smith and Glass). When they compared a smaller data set in which two active treatments were compared with each other, they found cognitive and certain multimodal behavioural treatments to be superior. However, they very clearly pointed out that much of this research was analogue and hence unrepresentative of clinical practice.

The extension of Generation I outcome research has been continued by its application in more clinically challenging problems. For example, the treatment versus no-treatment (i.e. wait-list) design has been used to evaluate the effect of CBT in the treatment of hypochondriasis. Warwick, Clark, Cobb and Salkovskis (1996) randomly assigned 32 patients to CBT or a no-treatment wait-list control. Results indicated that people receiving CBT showed significantly greater improvements than those in the wait-list control group on all therapist, assessor and patient – bar one – completed measures. These gains were maintained at three-month follow-up.

Generation II

Outcome research

The meta-analysis reported above (and limitations identified in it) led to a series of comparative studies evaluating different modes of therapies carried out by Shapiro and colleagues (see Shapiro et al., 1991). A programmatic series of studies was devised to evaluate both the outcome of these therapies as well as what was effective (i.e. processes) within each therapy. The first Sheffield Psychotherapy Project (Shapiro and Firth, 1987) compared eight-session phases of prescriptive (cognitive-behavioural) and exploratory (psychodynamic-interpersonal) therapy in which 40 professional and managerial workers diagnosed as depressed or anxious received either eight sessions of prescriptive followed by eight sessions of exploratory, or the same two therapies in the reverse order. All clients saw the same therapist throughout therapy. Findings showed a slight advantage to prescriptive therapy as well as an advantage to the initial phase (i.e. first eight sessions) of a 16-session therapy. This slight advantage to prescriptive over exploratory therapy was also obtained in the larger Second Sheffield Psychotherapy Project but only on one out of seven client self-report measures (SPP2; Shapiro et al., 1994). The design called for 120 white-collar workers, diagnosed as depressed, to be randomly assigned to one of the four treatment conditions: either psychodynamic-interpersonal (PI) or cognitive-behavioural (CB) therapy delivered in either eight- or 16-session durations. The study also found that 16 sessions was only superior to eight-sessions for those patients presenting with more severe levels of depression (as measured by the BDI). Follow-up data at one year showed that patients in the 8PI condition were faring worse than those in the other three treatment conditions (Shapiro et al., 1995). It was also found that clients presenting with cluster C personality disorders had significantly poorer outcomes than clients without a cluster C personality disorder following PI therapy but not CB therapy (Hardy et al., 1995). The SPP2 has been extended to NHS settings in a MRC/NHS collaborative study acting as a replication (Barkham et al., 1996). The effectiveness of treatments was found to be similar to that of SPP2 with the exception that patients had not maintained their gains at three-month follow-up. Scott (1995) has provided an update on psychological treatments for depression and on cognitive therapy for the treatment of depression (2001).

The effectiveness of psychotherapy has also been evaluated against other forms of clinical management. This applies particularly in clients diagnosed with anorexia nervosa or bulimia nervosa. In one study of severe anorexia nervosa, clients were randomly assigned to either 12 sessions of dietary advice or 12 sessions of combined individual and family psychotherapy (Hall and Crisp, 1987). At one-year follow-up, the dietary advice group showed significant weight gain. In contrast, while clients receiving the combined psychotherapy did not obtain a statistically significant improvement in weight gain, they did make significant improvements in their sexual and social adjustment. In another study of bulimia nervosa, 92 women diagnosed as bulimics were randomly assigned to one of three treatment conditions (cognitive-behavioural, behavioural, and group therapy) while a further 20 women were assigned to a waiting-list control group (Freeman et al., 1988). All three treatments were effective compared with the control group. The researchers predicted that cognitive-behavioural therapy would be superior to the other two active treatments. However, where differences did occur, they tended to favour behaviour therapy.

The efficacy of cognitive therapy has been extensively investigated. Teasdale has written extensively on a model of understanding depression within a cognitive-behavioural framework (Teasdale et al., 1984). Through both theoretical (Teasdale, 1985) and empirical (Fennell and Teasdale, 1987) work, Teasdale has developed a model of depression in which 'depression about depression' is a central component. Teasdale (1985) argues that depression about depression is best attacked by helping clients to view it as a problem to be solved rather than evidence of personal inadequacy. To test out this hypothesis, Fennell and Teasdale (1987) investigated the process of change in outpatients with major depressive disorder. Cognitive therapy was compared to treatment as usual. Cognitive therapy produced marked improvement within the initial two-week period which was maintained through the course of treatment. The study showed that when fast responders were analysed between the two treatment groups (cognitive therapy vs treatment as usual), only the good responders in the cognitive therapy group maintained their level of improvement. Establishing predictors of improvement is an important aim of psychotherapy research. By detailed session-by-session analysis, Fennell and Teasdale (1987) found the major differentiating factor between high and low responders to be clients' responsiveness to a booklet about depression. Clients who responded positively to the booklet improved most quickly. The authors argued that this was because the booklet addressed the issue of being 'depressed about their depression'.

Evaluations of the comparative effectiveness of cognitive therapy with pharmacotherapy have been carried out by Blackburn (for review, see Blackburn, 1995). Findings for hospital patients presenting with depression, although not statistically significant, tended to support the view that combined drug and cognitive therapy was more effective than cognitive therapy alone which was, in turn, more effective than drug treatment alone (e.g. Blackburn et al., 1981). However, this pattern of findings did not hold for general practice clients. Rather, patients receiving pharmacotherapy alone did significantly worse than the other two client groups, and further, there was little difference between the combined therapy and cognitive therapy groups. These findings suggested that drug and cognitive therapies failed to have the additive effect in the general practice group which occurred in the hospital patient group. Blackburn, Eunson and Bishop (1986) reported on the recurrence rate at two years for cognitive therapy, medication, and combined. Results showed appreciably lower rates of recurrence for cognitive therapy alone (23 per cent) and cognitive therapy/drug combination (21 per cent) as compared with medication alone (78 per cent).

A series of studies of cognitive therapy for anxiety have been carried out by Butler and colleagues. Butler, Cullington, Hibbert, Klimes and Gelder (1987a) treated a total of 45 clients meeting criteria for a diagnosis of generalised anxiety disorder (GAD), with 22 receiving anxiety management immediately while a further 23 received the same treatment after a three-month wait period. The results suggested that clients in the immediate treatment group improved significantly more than the matched group waiting for treatment. When the wait group received treatment, a similar improvement was obtained. A subsequent study treated 57 patients diagnosed with GAD and compared three treatment conditions: cognitive-behavioural therapy (CBT), behaviour therapy (BT), and a wait list (Butler et al., 1991). Results showed CBT to be superior to BT alone (relaxation training plus graded exposure), with both treatments superior to the wait-list control. Whilst the study had relatively low statistical power to detect differences between the two active treatments and the wait-list group (19 patients initially in each of the three conditions), the fact that differences were found for CBT over BT attests to the robustness of the findings. Hence, addressing the cognitions of those patients presenting with GAD is clearly beneficial. The authors note that this is one of the few examples where one form of psychological treatment has been found to be more effective than another as a treatment for GAD. However, inspection of the pre-post change effect sizes on one of the criterion measures of anxiety, the Beck Anxiety Inventory, suggests that it may not be so much a story of CBT being superior (the pre-post ES of 1.35 is standard) but more a story of BT being inadequate (as indicated by the pre-post ES of 0.65) and hence not a treatment of choice with GAD.

Salkovskis (1995) provides a summary of how cognitive-behavioural therapy has advanced in the area of panic disorder together with a very useful 'hourglass' model of how psychotherapy research progresses through various stages. Following on from Butler et al.'s (1991) assertion of the non-equivalence of psychotherapies, Salkovskis states:

> The myth of psychotherapy equivalence is not helpful in the process of refinement. Like the idea that all swans are white, the range of exceptions is now too striking to be ignored. As more knowledge is acquired about maintaining factors involved in different types of psychological problems, the rate of progress increases. Of course, where research is not guided by attempts to understand the idiosyncratic nature of the factors involved in the maintenance of such problems, outcome studies may show that there is no difference between therapies. (1995: 224)

In a comparative trial, Blowers, Cobb and Mathews (1987) studied a sample of 66 clients diagnosed as suffering from generalized anxiety. Clients were randomly assigned to one of three conditions: wait list, non-directive counselling, or anxiety management training (combined relaxation and brief cognitive therapy). Surprisingly, perhaps, there were few significant differences in outcome between non-directive counselling and anxiety management training. Blowers et al. summarized their findings as follows: 'A reasonable conclusion would therefore be that anxiety management training is indeed effective, but that its superiority to a less structured and less directive alternative remains to be proven' (1987: 500). However, as Morley (1988) suggests, it can be no surprise that such studies find little differences between anxiety management training and non-directive counselling. These studies are not really evaluating cognitive therapy but rather cognitive components divorced from their behavioural concomitants.

The comparative effectiveness of cognitive therapy (CT) and other interventions has been investigated (Clark et al., 1994). A total of 64 patients were allocated (the report does not state that this was carried out randomly) to either CT, applied relaxation therapy, imipramine or a waiting list. Patients on the waiting list received no treatment for the initial three months and were then randomly allocated to one of the three treatment conditions. Patients in the CT or applied relaxation conditions received up to 12 sessions in the first three months and up to three booster sessions in the next three months. Results showed CT to be the most effective treatment. However, as with the Butler study, finding CT to be superior is less impressive when the 'competing' therapy may not be as powerful as it should. Blanes and Raven (1995), in a review of psychotherapy of panic disorder, questioned the findings from Clark et al. given that over 80 per cent of their sample had some degree of agoraphobia and that the treatment of choice for this problem is systematic self-exposure with homework diaries.

A multinational study investigating treatments for panic disorder with agoraphobia has been carried out (Marks et al., 1993). The study compared the combination of alprazolam and exposure to either treatment alone for patients with a diagnosis of panic disorder. A total of 154 patient were randomly allocated to one of four treatment conditions: alprazolam and exposure, alprazolam and relaxation, placebo and exposure, placebo and relaxation. Patients in all four treatment conditions improved when evaluation of panic was used as the single outcome indicator. In brief, the findings indicated that while alprazolam and exposure were more effective than placebo, the effect size for exposure was approximately twice that for alprazolam, with the gains from exposure being maintained whilst those for alprazolam were not.

In a development of the Generation I design reported earlier (see Warwick et al., 1996), Clark and colleagues extended their investigations into the effective treatment of hypochondriasis (Clark et al., 1998). The study comprised 48 patients randomly assigned to one of three groups: cognitive therapy, behavioural stress management (BSM), or no-treatment wait-list control group. Patients in the last group were subsequently assigned randomly to one of the treatment conditions at the end of the waiting period. Both active treatments were more effective than the waiting list – a finding derived from a Generation I comparison. However, comparisons between the two active treatments showed that CT was more effective than BSM on specific measures of hypochondriasis but not for comparisons of general mood disturbance either at mid- or end of treatment.

There is an increasing empirically based literature on treatments for people presenting with psychosis. Studies have developed cognitive-behavioural strategies for problem-solving and coping (Tarrier et al., 1990, 1993). Cognitive-behavioural principles have also been developed and applied to aspects of psychosis (Chadwick and Lowe, 1990; Kingdon and Turkington, 1991). CT has been evaluated in the acute phase of psychosis in a trial carried out by Drury and colleagues (Drury et al., 1996). A total of 40 clients were assigned to either a multi-component CBT programme or a social recreational programme with informal support, both conditions acting as an adjunct to standard care. The social recreational programme provided clients with access to the same therapists as the CT group, thereby going some way towards controlling for common factors. Clients in the CT condition showed a significantly faster rate of decline in symptoms over the initial 12 weeks of the intervention and significantly fewer symptoms at weeks 7 and 12 compared with clients in the alternative condition. At nine months, only 5 per cent of clients in the CT condition showed moderate or severe residual symptoms compared with 56 per cent of clients in the social recreational programme (Drury et al., 1996). A follow-up at five years showed no significant differences in relapse rate, symptoms or insight between the groups. However, clients in the CT group did show significantly greater perceived 'control over illness'. In addition, for those clients who had experienced no more than one relapse in the follow-up period, self-reported residual delusional beliefs and observer-rated hallucinations and delusions were significantly less for those people in the CT group (Drury et al., 2000).

A pilot control trial of CBT for drug-resistant psychosis has been reported by Garety, Kuipers, Fowler, Chamberlain and Dunn (1994). Patients meeting a diagnosis of schizophrenia or schizo-affective psychosis and who presented with unremitting (i.e. for a period of at least six months) drug-resistant positive psychotic symptoms were assigned (but not randomly) to either the treatment group or a wait-list control group. Patients in the treatment group received on average 16 weekly sessions of cognitive-behavioural therapy (Fowler et al., 1994) and were found to report significantly less intense conviction in the delusional thoughts than the control group at end of treatment. Overall, the treatment group fared better than the no-treatment control group. Given that this was obtained using very low statistical power (a maximum of 13 treated vs 7 no-treatment patients), it is likely that this low power masks differences which might actually be found to exist, given adequate statistical power.

The results of the full trial have been published in a series of articles (see Freeman et al., 1998; Garety et al., 1997; Kuipers et al., 1997, 1998). A total of 60 subjects presenting with at least one positive and distressing symptom of medication-resistant psychosis were randomly allocated to one of two conditions: cognitive-behaviour therapy plus standard care, or standard care only. Hence, the study investigated the added value of CBT as an adjunct to routine standard care. Therapy lasted nine months and was targeted to the presentation of each individual patient. Results indicated that significant improvements were found only in the combined treatment group, with a 25 per cent reduction in scores on the Brief Psychiatric Rating Scale. No other measures suggested any significant change. There was a comparatively low drop-out rate (11 per cent) and a majority (80 per cent) expressed satisfaction with the treatment they received. Some of the design and analysis features of this series reflect Generation III research, such as consideration of treatment responders and drop-out rates. An overview of individual CBT in the treatment of hallucinations and delusions has been carried out (see Haddock et al., 1998).

Fairburn and colleagues have carried out a series of studies on the effects of psychotherapy on bulimia nervosa (e.g. Fairburn et al., 1991). Fairburn, Jones, Peveler, Hope and O'Connor (1993) compared cognitive-behavioural therapy (CBT) with interpersonal therapy (IPT) and also with behaviour therapy (BT; construed as a simplified version of CBT): 25 patients were allocated to each treatment condition, with patients receiving 19 sessions over 18 weeks. The results indicated a high rate of attrition and withdrawal (48 per cent) among patients assigned to BT with few patients in this condition meeting the criteria for a good outcome. By contrast, patients in the CBT and IPT treatments made substantial, lasting, and broadly equivalent changes across the various domains measured. Interestingly, while IPT showed the lowest percentage of patients meeting criterion at the end of treatment, the rate increased monotonically across the three post-treatment assessments such that it was the highest (44 per cent) at one-year follow-up compared with 36 per cent and 20 per cent for CBT and BT respectively. A follow-up study of 89 patients, assessed on average just under six years following treatment, from two consecutive studies (Fairburn et al., 1986, 1993) found that patients who had received either CBT or interpersonal therapy (IPT or focal) had a better prognosis than patients receiving behaviour therapy (Fairburn et al., 1995).

Roth and Fonagy (1996) identified psychotherapeutic interventions that have demonstrable benefit to patients (i.e. an evidence base) and also attempted to draw implications for their delivery within the NHS. In drawing attention to a number of limitations in the available research literature, they identified systemic and psychodynamic models as requiring research effort. They also identified a number of methodological limitations which should be noted, including generalizing results from highly controlled randomized controlled trials, the ambiguity of findings from less well-controlled studies, the relative absence of long-term follow-up, statistical analyses, and most importantly in their view, the complexity of mental health problems and issues of classification raised by such complexity. They concluded that meta-analyses and qualitative reviews of psychological treatments for depression strongly support CBT even for severe depression, and that they were superior to alternative psychotherapeutic treatments. However, they added the observation that 'the range of contrast therapies is sometimes rather limited and rarely includes psychodynamic treatments'. This reiterates the point made previously that some of the advantages shown for CBT may arise as a function of the weaker alternative treatment selected rather than the superiority *per se* of CBT.

The research reported so far has been based within a 'pure' treatment method (either CBT or PI [psychodynamic-interpersonal], or BT). However, there has also been an increase in integrative therapies. For example, a comparison between more traditional 'interpretative' therapy versus cognitive-analytic therapy (CAT: Ryle, 1990) has been carried out (Brockman et al., 1987). Although the overall findings reported no difference, one aim of this study was to evaluate effectiveness as carried out by trainees. Accordingly, it could be argued that the finding of no difference is a function of inexperienced therapists rather than similarly effective treatments. It is still valid to conclude that the two treatments are equally effective with trainee therapists. However, as the authors acknowledge, an unequal attrition (i.e. dropout) rate led to the two groups differing in severity level at intake. Because the two groups were not equivalent in severity at intake, rigorous comparisons of the comparative effectiveness of conditions is problematic. Subsequent reports on CAT have comprised single case studies showing the impact of CAT on patients presenting with borderline personality disorders (e.g. Ryle, 1995; Ryle and Beard, 1993).

Shapiro, Barkham, Reynolds, Hardy and Stiles (1992) combined prescriptive (cognitive-behavioural) and exploratory (psychodynamic-interpersonal) therapies by administering them as 'pure' therapies within a session but alternating within certain constraints across the course of therapy in response to a match between client requirements and a particular overarching integrative model (the assimilation model). The outcome for this single case was successful but requires replication. Overall, there is a dearth of direct evidence for the equivalence in efficacy, let alone superiority, of integrative therapies. Much of the argument in support of their use derives indirectly from the equivalence of outcomes. In addition, it is not clear that skills and expertise gained in one particular method of delivery transfer to a more integrated method without additional training. The current interest in, and articles emanating from, this area is considerable and reflects the fact that integrative therapies are probably more palatable to practitioners than pure treatment methods. Following a major workshop which focused on the research required to move this area forward, little empirical work has been carried out (Wolfe and Goldfried, 1988). Indeed, considerably more work is needed in order to provide hard data on the comparative effectiveness of integrative therapies.

Fonagy (1995) has provided a very useful summary of problems emanating from outcome research but states that without them we would not know what the optimal effects of treatments would be. Taking this forward, he argues for outcome studies (i.e. research from Generations I and II) to be enhanced by clinical audit, thereby bringing it into the realm of every practitioner: 'outcome studies and clinical audit should be performed in tandem. The first will identify potentially useful interventions which may be adopted by clinicians for specific disorders, and the second will show clinicians how effective they are in implementing these procedures' (1995: 176). He continues: 'Without outcome studies, the design of clinical services will lack strategic direction; without clinical audit, services may be massively distorted in unknown ways based on findings of little relevance to work at ground level' (ibid.). The domain of clinical audit is very much to the fore at present and it makes eminent sense that this agenda be carried forward collaboratively in the context of rigorous research in the area of psychotherapy.

Process and therapist skills

Generation II process research differs appreciably in Britain from the United States where Carl Rogers acted as a central motivator for research activity. A series of studies carried out by Shapiro (1969, 1970, 1973, 1976) which investigated the role of the facilitative conditions in psychotherapy offered little support for the view that they played a central role in accounting for change. However, later work investigating the role of various verbal response modes found 'exploration' (a response between interpretation and reflection) to be associated with client and helper experiences of perceived empathy (Barkham and Shapiro, 1986).

An ongoing programme of psychotherapy teaching and training has been implemented and evaluated in Manchester, largely through the work of Goldberg, Hobson, Margison and colleagues. This work has arisen as a result of its being a regional centre for psychotherapy. Consistent with its teaching priority, there has been considerable research into teaching specific psychotherapeutic methods to other caregivers, in particular, the development of the Conversational Model of psychotherapy, together with a comprehensive teaching programme (Goldberg et al., 1984; Maguire et al., 1984). The Conversational Model of therapy has been developed over the past 30 years as a therapeutic method for dealing with people who have experienced difficulties in their interpersonal relationships. Hobson, in some ways reflecting the impact of Rogers, not only developed the model, but has also been central in advocating its investigation through video-recording and research. This method has been packaged for teaching purposes and has been shown to be transferable to junior doctors (Goldberg et al., 1984). The development of teaching methods was paralleled by the development of manuals for specified therapies (a defining hallmark of Generation II research). For example, Startup and Shapiro (1993) carried out an adherence study on the Second Sheffield Psychotherapy Project in which each of 220 sessions (110 sessions from each of CB and PI therapies) were coded by two people according to a rating manual. These authors found that 97 per cent of sessions were correctly assigned.

The extension of psychotherapy skills to people in a primary care setting emphasizes not only the increasing adoption of a psychosocial model of presenting problems but also the notion that providing primary caregivers with psychotherapeutic skills results in an increase in the detection of psychological illness. For example, Gask (Gask and McGrath, 1989) has worked extensively on the application of psychotherapeutic skills by general practitioners dealing with issues such as AIDS. Research has also focused on therapist difficulties (Davis et al., 1987). These authors devised a taxonomy of nine categories: using these they were able to classify reliably therapists' difficulties. The three most commonly occurring difficulties were therapists feeling *threatened* (i.e. the therapist feels a need to protect self against the client), feeling *puzzled* (i.e. the therapist cannot see how best to proceed), and *damaging* (i.e. the therapist feels that he or she may be injuring the client). Most interestingly, therapists showed internal consistency in the patterns of difficulties experienced. This led the authors to argue that these profiles would be highly related to therapists' personalities and consequently might help identify potential counter-transference problems for different therapists. This work is ongoing.

Generation III

Cost-effectiveness and service delivery

There is currently considerable interest, both economically and clinically, in evaluating the cost-effectiveness of the psychotherapies (e.g. Healey and Knapp, 1995). For example, McGrath and Lawson (1987) have argued for the legitimacy of assessing the benefits of psychotherapy from an economic standpoint and conclude that it is possible to justify the provision of psychotherapy within the NHS on economic grounds. At a broad level, Parry (1992) has identified a range of issues which are pertinent in devising cost-efficient psychotherapy services.

A major feature of the studies detailed in Generation II is their attempt to combine both internal validity (i.e. the attempt to minimize bias, usually through random assignment of clients to particular conditions) and extrinsic validity (i.e. sampling a clinical rather than a student population). Perhaps the best single indicator of such attempts is the use of random allocation of clients to treatment conditions (RCT). Often, however, it is not possible to do this either for ethical or for practical reasons. When it is not possible to incorporate high components of both forms of validity, researchers face a choice: they must either employ analogue studies (e.g. studying students with test anxiety) in which internal validity is high but which are problematic in relation to generalizing the findings to clinical populations, or use more naturalistic studies (describing and evaluating clients referred to outpatient settings) which do not permit the researcher to manipulate specific variables. Naturalistic designs have been used and are a logical means for evaluating service delivery systems. A study using naturalistic design and studying inpatients has been carried out by Denford, Schachter, Temple, Kind and Rosser (1983). These workers completed a retrospective study of 28 successive admissions for inpatient psychotherapy at the Cassel Hospital, a community using a combination of both individual and community psychotherapeutic methods. Their findings suggested that 'to maximise the proportion of patients who improve, the hospital should be inclined to accept patients who have neurotic rather than borderline or psychotic psychopathology, those who appear considerably depressed, those with a history of minimal out-patient psychiatric treatment, and possibly those judged to be of superior intelligence' (Denford et al., 1983: 235–6). An important difference between successful clients when compared with clients rated as failures and dropouts was that motivation for insight and change was high in 50 per cent of successful cases and lower in both failed (38 per cent) and dropout clients (13 per cent). Blind ratings of motivation tended to distinguish success and failed groups at triage, a finding consistent with the results obtained by Malan (1963, 1976).

Another retrospective study was carried out by Keller (1984) who investigated the applicability of brief psychotherapeutic methods developed at the Tavistock Clinic in NHS outpatient psychotherapy clinics. Fifteen clients in all were treated but results did not obtain statistical significance. At non-significant levels, however, the results indicated that outcome was better for those clients who experienced high levels of distress subjectively but who functioned well externally. In addition, outcome was better for those clients who had a supportive relationship outside therapy and for whom a psychodynamic focus could be formulated. Keller argued that these findings generally substantiate Malan's (1976) work. Interestingly, this study exemplifies the difficulties of practitioners carrying out research. In their favour, these practitioners set up a workshop to provide a framework for the participating practitioners to adapt their methods to the clients they saw in their own practices as well as providing an environment for research to be implemented and carried out. However, from the researcher's viewpoint it is difficult to have much confidence in the findings: they are non-significant, based on a small sample, and contaminated by other influences (including rater bias). In addition, the finding that more distressed clients fare better (a finding also reported by Denford et al., 1983) may be a function of scores regressing to the mean. Accordingly, this phenomenon should always be borne in mind when considering improvement in high scorers.

Research has also occurred with specialized populations who are of particular concern to practitioners in service delivery settings. For example, the treatment of survivors of childhood sexual abuse (CSA) has been reviewed by Cahill et al. (1991), who concluded that virtually all publications in this area to date take the form of therapists' experience of treating patients. They conclude that what is needed is the application of empirical research methodology to establish the most effective treatments. In a study of six survivors of CSA, Clarke and Llewelyn (1994) report on the changes achieved by patients following cognitive-analytic therapy. Similarly, Birchwood (1992) has proposed practical intervention strategies to help reduce the occurrence of florid schizophrenic relapse where the emphasis is on providing an early intervention service.

The issue of cost-effectiveness has been addressed in several studies in which very brief interventions have been devised (i.e. therapy is construed as assessment). One model delivers therapy in the form of two sessions one week apart and a third session three months later. This generic model of therapy, termed two-plus-one therapy, has been evaluated in a large randomized controlled trial (Barkham et al., 1999). A total of 116 clients experiencing a range of sub-syndromal depression received two-plus-one sessions of either CB or PI therapy either immediately or after a four-week delay (the latter acting as a control condition). The initial advantage for patients in the immediate group disappeared once clients in the delayed condition received treatment (i.e. offering treatment immediately relieved distress quicker but the other clients 'caught up'). In terms of the comparative treatments, there were no significant differences in outcomes between CB and PI therapies at the end of treatment. However, at one-year follow-up, there was a significant advantage to CBT on the Beck Depression Inventory. Other features of the reporting in this study – for example utilizing reliable and clinically significant methods to show that approximately two-thirds of clients met such stringent criteria for change – reflect Generation IV research.

Other clinicians have devised variants of the original model; for example, a model of intervention comprising a three-plus-one design for patients presenting with greater severity (Aveline, 1995). Preliminary results based on analyses midway through this latter study, which compared a brief intervention and follow-up with a standard assessment for psychotherapy procedure, suggest that there are more discharges in the brief intervention model than in the standard assessment, together with greater change at the four-month follow-up. One consequence of the higher rate of discharge arising from the brief intervention model is that if this were adopted, it would help decrease the waiting time for patients prior to starting therapy. However, as Aveline (1995) correctly cautions, care should be taken in analysing results midway through a trial, particularly if those results themselves are less than clear-cut. Such models are informed by the dose-effect curve which, for example, would predict 30 per cent of clients to show improvement after two sessions. Interests in cost-effectiveness are therefore focused on identifying, like Fennell and Teasdale (1987), those clients who are able to respond beneficially to such treatment models. This is consistent with attempts to match treatment-specific delivery models with clearly defined presenting problems.

There have also been examples of established CT interventions being adapted to make them briefer (more cost efficient). Clark and colleagues adapted CT for panic disorder – normally comprising 12–15 one-hour sessions – to be administered in five one-hour sessions by making extensive use of inter-session work and self-study modules (Clark et al., 1999). A total of 43 patients were randomly allocated to one of three conditions: full CT, brief CT, or a three-month wait list. Both full and brief interventions were superior to the wait list – in itself a Generation I comparison – but it is the comparison between the full and brief versions which is of importance here. Clark and his colleagues found no significant differences between the two versions, both of which had large and very similar effect sizes.

However, cost-effectiveness is not synonymous with brevity. For example, while Freeman et al. (1988) acknowledged that improvement rate for bulimics in their study (77 per cent) was marginally less than in other studies, they argued that the greater intensity offered by other treatments (e.g. being seen several times a week or for half a day at a time) for marginally greater improvement was not necessarily cost-effective. Similarly, Peveler and Fairburn (1989) argued that while their treatment for a case of anorexia nervosa with diabetes mellitus lasted one year, 'the treatment was of relatively low intensity, amounting to just under 40 hours of therapist time in total'. More salient, perhaps, was the fact that the diabetes required only routine specialist input and no hospital admission, making the treatment cost-effective when compared with the potential cost of a single hospital admission.

Guthrie, Moorey, Margison, Barker, Palmer, McGrath, Tomenson and Creed (1999) evaluated the cost-effectiveness of brief psychodynamic-interpersonal therapy in 110 high users of psychiatric services. The sample was defined as patients who had made no improvement in their psychological symptoms. Their results showed that brief PI therapy for this particular patient sample resulted in significant improvement in their psychological status as well as a reduction in health care utilization and health care costs in the six months following treatment. The issue of cost-effectiveness has become an increasingly central issue in the design and delivery of psychotherapy services.

The impetus behind establishing effective psychological interventions in primary care has seen several programmes of research. One programme combining the issues of brief interventions and cost issues set in primary care has been carried out by Mynors-Wallis and colleagues (Gath and Mynors-Wallis, 1997; Mynors-Wallis, 1996). A series of studies have been carried out on problem-solving treatment (PST) and observations include that PST can be effectively delivered in primary care by a range of professionals (e.g. psychiatrists, nurses) but that it may be more expensive than usual treatment (by GPs) in primary care as indicated by direct costs. However, when indirect savings are considered, then greater cost savings are likely. A Cochrane review carried out by Rowland and colleagues (Rowland et al., 2000, 2001) found four randomized and controlled patient preference trials comparing *bona fide* counselling in primary care with usual general practitioner care. Findings suggested that clients receiving counselling had significantly better psychological symptom levels after their counselling compared with those receiving standard GP care, as indicated by an ES difference of 0.30.

A large outcome study – the London–Manchester trial – has compared non-directive counselling, CBT, and usual general practitioner care for the presentation of depression in primary care and is an exemplar of the combination of efficacy (Ward et al., 2000) and cost-effectiveness (Bower et al., 2000) issues that is a hallmark of Generation III research. A total of 464 patients took part in this prospective controlled trial which utilized both randomized and patient preference allocation arms. Patients who had a preference as to which treatment they preferred selected that treatment condition; those who stated they had no preference were randomized to one of the three treatment conditions. A total of 137 patients selected their own treatment, 197 patients were randomly assigned to one of the three treatment conditions, and 130 were randomized to one of the two psychological therapies (in which patients received upwards of 12 sessions). At four months, patients in the two psychological therapies showed greater gains on the BDI than those randomized to usual GP care (even though all groups improved over time). But interestingly, there were no significant differences between the two psychological therapies (i.e. non-directive counselling and CBT) at four months and no significant differences between all three conditions at 12 months. The additional cost-effectiveness analysis (Bower et al., 2000) showed that there were no significant differences in direct costs, production losses or societal costs between the three treatment conditions at either four or 12 months. It was concluded that the two psychological interventions were significantly more cost-effective in the short term (at four months) as patients showed greater improvement at no additional cost. However, all cost and clinical differences disappeared at 12 months.

The evidence drawn from both Generation II and Generation III has provided the basis for the development of the evidence-based approach to the psychological therapies. Rowland and Goss (2000) have presented the multifaceted components of an evidence-based approach to counselling and the psychological therapies. The main drivers for evidence-based health care are presented (Baker and Kleijnen, 2000), together with reviews of policy (Ferguson and Russell, 2000), economic issues (Maynard, 2000), as well as an overview of evidence-based psychotherapy (Parry, 2000). Methodological issues are presented, including those pertaining to RCTs (Bower and King, 2000), efficacy versus effectiveness (Barkham and Mellor-Clark, 2000), and the contribution of qualitative research (McLeod, 2000). The approach to clinical practice guidelines has been addressed by Cape and Parry (2000) and draws on the publication by the Department of Health of the *Treatment Choice in Psychological Therapies and Counselling: Evidence Based Clinical Practice Guideline* (2001). The *Guideline* was based on a systematic review of the literature and made recommendations on treatment of choice in relation to the following presenting problems: depression, anxiety, panic disorder, social anxiety and phobias, post-traumatic disorders, eating disorders, obsessive-compulsive disorders, and personality disorders. It also included psychological approaches to chronic pain, chronic fatigue, gastrointestinal disorders, and gynaecological presentations. A series of recommendations were made comprising generic points focusing on general principles, and specific points relating to therapies for specific presenting problems. Each recommendation was annotated according to four levels of evidence supporting it: meta-analysis or RCT (Level A); controlled or quasi-experimental study, or extrapolated from level A evidence (Level B), descriptive studies or extrapolated from level B evidence (Level C), and expert committee/clinical experience of respected authority, or extrapolated from level C (Level D). Examples of each level of evidence are presented here.

In relation to the area of initial assessment, it was recommended that 'Psychological therapy should be routinely considered as a treatment option when assessing mental health problems' (Level B evidence 2001: 34). For patient preference, it was recommended that 'Patient preference should inform treatment choice, particularly where the research evidence does not indicate a clear choice of therapy' (Level D evidence: 36). For depressive disorder, it was recommended that 'Depressive disorders may be treated effectively with psychological therapy, with best evidence for cognitive behaviour therapy and interpersonal therapy, and some evidence for a number of other structured therapies, including short-term psychodynamic therapy' (Level A evidence: 37). For personality disorder, it was recommended that 'Structured psychological therapies delivered by skilled practitioners can contribute to the longer-term treatment of personality disorders' (Level C evidence: 38). Of course, setting out recommendations – however scientifically sound – does not guarantee that they will be implemented in all settings, nor that they will be adhered to. So while the aim is to provide guidelines based on the best available evidence in an attempt to ensure that people in need are allocated to appropriate psychological interventions, the whole process requires auditing, evaluation and constant updating. More importantly perhaps, it also requires an educational process at the point at which clients are first assessed and the resources to provide the very interventions that are recommended.

Change pathways

In the study of 'psychotherapeutic process', work on psychoanalytic therapy has been, traditionally, the most difficult to carry out. However, there are studies worthy of note. For example, Moran and Fonagy (1987) carried out a non-experimental single-case study of a diabetic teenager who received psychoanalysis five times weekly for three and a half years. They investigated the relationship between psychoanalytic themes and glycosuria (the presence of sugar in the client's urine). They found that the working through of psychic conflict predicted an improvement in diabetic control, both in the short and in the long term. Of particular importance to the authors were the findings occurring in the short term where, they argued, other common factors could not be viewed as competing explanations. This view appears to counter research evidence attesting to the potency of common factors irrespective of time. Importantly, however, an aim of this study was to attempt to apply scientific rigour to psychoanalytic processes. As the authors state: 'the present study is viewed as an initial step towards the increased systematization of the treatment of psychoanalytic data and. . .other workers using similar methodologies may be able to explore psychoanalytic hypotheses which eluded the current authors' (Moran and Fonagy, 1987: 370).

In an attempt to ascertain how cognitive therapy works, Fennell (1983) drew together the purported mechanisms of change in cognitive therapy for depression. She asked three questions: How does cognitive therapy achieve its immediate effect? How does cognitive therapy affect depression over the course of the treatment as a whole? and How are treatment effects maintained over the longer term? In answer to the first question, Fennell (1983) concluded that active thought modification in itself can bring about significant change. In addition, where the intensity or frequency of depressive thinking is reduced, a reduction in severity of depression occurs. In answer to the second question, Fennell concluded that the most powerful strategy for achieving change is a 'close interweaving' of thought-change and behaviour-change. 'Thought-change allows behaviour-change to occur and behaviour-change in turn provides evidence to further counter distorted negative thinking' (1983: 102). The third question is answered by suggesting that long-term improvement will be most effectively achieved with the widest range of clients by training in generalized coping skills rather than modifying assumptions. This is because the modification of underlying assumptions is less easy to acquire and more difficult to implement when depressed. In a study of clients diagnosed as anxious, Butler, Gelder, Hibbert, Cullington and Klimes (1987b) attempted to determine the effective components of anxiety management. These researchers found evidence to suggest that treatment-specific components included the control of anxiety-related cognitions and the confronting of anxiety-provoking situations (as compared with the previous strategy of avoidance).

The attempt to discover the therapeutic ingredients responsible for the effectiveness of psychotherapy has been undertaken in a series of studies deriving from detailed analyses of the first Sheffield Psychotherapy Project (Shapiro and Firth, 1987). For example, Stiles, Shapiro and Firth-Cozens (1988) investigated the impacts of exploratory and prescriptive sessions. Impacts refer to the participants' evaluations of the immediate effects of the therapy session (their evaluation of the session, how they feel immediately afterwards, etc.). Both therapists and clients rated prescriptive sessions as smoother (i.e. smooth, easy, pleasant, safe) than exploratory sessions. However, while both therapists and clients rated exploratory sessions as rougher, therapists but not clients rated exploratory sessions as deeper (e.g. deep, valuable, full and special). Taken together, these results show different therapies to have different impacts. When these results are combined with the findings that there is a general equivalence of outcome, the most parsimonious explanation is that equivalence 'occurs' after the differing therapies have had their impact. That is, there are different routes (i.e. processes) to achieving broadly similar outcomes with the processes differing as a function of the different goals of therapy.

Common factors and integration

The above sections have addressed particular therapies which are based upon the assumption that they comprise specific techniques which can, or will, account for effective change. By contrast, research into common factors has provided a vehicle for arguing that the effective ingredients of therapy tend to be shared factors (i.e. the therapeutic relationship). Murphy, Cramer and Lillie (1984) asked clients to describe curative factors following individual therapy. Findings showed 'advice' and 'talking to someone interested in my problems' to be elicited from more than half the clients. Further, the study found that 'receiving advice' and 'talking with someone who understands' were both moderately correlated with outcome. The relationship of each of these to outcome accounted for approaching 20 per cent of the outcome variance.

In a study of phobic clients, Bennun and Schindler (1988) investigated therapist and client factors operative within behavioural treatments. Ratings on these factors by clients and therapists were positively correlated with outcome, suggesting that interpersonal variables may contribute to treatment outcome. The results showed that the more positive the participants' ratings of each other after the second session, the greater the amount of change achieved at the end of therapy. Bennun and Schindler concluded: 'Researchers and clinicians should not be too preoccupied with technique; favourable interpersonal conditions are also essential for therapeutic change' (1988: 151). In a study of clients' and therapists' views of therapy, Llewelyn (1988) sampled 40 therapist–client dyads participating in psychological therapy in standard British clinical settings. During the course of therapy, the most frequently reported helpful events for clients were 'reassurance' and 'problem evaluation', while at termination 'problem solution' was the most frequently rated as helpful. By contrast, therapists rated 'insight' as the most common helpful event both during therapy and at termination. These findings suggest that clients and therapists have quite different perceptions of what is helpful during the course of therapy. Clients appeared to value the common ingredients of reassurance and relief. In contrast, therapists valued both the cognitive and affective insight felt to be attained by their clients during therapy. Of course, if insight 'leads' to problem solution, at least in the sense of preceding it, it may be that clients are focusing on the consequences of their insight while therapists value the more personal and dynamic component of insight itself rather than the action arising from it. In the final analysis, it is to be expected that two differing perspectives on the therapeutic process will provide two differing perceptions.

Ryle has carried out research spanning some two decades into psychotherapy. Underlying his work is the aim of establishing an understanding of psychotherapy based within a cognitive framework. This was apparent in his early work using repertory grids. Ryle has developed three important constructs relevant to understanding change (Ryle, 1979): 'dilemmas' (the narrow way in which a client will see the possible alternatives), 'traps' (patterns of behaviour which are based upon and also serve to reinforce negative assumptions about the self), and 'snags' (the avoidance of change due to its effects, real or imagined). Ryle (1980) studied 15 cases in which clients received focused integrated active psychotherapy. The aim was to define therapeutic goals which were specific and individual to clients and yet which referred to underlying cognitive processes as well as to overt symptoms. In general, clients reported improvements both in target complaints as well as in target dilemmas, traps and snags. Results showed that when a change in target dilemmas in the predicted direction occurred, this change was invariably accompanied by a change in the client's cognitive structure as well as in problems targeted at the beginning of therapy. This provided support for Ryle's view that, first, a cognitive framework for understanding psychotherapeutic change is both feasible and informative. Further, Ryle argued that his research counterbalances the more narrow approaches to psychotherapy, stating that attending to deeper cognitive structures enables questions to be answered which have long interested dynamic therapists but which have eluded researchers. It is certainly true that psychotherapy research 'should attend with adequate subtlety. . .the fundamental but less easily demonstrated changes aimed for' (Ryle, 1980: 481). These findings have led to the formalization of Ryle's cognitive integration of theory and practice (Ryle, 1982), and more recently, to the development of a form of brief therapy termed cognitive-analytic therapy (CAT).

Generation IV

Clinically meaningful outcome research

In previous research generations, large-scale research studies addressed questions about the 'efficacy' of a particular intervention as delivered under optimal conditions. The results of such studies formed the basis for 'evidence-based practice' which is now required to substantiate the delivery of any psychological (or medical) intervention in service settings. As such, the evidence-based practice movement – which applies to all health-related professions – is now a central tenet in all health care delivery (see Parry, 2000). It is the basis upon which government health agencies make recommendations for treatment and is prem-ised on the view that the gold standards of research methodology lie in random-ized controlled trials (RCTs) and meta-analytic studies. The findings from these studies are then used to inform practice in routine settings. However, it is a questionable logic that findings derived from research studies carried out under optimal conditions should be adopted as policy and then directly transported 'down' into routine service settings. In contrast to the evidence-based paradigm, there has been an increased focus on developing an evidence base within routine practice. This focus has culminated in the development of a complementary paradigm for accumulating and presenting evidence: 'practice-based evidence'. In contrast to the 'top-down' paradigm of evidence-based practice in which RCTs inform policy, 'practice-based evidence' utilizes a 'bottom-up' paradigm in which 'routine clinical treatment' (RCT) is accumulated in practice settings to derive an evidence base in which practitioners are partners (see Barkham and Mellor-Clark, 2000; Margison et al., 2000). This process is summarized in Figure 15.1, which shows how these two paradigms can inform each other providing they are equally valued. This can also be seen to apply to process research which is grounded in the day-to-day and moment-to-moment work of practitioners. Because each paradigm can be viewed as representing the constituencies of researcher and practitioners respectively, it is likely that it is the combination of the two

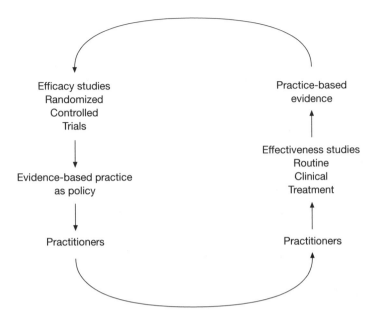

Figure 15.1   The efficacy-effectiveness model

paradigms which is most likely to form an effective bridge between practice and research in the future.

Within this practice-based paradigm, outcome research activity in the UK has been given real impetus from three differing perspectives. First, as with the field in general, there has been disquiet with the yield from the traditional outcome paradigm employing RCTs. Indeed, there are increasing criticisms of RCTs as the design of choice for investigating the psychological therapies (see Barkham and Mellor-Clark, 2000). Secondly, there are increasing directives from the Department of Health (DH) on monitoring outcomes as part of the broad agenda of clinical governance. And thirdly, there is a widening acceptance by practitioners of the potential utility of collecting routine outcome data to inform clinical practice and services.

The move towards adopting outcome measures in routine practice settings has grown from developmental work on a range of different but related instruments. These include the Health of the Nation Outcome Scales (HoNOS; Wing et al., 1998), the Functional Analysis of Care Environments (FACE; Clifford, 1999), and the Clinical Outcomes in Routine Evaluation (CORE) System (Evans et al., 2002; Mellor-Clark et al., 1999). Between them, these measures cover the range of people presenting from primary care settings through to those deemed to be experiencing severe and enduring mental illness. The availability of these measures provides a real incentive for services to generate data that will inform their service and will, in turn, increasingly generate large data sets that can be used to investigate variables associated with outcomes. However, the question as to whether routine outcome measurement is feasible in the broad domain of mental health (including psychotherapy) remains to be addressed. Three criteria have been identified that outcome measures would have to meet: (1) standardized, (2) acceptable to clinicians, and (3) feasible for routine use (Thornicroft and Slade, 2000). Hence, the agenda is very much that of determining the effectiveness of psychological therapies. Studies have reported falls in HoNOS scores of almost 50 per cent in people experiencing a range of mental illnesses (e.g. McClelland et al., 2000). Similarly, various studies using components of the CORE System have indicated that, for example, approximately 80 per cent of clients referred to secondary care services scored above a predetermined clinical cut-off point prior to therapy, a figure which halved to approximately 40 per cent at discharge (Barkham et al., 2001). Another study carried out in primary care settings reported that 58 per cent of clients showed both reliable and clinically significant change and a further 17 per cent achieved reliable change (Mellor-Clark et al., 2001). Further research is required into determining the range of possible contextual factors that influence outcomes in routine settings.

Clinically meaningful process research

The procedures employed in Generation IV process research can be described as either descriptive/exploratory or as aiming to link specific processes to theories of change. These two types of process work have been reviewed by Llewelyn and Hardy (2001) but not specifically within a model of psychotherapy research generations. Evidence of Generation IV process research can be seen as arising from the work employing the 'events' paradigm which has yielded findings that bridge the use of quantitative and qualitative approaches. Central to this approach has been interpersonal process recall (IPR) and its variants which can be used as the method for obtaining events to carry out comprehensive process analysis (CPA; Elliott, 1989; Elliott et al., 2001; Rees et al., 2001), as can having patients complete the Helpful Aspects of Therapy Form (HAT; Llewelyn, 1988). Llewelyn, Elliott, Shapiro, Hardy and Firth-Cozens (1988) investigated client perceptions of helpful impacts occurring in prescriptive and exploratory therapy. The most common impacts reported by clients as helpful at the session and phase level (i.e. after eight sessions) were (a) 'awareness' (the client getting in touch with feelings that may previously have been warded off) and (b) 'problem solution' (possible ways of coping being worked out or rehearsed in the session). Not surprisingly, 'awareness' was largely attributable to exploratory therapy and 'problem solution' to prescriptive therapy. As Llewelyn et al. (1988) argue, these findings suggest that clients are achieving the major types of therapeutic realization intended by the two different therapies. The least helpful was reported to be 'unwanted thoughts'. This latter finding raises the point that clients and therapists have differential perspectives, with the clients experiencing 'unwanted thoughts' as negative while therapists may well see this as a necessary stage for the client to progress through towards improved psychological health.

CPA was used to analyse six client-identified significant insight events in cognitive-behavioural (CB) and psychodynamic-interpersonal (PI) therapy (Elliott et al., 1994). Results suggested a general model of insight events which involved a 'meaning bridge' that linked the client's reaction to its context. Elliott et al. (1994) proposed the following five-stage sequential model: (1) contextual priming, (2) novel information, (3) initial distantiated processing, (4) insight, and (5) elaboration. However, the content of the insight events from the contrasting therapies were very different. CB events were primarily reattributional while PI events involved connection to a conflict theme from a previous session. Two further single-case studies combining outcome and process components have been drawn from the Second Sheffield Psychotherapy Project. The first study tested the assimilation model using a very stringent procedure and found support for successful assimilation of a problematic experience to be associated with a positive outcome (Field et al., 1994). The second study reported a task analysis of a single case in which a rupture and subsequent resolution of the therapeutic alliance was investigated (Agnew et al., 1994). While it may appear that this new generation of research is more grounded in clinical material, and hence more appropriate to the concerns of practitioners, it is probably too early, historically, within this research generation to be able to evaluate fully whether or not it is successful.

The concept of responsiveness has been employed to advance our understanding of the process of change. Recall that this concept suggests that the therapist needs to be responsive to the requirements of the individual client at a particular moment in therapy within the wider context of the client's presenting history and therapeutic progress. Hardy and colleagues have carried out research in this area and shown that therapists offered different moment-by-moment interventions to clients as a function of clients' particular interpersonal style (Hardy et al., 1998a, 1998b). This approach was applied to a study of 10 significant therapy events in psychodynamic-interpersonal therapy (Hardy et al., 1999). It was proposed that responsiveness would occur when therapists provided clients with a sense of security by responding to the moment-by-moment attachment needs of the clients. Moreover, appropriate responsiveness would occur when working with the clients in the zone of 'proximal development' whereby clients would feel safe to explore potential threats and dangers without being overwhelmed by them. Therapist responsiveness was classified into three categories: containment (i.e. made to feel safe), reflection (i.e. to be understood), and interpretation (i.e. challenged). Results showed nine out of the 10 events included containment strategies.

As in the international arena, a major tool of Generation IV process research has been the application of qualitative methodologies. For example, McLeod has written texts (McLeod, 1997) and carried out research (Grafanaki and McLeod, 1999) on the use of narrative as a means of understanding the therapy process. Similarly, examples of the potential of conversational analysis (Madill et al., 2001) and discourse analysis (DA; Madill and Barkham, 1997) have been presented. The study using DA addressed the question of how therapeutic change was achieved in one specified problem area for a client receiving psychodynamic-interpersonal therapy. Whilst providing an overall heuristic for researchers, the analysis focused on how the available linguistic resources and cultural meanings were used in both the construction of the client's presenting problem and also its solution. Conversational analysis and discourse analysis provide a perspective from outside the 'institution' of psychotherapy that offers considerable potential for practitioners to gain insight into their own work. This, ultimately, may be one of the major contributions of process work – providing a proxy to clinical supervision whereby other experts come to clinical material and apply their models and approaches in order to challenge the assumptions held by practitioners.

Conclusion

Future directions

The focus of this chapter has been on face-to-face individual therapy. It has not included research on group approaches nor on the growing area of self-help. Both these modalities have considerable potential in terms of the cost-effectiveness of delivering services to those who require them (Generation III research). The development of self-help interventions is also bolstered by the increased potential provided by computers. The ability to devise affordable computer-based packages (CD-Roms), easily updated, for individual use provides one means of ensuring widespread support of people in need. However, it might be argued that the voice and process of therapy is diminished in service of a more educational approach. Another perspective that has been increasingly heralded is that of the 'user' – the person receiving therapy. Researchers are now required to include the views of users, but much of this has been tokenism. While it appears absolutely right to incorporate users into the research domain, moving it to the point where they are equal partners in research activity requires considerable thought and effort.

In terms of outcome and process, outcomes research faces challenges to ensure that it does not become synonymous with generating league tables of therapies or services. Such procedures are ultimately divisive where so often like is not compared with like. And process research needs to ensure that it is seen to be central to the delivery of quality services through the mechanisms of training, supervision and continuing professional development. There remains a reluctance to focus on the practitioner. Studies are still designed and powered primarily according to client numbers rather than based on practitioners. Methodologically, ignoring therapist effects will inflate any estimate of treatment effects, so it is critical that the investigating of these effects becomes a central focus of research in the psychological therapies. Wampold (2001) has argued cogently for the case to replace the 'therapy' with the 'therapist' as the focus for future research.

Tensions and developments

In reviewing psychotherapy research over the past 50 years, it is striking how the field and the phenomena investigated tend to be presented in a dichotomous fashion: outcome vs process; qualitative vs quantitative methods; evidence-based practice or practice-based paradigms; client or practitioner perceptions; efficacy vs effectiveness; cognitive-behavioural therapy vs psychodynamic-interpersonal therapies; statistically significant findings vs no statistically significant findings; and so on. It would appear that this propensity to dichotomize phenomena, processes and methods is done in service of making the subject matter easier to research and, therefore, understand. However, has such a meta-paradigm yielded sufficient for the scientific and practitioner communities?

Over the past half-century, psychotherapy research has moved from establishing the efficacy of therapy via increasing specificity towards grappling with issues of service delivery and clinical meaningfulness for clinicians and patients. Yet it is interesting to note that by far the largest section of this chapter has been taken up by Generation II research, which may reflect the currency of 'specificity' at this point in time – an issue which underpins the evidence-based practice movement. However, while these generations can be placed in broad chronological and linear order, for some areas of clinical practice there is a cyclical order, with some areas only now moving towards Generation I-type research. These generations are conceptual and thematic and do not appear to have a definitive sell-by date. The cyclical phenomenon in which early issues are revisited by a new research generation or in which some political or social movement gives renewed salience to a paradigm from a prior research generation may suggest that there is a limit to the actual number of research generations. The accumulated evidence drawn from Generations I, II and III has provided a robust base for the broad activity of psychotherapy – and the evidence base is still growing. The hallmark of Generation IV research has been to move towards clinically meaningful research (process) and effectiveness in the field (outcome). In many ways these hallmarks reflect reworkings of process work prior to Generation I (see p. 375) and the outcome work comprising Generation I. It may be useful in the future to reflect on developments and trends in psychotherapy research equally as reworkings of earlier research generations rather than construing them as genuinely 'new' generations.

Some of the research strands reported in this chapter appear to be developmental (e.g. specificity leading on to empirically supported treatments) while others appear to reflect reactions to perceived past failures (e.g. the call for more qualitative research in response to the perceived failure of outcome research to identify significant differences between treatment approaches). In the efficacy versus effectiveness debate, there are developmental forces operating (e.g. the need to extend research from RCTs into field settings) as well as more reactionary forces (e.g. testing treatments in unrealistic conditions yield little for routine practice). The same tensions exist in relation to the debate concerning specific versus common factors in which some argue for increased efforts in the area of specificity whilst others argue that the influence of and evidence for common factors is so prevalent that this should be the focus of research efforts. Hence, while there is clearly a mounting knowledge base in the area of the psychological therapies, the products and positions taken reflect an art of science rather than any given single truth. In a personal reflection on the issues relating to psycho-therapy research, Goldfried has argued that: 'In order for psychotherapy to mature, we need to make use of our creative research and clinical energies to build upon, rather than rediscover, what we already know' (2000: 13–14). And therein lies the challenge to us all.

Further information on research

Further information on research on the psychological therapies can be obtained from the following websites:

Society for Psychotherapy Research (SPR)
www.psychotherapyresearch.org

Psychological Therapies Research Centre (PTRC)
www.psyc.leeds.ac.uk/ptrc/

British Association for Behavioural and Cognitive Psychotherapy (BABCP)
www.babcp.org.uk

Author note

This chapter is dedicated to the memory of Kenneth I. Howard, a founding father of the Society for Psychotherapy Research.

References

Agnew, R.M., Harper, H., Shapiro, D.A. and Barkham, M. (1994) 'Resolving a challenge to the therapeutic relationship: a single case study', *British Journal of Medical Psychology*, 67: 155–70.

Ahn, H. and Wampold, B.E. (2001) 'Where oh where are the specific ingredients? A meta-analysis of components studies in counseling and psychotherapy', *Journal of Counseling Psychology*, 48: 251–7.

Andrews, G., Guitar, B. and Howie, P. (1980) 'Meta-analysis of the effects of stuttering treatment', *Journal of Speech and Hearing Disorders*, **45**: 287–307.

Aveline, M. (1995) 'Assessing the value of brief intervention at the time of assessment for dynamic psychotherapy', in M. Aveline and D.A. Shapiro (eds.), *Research Foundations for Psychotherapy Practice*. Chichester: Wiley. pp. 129–49.

Aveline, M. and Shapiro, D.A. (eds) (1995) *Research Foundations for Psychotherapy Practice*. Chichester: Wiley.

Baker, M. and Kleijnen, J. (2000) 'The drive towards evidence-based health care', in N. Rowland and S. Goss (eds), *Evidence-based Counselling and Psychological Therapies*. London: Routledge. pp. 13–29.

Barker, C., Pistrang, N. and Elliott, R. (1996) *Research Methods in Clinical and Counselling Psychology*. Chichester: Wiley.

Barker, C., Pistrang, N. and Elliott, R. (in press) *Research Methods in Clinical Psychology*, 2nd edn. Chichester: Wiley.

Barkham, M. and Mellor-Clark, J. (2000) 'Rigour and relevance: practice-based evidence in the psychological therapies', in N. Rowland and S. Goss (eds), *Evidence-based Counselling and Psychological Therapies*. London: Routledge. pp. 127–44.

Barkham, M. and Shapiro, D.A. (1986) 'Counselor verbal response modes and experienced empathy', *Journal of Counseling Psychology*, 33: 3–10.

Barkham, M., Rees, A., Shapiro, D.A., Stiles, W.B., Agnew, R.M., Halstead, J., Culverwell, A. and Harrington, V.M.G. (1996) 'Outcomes of time-limited psychotherapy in applied settings: replicating the Second Sheffield Psychotherapy Project', *Journal of Consulting and Clinical Psychology*, 64: 1079–85.

Barkham, M., Shapiro, D.A., Hardy, G.E. and Rees, A. (1999) 'Psychotherapy in two-plus-one sessions: outcomes of a randomized controlled trial of cognitive-behavioral and psychodynamic-interpersonal therapy for subsyndromal depression', *Journal of Consulting and Clinical Psychology*, 67: 201–11.

Barkham, M., Margison, F., Leach, C., Lucock, M., Mellor-Clark, J., Evans, C., Benson, L., Connell, J., Audin, K. and McGrath, G. (2001) 'Service profiling and outcomes benchmarking using the CORE-OM: towards practice-based evidence in the psychological therapies', *Journal of Consulting and Clinical Psychology*, 69: 184–96.

Barlow, D.H., Hayes, S.C. and Nelson, R.O. (1984) *The Scientist-Practitioner: Research and Accountability in Clinical and Educational Settings*. Oxford: Pergamon Press.

Bennun, I. and Schindler, L. (1988) 'Therapist and patient factors in the behavioural treatment of phobic patients', *British Journal of Clinical Psychology*, 27: 145–51.

Bergin, A.E. and Garfield, S.L. (eds) (1971) *Handbook of Psychotherapy and Behavior Change*. New York: Wiley.

Bergin, A.E. and Garfield, S.L. (1994a) 'Overview, trends, and future issues', in A.E. Bergin and S.L. Garfield (eds), *Handbook of Psychotherapy and Behavior Change*, 4th edn. New York: Wiley. pp. 821–30.

Bergin, A.E. and Garfield, S.L. (eds) (1994b) *Handbook of Psychotherapy and Behavior Change*, 4th edn. Chichester: Wiley.

Bergin, A.E. and Lambert, M.J. (1978) 'The evaluation of therapeutic outcome', in S.L. Garfield and A.E. Bergin (eds), *Handbook of Psychotherapy and Behavior Change*, 2nd edn. New York: Wiley. pp. 139–90.

Birchwood, M. (1992) 'Early intervention in schizophrenia: theoretical background and clinical strategies', *British Journal of Clinical Psychology*, 31: 257–78.

Blackburn, I-M. (1995) 'The relationship between drug and psychotherapy effects', in Aveline, M. and D.A. Shapiro (eds), *Research Foundations for Psychotherapy Practice*. Chichester: Wiley & Sons. pp. 231–45.

Blackburn, I-M., Bishop, S., Glen, A.I.M., Whalley, L.J. and Christie, J.E. (1981) 'The efficacy of cognitive therapy in depression: a treatment trial using cognitive therapy and pharmacotherapy, each alone and in combination', *British Journal of Psychiatry*, 139: 181–9.

Blackburn, I-M., Eunson, K.M. and Bishop, S. (1986) 'A two-year naturalistic follow-up of depressed patients treated with cognitive therapy, pharmacotherapy and a combination of both', *Journal of Affective Disorders*, 10: 67–75.

Blanes, T. and Raven, P. (1995) 'Psychotherapy of panic disorder', *Current Opinion in Psychiatry*, 8: 167–71.

Blowers, C., Cobb, J. and Mathews, A. (1987) 'Generalized anxiety: a controlled treatment study', *Behavior Research and Therapy*, 25: 493–502.

Bordin, E.S. (1979) 'The generalizability of the psychoanalytic concept of the working alliance', *Psychotherapy: Theory, Research and Practice*, 16: 252–60.

Bower, P. and King, M. (2000) 'Randomised controlled trials and the evaluation of psychological therapy', in N. Rowland and S. Goss (eds), *Evidence-based Counselling and Psychological Therapies*. London: Routledge. pp.79–110.

Bower, P., Byford, S., Sibbald, B., Ward, E., King, M., Lloyd, M. and Gabbay, M. (2000) 'Randomised controlled trial of non-directive counselling, cognitive-behavioural therapy, and usual general practitioner care for patients with depression. II: Cost effectiveness', *British Medical Journal*, 321: 1389–92.

Brockman, B., Poynton, A., Ryle, A. and Watson, J.P. (1987) 'Effectiveness of time-limited therapy carried out by trainees: comparison of two methods', *British Journal of Psychiatry*, 151: 602–10.

Butler, G., Cullington, A., Hibbert, G., Klimes, I. and Gelder, M. (1987a) 'Anxiety management for persistent generalized anxiety', *British Journal of Psychiatry*, 151: 535–42.

Butler, G., Gelder, M., Hibbert, G., Cullington, A. and Klimes, I. (1987b) 'Anxiety management: developing effective strategies', *Behavior Research and Therapy*, 25: 517–22.

Butler, G., Fennell, M.J.V., Robson, P. and Gelder, M. (1991) 'Comparison of behavior therapy and cognitive behavior therapy in the treatment of generalized anxiety disorder', *Journal of Consulting and Clinical Psychology*, 59: 167–75.

Cahill, C., Llewelyn, S. and Pearson, C. (1991) 'Treatment of sexual abuse which occurred in childhood: a review', *British Journal of Clinical Psychology*, 30: 1–12.

Cape, J. and Parry, G. (2000) 'Clinical practice guideline development in evidence-based psychotherapy', in N. Rowland and S. Goss (eds), *Evidence-based Counselling and Psychological Therapies*. London: Routledge. pp. 171–90.

Chadwick, P. and Lowe, F. (1990) 'The measurement and modification of delusional beliefs', *Journal of Consulting and Clinical Psychology*, 58: 225–32.

Chambless, D.L. and Ollendick, T.H. (2001) 'Empirically supported psychological interventions: controversies and evidence', *Annual Review of Psychology*, **52**: 685–716.

Clark, D.M., Salkovskis, P.M., Hackman, A., Middleton, H., Anatasiades, P. and Gelder, M. (1994) 'A comparison of cognitive therapy, applied relaxation and imipramine in the treatment of panic disorder', *British Journal of Psychiatry*, 164: 759–69.

Clark, D.M., Salkovskis, P.M., Hackman, A., Wells, A., Fennell, M., Ludgate, J., Ahmed, S., Richards, H.C. and Gelder, M. (1998) 'Two psychological treatments for hypochondriasis: a randomised controlled trial', *British Journal of Psychiatry*, 173: 218–25.

Clark, D.M., Salkovskis, P.M., Hackman, A., Wells, A., Ludgate, J. and Gelder, M. (1999) 'Brief cognitive therapy for panic disorder: a randomized controlled trial', *Journal of Consulting and Clinical Psychology*, 67: 583–9.

Clarke, S. and Llewelyn, S.P. (1994) 'Personal constructs of survivors of childhood sexual abuse receiving cognitive analytic therapy', *British Journal of Medical Psychology*, 67: 273–89.

Clarkin, J.K., Koenigsberg, H.W., Yeomans, F., Selzer, M., Kernberg, P. and Kernberg, O.F. (1992) 'Psychodynamic psychotherapy of the borderline patient', in J.F. Clarkin, E. Marziali and H. Munroe-Blum (eds), *Borderline Personality Disorder: Clinical and Empirical Perspectives*. New York: Guilford Press.

Clifford, P.I. (1999) 'The FACE Recording and Measurement System: a scientific approach to person-based information', *Bulletin of the Menninger Clinic*, 63: 305–31.

Cohen, J. (1977) *Statistical Power Analysis for the Behavioral Sciences*. New York: Academic Press.

Consumer Reports (1995, November) 'Mental health: does therapy help?', 734–9.

Crits-Christoph, P., Cooper, A. and Luborsky, L. (1988) 'The accuracy of therapists' interpretations and the outcome of dynamic psychotherapy', *Journal of Consulting and Clinical Psychology*, 56: 490–5.

Davis, J.D., Elliott, R., Davis, M.L., Binns, M., Francis, V.M., Kelman, J.E. and Schroder, T.A. (1987) 'Development of a taxonomy of therapist difficulties: initial report', *British Journal of Medical Psychology*, **60**: 109–19.

Denford, J., Schachter, J., Temple, N., Kind, P. and Rosser, R. (1983) 'Selection and outcome in in-patient psychotherapy', *British Journal of Medical Psychology*, 56: 225–43.

Department of Health (2001) *Treatment Choice in Psychological Therapies and Counselling: Evidence Based Clinical Practice Guideline*. London: DH.

DeRubeis, R.J. and Crit-Christoph, P. (1998) 'Empirically supported individual and group psychological treatments for adult mental disorders', *Journal of Consulting and Clinical Psychology*, 66: 37–52.

DeRubeis, R.J., Evans, M.D., Hollon, S.D., Garvey, M.J., Grove, W.M. and Tuason, V.B. (1990) 'How does cognitive therapy work? Cognitive change and symptom change in cognitive therapy and pharmacotherapy for depression', *Journal of Consulting and Clinical Psychology*, 58: 862–9.

Docherty, J.P. and Streeter, M.J. (1995) 'Advances in psychotherapy research', *Current Opinion in Psychiatry*, 8: 145–9.

Drury, V., Birchwood, M., Cochrane, R. and MacMillan, F. (1996) 'Cognitive therapy and recovery from acute psychosis: a controlled trial. I. Impact on psychotic symptoms', *British Journal of Psychiatry*, 169: 593–601.

Drury, V., Birchwood, M. and Cochrane, R. (2000) 'Cognitive therapy and recovery from acute psychosis: a controlled trial. 3. Five year follow-up', *British Journal of Psychiatry*, 177: 8–14.

Dryden, W. (ed.) (1996) *Research in Counselling and Psychotherapy: Practical Applications*. London: Sage.

Eaton, T.T., Abeles, N. and Gutfreund, M.J. (1988) 'Therapeutic alliance and outcome: impact of treatment length and pretreatment symptomotology', *Psychotherapy*, 25: 536–42.

Elkin, I. (1994) 'The NIMH Treatment of Depression collaborative research study', in A.E. Bergin and S.L. Garfield, (eds), *Handbook of Psychotherapy and Behavior Change*, 4th edn. New York: Wiley. pp.114–39

Elkin, I., Shea, M.T., Watkins, J.T., Imber, S.D., Sotsky, S.M., Collins, J.F., Glass, D.R., Pilkonis, P.A., Leber, W.R., Docherty, J.P., Fiester, S.J. and Parloff, M.B. (1989) 'National Institute of Mental Health Treatment of Depression collaborative research program: general effectiveness of treatment', *Archives of General Psychiatry*, 46: 971–82.

Elliott, R. (1984) 'A discovery-oriented approach to significant events in psychotherapy: interpersonal process recall and comprehensive process analysis', in L.N. Rice and L.S. Greenberg (eds), *Patterns of Change*. New York: Guilford Press. pp. 249–86.

Elliott, R. (1989) 'Comprehensive process analysis: understanding the change process in significant therapy events', in M. Packer and R.B. Addison (eds), *Entering the Circle: Hermeneutic Investigation in Psychology*. Albany: State University of New York Press. pp. 165–84.

Elliott, R. (2001) 'Contemporary brief experiential psychotherapy', *Clinical Psychology: Science & Practice*, 8: 38–50.

Elliott, R. and Shapiro, D.A. (1988) 'Brief structured recall: a more efficient method for studying significant therapy events', *British Journal of Medical Psychology*, 61: 141–53.

Elliott, R., Hill, C.E., Stiles, W.B., Friedlander, M.L., Mahrer, A.R. and Margison, F.R. (1987) 'Primary therapist response modes: a comparison of six rating systems', *Journal of Consulting and Clinical Psychology*, 55: 218–23.

Elliott, R., Stiles, W.B. and Shapiro, D.A. (1993) '"Are some psychotherapies more equivalent than others?"', in T.R. Giles (ed.), *Handbook of Effective Psychotherapy*. New York: Plenum. pp. 455–79.

Elliott, R., Shapiro, D.A., Firth-Cozens, J., Stiles, W.B., Hardy, G.E., Llewelyn, S.P. and Margison, F.R. (1994) 'Comprehensive process analysis of insight events in cognitive-behavioral and psychodynamic-interpersonal psychotherapies', *Journal of Counseling Psychology*, 41: 449–63.

Elliott, R., Fischer, C. and Rennie, D.L. (1999) 'Evolving guidelines for publication of qualitative research studies in psychology and related fields', *British Journal of Clinical Psychology*, 38: 215–29.

Elliott, R., Shapiro, D.A., Firth-Cozens, J., Stiles, W.B., Hardy, G.E., Llewelyn, S.P. and Margison, F.R. (2001) 'Comprehensive process analysis of insight events in cognitive-behavioral and psychodynamic-interpersonal psychotherapies', in C.E. Hill (ed.), *Helping Skills: The Empirical Foundation*. Washington, DC: American Psychological Association. pp. 309–33.

Evans, C., Connell, J., Barkham, M., Margison, F., Mellor-Clark, J., McGrath, G. and Audin, K. (2002) 'Towards a standardised brief outcome measure: psychometric properties and utility of the CORE-OM', *British Journal of Psychiatry*, 180: 51–60.

Evans, M.D., Hollon, S.D., DeRubeis, R.J., Piasecki, J.M., Grove, W.M., Garvey, M.J. and Tuason, V.B. (1992) 'Differential relapse following cognitive therapy and pharmacotherapy for depression', *Archives of General Psychiatry*, 49: 802–8.

Eysenck, H.J. (1952) 'The effects of psychotherapy: an evaluation', *Journal of Consulting Psychology*, 16: 319–24.

Fairburn, C.G., Kirk, J., O'Connor, M. and Cooper, P.J. (1986) 'A comparison of two psychological treatments for bulimia nervosa', *Behavior Research and Therapy*, 24: 629–43.

Fairburn, C.G., Jones, R., Peveler, R.C., Carr, S.J., Solomon, R.A., O'Connor, M.E., Burton, J. and Hope, R.A. (1991) 'Three psychological treatments for bulimia nervosa: a comparative trial', *Archives of General Psychiatry*, 48: 463–9.

Fairburn, C.G., Jones, R., Peveler, R.C., Hope, R.A. and O'Connor, M. (1993) 'Psychotherapy and bulimia nervosa: the longer-term effects of interpersonal psychotherapy, behavior therapy, and cognitive behavior therapy', *Archives of General Psychiatry*, 50: 419–28.

Fairburn, C.G., Norman, P.A., Welch, S.L., O'Connor, M.E., Doll, H.A. and Peveler, R.C. (1995) 'A prospective study of outcome in bulimia nervosa and the longer-term effects of three psychological treatments', *Archives of General Psychiatry*, 52: 304–12.

Fennell, M.J.V. (1983) 'Cognitive therapy of depression: the mechanisms of change', *Behavioural Psychotherapy*, 11: 97–108.

Fennell, M.J.V. and Teasdale, J.D. (1987) 'Cognitive therapy for depression: individual differences and the process of change', *Cognitive Therapy and Research*, 11: 253–71.

Ferguson, B. and Russell, I. (2000) 'Towards evidence-based health care', in N. Rowland and S. Goss (eds), *Evidence-based Counselling and Psychological Therapies*. London: Routledge. pp. 30–43.

Field, S., Barkham, M., Shapiro, D.A. and Stiles, W.B. (1994) 'Assessment of assimilation in psychotherapy: a quantitative case study of problematic experiences with a significant other', *Journal of Counseling Psychology*, 41: 397–406.

Fonagy, P. (1995) 'Is there an answer to the outcome question? ". . .waiting for Godot"', *Changes*, 13: 168–77.

Fowler, D., Garety, P. and Kuipers, L. (1994) *Cognitive Behavioural Therapy for People with Psychosis: A Clinical Handbook*. Chichester: J. Wiley & Sons.

Frank, J.D. (1971) 'Therapeutic factors in psychotherapy', *American Journal of Psychotherapy*, 25: 350–61.

Freeman, C.P.L., Barry, F., Dunkeld-Turnbull, J. and Henderson, A. (1988) 'Controlled trial of psychotherapy for bulimia nervosa', *British Medical Journal*, 296: 521–5.

Freeman, D., Garety, P., Fowler, D., Kuipers, E., Dunn, G., Bebbington, P. and Hadley, C. (1998) 'The London–East Anglia randomized controlled trial of cognitive-behaviour therapy for psychosis IV: self esteem and persecutory delusions', *British Journal of Clinical Psychology*, 37: 415–30.

Freud, S. (1979) 'Notes upon a case of obsessional neurosis (the 'Rat Man')' (1909), *Pelican Freud Library*, Vol IX: *Case Histories II*. Harmondsworth: Penguin.

Gabbard, G.O., Lazar, S.G., Hornberger, J. and Spiegel, D. (1997) 'The economic impact of psychotherapy: a review', *American Journal of Psychiatry*, 154: 147–55.

Garety, P.A., Kuipers, L., Fowler, D., Chamberlain, F. and Dunn, G. (1994) 'Cognitive behavioural therapy for drug-resistant psychosis', *British Journal of Medical Psychology*, 67: 259–71.

Garety, P., Fowler, D., Kuipers, E., Freeman, D., Dunn, G., Bebbington, P., Hadley, C. and Jones, S. (1997) 'London–East Anglia randomised controlled trial of cognitive-behavioural therapy for psychosis II: Predictors of outcome', *British Journal of Psychiatry*, 171: 420–6.

Garfield, S.L. (1990) 'Issues and methods in psychotherapy process research', *Journal of Consulting and Clinical Psychology*, 58: 273–80.

Garfield, S.L. and Bergin, A.E. (eds) (1978) *Handbook of Psychotherapy and Behavior Change*, 2nd edn. New York: Wiley.

Garfield, S.L. and Bergin, A.E. (eds) (1986) *Handbook of Psychotherapy and Behavior Change*, 3rd edn. New York: Wiley.

Gask, L. and McGrath, G. (1989) 'Psychotherapy and general practice', *British Journal of Psychiatry*, 154: 445–53.

Gath, D. and Mynors-Wallis, L. (1997) 'Problem-solving treatment in primary care', in D.M. Clark and C.G. Fairburn (eds), *Science and Practice of Cognitive Behaviour Therapy*. Oxford: Oxford University Press. pp: 415–31.

Goldberg, D.P., Hobson, R.F., Maguire, G.P., Margison, F.R., O'Dowd, T., Osborn, M.S. and Moss, S. (1984) 'The clarification and assessment of a method of psychotherapy', *British Journal of Psychiatry*, 14: 567–75.

Goldfried, M.R. (2000) 'Consensus in psychotherapy research and practice: where have all the findings gone?', *Psychotherapy Research*, 10: 1–16.

Grafanaki, S. and McLeod, J. (1999) 'Narrative processes in the construction of helpful and hindering events in experiential psychotherapy', *Psychotherapy Research*, 9: 289–303.

Greenberg, L.S. (1986) 'Change process research', *Journal of Consulting and Clinical Psychology*, 54: 4–9.

Greenberg, L.S. (1994) 'The investigation of change: its measurement and explanation', in R.L. Russell (ed.), *Reassessing Psychotherapy Research*. New York: Guilford Press. pp. 114–43.

Greenberg, L.S. (1999) 'Ideal psychotherapy research: a study of significant change processes', *Journal of Clinical Psychology*, 55: 1467–80.

Greenberg, L.S. and Pinsoff, W.M. (eds) (1986) *The Psychotherapeutic Process: A Research Handbook*. New York: Guilford.

Grissom, R.J. (1996) 'The magical number .7+−.2: meta-meta-analysis of the probability of superior outcome in comparisons involving therapy, placebo, and control', *Journal of Consulting and Clinical Psychology*, 64: 973–82.

Gurman, A.S. and Razin, A.M. (eds) (1977) *Effective Psychotherapy: A Handbook of Research*. New York: Pergamon.

Guthrie, E., Moorey, J., Margison, F., Barker, H., Palmer, S., McGrath, G., Tomenson, B. and Creed, F. (1999) 'Cost-effectiveness of brief psychodynamic-interpersonal therapy in high utilizers of psychiatric services', *Archives of General Psychiatry*, 56: 519–26.

Haddock, G., Tarrier, N., Spaulding, W., Yusupoff, W., Kinney, C. and McCarthy, E. (1998) 'Individual cognitive-behaviour therapy in the treatment of hallucinations and delusions: a review', *Clinical Psychology Review*, 18: 821–38.

Hall, A. and Crisp, A.H. (1987) 'Brief psychotherapy in the treatment of anorexia nervosa: outcome at one year', *British Journal of Psychiatry*, 151: 185–91.

Hardy, G.E., Barkham, M., Shapiro, D.A., Stiles, W.B., Rees, A. and Reynolds, S. (1995) 'Impact of Cluster C personality disorders (Avoidant, Dependent, Obsessive-Compulsive) on outcomes of contrasting brief psychotherapies for depression', *Journal of Consulting and Clinical Psychology*, 63: 997–1004.

Hardy, G.E., Shapiro, D.A., Stiles, W.B. and Barkham, M. (1998a) 'When and why does cognitive-behavioural treatment appear more effective than psychodynamic-interpersonal treatment? Discussion of the findings from the Sheffield Psychotherapy Projects', *Journal of Mental Health*, 7: 179–90.

Hardy, G.E., Stiles, W.B., Barkham, M. and Startup, M. (1998b) 'Therapist responsiveness to client attachment issues during time-limited treatments for depression', *Journal of Consulting and Clinical Psychology*, 66: 304–14.

Hardy, G.E., Aldridge, J., Davidson, C., Reilly, S., Rowe, C. and Shapiro, D.A. (1999) 'Therapist responsiveness to client attachment styles and issues observed in client-identified significant events in psychodynamic-interpersonal psychotherapy', *Psychotherapy Research*, 9: 36–53.

Healey, A. and Knapp, M. (1995) 'Economic appraisal of psychotherapy', *Mental Health Research Review*, 2: 13–16.

Hill, C.E. (1989) *Therapist Techniques and Client Outcomes: Eight Cases of Brief Psychotherapy*. Newbury Park, CA: Sage.

Hill, C.E. (1990) 'Exploratory in session process research in individual psychotherapy: a review', *Journal of Consulting and Clinical Psychology*, 58: 288–94.

Hill, C.E. (1991) 'Almost everything you ever wanted to know about how to do process research on counseling and psychotherapy but didn't know who to ask', in C.E. Watkins, Jr. and L.J. Schneider (eds), *Research in Counseling*. Hillsdale, NJ: Lawrence Erlbaum Associates. pp. 85–118.

Hill, C.E. (ed.) (2001) *Helping Skills: The Empirical Foundation*. Washington, DC: American Psychological Association.

Hill, C.E. and Corbett, M. (1993) 'A perspective on the history of process and outcome research in counseling psychology', *Journal of Counseling Psychology*, 40: 3–24.

Hill, C.E., Thompson, B.J. and Williams, E.N. (1997) 'A guide to conducting consensual qualitative research', *Counseling Psychologist*, 25: 517–72.

Horvath, A.O. and Greenberg, L.S. (1989) 'Development and validation of the Working Alliance Inventory', *Journal of Counseling Psychology*, 36: 223–33.

Horvath, A.O. and Greenberg, L.S. (eds) (1994). *The Working Alliance: Theory, Research, and Practice*. New York: Wiley.

Horvath, A.O. and Symonds, D.B. (1991) 'Relation between working alliance and outcome in psychotherapy', *Journal of Counseling Psychology*, 38: 139–49.

Horvath, A.O., Marx, R.W. and Kamann, A.M. (1990) 'Thinking about thinking in therapy: an examination of clients' understanding of their therapists' intentions', *Journal of Consulting and Clinical Psychology*, 58: 614–21.

Howard, K.I., Kopta, S.M., Krause, M.S. and Orlinsky, D.E. (1986) 'The dose–effect relationship in psychotherapy', *American Psychologist*, 41: 159–64.

Howard, K.I., Lueger, R., Maling, M. and Martinovitch, Z. (1993) 'A phase model of psychotherapy: causal mediation of outcome', *Journal of Consulting and Clinical Psychology*, 61: 678–85.

Howard, K.I., Moras, K., Brill, P. L., Martinovitch, Z. and Lutz, W. (1996) 'Evaluation of psychotherapy: efficacy, effectiveness, and patient progress', *American Psychologist*, 51: 1059–64.

Huddleson, J.H. (1927) 'Psychotherapy in two hundred cases of psychoneurosis', *The Military Surgeon*, 60: 161–70.

Iliardi, S.S. and Craighead, W.E. (1994) 'The role of nonspecific factors in cognitive-behavior therapy for depression', *Clinical Psychology: Science and Practice*, 1: 138–56.

Jacobson, N.S. and Truax, P. (1991) 'Clinical significance: a statistical approach to defining meaningful change in psychotherapy research', *Journal of Consulting and Clinical Psychology*, 59: 12–19.

Jacobson, N.S., Follette, W.C. and Revenstorf, D. (1984) 'Psychotherapy outcome research: methods for reporting variability and evaluating clinical significance', *Behaviour Therapy*, 15: 336–52.

Jacobson, N.S., Follette, W.C. and Revenstorf, D. (1986) 'Toward a standard definition of clinically significant change', *Behavior Therapy*, 17: 308–11.

Jarrett, R.B. and Nelson, R.O. (1987) 'Mechanisms of change in cognitive therapy of depression', *Behavior Therapy*, 18: 227–41.

Journal of Consulting and Clinical Psychology (1993) Special Section: 'A briefing on curative factors in dynamic psychotherapy', 61: 539–610.

Journal of Consulting and Clinical Psychology (1995) Special Section: 'Efficacy and effectiveness in studies of child and adolescent psychotherapy', 63: 683–725.

Kazdin, A.E. (1994) 'Methodology, design, and evaluation in psychotherapy research', in A.E. Bergin and S.L. Garfield, (eds), *Handbook of Psychotherapy and Behavior Change*, 4th edn. New York: Wiley. pp. 19–71.

Keller, A. (1984) 'Planned brief psychotherapy in clinical practice', *British Journal of Medical Psychology*, 57: 347–61.

Kendall, P.C. and Sheldrick, R.C. (2000) 'Normative data for normative comparisons', *Journal of Consulting and Clinical Psychology*, 68: 767–73.

Kendall, P.C., Flannery-Schroeder, E.C. and Ford, J.D. (1999a) 'Therapy outcome research methods', in P.C. Kendall, J.N. Butcher et al. (eds), *Handbook of Research Methods in Clinical Psychology*, 2nd edn. New York: Wiley. pp. 330–63.

Kendall, P.C., Marrs-Garcia, A., Nath, S.R. and Sheldrick, R.C. (1999b) 'Normative comparisons for the evaluation of clinical significance', *Journal of Consulting and Clinical Psychology*, 67: 285–99.

Kiesler, D.J. (1966) 'Basic methodological issues implicit in psychotherapy research', *American Journal of Psychotherapy*, 20: 135–55.

Kingdon, D.G. and Turkington, D. (1991) 'Preliminary report: the use of cognitive behavior therapy with a normalizing rationale in schizophrenia', *Journal of Nervous and Mental Disease*, 179: 207–11.

Klee, M.R., Abeles, N. and Muller, R.T. (1990) 'Therapeutic alliance: early indicators, course, and outcome', *Psychotherapy*, 27: 166–74.

Koenigsberg, H.W. (1995) 'Psychotherapy of patients with borderline personality disorder', *Current Opinion in Psychiatry*, 8: 157–60.

Kopta, S.M., Lueger, R.J., Saunders, S.M. and Howard, K.I. (1999) 'Individual psychotherapy outcome and process research: challenges leading to greater turmoil or a position transition?', *Annual Review of Psychology*, 50: 441–69.

Kordy, H., Hannöver, W. and Richard, M. (2001) 'Computer-assisted feedback-driven quality management for psychotherapy: the Stuttgart-Heidelberg model', *Journal of Consulting and Clinical Psychology*, 69: 173–83.

Koss, M.P. and Shiang, J. (1994) 'Research on brief psychotherapy', in A.E. Bergin and S.L. Garfield (eds), *Handbook of Psychotherapy and Behavior Change*, 4th edn. New York: Wiley. pp. 664–700.

Krumboltz, J.D. (1966) *Revolution in Counseling: Implications of Behavioral Science*. Boston, MA: Houghton Mifflin.

Krupnick, J.L. and Pincus, H.A. (1992) 'The cost-effectiveness of psychotherapy: a plan for research', *American Journal of Psychotherapy*, 149: 1295–305.

Kuipers, E., Garety, P., Fowler, D., Dunn, G., Bebbington, P., Freeman, D. and Hadley, C. (1997) 'London–East Anglia randomised controlled trial of cognitive-behavioural therapy for psychosis I: Effects of the treatment phase', *British Journal of Psychiatry*, 171: 319–27.

Kuipers, E., Fowler, D., Garety, P., Chisholm, D., Freeman, D., Dunn, G., Bebbington, P. and Hadley, C. (1998) 'London–East Anglia randomised controlled trial of cognitive-behavioural therapy for psychosis III: Follow-up and economic evaluation at 18 months', *British Journal of Psychiatry*, 173: 61–8.

Lambert, M.J. (ed.) (in press) *Handbook of Psychotherapy and Behavior Change*, 5th edn. New York: Wiley.

Lambert, M.J. and Bergin, A.E. (1994) 'The effectiveness of psychotherapy', in A.E. Bergin and S.L. Garfield (eds), *Handbook of Psychotherapy and Behavior Change*, 4th edn. New York: Wiley. pp. 143–89.

Lambert, M.J. and Hill, C.E. (1994) 'Assessing psychotherapy outcomes and processes', in A.E. Bergin and S.L. Garfield (eds), *Handbook of Psychotherapy and Behavior Change*, 4th edn. New York: Wiley. pp. 72–113.

Lambert, M.J. and Hill, C.E. (in press) 'Assessing psychotherapy outcomes and processes', in M.J. Lambert (ed.), *Handbook of Psychotherapy and Behavior Change*, 5th edn. New York: Wiley.

Lambert, M.J. and Ogles, B.M. (in press) 'The efficacy and effectiveness of psychotherapy', in M.J. Lambert (ed.), *Handbook of Psychotherapy and Behavior Change*, 5th edn. New York: Wiley.

Lambert, M.J., Hansen, N.B. and Finch, A.E. (2001a) 'Patient-focused research: using patient outcome data to enhance treatment effects', *Journal of Consulting and Clinical Psychology*, 69: 159–72.

Lambert, M.J., Whipple, J.L., Smart, D.W., Vermeersch, D.A., Nielsen, S.L. and Hawkins, E.J. (2001b) 'The effects of providing therapists with feedback on patient progress during psychotherapy: are outcomes enhanced?', *Psychotherapy Research*, 11: 49–68.

Linehan, M.M. (1993) *Cognitive-behavioral Treatment of Borderline Personality Disorder*. New York: Guilford.

Linehan, M.M., Armstrong, H.E., Suarez, A., Allmon, D. and Heard, H.L. (1991) 'Cognitive-behavioral treatment of chronically parasuicidal borderline patients', *Archives of General Psychiatry*, 48: 1060–4.

Linehan, M.M., Heard, H.L. and Armstrong, H.E. (1993) 'Naturalistic follow-up of a behavioral treatment for chronically suicidal borderline patients', *Archives of General Psychiatry*, 50: 971–4.

Llewelyn, S.P. (1988) 'Psychological therapy as viewed by clients and therapists', *British Journal of Clinical Psychology*, 27: 223–38.

Llewelyn, S.P. and Hardy, G. (2001) 'Process research in understanding and applying psychological therapies', *British Journal of Clinical Psychology*, 40: 1–21.

Llewelyn, S.P., Elliott, R., Shapiro, D.A., Hardy, G.E. and Firth-Cozens, J. (1988) 'Client perceptions of significant events in prescriptive and exploratory periods of individual therapy', *British Journal of Clinical Psychology*, 27: 105–14.

Luborsky, L., Singer, B. and Luborsky, L. (1975) 'Comparative studies of psychotherapies: is it true that "everyone has won and all must have prizes"?', *Archives of General Psychiatry*, 32: 995–1008.

Lueger, R.J., Howard, K.I., Martinovitch, Z., Lutz, W., Anderson, E.E. and Grissom, G. (2001) 'Assessing treatment progress of individual patients using expected treatment response models', *Journal of Consulting and Clinical Psychology*, 69: 150–8.

Lutz, W., Martinovitch, Z. and Howard, K.I. (1999) 'Patient profiling: an application of random coefficient regression models to depicting the response of a patient to outpatient psychotherapy', *Journal of Consulting and Clinical Psychology*, 67: 571–7.

McClelland, R., Trimble, P., Fox, M.L., Stevenson, M.R. and Bell, B. (2000) 'Validation of an outcome scale for use in adult psychiatric practice', *Quality in Healthcare*, 9: 98–105.

McGinn, L.K. and Sanderson, W. (2001) 'What allows cognitive behavioral therapy to be brief: overview, efficiency, and crucial factors facilitating brief treatment', *Clinical Psychology: Science and Practice*, 8: 23–37.

McGrath, G. and Lawson, K. (1987) 'Assessing the benefits of psychotherapy: the economic approach', *British Journal of Psychiatry*, 150: 65–71.

McLeod, J. (1994) *Doing Counselling Research*. London: Sage.

McLeod, J. (1997) *Narrative and Psychotherapy*. London: Sage.

McLeod, J. (2000) 'The contribution of qualitative research to evidence-based counselling and psychotherapy', in N. Rowland and S. Goss (eds), *Evidence-based Counselling and Psychological Therapies*. London: Routledge. pp. 111–26.

McLeod, J (in press) *Doing Counselling Research*, 2nd edn. London: Sage.

Madill, A. and Barkham, M. (1997) 'Discourse analysis of a theme in one successful case of brief psychodynamic-interpersonal psychotherapy', *Journal of Counseling Psychology*, 44: 232–44.

Madill, A., Widdicombe, S. and Barkham, M. (2001) 'The potential of conversational analysis for psychotherapy research', *The Counseling Psychologist*, 29: 413–34.

Maguire, G.P., Goldberg, D.P., Hobson, R.F., Margison, F.R., Moss, S. and O'Dowd, T. (1984) 'Evaluating the teaching of a method of psychotherapy', *British Journal of Psychiatry*, 144: 576–80.

Malan, D.H. (1963) *A study of Brief Psychotherapy*. New York: Plenum Press.

Malan, D.H. (1976) *Toward the Validation of Dynamic Psychotherapy: A Replication*. New York: Plenum Press.

Malan, D.H., Bacal, H.A., Heath, E.S. and Balfour, F.H.G. (1968) 'A study of psychodynamic changes in untreated neurotic patients: I. Improvements that are questionable on dynamic criteria', *British Journal of Psychiatry*, 114: 525–51.

Malan, D.H., Heath, E.S., Bacal, H.A. and Balfour, F.H.G. (1975) 'Psychodynamic changes in untreated neurotic patients: II. Apparently genuine improvements', *Archives of General Psychiatry*, 32: 110–26.

Margison, F., Barkham, M., Evans, C., McGrath, G., Mellor-Clark, J., Audin, K. and Connell, J. (2000) 'Measurement and psychotherapy: evidence-based practice and practice-based evidence', *British Journal of Psychiatry*, 177: 123–30.

Marks, I.M., Swinson, R.P., Basoglu, M., Kuch, K., Noshirvani, H., O'Sullivan, G., Lelliott, P.T., Kirby, M., McNamee, G., Sengun, S. and Wickwire, K. (1993) 'Alprazolam and exposure alone and combined in panic disorder with agoraphobia', *British Journal of Psychiatry*, 162: 776–8.

Marmar, C.R. (1990) 'Psychotherapy process research: progress, dilemmas, and future directions', *Journal of Consulting and Clinical Psychology*, 58: 265–72.

Maynard, A. (2000) 'Economic issues', in N. Rowland and S. Goss (eds), *Evidence-based Counselling and Psychological Therapies*. London: Routledge. pp. 44–56.

Mellor-Clark, J., Barkham, M., Connell, J. and Evans, C. (1999) 'Practice-based evidence and need for a standardised evaluation system: informing the design of the CORE System', *European Journal of Psychotherapy, Counselling and Health*, 3: 357–74.

Mellor-Clark, J., Connell, J., Barkham, M. and Cummins, P. (2001) 'Counselling outcomes in primary health care: a CORE System data profile', *European Journal of Psychotherapy, Counselling and Health*, 4: 65–86.

Messer, S.B. (2001) 'What makes brief psychodynamic therapy time efficient', *Clinical Psychology: Science and Practice*, 8: 5–22.

Mitchell, K., Bozarth, J. and Krauft, J. (1977) 'A reappraisal of the therapeutic effectiveness of accurate empathy, nonpossessive warmth, and genuineness', in A.S. Gurman and A. Razin (eds), *Effective Psychotherapy: A Handbook of Research*. Oxford: Pergamon Press. pp. 482–502.

Moran, G.S. and Fonagy, P. (1987) 'Psychoanalysis and diabetic control: a single case study', *British Journal of Medical Psychology*, 60: 357–72.

Morley, S. (1988) 'Status of cognitive therapies', *Current Opinion in Psychiatry*, 1: 725–8.

Murphy, P.M., Cramer, D. and Lillie, F.J. (1984) 'The relationship between curative factors perceived by patients in their psychotherapy and treatment outcome: an exploratory study', *British Journal of Medical Psychology*, 57: 187–92.

Mynors-Wallis, L. (1996) 'Problem-solving treatment: evidence for effectiveness and feasibility in primary care', *International Journal of Psychiatry in Medicine*, 26: 249–62.

Nathan, P.E., Stuart, S.P. and Dolan, S.L. (2000) 'Research on psychotherapy efficacy and effectiveness: between Scylla and Charybdis?', *Psychological Bulletin*, 126: 964–81.

National Advisory Mental Health Council, National Institute of Mental Health (1999) *Bridging Science and Service: A Report by the National Advisory Mental Health Council's Clinical Treatment and Services Research Workshop* (NIH Publication no. 99–4353). Washington, DC.

Nietzel, M.T., Russell, R.L., Hemmings, K.A. and Gretter, M.L. (1987) 'Clinical significance of psychotherapy for unipolar depression: a meta-analytic approach to social comparison', *Journal of Consulting and Clinical Psychology*, 55: 156–61.

Norquist, G.S., Letowitz, B. and Hynam, S. (1999) 'Expanding the frontier of treatment research', *Prevention & Treatment*, 2: 1–10.

O'Farrell, M.K., Hill, C.E. and Patton, S. (1986) 'Comparison of two cases of counseling with the same counselor', *Journal of Counseling and Development*, 65: 141–5.

Ogles, M.M., Lunnen, K.M. and Bonesteel, K. (2001) 'Clinical significance: history, application, and current practice', *Clinical Psychology Review*, 21: 421–46.

Olfson, M. and Pincus, H.A. (1994a) 'Outpatient psychotherapy in the United States, I: Volume, costs, and user characteristics', *American Journal of Psychiatry*, 151: 1281–8.

Olfson, M. and Pincus, H.A. (1994b) 'Outpatient psychotherapy in the United States, II: Patterns of utilization', *American Journal of Psychiatry*, 151: 1289–94.

Orlinsky, D.E. (in press) 'Process and outcome in psychotherapy', in M.J. Lambert (ed.), *Handbook of Psychotherapy and Behavior Change*, 5th edn. New York: Wiley.

Orlinsky, D.E. and Howard, K.I. (1986) 'Process and outcome in psychotherapy', in S.L. Garfield and A.E. Bergin (eds), *Handbook of Psychotherapy and Behavior Change*, 3rd edn. New York: Wiley. pp. 311–81.

Orlinsky, D.E. and Russell, R.L. (1994) 'Tradition and change in psychotherapy research: notes on the fourth generation', in R.L. Russell (ed.), *Reassessing Psychotherapy Research*. New York: Guilford Press. pp. 185–214.

Orlinsky, D.E., Grawe, K. and Parks, B.K. (1994) 'Process and outcome in psychotherapy – Noch einmal', in A.E. Bergin and S.L. Garfield (eds), *Handbook of Psychotherapy and Behavior Change*, 4th edn. New York: Wiley. pp. 270–376.

Oxman, A.D. and Guyatt, G.H. (1988) 'Guidelines for reading literature reviews', *Canadian Medical Association Journal*, 138: 697–703.

Parry, G. (1992) 'Improving psychotherapy services: application of research, audit and evaluation', *British Journal of Clinical Psychology*, 31: 3–19.

Parry, G. (2000) 'Evidence-based psychotherapy: an overview', in N. Rowland and S. Goss (eds), *Evidence-based Counselling and Psychological Therapies: Research and Applications*. London: Routledge. pp. 57–75.

Paul, G. (1967) 'Strategy in outcome research in psychotherapy', *Journal of Consulting Psychology*, 31: 109–18.

Perry, C.J., Banon, E. and Ianni, F. (1999) 'Effectiveness of psychotherapy for personality disorders', *American Journal of Psychiatry*, 156: 1312–21.

Peveler, R.C. and Fairburn, C.G. (1989) 'Anorexia nervosa in association with diabetes mellitus: a cognitive-behavioural approach to treatment', *Behaviour Research and Therapy*, 27: 95–9.

Polkinghorne, D. E. (1994) 'Reaction to special section on qualitative research in counseling process and outcome', *Journal of Counseling Psychology*, 41: 510–12.

Porter, E.H. Jr. (1943a) 'The development and evaluation of a measure of counseling interview procedures: Part I', *Educational and Psychological Measurement*, 3: 105–25.

Porter, E.H. Jr. (1943b) 'The development and evaluation of a measure of counseling interview procedures: Part II', *Educational and Psychological Measurement*, 3: 215–38.

Quality Assurance Project (1984) 'Treatment outlines for the management of schizophrenia', *Australian and New Zealand Journal of Psychiatry*, 18: 19–38.

Rees, A., Hardy, G.E., Barkham, M., Elliott, R., Smith, J.A. and Reynolds, S. (2001) '"It's like catching a desire before it flied away": a comprehensive process analysis of a problem clarification event in cognitive-behavioral therapy for depression', *Psychotherapy Research*, 11: 331–51.

Rice, L.N. and Greenberg, L.S. (eds) (1984) *Patterns of Change*. New York: Guilford Press.

Robinson, F.R. (1950) *Principles and Procedures in Student Counseling*. New York: Harper.

Robinson, L.A., Berman, J.S. and Neimeyer, R.A. (1990) 'Psychotherapy for the treatment of depression: a comprehensive review of controlled outcome research', *Psychological Bulletin*, 108: 30–49.

Rogers, C.R. (1942) 'The use of electrically recorded interviews in improving psychotherapeutic techniques', *American Journal of Orthopsychiatry*, 12: 429–34.

Rogers, C.R. (1957) 'The necessary and sufficient conditions of therapeutic personality change', *Journal of Consulting Psychology*, 21: 95–103.

Rogers, C.R. and Dymond, R.F. (eds) (1954) *Psychotherapy and Personality Change*. Chicago: University of Chicago Press.

Rogers, C.R., Gendlin, E.T., Kiesler, D.J. and Truax, C.B. (1967) *The Therapeutic Relationship and its Impact: A Study of Psychotherapy with Schizophrenics*. Madison: University of Wisconsin Press.

Roth, A. and Fonagy, P. (1996) *What Works for Whom? A Critical Review of Psychotherapy Research*. New York: Guilford Press.

Roth, A. and Fonagy, P. (in press) *What Works for Whom? A Critical Review of Psychotherapy Research*, 2nd edn. New York: Guilford Press.

Rowland, N. and Goss, S. (eds) (2000) *Evidence-based Counselling and Psychological Therapies*. London: Routledge.

Rowland, N., Godfrey, C., Bower, P., Mellor-Clark, J., Heywood, P. and Hardy, R. (2000) 'Counselling in primary care: a systematic review of the research evidence', *British Journal of Guidance and Counselling*, 28: 215–31.

Rowland, N., Bower, P., Mellor-Clark, J., Heywood, P. and Godfrey, C. (2001) 'Effectiveness and cost effectiveness of counselling in primary care (Cochrane Review)', in *The Citroen Library*, issue 3. Oxford: Update Software.

Russell, R.L. and Orlinsky, D.E. (1996) 'Psychotherapy research in a historical perspective: implications for mental health care policy', *Archives of General Psychiatry*, 53: 708–15.

Russell, R.L. and Stiles, W.B. (1979) 'Categories for classifying language in psychotherapy', *Psychological Bulletin*, 86: 404–19.

Ryle, A. (1979) 'Focus on brief interpretative psychotherapy: dilemmas, traps, and snags as target problems', *British Journal of Psychiatry*, 134: 46–54.

Ryle, A. (1980) 'Some measures of goal attainment in focused integrated active psychotherapy: a study of fifteen cases', *British Journal of Psychiatry*, 137: 475–86.

Ryle, A. (1982) *Psychotherapy: A Cognitive Integration of Theory and Practice*. London: Academic Press.

Ryle, A. (1990) *Cognitive-analytic Therapy: Active Participation in Change*. Chichester: Wiley & Sons.

Ryle, A. (1995) 'Transference and counter-transference variations in the course of the cognitive-analytic therapy of two borderline patients: the relation to the diagrammatic reformulation of self-states', *British Journal of Medical Psychology*, 68: 109–24.

Ryle, A. and Beard, H. (1993) 'The integrative effect of reformulation: cognitive analytic therapy with a patient with borderline personality disorder', *British Journal of Medical Psychology*, 66: 249–58.

Safran, J.D., Greenberg, L.S. and Rice, L.N. (1988) 'Integrating psychotherapy research and practice: modeling the change process', *Psychotherapy*, 25: 1–17.

Salkovskis, P.M. (1995) 'Demonstrating specific effects in cognitive and behavioural therapy', in M. Aveline and D.A. Shapiro (eds), *Research Foundations for Psychotherapy Research*. Chichester: Wiley & Sons. pp. 191–228.

Scheel, K.R. (2000) 'The empirical basis of dialectical behaviour therapy: summary, critique, and implications', *Clinical Psychology: Science and Practice*, 7: 68–86.

Scott, J. (1995) 'Review of treatments for depression', *British Journal of Psychiatry*, 167: 289–92.

Scott, J. (2001) 'Cognitive therapy for depression', *British Medical Bulletin*, 57: 101–13.

Seligman, M.E.P. (1995) 'The effectiveness of psychotherapy: the Consumer Reports study', *American Psychologist*, 50: 965–74.

Sexton, T.L. and Whiston, S.C. (1994) 'The status of the counseling relationship: an empirical review, theoretical implications, and research directions', *The Counseling Psychologist*, 22: 6–78.

Shadish, W.R., Matt, G.E., Navarro, A.M., Siegle, G., Crits-Christoph, P., Hazelrigg, M.D., Jorm, A.F., Lyons, L.C., Nietzel, M.T., Prout, H.T., Robinson, L., Smoth, M.L., Svartberg, M. and Weiss, B. (1997) 'Evidence that therapy works in clinically representative conditions', *Journal of Consulting and Clinical Psychology*, 65: 355–65.

Shadish, W.R., Matt, G.E., Navarro, A.M. and Phillups, G. (2000) 'The effects of psychological therapies under clinically representative conditions: a meta-analysis', *Psychological Bulletin*, 126: 512–29.

Shapiro, D.A. (1969) 'Empathy, warmth and genuineness in psychotherapy', *British Journal of Social and Clinical Psychology*, 8: 350–61.

Shapiro, D.A. (1970) 'The rating of psychotherapeutic empathy: a preliminary study', *British Journal of Social and Clinical Psychology*, 9: 148–51.

Shapiro, D.A. (1973) 'Naive British judgements of therapeutic conditions', *British Journal of Social and Clinical Psychology*, 12: 289–94.

Shapiro, D.A. (1976) 'The effects of therapeutic conditions: positive results revisited', *British Journal of Medical Psychology*, 49: 315–23.

Shapiro, D.A. and Firth, J.A. (1987) 'Prescriptive vs. exploratory psychotherapy: outcomes of the Sheffield Psychotherapy Project', *British Journal of Psychiatry*, 151: 790–9.

Shapiro, D.A. and Shapiro, D. (1982) 'Meta-analysis of comparative therapy outcome studies: a replication and refinement', *Psychological Bulletin*, 92: 581–604.

Shapiro, D.A., Barkham, M., Hardy, G.E., Morrison, L.A., Reynolds, S., Startup, M. and Harper, H. (1991) 'Sheffield psychotherapy research program', in L.E. Butler (ed.), *Psychotherapy Research Programs: An International Review of Programmatic Studies*. Washington, DC: American Psychological Association.

Shapiro, D.A., Barkham, M., Reynolds, S., Hardy, G.E. and Stiles, W.B. (1992) 'Prescriptive and exploratory psychotherapies: toward an integration based on the assimilation model', *Journal of Psychotherapy Integration*, 2: 253–72.

Shapiro, D.A., Barkham, M., Rees, A., Hardy, G.E., Reynolds, S. and Startup, M. (1994) 'Effects of treatment duration and severity of depression on the effectiveness of cognitive-behavioral and psychodynamic-interpersonal psychotherapy', *Journal of Consulting and Clinical Psychology*, 62: 522–34.

Shapiro, D.A., Rees, A., Barkham, M., Hardy, G.E., Reynolds, S. and Startup, M. (1995) 'Effects of treatment duration and severity of depression on the maintenance of gains following cognitive-behavioral and psychodynamic-interpersonal psychotherapy', *Journal of Consulting and Clinical Psychology*, 63: 378–87.

Shefler, G., Dasberg, H. and Ben-Shakhar, G. (1995) 'A randomised controlled outcome and follow-up study of Mann's time-limited psychotherapy', *Journal of Consulting and Clinical Psychology*, 63: 585–93.

Silberschatz, G. and Curtis, J.T. (1986) 'Clinical implications of research on brief dynamic psychotherapy: 2. How the therapist helps or hinders therapeutic progress', *Psychoanalytic Psychology*, 3: 27–37.

Sloane, R.B., Staples, R.F., Cristol, A.H., Yorkston, N.J. and Whipple, K. (1975) *Psychotherapy versus Behavior Therapy*. Cambridge, MA: Harvard University Press.

Smith, M.L. and Glass, G.V. (1977) 'Meta-analysis of psychotherapy outcome studies', *American Psychologist*, 32: 752–60.

Smith, M.L., Glass, G.V. and Miller, T.I. (1980) *The Benefits of Psychotherapy*. Baltimore: Johns Hopkins University Press.

Startup, M. and Shapiro, D.A. (1993) 'Therapist treatment fidelity in prescriptive vs. exploratory psychotherapy', *British Journal of Clinical Psychology*, 32: 443–56.

Steinbrueck, S.M., Maxwell, S.E. and Howard, G.S. (1983) 'A meta-analysis of psychotherapy and drug therapy in the treatment of unipolar depression with adults', *Journal of Consulting and Clinical Psychology*, 51: 856–63.

Stiles, W.B. (in press) 'Assimilation of problematic experiences', in J.C. Norcross (ed.), *Psychotherapy Relationships That Work*. New York: Oxford University Press.

Stiles, W.B. and Shapiro, D.A. (1989) 'Abuse of the drug metaphor in psychotherapy process-outcome research', *Clinical Psychology Review*, 9: 521–43.

Stiles, W.B., Shapiro, D.A. and Elliott, R. (1986) '"Are all psychotherapies equivalent?"', *American Psychologist*, 41: 165–80.

Stiles, W.B., Shapiro, D.A. and Firth-Cozens, J.A. (1988) 'Do sessions of different treatments have different impacts?', *Journal of Counseling Psychology*, 35: 391–6.

Stiles, W.B., Elliott, R., Llewelyn, S.P., Firth-Cozens, J.A., Margison, F.R., Shapiro, D.A. and Hardy, G.E. (1990) 'Assimilation of problematic experiences by clients in psychotherapy', *Psychotherapy*, 27: 411–20.

Stiles, W.B., Shapiro, D.A. and Harper, H. (1994) 'Finding the way from process to outcome: blind alleys and unmarked trails', in R.L. Russell (ed.), *Reassessing Psychotherapy Research*. New York: Guilford Press. pp. 36–64.

Stiles, W.B., Honos-Webb, L. and Surko, M. (1998) 'Responsiveness in psychotherapy', *Clinical Psychology: Science and Practice*, 5: 439–58.

Strupp, H.H. (1980a) 'Success and failure in time-limited psychotherapy. A systematic comparison of two cases: Comparison 1', *Archives of General Psychiatry*, 37: 595–604.

Strupp, H.H. (1980b) 'Success and failure in time-limited psychotherapy. A systematic comparison of two cases: Comparison 2', *Archives of General Psychiatry*, 37: 708–16.

Strupp, H.H. (1980c) 'Success and failure in time-limited psychotherapy. With special reference to the performance of a lay counselor', *Archives of General Psychiatry*, 37: 831–41.

Strupp, H.H. (1980d) 'Success and failure in time-limited psychotherapy. Further evidence (Comparison 4)', *Archives of General Psychiatry*, 37: 947–54.

Strupp, H.H., Horowitz, L.M. and Lambert, M.J. (1997) *Measuring Patient Changes in Mood, Anxiety, and Personality Disorders: Towards a Core Battery*. Washington, DC: American Psychological Association.

Talley, P.E., Strupp, H.H. and Butler, S.F. (eds) (1994) *Psychotherapy Research and Practice: Bridging the Gap*. New York: Basic Books.

Tarrier, N., Harwood, S., Yusopoff, L., Beckett, R. and Baker, A. (1990) 'Coping strategy enhancement (CSE): a method of treating residual schizophrenic symptoms', *Behavioural Psychotherapy*, 18: 283–93.

Tarrier, N., Beckett, R., Harwood, S., Baker, A., Yusopoff, L. and Ugarteburu, I. (1993) 'A trial of two cognitive behavioural methods of treating drug-resistant residual psychotic symptoms in schizophrenic patients: I Outcome', *British Journal of Psychiatry*, 162: 524–32.

Taube, C.A., Burns, B.J. and Kessler, L. (1984) 'Patients of psychiatrists and psychologists in office-based practice: 1980', *American Psychologist*, 39: 1435–7.

Teasdale, J.D. (1985) 'Psychological treatments for depression: how do they work?', *Behaviour Research and Therapy*, 23: 157–65.

Teasdale, J.D., Fennell, M.J.V., Hibbert, G.A. and Amies, P.L. (1984) 'Cognitive therapy for major depressive disorder in primary care', *British Journal of Psychiatry*, 144: 400–6.

Thornicroft, G. and Slade, M. (2000) 'Are routine outcome measures feasible in mental health?' *Quality in Healthcare*, 9: 84.

Truax, C.B. and Mitchell, K.M. (1971) 'Research on certain therapist interpersonal skills in relation to process and outcome', in A.E. Bergin and S.L. Garfield (eds), *Handbook of Psychotherapy and Behavior Change*. New York. Wiley. pp. 299–344.

US Department of Health and Human Sciences (US DHHS) (1993) *Depression in Primary Care: Treatment of Major Depression*. Depression Guideline Panel. Rockville: AHCPR Publications. pp. 71–123.

Wampold, B.E. (1997) 'Methodological problems in identifying efficacious psychotherapies', *Psychotherapy Research*, 7: 21–43.

Wampold, B.E. (2001) *The Great Psychotherapy Debate: Models, Methods, and Findings*. Mahwah, NJ: Lawrence Erlbaum Associates.

Wampold, B.E., Mondin, G.W., Moody, M., Stich, F., Benson, K. and Ahn, H. (1997) 'A meta-analysis of outcome studies comparing bona fide psychotherapies: empirically, "all must have prizes"', *Psychological Bulletin*, 122: 203–15.

Ward, E., King, M., Lloyd, M., Bower, P., Sibbauld, B., Farrelly, S., Gabbay, M., Tarrier, N. and Addington-Hall, J. (2000) 'Randomised controlled trial of non-directive counselling, cognitive-behaviour therapy, and usual general practitioner care for patients with depression. I: Clinical effectiveness', *British Medical Journal*, 321: 1383–8.

Warwick, H.M.C., Clark, D.M., Cobb, A.M. and Salkovskis, P.M. (1996) 'A controlled trial of cognitive-behavioural treatment of hypochondriasis', *British Journal of Psychiatry*, 169: 189–95.

Waskow, I.E. and Parloff, M.B. (eds) (1975) *Psychotherapy Change Measures* (DHEW Pub. no. (ADM) 74–120). Washington, DC: US Government Printing Office. pp. 245–69.

Whiston, S.C. and Sexton, T.L. (1993) 'An overview of psychotherapy outcome research: implications for practice', *Professional Psychology: Research and Practice*, 24: 43–51.

Whitehorn, J.C. and Betz, B. (1954) 'A study of psychotherapeutic relationships between physicians and schizophrenic patients', *American Journal of Psychiatry*, 3: 321–31.

Wing, J.K., Beevor, A., Curtis, R.H., Park, S.B.G., Hadden, S. and Burns, A. (1998) 'Health of the Nation Outcome Scales (HoNOS): research and development', *British Journal of Psychiatry*, 172: 11–18

Wolfe, B. and Goldfried, M.R. (1988) 'Research on psychotherapy integration: recommendation and conclusions from an NIMH workshop', *Journal of Consulting and Clinical Psychology*, 56: 448–51.

16 The Training and Supervision of Individual Therapists

Mark Aveline

Overview

The purpose of training in psychotherapy is to facilitate the exercise of natural abilities and acquired skills to best effect. This statement, which is based on my experience as a practitioner and trainer in psychotherapy in the National Health Service in the UK over 27 years, asserts two propositions, each of which is central to this chapter. First, that therapists bring to their work a greater or lesser degree of natural talent for psychotherapy. Two subsidiary propositions are that the possession of talent is an essential foundation on which expertise can be built in training and that the talent is not a unitary predisposition; it may be for one of the individual therapies or for some other form such as group or family therapy. Secondly, psychotherapy is a purposeful activity in which trainees and trainers share a professional and ethical commitment to evaluate and refine their work. Thoughtful therapists will ask themselves three questions again and again: (1) What in the therapy and this person's life actually helped the patient?[1] (2) Could the end have been achieved more expeditiously? and (3) Was anything done that was to the patient's ultimate detriment?

In this chapter, it is impossible to do justice to the fine detail of training in each of the many forms of individual therapy. Instead, attention is drawn to important issues in each area of training. After the introduction, I present a checklist of training objectives, then discuss motivating factors in therapists and selection for training before considering the sometimes neglected but universally important dimensions of counter-transference and the abuse of power. The three cardinal elements of theoretical learning, supervised clinical work, and personal therapy are discussed in turn. The move towards National Vocational Qualifications (NVQs), the registration and statutory registrations of psychotherapists, and the need for continued education is then considered. A section on supportive therapy concludes the review.

Introduction

'In what is called "individual psychotherapy" two people meet and talk to each other with the intention and hope that one will learn to live more fruitfully.' This deceptively simple statement by Lomas encompasses the central dimensions in psychotherapy practice – meeting, talking (I prefer the form 'talking with' rather than 'talking to') in a hopeful spirit and the purposeful intention of achieving more fruitful living in the patient's everyday life (Lomas, 1981). The statement sets out in ordinary language the parameters of a kind of psychotherapy with which I can identify, a rather ordinary encounter between two people but one of exceptional promise. However, as is so often the case, the results of our intentions frequently do not measure up to our hopes. Training is intended to enhance the competence of the therapist but in itself is no guarantee of success. Please note that types of training that emphasize the apparent substantial difference in form between therapies may obscure underlying, powerful similarities.

Luborsky and Singer (1975) in a survey of the effectiveness of different approaches to psychotherapy subtitled 'Is it true that "Everyone has won and all must have prizes"?' call attention to the fact that in research studies all the psychotherapies are similarly effective and none pre-eminent, a sobering conclusion for partisans of any school or faction. In other words, what effective therapies across schools have in common is more important than what divides them, a theme I return to later. This is not to say that certain therapies are not particularly suitable for a given person or problem, nor that a therapist will not function especially well in the approach that she finds most congenial. What are the best applications of the different therapies is a matter for research (Roth and Fonagy, 1996), while the natural affinity of a trainee with particular approaches is a key aspect to be identified in training.

The findings of Luborsky and other researchers certainly have not stilled debate about who is or is not a psychotherapist or which theoretical system, if any, approximates most closely to the complexity of being human. Or can one variant, for example psychoanalysis and psychoanalytic psychotherapy that share so many features, consistently and with enhanced therapeutic effect be distinguished from the other? Sandler (1988), a distinguished psychoanalyst, thinks not. In such debates, questions of power, prestige and authenticity lurk in the shadows and threaten to upstage the essential question of how appropriate and effective are the different approaches with which patients and what problems. When, as all too often, the tribes in the psychotherapy nation go to war with one another, they yield to the temptation of vested interest in promoting ascendancy over competitors and, within their own ranks, in stilling dissident voices; in such struggles, the pursuit of truth may be neglected. They neglect the communality of interest on the larger stage of developing a profession of psychotherapy where effective practice may be refined through the twin, opposite processes of differentiation and integration. In selecting a training programme, trainees need to bear these points in mind.

Given the wide range of approaches that may be gathered under the generic title of individual psychotherapy, and the partisanship that goes with differences that are often more apparent than real, I am mindful of the hazard of this chapter being dismissed by adherents of one approach on the grounds of irrelevance to their practice, ignorance of what they do or believe, and partiality to my own bias. In contrast, my intention is to address important issues for trainees and trainers which I hope will be heard across the spectrum. But first I must state what is central to my approach. I will be declaring my bias and setting out a synthesis, derived from my experience as a therapist, with which readers may compare their own conclusions (Aveline, 1979).

Psychotherapy attends both to the vital feelings of hope, despair, envy, hate, self-doubt, love and loss that exist between humans and to the repeated pattern of relationships that a person forms; in particular, to those aspects of the patterns for which that person has responsibility and over which they can come to exercise choice. As a therapist, I encourage my patient to take personally significant action in the form of new ways of relating, both in the consulting room and in his relationships outside, which, once succeeded in, will begin to rewrite the cramped fiction of his life. This therapeutic action challenges the determining myths that a person has learned or evolved to explain his actions; commonly, these myths are restrictive and self-limiting. I work with the psychological view that a person takes of himself, his situation and the possibilities open to him; essentially, this is the view that has been taken of him by important others and that he has taken of himself in the past, and it will go on being the determining view unless some corrective emotional experience occurs. The view that the person takes of himself is illuminated by the relationship patterns that form between the patient and the people in his life, including me; jointly, the patient and I examine the meaning of the patterns. Importantly, it is change in the external world of the patient, rather than inferred intrapsychic change, against which I judge the success of our mutual endeavour. Lest this sound too demanding, let me balance the statement by the recognition that many patients with deep problems of self-doubt and a negative world view need sustained care in order to gather the courage to change.

On one level, I make no distinction between enlightened analytic and cognitive-behavioural theory and practice; both recognize and utilize the therapeutic factors they have in common; both offer encouragement, the one covertly, the other overtly. In the former, intrapsychic terrors are faced and the treatment proceeds by analogy; if a new end to the old sad story can be written in the relationship with the therapist, the same new chapter can be written in the natural relationships outside the consulting room. In the latter, direct action is taken, perhaps after a period of rehearsal, often undertaken with the therapist. What characterizes good psychotherapy of any sort is a sustained, affirmative stance on the part of an imaginative, seasoned therapist who respects and does not exploit (Schafer, 1983). I hope that my relationship with the patient is both passionate and ethical, for both these elements are necessary if personal change is to occur. In the interplay of therapy, I influence and am influenced by what passes between us. It is the other person's journey in life, but it is a journey for us both and one in which I may expect to change as well as the patient. It is a journey and not an aimless ramble: though the ultimate destination may be unknown, the way stations are known by the therapist and aimed for; the therapist has expertise in guiding the other through terrain which is new to them and has some responsibility for the choices made (Aveline, 2001). It is, also, a journey in which I do not expect to be the guide for the whole way; someone may enter therapy for a while, gain what they require to get their life moving, go away to try their modified approach and return later if they need; in this, I am a minimalist. I do not aim, even if it were possible as early psychoanalysts hoped, to exhaust through the psychotherapy the patient's potential for neurosis or, necessarily, to locate the locus of change wholly in the relationship with me.

I have presented my conclusions in summary form. The constraint of space means that I cannot spell out the significance of each point, but I offer these conclusions as a personal point of reference for the following discussion of the elements in training. Let us begin by recognizing the formidable task that awaits the trainee therapist.

What the individual therapist has to learn

Despite the plethora of texts and manualized procedures whose clinical purpose is to lend assistance to both experienced and novice therapists, the practice of psychotherapy is challenging in its elusive complexity, ambiguity and frustratingly slow pace of change. Even in the more procedure-dominated cognitive and behavioural therapies, the ambiguous, uncertain reality of practice is disconcerting to those (and this includes many with medical, nursing and psychology backgrounds) who are used to the predictable clarity in the physical sciences of structure, intervention and consistent outcome. In physical science at a macro level, linearity is the rule. In psychotherapy, chaos theory is a more apt model; change being the product of a complex and uncertain interaction between the form and severity of problems, the patient's personality, developmental stage and motivation, the appropriateness, intrinsic power and dose of the therapy, the skill, motivation and healing capacity of the psychotherapist, the malleability of the life situation and the operation of chance and good or ill-fortune.

Furthermore, what happens between therapist and patient is complicated by the often unrecognized involvement of the therapist during therapy in the patient's self-limiting fiction and by the arousal in the therapist of unresolved personal conflicts; this phenomenon of transference and counter-transference has the central place in the analytic therapies (and, of course, is fostered by their techniques) but to a greater or lesser extent is also part of any human interaction and, certainly, of any therapy where the participants have a close relationship. Yet, I trust, for readers of this volume, the struggle to become proficient therapists is worth while, not least because psychotherapy is a fundamentally important activity in our technological and materialistic age: it attends to individual and shared experience and meaning and it attests to the ability of people to support and help each other. But this practical discipline and creative art is not easily learned.

What a therapist has to learn depends on the level and intensity at which she has to practise, be it at the level of beginner gaining a limited appreciation of what psychotherapy is or of qualified professional who as a generalist needs psychotherapeutic skills as part of her work, or of career psychotherapist and future trainer of therapists. The caveat is that, at all levels, the same lessons are repeated again and again. The individual therapies vary substantially in theory, focus and technique and there is much to be learned. However, the trainee who quite appropriately immerses herself in one approach risks being ignorant of others.

437

The alternative, when faced with such variety, is to attempt to learn simultaneously two dissonant approaches, which may cause trainee confusion and a degree of trainer alienation. Yet not to look widely at the therapy spectrum during the formative period of training is to risk premature closure in thinking and mental ossification, an eventuality to be guarded against.

From the point of view of the trainee therapist, the objectives in training can be stated as follows:

General

- to make progress towards the optimal use of natural ability and acquired skills;
- to identify the type(s) of therapy and range of patient problem and personality with which the therapist can work effectively.

Specific (in approximate order of priority)

- to learn to listen to what is said and not said by patients and to develop with them shared languages of personal meaning;
- to develop the capacity to keep in contact with patients in their pain and anger-filled explorations;
- in interaction with patients, to learn to move between participation and observation; to get a sense of when and when not to intervene;
- to gain a coherent conceptual frame within which to understand what happens and is intended to happen in therapy;
- to study human development, the process of learning, and the functioning of naturally occurring personal relationships between friends, couples and in families and the artificial, constructed relationships in psychotherapy where strangers are brought together;
- to understand and bring to bear both the therapeutic factors that types of therapy have in common (these, which are often referred to as non-specific or common factors, are detailed in the section on theoretical learning) and those that are approach specific;
- to gain confidence in the practice of the preferred type of therapy; to make full use of the therapist's emotional responses, theoretical constructs and techniques in resolving the patients' problems; to become adept in working briefly and long term, and at different frequencies;
- to commit to evidence-based practice;
- to increase the therapist's level of self-awareness and to work towards the resolution of personal conflicts which may interfere with the process of therapy;
- to come to know personal limitations and be able to obtain and use supervision;
- to know the features of major psychiatric illness and the indications and contra-indications for psychotropic medication; to make valid diagnostic assessments psychiatrically, psychologically and dynamically (Malan, 1995: Chs 18–23; Aveline, 1997a);
- to be sufficiently knowledgeable about other types of therapy so as to match therapy to patient need by referring on; to consider ethical dilemmas and internalize high ethical standards; to cultivate humility, compassion and modesty as well as a proper degree of self-confidence;
- to be familiar with the chosen theoretical system and aware of its areas of greatest utility and its limitations; to appreciate the significance of cultural and social factors and to adjust therapy accordingly; to evaluate critically what is enduring truth and what is

mere habit or unsubstantiated dogma in the practice of psychotherapy through (a) the experience of clinical practice, (b) being supervised, and (c) studying the research literature; to be able to evaluate outcome; to set standards of practice and systematically evaluate these by clinical audit;

- to understand the implications of the employment context in which practice is to occur (philosophical, political, institutional, economic and contractual);
- to commit to continuous professional development; at the level of career psycho-therapist, to acquire that professional identity.

For the trainer, the objectives are:

- to assess accurately (a) the stage at which trainees are in their development as therapists and (b) their strengths and weaknesses. At different stages, this may involve the normative functions of selection for training and evaluation for graduation (in educational terms, 'normative' refers to entry/exit, pass/fail criteria, whereas 'formative' refers to non-examined elements that enrich the educational experience of training);
- to help trainees secure the formative learning experiences which will clarify and develop their natural affinity with particular types of therapy and problem;
- to hold the balance of interest between the learning needs of trainee therapists and the clinical needs of their patients until such time as the trainee therapists can do this for themselves.

This long list is not intended to be intimidating but it does serve to underline the seriousness of embarking on training to be a therapist. It provides a framework with which to assess training needs, progress and the suitability of the training programme for a particular trainee.

Training has no end-point or single path. An individual's training over time is the result of personal and occupational choices. The choices may mark a progression from the expertise needed by a generalist with an interest in the subject to that required by a career psychotherapist, and within psychotherapy from one type to another as the trainee's interest changes. Further training will be necessary to update the therapist with advances in practice and to maintain existing expertise at a good level. Just as therapy should meet the needs of the patient, so should training meet the requirements of the therapist's practice, those that stem both from the type of therapy and from the work setting. What a therapist working in brief therapy in a clinic with a long waiting list needs to know is very different from one specializing in long-term therapy in independent practice who only takes on new work when she has a vacancy.

The reader at this point may be eager to plunge into the detail of the three cardinal elements of training, namely theoretical learning, supervised clinical work, and personal therapy. To accede to this wish would be premature. It would collude with the view that proficiency in psychotherapy is a simple, acquired technical skill. Instead, I argue that the wish to train in psychotherapy arises from events in the trainee's personal history and their consequent effect on character structure. The reflective therapist will want to take stock of what she brings from her inheritance and experience of life to this work before she becomes deeply committed to it. Two things are certain. In the work of psychotherapy, whatever the type, the personal, unique reactions of the therapist will complicate and illuminate the relationship that she and the patient have, and being a therapist will expose her to the temptation of abusing that powerful position. What I mean by these strong statements is spelt out in the next four sections that deal with motivating factors in therapists, selection for training, counter-transference and the abuse of power.

Motivating factors in the therapist

The trainee therapist has been long in the making before he or she formally enters training. Family circumstance, life events, gender, race and culture combine with inherited predisposition to form a unique individual who may or may not be suited to the practice of some or all of the psychotherapies. Each potential therapist will be special in their values, expectations and sensitivities; each will have natural ability in different measure for the work and a natural affinity with particular types of therapy and patient problems.

Being a psychotherapist offers many satisfactions: the opportunity to develop a unique personal style of practice with a substantial degree of professional independence, to share at close hand an endless variety of human activities far beyond that generally encountered in the therapist's own life, to satisfy the desire to help others, to be intellectually stimulated, to gain in emotional growth. . .and to have prestige and be paid! (Bugental, 1964; Burton, 1975; Greben, 1975; Farber and Heifetz, 1981; Farber, 1983).

Guy (1987) distinguishes between functional and dysfunctional motivators. In fact, his items encompass both motivating factors and functional attributes of effective therapists. Functional motivators include a natural interest in people, the ability to listen and talk, the psychological-mindedness of being disposed to enter empathically into the world of meaning and motivation of others, and the capacities of facilitating and tolerating the expression of feelings, being emotionally insightful, introspective and capable of self-denial, as well as being tolerant of ambiguity and intimacy and capable of warmth, caring and laughter (see also Greben's six functional attributes in the next section).

Dysfunctional motivators draw people to the role of therapist and may prove to be functional, but when present to excess subvert the process for the therapist's own ends. There is a well-established tradition in dynamic psychotherapy, clearly articulated by Jung, that only the wounded healer can heal. Thus, Storr writes: 'Psychotherapists often have some personal knowledge of what it is like to feel insulted and injured, a kind of knowledge which they might rather be without, but which actually extends the range of their compassion' (Storr, 1979: 173). Guy (1987) lists six dysfunctional motivators, the first of which is the most common:

1 emotional distress: therapists may seek – and gain – self-healing through their work; the crucial question is one of magnitude. Some acquaintance with emotional pain is essential; an over-preoccupation with unresolved personal needs hinders the therapist from giving full attention to the patient;
2 vicarious coping as a lifestyle which imparts a voyeuristic quality to the therapy relationship;

3   conducting psychotherapy as a means of compensating for an inner sense of loneliness
and isolation; this is self-defeating as it is life lived at one remove;
4   fulfilling the desire for power and fostering a false sense of omnipotence and
omniscience (Marmor, 1953; Guggenbuhl-Craig, 1979);
5   a messianic need to provide succour; one positive aspect of psychotherapy is that it is
an acceptable way for a person to show their love and tenderness, but this becomes
dysfunctional when it is carried to excess;
6   psychotherapy as a relatively safe way of expressing underlying rebellious feelings in
the therapist through getting the patient to act them out.

These dysfunctional motivators give rise to counter-transference problems which
are considered later (counter-transference means distortions derived from unresolved conflicts in the therapist's life which she unconsciously introduces into the
therapy relationship).

The prevalence of dysfunctional motivators among psychotherapists is not
known. In a major survey of 4,000 American psychotherapists (Henry, 1977),
most reported good relationships with their families though 39 per cent said that
their parents' marriage was not good. Childhood separations, deaths and incidence of mental illness were similar to that of other college-educated populations.
These global statistics doubtless conceal much individual variation. Thus Storr's
(1979) impression may be true that many therapists (and here he means
dynamically oriented therapists) have had depressed mothers to whose feelings
they may have developed a special sensitivity, together with an urge not to upset
or distress; their childhood experiences may well prompt them to seek out in adult
life the role of therapist. In Kleinian terminology, the need to make reparation will
be great in these therapists; they may be especially adept at making contact with
timid and fearful patients. There is some evidence that within the occupation of
psychotherapy a history of personal conflicts and a greater experience of mental
illness in the family of origin inclines practitioners more towards dynamic rather
than behavioural orientations (Rosin and Knudson, 1986). I know of no research
that distinguishes between the personal backgrounds of therapists choosing to
work in individual therapy and those choosing family and group therapy.

These factors and attributes constitute the natural ability for which selection has
to be made and which is built on in training.

The selection of therapists for training

Trainers have a dual responsibility in selecting their trainees: the responsibility to
help that person avoid taking on work for which she is not suitable; and the
responsibility to the patients – from whom the trainee will learn – to ensure that
they have optimal care.

Selection is a matter for both the trainee and the trainer: the trainee will want
to test out what is on offer and the trainer will test the trainee's readiness for each
level of training. Introductory trainings offer the trainee, through workshops and
brief courses, the opportunity to try different types of therapy and to discover the
ones with which she has a natural affinity. Little or no attempt is made to select at

this level. Another formative route into formal psychotherapy training is to be supervised by therapists whose style and orientations vary and, either before or as a supplement to this, to be in personal therapy; both experiences form and clarify aptitude. With advancing level, selection procedures become correspondingly complex. Commonly, for analytic training, candidates will have to complete an autobiographical questionnaire and undergo two extended interviews with different assessors, one more factual and the other explorative in the analytic style; the results will be considered by a panel of assessors so as to reduce individual bias (a detailed explication of the process and criteria used in one institute can be found in Fleming (1987: Chs 3 and 7). Later, the candidate's progress will have to be approved before entry to each further stage of training is allowed. In the case of psychoanalysis, this would commence with the candidate beginning their five times a week training therapy, being in therapy for at least a year, and having to secure satisfactory reports from their therapist before proceeding to the next stage of participating in theoretical seminars, and, then at a later date, embarking on their training cases, a meticulous and extended procedure. Educationally, having reports from the therapist helps exclude the unsatisfactory trainee but may have the negative effect of compromising the neutrality of the therapy and further enhancing the asymmetry of the relationship (see the section on abuse of power).

In the public sector, acquisition of a core health profession qualification, in-service training in psychotherapy, appraisal and competitive interview serve the twin purposes of preparation and exclusion.

Sadly, the correlation between length of training and effectiveness as a therapist is low (Auerbach and Johnson, 1977); this finding may reflect deficiencies in research methodology but is also a function of the overwhelming importance in promoting personal change of pre-existing personality factors such as decency, a respectful, empathic concern with others, neutrality, persistence and optimism. Reflecting on my own experience as a therapist and trainer, a therapist's effectiveness over the years of her career often seems to follow a U-curve and is a function of different attributes. Early on, patients benefit especially from the therapist's energy and enthusiasm and later from her acquired wisdom and skill as a therapist (Orlinsky and Howard, 1980; see also the forthcoming book on the longitudinal development of psychotherapists: Orlinsky and Ronnestad, forthcoming). In the middle phase, as therapists become more self-conscious and aware of the complexity of the subject, performance may decline temporarily. Later, therapists may work with patients whose problems are more severe and entrenched; gains may be slow and hard-won. Trainees should not feel dismayed by feeling de-skilled when they enter the next level of training, and may with justice on their side ask the training organizers what help they propose to provide in overcoming this common reaction.

The above should not be taken to imply that putting effort into selection is worthless. Personality is all-important. 'The greatest technical skill can offer no substitute for nor will obviate the pre-eminent need for integrity, honesty, and dedication on the part of the therapist' (Strupp, 1960). As a selector, I look for the functional motivators listed by Guy (1987), and also the six qualities identified by Greben: empathic concern, respectfulness, realistic hopefulness, self-awareness, reliability and strength of character (Greben, 1984). These are the qualities that are necessary if the therapist is to win the patient's trust; they give him the sense of being tended to and valued. Women often seem to have these qualities in greater abundance than men. It must be stressed that no one is perfect: what is required for this work is a sufficiency of these qualities. In addition, I look for two markers of maturity in life: that the trainee has struggled with some personal emotional conflict and achieved a degree of resolution, and that she has enjoyed and sustained over years a loving, intimate relationship. The first may bring in its wake humility and compassion, the second an active commitment to and capacity for good relationships, so well summed up in Fairbairn's concept of mature dependence (Fairbairn, 1954). I am wary of aspiring therapists who have a scornful, rejecting or persecutory cast to their nature or who are not emotionally generous in their interaction.

My impression is that therapists who prefer to work in individual therapy rather than in, for example, group therapy have a number of identifying characteristics. They seem to have a greater interest in the vertical or historical axis of there-and-then exploration into the childhood origins of adult problems and their re-creation within the therapy relationship, as opposed to the horizontal axis of here-and-now interactions that is central to the focus of the group therapist (and increasingly of the modem psychodynamic therapist). They are more interested in fantasy, prefer to take a passive role and like the immediacy of the one-to-one relationship and the scope to work in depth. These impressions may help the trainee in the choice of which type of therapy to train in, though other factors will also be influential. Cognitive-behavioural therapy has seized the high ground in the competition for legitimacy through research and is favoured by purchasers. In addition, the high patient demand for individual therapy and its greater economic viability in private practice, especially with the advent of powerful, brief therapy (Ryle, 1990), may strongly reinforce natural affinity for individual ways of working.

A controversial issue concerns whether or not a therapist should have as a prerequisite for being a psychotherapist a qualification in one of the core mental health care professions; these are generally taken to be medicine, psychology, nursing and social work, all degree occupations, and occupational therapy and, perhaps, the new categories of art and drama therapy. Talent as a psychotherapist is not the exclusive preserve of any profession. The development in the UK within the NHS of the new *ad hoc* grade of Adult Psychotherapist, open to all with aptitude and training, testifies to the truth of this proposition. However, the possession of a core qualification indicates that the trainee has a certain level of intelligence and ensures familiarity with the symptoms and signs of major psychiatric illness. It will also have offered the trainee the opportunity to internalize high ethical standards and, through membership of a professional group, ensures that she is subject to disciplinary procedures that help maintain good practice. Qualifications in literature, philosophy and religion are relevant but trainees with these backgrounds will need special training in the features of major psychiatric illness and in what may be gained from pharmacological treatments, especially if they intend to practise independently. I return to this question in the sections on theoretical learning, supervised clinical practice, and registration.

I have written at some length about the personal qualities and qualifications that a trainee therapist brings to the work. In order to bring out two important consequences that stem from the intensity of the closed, asymmetrical personal relationship between patient and therapist that lies at the heart of individual therapy, the next two sections deal with the importance of counter-transference reactions and the temptation for the therapist to abuse her power in all types of psychotherapy.

Counter-transference

Unconsciously mediated transference and counter-transference reactions inevitably feature in any relationship, and especially in the intimate, prolonged relationship of individual therapy. These powerful distortions are present even in the symptom-oriented, individual cognitive and behaviour therapies. Increasingly, cognitive-behavioural training programmes pay attention to these processes (as they should!).

The term 'counter-transference' is used in two senses; it may refer (a) to feelings that are the counterpart of the patient's feelings and (b) to feelings that are counteractions to the patient's transference (Greenson, 1967). Counterpart feelings are part of empathy; they provide valuable information about the other, as when the therapist feels in herself the disowned, hidden sadness or anger of the other, technically a manifestation of projective identification in Kleinian parlance. Thus the therapist's unconscious mind understands that of her patient (Heimann, 1950). 'Counteractions' are situations where the patient's communications stir up unresolved problems of the therapist. An example would be a therapist who fears her own aggression and placates the patient whenever she detects hostile feelings towards her. In addition, the patient, through some combination of age, gender or other characteristics, may be a transference figure for the therapist; examples would be as parent or rival. Furthermore, the dependence and intimacy of the role relationship of therapist and patient will have a personal meaning for the therapist for good or for ill, based on past and childhood experiences of psychologically similar situations.

Consider the following list of counter-transference reactions and their consequences (Bernstein and Bernstein, 1980: 48) and see how each limits the therapeutic potential of the encounter.

1. Do I require sympathy, protection and warmth so much myself that I err by being too sympathetic, too protective toward the patient?
2. Do I fear closeness so much that I err by being indifferent, rejecting, and cold?
3. Do I need to feel important and therefore keep patients dependent on me, precluding their independence and assuming responsibility for their own welfare?

4. Do I cover feelings of inferiority with a front of superiority, thereby rejecting patients' need for acceptance?
5. Is my need to be liked so great that I become angry when a patient is rude, unappreciative, or uncooperative?
6. Do I react to the patient as an individual human being or do I label him with the stereotype of a group? Are my prejudices justified?
7. Am I competing with other authority figures in the patient's life when I offer advice contrary to that of another health professional?
8. Does the patient remind me too much of my own problems when I find myself being overly ready with pseudo-optimism, and facile reassurance?
9. Do I give uncalled-for advice as a means of appearing all-wise?
10. Do I talk more than listen to a patient in an effort to impress him with my knowledge?

Counter-transference problems are signalled by intensifications or departures from the therapist's usual practice. At the time, they seem plausible, even justifiable; yet, when considered in supervision or in the routine self-scrutiny ('internal supervision': Casement, 1985) that is the mark of responsible psycho-therapy, their obstructive nature becomes apparent. Menninger (1958) lists among the items that he has 'probably experienced': repeatedly experiencing erotic feelings towards the patient, carelessness in regard to appointment arrangements, sadistic unnecessary sharpness in formulating interpretations, getting conscious satisfaction from the patient's praise or affection and sudden increase or decrease in interest in a certain case.

Items like the above can serve as a checklist to help identify counter-transference problems that arise from conflicts in the therapist's unconscious mind. This is different from the equally problematic feelings that are manifesta-tions of the therapist's involvement in the patient's determining fiction or, in language of psychoanalysis, the transference and transference neurosis. One example of these processes is the way in which a patient who has been brought up in a persecutory environment expects others to persecute him, perceives the therapist as being persecutory (transference) and actually prompts the therapist to act in a persecutory way (transference neurosis); another example is when the therapist finds herself not respecting the boundaries of a patient whose bounda-ries as a child have been breached by a parent in incestuous acts. This is an acting-out of counter-transference feelings, an enactment of formative events from the patient's past, re-created by the interaction of patient and therapist. A golden route for promoting change lies in identifying these involvements, explor-ing their meaning and disentangling both therapist and patient from them. Both sets of involvements are encompassed within a taxonomy of therapist difficulty devised by Davis, Elliott, Davis, Binns, Francis, Kelman and Schroder (1987). This allows therapists to compile their own distinctive profile of difficulty on nine categories. Trainees might benefit from plotting their profile and using this to highlight their idiosyncrasies; these could then be focused on in training, including their work in personal (training) therapy.

A particularly common form of noxious therapy relationship results from the abuse of power.

The abuse of power

Therapists are all too easily seduced into abusing the therapy relationship. When this occurs, the relationship is no longer therapeutic. During training, trainees need to learn how to recognize when abuse is likely to happen and is happening and take corrective action. In this respect, the work that is done in supervision is crucial. How does the abuse of power come about? It results from the conjunction of the patient's transference wishes and dysfunctional motivators in the therapist; it is encouraged by the inequality of power between the pair.

Essentially the therapist constructs the arena in which individual therapy takes place. Though it is subject to negotiation, the therapist decides the duration, frequency and form of the therapy. Ultimately, beginning and ending is in her hands, ending being a powerful threat to the patient who is dependent or not coping. With rare exceptions, the meetings take place on the therapist's territory. The therapist, whether trainee or trained, is held to be expert in what goes on in the arena, certainly by the patient who is relatively a novice in this setting. Whatever procedures the therapist propounds, the patient is predisposed to accept. Because the sessions take place in private, the therapy is not subject to the natural regulation of the scepticism, and even incredulity, of outsiders. All this gives the therapist great power and, consequently, exposes her to great temptation.

Ideological conversion through a process analogous to brainwashing is one hazard. When Scientology was investigated (Foster, 1971), its practices of 'auditing' and 'processing' were seen to be so dangerous that statutory regulation of psychotherapy was called for (see section on registration, p. 460). More commonly, eccentric, unsubstantiated beliefs are peddled as truths by those with power and clung on to by vulnerable, uncertain people who deserve better.

Another hazard for the patient is the conjunction of his need for an ideal parent who will protect, guide and succour with the therapist's wish to be idealized. What Ernest Jones (1913) termed the 'God-complex' lies in wait for the unwary (Marmor, 1953). The therapist's ego is boosted by transference admiration; this seductive pitfall is compounded by the common tendency in psychotherapy and especially in individual therapy for therapists to mystify the process through the use of esoteric jargon and the adoption of an aloof, all-knowing stance. Therapists run the risk of coming to feel superior, free of the struggles, conflicts and defeats of their patients. From a detached position – which may be bolstered by viewing all the patient's communications as manifestations of transference and, as such, only needing to be put back to the patient for his sole consideration – the therapist is tempted to be a bystander in life, vicariously involved but spared the pain and puffed up by the patient's dependent approval. Progress towards separation and individuation is obstructed. In the artificial, time-limited world of the therapy session, the therapist may have the pretence of having all the answers.

Guggenbuhl-Craig (1979) asserts that within us all is the archetype of the patient and healer. In order to reduce ambivalence, the archetype may be split and either polarity projected on to others. But both are necessary for healing. The sick man needs an external healer, but also needs to find the healer in himself; otherwise he becomes passive through handing over his healing ability to the other. This is obviously antithetical to the spirit of good psychotherapy. For the healer, the danger is to locate the polarity of the 'patient in her' in her patients and not recognize it in her own self. Then, she will come to see herself more and more as the strong healer for whom weakness, illness and wounds do not exist. As a healer without wounds, she will be less able to engage the healing factor in her patients. Traditional medical education can reinforce the division (Bennet, 1987).

The therapist who locates weakness in others becomes powerful through their failure. In Jungian language, the charlatan shadow of the therapist has been constellated. Guggenbuhl-Craig doubts that personal therapy or case discussions are sufficient to reduce the split in the archetype. The analytic shield carefully acquired in training is too effective, the risk of loss of self-esteem or prestige too great, the need to maintain one's allegiance to a school of therapy against outside attack too pressing. In some therapists, the split in the archetype is minimal; their patients' problems illuminate their own and are consciously worked on; they remain a patient as well as a healer. The best way of reducing the split is through involvement in ordinary life in un-analytic, symmetrical relationships that have the power to touch deeply, and to throw off balance, relationships which are quite different from the asymmetrical ones of therapy. Friendships – loving, forceful encounters with equals – develop the therapist as a whole person. What the therapist advocates for others is good for her.

Not surprisingly, given the intensity and privacy of individual therapy, some therapists become sexually involved with their patients. It is hard to conceive of circumstances when this is not abusive in its impact or a dereliction of the responsibilities of being a therapist. One can understand how it happens but it should not be condoned. Many more male therapists have sexual involvement with female patients than do female therapists with male patients but all combinations do occur, including with the same sex. Eroticized transference and counter-transference are common in therapy and may be acted out (Holroyd and Brodsky, 1977). In the transference, the patient may be looking for a loving parent. This wish may connect with the therapist's need to be a helping figure but subsequent sexual action represents a confusing of childhood wishes, albeit expressed in adult language, with mature intent; sexual action fractures the boundaries that are necessary if the therapy arena is to be psychologically safe.

Lust is a relatively straightforward motivation in acting-out; its intensity depends on the urgency of the therapist's biological drive, age, state of health, recency of drive satisfaction, general satisfaction with personal life and, of course, the attractiveness of the patient. Darker motivations such as unconscious hostility to women or reaction formations against feared homosexuality or gender inadequacy may be present (Marmor, 1972). Sexual action may be rationalized as being for the patient's benefit, but this self-deception should not survive the monitoring of self-scrutiny, supervision and personal therapy.

Occasionally, therapist and patient fall in love and form a long-term relationship. Though one may wonder about the basis of a personal relationship founded in the strange circumstances of the therapy room, when the two are in love the ethically correct action is to suspend the therapy and arrange for it to be continued by a colleague if necessary.

Cardinal elements in training

Theoretical learning, supervised clinical practice and personal therapy are the cardinal elements in training. It is difficult to discuss one without making an artificial distinction from others, as the three are so interrelated. The section on each should be read with the others in mind. The reader is also invited to refer back to the section on what the individual therapist has to learn. The order of discussion reflects my priority. Many analytic therapists might wish to give primacy to personal therapy; many cognitive-behaviourists might dispute its relevance to their work. Academic courses awarding certificates, diplomas and Master's degrees are likely to emphasize theory and research, though this is a changing scene as universities realize that they have to incorporate supervised practice if their graduates are to be registered as practitioners by one of the national registering bodies. Many of the points made here are also relevant to training in other modalities of psychotherapy such as group therapy (Aveline and Ratigan, 1988).

Theoretical learning

Purpose and content

The purpose of training is to facilitate the exercise of natural abilities and acquired skills. To do this the therapist needs to gain extensive experience in the type(s) of therapy required for her practice and for which affinity has been shown, in this case individual therapy. But to begin with the trainee needs to acquire a conceptual framework of what therapy is about, how people mature and learn, and the role of the therapist. Later in training, theory will be critically examined to discover its areas of greatest applicability and limitations. Studying theory means that therapists do not reinvent the wheel. Assimilating theory into practice provides the therapist with an internalized rationale for the comprehension of clinical phenomena, the derivation of technique and the formulation of testable, clinically relevant hypotheses.

Learning theory is part of a broad educational process in which, in enlightened training, the development of informed critical thinking is being encouraged. Theory tends to be taught in an approach-specific way but general, overlapping and complementary perspectives also ought to be studied. Both specific and general learning need to be presented in the quality and level appropriate to the trainee's need and ability. Ideally, theoretical learning would encompass the following:

Theory and techniques specific to the therapy approach being learned. In most types of training this is the major component but, as has been indicated, the well-educated therapist needs to consider the range of approaches.

The common therapeutic factors. Frank (1973) has argued convincingly that in all effective therapies six influential factors are operative. The therapy provides (1) an exploratory rationale and (2) facilitates the exploration of traumas and conflictual issues in a state of emotional arousal. The effect is strengthened (3) when the therapist is sanctioned as a healer by the society. Responding to the patient's request for help (4) encourages that person to be hopeful about themselves and counters the demoralization which typifies most patients' state. Therapy provides or prompts (5) success experiences, which enhances a sense of mastery, thus countering demoralization. Finally psychotherapy provides (6) an intense confiding relationship with a helping person. These factors have a much greater influence on outcome than the contribution made by approach-specific theory and technique; in Lambert's review of empirical studies, common therapeutic factors accounted for 30 per cent of the therapeutic effect, technique 15 per cent, expectancy (placebo effect) 15 per cent and spontaneous remission 40 per cent (Lambert, 1986).

The necessary conditions. Rogers (1957) promoted research studies to support his proposition that three therapist conditions were necessary and sufficient for personality change: genuineness, unconditional positive regard and accurate empathy. The contention that these conditions are sufficient in themselves, are always helpful and should be taken as absolutes has been much investigated and caveats placed on the original proposition. However, a sufficiency of each constitutes the basis of a helpful relationship. In passing, it should be noted that Freud took it as read that the analyst would be a decent, understanding, non-judgmental, respectful and neutral person. These qualities formed the basis of the therapeutic alliance and gave, in Sandor Ferenczi's word, 'stability' (*Tragfestigheit*) to the relationship (Strupp, 1977).

Natural capacity for healing. Hubble and his colleagues see successful therapy as being that which assists the person's natural capacity for healing (Hubble et al., 1999). Each person has their own theory of change which is an emergent reality in the therapy, there to be prized and learned from. The therapist has to be sufficiently flexible to work congruently and creatively with the patient's world view. Technique acts, then, like a magnifying glass, focusing the forces for change and causing them to ignite into action.

The evolution of psychotherapy ideas. How the concepts of psychoanalysis, analytical psychology, individual psychology, existentialism, humanism, Gestalt psychology, psychodrama, cognitive, learning and systems theory have developed, their interrelationship and the implications for practice. In the analytic tradition, how an instinct-based theory has evolved to ego-psychology and then to self-psychology with increasing emphasis on object relations (human relations) and, especially in North America, on cultural and interpersonal aspects.

Human development. How individuals develop over the life span with particular reference to maturational tasks, attachment theory, and the elements that contribute to being able, in Freud's definition of maturity, to love and to work.

Mental mechanisms, character structure and the concept of conflict. How to make a dynamic formulation of the origin and meaning of the patient's problems (Aveline, 1980). The meaning and significance in clinical practice of the technical terms: process, content, therapeutic alliance, transference, counter-transference and resistance. When and how to make effective interpretations and other interventions. Good examples of the practical application of these concepts may be found in Malan (1995) and Casement (1985).

Learning and systems theory. The role of shaping, modelling, generalization and *in vivo* learning and faulty cognitions in determining human behaviour. The importance of problem definition and behavioural analysis in making a diagnostic assessment. How behavioural, system and dynamic processes operate in marriage and in families and result in disturbed functioning. The contribution of psychological theory on cognitive dissonance, attribution theory and crisis theory to the understanding of change and resistance to change.

Ways in which therapists need to take account of linguistics, philosophy, religion and ethics in formulating a comprehensive model of human aspirations and functioning.

Cultural relativity, with special reference to race, gender, sexual orientation, age and culture itself. The specific contribution made to 20th-century understanding of role relationships and psychology by feminist psychology.

Physical disease presenting as mental disorder. In addition, the trainee will need to know the signs and symptoms of major psychiatric illness, the likely benefits and side-effects of psychotropic medication and when and to whom to refer on. As a counterpart of this medical knowledge, the ways in which the sociological concepts of stigma and labelling further our understanding of alienation and isolation.

Indications and contra-indications for different kinds of psychotherapy.

The vital role of support in psychotherapy.

Preparation for therapy and patient–therapist matching. How negative effects arise through therapy and may be minimized. Taking into account available alternatives, does the therapist have the necessary interest, skills and time to help this patient?

Research methodology and classic studies. How to evaluate the research literature and derive implications for clinical practice (see Roth and Fonagy, 1996; Parry, 2001 for current statements of evidence-based practice).

Clinical audit. How to set standards for practice and systematically monitor them through the audit cycle.

Clinical governance, the profession-long responsibility for the quality of one's own work and the work of other psychotherapists (Department of Health, 1998). Identifying and implementing needs for continuing professional development (CPD). Delineation of system errors.

Ethics. Practice dilemmas, conflicts of interest, duty of care, informed consent and confidentiality.

Supervised clinical practice

Clinical practice

Appropriate supervised practice is the central learning experience in training. The trainee needs to learn what can be achieved in brief (up to 10 sessions), focal work (16–25 weekly sessions), medium (40–70 sessions) and long-term therapy (upwards of 2–3 years). Weekly therapy is the most common mode in NHS psychotherapy and in many other settings; this has its own rhythm and intensity and is quite different from more frequent therapy, where intensity may accelerate the process of change or be necessary in order to contain major personal disturbance. Weekly therapy tends to be more reality oriented; two, three or five times a week therapy affords greater scope for exploration and regression. The two ends of the spectrum present different learning experiences and need to be sampled.

The supervisor has a key role in ensuring that patients with a wide range of problems and character structure are seen during the training period. Both breadth and depth of experience are important for the development of trainees. Breadth develops flexibility and highlights to the trainee problematic counter-transferences and personal limitations that need either to be addressed in supervision, further experience and personal therapy or to be avoided. Depth fosters stamina, the ability to contain intense feelings and to have the patience to move at the pace of someone whose sense of basic trust and confident autonomy is poorly developed; often this will mean enduring feeling powerless and helpless as the reality of the patient's inner world is engaged (Adler, 1972).

In intermediate and advanced training, the trainee should gain supervised experience in making assessments. While the thrust of this chapter is towards individual therapy, I strongly favour a required element in training being the conduct of therapy groups, e.g. a small group over 18 months. A degree of competence in group therapy or, at the very least, a favourable familiarity with the approach should be part of the skills of an individual therapist. This can only be gained through direct experience.

What is judged to be an adequate training for a fully trained, autonomous practitioner in terms of duration, frequency and amount of clinical practice varies between the psychotherapies. At the level of career psychotherapy, it is hard to see that less than 900 hours of conducting therapy over three whole time equivalent years plus 300 hours of supervision divided between one main and two subsidiary supervisors could be sufficient, and this would need to be built on a foundation of less intensive, preliminary training in psychotherapy over two or more years; to learn well, one needs to immerse oneself in the subject. This is the standard set by the Royal College of Psychiatrists for the training of consultant medical psychotherapists. In addition, the College specifies that of the 900 hours, 700 should be in the main branch of psychotherapy being studied and 100 in each of the other two branches; currently, the branches recognized are psychodynamic/interpersonal, cognitive-behavioural and systemic (JCHPT, 1996). The British Association for Counselling and Psychotherapy specifies 450 hours of practice and 250 hours of supervision for accreditation as a counsellor. The United Kingdom Council for Psychotherapy requires a full programme of training over four years at degree level for registration and is moving towards objective-led training.

Format

Theory orders the great mass of clinical information and helps orientate the therapist in finding a way forward. This useful function should not curtail curiosity and the spirit of enquiry that is necessary for the development of the professional and the profession. Theory should always be relevant and, dependent on the level at which the training is pitched, comprehensive in coverage.

How theory is presented varies greatly. Commonly the span of knowledge to be studied is set by the training organizers, which has the virtue of making it clear what is to be learned. Then, there may be set readings either by author or topic, an approach that specifies the route of study and makes it easy for trainer or trainee to spot omissions. Curriculums, while reassuringly solid for trainers and trainees, may not engage the student's active participation. An alternative, which we employed for a time in the South-Trent Training in Dynamic Psychotherapy, a specialist NHS training, is to have a planning event each year where the trainees and seminar leaders jointly decide what is to be studied and how this is to be done. Instead of the conventional study of topics and authors, the question may be posed: 'What do I need to know in order to understand a specified psychotherapy process or problem?' This is the approach of researching a topic rather than simply reading someone else's selection of what is relevant. Another way is to specify learning objectives and, then, pose practice-dilemmas for exploration and debate.

At the advanced level, when many topics will have to be studied, teacher enthusiasm may be retained by offering a menu of courses in the teachers' areas of expertise; the trainee may select from these, with the training committee having the responsibility of ensuring that a balanced choice has been made. Here, an over-inclusive curriculum can be helpful. When every subject listed manifestly cannot be studied formally within the time available, a trainee in conjunction with a personal tutor can plan a more personal course of learning that takes account of prior learning and present interest. Self-directed learning and discovery is the adult way of learning. Didactic teaching soothes curriculum anxiety but at the cost of regression and passivity.

Theory is not just to be found in textbooks. Novels, plays, films and poems portray the human condition more vividly, complexly and, often, more sensitively than do dry texts. Biographies and autobiographies trace individual lives (Holmes, 1986). All these should be studied.

Whatever the format, the trainee should return again and again to the fundamental, practical question: *what are the implications of this theory or portrayal of life for my practice in my working environment with the patients that I see?*

The same principle of breadth and depth in practice adduced above applies to supervision. To gain alternative perspectives against which the trainee's own view may develop, several supervisors need to be worked with for a year at a time. In order for the trainee to know one perspective in depth and to feel safe enough to explore certain doubts and conflicts, one main supervisor needs to be engaged with over two or three years. The choice of main supervisor is clearly a matter of great import.

In addition, trainees who are not qualified in one of the core mental health care professions need to gain through clinical placements sufficient acquaintance with major psychiatric illnesses to be able to recognize their presence; knowledge of the effects and likely benefits of pharmacological and physical treatments is also necessary. One example of why therapists need to be familiar with such matters is the high risk of suicide and depressive homicide in severe depressive illness; in such cases, antidepressants or ECT (electro-convulsive therapy) can be life-saving measures that restore normal functioning. Psychotherapists should not persist in interpreting psychopathology when a speedier and more effective biological remedy is at hand. When the patient is once more accessible to verbal interaction and the risk of harm to himself and his family has receded, the precipitants and psychological vulnerabilities can then be explored in psychotherapy with the benefit of greater self-understanding and reduced likelihood of recurrence.

The role of the supervisor

The supervisor has a privileged, responsible position as mentor, guide and, often, assessor. From the advantageous position of hearing about therapy at second hand and generally after the event, the supervisor places his accumulated experience and knowledge at the service of the trainee. He helps the trainee work out with the patient the meaning and significance of the patient's communications, the nature of the conflicts and, certainly in the more dynamic therapies, brings into sharp focus the way in which patient and therapist engage and how this may be turned to good account. In the beginning, the trainee may feel an ambivalent mixture of excitement and dread in taking on a new role. During this time of insecurity, and fearing being inadequate, she will need the support of the supervisor. As training progresses, the supervisor has to encourage the trainee to let go of the early, perhaps necessary, idealization of the supervisor so that identification can be replaced by an internalization of professional skills (Gosling, 1978). In successful training, the trainee moves through the stages of inception, skills development and consolidation to mutuality of expertise with the trainer (Hess, 1986).

When patient and therapist concur in their appreciation of the aims of therapy *and* when there is clarity in understanding accurately the structure of the conflicts and the process of the session, two major contributions have been made to the success of the endeavour. Many psychotherapy centres use a pre-assessment interview questionnaire to help clarify the purpose of the therapy and, incidentally, to test motivation; in Nottingham, this has questions on what the problems are, how the patient thinks they have come about and in what ways they have been shaped in their life, their self-concept, the characteristic form of their relationships, what they have found helpful and unhelpful in the past, what has prompted them to seek help now, and what change they want to make through psychotherapy. Of course, in cognitive-behaviour therapy, goal definition and objectification of problem severity as a baseline for therapy is an integral part of the approach. In every type of individual therapy, a formulation of the underlying dynamics is beneficial and, I would argue, necessary and more useful than categorical diagnosis (Aveline, 1999). Though different approaches will use their own vocabulary, schemas for the content are to be found in Aveline (1980), Cleghorn et al. (1983), Friedman and Lister (1987), Perry et al. (1987), Aveline (1995), Mace (1995) and Eells (1997). I now favour an interpersonal formula that identifies a personally characteristic narrative of recurrent acts of self. This is an adaptation of Strupp and Binder (1984) and Luborsky's (Luborsky and Crits-Christoph, 1990) approach: it records conscious and unconscious wishes, formative acts by others, and responses to self and to others as well as restorative actions, risk factors and prediction of clinically significant patterns in therapy (Aveline, 1995); though derived from analytic and cognitive approaches, the formula is atheoretical and may be used by all.

Whichever conceptual schema is used, the supervisor helps the supervisee to make fuller use of the session and, crucially in my view, to see how she is getting caught up in the self-limiting relationship patterns of the patient. Getting caught up is inevitable; the skill in psychotherapy is in recognizing what is happening and using it constructively (Aveline, 1989). In the phenomenon called 'negative fit', therapists act in ways that fit the patient's negative preconceptions, which have been formed by how important people in his past have responded to him. Luborsky and Singer (1974) demonstrated two major patterns of negative fit when the tape recordings of experienced therapists were studied. One pattern was confirming the patient's fear of rejection by being critical, disapproving, cold, detached and indifferent, and the other was confirming the patient's fear of being made weak by being too directive, controlling and domineering. Clearly every effort should be made in supervision to identify these two patterns and to turn the potentially negative impact to therapeutic effect. Often the supervisor will be able to guide the trainee in selecting suitable patients for her stage in training. In this situation, the supervisor may consider selecting pairings that promise well e.g. when the therapist has successfully resolved in her life a similar conflict to the patient's *or* avoiding pairings where the therapist seems likely only to reinforce the patient's maladaptive pattern (Aveline, 1992).

Ways of supervising

Pedder sees supervision in three ways: (1) as being analogous to gardening, that is as a process of promoting growth, (2) as a place for play in the Winnicottian[2] sense, and (3) as being like therapy in that it provides a regular time and place for taking a second look at what happened in the therapy session (Pedder, 1986). Supervision aims to bring to the fore the creative potential of the therapist. It should be noted that supervision is not the same as therapy, though at times the distinction may become blurred.

Broadly speaking, the focus of supervisory interest can be on one of four areas: the process and content of the patient's concerns and communications, theoretical understandings and technique, transference and counter-transference reactions between therapist and patient, and the supervisee–supervisor relationship. The focus on the last is justified by Doehrman's classic study (Doehrman, 1976), which demonstrated the re-creation in the supervisee–supervisor relationship of the dynamics between patient and therapist. At least theoretically, this supports the view that, if the dynamics in supervision can be comprehended and resolved, blocks in the therapy relationship will be undone (for an example see Caligor, 1984). In practice, all these focuses are useful though, in my practice, I incline towards the first, as it is the patient's life that is my primary concern.

Much debate rages in psychotherapy circles about how the supervisory material should be presented. Classically in psychoanalytic training, a free-flowing account of the session is given with much attention being paid to what is said and not said and the elucidation of counter-transferences and associations as ways of illuminating unconscious processes. This is listening with the 'third ear' (Reik, 1949). That the report may factually correspond poorly to the observable events of the session is held to be of little importance; indeed some supervisors argue that factually precise reporting misses the point and, furthermore, may positively obscure it. I cannot accept this position. All ways of capturing the facts and essence of what went on are useful. Aids to supervision are just that: servants, not masters. They can be adapted to meet the needs of the moment.

After each session, trainees will write notes detailing content, process and feeling issues. It is advantageous to have audio or video recordings of the session, which may be viewed from the beginning or at a point of difficulty or interest. . . or not at all. Such recordings document the actual sequence of events and bring the dimensions of non-verbal and paralinguistic communication and change in emotional tone into the arena of supervision (Aveline, 1997b). Other means may be utilized. Transcripts allow the leisurely study of process and form of verbal intervention; as a semi-research exercise, the method of brief structured recall (Elliott and Shapiro, 1988) may be used to go over the most significant events in a session with the patient; the patient identifies significant events immediately after the session, then therapist and patient listen to the tape just before, during and after the event, and amplify through discussion the associated feelings, meaning and impact of that segment of interaction. New technology such as Code-A-Text (see www.code-a-text.com) offers flexible ways of classifying and examining the micro process of therapy. Live supervision from behind a screen with either telephone contact or a 'bug in the ear' may also be employed, though such measures reduce the scope for the therapist to grapple on her own as a person with the patient's issues. There is more to be said for the supervisor leading the way in openness by occasionally putting his own tapes forward for discussion.

Being supervised is supposed to be helpful, but it can be persecutory (Bruzzone et al., 1985) and intrusive (Betcher and Zinberg, 1988). The trainee's self-esteem is vulnerable and there needs to be room in the training for privacy and for mistakes to be made and discussed without dire penalty or excessive shame. Counter-transference reactions on the part of the supervisor must not be forgotten. The trainee may represent the coming generation that may equal or overtake the supervisor in skill and knowledge. Rivalry and the struggle for power may constitute a subtext for the supervisory meetings and, if not resolved, prove detrimental to professional development. Training for supervisors and a forum for them to discuss problems in supervision are beneficial (Hawkins and Shohet, 1989). In the training, it is also sensible and desirable in its own right to have group supervision as well as individual supervision, since the former provides multiple perspectives, peer support and the morale-enhancing opportunity of being of assistance to colleagues.

Skills development

While I favour weekly supervision over months and years as the best complement to the work of individual therapy, workshops and role-plays quickly lead to the acquisition of fundamental skills (structured examples of exercises are to be found in Egan, 1982a, 1982b; Jacobs, 1985, 1991; Tolan and Lendrum, 1995). Without risking any harm to the patient, difficult situations that therapists commonly face can be practised, the effects of different interventions observed and the model presented by more experienced therapists evaluated. Micro-counselling training courses, first described at the end of the 1960s, have retained their promise for the relatively inexperienced trainee; they provide structured, focused learning over periods of one, two or three days with a strong emphasis on skills acquisition through role-play. At the more advanced, approach-specific level, the use of detailed treatment manuals for such diverse approaches as supportive-expressive psychoanalytic psychotherapy, cognitive and interpersonal therapy of depression and short-term therapy is an interesting, effective new method of skill development (Matarazzo and Patterson, 1986).

Personal therapy

'The therapist can only go as far with the patient as he can go himself', so the maxim runs. What the therapist can bear to hear in herself, she can hear in the patient. What the therapist can find in herself, she can recognize in the other. Thus in addition to the resistance by the patient to dismantling defensive, outmoded but originally adaptive patterns, the therapist contributes a resistance of her own to free exploration. The therapist's resistance may take the form of avoidance or over-interest; the former limits the opening up of areas of concern for the patient, the latter diverts the focus of the discourse to the therapist's own conflictual issues; these processes largely take place out of consciousness. Examples have been given in the sections on counter-transference and the abuse of power of some common personal conflicts, which may limit or adversely distort the engagement of the therapist. All therapies at some stage confront the reflective therapist with the dilemmas in her own life and the partial solutions that she has adopted. An overlap of conflictual issue between therapist and patient often results in a blocked therapy, but may generate a particularly fruitful dyad when the therapist's conflict is not too great and the overlap enhances empathic contact (Aveline, 1992).

Life experience and the practice of psychotherapy educate the therapist about herself. Self-scrutiny takes the learning about conflicts and their resolution one step further but the therapist's own internal security measures operate to maintain blind spots and protect self-esteem from sobering self-realizations; these defences limit what can be done alone. Personal therapy offers the therapist the same opportunity as the patient has to explore, understand and resolve inner conflicts. It brings together theoretical learning and psychotherapy practice in an experience that makes personal sense of the two. At a practical level, personal therapy provides a means through which sufficient self-understanding can be gained for the therapist to recognize how her personality and life experience affect her ability to be objective and to reduce her tendency to impose her own solutions on the life problems of the patient. The nature of the conflicts that interfere with the therapist's work predicate her requirement for therapy in terms of type, duration and frequency; and the achievement of sufficient resolution in order to work more effectively indicates the end-point of personal therapy on the practical level. At the next level, therapy aims to enhance the therapist's ability to relate, empathically and creatively, to her patients. One element in this is knowing at first hand what it is like to be a patient; another is the loosening through therapy of the self-limiting grip of personal conflicts. Beyond that, as was detailed in the section on motivating factors in the therapist, therapy offers an opportunity for the therapist to heal herself, an unmet need which may have been of prime importance in the selection by the trainee therapist of this kind of work. At a sociological level, personal therapy has the function of a rite of passage, forming and affirming her identity as a psychotherapist and as a member of her professional group. Importantly, personal therapy offers support with difficult work.

Perhaps the most compelling argument in favour of personal therapy is that every therapist, like every patient, sees the world from the perspective of her guiding fictions and is impelled to impose that order, those patterns and her solutions on others. Thus, the more the therapist is aware of her personal, determining fictions, the more likely she will be able to engage with the reality of the other.

Personal therapy in varying intensity and duration is a required component of most formal, advanced trainings in psychotherapy. In psychoanalysis, full personal analysis is mandatory: the sequence of engagement in training is being in therapy, then theory seminars and finally conducting analyses. In Henry's (1977) survey of 4,000 North American psychotherapists 74 per cent had been in personal therapy and nearly 50 per cent had re-entered therapy for two to four periods; conversely, 26 per cent had chosen not to pursue that course. Despite the consensus in favour of personal therapy, especially at the psychodynamic end of the spectrum, there is little published evidence of its efficacy in enhancing therapeutic ability. Surveys of the literature (Greenberg and Staller, 1981; Macaskill, 1988; Macaskill and Macaskill, 1992) conclude that (a) 15–33 per cent of therapists have unsatisfactory personal therapy experiences, e.g. damage to marriage, destructive acting-out and excessive withdrawal from the outside world; (b) therapy early in the therapist's career may have deleterious effects on work with patients; and (c) there is no positive correlation between either the fact of having been in therapy or its duration on outcome of the therapist's professional work. The level of reported dissatisfaction is in line with that generally expected for negative effects in psychotherapy, and, as such, emphasizes the importance of the trainee's making a sage choice of therapist. The research base is slight but suggests that therapy may enhance counter-transference awareness and containment; more rigorous studies are needed (Macran and Shapiro, 1998).

When personal therapy is decided upon, its form, intensity and duration should parallel the form of psychotherapy that the therapist is going to practise. This follows the educational principle of congruence. Generally for training in individual therapy, this will be one or more times a week for three or more years. It is important that the therapist enters therapy not just because the training requires it but to resolve personal conflicts or difficulties that are being encountered in her work and life. Advice on whom to consult should be sought from an experienced adviser who can steer the trainee away from pairings that are less than optimal and towards those of greater promise (Coltart, 1987). A balance needs to be struck between comfortable similarity and challenging difference. Exploratory sessions should be held with several potential therapists before the choice is made. This counsel of perfection could well apply to patients if ever they were in the position of being able to choose whom to see.

Evaluation

During training, there should be opportunities for evaluation, both formative and normative. The reader may recall that, in educational terms, 'formative' evaluation refers to non-examined elements that enrich the educational experience of training, whereas 'normative' refers to entry/exit, pass/fail criteria. The aims of the training should be clearly stated and be attainable within the learning experiences of the scheme. A system for monitoring progress both by self-assessment and by the trainers is necessary, as is the giving of feedback so as to help the trainee improve the quality of her psychotherapy. Individual and psychometric assessments of severity of patient problem can form a baseline for the evaluation of the success of therapy. Casebooks recording progress and any alteration in formulation of the patient's problems document the range of therapy experience and the lessons to be learned from actual practice as opposed to the fine rhetoric of texts. Detailed written case accounts of one or more psychotherapies carried out by the trainee demonstrate the degree of the trainee's development and bring into focus how difficulties have been encountered and struggled with. A personal tutor has a key role as adviser and appraiser to the trainee finding her way through the training. Ultimately, evaluation should address the question of therapist competence: how effective is this therapist in aiding the quest of her patients for more fruitful living? The methodology to assess this does not yet exist. Only partial progress has been made towards the subsidiary but important question of what this training has added to the therapist's ability; one example is the quantification of the improvement in interviewing skills acquired through micro-counselling courses (Matarazzo and Patterson, 1986).

National Vocational Qualifications

Since 1987, the British government has been committed to introducing National Vocational Qualifications (NVQs) for as many occupations as possible. NVQs are based on a functional analysis of what a competent worker does. They describe competencies at five levels of increasing complexity of activity. Level one describes routine and predictable tasks where the worker follows rules set by superiors, and level five the application of fundamental principles or complex techniques across a wide range of unpredictable contexts by someone operating with substantial, personal autonomy. Level five would equate to the standards of the established professions like law or medicine, though these occupations have yet to be mapped by this process. The declared purpose of NVQs is to provide an alternative pathway to qualification other than traditional university courses and to help employers judge that their employees have the competencies to discharge the duties of a specific post.

After much deliberation, the British Association for Counselling (BAC, now BACP: see next section) joined with the Department of Employment in 1992 to map and devise standards in the fields of work covered by BAC. The organ for this project was the Lead Body for Advice, Guidance, Counselling and Psychotherapy. After an ambivalent period, the United Kingdom Council for Psychotherapy (again see next section) voted to join the Lead Body in 1994. Competency statements were agreed for advice, guidance, and counselling and contracts placed with awarding bodies to turn these into NVQ qualifications for advice and guidance. Joint work began on mapping competencies for therapeutic counselling and psychotherapy but that concordat fell apart. The development of functional standards aroused many anxieties. Critics argued that the approach is atomistic, and risks losing the sum of the parts by splitting the whole into so many elements, slavishly to be checked off during training. They fear that it will emphasize action over reflection, 'doing to' over 'being with', and is all too cognitive, rather than emotional. They say that the method misses out synthesis and intuition and suggests falsely that the practice of psychotherapy is algorithmic when, truly, it is heuristic. The participating sceptics, myself among them, value the healthy emphasis on outputs and anticipate that it will bring out commonalties and differences between the psychotherapies. It has the potential to clearly define the competencies to be developed through training and promote the equivalence of trainings.

It now seems unlikely that NVQs will become another route to qualification for psychotherapists. This is partly because the last decade has seen a huge expansion of university diplomas, MScs and doctorates that provide externally validated qualifications and have proved very popular. Educationally, these are objective-led and bring a welcome level of critical enquiry to the field. Sometimes they are light on clinical practice.

Registration

At present, anyone in Britain may practise as a psychotherapist and advertise their services as such. Unlike the situation in North America and many European countries, psychotherapy is not a regulated profession. No formal training or subscription to a code of ethics is required by statute. Some titles such as psychoanalyst and child psychotherapist are protected. Within institutions such as the NHS, and university counselling services, the patient as consumer of psychotherapy has the protection of knowing that for the most part the therapist will have been appointed in open competition with other applicants, and has the sanction of being able to initiate an official complaint through the institution's code of practice and complaints procedure. Membership of professions that are regulated by statutory bodies (as for example is medicine by the General Medical Council) or have chartered status, such as psychology, or of training institutes with regulatory powers affords some assurance that the standards of the therapist are adequate and will be maintained. But in the private sector, members of the public have little protection against the misinformed or unethical therapist. This is bad for the consumer and bad for the profession.

The Foster Report (Foster, 1971), the result of a government-appointed inquiry, recommended that the profession of psychotherapy be regulated by statute. Seven years later, the Sieghart Report (Sieghart, 1978) proposed the establishment of a council that would draw up and enforce a code of professional ethics and approve training courses. Registration of individuals as psychotherapists would be indicative rather than functional, that is, on the basis of titles associated with various forms of psychotherapy in which the therapist was qualified rather than the content of the work. The desirable goal of registration as some guarantee of integrity and competence, at present on a voluntary basis, has since made significant progress, especially in the last five years.

During the 1980s, psychotherapists and psychotherapy organizations from across the spectrum of practice met each year in Rugby (the Rugby Conference), initially under the auspices of the British Association for Counselling, and latterly in Canterbury. In 1989 the conference adopted a formal constitution as the United Kingdom Standing Conference for Psychotherapy (UKSCP), metamorphosing into the United Kingdom Council for Psychotherapy (UKCP) in 1993. UKCP is an organization of organizations, grouped into eight sections: Analytical

Psychology; Behavioural and Cognitive Psychotherapy; Experiential Constructivist; Family, Marital and Sexual Therapy; Humanistic and Integrative Psychotherapy; Hypnotherapy; Psychoanalytic Psychotherapy; and Psycho-Analytically based Therapy with Children. In 1993 UKCP established a register of its qualified members, now some 4,000, grouped for competence by the title of the section in which they are registered. Registrants have to meet a common standard of training and ethics and are subject to disciplinary procedures (Pokorny, 1995). Having successfully launched the register, the next step is to define criteria for re-registration.

UKCP is committed to seeking statutory registration. Achieving this goal depends on all the major psychotherapy organizations speaking with a common voice and showing evidence of being able to uphold high standards, investigate complaints and discipline registrants who engage in malpractice. A bill to regulate psychotherapy was introduced by Lord Alderdice in the House of Lords in 2000 but failed. It now seems likely the government will regulate psychotherapy and a wide range of related therapies in the NHS alone through an Order in Council. This will have the benefit of recognizing the status and training of registered NHS therapists but, in my view, misses the point that patients are more at risk in the unregulated private sector than in the public sector with all its inbuilt safeguards.

At the moment when UKSCP was preparing to vote UKCP into existence, a substantial proportion of the organizations from the psychoanalytic end of the spectrum withdrew from the conference. They were unhappy about the breadth of psychotherapy approach represented in UKSCP and, it would appear, about being one voice among many. They preferred to cluster round a psychoanalytic identity and formed the British Confederation of Psychotherapists in 1992. In 1994 they launched their register of 1,200 practitioners (Balfour and Richards, 1995). I regret that they turned away from the greater good of a representative profession of psychotherapy. Doubtless, a *rapprochement* will be necessary if statutory registration for all is to be achieved.

For many years, the British Association for Counselling, a substantial organization with 19,000 mmbers, has operated a system of individual accreditation of counsellors. In 1996, the counselling organizations launched the United Kingdom Register of Counsellors; BAC holds the register. As well as individual registration, counsellors may be registered by sponsoring organizations that will guarantee the counselling that they do within that organization. Thus, a counsellor might be registered for independent practice and/or for work in, for example, Relate or Cruise. In 2000, BAC altered its name to include psychotherapy, i.e. BACP.

All these moves help identify areas of competence among psychotherapists and in therapeutic counselling and provide a useful measure of protection for the public and for employers of therapists.

Implicit in the above is the proposition that continued attention to maintaining and extending competence is part of the professional attitude of the psychotherapist. The rubric for this further education is continuing professional development (CPD); it can help guard against burnout (Grosch and Colsen, 1994). This is particularly important for the individual therapist, who tends to work in relative or absolute isolation and, in the absence of challenging opportunities for further learning, may develop poor working practices. Feedback from colleagues in peer group supervision of actual clinical work is especially helpful.

Supportive psychotherapy

The rhetoric of psychotherapy is towards fundamental change in people's feelings, attitudes and interactions; this has been the type of individual therapy for which training has been described in this chapter. The trainee therapist in her enthusiasm and inexperience of the struggle to survive that many patients face may be tempted to press for a pace and depth of change for which her patient is not ready. Fundamental change will not be possible or desirable for all or, if possible, the patient may not be given authorization for deep exploration that may profoundly challenge his view of himself. This situation has to be explicitly respected and the value of support recognized and taught in training. All therapy has to have in it a sufficiently supportive element in order to help the patient contend with the upheaval of change: most therapies will move between challenging and supportive phases. Furthermore, supportive psychotherapy is a subject in its own right. It is indicated for the many individuals who need sustained support in order to return to their optimal level of adjustment and maintain themselves there. It has its own complex skills and needs to be learned by even the most therapeutically ambitious therapist.

Conclusion

The current practice of psychotherapy distils what is known about human healing. In its practice, it is both an art and a science; both elements need to be borne in mind in training. Training may occur in phases but is a lifelong commitment. Competence is achievable but there is always more for the therapist to learn. No end-point has been reached in the development of individual therapy as an agent of personal change. Further refinement in theory, scope and practice can be expected, especially if the practitioners of the different individual psychotherapies learn to speak with one another in pursuit of the common goal of assisting their fellow human beings to lead more fruitful lives.

Notes

1 In this chapter, I use the word patient as a generic term for someone who suffers and is seeking help. Also, to avoid the cumbersome form of he/she, the male form is used unless a named authority is being referred to. The female form is used for the therapist.
2 Winnicott derived many of his ideas from his work with children. He saw psychotherapy taking place in the overlap of two playing areas, that of the patient and that of the therapist. The therapist's job is to help the patient move from a state of not being able to play into one of being

able to play. Playing is an especially creative, intensely real activity, which allows new syntheses to emerge.

References

Adler, G. (1972) 'Helplessness in the helpers', *British Journal of Medical Psychology* 45: 315–25.

Auerbach, A.A. and Johnson. M. (1977) 'Research on the therapist's level of experience', in A.S. Gurman and A.M. Razin, *Effective Psychotherapy*. Oxford: Pergamon Press. pp. 84–302.

Aveline, M. (1979) 'Towards a conceptual framework of psychotherapy – a personal view', *British Journal of Medical Psychology*, 52: 271–5.

Aveline, M. (1980) 'Making a psychodynamic formulation', *Bulletin, Royal College of Psychiatrists*, December: 192–3.

Aveline, M. (1989) 'The provision of illusion in psychotherapy', *Midland Journal of Psychotherapy*, 1: 9–16.

Aveline, M. (1992) 'Parameters of danger: interactive elements in the therapy dyad', in *From Medicine to Psychotherapy*. London: Whurr.

Aveline, M. (1995) 'Assessing the value of intervention at the time of assessment for dynamic psychotherapy', in M. Aveline and D. Shapiro, *Research Foundations for Psychotherapy Practice*. Chichester: John Wiley & Sons.

Aveline, M. (1997a) 'Assessing for optimal therapeutic intervention', in S. Palmer and G. McMahon (eds), *Client Assessment*. London, Sage. pp. 93–114.

Aveline, M. (1997b) 'The use of audiotapes in supervision of psychotherapy', in G. Chapman (ed.), *Supervision of Psychotherapy and Counselling. Making a Place to Think*. Buckingham: Open University Press.

Aveline, M. (1999) 'The advantages of formulation over categorical diagnosis in explorative psychotherapy and psychodynamic management', *European Journal of Psychotherapy, Counselling and Health*, 2(2): 199–216.

Aveline, M. (2001) 'Complexities of practice: psychotherapy in the real world', in F. Palmer-Barnes and L. Murdin (eds), *Values and Ethics in the Practice of Psychotherapy and Counselling*. Buckingham: Open University Press. pp. 128–43.

Aveline, M. and Ratigan, B. (1988) 'Issues in the training of group therapists', in M.O. Aveline and W. Dryden (eds), *Group Therapy in Britain*. Milton Keynes: Open University Press. pp. 317–36.

Balfour, F. and Richards, J. (1995) 'History of the British Confederation of Psychotherapists', *British Journal of Psychotherapy*, 11(3): 422–6.

Bennet, G. (1987) *The Wound and the Doctor*. London: Secker & Warburg.

Bernstein, L. and Bernstein, R.S. (1980) *Interviewing: a Guide for Health Professionals*. New York: Appleton-Century-Crofts.

Betcher, R.W. and Zinberg, N.E. (1988) 'Supervision and privacy in psychotherapy training', *American Journal of Psychiatry*, 145: 796–803.

Bruzzone, M.E., Casaula, J.P. and Jordan, J.F. (1985) 'Regression and persecution in analytic training: reflections on experience', *International Review of Psychoanalysis*, 12: 411–15.

Bugental, J.F.T. (1964) 'The person who is the psychotherapist', *Journal of Counseling Psychology*, 28: 272–7.

Burton, A. (1975) 'Therapist satisfaction', *American Journal of Psychoanalysis*, 35: 115–22.

Caligor, L. (1984) *Parallel and Reciprocal Processes in Psychoanalytic Supervision*. New York, Plenum.

Casement, P. (1985) *On Learning from the Patient*. London: Tavistock.

Cleghorn, J.M., Bellissimo, A. et al. (1983) 'Teaching some principles of individual psychodynamics through an introductory guide to formulations', *Canadian Journal of Psychiatry*, 28: 162–72.

Coltart, N. (1987) 'Diagnosis and assessment for suitability for psycho-analytical psychotherapy', *British Journal of Psychotherapy*, 4: 127–34.

Davis, J.D., Elliott, R. et al. (1987) 'Development of a taxonomy of therapist difficulties: initial report', *British Journal of Medical Psychology*, 60: 109–19.

Department of Health (1998) *A First Class Service*. London: DoH.

Doehrman, M.J.G. (1976) 'Parallel processes in supervision and psychotherapy', *Bulletin of the Menninger Clinic*, 40: 1–104.

Eells, T.D. (ed.) (1997) *Handbook of Psychotherapy Case Formulation*. New York: Guilford Press.

Egan, G. (1982a) *Exercises in Helping Skills*. Belmont, CA: Wadsworth.

Egan, G. (1982b) *The Skilled Helper*. Belmont, CA: Wadsworth.

Elliott, R. and Shapiro, D.A. (1988) 'Brief structured recall: a more efficient method for studying significant therapy moments', *British Journal of Medical Psychology*, 61: 141–53.

Fairbairn, W.R.D. (1954) *An Object-Relations Theory of the Personality*. New York: Basic Books.

Farber, B.A. (1983) 'The effects of psychotherapeutic practice upon psychotherapists', *Psychotherapy: Theory, Research and Practice*, 20: 174–82.

Farber, B.A. and Heifetz, L.J. (1981) 'The satisfactions and stresses of psychotherapy work: a factor analytic study', *Professional Psychology*, 12: 621–30.

Fleming, J. (1987) *The Teaching and Learning of Psychoanalysis*. New York: Guilford Press.

Foster, J.G. (1971) *Enquiry into the Practice and Effects of Scientology*. London: HMSO.

Frank, J.D. (1973) *Persuasion and Healing*. Baltimore, MD: Johns Hopkins University Press.

Friedman, R.S. and Lister, P. (1987) 'The current status of the psychodynamic formulation', *Psychiatry*, 50: 126–41.

Gosling, R. (1978) 'Internalization of the trainer's behaviour in professional training', *British Journal of Medical Psychology*, 51: 35–40.

Greben, S.E. (1975) 'Some difficulties and satisfactions inherent in the practice of psychoanalysis', *International Journal of Psycho-Analysis*, 56: 427–33.

Greben, S.E. (1984) *Love's Labor*. New York: Schocken Books.

Greenberg, R.P. and Staller, J. (1981) 'Personal therapy for therapists', *American Journal of Psychiatry*, 138: 1467–71.

Greenson, R.R. (1967) *The Technique and Practice of Psychoanalysis Vol. 1*. New York: International Universities Press.

Grosch, W.N. and Colsen, D. (1994) *When Helping Starts to Hurt: a New Look at Burnout among Psychotherapists*. New York: W.W. Norton.

Guggenbuhl-Craig, A. (1979) *Power in the Helping Professions*. Irving, TX: Spring Publications.

Guy, J.D. (1987) *The Personal Life of the Psychotherapist*. New York: John Wiley & Sons.

Hawkins, P. and Shohet, R. (1989) *Supervision in the Helping Professionals*. Oxford: Oxford University Press.

Heimann, P. (1950) 'On counter-transference', *International Journal of Psychoanalysis*, 31: 81–4.

Henry, W.A. (1977) 'Personal and social identities of psychotherapists', in A.S. Gurman and A.M. Razin (eds), *Effective Psychotherapy*. Oxford: Pergamon Press.

Hess, A.K. (1986) 'Growth in supervision: stages of supervisee and supervisor development', in F.W. Kaslow (ed.), *Supervision and Training: Models, Dilemmas, Challenges*. New York: Haworth Press.

Holmes, J. (1986) 'Teaching the psychotherapeutic method: some literary parallels', *British Journal of Medical Psychology*, 59: 113–21.

Holroyd, J.C. and Brodsky, A.M. (1977) 'Psychologists' attitudes and practices regarding erotic and non-erotic physical contact with patients', *American Psychologist*, 32: 843–9.

Hubble, M.A., Duncan, B.L. et al. (1999) *The Heart and Soul of Change: What Works in Therapy*. Washington, DC: American Psychological Association.

Jacobs, M. (1985) *Swift to Hear. Facilitating Skills in Listening and Responding*. London: SPCK.

Jacobs, M. (1991) *Insight and Experience*. Milton Keynes: Open University Press.

JCHPT (1996) *Requirements for Specialist Training in Psychotherapy*. London: Royal College of Psychiatrists.

Jones, E. (1913) *The God Complex. Essays in Applied Psychoanalysis Vol. 2*. London: Hogarth Press.

Lambert, M.J. (1986) 'Implications of psychotherapy outcome research for eclectic psychotherapy', in J.C. Norcross (ed.), *Handbook of Eclectic Psychotherapy*. New York: Brunner Mazel.

Lomas, P. (1981) *The Case for a Personal Psychotherapy*. Oxford: Oxford University Press.

Luborsky, L. and Crits-Christoph, P. (1990) *Understanding Transference. The Core Conflictual Relationship Theme Method*. New York, Basic Books.

Luborsky, L. and Singer, B. (1974) *The Fit of Therapists' Behavior into Patients' Negative Expectations: a Study of Transference-Countertransference Contagion*. University of Pennsylvania Press.

Luborsky, L. and Singer, B. (1975) 'Comparative studies of psychotherapies. Is it true that "Everyone has won and all must have prizes?"', *Archives of General Psychiatry*, 32: 995–1008.

Macaskill, N.D. (1988) 'Personal therapy in the training of a psychotherapist: is it effective?' *British Journal of Psychotherapy*, 4: 219–26.

Macaskill, N.D. and Macaskill, A. (1992) 'Psychotherapists in training evaluate their personal therapy: results of a UK survey', *British Journal of Psychotherapy*, 9(2): 133–8.

Mace, C. (1995) *The Art and Science of Assessment in Psychotherapy*. London: Routledge.

Macran, S. and Shapiro, D.A. (1998) 'The role of personal therapy for therapists: a review', *British Journal of Medical Psychology*, 71: 13–25.

Malan, D.H. (1995) *Individual Psychotherapy and the Science of Psychodynamics*. Oxford: Butterworth Heinemann.

Marmor, J. (1953) 'The feeling of superiority: an occupational hazard in the practice of psychotherapy', *American Journal of Psychiatry*, 110: 370–3.

Marmor, J. (1972) 'Sexual acting-out in psychotherapy', *American Journal of Psycho-Analysis*, 22: 3–8.

Matarazzo, R.G. and Patterson, D.R. (1986) 'Methods of teaching therapeutic skill', in S.L. Garfield and A.L. Bergin, *Handbook of Psychotherapy and Behavior Change*. New York: John Wiley & Sons.

Menninger, K. (1958) *Theory of Psychoanalytic Technique*. New York: Basic Books.

Orlinsky, D. and Howard, K.I. (1980) 'Gender and psychotherapeutic outcome', in A.M. Brodsky and R.T. Hare-Mustin, *Women and Psychotherapy*. New York: Guilford.

Orlinsky, D.E. and Ronnestad, M.H. (forthcoming) *The Psychotherapist's Perspective: Therapeutic Work, Professional Development, and Personal Life*, Washington: American Psychological Association.

Parry, G. (2001) *Treatment Choice in Psychological Therapies and Counselling*. London: Department of Health.

Pedder, J. (1986) 'Reflections on the theory and practice of supervision', *Psychoanalytic Psychotherapy*, 2: 1–12.

Perry, S., Cooper, A.M. et al. (1987) 'The psychodynamic formulation: its purpose, structure, and clinical application', *American Journal of Psychiatry*, 144: 543–50.

Pokorny, M.R. (1995) 'History of the United Kingdom Council for Psychotherapy', *British Journal of Psychotherapy*, 11(3): 415–21.

Reik, T. (1949) *Listening with the Third Ear*. New York: Farrer & Strauss.

Rogers, C.R. (1957) 'The necessary and sufficient conditions of therapeutic personality change', *Journal of Consulting Psychology*, 21: 95–103.

Rosin, S.A. and Knudson, R.M. (1986) 'Perceived influence of life experiences on clinical psychologists' selection and development of theoretical orientations', *Psychotherapy*, 23: 357–63.

Roth, A. and Fonagy, P. (1996) *What Works for Whom? A Critical Review of Psychotherapy Research*. New York: Guilford.

Ryle, A. (1990) *Cognitive-analytic Therapy: Active Participation in Change*. Chicester: John Wiley & Sons.

Sandler, J. (1988) 'Psychoanalysis and psychoanalytic psychotherapy: problems of differentiation'. Paper presented at the Psychoanalysis and Psychoanalytic Psychotherapy Conference (Association of Psychoanalytic Psychotherapy in the NHS), London 22–23 April.

Schafer, R. (1983) *The Analytic Attitude*. London: Hogarth Press.

Sieghart, P. (1978) *Statutory Registration of Psychotherapists*. London: Tavistock Clinic.

Storr, A. (1979) *The Art of Psychotherapy*. London: Secker & Warburg.

Strupp, H.H. (1960) *Psychotherapists in Action*. New York: Grune & Stratton.

Strupp, H.H. (1977) 'A reformulation of the dynamics of the therapist's contribution', in A.S. Gurman and A.M. Razin (eds), *Effective Psychotherapy*. Oxford: Pergamon Press.

Strupp, H.H. and Binder, J.L. (1984) *Psychotherapy in a New Key*. New York: Basic Books.

Tolan, J. and Lendrum, S. (1995) *Case Material and Role Play in Counselling Training*. London: Routledge.

Appendix 1: Chapter Structure (for Authors of Chapters 2–14)

1 Historical context and development in Britain (1,000 words)

1.1 Historical context

Your aim here should be briefly to acquaint the reader unfamiliar with your approach with its *historical context*. Examine its historical origins, its intellectual roots and explain why it is called what it is.

1.2 Development in Britain

Your aim here should be to treat briefly the development of the approach in Britain (where this is different from 1.1 up to the time of writing).

2 Theoretical assumptions (2,500 words)

2.1 Image of the person

Outline the basic assumptions made by the approach about the person and human nature.

2.2 Conceptualization of psychological disturbance and health

Outline how the approach conceptualizes both psychological disturbance and psychological health. Explain in detail the *major concepts* utilized by the approach in accounting for psychological disturbance and health.

2.3 Acquisition of psychological disturbance

Explain the approach's view on how psychological disturbance is acquired.

2.4 Perpetuation of psychological disturbance

Explain the approach's position on how psychological disturbance is perpetuated. What *intrapersonal mechanisms* are utilized by individuals to perpetuate their own psychological disturbance; what *interpersonal mechanisms* are recognized as important in the perpetuation process; what is the role of the *environment* in the perpetuation process?

2.5 Change

You should use this section to outline briefly the approach's view on how humans change with respect to movement from psychological disturbance to psychological health. This section should orient the reader to what follows under 'Practice' but should not be limited to the change process in therapy (i.e. it should not duplicate section 3.6). Thus it should both complete the 'Acquisition–Perpetuation–Change' cycle and orient the reader to what follows.

3 Practice (5,500 words)

3.1 Goals of therapy

Your aim here is to set out the goals of the approach.

3.2 Selection criteria

What selection criteria are used to determine whether or not clients will benefit from the approach in its *individual therapy format*? There are two issues here: first, what clients (if any) are deemed unsuitable for the particular approach under consideration (refer back to 3.1 here where relevant), and secondly, what criteria are employed in deciding whether or not clients who are suitable for the approach would benefit from individual therapy (as opposed to couples, family and group therapy) at the outset. What criteria are employed when decisions concerning transfer from one modality (e.g. individual therapy) to another (e.g. group therapy) become salient? Indeed when do these issues become salient? What are the approach's views on the use of concurrent therapeutic modalities (e.g. where the client is seen in both individual and group therapy)?

3.3 Qualities of effective therapists

From the point of view of the approach under consideration, what qualities do effective therapists have? Focus on both personal qualities and skill variables. In writing this section what is the relative importance of personal characteristics vs skill factors here?

3.4 Therapeutic relationship and style

Here you should outline the type of therapeutic relationship that therapists of your orientation seek to establish with their clients. You should also characterize the interactive style of the therapist in the conduct of the approach in action. (While you will no doubt use your own dimensions the following might be kept in mind: action–passive; formal–informal; self-disclosing–non-self-disclosing; humorous– serious.) How does the interactive style of the therapist change during the therapeutic process?

3.5 Major therapeutic strategies and techniques

List and describe the major strategies and techniques advocated as therapeutic by the approach. According to Marvin Goldfried, strategies lie at a level of abstraction between theory and techniques, so techniques are more *specific* than strategies. Please use this formulation in preparing this section and list the strategies first, showing how the techniques are specific ways of operationalizing the strategies. I am quite aware that some approaches cannot easily be described in these terms. Contact me if this is the case and we'll discuss how best to write this section.

3.6 The change process in therapy

Here outline the process of therapeutic change from beginning to end. What reliable patterns of change can be discerned in successful cases? Outline the major sources of lack of therapeutic progress and how these are addressed in the approach.

3.7 Limitations of the approach

Here describe the limitations of the approach. Where is there room for improvement? How should the approach develop in the future to rectify such deficiencies?

4 Case example (1,500 words)

Fully describe a case (a British client) which shows the approach in action, referring whenever possible to the above framework and dividing the section thus:

4.1 The client

Briefly describe the client and his/her presenting concerns.

4.2 The therapy

Here the emphasis should be on describing the process of change (i.e. how the therapy unfolded over time). Speculate on the sources of the therapeutic change. What, with hindsight, might you have done differently?

Please resist the temptation to select a 'brilliant success'. Choose a case that readers can relate to, i.e. one that had its difficulties and where the client had a realistic (not an idealistic) outcome.

NB: Those of you who contributed a chapter to *Handbook of Individual Therapy* should present a *new* case.

Appendix 2: Useful Addresses

Contributors were asked to provide not more than two addresses for those wishing for information on therapy services and training opportunities in a particular approach. The organizations listed below will often give details of others not shown here.

Psychodynamic Therapy: The Freudian Approach

Therapy and training

British Association of Psychotherapists
37 Mapesbury Road
London
NW2 4HJ
Tel: 020 8452 9823

Psychodynamic Therapy: The Kleinian Approach

Therapy and training

Institute of Psycho-Analysis
Byron House
112a Shirland Road
London
W9 2QE

Psychodynamic Therapy: The Jungian Approach

Therapy and training

Association of Jungian Analysts
7 Eton Avenue
London
NW3 3EL
Tel/fax: 020 7794 8711
aja@dircon.co.uk

Society of Analytical Psychology
1 Daleham Gardens
London
NW3 5BY
Tel: 020 7435 7696
Fax: 020 7431 1495
sap@jungian-analysis.org

Adlerian Therapy

Therapy and training

The Adlerian Society (of the United Kingdom) & The Institute for Individual
Psychology
73 South Ealing Road
London
W5 4QR
www.adleriansociety.co.uk

Adlerian Workshops and Publications
Wendover
Buckinghamshire
lilain@beattie.alcom.co.uk

Person-Centred Therapy

Therapy and training

The British Association for the Person-Centred Approach (BAPCA)
BM BAPCA
London
WC1N 3XX

Association for Person-Centred Therapy, Scotland
40 Kelvingrove Street
Glasgow
G3 7RZ

Existential Therapy

Therapy and training

Society for Existential Analysis
BM Existential
London
WC1N 3XX
Tel: 07000 473 337
www.existentialanalysis.co.uk

New School of Psychotherapy and Counselling
Royal Waterloo House
51–55 Waterloo Road
London
SE1 8TX
Tel: 020 7928 4344
admin@nspc.org.uk
www.nspc.org.uk

Gestalt Therapy

Therapy and training

The Administrator
GPTI
PO Box 2555
Bath
BA1 6XR
Tel/fax: 01225 482135

Personal Construct Therapy

Therapy and training

20 Cleveland Avenue
Chiswick
London
W4 1SN

Transactional Analysis

Therapy and training

The Administrator
Institute of Transactional Analysis
6 Princes Street
Oxford
OX4 1DD
Tel/fax: 01865 728012
admin@ita.org.uk

Cognitive Analytic Therapy

Therapy and training

Association for Cognitive Analytic Therapy (ACAT)
Academic Psychiatry
5th Floor
Block 8
South Wing
St Thomas's Hospital
London
SE1 7EH
Tel: 020 7928 9292 x 3769
Fax: 020 7928 0981

Cognitive Therapy

Therapy and training

British Association for Behavioural and Cognitive Psychotherapy
General Office
PO Box 9
Accrington
BB5 2GD
Tel: 01254 875277
Fax: 01254 875277
info@babcp.com

Behaviour Therapy

Therapy and training

British Association for Behavioural and Cognitive Psychotherapy
General Office
PO Box 9
Accrington
BB5 2GD
Tel: 01254 875277
Fax: 01254 875277
info@babcp.com

Rational Emotive Behaviour Therapy

Therapy

The Honorary Secretary
Association of Rational Emotive Behaviour Therapists
Behavioural Psychotherapy
Sir Michael Carlisle Centre
75 Osborne Road
Sheffield
S11 9BF

Training

Professor W. Dryden
PACE
Goldsmiths College
New Cross
London
SE14 6NW

Further information

In addition, useful referral and training directories are available from:

British Association for Counselling and Psychotherapy
1 Regent Place
Rugby
CV21 2PJ

United Kingdom Council for Psychotherapy
167–169 Great Portland Street
London
W1N 5FB

British Confederation of Psychotherapists
37 Mapesbury Road
London
NW2 4HJ

Feedback

The editor welcomes feedback on the present volume. Correspondence should be addressed:

Professor W. Dryden
PACE
Goldsmiths College
New Cross
London
SE14 6NW

Index